THE ENGLISH HORACE
Anthony Alsop and the Tradition of British Latin Verse

PORTRAIT OF ANTHONY ALSOP
by an unknown artist
(*courtesy of the Governing Body, Christ Church, Oxford*)

THE ENGLISH HORACE
Anthony Alsop and the Tradition of British Latin Verse

by
D. K. Money

*A British Academy
Postdoctoral Fellowship Monograph*

Published *for* THE BRITISH ACADEMY
by OXFORD UNIVERSITY PRESS

Oxford University Press, Great Clarendon Street, Oxford OX2 6DP

Oxford New York
Athens Auckland Bangkok Bogota Bombay
Buenos Aires Calcutta Cape Town Dar es Salaam
Delhi Florence Hong Kong Istanbul Karachi
Kuala Lumpur Madras Madrid Melbourne
Mexico City Nairobi Paris Singapore
Taipei Tokyo Toronto Warsaw

and associated companies in
Berlin Ibadan

Published in the United States by
Oxford University Press Inc., New York

© The British Academy 1998

British Library Cataloguing in Publication Data
Data Available

ISBN 0-19-726184-1

Typeset by J&L Composition Ltd, Filey, North Yorkshire
Printed in Great Britain
on acid-free paper by
Bookcraft (Bath) Ltd.
Midsomer Norton, Avon

UXORI, PARENTIBUS, FAUTORIBUS, AMICIS

Contents

Preface

The first section of my first chapter is devoted to an explanation of the subject matter of this book. I will therefore confine myself, in the preface, to expressing my gratitude to the many individuals and institutions without which it would not have appeared. The book owes its publication to the British Academy's first Postdoctoral Fellowship Monograph Competition, and I am naturally grateful to the Academy not only for making me a Postdoctoral Research Fellow, but also for helping the results of my research to reach what may (I hope) be a wide and sympathetic audience, at least by the standards of academic publications.

Some of the material used in the book previously appeared in my Ph.D. thesis (Cambridge, 1992); it is a pleasure to repeat the thanks that I then gave to all those who had supported my studies. Since completing that thesis, I have enjoyed the hospitality of Darwin College (as Munby Fellow in Bibliography at Cambridge University Library) and Wolfson College, Cambridge (as a Senior Research Fellow). Several scholars have offered kind and invaluable advice at all stages of the book's preparation, chief among them James Diggle and Howard Erskine-Hill; I would also like to thank James Binns, Elisabeth Leedham-Green, John K. Hale, Hilton Kelliher, Simon Corcoran, Jeremy Maule, and Richard Luckett for helping in various ways. Conversations with a number of others, in many cases in the convivial surroundings of colleges or the Cambridge Society for Neo-Latin Studies, have also proved stimulating. The staff of many libraries have either facilitated my visits or responded to my written queries; my thanks are due to them all, for their courtesy, knowledge, and efficiency. Much practical assistance was provided by my wife.

D. K. M.

List of Abbreviations

Bradner – L. Bradner, *Musae Anglicanae* (1940)

Grove – S. Sadie, ed., *New Grove Dictionary* (1980)

Hearne, *Coll.* – C. E. Doble, *et al.*, eds., *The Remarks and Collections of Thomas Hearne* (1885–1921)

Hearne, *Reliquiae* – P. Bliss, ed., *Reliquiae Hearnianae* (1857; rev. J. Buchanan-Brown, 1966)

HMC Portland 7 – R. Ward, ed., *Historical Mss. Commission, Report on the Mss. of his Grace the Duke of Portland, K.G., at Welbeck Abbey* vol. 7 (1901)

ms. – manuscript

Nichols, *Anecdotes* – J. Nichols, *Literary Anecdotes of the 18th century* (1812–16; repr. 1966)

Nichols, *Corresp.* – J. Nichols, ed., *The Epistolary Correspondence of Francis Atterbury* (1789–90)

Nichols, *Illustrations* – J. Nichols, *Illustrations of the Literary History of the 18th century* (1817–58; repr. 1966)

Sutherland and Mitchell, *Oxford* – L. S. Sutherland, L. G. Mitchell, eds., *History of the University of Oxford, vol. 5, the 18th century* (1986)

Wood, *Athenae* – A. à Wood (ed. P. Bliss), *Athenae Oxonienses* (3rd edn., 1813–20)

Wood, *Life & Times* – A. Clark, ed., *The Life & Times of Anthony à Wood* (1891–2)

Abbreviations for works by classical authors should be self-evident; e.g., Hor., *Carm.* = Horace, *Carmina* (i.e. *Odes*).

Within each chapter, sources are cited in full in the first instance; thereafter, only the author's name is used (unless confusion seems possible, in which case a short title is also given).

English dates before 1752 appear in the old style. Original spelling is used in quotations; some Latin words may look a little different to their conventional modern form, but there should be no real difficulty in identifying them. Some features of archaic spelling are even helpful: the distinction between 'i' and 'j', for example, has some value. I find that many students, using philologically correct modern texts, have no idea that 'i' or 'u' can act as consonants, which makes it hard to identify elisions. With some regret I abandon the Latin accents also regularly used in old texts; the circumflex is particularly useful as a mark of a long vowel (*mensâ*, ablative; *mensa*, nominative); no doubt readers will be able to spot cases without it.

PART I

I
Introduction

Anthony Alsop is one of Britain's major poets. He lived in what is often described as our 'Augustan age' (born in 1669 or 1670, he died in 1726), and made a major contribution to the literature of the early eighteenth century. He was not much concerned with fame or publication, and his output was not vast; it is nevertheless of a quality and historical significance that should command respect. Why is he not famous? Simply because he chose to write not in English but in Latin, a choice that was perfectly reasonable in his day, but which appears mysterious, eccentric, and off-putting to the anachronistic judgements of our own very different age. We can still appreciate him; if we take the trouble to try, we are rewarded with a new insight into an elegant, brilliantly witty, and combative world.

What this book is about

Alsop's poems are not unknown, and I do not claim to have 'discovered' him. Nor does he enjoy a place at the centre of our canon of 'great writers', or even in its smarter suburbs. He languishes in that literary Siberia to which good students are never sent, unless they rebel against their tyrannical syllabus, and which brings shivers to the spine (if any) of a commercially-minded publisher. Yet he would not be out of place among other major writers of the century, alongside Addison, Swift, Pope, Gray or Johnson. That, at least, is one of my arguments; the reader may agree wholly with me, or disagree violently, or remain incompletely convinced. To have an opinion, it is necessary to look at the poems themselves. These are presented in Part II of this book, a new edition of Alsop's works (with translation and brief commentary). It does not attempt to provide the last word on Alsop's works; it is intended as a companion to the chapters that precede it, allowing the reader to explore his works more widely, and form an independent judgement of them.

The book is not just an edition of Alsop. The majority of twentieth-century century scholars (and I imagine also those of the new millennium soon to be upon us) would want more than an annotated text to convince them of a Latin writer's value. The central section of the book (Chapters 3–7) looks at different aspects of Alsop's life and works, and offers some answers, albeit incompletely, to some of the questions that a reasonably sceptical enquirer might pose about his achievement. Chapter 3 deals with his early life and university career, and some assessments of his poetic quality; Chapter 4 turns to literary quarrels, and Chapter 5 to a humorous personal attack on a leading Oxford figure. Chapters 6 and 7 examine the fascinating poems he wrote to various friends; Chapter 7 also covers the later part of his life, including his time in exile (a prime cause of personal unhappiness and wonderful verse).

The book is aimed at scholars in various disciplines. Latin is the natural preserve of the classicist. Many classicists are not especially interested in later Latin literature, some of them being inclined to be dismissive of its value, in comparison to the sacred ancient canon. The merit of Alsop's odes, from a technical point of view, is discussed in Chapter 3. It may be that few modern authors are quite as good as Virgil or Horace; few ancient authors were, either. Good modern authors are better than mediocre ancient ones (and there are far more of them, far less intensively studied at present). At a time when the Classics are under some threat in schools and universities, there seems something to be said for a field which stresses interdisciplinary links: the Classics are actually useful outside their own traditional boundaries.

For the historian, literature is a valuable source of evidence. Many issues touched upon here are of historical significance. The history of universities (see especially Chapter 5) and the history of scholarship (Chapter 4) are interesting subjects in themselves, and also vital parts of national cultural history. The eighteenth-century universities have often been seen as places of little account, unreformed and uninspiring; a look at the health of their Latin culture may help to dispel that image. The literary quarrels in which Alsop was engaged raise fundamental questions about the function of scholarship, and its place in society. Historians of science might be interested in the relationship between science, politics, and literature (see Chapter 6; also Chapter 2). Members of Alsop's circle were leading scientific figures; they were also users of Latin, and leaders of Jacobite sedition. Jacobitism is an essential issue in eighteenth-century political and social history, one that has received considerable recent attention from historians. The Jacobite theme recurs in this book, especially in Chapters 6 and 7; many parts of Chapters 2–9 have some political angle. Other aspects of social history are mentioned (such as attitudes to homosexuality, in Chapters 2 and 7, and slavery, in Chapter 9). The aristocracy, the church, and the poor, music and hard-nosed business-men, all make their appearance.

Scholars of English literature will, I hope, want to examine Alsop's work, in the context of his times. He cannot be studied in isolation from his contemporaries, and from the whole tradition of British Latin verse. That tradition includes several authors whose English works entitle them to a prominent place in the existing canon. Accordingly, I devote Chapter 2 to the half-century before Alsop's career begins (with some thoughts on Milton and Marvell), and Chapter 8 to the period after Alsop's death, with coverage of Thomas Gray and Samuel Johnson. Gray makes a particularly interesting comparison with Alsop, since he also wrote relatively little (and much of that in Latin); if Gray merits a place in the canon, Alsop should certainly join him. The relative weight of English and Latin in Britain's literary culture is debatable. Scholars have tended to ignore or undervalue the Latin, giving undue stress to the English; I am aware of the opposite danger, of overemphasising the Latin while trying to redress the balance. In Chapter 9, I look at a wide range of university authors (giving a fair amount of space to English poems), and try to assess the overall place of Latin culture in society.

I consider Alsop to be the most interesting individual writer of British Latin. He is pre-eminent in one particular genre, the Horatian lyric. For that reason, I call him 'the English Horace', in the belief that he has a better claim to the title than any other possible candidate. Unlike writers of English poetry, he is genuinely devoted to Horace's Latin forms. He is not a slavish imitator of Horace, but an original poet making use of the Horatian tradition to express his own lively thoughts on contemporary life; in other words, he is fit to be seen as an English equivalent to Horace, admittedly not as great as the Roman master (for no one has ever really equalled Horace's lyric poetry), but a worthy modern successor.

An author can never know who all his readers might be, and must try to cater for them blindfold. In the eighteenth century, few works of literary criticism were published, but an intelligent public took up and discussed, often heatedly, both old and new literature, and found scholarly battles invigorating. Of all the twentieth century's literate millions, hardly any find enjoyment in reading today's literary critics (proportionately fewer, I would estimate, than took part in eighteenth-century Latin culture). The jargon used by some critics may have tended to alienate the non-specialist reader: I try to avoid confusing jargon in this book, wherever possible, in the hope that an interested non-specialist (if such a rare animal is not yet extinct) might not be put off. The main exception may be in the use of technical terms for Latin verse forms. Latin poetry is written in quite strict rhythmical patterns, which nevertheless allow a great deal of scope for fascinating and sophisticated variations. One cannot read and comment properly on poetry without understanding the author's chosen metrical restrictions, and the metre is best described in traditional terms ('dactyl', 'spondee', 'caesura', 'hexameter', 'elegiac', 'sapphic', and so on). I do not define these terms here, since they may readily be found in a large number of basic reference books, in addition to specialised works on metre; any reasonably detailed Latin grammar should supply a beginner with ample information.[1] For the lyric metres, annotated editions of Horace can be consulted.[2] Some effort is required for a beginner to become familiar with the subject. The basic rules of scansion are not very hard to learn, but occasional exceptions and difficulties can be frustrating. It is worth the effort, for it reveals the real beauty of a supremely beautiful language. No student of classics should ever neglect metre; nowadays, unfortunately, many stop at a nodding and distant acquaintance with the Virgilian hexameter, from which few intimate secrets are extracted (the lyric metres are actually easier to scan, having a less flexible scheme).

On the other hand, I can well appreciate that scholars in English literature, History, or other disciplines will not be able or willing to devote time to Latin metre; they may still, I hope, find the book of interest, and may perhaps take my word that metre matters, while skipping over the technicalities. For the benefit of those with little or no Latin, I offer translations of passages quoted (with the exception of some book titles, and classical quotations in notes, which should be clear). This sort of translation is a tedious and thankless task. If done properly, it attracts no credit. Any blemish can be seized upon by critics claiming that the original has been scandalously misunderstood. My aim has been to provide readable English versions, without striving for great elegance. A too literal translation can make Latin sound unbearably stilted, and thus give a misleading impression of its effect on the reader. In an attempt to avoid that problem, I favour free renderings; if my version looks wrong, it may be that I am trying to interpret the original in such a way as to emphasise its essence (or, I may have scandalously misunderstood it). Non-classicists are warned not to assume that every word of the Latin is fully translated; it can be rash to rely on a translation from any language for detailed analysis of the text.

We should at no point forget how different from our own were the intellectual expectations of the eighteenth century. I do not suppose that many teachers of English (or, now, of Classics) in British and American universities can write good Latin verse; they would therefore not perform very impressively at the regular exercises of an eighteenth-century school. An ordinary schoolboy at a major English school, by the age of twelve or thirteen, would then have known the techniques of verse-writing, and have been capable of producing dozens of lines in an afternoon. It may not have been high art, but it laid the foundation for a lifetime's poetic appreciation. He did not follow a modern curriculum, yet could probably write as good an essay, in Latin, on a scientific or philosophical topic as an average modern pupil would manage in English. The

[1] B. L. Gildersleeve, G. Lodge, *Latin Grammar* (London, 1895: often reprinted) gives a thorough explanation: the metres described, sections 757–827 (pp. 464–90, in 3rd edn., 1957).
[2] Detailed analysis in R. G. M. Nisbet, M. Hubbard, *Commentary on Horace: Odes Book* I (Oxford, 1970).

Latin essay, or 'theme', would be rounded off with a set of Latin verses offering an alternative, and often witty, view of the question. Modern scholars may affect to despise what they cannot do. Our eighteenth-century boy could not have the inestimable pleasure of today's literary theory, and had to subsist on less exalted forms of creativity.

The place of Latin in European culture

Latin has been the chief intellectual language of western and central Europe for most of the last two thousand years. Writings that mattered, were intended to last, and sought an international audience, were best entrusted to the language of the Romans. An important book that happened not to have been written in Latin might be translated. Trivia and ephemera might be in a local tongue (though they, too, could amuse a wide audience in Latin). Latin gradually lost its pre-eminence; by the late eighteenth century, although its prestige remained, the vernacular had taken over in most spheres of European culture. In the last couple of centuries, that decline has accelerated to the point where previous Latin achievements have been regularly ignored, and the study of Latin has no particular prestige in society. Yet no sensitive historian or literary critic should ignore such a central feature of our cultural heritage. Much of the writing of the last two thousand years can be described as 'medieval'; but this will not do for the huge flood of creativity released by the Renaissance, and not exhausted for several centuries. The term used to describe this vast amount of writing is 'Neo-Latin' (more commonly left without an initial capital, 'neo-Latin'); the term is not wholly satisfactory, in that it might suggest, to some people, something rather minor, derivative, ersatz, or second-rate. The 'neo-' prefix invites comparison with 'neo-classical', not always a term of praise: its regular use in architecture and other fields (including even economics) tends also to reduce its helpfulness as a literary term.

Neo-Latin is not an inferior language to ancient Latin. It is, in effect, the same language, with minor variations (much less obtrusive than the medieval version) and an enlarged vocabulary, used by very different people for different purposes. To call it 'Renaissance Latin' is to place undue emphasis on the earlier part of the tradition; to call it 'modern Latin' perhaps suggests something incongruously trivial. It is 'modern' in the historian's sense of 'post-medieval', not the colloquial sense of 'up-to-the-minute'. There is some extremely modern Latin (some of it well worth reading); this book is primarily concerned with the Latin of two or three centuries ago, which is not quite so modern. Hence, the term Neo-Latin seems the most appropriate way of referring to the whole field. For a general introduction to the Neo-Latin of all nations, one can consult the *Companion* of Josef IJsewijn.[3]

Students of British Latin verse over the last half-century have had as their guide the estimable Leicester Bradner. His *Musae Anglicanae: A History of Anglo-Latin Poetry, 1500–1925* (which I cite as 'Bradner') was published by the Modern Language Association of America in 1940, and remains an impressive piece of work. It has long been out of print. Major libraries, and some fortunate individuals, have copies; I have never seen one offered for sale in an English bookshop.[4] A new edition would be most welcome. The text would merit reprinting as it stands (with only those corrections and additions to the bibliography that Bradner himself later made); alternatively, it might usefully be revised, to take into account some more recent scholarship, and to make Bradner's own generous quotations more accessible to a less learned audience. It is a fair indication of the changes in educational standards that Bradner (himself a scholar of English literature, rather than Classics) could think it useful to quote long passages of Latin (often 20 lines or more) without translation. Few scholars, let alone students, of English would today be willing to wade through such forbidding blocks of foreign-sounding material, nor are they (in general) properly equipped to appreciate the beauties of the verse. If the quotations were translated, and perhaps trimmed in places, they might now receive more attention.

Bradner does tend to offer these extended quotations without much critical comment: the reader is expected to be able to assess them without further guidance. Since he covers a long and varied tradition in a single volume, the space available for any one author is inevitably limited. Good use is made of that space, to give the reader a flavour of each significant poet's work, and a judgement of its value. Alsop, for example, receives a solid treatment in about six pages (pp. 230–6), in which 58 lines of his odes are quoted; he is also mentioned in passing elsewhere. Bradner's judgements tend to be measured, sensible, and straightforward; one may occasionally quibble with him for blandness, or for being too ready to dismiss an author as weak. These are relatively minor criticisms, and more often than not I am happy to agree with Bradner's opinions, and admire the splendid breadth of his research. In covering part of the same ground, I have tried to avoid duplication wherever possible, often by citing the appropriate pages of his work, and leaving it at that. Sometimes I examine different material. In the central chapters of the book I am able to go into far greater detail, but in the more rapid surveys of earlier and later periods, I offer a complement, rather than a replacement, to Bradner.

---

[3] J. IJsewijn, *A Companion to Neo-Latin Studies* (Amsterdam, 1977; 2nd edn., as *Humanistica Lovaniensia*, supplement 5, Louvain, 1990).
[4] I have seen references to a 1966 reprint (but copies do not seem to be easily available, at least in Britain).

Among more recent works on British Latin, the outstanding book is *Intellectual Culture in Elizabethan and Jacobean England: the Latin Writings of the Age*, written by J. W. Binns and published by Francis Cairns (as no. 24 in the 'ARCA' series). No serious student of the history or literature of the sixteenth and seventeenth centuries should be unaware of this work. Binns analyses the various genres of Latin literature (in both prose and verse) found in printed books from *c.* 1550 to 1640, and convincingly demonstrates their central place in the culture of the time. It is a storehouse of detailed information, in nearly 800 pages (more than a third of which are devoted to notes, indices, a substantial bibliography of original sources and modern scholarship, and a biographical register giving brief details, and bibliographical references, for hundreds of significant figures).[5] Binns does provide translations, and in that respect is more accessible, as well as more thorough, than Bradner; Binns' quotations also tend to be shorter, and chosen to illustrate a particular point (thus, he makes much use of Latin prose prefaces to examine authors' attitudes to their work, and printing-house practice). Despite his greater length and smaller timespan, Binns cannot treat most of his large number of authors in any detail; some receive a section of up to four or five pages, others are merely cited as examples of a genre. Only John Case, the Oxford philosopher, has a chapter to himself (pp. 366–77). The book is therefore an essential work of reference for the period, with room for critical examination of some subjects.

My own period really begins as Binns' ends, in about 1640 (although I occasionally stray earlier, in this chapter and in Chapter 9). I do not offer an equivalent to Binns' thorough treatment. Arguably, that approach would be less appropriate for a later age, when Neo-Latin becomes less obviously central to intellectual culture (although it is my contention that it remains of considerable importance). Nor have I yet had the time, or learned the patience, to assemble and assimilate such a mass of information. Instead, I offer a different type of study, taking a single author as the centre of a wide context, in the hope that I might be able to explain some of the fascinating historical and literary issues raised by the later part of the tradition.

The question of permanence

The place of Neo-Latin in seventeenth-century British culture can be illustrated by a significant English poem, Edmund Waller's *Of English Verse*. It is one of his

---

[5] It can take a minute or two to find a reference, with the text referring to endnotes, the notes in turn requiring consultation of one of the bibliographies; but it is well worth the effort.

finest and (ironically) most lasting pieces, deservedly anthologised;[6] I first
encountered the poem long before I had thought of Neo-Latin as a subject
for serious study (since it is far removed from a student's syllabus), and knowing
little more of it than the works of Milton. Despite the poem's relative familiarity,
it may be worth quoting it, and considering the points made therein:

> Poets may boast (as safely vain)
> Their work shall with the world remain
> Both bound together, live, or dye,
> The Verses and the Prophecy.
>
> But who can hope his lines should long
> Last in a daily changing Tongue?
> While they are new, envy prevails,
> And as that dies, our Language fails;
>
> When Architects have done their part
> The Matter may betray their Art,
> Time, if we use ill-chosen stone,
> Soon brings a well-built Palace down.
>
> Poets that lasting Marble seek
> Must carve in *Latine* or in *Greek*,
> We write in Sand, our Language grows,
> And like the Tide our work o'erflows.
>
> *Chaucer* his Sense can only boast,
> The glory of his numbers lost,
> Years have defac'd his matchless strain,
> And yet he did not sing in vain;
>
> The Beauties which adorn'd that age
> The shining Subjects of his rage,
> Hoping they should immortal prove
> Rewarded with success his love.
>
> This was the generous Poets scope
> And all an *English* Pen can hope,
> To make the fair approve his Flame
> That can so far extend their Fame.
>
> Verse thus design'd has no ill fate
> If it arrive but at the Date

[6] E.g. as no. 354 in H. J. C. Grierson, G. Bullough, eds., *The Oxford Book of Seventeenth Century Verse*
(Oxford, 1934). The fourth stanza is quoted (as illustration of Latin's lapidary qualities) by M. Storey, in
J. W. Binns, ed., *The Latin Poetry of English Poets* (London, 1974), pp. 130–1. The poem first appears in 1668,
in a prominent position at the end of the vol. (pp. 234–5): the mature Waller clearly thought it worth
adding to his published oeuvre.

Of fading Beauty, if it prove
But as long liv'd as present love.

The message is unambiguous: Latin and Greek are the languages for serious
poetry, not only in the classical past but the seventeenth-century present. Their
suitability is the result of their permanence, which contrasts with the rapid
fluctuation of vernacular idioms. The example of Chaucer is telling. He had
long been something of a mystery to English readers. Before the civil war, he
had been translated into Latin, for the benefit of Englishmen as much as
foreigners. This poetic jewel, according to the translator, 'fere amissa erat, et a
nostratibus vix intellecta, (saltem nemini in deliciis) ob verborum in ea obsole-
torum ignorantiam . . .' [had almost been lost, and was hardly understood (or at
least never enjoyed) by our compatriots, since they did not know the obsolete
words in it.][7] Even in the early nineteenth century, this Latin version was more
widely understood than the original.[8]

Waller does not here follow his own advice, and write in Latin (as he
sometimes, though rarely, did). This does not mean that the advice is insincere.
He is not attempting to carve 'lasting Marble', to delight and satisfy the learned
of future generations. He merely wishes to ease his way into the arms and
bedchambers of some contemporary ladies, as Chaucer had done before him.
Human beauty is notoriously evanescent, and verse that is designed to impress
the beautiful need be no less ephemeral. Rash promises of immortality need not
be fulfilled, nor will the poet live to see them broken. English vernacular poetry
is more of a sexual aid than a serious literary endeavour.

The issues raised by Waller were of the greatest relevance to the period of
Alsop. There was not, in fact, a firm division between serious Latin and
transitory English. Alsop himself does not seem to have cared whether his poems
lasted for ever, and his choice of Latin is not dictated by a lust for immortality.
Most of the contemporary English works which are now canonical would not
then have seemed particularly liable to last. Waller's poem was associated with a
debate about the concept of Augustanism, as applied to Stuart England. The
term 'Augustan Age' was perhaps coined by Francis Atterbury (who is discussed
below, in Chapter 4), in his preface to the second part of Waller's poems (1690).[9]
These considerations form part of the background to Alsop's poetry; to them
must be added some notes on the previous development of lyric poetry, and the
long tradition of Latin in Britain.

---

[7] Sir F. Kynaston, *Amorum Troili et Creseidae* . . . (Oxford, 1635): cited in Binns, p. 254.
[8] Binns, p. 257, citing C. Spurgeon, *Five Hundred Years of Chaucer Criticism and Allusion, 1357–1900* (Cam-
bridge, 1960), 2. 159.
[9] See H. H. Erskine-Hill, *The Augustan Idea in English Literature* (London, 1983), pp. 223, 244–5, 247.

Some Horatian predecessors

Horace was surprisingly little imitated in antiquity, at least among surviving authors. Statius, in a few of his *Silvae*, and the fourth-century poet Ausonius, are the most significant borrowers of his lyric metres. Neither of them was primarily concerned with following Horace's lead. The Renaissance produced rather more Horatian imitators, both foreign and English. None is more impressive than Alsop, but they do offer precedents and parallels for his poetry. He was not creating a new form of Neo-Latin, but transforming an existing genre. There is some lyric verse in Elizabethan Latin. Even Alsop's favourite literary form, the lyric epistle, is found in the work of John Brownswerd (d. 1589), an influential schoolmaster.[10] William Gager (1555–1622) was the centre of a cultured literary group at Christ Church, which can be compared to Alsop's later circle. 'Almost alone among his contemporaries Gager cultivated the forms of the alcaic and sapphic odes and the Horatian style.'[11] An oddity, from rather later than Gager, is Andrew Melville's use of the sapphic metre for an extended polemic, *Anti-Tami-Cami-Categoria* (written *c.* 1603, published 1620).

The ode was also important in Continental Neo-Latin; lyric verse was written, for example, by Campano, Filelfo, Pontano, Marullo, Navagero, Ariosto, Flaminio, Celtis, and Macrin.[12] Campano made good use of repetition (a technique that Alsop also favoured); direct influence on Alsop seems unlikely, although Campano was printed in Alsop's lifetime (e.g. a Leipzig edition, 1707). Pontano, like Alsop, had a strong preference for sapphics. Macrin's eroticism is an interesting parallel to Alsop; again, it is probably not a direct influence. Much foreign Latin was read in England; although it is rarely possible to identify borrowings from Neo-Latin authors with any confidence, their work will have encouraged Englishmen to write in Latin. The most influential of the Neo-Latin lyric poets was Casimir Sarbiewski, sometimes called 'The Polish Horace'. His popularity exerted a general influence on the lyricists of late seventeenth-century England: Alsop himself was no doubt aware of Casimir, but did not choose to follow him closely.[13]

[10] Bradner, pp. 33–4.
[11] Bradner, p. 62 (Gager's odes quoted, pp. 62–4; an asclepiadic ode by W. Whitlock, another member of Christ Church, pp. 66–7). Gager as dramatist: Binns, pp. 127–31; C. F. T. Brooke, 'The Life and Times of William Gager', *Proceedings of the American Philosophical Society* 95 (1951), pp. 401–31.
[12] See Ijsewijn's *Companion* for brief discussion and bibliography; examples in A. Perosa, J. Sparrow, eds., *Renaissance Latin Verse* (London, 1979) or F. J. Nichols, *Anthology of Neo-Latin Poetry* (New Haven, 1979). On the ode, see C. Maddison, *Apollo and the Nine* (Baltimore, 1960).
[13] M. S. Røstvig, *The Happy Man* (Oslo, 1954–8); A. O'Malley, 'Sarbiewski, poet and Priest', *Ecclesiastical Review* 55 (1916), pp. 145–54 (p. 146: used as a textbook); H. E. Wedeck, 'Casimir, the Polish Horace', *Philological Quarterly* 16 (1937), pp. 307–16; G. Starnawski, 'De Matthia Sarbievio in Britannia recepto quaestiones selectae' in O. Dilke, G. Townend, eds., *Acta . . . Conventus Sexti Latinis Litteris Linguaeque Fovendis* (Kendal, 1986), pp. 158–60.

The issue of possible influences is something of a minefield, through which a scholar might be well advised to travel with caution. It is central to the study of Neo-Latin, since a large proportion of later Latin writers imitate their predecessors in some respects. This imitation is often combined with considerable originality. Very often, the debt is general, to a traditional genre or subject; very often, also, it takes the form of an allusion to a specific passage of ancient or modern literature. It is wise to be sceptical: 'one must not too rashly leap in to identify allusion on the basis of verbal similarity or identity. One tends to forget too easily that the strict prosodic and metrical rules and the selected vocabulary with which Latin poets usually operate will almost inevitably generate the same expressions in the same places in the verse . . .'.[14] In other words, there need be no reason to attach particular significance to a few words in a Neo-Latin poet that happen also to have been used by an earlier writer. The 'borrowings' may be wholly coincidental. They may have been the result of a vague memory of earlier reading, perhaps in a commonplace book, a *florilegium*, or another aid to composition, rather than in the original author. Large amounts of Virgil, Horace, Ovid, or indeed a modern poet such as Mantuan, once absorbed at school, might remain in the recesses of the mind, to be dredged up unconsciously for later use. A conscious, deliberate allusion is quite another matter; the search for allusions can tell us much about the poet's aims and technique, so long as we have not only identified its source, but also demonstrated its familiarity.

One can be fairly confident about allusions to classical 'tags', phrases made familiar by regular quotation. Having demonstrated that an allusion was intended, one may then speculate about its function. There have been some interesting attempts to show that Neo-Latin poetry can be a source of deliberate allusions; Pope Urban VIII, for example, could have been echoed in seventeenth-century England.[15] Another possible, but unverifiable, Continental influence is the 'vast quantity of lyric poetry' of the Arcadian societies formed in memory of Queen Christina of Sweden.[16] Marvell's Latin tribute to Queen Christina (while she was still on the throne) is discussed in Chapter 2. One may reasonably doubt individual assertions of influence, but 'it must not be forgotten that renewed interest in Neo-Latin poetry is part of the Augustan scene'.[17]

[14] J. Ijsewijn, in P. Godman, O. Murray, eds., *Latin Poetry and the Classical Tradition* (Oxford, 1990), p. 222.
[15] J. Sparrow, 'A Horatian ode and its descendants', *Journal of the Warburg and Courtauld Institutes* 17 (1954), p. 359. Urban is praised by J. Duport, *Musae Subsecivae* (Cambridge, 1676), p. 75, and E. Hannes, in *Musarum Anglicanarum Analecta* 1 (1692), pp. 292–4 (mentioned in Ch. 2). Cf. A. Moss, *Printed Commonplace-Books and the Structuring of Renaissance thought* (Oxford, 1996).
[16] G. Highet, *The Classical Tradition* (Oxford, 1949), p. 176.
[17] I. D. McFarlane, *Renaissance Latin Poetry* (Manchester, 1980), p. 12.

From a medieval tradition to the Renaissance

There is no space here for more than the briefest summary of a huge subject. Some awareness of medieval Latin is helpful for the study of what follows. The distinction between Neo-Latin and medieval writing is important, but not always clear-cut. Medieval-style poetry, in rhyming and accentual verse forms, is sometimes written after the Renaissance (although generally confined to minor pieces of archaising wit).[18] Quantitative poetry (in which the length of syllables is determined by a fixed set of rules, not a stress accent), as practised in ancient and modern Latin, did not disappear in the medieval world. The Leonine hexameter combines quantitative rhythm with internal rhyme; although characteristic of medieval verse, it can be found later (isolated examples are probably accidental).

The Latin literature of the European Middle Ages was varied and vigorous.[19] Much of the best British writing was in prose, from the sixth-century historian Gildas, through Bede, to William of Malmesbury, Geoffrey of Monmouth, John of Salisbury (also a didactic poet), Matthew Paris, and Gervase of Tilbury. Roger Bacon exemplified the aggressive and inquisitive philosophy of the thirteenth century. Not all the early verse writers are entertaining; Aldhelm wrote Latin 'with little trouble and no distinction . . . it is useless to give quotations, for they could not convey an impression of interminable dullness.'[20] Alcuin, in the eighth century, wrote copiously in verse and prose. Latin verse satire flourished in twelfth-century England. Joseph of Exeter wrote an epic on the Trojan war, based not on Homer but on 'Dares Phrygius', that includes some fine writing. Christian 'sequences' produced memorable outpourings of lyric poetry (though a very different sort of lyric poetry to Horace's quantitative stanzas). Serlon of Wilton, on the other hand, wrote licentious verse in his youth, using Leonine hexameters and brilliantly immoral, Ovidian, elegiacs.

The Renaissance affected northern Europe rather later than Italy; in England, the middle of the sixteenth century marks the beginning of a vigorous Neo-Latin literary culture. Thomas More was not only a great man in the state, but also a great Latin author, a friend of Erasmus, through whom the Renaissance spirit was strengthened. By the end of that century, several Latin writers of real distinction had arisen. All parts of Britain were affected; in the kingdom of England, one of the leading authors was the Welshman, John Owen, whose

---

[18] See Binns, pp. 57–8, on survivals of medieval Latin verse forms.
[19] A readable introduction, continuing to the age of Milton: F. A. Wright, T. A. Sinclair, *A History of Later Latin Literature* (London, 1931); much drier and more technical: K. Strecker (trans. R. B. Palmer), *Introduction to Medieval Latin* (Dublin and Zurich, 1968); see also various anthologies, and the works of F. J. E. Raby on *Christian* and *Secular Latin Poetry* (Oxford, 2nd edn. 1953, and 1934). A recent study: A. G. Rigg, *A History of Anglo-Latin Literature* (Cambridge, 1992).   [20] Wright and Sinclair, p. 125.

epigrams were frequently reprinted, and circulated widely on the Continent as well as in Britain.[21] In Scotland, the outstanding Latin poet was George Buchanan, who spent much of his life abroad, and also gained an impressive European reputation.[22] Poets who also wrote in English, such as Thomas Campion,[23] often chose Latin for their most substantial work.

William Shakespeare and Ben Jonson

For a modern audience, there is no question that Shakespeare is the most celebrated author of his (or any) age. This is an anachronistic judgement. On the continent of Europe, English vernacular writing was then an incomprehensible irrelevance, and the high culture of England was more deeply concerned with Neo-Latin than the popular theatre (which is not to deny the value of theatre as a relaxation for the noble and learned).[24] Nor did the seventeenth century accord Shakespeare the prominence that has since become orthodox. The more obviously classical Ben Jonson had an equal, if not greater, reputation as a dramatist.[25] It is in a poem of Jonson's in praise of Shakespeare's great achievement that we find the most celebrated quotation about Shakespeare's modest learning. There is little doubt that Shakespeare was actually equipped with a respectable classical education.[26] Jonson sees the great Greek tragedians as fit company for his friend:

> . . . And though thou hadst small *Latine* and less *Greeke*,
> From thence to honour thee, I would not seeke
> For names; but call forth thund'ring *Aeschilus*,
> *Euripides*, and *Sophocles* to us . . .[27]

While full of genuine admiration for another's theatrical talent, Jonson does hint that his own Latin and Greek are far superior. The tradition that Shakespeare

[21] Bradner, pp. 86–90; Binns, p. 109, etc.; modern edition by J. R. C. Martyn (Leiden, 1976–8). Cf. J. Powell, 'De Iohanne Audoeno, scriptore epigrammatum Cambrobritannico', in O. Dilke, G. Townend, eds., *Acta . . . Conventus Sexti Latinis Litteris Linguaeque Fovendis* (Kendal, 1986), pp. 130–4.

[22] Bradner, pp. 130–48; Binns, p. 100, etc.; I. D. McFarlane, *Buchanan* (London, 1981); P. J. Ford, *George Buchanan, Prince of Poets* (Aberdeen, 1982).

[23] J. W. Binns, in J. W. Binns, ed., *The Latin Poetry of English Poets* (London, 1974), pp. 1–25.

[24] The Latin university drama was a major influence in the development of vernacular plays, and hence on Shakespeare; cf. Binns, pp. 120–40.

[25] See, e.g., D. H. Craig, *Ben Jonson: the Critical Heritage, 1599–1798* (London, 1990); G. E. Bentley, *Shakespeare & Jonson: their Reputations in the 17th century Compared* (Chicago, 1945); A. Barton, *Ben Jonson, Dramatist* (Cambridge, 1984).

[26] See the thorough study of T. W. Baldwin, *William Shakspere's Small Latine and Lesse Greeke* (Urbana, IL, 1944); also J. E. Hankins, *Backgrounds of Shakespeare's Thought* (Hassocks, 1978).

[27] Cited and discussed by Baldwin, vol 1, p. 2; it implies at least some Greek, which in turn requires good Latin, pp. 12–13; cf. ch. 49, 'Shakspere's lesse Greeke', 2. 617–61.

was actually ill-educated was formed after the Restoration, and grew to be generally accepted in the following century.[28] Terence, Mantuan, and Palingenius (an ancient dramatist, and two Neo-Latin poets) were commonly read in the Elizabethan classroom, and the young Shakespeare must have encountered them.[29] He will also have looked at Ovid, a major influence on his later works, and tried his hand at the composition of Latin verse.[30] If such exercises were to be done well, more than mere imitation was required: some real poetry was created.[31] Nevertheless, it was Jonson rather than Shakespeare who cultivated a truly classical taste.

Ben Jonson saw himself, and was seen by his contemporaries, as an author deeply imbued with the classics. He borrowed classical phrases, redolent of Augustan authority, for display on triumphal arches, and for other purposes.[32] One such was not strictly speaking Augustan (except in the sense that a long succession of later emperors added *augustus* to their titles): he quotes Martial's sycophancy towards Domitian (8. 36. 11–12), presumably without intending to link the king too closely to that widely detested emperor. Observers might recall that Martial began his poem with a nod to Horace's famous claim to poetic immortality.[33] Horace was, alongside Virgil, the great Augustan model. Jonson's general Augustanism (and presentation of himself as Horace in *Poetaster*), rather than any exclusive devotion to Horace as compared with other models for imitation, led to him being dubbed 'the English Horace'; it is not necessarily a compliment, but a term used ironically by his enemies (often both bitter and facetious), and in jest by his friends.[34] Jonson's translation of Horace's *Ars Poetica*, together with some imitations of Horatian lyric, is evidence of respect for Horace; yet other models also affect his non-dramatic verse, and he is in any case chiefly a dramatist, the English Plautus rather than the English Horace.

The collection of poetry issued to commemorate Jonson's death, *Jonsonus Virbius* (1638), contains Latin as well as English. Of thirty-three items, the last seven are in learned languages, by six Oxford men.[35] Other Latin tributes had

---

[28] Baldwin, 1. 19–74.   [29] Baldwin, 1. 641–81.
[30] Baldwin, 2. 417–55 ('Ovid'); 2. 380–416 ('Shakspere's exercise of versifying').
[31] Baldwin, 2. 406–7, citing Holofernes in *Love's Labours Lost*, 4. 2. 125–31.
[32] Erskine-Hill, pp. 125–6.
[33] Martial 8. 36. 1, 'Regia pyramidum . . .'; Horace, *Carm*. 3. 30. 2, 'Regalique situ pyramidum altius'.
[34] Erskine-Hill, p. 169. Cf. W. D. Kay, *Ben Jonson: A Literary Life* (London and Basingstoke, 1995), pp. 59, 62 (also ch. 3, 'The emerging classicist', pp. 27–42); K. E. Maus, *Ben Jonson and the Roman Frame of Mind* (Princeton, 1984); cf. T. G. S. Cain, ed., *Poetaster* ('The Revels plays', Manchester, 1995). Jonson's admirers could also compare him seriously to Horace: their reasons are worth examination, but fall outside the scope of this survey. Cf. also J. H. Martindale, 'The Response to Horace in the 17th century', unpublished D.Phil. thesis (Oxford, 1977).
[35] One from Magdalen, two from Christ Church, and three from New College (assuming that the last poem, in Greek elegiacs, is also by R. Brideoake of New College); the collection is reprinted in vol. 11 of C. H. Herford, P. & E. Simpson, eds., *Ben Jonson* (Oxford, 1952), pp. 428–81.

been received in his lifetime, including mentions in two sets of liminary verses (i.e., poems on the threshold of a volume) for a Latin play, Hausted's *Senile Odium*.[36] John Selden wrote 67 Latin hendecasyllables for Jonson's folio.[37] These suggest that Jonson was part of a world in which Neo-Latin literature was perfectly familiar, and as natural a medium as English. He was remembered by Neo-Latin writers later in the century; James Duport devotes 70 hexameters to his praise.[38] Jonson himself was well aware of the Continental tradition of Neo-Latin; his library included a good selection of modern writers (with Gruter's anthologies, Buchanan, Secundus, etc.). He may have arranged collections of his English verse in deliberate homage to books of Neo-Latin epigrams.[39]

Although he participated in Latin culture, Jonson's own Latin poetry is not impressive. A few elegiac couplets accompanied his friend Thomas Farnaby's *Juvenal* and *Persius* (1612), twelve iambic lines (along with verses by other friends) ushered in Farnaby's *Seneca* in the following year. Swinburne thought them so bad that they could not be Jonson's: a poor argument, and a harsh judgement on some ordinary pieces of compliment.[40] They do not give him a claim to be a serious Neo-Latin poet. Jonson praised Thomas May's translation of Lucan (1627) in English verse that reads rather more convincingly than his Latin.[41] About half of the funerary inscriptions that he composed are in Latin prose (as one might expect); he was also responsible for the Latin *Leges Convivales*, rules for the good conduct of a drinking club.[42]

The use of Latin for dedications and liminary verses is an important sign of its place in intellectual culture, and also a means of charting the relationships of scholarly friends. Farnaby, for whom Jonson ventured into Latin verse, in turn offered warm support to the Neo-Latin productions of others.[43] John Donne used Latin hendecasyllables to praise Jonson's *Volpone* (1607), and wrote in elegiacs to George Herbert, and to the Oxford scholar Richard Andrews (on the mutilation of a book by children, and its replacement, an unusual reason for academic flattery).[44] Latin was a natural medium for flattery, whether of one's

---

[36] Herford and Simpson, *Jonson*, 11. 349–50; cf. p. 370 (C. Fitzgeoffrey, *Affaniae*: on whom see Binns, p. 393, etc.), p. 383 (manuscript of T. Porter).   [37] Herford and Simpson, *Jonson*, 11. 326–8.

[38] *Musae Subsecivae* (1676), pp. 8–9; repr. in Herford and Simpson, *Jonson*, 11. 536–7 (Duport is mentioned in Ch. 2).

[39] See S. P. Revard, 'Classicism & Neo-Classicism in Jonson's *Epigrammes* & *The Forest*', in J. Brady, W. H. Herendeen, eds., *Ben Jonson's 1616 Folio* (Newark, DE, 1991), pp. 138–67; D. McPherson, 'Ben Jonson's Library and Marginalia', *Studies in Philology* 71 (1974), pp. 3–106.

[40] Texts in vol. 8 of Herford and Simpson, *Jonson* (Oxford, 1947), pp. 381–2; commentary, 11. 135.

[41] Herford and Simpson, *Jonson* 8. 395. On May, see Ch. 2.

[42] Herford and Simpson, *Jonson* 8. 661–6 (inscriptions), 656 (*Leges*).

[43] Binns, pp. 132, 224; the genre of liminary verse, pp. 165–71.

[44] J. Hayward, ed., *Donne: Complete Poetry and Selected Prose* (London, 1962), pp. 325–7; cf. R. C. Bald, *John Donne: a life* (Oxford, 1970; repr. 1986), p. 195, 250.

fellow authors or of the powerful; it could be used and understood by a large proportion of the literate population, including many women, to whose contribution it is instructive to turn.

Female authors

One of the most fascinating prodigies of the seventeenth century was Bathsua Makin, daughter of the London schoolmaster Henry Reginald (or Reynolds, Rainolds: Reginaldus), who married Richard Makin in 1621.[45] At the age of sixteen she published her works, as *Musa Virginea Graeco-Latino-Gallica . . . anno aetatis suae decimo sexto edita* (London, 1616). The book contains a total of more than 250 lines of Latin and Greek poetry. She takes scriptural precedents (*S. Petri* or *S. Pauli Norma . . .*), turned into a variety of languages to show that her breadth of learning includes Hebrew, Italian, Spanish, French, and German,[46] and follows them with poems in Greek, Latin, or (in two cases) French. There are two mottoes on the title page, a couple of cryptic French alexandrines,[47] and a rather more straightforward Greek statement that everything therein has its origin in the Bible. The abiding theme is the divine right of kings, and the subject's duty of obedience. The last poem in the book is typical, celebrating the king's power to punish:

> . . . Nam Princeps scelerum vindex est, ultor ad iram.
> Quisquis iniqua studet, quisquis scelerata tuetur,
> Quisquis in illicitis rebus sua tempora perdit,
> Principis ut gladium timeat paenamque necesse est . . .
>
> For the monarch punishes crimes, avenging them wrathfully; whoever plans injustice, whoever looks kindly upon wickedness, whoever wastes his time in forbidden actions, must fear the monarch's sword and punishment. (lines 5–8)

She ends the poem thus:

---

[45] F. Teague, 'The Identity of Bathsua Makin', *Biography* 16 (1993), pp. 1–17; J. R. Brink, 'Bathsua Reginald Makin: "Most Learned Matron"', *Huntington Library Quarterly* 54 (1991), pp. 313–26. She is mentioned by Binns, pp. 58–9. Bathsua Reginald was first identified with Makin by V. Salmon, 'Bathsua Makin; a Pioneer Linguist & Feminist in 17th century England', in B. Asbach-Schnitker & J. Roggenhofer, eds., *Neuere Forschungen zur Wortbildung und Historiographie der Linguistik: Festgabe für H. E. Brekle* (Tübingen, 1987), pp. 303–18: her poems mentioned, but not discussed, p. 305. Cf. Salmon's *Language and society in early modern England* (Amsterdam, 1996).
[46] Teague calls it Dutch, Brink German; it looks German to me (though most people in 17th century England would not distinguish between the two).
[47] 'The [French] couplet is characteristic of the volume: although ambitious in scope, the poems are not particularly skilful' (Teague, p. 4). I presume her criticism refers only to the French, since she does not quote from a Latin or Greek poem (and gives no evidence of having read them). The use of Latin and Greek is very skilful.

> Scilicet est Regum gladio punire malignos,
> Parcere subjectis et debellare superbos.
>
> Indeed it is the task of kings to punish rebels with the sword, to spare the
> conquered and beat down the proud. (lines 19–20)

The last line is a famous quotation from Virgil,[48] neatly tied to her own
preceding verse.

When she praises Frederick, Elector Palatine, who had married King James'
daughter, Elizabeth, she sees the wedding as a triumph of Protestantism:

> . . . Papa tremis, quidni? tremat hic, timeatque Leonis
>   Rugitum; duplicem qui facit inde metum.
> . . . Roma cave; blanda es meretrix, jam sumere paenas
>   Incipit hoc facto foedere, spretus Hymen;
> Laetus Hymen nobis quos unit pace cupita,
>   Laethifer Italidis, Papicolisque tuis; . . .
>
> You tremble, Pope: and why not? Let him tremble, and fear the roar of the
> lion, who makes a double cause for fear. Rome, beware: you are an
> alluring harlot; now the scorned marriage-god begins to punish you
> with this marriage-treaty; happy is the god who unites us in welcome
> peace, but deadly to the Italians, and your Papists. (lines 7–8, 19–22)

The Thirty Years' War (in which Frederick was soon to lose his throne) was
imminent, and the passionate hatreds of that conflict are foreshadowed by this
young woman, from whose mouth the familiar image of Rome as the whore of
Babylon appears especially shocking. The first of the poems, an encomiastic
dedication to King James, stresses the evils of *Pontifices* and *Papicolae* [Popes and
Papists (lines 7–10)]. The king's supreme spiritual authority is upheld against the
arrogant claims of Rome:

> Cedite sceptrigeris Primatum; ponite larvas
>   Mitrigerique senes, Nitrivomique Lupi . . .
>
> Give up the chief place to monarchs; set aside your hobgoblins, you mitre-
> wearing old men, and gunpowder-spewing wolves. (lines 19–20)

The gunpowder plot (the theme of much Latin verse throughout the century, a
topic regularly set in schools and colleges)[49] naturally receives an allusion,
although she does not dwell on its horror. The four-word pentameter is bold
and vigorous, with two powerful and matching epithets (mitre rhyming with
nitre, skilfully hinting at a logical link).

The message of passive obedience to royal authority recurs again and again; it
provides the opening for the first of the Greek poems:

---

[48] *Aen.* 6. 853.   [49] Some major Latin poems on the plot listed by Binns, p. 457.

Ἄνθρωπον δεῖ πάντα ὑπὸ σκηπτροῖσιν ἀκούειν . . .[50]
A man must obey the monarch in everything.

And a later poem starts similarly:

Ἀρχοῖσιν πρόσεχειν ἐστ' ἀνθρωποῖσιν ἀναγκή . . .
It is necessary for men to obey their rulers.

As a celebration of fanatical loyalty to the throne, the *Musa Virginea* is a splendidly successful production (especially if one considers the author's age and sex). George Eglisham, a Scottish physician at James's court, commended her work in an epigram; he could be a harsh critic, deriding Buchanan's style in his *Poeticum Duellum* (1618).[51] The young Makin also wrote on shorthand.[52] She remained a royalist, and her devotion was rewarded, in the 1640s, by the post of tutor to Princess Elizabeth; at the age of nine, her young pupil could read Latin, Greek, Hebrew, French, and Italian, a tribute to Makin's learning and teaching ability.[53] She was still teaching in her seventies, when her influential *Essay to Revive the Antient Education of Gentlewomen* (1673) acted as an advertisement for her school.

As an octogenarian, Bathsua Makin continued to write Latin verse, sending a poem in twelve lines of elegiacs (with a title in Greek) to Robert Boyle, the natural philosopher.[54] She alludes to Horace's famous opening to *Carmina* I. I, in praise of his great patron, changing the last word to fit a pentameter rather than an asclepiadic line: 'Maecenas atavis edite nobilibus' [you are a Maecenas, descended from noble ancestors (line 2)]. A remarkable woman, she is wholly at home in Neo-Latin culture.

Other seventeenth-century women were also quite capable of using Latin poetry. Among fourteen sets of liminary verses for a beautifully illuminated Italian astronomical treatise are at least four pieces by English women, including six lines of Greek elegiacs by Mildred Burghley, and twenty of Latin elegiacs by Catherine Chilligrew (or Killigrew).[55] Another remarkable female author was Elizabeth Weston,[56] whose works were published and much celebrated on the Continent (she lived and wrote in Prague). A few women, such as Anne Conway, took an active interest in natural philosophy, at a time when Europe's chief

---

[50] Her Greek accents are erratic (as was common at the time); I leave them uncorrected. In other respects, her competence is remarkable.
[51] Brink, p. 317; cf. Binns, pp. 58, 103–4.   [52] Date uncertain, but before 1619: Salmon, p. 305.
[53] Teague, pp. 6–7.   [54] Royal Society, *Boyle Mss.* 4. 6–7.
[55] Cambridge University Library, ms. Ii. 5. 37. Another of the contributors is Pietro Bizarri (Peter Perusinus), a writer of verses on Bucer in 1551 (Binns, p. 459). On the women's verses, see L. Schleiner, *Tudor & Stuart Women Writers* (Bloomington and Indianapolis, 1994), pp. 41–2: Lady Hoby's Greek quoted (with erratic breathings and accents), and 'Lady Bacon's Latin hexameters', by which she means elegiac couplets; other Latin and Greek poems by women in appendix, pp. 205–49.
[56] Binns, pp. 110–14; Schleiner, pp. 96–106.

medium for intellectual exchanges was Latin. While the vast majority of British Latin authors were men, as is inevitable given the predominant position of male schools and universities, one should not forget that both sexes could be part of the tradition.

Intellectual culture under Charles I

As Binns has shown, the reigns of Elizabeth (herself a learned woman, the composer of Latin speeches) and of James I were ages of predominantly Latin culture at the highest levels of society and literary achievement. The same is true of the following reign (with which, up to 1640, Binns also deals). In these years Latin verse was flourishing at the universities; a host of young men saw their commendatory poems in print (as discussed in Chapter 9), and the Latin panegyric was a significant part of the divine mystique that surrounded royalty. The young Milton was composing freely at Cambridge; his poems, published after the civil war had brought about the collapse of that royal image, are discussed in Chapter 2.

Major, serious English poets continued to turn to Latin for deeply felt poetic statements. Chief among these were Herbert and Crashaw,[57] both of whom displayed their Christian devotion in passionate Latin epigrams. Herbert also engaged in controversial debate, attacking the Scot Andrew Melville in verse. As Cambridge's public orator, he had written numerous Latin speeches and letters. Crashaw admired the pastorals of the schoolmaster William Hawkins;[58] Phineas Fletcher wrote marine eclogues (in the Neo-Latin tradition of Sannazaro) in both Latin and English. Important medical and philosophical writing remained in Latin. Francis Bacon, who lived to see the start of Charles' reign, had been a truly bilingual philosopher; his Latin is clearer and more elegant than his English, a more natural medium for the fluent expression of his thought, and 'usually much easier to read'.[59] This is an indication of the essential place of Neo-Latin in intellectual life. When we turn, in the next chapter, to an examination of the writers of the latter part of the seventeenth century, we can observe the development of a tradition that was already firmly established.

[57] See W. H. Kelliher, 'The Latin Poetry of George Herbert', and K. J. Larsen, 'Richard Crashaw's *Epigrammata Sacra*', in J. W. Binns, ed., *The Latin Poetry of English Poets* (London, 1974), pp. 26–57 & 93–120. In Scotland, under Charles I, Arthur Johnston established a great reputation, his psalm paraphrases rivalling those of Buchanan.   [58] Bradner, p. 76.   [59] Binns, p. 298.

2
From the Rebellion to the Revolution

Two periods of political upheaval dominate the history of the seventeenth century, the Great Rebellion and the Glorious Revolution. The first of these periods lasted for almost twenty years, with a series of civil wars followed by Cromwell's republican (or pseudo-monarchical) government, and finally the Restoration of 1660. The Revolution might seem to have been over much more rapidly, its civil war largely confined to Ireland, and its changes more enduring because less extreme. Had there been a second Stuart restoration, as so many Jacobites wished, appearances would have been different. The Revolution might then have seemed, like the Rebellion, no more than a lengthy episode of chaos, before the return of normality. As will be seen in the following chapters, Jacobitism was a vital factor in British Latin culture. The beginning of the Rebellion and the Revolution settlement lie approximately fifty years apart, and this half-century (c. 1640–90) forms a convenient period for the examination of Latin poetry. It is particularly convenient for the present study, since at the end of it we reach the start of Anthony Alsop's university career.

Prelude to war: May's continuation of Lucan

The significance of Latin verse in the turbulent years leading up to the civil war may well be illustrated by Thomas May's *Supplementum Lucani*. May translated Lucan's unfinished epic into English, adding his own version of the later stages of Caesar's career, his victory and murder. Yet more could reasonably have been added, to cover the further conflicts that ensued, before Octavian could become the unchallenged master of the Mediterranean world, and focus of the Augustan age. May's stopping-point, while not the end of the story, is far more satisfactory than that of the ancient poem. The comparison of the English and Latin versions of the *Supplementum* is an interesting exercise, that helps to demonstrate the importance of the Latin.[1] There are many places where the texts are significantly

---

[1] See R. T. Bruère, 'The Latin and English versions of Thomas May's *Supplementum Lucani*', *Classical Philology* 44 (1949), pp. 145–63.

different; in general, the Latin version is more tightly organised, with some of the less dramatic passages severely pruned, and effective *sententiae* in Lucan's manner used to conclude some sections: 'the *Supplementum* is the mature and definitive version of May's work.'[2]

The English *Continuation* appeared in London in 1630, and had reached a third edition, 'corrected by the author',[3] by 1635; the Latin *Supplementum* was printed in Leyden in 1640, and in London in 1646. Momentous events had occurred between these two Latin editions, making the subject of civil war of immediate topical relevance to English readers. Further drama was to follow, with the execution of the king. May's description of Caesar's end is also relevant to that crisis. Both monarchists and republicans could gain some comfort from the story; the deserved end of a tyrant would appeal to the latter, while the ensuing revenge of Octavian (not covered by May, but familiar to all educated people) provided a parallel for Charles II. Literary interest in Caesar and Augustus, as models for modern kings, long predates the English 'Augustan age'.[4] The seeds of May's growing republicanism can be charted in the harsher attitude towards Caesar, and greater stress on *libertas*, that are found in the Latin.[5] The English was dedicated to the king: '. . . your Maiesties renowned worth, and Heroical virtues (the perfection of mind meeting in you with the height of Fortune) may make you securely delighted in the reading of great actions . . .'. A few years later he was neither secure nor delighted, and May had joined his enemies. May's final lines do not show a striking change of tone between the two versions, but are nevertheless interesting in several respects for a reader of 1648/9 and thereafter; Caesar considers, as he perishes, the positive side of his sudden calamity:

> Interea tacito secum haec in pectore volvens:
> 'Hoc saltem, Fortuna, placet, quod nulla superbo
> Victori capitis nostri est concessa potestas,
> Nec domini jussu pereo. Mactatus iniquis
> Insidiis, quas Roma mihi subjecta paravit,
> Occumbo princeps orbis, numerumque Deorum
> Aucturus posthac.' Tandem, per vulnera mille,
> Spiritus erumpit: saevis qui semper in armis
> Inviolatus erat, violatae victima pacis

---

[2] Bruère, p. 163. There are some interesting passages found only in the English, e.g. the simile of the circulation of the blood in b. 1, written only a few years after Harvey's treatise: Bruère, p. 149.

[3] Bruère, p. 148, n. 17, states that the 2nd edn. (1633) 'is the last revised by the author'. The claim of authorial attention to the 3rd edn. is on the title page of the translation, but may also apply to the continuation.

[4] See H. H. Erskine-Hill, *The Augustan Idea in English Literature* (London, 1983). Cf., on Lucan's influence, N. Smith, *Literature and Revolution in England, 1640–60* (New Haven and London, 1994); K. Sharpe, P. Lake, eds., *Culture and Politics in early Stuart England* (Basingstoke, 1994).   [5] Bruère, pp. 160–2.

Hic cadit: atque togae, quas bello laeserat, aedes
Ipse suo moriens perfundit sanguine Caesar.

In the English version, Caesar had died thus:

Of those great deeds through all the world exprest,
These silent thoughts revolving to his breast:
'Yet has not fortune changed, nor given the power
Of Caesar's head to any Conquerour;
By no Superiours proud command I die,
But by subjected Romes conspiracie;
Who to the World confesses by her fears,
My State and strength to be too great for hers,
And from earths highest Throne sends me to be
By after ages made a Deitie;'
Through many wounds his life disseized, fled
At last; and he, who never vanquished
By open war, with blood and slaughter strew'd
So many lands, with his own blood embrew'd
The seat of wronged Justice, and fell down
A sacrifice to appease th' offended gown.

Charles I did not die after having subdued the world; but he did fall to a conspiracy of his subjects, never owning any superior who might have the right to condemn him. The regicides confessed their fear of him, of his divinely-endowed 'state and strength', when they declared the execution necessary. Most significantly, he was 'made a Deitie' by the Anglican Church. The language of pagan gods is often applied to Christian saints, and the deified emperors are models for dead monarchs in Neo-Latin writing; Charles the Martyr is the perfect example of ancient ideas meeting politicised modern theology. Charles, like Caesar, had been inviolate in war (though much less successful), only to fall in peacetime. The Latin makes this point forcefully, with its powerful alliteration, and juxtaposition of *inviolatus* and *violatae*,[6] in the antepenultimate line. The Latin also gains by ending with Caesar's name. The last word of Lucan's (unfinished) book 10 is *Magnum* (Caesar's opponent Pompey, *Pompeius Magnus*), so there is a neat parallel, as well as the dramatic value of the line itself. The ending of Lucan's book 2 is also close: '. . . Romanaque tellus/Immaculata sui servetur sanguine Magni.' [and the Roman land/Cleare from the bloud of her deare Pompey stand. (May's translation)]. Earlier, 'concessa potestas' may recall two passages of Lucan.[7]

---

[6] Cf. Lucan 7. 94, 'violatae . . . paci'; the juxtaposition with 'inviolatus' seems to be May's idea, not a borrowing from Lucan.
[7] Cf. Lucan 2. 76, 'concessa potestas'; 4. 823–4, 'potestas/concessa est'. The latter is in a prominent position at the end of a book.

From the regicides' point of view, the stress in the final lines on Caesar's crimes against Justice, his attack on the peaceful toga, could be related to the crime of a king who makes war on his Parliament. He is not an innocent sacrificial victim, but the rightful victim of a sacrifice that is inevitable to appease the 'offended gown'. And he violated the peace, by his incessant intrigues. Of all the various literary versions of Caesar's story, May's *Continuation* or *Supplementum* is perhaps the most likely to have been in the pockets of the regicides: certainly it is a more probable influence than Shakespeare's *Julius Caesar*. The Latin version could also circulate widely on the Continent, helping to focus people's minds on issues that were of vital international interest.

One of the most remarkable aspects of the *Supplementum*, as a literary phenomenon, is its regular reprinting in Continental editions of Lucan, from the seventeenth to the nineteenth century.[8] The last of these noted by Bruère is Lemaire's (Paris, 1832); I have a pocket edition of Lucan and Suetonius (London, 1820) that includes it as a matter of course.[9] It could also be read in the elegant Elzevir, edited by Cornelius Schrevelius (Amsterdam, 1658; reprinted 1669).[10] This piece of British Neo-Latin was thought worthy to accompany Lucan's original. May was modest about his *Continuation*, in a Latin epigram prefixed to the English version:

> . . . Desine mirari, Lector, si carmina forsan
>   Ista videbuntur frigidiora tibi.
> Impetus Ingenii felix, ardensque recessit.
>   Hoc tibi defuncti debilis Umbra canit.
>
> Do not be amazed, reader, if this poem should perhaps seem rather cold; the mind's happy and ardent force has gone. The weak shade of a dead man sings this to you.

But it was the living May, not the dead Lucan, who provided the impetus; and the potentially frigid work was soon to be warmed in the flames of war. May's *Supplementum* was his most enduring work: better poetry than his early plays, or narrative poems on historical subjects. As a historian of the Parliament, his influence was inevitably eclipsed at the Restoration. His international reputation for Neo-Latin could survive that, as it could survive the vernacular ridicule of Marvell (a lesser Latin poet, as will be seen below), whose *Tom May's Death* stresses the inept comparisons between Rome and England in which May indulges.

---

[8] Bruère, pp. 145–6; Bradner, p. 71; J. W. Binns, *Intellectual Culture . . .* (Leeds, 1990), pp. 195, 508; A. G. Chester, *Thomas May, Man of Letters* (Philadelphia, 1932).
[9] This edn. numbers the lines of the *Supplementum*, *pace* Bruère's statement, p. 145, that Lemaire was the first to do so.
[10] In the 1669 edn., pp. 531–614; there is also the *Specimen Belli Civilis*, attributed to Petronius, pp. 519–28.

If May's work acts as a literary prelude to the civil war of the 1640s, it is interesting to note that Neo-Latin is used by a passionate partisan to record further civil war about fifty years later. James Philip's *Grameid*, written in 1691, was not printed (as being blatantly seditious) until nearly a hundred years after the events it describes,[11] the campaign of John Graham of Claverhouse, Viscount Dundee, in 1689; Graham died heroically, leading his men in the Jacobite victory of Killiecrankie, and therefore provided a fit subject for a Jacobite epic. Philip begins his work with a clear allusion to Lucan's famous opening, when he sings of 'Bella Caledonios civiliaque arma per agros . . .' [war and civil strife through Scottish fields]. His five substantial books (and part of a sixth) are a comparable achievement to May's, evidence of the continuing vitality of his poetic genre.

Milton's imperfect genius

Although written some years earlier, most of Milton's Latin poetry was offered in 1645 to a public that had experienced civil war. There is no doubt that Milton is the most famous and important writer of English who also wrote significant amounts of Latin verse. The present work is not the place for a detailed reassessment of his Latin.[12] Nevertheless it is appropriate to consider briefly here the nature and extent of his Latin, in the context of other seventeenth century writings, and to compare his achievement with that of Alsop. I believe that Alsop can well sustain the comparison, and is indeed a considerably better and more interesting Latin poet. They did not attempt directly comparable genres: the vast majority of Milton's work is in elegiacs or hexameters, his lyrics quite insignificant compared to Alsop's. But Alsop masters his chosen form, and uses it brilliantly throughout his poetic career, in a way that Milton cannot quite match, despite the fine qualities that he occasionally displays. If we add the English poetry to the scale, it naturally swings back in Milton's favour; yet the weight is by no means all on one side. If Alsop were to receive even a tenth of the scholarly attention lavished on Milton, it would be less than he deserved, but more than the imbalanced canon has previously allowed. I do not wish to

---

[11] Ed. A. D. Murdoch, for the Scottish History Society (Edinburgh, 1888).
[12] I hope soon to make a contribution elsewhere to the enormous Milton industry. D. Bush, 'Latin and Greek poems', is vol. 1 of M. Y. Hughes, *et al.*, eds., *Variorum Commentary* (New York, 1970). *Milton Studies* 19 (1984) is devoted to the Latin poetry: n.b. esp. J. G. Demaray on *In Quintum Novembris*, pp. 3–19; G. Campbell, on imitation in *Epitaphium Damonis*, pp. 165–77; J. B. Dillon compiled the valuable bibliography, pp. 227–303. For some of the industry's more recent efforts, see *Milton Quarterly* 28 (1994), pp. 74–6; from which n.b. M. A. DiCesare, ed., *Milton in Italy* (Binghamton, 1991).

disparage Milton's Latin; it is Alsop's vibrancy, rather than any feebleness of Milton's, that leads to that judgement of their relative merit.

Milton can produce some passages of impressive Latin poetry, whether drawing wholly on his own imagination or adapting phrases from classical models. He realises the importance of grandly rolling language, a characteristic that he transferred to his mature style in English. He describes the music of the spheres as 'immortale melos et inenarrabile carmen'[13] [an immortal melody, a song that one cannot fully describe]. He strives for something comparable himself. At its best, the style is heavenly. Things which are indescribable can sometimes be indescribably bad. Milton's periodic badness tends to be describable, and is described harshly by modern critics.[14] The chief flaws are the result of youthful exuberance: a poorly planned structure (e.g. the relatively feeble conclusion of *In Quintum Novembris*) and excessive use of pagan mythology. Some of the poems seem too long, pointlessly extended (and then abruptly concluded), displaying an array of mythological learning that has little application to the subject at hand. In this he is probably imitating, with rather more enthusiasm than wisdom, the Alexandrian style found in Catullus, Ovid, and other distinguished models (as well as Renaissance notions of *copia*). Careful study of each allusion, indeed, might well throw up a few clever reasons for its presence; such arguments are deployed to elucidate the classics. One may reasonably doubt that the young Milton invariably devoted deep thought to such matters.

Equally, it is at least worth considering whether or not he cared about the possible implications of his allusions. An interesting example is the last line of *Elegia Tertia*: 'Talia contingant somnia saepe mihi' [may such dreams often seize me]: 'a most un-Miltonic howler. It echoes a line from Ovid's *Amores* (1. 5. 26). But while Milton's vision is of the saintly Bishop of Winchester in Heaven, Ovid's was of Corinna in the nude.'[15] Is this simply a howler? Should we howl with laughter at Milton's maladroitness? Or was it Milton who giggled as he wrote it, well aware of its humorous potential? First, one should note that the 'echo' is not particularly close to the Ovid, so that the link may be accidental, no more than a half-remembered idea; the only word that occurs in both is *saepe* [often]. The Ovidian passage is famous enough to make the connection plausible, but commentators have been too eager to treat it as proven. If we do find it plausible, it may not be an isolated reference to sex.[16]

---

[13] *Ad Patrem* 37.
[14] E.g. R. W. Condee, in J. W. Binns, ed., *The Latin Poetry of English Poets* (London, 1974), pp. 58–92; on faults, see pp. 63, 65, etc.   [15] Condee, p. 91, n. 13.
[16] Cf. J. K. Hale, 'Milton playing with Ovid', *Milton Studies* 25 (1989), pp. 3–19; this line is discussed, pp. 10–12, with emphasis on the selection of phrases from Ovid earlier in the poem, on the popularity of *Amores* 1. 5 (e.g. in Marlowe's version), and on Milton's acceptance of the challenge to Christian humanism that is implicit in the imitation of Ovid.

Milton's penultimate line is 'Flebam turbatos Cephaleia pellice somnos' [I wept for the sleep that had been disturbed by Cephalus' whore]. The *pellex* (a fairly strong word for 'mistress') is Aurora, goddess of the dawn. The reference appears a pretentious Alexandrian circumlocution. Dawn may certainly be described without hauling in Cephalus (*Aurorae lumine*, for example, would have filled this particular gap more straightforwardly). Elsewhere, Milton alludes to the story without Cephalus' name, but with sufficient additional detail to indicate his interest in the myth.[17] The story of Cephalus and Procris, their relationship tragically disturbed by the intervention of Aurora, would be familiar from Ovid's *Metamorphoses*; the themes of passion, jealousy, and death are suggested by an allusion to the myth. The word *pellex* (or rather *paelex*) is common in Ovid; we find it in another witty retelling of the Cephalus and Procris story, with the moral that one should not believe too readily in the existence of a rival, who is in this version not the goddess Aurora, but merely Aura, the insubstantial breeze: 'Procris ut accepit nomen, quasi paelicis, Aurae . . .' [when Procris heard the name of the breeze, spoken as if it were a whore's . . .].[18] Her jealousy, this time over nothing at all, causes her death. A reminder of such folly may have been a lesson to Milton's circle.

Of the ideas suggested by Ovid, only the theme of death seems appropriate to Lancelot Andrewes, the cleric lamented in *Elegia Tertia*.[19] Are the others not intended? Milton may be using the phrase loosely, searching only for something exotic. If it is meant to make us think of Ovidian sex, it would prepare us for the possible allusion in the final line. The goddess of love has been rather gratuitously introduced at line 20. The poem begins with Milton's loneliness, without any (male) companion, and is as much concerned with his thoughts and feelings on death as with the bishop. The ecstatic vision of heaven, a precursor to *Lycidas*, is linked to him, but could apply more generally to the poet's emotional state.

Some of his thoughts seem at odds with the pious commemoration of a bishop. Unless he was most insensitive to the resonance of his words, he must have meant an obscure hint at other things; such a hint would have to remain

---

[17] *Elegia Quinta* 49–52; *Il Penseroso* 122–4. He is *Aeolides*/'The Attick Boy'. The former is discussed by Hale, pp. 12–13 ('Paganism is unwavering in this poem', p. 13).

[18] Ovid, *Ars Amatoria* 3. 701 (the story retold, 685–746).

[19] On Milton and death, cf. D. Clay, 'Milton's early poems on death', *Milton Studies* 26 (1990), pp. 25–57. Dillon's bibliography cites (p. 263), on erotic undertones in the second, third, and fifth elegies: W. M. Card, *Milton's Coming of Age* (unpublished Ph.D. thesis, University of Wisconsin, 1936), which I have not seen; other discussions of *Elegia Tertia* listed at Dillon, p. 278. A glib mention in J. Bate, *Shakespeare and Ovid* (Oxford, 1993), p. 25: when Milton 'converted one of Ovid's cries of post-coital bliss into the climax of a vision of Lancelot Andrewes . . . entering into heaven, he was doing something very traditional.' The preceding parallels from Prudentius and Venantius Fortunatus are neither close in time nor particularly convincing. It is a despicable habit to write in library books, but I have some sympathy for the reader who placed an exclamation mark in the Cambridge University Library copy (and added 'tone of embarrassment over self-indulgence' on p. ix); *quod in meo scribas libello, lector benevole, sit saltem non infacetum.*

obscure, if the poem was not to be disgracefully improper, but a friend might notice it. In choosing the word *Cephaleia*, was he aware of the very similar sound of *cephalaea* [a headache]? The word, from the same Greek root as the proper name, occurs in Pliny the elder; it is a more prosaic reason for sleep to be disturbed. With very little alteration we might read 'Flebam turbatos cephalaea et pellice somnos' [I wept for the sleep that had been disturbed by a headache and a whore]: the sort of joke that witty youths of seventeen might enjoy, a subversive misreading of a dull and worthy original. It might also be 'a whore in the head' (from the Greek adjective, *cephalaios*), an imaginary fantasy that keeps the young man awake, or even 'my chief whore', out of an imaginary harem (taking *cephalaios* in its common Greek sense of 'principal, most important'). Is there any significance in the choice of *contingant* in the final line? It can have various nuances of meaning, like most verbs; among them, the idea of being defiled by touch, or tasted, or moistened. These senses are not incompatible with immoral amusements in the night, with or without female assistance.[20] Ovid uses *proveniant* [happen, turn out well], a slightly different expression, for his hopes of further sleazy afternoons: Milton is at least choosing a new word, even if the choice is random.[21]

If the link with the *Amores* is intentional, Ovid's penultimate line repays some attention: 'Cetera quis nescit? Lassi requievimus ambo.' [Who does not know the rest? We both lay back, exhausted.] He wittily avoids a description of sex itself, leaving it to the reader's by now excited imagination. The poet relies on the reader's sophistication, and ability to supply what the poet has omitted: in effect, the most essential part has been left out, and an inexperienced reader is left in deserved ignorance. Milton seems to be asking his own reader the same question, 'Cetera quis nescit?'; by implication, there is more here than meets the eye, but sexual details must be left to those who already know them.

These speculations about the potential implications of a few lines are somewhat fanciful, and I do not put them forward as a coherent theory. How sophisticated can we assume a young poet to be? He is not himself wholly coherent; his poems may contain separate ideas, incoherently juxtaposed. In reading a brief passage as a possible hint of eroticism, one need not assume elaborate sub-texts throughout his work. Nor is it wholly safe to accuse him of a childish howler, if his words seem to imply a surprising link with an alternative literary genre. A healthy erotic interest in Britain's native talent appears in *Elegia Prima*.[22] There is an obvious sexual charge to *Comus*, in which he can enjoy the presentation of immoral doctrines (as well as their refutation): 'mutual and

[20] *Turbatos* may even have its resonances; cf. Martial 14. 203. 2, 'Masturbatorem fecerit Hippolytum.'
[21] He may be recalling Tibullus 1. 1. 49 (not 48, as in Bush *Variorum*, p. 14).
[22] Lines 53–72; cf. Condee, pp. 61–2.

partaken bliss'.[23] Similar exuberance of emotion characterises his friendships, as presented in poetry. Both *Lycidas* and *Epitaphium Damonis* are set in the imaginary world of the eclogue, familiar from Renaissance Latin as well as Virgil.[24] When he alludes to Virgil's 'hic gelidi fontes . . .' [here are cool springs],[25] it may therefore be significant that, in Virgil, we are concerned with sex, the cool springs providing the environment for love, with which Gallus tries to attract the girl, Lycoris. Love in the *Eclogues* is as much homosexual as heterosexual; the second eclogue notoriously dwells on Corydon's passion for beautiful (and male) Alexis, and in the tenth we have a parenthesis explaining that Amyntas, though *fuscus* [dark], is still attractive. Milton must certainly have remembered this, when he calls Amyntas *pulcher* [beautiful], the only one of the four male shepherds mentioned immediately before 'hic gelidi fontes . . .' to be given an epithet. Amyntas ends three lines in Virgil; the prominent position is virtually dictated by the name's metrical value, but it is nevertheless striking that Milton also uses it.

Are we to think that the beautiful Amyntas is paralleled among Milton's friends? The invitation to Lycoris, in this sexually ambiguous world, can be made to a man as well as a woman. The closeness of Milton's friendship for 'Damon', Charles Diodati, is obvious; its precise nature is unclear, but the subtle use of Virgil does suggest an intentional homoerotic undercurrent to the poetry.[26] If so, yet another possible reading of *Elegia Tertia* arises. 'Cephaleia pellice' might mean 'a Cephaleian whore', i.e. 'a (male) whore like Cephalus'; *pellex* can be used of men (most famously of Julius Caesar, in a text that Milton's contemporaries were quite likely to know).[27] Again, the interpretation must not be stressed. Milton's Latin poetry is sufficiently varied to convey a wide range of ideas, not necessarily consistent with each other or with his English verse, in a variety of forms.

Some experimentation with form can be seen at the very beginning and end of his published Latin verse. He begins, at the age of sixteen, with an ode in twelve alcaic stanzas, *In obitum procancellarii medici*; he does not persevere with the Horatian lyric, but turns thereafter to iambic forms, as well as the more conventional dactylic ones. *De Idea Platonica*, in 39 iambic lines, is more substantial

---

[23] *A Maske presented at Ludlow Castle . . . (Comus)* 740. Discussion of *Comus* can sometimes stress the purer aspects, e.g. A. Guibbory, 'Donne, Milton, and Holy Sex', *Milton Studies* 32 (1995), pp. 3–21.

[24] On Milton and the bucolic genre, cf. W. C. Watterson, '"Once more, O ye Laurels": *Lycidas* and the Psychology of Pastoral', *Milton Quarterly* 27 (1993), pp. 48–57.

[25] *Epitaphium Damonis* 71–2; *Eclogue* 10. 42–3; cf. Condee, pp. 84–5, praising Milton's subtlety.

[26] On Milton's confused sexual identity, and homoerotic links to Diodati, see J. T. Shawcross, 'Milton and Diodati: an essay in Psychodynamic Meaning', *Milton Studies* 7 (1975), pp. 127–63; Watterson is sceptical of his approach (p. 56, n. 12). Indeed, one might as a general rule be wary of anything with 'psycho-' in its title. Cf. also M. Adams, 'Fallen Wombs: the origin of Death in Miltonic Sexuality', *Milton Studies* 29 (1992), pp. 165–79.   [27] Suetonius, *Julius* 49; also found in Martial.

than the normal student's attempt at a philosophical theme, and in a less usual metre for such work. But Milton's Cambridge contemporaries were equally capable of varied writing, as is impressively clear from the Latin portion of *Justa Edovardo King* (1638), the commemorative volume in which Milton published his *Lycidas*.[28] Nicholas Felton's huge alcaic ode in that volume, with its 284 lines, rather dwarfs Milton's youthful attempt at the metre. With his final Latin poem, *Ad Joannem Rousium* (written in 1646, published in 1673), we find him experimenting with the irregular ode: not, indeed, his invention, but a type of poetry in which he could seek novel combinations of rhythms.[29] Novelty and ambition remain central to his outlook.

At the end of *Mansus*, Milton declares his intention of recalling *indigenas . . . reges* [native kings], King Arthur and his great-hearted heroes, in all their Saxon-smiting splendour. Opinions on this differ. Bradner sees a 'splendid conclusion', while for Condee: 'It would be difficult to defend the tone of these closing lines, and especially the last line, where Milton is so enraptured by his own apotheosis that he bursts into applause for himself.'[30] One may try to defend them on two counts. First, the triumphant end is arguably still dependent on the earlier conditional clause: all this is only possible if one has *talem . . . amicum* [such a friend] (and has thus not quite forgotten the poem's complimentary function). Secondly, the apotheosis is a classical device that Milton may be adopting with some humour; even if he is entirely serious, he is at least being nauseatingly smug in the company of Horace, and no more mawkishly sentimental than Propertius.

Milton's consideration of the best subject, and language, for his new epic is an important turning point of his career. His choice of English is, notoriously, signalled in the Latin *Epitaphium Damonis*: he is happy to be read by the banks of Britain's native rivers.[31] Here he protests a little too much. To be read by the Thames may be a worthy ambition. He would have had as much chance of making an impact on the Orkney islanders in Latin, and in any case their attention scarcely seems worth the abandonment of a European audience. The *Orcades* are cited more from classical models than from vernacular enthusiasm. For the Romans, they are one end of the known world. To be read there is a marvellous thing, as long as one is also read at other far-flung corners, and in

---

[28] On King's own work, see N. Postlethwaite, G. Campbell, 'Edward King, Milton's *Lycidas*: Poems and Documents', *Milton Quarterly* 28 (1994), pp. 77–111. Cf. also A. T. Turner, 'Milton and the Convention of the Academic Miscellanies', *Yearbook of English Studies* 5 (1975), pp. 86–93. Facsimile edition of *Justa Edovardo King*, with translation and some notes, ed. E. LeComte (1978).

[29] See Bradner pp. 116–17 (on Milton's ode), 102–10 (on other irregular verse); S. P. Revard, 'Ad Jo. Rousium: Elegiac Wit and Pindaric Mode', *Milton Studies* 19 (1984), pp. 205–26.

[30] Bradner, p. 114 (quoting *Mansus* 78–84, 94–100: the gap makes the link less clear); Condee, p. 80. Cf. A. D. Nuttall, 'Milton's Arthurian Epic: *Mansus* 80', *Notes & Queries* 233 (1988), p. 161.

[31] *Epitaphium Damonis* 175–9 (quoted with discussion: Condee, p. 87).

the great empire that lies between; to be read only in the farthest province is merely pathetic. Milton attempts to cover up this disadvantage, but his rhetoric is not quite convincing. We have seen that he was thinking of celebrating the Arthurian legend; his reaction against this earlier thought is seen in the protestation that he is

> Not sedulous by Nature to indite
> Warrs, hitherto the onely Argument
> Heroic deem'd, chief maistrie to dissect
> With long and tedious havoc fabl'd Knights
> In Battels feign'd; . . .[32]

He again protests too much, since this is exactly what he had been intending to do. The zealous literary convert parades his contempt for his previous position. Not content with betraying his own past, he is keen to show his superiority to his ancient models, and has few scruples about the use of distorted plot summaries to do so. A few lines before that attack on Arthurian romance, he has a similarly aggressive defence of his material:

> . . . Sad task, yet argument
> Not less but more Heroic than the wrauth
> Of stern Achilles on his foe pursu'd
> Thrice Fugitive about Troy Wall; or rage
> Of Turnus for Lavinia disespous'd,
> Or Neptun's ire or Juno's, that so long
> Perplex'd the Greek and Cytherea's Son; . . .[33]

He is here deliberately simplifying the plots of Homer and Virgil, so as to make them seem less heroic than his own. He was well aware that there is more to the *Iliad* than Achilles' mistreatment of Hector (the last eighth, roughly speaking, of a very long poem); yet the wrath of Achilles against his own side, a theme interestingly relevant to Milton's own character, Satan, is present from Homer's very first line, and must be implicit in Milton's abbreviated description. The link between the *Odyssey* and the first half of the *Aeneid* is made to seem even closer. The language is more allusive: 'the Greek' must, from the context, be Odysseus, but is otherwise a remarkably unhelpful epithet, applicable to virtually the whole mythological bedlam; 'Cytherea's son' is a rather pointless piece of Alexandrian allusion, saying not 'Aeneas', not 'the son of Venus', but 'the son of the goddess of the isle of Cythera'. Why this particular circumlocution? One might have said the same thing in other ways, without ruining the metre: e.g., 'Perplex'd Aeneas and Laertes' Son'. Does it matter that we mention Aeneas' divine parentage, rather than Odysseus' human origins, in proximity to the

---

[32] *Paradise Lost* 9. 27–31.   [33] *Paradise Lost* 9. 13–19.

wrath of heathen heroes and deities? There is potential significance in every choice of phrase. The links he makes, and implies, between the ancient epics are clever; 'disespous'd', apart from being an impressive word, is as applicable to Menelaus as to Turnus, and so he need not mention that other prime mover of the *Iliad* story, leaving the reader to remember the unedifying details. However he puts it, he is in danger of seeming to protest too much. *Paradise Lost* is a great poem, but it is not better than the *Iliad*; the putative superiority of a Christian 'argument' is not necessarily sufficient to raise his work up to, or beyond, the level of his classical models. The mature Milton is still concerned with the issues raised in his Latin verse, and no closer to solving them.

Andrew Marvell

Marvell, like Milton, established a reputation for Latin verse: 'For Latin verses there was no man could come into competition with him'.[34] One may legitimately doubt this judgement, when looking with hindsight at his whole career. The majority of his Latin poetry is of no more than moderate quality, less interesting than that of some other contemporaries. His status as an English poet does make him significant; Bradner barely mentions him, which is perhaps to neglect his modest achievement. He is very much a bilingual author, deeply imbued with the spirit of Neo-Latin literature. His English work should not be examined in isolation from the Latin; indeed, several of his major English poems were also written in Latin versions (as in the case of Cowley, and others). Scholars have argued about which came first, without reaching any very firm conclusions.[35] In either case, Latin is of the utmost importance to him, whether as the original vehicle for his ideas, or as an alternative medium for their circulation. The different requirements of his chosen forms in each language account for much of the expansion or compaction (characteristic 'economy and allusiveness', in Bain's words) that have exercised the minds of commentators. When the two languages are fairly close, as in the second stanza of *The Garden*, and *Hortus* (lines 7–11), the comparison can still be instructive:[36]

> Alma Quies, teneo te! et te Germana Quietis
> Simplicitas! Vos ergo diu per Templa, per urbes,

[34] Aubrey, ed. A. Clark, *Brief Lives* (Oxford, 1898) 2. 53 (= ed. O. L. Dick (London, 1949), p. 196); cited in C. E. Bain, 'The Latin Poetry of Andrew Marvell', *Philological Quarterly* 38 (1959), pp. 436–49.
[35] E.g. Bain, p. 442 (thinks English first); his flimsy reasoning rejected by W. A. McQueen, K. A. Rockwell, *The Latin Poetry of Andrew Marvell* (Chapel Hill, NC, 1964), pp. 13, 20 (though it is only their 'opinion that the Latin was composed first'). On Marvell in general, see bibliography compiled by J. S. Dees, 'Recent Studies in Andrew Marvell (1973–90)', *English Literary Renaissance* 22 (1992), pp. 273–95.
[36] *Poems*, ed. H. M. Margoliouth, 3rd edn. rev. P. Legouis (Oxford, 1971), pp. 53, 51.

> Quaesivi, Regum perque alta Palatia frustra.
> Sed vos Hortorum per opaca silentia longe
> Celarant Plantae virides, et concolor Umbra.

The short lines of the English immediately give a different effect:

> Fair quiet, have I found thee here,
> And Innocence thy Sister dear!
> Mistaken long, I sought you then
> In busie Companies of Men.
> Your sacred Plants, if here below,
> Only among the Plants will grow.
> Society is all but rude,
> To this delicious Solitude.

The Latin passage opens with a neat rhetorical effect, the chiasmus made possible by the repetition of *te*. While the English begins its second sentence with 'Mistaken long', the Latin saves *frustra* for the end of the sentence. Both are dramatic positions, neither necessarily better than the other. The Latin word could well have come earlier (e.g. in the place of *Regum*). He follows that final adverb with another, *longe*, in the next line, emphasising them both by the juxtaposition. The 'busie Companies of Men' and 'Society' appear in the Latin as churches, cities, and royal palaces: conventional language, nodding to the ancients (and a rhetorical tricolon, with repeated *per*), but also more specific than the English, and in a potentially significant way. Religion and politics were the great enemies of quiet, a thought which gives the Latin version a slightly sharper edge. In the Latin, too, the plants had hidden their precious quiet (*celarant*, a shortened form of *celaverant*); the idea of secrecy and concealment is appropriate for a turbulent age. The Latin avoids the repetition of 'Plants' ('sacred Plants' is in any case rather contrived). Without venturing too deeply into the tangled thickets of modern interpretation,[37] one may safely say that the two versions are indeed independent (though related), even in their closer passages, and that the Latin has as much to say as the English.

Marvell's most substantial Latin poem (and one without an English version) is the *Letter to Dr Ingelo*. Nathaniel Ingelo was chaplain to Bulstrode Whitlocke, ambassador to Sweden (1653–4), and the majority of the poem is devoted to Sweden, and its Queen, Christina (who was very shortly to abdicate). The poem has the Queen in full control, and likely to remain so:

> Nam regit Imperio populum Christina ferocem,
>   Et dare jura potest regia Virgo viris . . .
> At, si vera fides, Mundi melioris ab ortu,
>   Saecula Christinae nulla tulere parem.

---

[37] See Margoliouth, pp. 267–71, for some views on the English.

Ipsa licet redeat (nostri decus orbis) Eliza,
  Qualis nostra tamen quantaque Eliza fuit.[38]

For Christina rules over a fierce people, and the royal maiden can give
laws to men . . . But (if one can believe it) no age since the beginning of
this better world has ever produced her equal—not even if Elizabeth, the
glory of our own sphere, were to return, though our Elizabeth was so
good and great.

The comparison with Elizabeth is inevitable, and not unreasonable at the time of
writing, even if it looked a little ridiculous a few months later. The poem
becomes more extravagant as it extends itself to 134 lines. The overall verdict
of scholars has not been kind: 'None of these far-fetched comparisons suggests
great originality in the handling of the complimentary epigram.'[39] That is too
much to expect; the mere fact that he thought it worth while to write a Latin
complimentary poem (epigram is hardly the word) on such a scale is interesting
enough. The poem is primarily for Christina's attention, and that of other
important figures; Marvell did not know Ingelo well. Latin was essential for
communicating with foreigners, and could serve just as well with Englishmen.
Such poetry could have a real political purpose, as part of Whitlocke's diplo-
matic effort, especially when directed to a learned and susceptible Queen. The
Latin culture of Sweden, under Christina's patronage, is a source of wonder:

Transpositos Suecis credas migrasse Latinos,
  Carmine Romuleo sic strepit omne Nemus.
Upsala nec priscis impar memoratur Athenis,
  Aegidaque et Currus hic sua Pallas habet.

You would believe that the Romans had migrated, changed into Swedes,
since there is Latin song in every grove; nor is Uppsala spoken of as
unequal to ancient Athens, and her own Athena keeps her aegis and
chariot here. (lines 75–8)

This northern Athena is, naturally, the Queen: a piece of flattery, but a well-
judged one. The intellectual revival of the north was real (Marvell did not need
to say how much grander Uppsala was than the Athens of the 17th century), and
to celebrate it in such words is no more far-fetched than any other commem-
orative verse of the period. The hope that Christina might emulate the recent
heroism of Gustavus Adolphus is also reasonable (if not to be fulfilled):

Ingens Virgeneo spirat Gustavus in ore:
  Agnoscas animos, fulmineumque Patrem.

[38] Lines 15–16, 21–4; Margoliouth pp. 104–7 (text), 314–19 (notes).
[39] Bain, p. 449. See also M. Stocker, 'Remodeling Virgil: Marvell's new Astraea', *Studies in Philology* 84 (1987), pp. 159–79.

> The great Gustavus breathes in this maiden's face: see the spirit of her
> thunderous father. (lines 29–30)

Christina was certainly spirited; it is only when he trawls through mythology
that Marvell becomes less impressive, and this again is a common feature of such
poetry.

In some of his later writing, under Charles II, Marvell uses Latin to express
strong opinions. In *Bludius et Corona* and *Scaevola Scoto-Brittannus*, 'Marvell
presents criminal acts in a favourable light while castigating the evils of prelatry
and priesthood'.[40] The epigram (of eight lines) on Colonel Blood is very close
to *The Loyall Scot*, lines 178–85, indicating that the sentiment, though strongly
anti-clerical, can be expressed in English. The parenthesis in the fourth line is
more pointed in the Latin:

> (Larva solet Reges fallere nulla magis)
> (No mask is more accustomed to deceiving kings).

The vestments of priests can deceive kings, as Laudian priestcraft led to the
downfall of Charles I; in the English, without an equivalent to *fallere*, we have
merely:

> The fittest Mask for one that Robs a Crown.[41]

Scaevola Scoto-Brittannus is longer (36 lines of elegiacs) and fiercer, without an
English equivalent. Blood was pardoned, and no individual cleric is satirised in
that epigram; from the beginning of the longer piece, we have no doubt of
Marvell's feelings on James Sharp, Archbishop of St Andrews, held responsible
for the torture of his would-be assassin, the 'Scaevola' of the title (compared to
the Roman hero of that name):

> Sharpius exercet dum saevas perfidus iras,
>   Et proprii Pastor fit Lupus ipse gregis . . .
> While faithless Sharp exercises his savage wrath, and the shepherd himself
> becomes the wolf savaging his own flock . . .[42]

This is a violent piece of political invective: throughout his career, Marvell could
turn to Latin to express strong feelings (in this case also seditious ones). The
poem circulated in manuscript: it remained unprinted until Captain Edward
Thompson's edition of 1776, when sufficient time had passed to make it less
controversial. With the Americans even then revolting (and the French soon to
guillotine some of their priests), the fervour of Marvell could still be relevant to
a later age.

---

[40] McQueen and Rockwell, p. 67.   [41] Margoliouth, pp. 178, 184–5 (text), 379 (notes).
[42] Margoliouth, pp. 213–4 (text), 419–20 (notes).

The Horatian influence on Marvell's English lyric poetry is clear, especially in his well-known *Horatian Ode upon Cromwel's Return from Ireland*. He did not choose to imitate Horace in Latin, except in his youthful *Ad Regem Carolum Parodia* (in 13 sapphic stanzas), from the Cambridge collection of 1637, to which he also contributed ten Greek elegiacs.[43] The *Parodia* is a very close adaptation of Horace, *Carmina* 1. 2, a witty gesture of loyalty, demonstrating how applicable the ancient poet's words are to a new Augustus. It cannot, however, be called an independent lyric production; this gap in the range of Marvell's work is symptomatic of the lower place of lyric in British Latin, until its rise towards the end of the seventeenth century. We have seen that Milton, too, attempted Latin lyric only very rarely.

Payne Fisher, congratulating Cromwell

A colourful, if not wholly attractive, figure of the Commonwealth is Payne Fisher, who published various volumes of Latin verse in London;[44] he continued to write after the Restoration, and also later produced studies of church monuments, but is most interesting for his praise of Cromwell and other Parliamentary leaders. He had been educated at Hart Hall, Oxford, and Magdalene College, Cambridge, before joining the king's forces. He changed sides in 1644, shrewdly guessing the direction of the conflict and deserting at Marston Moor.

Fisher's *Irenodia Gratulatoria* (1652)[45] is a good example of his Latin productions during the Commonwealth. It is an attractively produced volume, with two fine engravings of Cromwell; the first offers a reference to Psalm 91: 13, 'Thou shalt tread upon the lion and adder: the young lion and the dragon shalt thou trample under feet', and a Latin motto, 'Duce, et Auspice Christo' [with Christ as leader and director], altering a famous Horatian tag[46] (the reader will remember the preceding *nil desperandum*, and realise that there is no cause to despair in the English republic), and stressing the religious basis of Cromwell's government. The other engraving faces Fisher's grand ode, in 29 alcaic stanzas, *Ad Illustrissimum Britanniarum Polimarchum* [*sic*, for *polemarchum*, 'leader in war'] (sig. K), a more Horatian offering than Marvell's *Horatian Ode*; the motto here is taken from Claudian's *De Laudibus Stilichonis*. Fisher's series of Cromwellian poems looks back to Claudian's celebration of Stilicho, the great general of

---

[43] Margoliouth, pp. 1 (text), 238–9 (notes).
[44] See list in Bradner's bibliographical appendix, pp. 359–62; there is no discussion of him in Bradner's text.
[45] *Aera Salutis Humanae MDCLII, Libertatis Angliae IIII*: a nice example of the new, revolutionary era (which one may compare with French books in the years after their Revolution).
[46] Horace, *Carm.* 1. 7. 27: 'Nil desperandum Teucro duce, et auspice Teucro'.

that age, and forms a modern equivalent.[47] Fisher, who Latinises his name as
'Fitzpaganus Piscator', is himself praised as *Virgilii aemulum vel Virgilium Angligenum* [a rival to Virgil, or the English Virgil] by B. Denham (who follows his
Latin title with thirteen Greek hexameters, a learned piece of liminary verse).

Not unlike Milton (in the passages of *Paradise Lost* quoted above), Fisher
declares his subject to be nobler than those of ancient epic. Cromwell is also
greater than the heroes of prose history: greater than Romulus, Fabius, Themistocles, Hannibal, Hector, Aeneas, *Penelopeus Ulysses*, and Priam (sig. B4):

> . . . licet hos fama inclyta cantu
> Maeonio, procul in totum vulgaverit orbem:
> Fortunate Heros! cui temperat omnia candor:
> Qui virtute animi pompa meliore triumphans,
> Mobile suffragium,[48] populi et plaudentis honores
> Despicis, aeriae damnans crepitacula famae.
> Sic hostes, sic Te, Ductor fortissime vincis: . . .

> . . . although fame has spread their names far and wide, through Homeric
> poetry, to the whole world. Fortunate hero, for whom candour tempers
> everything, who triumphs with virtue of soul, better than pomp, despises
> the mob's fickle votes and the honours that accompany its applause,
> condemning the rattle of airy fame. Thus you conquer your enemies,
> bravest of leaders, and conquer yourself.

Vigorous language is used to illustrate the perennial theme of fame's unreliability: *crepitacula* is an unusual and evocative word. The image of Cromwell's
heroic self-control is powerful, and appropriate for imminent political difficulties. The remaining Rump of the Long Parliament was to cause Cromwell
further irritation, before he did away with it. On that occasion, Cromwell
was to clash with the dedicatee of Fisher's *Irenodia*, John Bradshaw;[49] with
that conflict still in the future, Fisher was keen to link his fortunes not only
with Cromwell, but also with Bradshaw, President of the Council of State, and
the other thirty-nine magnates of the new régime whose names he carefully lists
(sig. A2[v]). Unlike Milton, Fisher is not claiming that his own poetry must be
better than Homer's, merely that his hero is greater than other heroes of verse
and prose; arguably he is right.

The Restoration of 1660, as one might expect, produced Latin verse tributes

---

[47] On classical models, including Claudian, for the English 'Augustans' cf. J. D. Garrison, *Dryden and the tradition of panegyric* (Berkeley, 1975).
[48] The short 'a' is a false quantity by classical standards; but it is found in later authors, and in a variant reading in Ovid, that might act as respectable models: see, e.g., Heinrich Smetius' *Prosodia* (pp. 462, 535 in the London edn. of 1672; an earlier edn., London, 1640, may well have been in Fisher's hands).
[49] See, e.g., G. Davies, *The Earlier Stuarts* (London, 1937; repr. 1945), p. 172. On Cromwellian panegyric, see H. H. Erskine-Hill, *Poetry and the Realm of Politics* (Oxford, 1996), pp. 133–67 (on Marvell's *Horatian Ode*, pp. 160–1).

to the king.[50] While Fisher's career continued after 1660, his greatest days were as Cromwell's Claudian, if not quite his Virgil. Many other writers of the mid-century also deserve notice; one such is James Duport, a leading Cambridge scholar (successively Vice-Master of Trinity and Master of Magdalene), and a fluent producer of Greek verse, as well as Latin. Duport's numerous paraphrases of parts of the Bible in Greek hexameters appeared both during and after the Commonwealth, a sign of continuing interest in such modern literary treatments of sacred texts.[51] Duport also greatly encouraged the production of Latin verse by others; under his mastership, Magdalene became a much more prominently poetic college.[52] Among poets whose main work is in English, we may continue to note both a strong interest in the classics and an occasional use of Latin; thus John Oldham wrote 12 elegiac lines on the death in 1672/3 of John Freind of St Edmund Hall, one of a number of manuscript funeral tributes.[53]

William Dillingham's anthology, and the archbishop

Anthologies provide some useful evidence for the place of Neo-Latin in literary culture. If poems were considered worth reprinting, they had probably also been enjoyed for some time in manuscript form. There were several significant anthologies in the last two decades of the seventeenth century: most notably, *Musarum Anglicanarum Analecta* in the 1690s (and in further editions in the 18th century),[54] and the collection edited by Francis Atterbury in 1684 (discussed in Chapter 4). These were preceded by William Dillingham's *Poemata varii argumenti* [poems on various subjects] of 1678, the first such anthology in England. There had been several major Continental anthologies towards the beginning of the century, the *Delitiae*, edited by J. Gruter (1560–1627), whose English mother taught him Latin, and who studied at Cambridge before returning to the Continent.[55] For Scotland, and a Continental audience appreciative of Scottish Latin, there was J. Scot, ed., *Delitiae Poetarum Scotorum* (Amsterdam, 1637). Some English equivalent was therefore long overdue.

    Dillingham included much of his own work in the book, as well as that of

---

[50] Bradner, p. 360.
[51] He is mentioned prominently, though not praised (no one is) by Dr James Gibbs [not to be confused with the Latin poet discussed below], *The First Fifteen Psalms . . . with a preface . . . on the great and general Defectiveness of former versions in Greek, Latin, and English* (London, 1701).
[52] E. Duffy, in R. Hyam, ed., *A History of Magdalene College, Cambridge, 1428–1988* (Cambridge, 1994), p. 150 (information supplied by myself, as is kindly acknowledged, n. 36, p. 288).
[53] H. F. Brooks, R. Selden, eds., *Poems* (Oxford, 1987), p. 351. This John Freind was from the Bristol area, and was not (as far as I know) a close relative of Alsop's friend (on whom see Ch. 6).
[54] Bradner, pp. 212–16, 363–4.
[55] Bradner, p. 213; J. E. Sandys, *History of Classical Scholarship* (Cambridge, 1903–8), 2. 361.

other British and foreign authors; according to Bradner (p. 205), these were chosen 'without any guiding principle of selection'. He did, in fact, explain his aims in a letter, dated from Oundle, 18 September [16]71, to William Sancroft, then Dean of St Paul's. He intended to make 'a collection of such poems as for variety of matter and elegancy of verse might be profitable and delightfull to scholars of all conditions; and in so doing to revive some pieces of worth yet not like otherwise to be reprinted; to communicate others which are *non tam in vulgus nota* [not so publicly known]; to collect some which lay dispersed, and to publish others not yet printed. In the whole I have regard to the delicacy of the present age, by making choice only of such as have clearness and facility of expression.'[56] His procedure, then, is not quite haphazard. He presupposes the wide availability of much Neo-Latin literature, since he deliberately searches for rare pieces, on the assumption that there is no need to offer pieces already familiar to his intended audience. While many publishers tended to be piratical, he was scrupulous in obtaining the consent of living authors; he was attempting to be a careful and scholarly editor, concerned to provide as correct a text as he could. In the case of his own pieces, this led him to urge Sancroft, on 4 December 1671, to use '*aut limam aut Spongiam* [file or sponge: i.e. polish or rub out where necessary] for though it be printed in a few copyes, yet it is not publick, and so is capable of due correction or reformation, to prevent a more publick Blush'.[57] In the case of a poem by Hobbes, 'by reason of a blott having lost a word', he prefers to omit a line rather than risk a bad conjecture, 'but if you think it fitt, it may be restored (I suppose) out of another copy; for though I could gett no other but this, I heare lately that it is reprinted'.

He places ancient, Renaissance, and contemporary work on an equal footing. He includes the pseudo-Virgilian *Moretum*, and part of Lucan; among later writers we find Grotius, Vida, Erasmus, Beza, Thomas More, and Phineas Fletcher. He proposes to print an epigram of Sancroft with one of Buchanan, 'with whom yours will pare very well . . . and [I] shall be directed by you how much of your name you will give way to have appeare with it'.[58] In the same letter he considers the title *Herberti Poemata* for the book, in recognition of the fact that about a quarter of the final version consists of Dillingham's translations from Herbert (and that quarter 'will be most known'); he also suggests the mixed collection could come under his own name, 'or else under some more general title to comprehend all in one'. These details were being discussed in the later months of 1677, the year in which Sancroft became Archbishop of Canterbury (he was to be ejected, as a non-juror, in 1689); six years after the project

---

[56] Bodleian, ms. Tanner 44, fo. 274.   [57] Bodleian, ms. Tanner 44, fo. 278.
[58] Bodleian, ms. Tanner 40, fo. 109.

had first been proposed, it was still capable of attracting the regular attention of so senior a churchman.[59]

As well as his own Latin versions of Herbert, Dillingham was interested in printing other translations; one that Sancroft sent (of John Denham's *Cooper's Hill*) he thought 'excellent in itself, though having never seen that which it translates I must needs want much of the delight, which I presume would arise from the harmony between the translation and the original. But as it is it may passe for a native of Old Rome were not the subject modern.'[60] Here we see that a fairly significant modern English poem is known to Dillingham only in a Latin version, which he can appreciate for its own virtues, while being curious about its relationship with the English model. Translations had long appealed to Dillingham, who had in 1653 been responsible for publishing Theodore Bathurst's version of Spenser's *Shepherd's Calendar*.[61] Both he and Sancroft continued to be fascinated by a wide range of Neo-Latin literature.

Dillingham's original poems include some very substantial sets of hexameters. *De Moribus Puerorum* runs for all of eleven pages, more than twice as long as his *Campanae Undellenses*, on the Oundle church bells, or *Sphaeristerium Suleianum*, on the bowling green at nearby Sulehay (which may have influenced Addison). He is a rather more serious poet, as well as a more thoughtful anthologist, than Bradner acknowledges.[62]

Sancroft and Dillingham were linked by their membership of Emmanuel College, Cambridge, of which Dillingham had been master, until his ejection in 1662; Sancroft followed him in that post, and their friendship survived their different fortunes thereafter, with Dillingham remaining in retirement at Oundle while his former colleague received further promotion. Archbishop Sancroft's gift to Emmanuel included his personal manuscript copy of a Latin play, *Valetudinarium*, by William Johnson of Queens' College, and also, more interestingly, his commonplace book of miscellaneous epigrams, nearly all in Latin.[63] This book is in Sancroft's hand throughout, but the writing and ink change at times, suggesting that he continued to collect poems at various stages in his life. One poem, on a comet, cannot have been copied earlier than 1680, when Sancroft had already been Archbishop for two years. About a quarter of the book was left blank. Two-thirds of the epigrams were copied from the Latin of the Welshman John Owen, who was enormously popular throughout Europe. The rest include some interesting oddities: extempore

---

[59] Sancroft's own *Soteria Regi et Ecclesiae Anglicanae* (1678) appears in L. Bradner, 'Musae Anglicanae: A Supplemental List', *The Library* 5th ser., 22 (1967), pp. 93–103.
[60] Bodleian, ms. Tanner 40, fo. 14 (cf. fo. 7, 10, 29, 112, 118: further correspondence with Sancroft, exchanging manuscript copies of Latin verse).   [61] Bradner, p. 205.
[62] Bradner, pp. 204–5; he there praises the others, especially *Campanae*, but ignores *De Moribus* (on which see ms. Tanner 40, fo. 112).   [63] Emmanuel ms. 52 (play); ms. 105 (commonplace book).

verses, for example, by a Westminster schoolboy and an undergraduate of St John's, Oxford, the latter's four couplets supposedly being composed in less than half a quarter of an hour, which makes more than a line a minute.

Sancroft's tastes in epigrams are not always holy. The 402nd epigram, for example, which must have been copied when he was archbishop, is about Venice: 'Urbe tot in Veneta scortorum milia cur sunt?/In promptu causa est. Est Venus orta mari.' [Why are there so many thousands of whores in Venice? The reason is simple: Venus was born from the sea.] Eighteen epigrams later we find Stephanus' humorous battle of the sexes: '. . . Quid de me queritur coniux? quod vult, volo (dixit)/Imperium sibi vult: id volo et ipsa mihi.' [Why does my husband complain about me? I want what he wants (she said). He wants to wear the trousers: that's what I'm after as well.] Epigram number 432 is by the English Roman Catholic exile in Rome, James Alban Gibbs, attacking British regicide tendencies: an appropriate choice for a man whose conscience was to prevent him serving William III, but also useful evidence of Gibbs' reputation in High Church Anglican circles. There are a few poems in English, and a macaronic couplet (mixing English and dog-Latin, but preserving the metre) on 'Mr L., one of Oliver's Itinerants in Wales': 'Qui sermonavit vivus sine think, sine thanko/Mortuus in foveam iacitur sine clink, sine clanko.' [Who spoke when alive without thinking or thanking/Is dumped in a pit without clinking or clanking].

The English abroad

Not all the significant Latin writings of English authors appeared in Britain; many arranged publication on the Continent, for a variety of reasons. May's *Supplementum*, as noted above, first appeared in Leyden, and Holland was one natural home for Neo-Latin.[64] Travellers and political exiles alike were also drawn farther afield, especially to Italy. Milton as a youthful poet, or the Earl of Arundel as a collector of art and antiquities, were parts of a long tradition of travel, that culminated in the Grand Tour of the eighteenth century. The most prolific writer of Latin among the exiles was James Alban Gibbs (or Gibbes, Ghibbesius), whom we have seen in Sancroft's book. He is a major poet, entirely overlooked by Bradner.[65] From the 1650s to the 1670s he published poems and orations in Rome, mainly concerned with the life of the Church, and of his medical, scholarly, and ecclesiastical friends. In *Astraea Regnans* (1655), he prints three alcaic odes (from 1652–5), a poem in 64 hendecasyllables (from 1653), and

[64] Although Alsop, in the early eighteenth century, did not find it congenial: see Ch. 7.
[65] Publications noted, but not discussed, in his 'Supplemental List'.

some prose, dated December 1651, all in praise of various papal virtues. The hendecasyllables, *Clementia: de custodia Bibliothecae Vaticanae negata* ['Clemency': on being denied the post of keeper at the Vatican library], are a lively Catullan complaint:

> . . . Quid Romae facerem, tot albus annis
> Fortunae scopus et petitor atrae?
> Iam non blanditias, precesve mitto:
> Turget felle iecur; stat ulceroso
> Sic pulmone frui malos in hostes.
> Huc, huc Hendecasyllabi dicaces . . .

> What am I to do at Rome, a white man[66] for so many years an applicant, a target of black fortune? Now I am not sending flattery and pleadings; bile rises in my liver; I am resolved to enjoy venting an ulcerous lung upon evil enemies; come hither, satirical verses.

The poem concludes with a recantation, since the Pope's decision cannot be seriously criticised; one wonders, though, how sincere he is in suggesting that he did not really want the job anyway:

> . . . Hic tum quae mihi mens benigna venit!
> Quam diversus agor furore primo!
> Quicquid constitui mali, retracto:
> Quicquid perstrepui, dolens recanto:
> Iusti Romulidae; beata Roma;
> Et qui Romulidas, regitque Romam,
> Felix, innocuus, vigilque custos . . .

> Then, what kindly thoughts have come to me here! How different from my first anger! Whatever evil I decided upon, I retract; whatever fuss I made, I sorrowfully withdraw. The Romans are just, Rome is happy; and he who rules Rome and the Romans is fortunate, innocent, and a watchful guardian.

This may be read as Catullan irony.[67] Gibbs is more than a simple sycophant, and can combine panegyric with criticism. Praise of cardinals and bishops, nevertheless, figures prominently in his output, and can include substantial hexameter pieces as well as odes.[68] The English Catholic community is well represented, and he devotes a whole volume of miscellaneous poems to his excitement at the promotion to cardinal of Philip Thomas Howard, poems that he hopes might last longer than the famous marbles of Howard's grandfather.[69]

---

[66] *Albus* is perhaps a pun on his middle name, *Albanus*.
[67] Cf. Catullus' insincere deference to Cicero (poem 49).
[68] E.g. *Iter Barberinum*, about 700 lines, appended to *Astraea Regnans*, pp. 15–38; *Novum Sidus* (Rome, 1656: not in Bradner's 'Supplemental List'), over 300 lines.
[69] *Carmina marmoribus Arundelianis fortasse perenniora* (Rome, 1676).

The anticipation of immortality is characteristic of Horace, and might be expected from a poet who had consciously modelled himself on the ancient master. His lyric poetry appeared in 1665 (and again in 1668), arranged in a format designed to imitate Horace as closely as possible.[70] There are four books of odes, one of epodes, and a *Carmen Saeculare* written for the Jubilee of 1650; even the numbers of odes in each book are chosen to reflect Horace's proportions.[71] The plan is somewhat contrived: he includes in the four books of odes numerous poems in epodic metres that might more naturally have joined the epodes. Nonetheless, the lyric poems are a splendid achievement. The prefatory matter includes the judgement of a critic that 'facile tibi persuaseris, Horatium fuisse superiorum temporum Ghibbesium; Ghibbesium nostri huiusce aevi Horatium.' [you might easily persuade yourself that Horace was the Gibbs of the past, Gibbs the Horace of our age.] The English in his circle included Sir Kenelm Digby and Thomas Farnaby; among the Italians was the painter and satirist Salvator Rosa.

Gibbs had received the degree of MD from Oxford, and the title of laureate from the Emperor Leopold. Ralph Bathurst, MD and President of Trinity College, Oxford, celebrated his glory:

> . . . Et Vaticanae feriant licet aethera Turres.
> Altior ipse tamen . . .
>
> Even though the towers of the Vatican might reach the sky, he is still higher.[72]

That exalted praise was read in the eighteenth century, as the last poem in volume three of *Musarum Anglicanarum Analecta* (Oxford, 1717). Does he rival Alsop as the 'English Horace'? For sheer effort, he is unsurpassed: Alsop never tried so hard. His collection is perhaps too artificially Horatian, while Alsop's approach is natural and unaffected. Gibbs scattered his energies in many other directions; Alsop remained devoted to his own Horatian style. Alsop is wholly and quintessentially English; Gibbs does not quite abandon his English identity, but is primarily a Continental figure. He might be called the European, and Alsop the English, Horace.

Although Gibbs was the most important poet, other Englishmen abroad also

---

[70] 1st edn., Rome (which I have not seen: Bradner's 'Supplemental List', p. 95); 2nd edn.: *Carminum Iacobi Albani Ghibbesii, Poetae Laureati Caesarei, Pars Lyrica: ad exemplum Q. Horatii Flacci quamproxime concinnata* (Rome, 1668).

[71] Book 1 (pp. 1–46), 40 poems; book 2 (pp. 47–80), 25 poems; book 3 (pp. 81–126), 35 poems; book 4 (pp. 127–55), 19 poems; *Epodon liber* (pp. 156–84), 21 poems; *Carmen Saeculare* (pp. 184–7); cf. Horace, with 38, 20, 30, 15, and 17 poems respectively: Gibbs has a few more in each book, but preserves the relative sizes. The rest of the book contains *Clarorum Virorum Symphonia* (pp. 187–220), poems in praise of Gibbs; and an ambitious *Declaratio* (p. 221) of planned publications.

[72] *Carmen in honorem Viri Celeberrimi et Principis Poetarum Domini Doctoris Gibbesii*, lines 13–14.

cultivated literary Latin. William Cartwright, the Oxford poet and dramatist, was among those contributing to foreign collections of commemorative verse.[73] Even more interesting, perhaps, is the occasional organisation of a collection on the initiative of British students and travellers, as in the case of those who found themselves at Padua (whether to study or simply to escape Cromwell) in the early 1650s, and were entranced by the theatrical dissections that they witnessed.

Antonio Molinetti, Professor of Anatomy and Surgery at Padua, was publicly honoured in the years 1650, 1653 and 1654 by the English and Scottish *nationes* of his university.[74] These tributes were probably inspired both by the tradition of commemorative verse in Britain, and, more immediately, by the volume issued in 1646 by the *inclita natio Germana medicorum* [distinguished community of German medical students] in praise of Joannes Veslingius,[75] Molinetti's predecessor. The Germans seem to have been the most prominent, or at least the most efficiently organised, of the foreigners at Padua; thus, they are given pride of place in a contemporary account of the *nationes*, which records one definite instance of the British following a German lead, in their decision to establish a library in 1649.[76] Veslingius himself was a competent poet, who wrote in praise of the Doctoral laureate Joseph Colston of London: 47 lines of Latin iambics, naming Colston in line 26—Tomasinus tells us that Veslingius also praised Peter Videmann of Salzburg at the same New Year's ceremony, but his name is not mentioned in the quoted verses. Tomasinus also quotes a sapphic ode of 20 lines by Veslingius in praise of Padua University and of its Venetian masters, recited on the same occasion.[77] He is one of the contributors to the *Symphonia*, or extended group of commendatory verses, appended to the poems of Gibbs.[78] Veslingius appears to have been a man of remarkable culture, even at a time when it was common to combine an interest in science with some poetic flair; another historian calls the verse quoted by Tomasinus 'elegantissimum, ex quo licet colligere Weslingium non minorem Philosopho fuisse Poetam' [. . . most elegant: from which one can perceive that Veslingius was no less a poet than he was a philosopher].[79]

These poetic tributes, delivered as a part of a festive ceremony, were no doubt a regular part of Paduan academic life. But the collection of laudatory

---

[73] T. Raylor, 'English responses to the death of Moritz the Learned: John Dury, Sir Thomas Roe, and an unnoticed Epicede by William Cartwright', *English Literary Renaissance* 25 (1995), pp. 235–47 (with text and translation by J. W. Binns).

[74] D. K. Money, H. T. Swan, 'Doctors as poets: laudatory verses addressed to Antonio Molinetti by British medical students at Padua, 1650–4', *Journal of Medical Biography* 3 (1995), pp. 139–47. See also, on the British at Padua and elsewhere, A. L. Lytton Sells, *The Paradise of Travellers* (London, 1964).

[75] J. Vesling (1598–1649), originally from Westphalia. Gibbs studied under him.

[76] J. P. Tomasinus, *Gymnasium Patavinum* (Udine, 1654), p. 52.   [77] Tomasinus, pp. 165–7.

[78] Gibbs, *Carmina* (Rome, 1668), p. 204.

[79] N. Comnenus Papadopolus, *Historia Gymnasii Patavini* (Venice, 1726), I. 365–6.

poems addressed to a professor suggests an unusual degree of enthusiasm. Was this enthusiasm, in Molinetti's case, generated wholly by the brilliance of his teaching of anatomy, or by his skill in curing disease? Papadopolus has an interesting note on his career: '. . . Vir fuit plane in arte, quam profitebatur, doctus et felix, quae duo Medicum maxime venerabilem faciunt, ac necessarium vel invitis. Quamobrem Molinettus, quamvis natura dicax, et indole ad quamlibet aliorum censuram liberrimus, passim in usu fuit, evocatusque extra Italiam saepe, muneribus ac beneficiis semper, praesertim a Duce Bavariae cumulatus Patavium rediit . . .' [In the art that he practised, he was clearly endowed with both learning and luck, which two qualities make a doctor revered, and necessary even to those who would prefer to do without him. For this reason Molinetti, despite being naturally sarcastic, and disposed to be very free in his criticism of other people, was continually employed, and was often called away from Italy: he always returned to Padua weighed down with gifts from his patrons, particularly the Duke of Bavaria . . .].[80]

Since Papadopolus is not normally given to making criticisms of the characters of his subjects, his remarks about Molinetti's sharp tongue are particularly interesting (and, since Papadopolus probably conversed with people who had known Molinetti, they are also likely to have some factual basis). It seems, furthermore, that Molinetti was involved in controversy within a short time after his appointment as Veslingius' replacement at the end of 1649. Tomasinus records the following summary of the dispute: '1650. Die 20 Septembris controversia inter Anatomicum, et primae Sedis Philosophum a Senatu Veneto decisa est, ut hoc ordine Cathedrae procedant. Nimirum, Primum locum obtineat Medicinae Theoricae Professor primarius. Secundum Medicinae Practicae. Tertium Primae Sedis Philosophum. Quartum Anatomes professor.' [On 20 September 1650 a dispute between the anatomist and the senior philosopher was decided by the Venetian senate, which ordered that the professorial chairs should have the following order of seniority: the senior professor of theoretical medicine should have the first place; second, should come that of practical medicine; third, should come the senior philosopher; fourth, the professor of anatomy.][81]

Thus, it appears that Molinetti lost his dispute over precedence with his philosophical colleague. The senior philosopher at the time was 'Ioannes Cotunius . . . vir voce et scriptis celeberrimus, cuius copiosa, et erudita Commentaria extant . . . ac de conficiendo Epigrammate Liber, cuius rationem se optime novisse ostendunt Epigrammata Graeca nuper emissa; eloquentiam Viri testantur Orationes diversae; omnia Cedro digna.' [John Cot[t]unius (or Cotugno ?): a man most celebrated both for his speech and for his writings; substantial and

---

[80] Papadopolus, 1. 370.   [81] Tomasinus, p. 465.

learned treatises by him are in existence, as well as a book on the writing of epigrams: the Greek epigrams that he has recently published demonstrate that he understood this art very well; his various speeches prove his eloquence; and all his works are worthy of preservation.][82]

Since Cottunius was notoriously witty, and Molinetti notoriously outspoken, it would be surprising if there was not some battle of words between them, in their clash over status. Cottunius had been appointed in 1637 at a salary of 1,000 florins; this was increased to 1,300 in 1645, and to 1,600 in 1650, the year of the dispute; Molinetti, by contrast, earned only 800 florins at this time. Salary is not the only indication of status, but it does suggest the relative importance accorded by the university to its professors. Fortunius Licetus, senior professor of theoretical medicine, received 1,300 florins; Benedictus Silvaticus, senior professor of practical medicine, 1,200: both slightly less than Cottunius, whom they outranked, but more than Molinetti. One can chart Molinetti's own increasing status in the records of his salary rises: '. . . anno 1652 29 Decembris concessum fuit stipendio quinquaginta Florenorum, ut juvenem sibi auxiliarem eligeret . . .' [On 29 December 1652 he was allowed a salary increase of 50 florins, so that he could choose a young assistant.][83] With increasing responsibilities, his salary continued to rise, until in 1667 he was receiving 1,650 florins, and was among the highest-paid professors. Cottunius, however, also received further increases, and ended on a salary of 1,900 florins (which was exceeded only by the medical scholar Zanfortius, and the literary scholar and orator Ferrarius, who both received 2,000).[84]

Molinetti, therefore, may have been feeling bruised by his battle with Cottunius, and may have welcomed the moral support of the British *nationes*. If the 1650 volume was published before the adjudication from the Venetian senate, it may even have been intended to influence the senators in Molinetti's favour; and if it appeared after Molinetti's defeat, its purpose may have been to demonstrate that he, as well as Cottunius, had his partisans, and that they, like Cottunius himself, could produce elegant verses. At any rate, the British could show that they held Molinetti in the same high esteem as the Germans had held Veslingius. If Molinetti's rivalry with Cottunius continued beyond 1650, it may be significant that Cottunius' Greek epigrams, with Latin versions, were published in Padua in 1653 (this is the recent work referred to by Tomasinus; his *De conficiendo epigrammate* had appeared in Bologna as long ago as 1632). Gibbs wrote an ode, in six alcaic stanzas, in praise of Cottunius, calling him *Alcidem Philellenum* [a Hercules in his love of Greece].[85]

Nearly all of the poems in praise of Molinetti are in Latin. William Sydenham

[82] Tomasinus, p. 307. [83] Tomasinus, p. 304. [84] Papadopolus, 1. 12.
[85] Gibbs, *Carmina* (Rome, 1668), p. 21: book 1, ode 18.

contributed English verses that at times achieve an attractively vigorous effect.
The second half of his poem suggests dramatically that printing should be
overthrown:

> . . . Why should those vast volumes see
> A longer welcome or revived be
> From their decaying ashes? When their owners lie
> Wrapped in the Urns of their mortality?
> No—we'l no longer be enslav'd or tied
> To books enveloped with their authors' pride . . .[86]

This suggests that Molinetti (whose own publications were some distance in the
future) may have been frustrated by the weight of previous, faulty scholarship;
or, at least, that his students felt that they could safely ignore written texts in
favour of the new information in his lectures. Additionally, if the dispute with
Cottunius had anything to do with the collection, this may be an oblique attack
on Molinetti's rival, already distinguished for his publications.

William Pound (in the same book, of 1650) compares both Veslingius and
Molinetti to the phoenix, thus linking them closely together, and emphasising
that the one is the other's natural and fitting successor: the conceit here seems
both appropriate and well executed, and the verse is lively. Pound expresses
modesty about his own powers, towards the end of the poem:

> Anseris at calamo Phoenicis scribere laudes
> Fata vetant. Tanti ac tam clari luminis ictus
> Lumina Bubonis perstringunt sueta tenebris.
>
> But the fates forbid me to praise a phoenix with a mere goose quill pen.
> The beam of so great and so distinguished a light blinds the owl's eyes,
> used as they are to darkness.

Anser implies not only a pen, but also a dreadful poet.[87] This is not the modesty
of youth: Pound, too, was a well-established figure, first inscribed among the
members of Padua University in 1641. The following lines, about the owl, might
be read as continuing the theme of the poet's modesty; they might also be an
attack on Molinetti's owl-like rival, Cottunius. The owl is commonly a bird of ill-
omen in ancient literature; but it is also the bird of Athena, and thus appropriate
for a pedantic Greek scholar, used to the darkness of his antique philosophy.

'N. N.'[88] concentrates wholly on the dissection of the penis, and the tone is

---

[86] [English and Scottish *nationes*], *Absolutissimae humani corporis dissectioni* . . . (Padua, 1650).
[87] Virgil, *Eclogue* 9. 36, 'argutos inter strepere anser olores' [to honk like a goose amid melodious swans].
[88] [English *natio*], *In accuratissimam humani corporis dissectionem* . . . (Padua, 1653). There are no good clues to
identify him; one Nicholas (forename or surname?) was inscribed at Padua in 1648. It may be a deliberately
obscure pseudonym for an important personage dabbling in risqué verse: cf. F. B. Williams, 'An Initiation
into Initials', *Studies in Bibliography* 9 (1957), pp. 163–78 ('N.' [*nomen*] so used, p. 165).

ribald throughout: it is perhaps the funniest of the verses (and is excellent as a poem in its own right, though as panegyric its value is more doubtful). The opening is direct: 'Pars ea, vel Patavis ambita et amata Puellis . . .' [That part, encircled and beloved by Paduan girls . . .]. *Ambio* is to be taken in two senses: 'solicit' or 'surround'. The latter sense is gleefully obscene. He also gains a powerful humorous effect by the repetition of *pars* at the beginning of the first three couplets. The unfortunate member was once 'ferro durior ipsa tuo' and a 'crassa columna' [harder than your scalpel . . . a thick column]; '. . . plauditque iuventus/Imberbis, merito consulit atque sibi.' [the young men applaud, and rightly look to themselves]—this too is deliberately ambiguous, and another fine touch: they no doubt looked to that essential part of their own anatomy with nervousness, embarrassment, or pride, perhaps combined with some natural queasiness at the sight before their eyes. But it is the women who object to this dissection; he could have done more, 'contenta fuisset/Si matronarum Luxuriosa cohors'. [if the pleasure-loving horde of women had allowed it]: this striking four-word pentameter makes a most effective end to the poem, and is suggestive to the last.

George Wakeman, a zealous Roman Catholic and royalist, was in exile under the Commonwealth;[89] he was to be created a baronet in 1661, and was physician to Catherine of Braganza. His poem addresses 'Laurentius Gallus' (the French scholar, André du Laurens, dead for 45 years), who claimed that the *hymen virgineus* did not exist, and triumphantly records Molinetti's demonstration of its existence.[90] It is thus an interesting document, illustrating scientific rivalries; it is also a lively poem, exploiting (like N. N.'s bawdy verses) the natural humorous potential of the subject. The hymen is broken, often enough, before the wedding night: '. . . Hinc tuus invidiae debetur forsitan error,/Defuit uxori pars ea nempe tuae.' [thus your mistake (i.e. Laurentius' position)[91] perhaps stems from envy: I'm sure your wife lacked that part herself.] This sort of personal attack was not an uncommon feature of serious academic debate, and it fits well in this context. There are many nice touches, including the end: '. . . Tu quoque quae Phoebum metuebas, innuba Daphne,/Haerebis doctis ambitiosa comis.' [and you, virgin Daphne (i.e. laurel), who feared Apollo, will stick closely to his learned locks]. There is a clever use of the Daphne myth, and perhaps *ambitiosa* [encircling?] hints at Molinetti's own interest in sex, echoing the use of the word by N. N.; there may be a similar idea at the end of Robert

[89] Cf. Thomas Wakeman, *Regiis Angliae divis dithyrambus* (Rome, 1627): an earlier generation of recusant Latin verse.

[90] [English *natio*], *In exactissimam humani corporis anatomen . . .* (Padua, 1654); on Wakeman's colourful career see *DNB*.

[91] See A. du Laurens, *Historia Anatomica* (Frankfurt, 1599), pp. 273, 279.

Henchman's poem in the 1653 volume: '. . . quod superest det Venus ipsa tibi' [for the rest, let Venus herself reward you].

There are 22 Latin poems addressed to Molinetti in these three books.[92] They are a varied collection, both in literary quality and in their approaches to the subject. They offer a picture of Molinetti as a masterly lecturer, captivating his audience with theatrical brilliance, and revealing hitherto unsuspected secrets of the human body. He is at least the equal of his distinguished predecessors, able to hold his own in a scientific controversy. The most natural medium for these students to express their delight at scientific discovery, and stake a claim for their professor's promotion in status, was elegant Latin poetry. Some of them became men of considerable reputation, notably Sir John Finch, as Professor of Anatomy at Pisa, and ambassador at Constantinople.[93] He and Gibbs may be taken as fine examples of British Neo-Latin abroad.

Abraham Cowley, and poetry for philosophers

Cowley is a significant Latin poet, particularly so because, unlike Milton, he remained equally interested in Latin and vernacular writing throughout his mature career. In youth, at Trinity College, Cambridge, he had produced a Latin play;[94] one wonders if the subject of a cheerful shipwreck was a little tactless in Cambridge that year, when Milton and others were lamenting the shipwreck of Edward King. His most substantial Latin work is an ambitious didactic poem on botany (a subject of great relevance to medicine, which he had studied); in the *Sex Libri Plantarum* he uses both classical and Mexican mythology to add colour to the botanical information.[95] The first two books appeared in 1662, the year after his election to the Royal Society; the full version forms the chief part of his *Poemata Latina* (London, 1668). There are a few quite long sapphic odes in the *Poemata*: *Solitudo* in 15 stanzas, and *In Lucem* with 25 stanzas. Cowley is better known for his English odes, in the irregular or 'Pindaric' style; this genre (as noted above) flourished in Latin, and included Milton's last Latin poem. The year after Cowley's *Poemata*, a long irregular ode was recited in the Oxford theatre.[96] Cowley was no more than an occasional user of the Latin lyric, but he shows that he is capable of handling Horatian forms.

---

[92] Discussed at Money and Swan, pp. 143–6.   [93] Money and Swan, p. 144; Lytton Sells, pp. 119–25.
[94] *Naufragium Joculare* (London, 1638); cf. Binns, *Intellectual Culture*, pp. 125, 140; A. H. Nethercot, *Abraham Cowley: the Muse's Hannibal* (London, 1931), pp. 63–5.
[95] See Bradner, pp. 118–22; more generally, J. G. Taaffe, *Abraham Cowley* (New York, 1972).
[96] Corbett Owen, *Carmen Pindaricum* (Oxford, 1669); cf. Bradner, pp. 102, 110 (discussing the strictures of Johnson's *Life of Cowley*).

He was reasonably successful in the didactic genre, less so in the epic. Only one book of his *Davideis* received a Latin version (as opposed to four books in English).[97] That single book is competently written; he can compress the meaning of an English couplet into a hexameter, for example in the opening three lines:

> Bella cano, fatique vices, Regemque potentem
> Mutato qui Sceptra pedo Solymaeia gessit,
> Rex olim et vates, duo maxima munera coeli.

This covers four lines of English:

> I sing the Man who Judah's Scepter bore
> In that right Hand which held the Crook before;
> Who from best Poet, best of Kings did grow;
> The two chief gifts Heaven could on man bestow.

In the first two lines he manages to say more than the corresponding English couplet, beginning with *bella* and *vices* (sounding suitably epic and Virgilian). In the third, he loses the repeated 'best' (superlatives that may the easier be dispensed with, in proximity to another, *maxima*), and the sense of growing from poet to king; 'grow' may be introduced largely for the rhyme. On the other hand, he does not always condense: the Latin book has 1088 lines, the English only 934. Though it is not a close rival to Virgil in Latin, or Milton in English, students of Cowley might do well to take the Latin *Davideis* more seriously. The *Sex Libri Plantarum* certainly deserves attention, if only as the major work of a serious literary figure, for whom natural philosophy was at least as important as writing the *Mistress* or poetical *Miscellanies*. Membership of the Royal Society, or wide philosophical interests, often accompanied participation in Latin intellectual culture. New ideas still circulated in Latin prose; even those philosophers who preferred the vernacular regularly wrote and received letters in Latin. The correspondence of Robert Boyle, for example, includes an amazing variety of Latin letters addressed to the philosopher. Foreign adventurers try to sell him the philosopher's stone, with implausible details of its acquisition given at preposterous length; impoverished Englishmen beg for a few shillings, convinced that an extended display of learning will be more effective than their native tongue; alchemical recipes,

---

[97] Brief discussion of b. 1, at G. Shadduck, *A critical edition of Cowley's Davideis* (New York and London, 1987), p. 5 (her rather thin commentary does not say much about the Latin); J. M. McBryde, *A Study of Cowley's Davideis* (Johns Hopkins Dissertation, reprinted from *Journal of Germanic Philology*, n.d. [Baltimore, 1901]) is not informative on the Latin version, but has some discussion of other works on the David story, e.g. Fracastoro's *Joseph*, p. 66.

physicians' case histories, and proposals for the advancement of Christianity all pass through the medium of Latin.[98]

The most striking example of a philosopher-poet is Thomas Hobbes.[99] Like Cowley, he retained a life-long facility at Latin verse; he chose Latin, too, for several of his prose treatises. His youthful poem on the Peak District, *De Mirabilibus Pecci* (1636), displays powers of straightforward description, and interest in the drama of mountain scenery, that anticipate later poetical trends. In extreme old age he turned to Latin elegiacs for his autobiography;[100] *Historia Ecclesiastica* (London, 1688), written twenty years before its publication, was issued posthumously for its relevance to the anti-Catholic sentiments of the Revolution. The characteristic qualities of the author of *Leviathan* shine through in his sternly eloquent Latin. It was not for the sage of Malmesbury to indulge in too much pseudo-intellectual Ovidian trickery.

Edward Hannes and the Christ Church poets

In the years leading up to, and beyond, the Revolution there were many fine writers of Latin in British schools and universities. One of the most interesting groups flourished in Christ Church, Oxford, around the figure of Dr Edward Hannes (*c.* 1664–1710), another learned physician and natural philosopher.[101] There is something of a medical theme running through seventeenth-century Latin, with Hannes, Gibbs, and others here discussed: it recurs in Chapter 6. Hannes was among those poets who gave priority to the Horatian ode, a less popular form in England (if not in Gibbs' Rome) earlier in the century. His alcaic odes offer elegant compliments to various addressees, and draw effectively on his medical experience. He is a far less brilliant poet than Alsop; yet the existence of such a group on Alsop's arrival at the college must have facilitated the creation of a younger and still livelier circle. Physicians continued to play a part in Christ Church poetry; John Wigan,[102] editor of the medical works of Alsop's addressee John Freind, MD, is a further example of this combination of talents.

Also from Christ Church was John Philips, whose celebrated ode to Henry

[98] Royal Society, *Boyle Mss.*, *passim*; M. Hunter, A. Clericuzio, D. K. Money, *et al.*, eds., *The Correspondence of Robert Boyle* (forthcoming). A letter to Boyle in Greek, with 6 Greek hexameters: 1. 20. See also Bathsua Makin, Ch. 1.   [99] Cf. Bradner, pp. 202–4.
[100] *Vita carmine expressa autore seipso* (London, 1679).
[101] Professor of chemistry, 1690–1704 (after which the chair lapsed, though teaching continued, in the hands of Keill and Freind); royal physician, 1702; knighted, 1705. See Sutherland and Mitchell, *Oxford*, pp. 663, 703 (without mention of his poetry). Bradner, pp. 208–10; on medical learning and literature, cf. M. L. Clarke, *Greek Studies in England, 1700–1830* (Cambridge, 1945), pp. 4–5.
[102] Bradner, pp. 230, 235–6.

St John was described as 'certainly a masterpiece: the style is pure and elegant, the subject of a mixt Nature, resembling the sublime spirit, and gay, facetious Humour of Horace . . .'[103] The poem, in fifteen alcaic stanzas, begins with the praise of tobacco and wine; it ends with those same essential products, now unable to procure sleep for the lovesick poet. The central stanzas have praise for St John, the patron and Tory politician, as a new Maecenas, whose health is drunk before we turn to the poet's own affairs. The style is smooth, and the whole (if not quite a masterpiece) is attractive in its handling of the insubstantial subject matter. The preface asserts that his Latin is 'not inferior' to his English works; the latter are much longer, but the *Splendid Shilling*, parodying Milton, and *Cyder* (with more alcoholic material), are equally light in tone, while *Blenheim* is dedicated to Harley, the other leading Tory politician. Newcomb's preface to his translation, printed after the Latin, compares Philips to Swift and King,[104] in their talent for pompous solemnity about ludicrous trifles, 'which they have all borrowed from Virgil's manner of describing the oeconomy of bees'. I am not sure that even Virgil would have appreciated all the lessons that the *Georgics* could teach.

[103] J. Philips, *Works* (Tonson's 1720 edn., with the place of publication misprinted as 'Loldon'), p. xxvii; first printed separately, 1707; in *Works*, 1712; pirated by Curll, *Musae Britannicae*, 1711 (see Bradner, p. 281), etc.
[104] William King (1663–1712), also of Christ Church: not to be confused with the Principal of St Mary Hall (discussed in Ch. 8) or others of the same name.

3
The Greatest Lyric Poet

A sad and rather farcical accident brought to an end the career of one of the most fascinating of England's literary figures. The description of a local newspaper, the *Reading Post, or Weekly Mercury*, for 20 June 1726, was recorded in the diary of Thomas Hearne, the Oxford antiquary: 'On Friday night last (June 10th), about 11 o'Clock, as the Rev Mr Anthony Alsop . . . was walking by a small Brook called the Lock Bourne, near the College of Winchester, the Ground gave way under his Feet, which threw him into the Brook, where he was found dead the next Morning.'[1] The date of his death was a significant one, a cause for celebration among Jacobites: the Pretender, 'James III', had been born on 10 June 1688, and to commemorate the event was a duty as well as a pleasure for his supporters.

Canon Stratford of Christ Church, an acerbic commentator on the failings of his current and former colleagues, suggests that Alsop was drunk when he fell, his 'condition' making 'it still more deplorable'.[2] This is plausible enough; but for a middle-aged Tory cleric in the early 18th century to imbibe freely on a day of special note for himself and his friends is far from remarkable, and while contemporary opponents might well have felt that God had declared his disapproval of drunken sedition, it would take a sour theologian today to agree. Thomas Hearne adds his own affectionate obituary to the newspaper account:

> He was one of the oldest, and one of the most ingenious, Acquaintance I had. He was a man of most ready wit, of excellent Learning, a fine Preacher, and of rare good nature. He was looked upon to be the best Writer of Lyric Verses in the World. . . . He was about 55 years of age when his unfortunate Death happened, which was occasioned by the Workmen's having loosened the Ground in order to new Pitch it, what Mr Alsop did not know of. He was going that byway to his Lodging, having parted (I am told) with a friend at the College great Gate, which being not readily opened, Mr Alsop said he would not stay, but go the by way, which he unhappily did. His Death is much lamented.

[1] Hearne, *Reliquiae*, p. 302 (23 June 1726).
[2] *HMC Portland* 7. 439 (13 June 1726: the news travelled fast).

There is one phrase in this account that stands out, and turns an ordinary man's personal tragedy into a moment of historical significance: 'He was looked upon to be the best Writer of Lyric Verses in the World.' He does not even say the best contemporary, or the best Latin poet, though these qualifications may be implied; or he may mean that Alsop was thought to be the greatest lyric poet in any language, at any time. This sounds a ridiculous exaggeration, to a modern scholarly audience for whom he is at best a name among dozens of other so-called minor poets. Our modern ideas of a literary canon (even if that canon were universally agreed) are not necessarily of much help in assessing what was felt to be important two or three hundred years ago. Nor was there agreement in the past on such subjects. Hearne does not say who 'looked upon' Alsop as being superior to all others. The implication is that everyone did, or if not everyone, at least every sensible connoisseur of the art. To be sensible was no doubt, in Hearne's opinion, not unconnected with sharing Hearne's own point of view. This is so in matters of politics. Hearne was a Jacobite of quite extreme views, very ready to think ill of a Whig; the fact that he shared his opinions with Alsop may well have led to his approval of the man or the preacher, but it is not sufficient to explain away his judgement of the poet. Hearne was an acute critic of literature, and did not let political bias colour his criticism. He was interested in what other people were thinking, and if he had not known his views of Alsop to be widely shared, he would not have phrased his verdict in such a way.

Other recorded views of Alsop's achievement seem thin on the ground. Most connoisseurs of poetry did not necessarily discuss their preferences in letters or journals that have survived (nor have I been able to examine all that there is: further research may throw up interesting material on the reception of Neo-Latin in this period). Authors whose work was read in manuscript are less likely to be the subject of public criticism, but could still have had a large body of private admirers. When, after his death, individual works of his are printed by the *Gentleman's Magazine* or by Dodsley, he is spoken of with great respect, as an author whose brilliance the public will wish to see.

Birth, family and education

Alsop was born late in December 1669, or in the first few days of January 1670. This is a good two years earlier than the date of 1672 that is found in nearly all reference books; the source of the error is probably the statement that he was aged 18 in 1690, on matriculation at Christ Church, as published from the college archives by Joseph Foster in his *Alumni Oxonienses*. The records of Westminster School note that he was the son of another Anthony Alsop, of

Darley in Derbyshire.[3] This Anthony Alsop did have a son in 1672, but he was christened George. Anthony was baptised on 4 January 1669/70, according to the parish register of St Helen's, Darley.[4] His father married Anne Lowe on 13 August 1660. He is an obscure figure; the county record office contains no other documents that can be tied to him.[5] The poet's family was not an eminent one.

He became a King's Scholar at Westminster School in 1686. This event set him on course for a successful academic career, since Westminster was the leading school of the day, with close links to Christ Church in Oxford, and Trinity College in Cambridge. These two colleges held an annual election of the best Westminster scholars; most preferred to go on to Christ Church rather than Trinity. Each was the largest college in its university. Christ Church had an unusual system of government, since it was a cathedral as well as a college. The Dean and Chapter formed the college's governing body, but the Students (who were the equivalent of the fellows of other colleges) undertook the teaching and discipline of the undergraduates. These included both recently appointed Students, and the other classes of member, which were, in descending order of social status: noblemen, gentlemen-commoners, commoners, and servitors. A Student was entitled to remain in college as long as he wished, provided that he took his degrees and holy orders at the appropriate times, and refrained from matrimony or other serious misdemeanours. The restriction on marriage applied to fellows of all colleges, with the exception of heads of houses and professors, whose positions were therefore particularly desirable. It helped to ensure a healthy turnover in the university, since the majority of fellows preferred to accept a church living rather than remain perpetual bachelors. There were 101 Students of Christ Church; those vacancies not filled at the Westminster elections went to 'Canoneer Students', appointed in rotation by the Canons (and the Dean), often from the ranks of Westminster School. There was considerable continuity in this system: a young Westminster Student would find himself taught by an older product of the same school. Academic competition in the election was high. Richard Busby was a formidable headmaster of Westminster, and his standards were matched by those of two outstanding Deans of Christ

---

[3] G. F. R. Barker, A. H. Stenning, *Record of Old Westminsters* (1928). They put his baptism a year early (1668/9).   [4] Derbyshire Record Office, XM 1/109.

[5] He may possibly have been the 'Antho: Allsop' who paid the largest hearth tax in the parish of Eaton and Alsop, or the 'Antho: Allsop' who paid a lower amount in Wensley and Snitterton; or, if a man of substantial property, he may have been both. Alsop is a common name in Derbyshire, largely concentrated in the hundred of Wirksworth; Darley is outside this area, but not far away. Fifty families of that name paid hearth tax in the county in the decade before the poet's birth, not one of them listed under Darley. The leading family in Darley was named Columbell. Apart from the parish register, the only evidence I found for Alsops living there is a field name, 'Alsop alias Cooks', on an 18th century map: Derbyshire Record Office, 8792/P1.

Church, John Fell and Henry Aldrich. Verse composition was encouraged, with most emphasis placed on 'themes', subjects set for witty and original elegiacs.[6]

Alsop did well at Westminster, and in 1690 was head of the list of boys elected to studentships at Christ Church.[7] It was slightly unusual for a youth of twenty to matriculate, and he may have wished to seem younger, thus causing the confusion about his date of birth. Most Westminster Students arrived aged between 17 and 19; aristocratic undergraduates tended to be younger, about 15 or 16. A number of older entrants are also recorded: two such came in 1705, to be taught by Alsop, Thomas Wigfall aged 20 and Matthew Randolph aged 21. Alsop's university career began at a later age than was normal, but only by a year or two, and his relatively modest, rustic origins may have delayed his appearance at Westminster, after which his progress followed the regular pattern.

He obtained his BA on 1 January 1694/5, and his MA on 23 March 1696/7; he took the degree of BD in 1706, having it incorporated at Cambridge in the following year (possibly to impress a wider range of potential patrons). He never took the highest theological degree of DD; it was an expensive business, and undertaken only reluctantly by many academic clergymen, to preserve their college seniority. By the time that he might have expected to take it, he had left Oxford, and did not choose to signify further ambitions in this way. While at Christ Church he played a full part in the college's academic life, and was appointed to various positions of responsibility: 2nd praelector (1695), tutor (1698–1709), Greek praelector (1700), junior censor (1701–2), senior censor (1703–5), and catechist (1706–7, 1711). Of these, the senior censor's post was the most important, from the point of view of college discipline; censors at Christ Church fulfilled the role of deans elsewhere, attempting to keep the young gentlemen in order. While holding other offices he continued to act as a tutor, supervising the education of a varying number of pupils from the college. He also played a full part in other aspects of college life.[8]

Dean Aldrich is said to have entrusted to Alsop 'the principal noblemen and gentlemen' of the House.[9] Other tutors shared these prestigious duties, but the college caution books, in which some tutors' signatures are to be found, support the assertion that Alsop's role was important. He was almost certainly responsible

---

[6] On the system under Fell and Aldrich, see E. G. W. Bill, *Education at Christ Church, Oxford, 1660–1800* (Oxford, 1988).

[7] J. Welch, *List of Scholars of St Peter's College, Westminster* (1788), p. 70; Barker and Stenning. Alsop's tutor, initially, was Roger Altham, who soon afterwards became a canon and Regius Professor of Hebrew (Christ Church archives). Altham probably continued to influence Alsop (cf. Hebrew in the *Aesop* edition, discussed in Ch. 4); he was vicar of Finedon, 1688 (cf. Alsop's Northamptonshire connections, especially Dolben, discussed in Ch. 7).

[8] There is a Latin speech in praise of Fell, possibly by Alsop: Bodleian, ms. Ballard 29. 102 [fo. 147] (originally attributed to 'Adams', altered to 'Alsop' in another hand).

[9] Nichols, *Corresp.* 2. 42, n.: quoted in *DNB*.

for the teaching of at least 4 noblemen, 5 gentlemen-commoners, 7 commoners, and 13 students.[10] One of them, John Addenbrooke, must have caused some trouble to Alsop as censor, being degraded a year for misbehaviour in 1705, and expelled in 1706. Some of the rest remained in the college for many years. In a single year, 1705, he seems to have been entrusted with at least twenty pupils, a substantial proportion of the college's undergraduates.

To those pupils identified from the caution books must be added one important nobleman; there may have been more. James Cecil, 5th Earl of Salisbury (1691–1728), had succeeded to the title at the age of three; on his fourteenth birthday he matriculated at Christ Church. A few weeks later he was praised by Arthur Charlett as a 'gentleman of excellent parts, principles and temper'.[11] In his time there (1705–9), he appears to have been in Alsop's care, and also that of John Savage. He was created MA in 1707, and married in February 1708/9. He took his seat in the Lords in 1712; although a Tory, he was loyal enough to bear a staff at George I's coronation. He is one of three members of the college whom Alsop praises in his ode for the university collection of 1708:

> . . . sic tibi moenia
> Superba surgant, sospitante
> Aldrichii genio penates.
> Sic te faventis Cecilii integra
> Virtus honestet; sic aveat Tuus
> Dici Trelaunus Wintonensis
> Grande decus columenque mitrae.

> Thus may your proud walls rise, with the genius of Aldrich preserving the household gods. Thus may the unblemished goodness of your patron Cecil bless you; thus may Trelawny, the great glory and support of the see of Winchester, desire to be called one of your own.[12]

The rising walls are those of the new Peckwater Quad, in which Salisbury set up this inscription: 'Jacobus, comes Salisburiensis,/Hunc Lapidem locavit,/Gratitudinis suae et Gaudii testem,/quod ipse, dum haec surgerent moenia,/

---

[10] Pupils identified in this way, with the dates of their membership of the college (which, in some cases, continued after Alsop's tuition of them will have ceased) are: noblemen: Lord Arthur Altham (1703–6), Langham Booth (1701–3), Lord John Finch (1703–5), Lord Charles Somerset (1704–8); gentlemen-commoners: Jonathan Cope (1708–10), Thomas Frewen (1703–6), John Guise (1700–4), William Kingsmill (1703–5), Francis Wollaston Wilkins (1705–9); commoners: William Adams (1698–1706), Roger Chapman (1705–15), Edward Dennys (1702–13), William Feilde (1705–6), Humphrey Persehouse (1702–10), John Treise (1702–4), Francis Tucker (1702–9); students: John Addenbrooke (1702–6), John Bedford (1702–14; 2nd praelector, 1707), Samuel Chittle (1703–18), Richard Clutton (1702–3), Charles Fairfax (1702–19; tutor, 1711–15), Edward Hammond (1707–32), Thomas Hawes (1705–17), Richard Jenkinson (1704–14), Charles Long (1703–19), Matthew Randolph (1705–25), Thomas Ward (1705–13), John Wheeler (1702–49), Thomas Wigfall (1705–7).

[11] *HMC Ormonde*, new ser. 8. 162: quoted in G.E.C., *Peerage*.

[12] I. 3. 42–8. (See further discussion in Ch. 9.)

sub auspiciis Decani,/Eorundem Architecti,/De se optime meriti,/Feliciter adolesceret,/Praeceptoribus usus/Antonio Alsop A.M./Joanne Savage A.M./ Quorum dulcem memoriam/Tam conservatam voluit quam suam'[13] [James, Earl of Salisbury, placed this stone as a witness to his gratitude and joy that, while these walls arose, he himself grew up and prospered under the auspices of the Dean, their architect, to whom he owed much, and under the tuition of Anthony Alsop MA and John Savage MA, whose sweet memory he wished to be preserved as much as his own].

Alsop may well have written the inscription, and his verses echo some of its language. The ode is a polite form of flattery to three important people, the Dean, the Bishop, and his noble pupil. Its last line is an allusion to Horace,[14] suitably altered to reflect Trelawny's status; Horace is addressing his own patron, Maecenas, and the allusion is a subtle plea for similar patronage. While a scholar is expected to praise his potential patrons, it is less usual to find an aristocratic pupil praising his tutors so publicly. Salisbury could easily have confined his compliments to the Dean, and the inclusion of Alsop and Savage on the inscription indicates his real affection for them, and satisfaction with the education he received.

Not everyone was satisfied by Alsop's performance. Canon Stratford, writing to Edward Harley on 7 September 1712, discusses the prospects of young Lord Huntingdon, who was 'designed' for Christ Church: '. . . Alsop has a sister who lives with Lady Betty Hastings, she has been made use of . . . to recommend Mr Alsop . . . for [Lady Betty's] brother's tutor . . . His enemies could not wish him [Atterbury] to do anything more to his disadvantage than to put one of that quality into Alsop's hands, who, as your Lordship knows, is so infamous for his neglect of Lord Salisbury and all others that ever were entrusted to him . . .'.[15] What an unfriendly observer saw as infamous neglect was doubtless welcome indulgence to many pupils. By 1712, Alsop was in any case shortly to leave the college for a country living, and his enthusiasm for teaching may have waned; the inscription at least suggests that he had not treated Salisbury as badly as Stratford would have us believe.

Patrons and friends

Aldrich was succeeded as Dean of Christ Church by Francis Atterbury, a fiercely ambitious and abrasive character (discussed in Chapter 4), much to Stratford's disgust. Alsop was a firm supporter of Atterbury, and Atterbury in turn fostered

[13] Bodleian, ms. Lat. misc. e. 19, fo. 152–3.
[14] *Carm.* 2. 17. 3–4: 'mearum/grande decus columenque rerum'. [15] *HMC Portland* 7. 87–8.

Alsop's career. He represented Atterbury in welcoming the Dutch ambassador, Mr Buys, in 1711; Stratford had already selected another Student, Thomas Terry, for the task, and thought that Atterbury was trying to steal credit from himself.[16] In the following year, when he was 'the senior divine of the students now resident', Alsop was summoned to assist Atterbury at the election for Convocation (a matter of importance for politically minded clergymen), and passed on messages for the Dean.[17]

It was through Atterbury that he secured the good wishes and repeated patronage of Sir Jonathan Trelawny. As Bishop of Winchester, from 1707, he had many desirable livings in his gift. He first appointed Alsop his chaplain, and then gave him a succession of benefices, the first being Nursling in Hampshire. Atterbury continued to press his case to Trelawny, even after he had received this mark of favour: 'I need not mention Mr Alsop to your Lordship; because I know your Lordship cannot be unmindful of him. However . . . give me leave to repeat . . . that no man ever came under your roof, of more worth, or a better nature, or more likely to be in every way acceptable . . . It is the first and last request of this kind I shall ever make to your Lordship; and therefore I urge it the more freely.'[18]

Nursling was followed by Alverstoke, in the same county.[19] The culmination of Trelawny's patronage came in 1715, with the gift of Brightwell, in Berkshire, and a prebend at Winchester. In these two posts Alsop remained for the rest of his life; they provided the means for a very comfortable existence. Hearne quotes an estimated value of £500 per annum for Brightwell, which would make it a most desirable living. A lower estimate of £300 is still a substantial sum. It was perhaps twice as rich as Alverstoke, which was in turn one and a half times as valuable as Nursling. The prebend was worth about £250 per annum.[20] He could reside at Winchester or at Brightwell; the latter was conveniently close to Oxford, which helped him to keep in contact with those of his old friends who remained there. It was necessary for Students receiving a living to vacate their studentships; it was traditional for them to be allowed a year of grace, in which they could continue to take their emoluments from the college. Atterbury wished to grant this on his own authority, without the Chapter's formal permission. Thus Alsop became involved in one of the Dean's trials of strength with his colleagues, over whom he was determined to assert his authority, using routine matters such as this, or minor opportunities for patronage like the

[16] *HMC Portland* 7. 73 (15 November 1711).
[17] Nichols, *Corresp.* 1. 454 (9 May 1712), 1. 458 (December 1712), 2. 9 (December 1713).
[18] Nichols, *Corresp.* 2. 6–8 (11 September 1713).   [19] *Victoria County History, Hampshire* 3. 202, 439.
[20] Hearne, *Reliquiae* p. 302; J. Ecton, *Thesaurus Rerum Ecclesiasticarum* (ed. B. Willis, 1754); B. Williams, *Whig Supremacy* (1960 edn.), map 1. On the village and church of Brightwell: *Victoria County History, Berkshire* 3. 464 (not accurate on Alsop).

appointment of a chapter clerk instead of a rival candidate favoured by Stratford.[21]

Not all Alsop's friendships had been academic. His fondness for beer and conversation brought him into contact with the publican John Freeman, land-lord of the King's Head, whom he recommended as a JP in March 1713/4 (a recommendation about which Stratford is predictably sarcastic).[22] This was during his time at Alverstoke, a period when he may have continued to spend much of his time in Oxford. This same Freeman had commissioned 'the ingenious Mr Alsop' to write the epitaph of Mr Richard Walker, in St Michael's Church, Oxford; Walker was an *oenopola* [vintner].[23] Music formed an impor-tant part of his social life, both within the college and outside it. Dean Aldrich was extremely fond of music, and added the composition of catches to his many other accomplishments. A younger Christ Church man, John Dolben, later a close friend (discussed in Chapter 7), was devoted to church music. Alsop himself was one of the 41 members of the Oxford musical club that met 'every last Thursday in the month at Mr Hall's tavern at five of the clock precisely in the evening . . . till ten'. The publican, Anthony Hall, was a musician, and the club included Daniel Purcell, organist of Magdalen and brother of Henry, as well as Alsop's colleagues John Pelling and Charles Woodruffe, and the young James Brydges, later Duke of Chandos, who was to prove a most valuable acquaintance (as discussed in Chapter 7).[24]

One of the earliest of Alsop's odes to which a date can be assigned was written to be set to music. The 1693 Act song, *Britannia* (3. 6), published as part of the Encaenia programme, is attributed to him in a musical manu-script;[25] it celebrates British military achievements, in particular the recent naval victories of Barfleur and La Hogue. Music and Latin lyric poetry can be combined effectively, though with the risk of so much damage being done to the metre that the words are difficult to distinguish from prose; the repetitions expected of a baroque song wreak some havoc with the alcaic rhythm. The copyist of the vocal parts, and probably the singers, showed little understand-ing of the Latin. Nevertheless, Alsop will have enjoyed providing the text for another artistic medium that he loved, and hearing it performed at a presti-gious university celebration. The vast majority of his later work was intended to be read rather than sung; but he may have been involved in writing an ode to be set for music at the 1706 Encaenia, and he certainly wrote the words to an English song for the wedding of his friend John Dolben (see Chapters 4 and 7).

---

[21] *HMC Portland* 7. 117, 134 (2 and 25 Dec. 1712).   [22] *HMC Portland* 7. 183.
[23] Hearne, *Coll.* 1. 88 (21 Nov. 1705). Dr Hudson gave Hearne a copy.
[24] Bodleian, ms. Top. Oxon. a. 76. Cf. M. Crum, 'An Oxford Music Club, 1690–1719', *Bodleian Library Record* 9 (1974), pp. 83–99.   [25] Bodleian, ms. Mus. Sch. c. 121.

The 1693 Encaenia, like most celebrations of that festival in the period, had its lively as well as its solemn aspects. From the day after the formal, Latin, programme we may note the risqué 'Musick-Speech spoken by Mr Smith of University College in the Theatre: July 8, 1693', addressing the female part of his audience:

> . . . For how could we this Subject justly handle,
> Did you not carefully provide for Scandal.
> And in the first Place, know my Occupation,
> I've learn'd Anatomy; and on Occasion
> Can tolerably dissect your Reputation:
> And tho' unlearn'd in *Hans's* deeper Arts,
> Yet sure I've Skill enough to know your Hearts,
> And to lay open too some other Parts.
> My knowledge goes beyond external Beauty,
> For Gad I know Ye *intus & in Cute*.
> And here I'll spare some Ladies of the Town,
> Their Frailties every day enough are known:
> For some of them, as I have understood,
> Have oft been try'd, and found true Flesh and Blood.
> In vain before his Door does *Astrey* waddle
> With gauntlett Fist, & on his shoulder paddle;
> In vain, in vain, he strives to keep out Sin,
> Whilst *Bungee* and his Spouse solace within.

The loose morals of the Astrey family were to have more than a little effect on Alsop's later career (see Chapters 6 and 7); Smith's 'Epilogue' mentions another name that may appear in Alsop's own satire (depending on whether we take Jenny here to be a surname, related to the coffee-house-keeper of his 1. 9 and 1. 10: see Chapter 5):

> . . . Yet East-Gate *Jenny* shan't neglected pass,
> Whose early Lewdness may in time encrease,
> And be the only Entertainment of this Place.
> But since in Privacy her Pleasure lies,
> We'll leave her to her Closet Exercise.[26]

The Oxford atmosphere fostered light verse on scandalous local themes, and Alsop gained much from this tradition, while transforming it into grander Latin poetry.

Another ode dates from 1693: the lament for James Harrington (1664–93), the lawyer and Latin poet (3. 7). This was no doubt part of a tribute by several members of the college to a former student who died tragically young, after

---

[26] Bodleian, ms. Eng. poet. f. 13, pp. 116–8 [fo. 61–2] and pp. 119–20. Cf. Persius 3.30, 'intus et in cute'.

having achieved considerable distinction.[27] One cannot tell the depth of Alsop's own emotion from the poem, but it is an accomplished piece of public funereal verse, and a good preparation for future excellence, with some telling phrases and effective progression from Orpheus to Harrington's skill in law (at which the judges are amazed, and for which the multitude thirsts) and in poetry. The ending, turning to praise of Ormonde, is perhaps rather too abrupt; he learned to manage such flattery of the living with superior skill by the time he wrote 1. 3, quoted above.

A year and a half after the performance of *Britannia*, Alsop had his first opportunity to contribute to a university verse collection, an important way for a poet to further his career (the genre is discussed in Chapter 9). This early poem on Queen Mary's death (1. 2) does not stray so far from its subject as 1. 3, but it may well have a subversive undertone. There is emphasis on the disasters suffered by William; ostensibly, this is a cause for sympathy, but it is also encouraging to a Jacobite. Alsop was certainly a Jacobite by 1695 (see Chapter 6). The poem reads loyally enough on the surface, and could not otherwise have been printed; certain nuances seem susceptible to an alternative interpretation.[28] The Jacobitism (if it is indeed there) is combined with pride in Britain's success against the French. A similar mixture of feelings may underlie *Britannia*; the victories there celebrated had been disastrous for the Jacobite cause, and natural patriotic enthusiasm for the humbling of a traditional foe was tinged with regret that the rightful king had to rely on such worthless allies (James II himself, the former admiral of England, shared this ambivalence).[29] The stress on the horror of war in the poems may be intended to remind the audience that none of this need have happened, if Britain had remained loyal. A similar sense of horror (as well as much humour) permeates another of Alsop's poems for public recitation during this nine years' war, *Givetta Ardens* (3. 8: discussed in Chapter 4).

Bernard's publication of the Odes

Although a few of Alsop's poems appeared in print during his lifetime, he was not interested in publishing a collection of his work that would provide a record of his achievement. The decision to produce an edition was made some twenty years after his death, by his stepson, Francis Bernard (1712–79). Shortly before he died, Alsop had sent Bernard to Westminster, whence the young man

[27] There is another poem on his death, in 12 alcaic stanzas, attributed to 'Adams', now bound in the same ms. vol.: Bodleian ms. Lat. misc. c. 14, fo. 121ʳ; a Latin letter from Harrington to Aldrich, fo. 147.
[28] See 1. 2. 35, 44, 73–5.
[29] On these battles and their crucial significance, see P. Aubrey, *The Defeat of James Stuart's Armada, 1692* (Leicester, 1979).

proceeded to Christ Church. He became a lawyer, and was called to the bar in
1737; he married in 1741, and his wife's cousin, Lord Barrington, obtained for
him the governorship of New Jersey in 1758. In 1760 he was transferred to
govern Massachusetts, where he remained for nine turbulent years. He was
created baronet in 1769, shortly before the home government removed him
from office, in an attempt to placate the Boston assembly. He continued to
promote Neo-Latin literature while in America, by the giving of prizes, and by
suggesting that Harvard should join the tradition of Latin commemorative
volumes that was still flourishing at Oxford and Cambridge; that Harvard *Pietas
et Gratulatio* (1761) is one of the colonies' most significant literary productions.
Bernard wrote verses himself, and a set of his sapphics, in the spirit of Alsop, is
included in the Harvard volume.[30]

On 27 July 1748 Bernard issued a proposal to publish Alsop's odes. The
printer was William Bowyer, one of the leading London tradesmen; his father's
business had included much Latin literature, and he himself was known as the
'learned printer'. As well as Bowyer's learning, his family's links with non-jurors
and Jacobites may have made him a suitable printer to choose. The Bowyer
firm's ledgers can be used to chart the progress of the project. The proposal, *To
be published by subscription, Antonii Alsopi odarum libri duo*, was printed in 500
copies.[31] The price of the book was to be 6/- (on small paper) or 10/6 (large
paper); subscriptions were to be taken by a number of booksellers, in the various
places frequented by lovers of modern Latin. These were Knapton, Davis and
Dodsley in London, Fletcher in Oxford, Thurlbourn in Cambridge, and Leake
at Bath. A few months later 200 copies were printed of a list of the odes,
Poematum Antonii Alsopi adhuc ab editore collectorum catalogus;[32] the purpose of
this was to solicit further manuscript contributions from the private collections
of interested connoisseurs. This list is dated 25 February, 1748/9. When the
book did appear, Knapton advertised the fact in the *Gentleman's Magazine* and
London Magazine.[33] Bowyer printed 400 copies on small paper, and 200 on large
paper (called fine in the ledger), for Francis Barnard [*sic*] at Lincoln; the ledger
also notes the use of blue paper (for wrappers?).[34]

The ostensible reason for the publication, according to Bernard's proposal,
was to support a 'near relation in advanced age, by unexpected losses greatly
reduced'. He briefly describes Alsop's career, as 'a principal ornament of [Christ

[30] L. M. Kaiser, *Early American Latin Verse* (Chicago, 1984), p. 141; see also A. Johnson, ed., *Dictionary of American Biography* (1928–37).
[31] K. Maslen, J. Lancaster, *The Bowyer Ledgers* (London and New York, 1991), p. 265 [no. 3485].
[32] Maslen and Lancaster, p. 268 [no. 3529].
[33] A copy of the proposal, and list of poems: Bodleian, ms. Rawl. J. fol. 2, fo. 58. Advertisements: *Gentleman's Magazine* 22 (March 1752), p. 146; *London Magazine* 21 (March/April 1752), p. 194 (item 114: 'pr. 6s. Knaptons').   [34] Maslen and Lancaster, p. 286 [no. 3742].

Church] at a time when it was in the highest repute'. He praises the poet's 'uncommon facility', and 'style so natural and easy, that he has been not unjustly esteemed inferior only to his master Horace'. Alsop's modesty prevented him from promoting their circulation, even in manuscript, 'but these odes, deserted by their parent and left exposed to the wide world, have, by the strength of their constitution, without the assistance of the press, lived some to forty, and most above thirty, years'. He might indeed have said that a few had circulated in manuscript for fifty years, since the earliest works in Bernard's edition date from the 1690s.

The edition took some four years to prepare. One reason for delay is the request for collectors of manuscripts to send additional poems to the editor. But in fact Bernard prints no poems that are not included in his preliminary list; if he received any others, he must have thought them unsuitable. He also chose to confine the edition to the lyric poetry, omitting the hexameter works that he had earlier listed. This is a sensible decision, concentrating on the work that had made Alsop's reputation unique. The addition of miscellaneous works in other metres would also fit uneasily with the title, *Antonii Alsopi, Aedis Christi olim alumni, Odarum libri duo* [two books of odes by Anthony Alsop, sometime Student of Christ Church]. The division of the poems into classical books is a device used for some parts of the works of distinguished Neo-Latin predecessors such as Milton and Buchanan. The two books are of uneven length, with 12 numbered odes in the first and 26 in the second, together with the final ode to Ezechiel Spanheim which he left unnumbered. The division seems to be between epistolary odes, all in the sapphic metre, in book 2 and miscellaneous odes (some also sapphic or epistolary) in book 1. The odes in book 2 have the names of their addressees as titles. It may be that 1. 4, a sapphic letter to Dr John Freind, appears in the first book because it has been given a separate title, *In obitum uxoris*; a personal poem on his wife's death, it is also suitably placed after poems published in university collections, and without it the first book would have been even thinner by comparison with the second. This lack of proportion does have a parallel in Horace: of the first three books of *Carmina* [Odes], originally issued together, the second has significantly fewer poems than the first and third; the fourth, issued much later, is shorter still, and provides an excuse, if one is needed, for Alsop's short book 1. Bernard doubtless places his shorter book first so that we may begin with religion and royalty, rather than with a circle of friends whose names the casual reader might not know.

The motto which Bernard chose for the title-page, 'nascentem placido lumine viderat' [she had looked kindly upon his birth], is an allusion to Horace:[35] not quite a quotation, since the ending of the verb is changed, but

---

[35] *Carm.* 4. 3. 1–2, 'Quem tu, Melpomene, semel/ nascentem placido lumine videris . . .'

ANTONII ALSOPI

AEDIS CHRISTI OLIM ALUMNI

ODARUM

LIBRI DUO.

C. Grignion sculp.

LONDINI,

MDCCLII.

Figure 1   Title page of Bernard's edition, 1752

nearly so. The alteration makes a firm statement about Alsop's status as the Muse's favourite, and as a worthy successor to Horace. The Horace ode (from that shorter, more mature fourth book) sums up the poet's view of his own individual position, separated from the ambitions of other men (a favourite theme, introduced in the first ode of book 1), and happy with his achievement, 'quod monstror digito praetereuntium/Romanae fidicen lyrae' [since I am pointed out by passers-by as the player of the Roman lyre (lines 22–3)]. Alter *Romanae* to *Anglorum*, and we would have Alsop's claim to be the English Horace: a claim that he would be too modest to make for himself, but which his admirers might well make on his behalf. Horace is immodest in this one respect, the desire for attention. His avoidance of public office, his preference for rural retirement, are both paralleled by Alsop's behaviour. The modern poet's character, as well as his importance, can thus be indicated by the choice of a significant motto.

Bernard imposed his own personality on the works of his stepfather with his dedication of them to Thomas Pelham-Holles, Duke of Newcastle (1693–1768). Newcastle was a Secretary of State, the Chancellor of Cambridge University, and a trustee of Westminster School, where he had been educated. He controlled a vast system of patronage.[36] Apart from the Westminster connection, there was little to link him to Alsop, and much of which Alsop would have disapproved. Bernard may have wished to bring his own merits to the attention of government; and, with a less self-interested motive, to ensure the wider circulation of Alsop's poetry by associating it with a leading public figure. For the dedication, Bernard wrote a pleasant piece of flattery, in 20 hendecasyllables; this metre is not used by Alsop, the closest approximation being his iambic dedicatory verses (1. 5, 1. 6). It is not uncommon in eighteenth century Latin, and is suitable for anything light-hearted or Catullan in character, allowing the dedication to sound fresh and charming, rather than merely exaggerated, as is the case with so many such pieces, particularly when senators are lauded in empurpled prose. Bernard reminds Newcastle of his patronage of Westminster, founded by the great Queen Elizabeth:

> . . . Non doctae tamen immemor juventae
> Queis interfuit, atriis Elisae
> Artes ingenuas amat fovere . . .

> But he does not forget learned youth, and loves to foster honest arts in Elizabeth's halls, among which he once took his place (lines 11–14).

The last five lines repeat the sentiment of his 1748 proposal:

---

[36] B. Williams, *Whig Supremacy* (1960 edn.), pp. 16, 28, 77–80, 428; P. Langford, *A Polite and Commercial People* (Oxford, 1989), pp. 43, 292–3, etc.

> . . . Non affers rudis ingeni labores:
> Alsopi lyra, vel suo vigore,
> Ter denos superasse jactat annos.
> Sed, si nomine gaudeat Pelhami
> Non ullo metuet perire saeclo.

> You do not bring the labours of an uncultivated mind; Alsop's lyrics can boast
> of lasting thirty years, even by their own unaided strength. But, if they rejoiced
> in the addition of Pelham's name, they would not fear to die in any age.

The final compliment to Pelham's eternal eminence is a necessary part of the
dedication, and handled prettily enough to avoid absurdity. Alsop's reputation is
robust, having stood by itself for so long, but who could deny the value of a
great name? That Newcastle is now remembered only by historians, who are
generally scathing about his behaviour, might have been foreseen by Bernard,
although he could hardly have said so.

The link with Newcastle is perhaps intended to defuse the most politically
explosive aspect of Alsop's life, his Jacobitism. This is effectively smothered by
Bernard in his editing of the text, by the omission of passages that would make it
clear, or even of a whole poem (3. 3: of which we know he was aware, from his
earlier list). Other odes listed, but eventually omitted, are more puzzling. The
religious paraphrase *Epinicium Deborae* [*sic* in list] is not overtly Jacobite, even if a
Jacobite might hope that his own side could sing such a song of victory. One ode
he lists appears to have been lost: at least, it was not found by Bradner, and my
own incomplete searches have not as yet turned it up, although it may well be
somewhere, in one of the many manuscript miscellanies that I have not seen.
The list offers some tantalising details: a title, *Josepho Taylor, Henrico Bridges*, and
the opening, 'Se parat tandem . . .'. Taylor and Bridges [or Brydges] are familiar
names to a reader of Alsop (discussed in Chapter 7). No other ode is addressed to
two people (though there is no reason why one should not be, since they are all
meant for a wider audience than a single addressee). It is just possible that
Bernard was mistaken, and omitted the poem on discovering the mistake: that
the ode was not by Alsop, but another member of the circle (by Bridges to
Taylor, for example, rather than to them both). Even so, copies would still have
circulated and might survive; the poem would certainly be an interesting addi-
tion to the Alsopian corpus. If it were Jacobite, two more of Alsop's friends
could be added to the list of definite sympathisers.

There can be no doubt that Jacobitism was still controversial, and that
Bernard was right to be cautious. The proposal of 1748 came only a few years
after the dangers of the 1745 invasion, that most famous of Jacobite enterprises;
plots continued to be made thereafter, and many of the Pretender's supporters
retained their sympathies, even as practical hopes faded. In 1752, the year of
publication, a medal was struck with the Jacobite slogan, 'Redeat magnus ille

genius Britanniae' [may that great guiding spirit of Britain return], an allusion to the notorious *Redeat* speech of the Oxford Jacobite William King, Principal of St Mary Hall.[37] These considerations will have been fresh in Bernard's mind; if he wished to gain a London audience for Alsop, and to see the book sold to Whigs as well as Tories, he was well advised to treat the text as if it had been politically neutral. The excisions, and the dedication, are both necessary camouflage.

Alsop's lyric style

Much of Alsop's work is as fascinating for its historical significance as for its literary quality. In the following chapters I examine several of his poems in detail, exploring their context, and the skill with which he makes a variety of subtle points. The full scope of his lyric style will, I hope, thus gradually emerge. But it may be worth while to prepare for those discussions, and attempt to convey something of his essential quality, with a critical assessment of one of the odes (2. 18): not necessarily his finest production,[38] but a typical example of his most typical form, the intimate personal epistle. A prose translation cannot easily convey its effect; and a verse translation, though it might be fun to do, would also produce something rather different, and no more helpful for understanding the original. So much of the beauty of his Latin lies in the interplay of language and meaning. The opening line illustrates this well. He addresses his friend John Dolben (see Chapter 7 for his biography), 'bound up in a delightful chain', the chain of marriage. This could be no more than a cliché; in Alsop's hands, the sound reinforces the sense, making it original and memorable. In the three words 'vinc'lo implicitus suavi', there is alliteration and chiasmus (v–c–l/l–c–v; –us/su–); the reversal is not crudely obvious, but adds a subtle link. The linkage is stressed by the elision at the middle of the line (see below for more on this stylistic feature); the highly unusual treatment of 'suavi', in three syllables rather than two, is arresting, making us linger over a significant word. The sensuousness of the poetry and of Dolben's marriage are intertwined. Later lines in the stanza echo the 'v' and 's' sounds, and 'invidendus' at the end of the second line balances 'implicitus' before the end of the first.

The second and third stanzas explore the marriage relationship further. There is more alliteration (especially 'pudentem . . . placidisque . . . palam'), and 'seu . . . seu' in line 7 echo the same words in line 2, and look forward to 'sive . . . sive' (9 and 13), offering an alluring series of alternatives. Even against

---

[37] D. Greenwood, *William King, Tory and Jacobite* (Oxford, 1969), pp. 237–8. See Ch. 8.
[38] These value judgements can be difficult, but I feel that other odes are even better than this one: e.g. 1. 4; 1. 9; 1. 10; 2. 2; 2. 5; 2. 7; 2. 12; 2. 24; 2. 26 (all examined in later chapters: see index of passages cited from Alsop).

his will, Dolben reveals his love; at one moment 'furtivo intuitu pudentem/ Nequiter spectas' [you look wickedly at the modest woman with a furtive glance].[39] The juxtaposition of 'pudentem' [modest] and 'nequiter' [in a wicked, wanton, or worthless fashion] over a break between lines catches the delicate tension between lust and politeness in an eighteenth-century household. The coming whisper in her ear (lines 12–13) is sexually charged, and again uses gloriously sensuous language. As so often in Alsop's writing, the final, short line of a sapphic stanza (the 'adonic') is used to round off the stanza to powerful effect. The end of the fourth stanza is the first occasion in the poem where the sense runs on into the following stanza; the variety is explosive: 'Eripis ardens/ Osculum' [you ardently steal a kiss (16–17)]. The kiss, 'osculum', stands at the start of the stanza, the snatching movement joining it to the previous line; it is repeated at the start of the next line, with dramatic emphasis. And that bold repetition is echoed in lines 26–7, with the doubled 'poscimus' [we ask, we demand] in a parallel position.

The drama of the kiss is followed by a pair of sophisticated classical allusions, to the story of Endymion, and to Catullus' sugary-sweet pair, Septimius and Acme; 'suavius' in line 20 looks back to the opening line (the 'ua' now slurred, as usual, into a single syllable). The allusions reinforce the sense of drama, but also add another level of meaning; there is some hyperbole (are these modern kisses really better than their ancient models?), and that exaggeration may reflect the poet undermining his blissful picture with a sly laugh. Acme is too good to be true, the highest point of perfection; and Endymion's tale is not wholly positive. After these witty allusions, we are ready for the references to Orcus (the god of death, 24), and to the goddess of childbirth, who will allow Dolben to have an heir. These could be dull pieces of classical wallpaper, but here they are invested with more point. We see how much the heir matters to Dolben; with a son, he will no longer be 'Ex-/trema domus spes' [the last hope of the house (39–40)]. He stresses the vital word, 'extrema', by dividing it between the lines; the other occasion in the poem where that technique had been used was in lines 23–4 'extra im-/mitius Orci' [outside the harsh (power) of the underworld]. This parallel reminds us that it was death that threatens to cut off Dolben's line, and which might still destroy the hopes of his new family. For Alsop's own hopes have been shattered in just that fashion; the last stanza turns to the poet himself, in a poignant comparison between his affectionate hopes for Dolben and his own lost chance of similar happiness. He ends by stating his general content-ment: 'Hoc miser uno' [sad in that one respect (i.e., his wife's death)]. The emphatic position of the last word, 'uno', may suggest his isolation (though he has friends like Dolben); it also suggests the devastation caused by this one small

---

[39] 2. 18. 9–10, translated literally (I offer a looser version in Part II).

thing, a person's death. As for the poem as a whole, any reader must judge it fairly on its merits, and come to a personal conclusion. As a result of the qualities discussed above, this poem should be considered (in my own opinion) one of the very best lyric poems of the English Augustan age.

The assessment of Alsop as a superb lyric poet depends primarily on the content of the odes: the wit, the variety, the vivid treatment of contemporary themes. The elegance of the Latin is an important secondary consideration, without which the poems would be much less effective. This is not, on its own, sufficient for great poetry. The work of many other Neo-Latin poets is, from a purely technical point of view, equal or even superior to Alsop's, although few can match him in other respects. He is both elegant and lively, with many passages of sustained humour, and innumerable other humorous touches. As well as producing entertainment, he can on occasion create passages of great power. Some details of his technique are analysed here, as a prelude to the discussion of the poems in the context of the poet's life and times (see Chapters 5, 6, and 7). What follows is necessarily somewhat technical, for which I apologise to the non-Latinate reader, who may wish to skip over some of the metrical details; the overall conclusion, that Alsop is not totally or slavishly Horatian, but lively and inventive on his own terms, is nevertheless important.

For much of the time his language is purely classical. He does allow himself frequent excursions into more exotic vocabulary, occasionally producing his own neologisms. These are mostly humorous combinations such as *Medico-Senator* (2. 1. 61), or Latinisations of English words, such as *alla* for ale (2. 21. 19, 2. 26. 8). Even if it happens that these expressions are found elsewhere (and I have not seen them myself), it is likely that the poet coined them for himself, rather than looking for them in other Neo-Latin works. He is treating Latin as a living language, and is prepared to be original and creative in his use of it.

A favourite technique, employed in numerous odes (including 2. 18) to good effect, is repetition. This often produces a pleasing rhetorical solemnity. As well as repeating a phrase in successive lines, he sometimes returns to it a few lines later (e.g. 2. 1. 1, 5). Certain phrases appealed to him particularly, and are reused with some regularity, both at the opening and in the middle of odes. One recurrent opening is the interrrogative, 'estne quis . . . ?' [is there anyone . . . ?], and variations on it. This also appears later in some odes.[40] Most of his odes are letters to friends, often beginning with a name in the vocative, or the adjective 'chare . . .' [dear . . .] (as in 2. 18). Within an ode, he

[40] See 1. 8. 1–2; 2. 2. 21; 2. 6. 13; 2. 20. 1, 3; 2. 23. 1.

can rouse himself or his addressee with 'quare age . . .' [come, then . . .], a natural expression for him.[41]

Some general features of versification deserve comment, for differing from the classical norm. This does not make them inferior, merely different. The issue is potentially difficult, since there is a tendency in some classicists to scorn post-classical developments; and those without extensive classical training can find metrical points understandably mystifying. To understand Alsop one must try to appreciate the metrical restrictions he accepts, and the freedoms that he allows himself within those rules. In common with most Neo-Latin writers, he is entirely happy to place a short syllable before double consonants in the following word (*sc*, *sp*, *st*, etc.) without lengthening it. Classical poets were very reluctant to do so, although a few examples exist.[42] There are more than 30 cases in Alsop. The results are not unpleasing to the ear: typical examples are *utrumque spectas* (1. 2. 6), and *bona Scotico* (1. 11. 10). This would have sounded quite acceptable. If this common practice is unclassical, another is not: the frequent shortening of a final 'o', usually (but not always) in verbs. This is the continuation of a process that began with the period of Horace and Ovid.[43] There are over 20 instances in Alsop; in the phrase 'edo, poto, scribo' (2. 22. 14) the short syllables are repeated, and found before three consonants.

Two of the poems in Bernard's edition are in iambics (discussed in Chapter 4), three are in alcaics, and the remaining thirty-four are in sapphics. Most of the additional odes found in manuscripts are also in sapphics. Thus the sapphic metre is overwhelmingly predominant, and is Alsop's automatic choice for a personal, epistolary ode, his chief literary form. The alcaic odes[44] are nevertheless of considerable interest. In the first two lines of the alcaic stanza, there are a few instances where he fails to observe the Horatian caesura. Horace did not do so with absolute rigidity, but exceptions are rare.[45] Alsop sometimes admits a short syllable as the fifth syllable of the third line, which is not Horatian.[46] It may be significant that he avoids this more doubtful practice in the odes for publication in university collections. There are also some unusual word divisions in the third line.[47] I do not suppose that any of these subtleties would have

---

[41] See 2. 1. 61; 2. 2. 23; 2. 7. 25; 2. 11. 33; 2. 15. 17; 2. 19. 9; 2. 20. 17; 2. 21. 5; 2. 27. 5 (*eia age*); 3. 2. 17. He probably took the phrase from Virgil: *Aen.* 7. 429, 'quare age, et armari pubem . . .' and 'quare agite . . .' four times.
[42] E.g. Virgil, *Aen.* 11. 309; Horace, *Serm.* 1. 5. 35, 1. 10. 72; Propertius 3. 19. 21, 4. 5. 17; see J. P. Postgate, *Prosodia Latina* (Oxford, 1923), pp. 31–2; D. S. Raven, *Latin Metre* (1965), pp. 24–5.
[43] Postgate, pp. 42–3.   [44] 1. 2, 1. 3, 1. 11, 3. 5, 3. 6, 3. 7.
[45] *Carm.* 1. 37. 14, 4. 14. 17; with a prefix, perhaps a lesser aberration, at 1. 16. 21, 1. 37. 5, 2. 17. 21; see Postgate, p. 97.   [46] 1. 11. 3, 51, 63; 3. 5. 3 (probably), 7.
[47] On Horace's preferred arrangements, see R. G. M. Nisbet, M. Hubbard, *Commentary on Horace: Odes Book 1* (Oxford, 1970), p. xli. (A more detailed essay, but confusing, in N. A. Bonavia-Hunt, *Horace the Minstrel* (1969), pp. 55–6.) Quadrisyllabic endings (Alsop 1. 2. 27, 1. 11. 11 etc.) are infrequent (eleven

seriously troubled a contemporary, and they need only concern us in passing. He allows some heavy elisions of long by short syllables: perfectly classical, but potentially awkward or harsh-sounding.

The sapphic poems, too, contain some harsh elisions. The total number of elisions is high, and there can be two or even three in a single line (e.g. 2. 21. 7, 31). On average, there is one elision approximately every three lines (more frequently if one leaves the adonics out of the calculation). He readily allows elision in the adonic, the short fourth line of the stanza; but it is much less common there than elsewhere. Horace seems to avoid it.[48] A substantial number of the elisions occur at the caesura, tending to obscure it: by an obscured caesura, I mean an instance where there would be a satisfactory break, but for an elision at the fifth syllable, e.g. 'Filium Patri aequiparem . . .' (1. 1. 27). There are also a few lines where the caesura is non-existent, not merely obscured by elision, e.g. 'Pectinis; non Elysias timerem' (1. 4. 55). Overall, about one line in thirteen has an obscured or non-existent caesura. This phenomenon is not evenly distributed; most odes have at least one line without a proper caesura, and a few have an unusually large number.[49]

In this respect, Alsop's sapphic writing is nearer to Catullus than Horace. Horace invented the caesura in this metre, one of his many refinements of the lyric forms he adopted from his predecessors. Catullus, following Greek models, feels no such requirement; some of his lines happen to have a caesura, but many do not.[50] The third and fourth lines were treated as a single metrical unit, and thus Sappho, Catullus and Horace split words between them. Alsop regularly follows this practice, with more than thirty instances; it is used to good effect, to draw attention to the word that straddles the break between lines. On three occasions[51] he extends this licence to the rest of the stanza, in breach of classical restrictions. When used so sparingly, it does not become an irritating affectation; he is prepared to bend the rules, when it suits him to do so, with rather more freedom than most Neo-Latin authors. He employs synaphea to allow elision between lines (which is classical); but he also freely allows hiatus between lines, which is rare but legitimate in Horace.[52] Very occasionally he has a false quantity.[53] No

examples in Horace *Carm.* 1 and 2, none in 3 and 4); double dissyllable (Alsop 1. 2. 19, 59) very rare, twice in Horace; Alsop freely admits a trisyllable preceded by a disyllable (1. 2. 23, 1. 3. 11 etc.), a combination not listed by Nisbet and Hubbard.

[48] Possibly at *Carm.* 2. 16. 8, if one reads *neque* rather than *nec*.

[49] 11 in 3. 1: about 25% (depending on the version); 6 in 2. 12 (12.5%); 6 in 2. 15 (18%).

[50] Catullus 11 has 5 examples (28%), both with and without elision. Elision at the caesura (without its being obscured) is rare in Horace, but does occur: e.g. *Carm.* 2. 4. 10.

[51] 2. 1. 45–6; 2. 4. 30–1; 2. 12. 13–14.

[52] Postgate, p. 111. Hiatus can occur between the third and fourth lines in Alsop: e.g. 2. 1. 11–12.

[53] See commentary on 1. 10. 13; 2. 27. 47; 3. 3. 16; 3. 5. 3.

doubt he relied on his memory and ear, which fail most of us from time to time.

The creative use of classical allusions forms an important part of Alsop's style. It is a regular feature of Neo-Latin poetry to allude to past authors; Renaissance authors naturally wished to show homage in some way to the classics. Ancient authors themselves are always doing so, and awareness of a literary tradition in no way precludes originality. What matters is the function and purpose of the allusion. Neo-Latin allusions can be rather superficial. Sometimes a famous phrase is copied, almost as a private joke between author and reader, who share this piece of learning. Allusion can even be an act of laziness or desperation, to fill out or revive an unpromising subject. Much mythological allusion in Neo-Latin is of this unpromising character, from the pens of famous poets as well as less familiar ones; some of Milton's Latin verse is open to this criticism.[54] The same might well be said of huge masses of vernacular poetry. But occasionally an allusion can make a significant contribution to a poem's value, by encouraging the reader to think about the source and its relationship to the modern poem; this may enhance his understanding of the latter, or even offer another level of meaning for it. This one might term a creative, or constructive, allusion: the allusion is either adding much to the poem, or is quite integral to it. A superficial allusion, on the other hand, adds little; by becoming wearisome, it can detract from the reader's appreciation.

Not all of Alsop's allusions are of this constructive nature. His biblical paraphrase, *Epinicion Deborae* (3. 5), which contains the largest number of clear allusions in his *oeuvre*, has a number of references that seem to be fairly superficial. A different case is 3. 3 which, alone of Alsop's works, depends entirely on allusion to a single model. This approach is one of creative imitation, in which Alsop makes some interesting variations on his theme. The poem is a good deal more inventive than most such attempts: much more interesting, for example, than Marvell's sapphic *Ad Regem Carolum, Parodia*. Most of Alsop's allusions are neither pointlessly superficial nor especially constructive. They add considerable interest, but do not radically alter the message of most poems. Some are easily spotted, then passed over as the reader comes to more original ideas. A few are to phrases familiar enough to be 'tags': to Ennius (via Virgil: on the Cunctator), to the opening of the *Aeneid*, and to Juvenal's 'mens sana . . .'. Most, though not obscure, are not in this category; the poet could generally expect readers to recognise them, but they are not so hackneyed as to be tedious. Some of the allusions that I consider constructive cannot be proved to be deliberate; when they are probably intentional, but not certainly so, the potential ramifications are

[54] See, e.g., R. W. Condee, in J. W. Binns, ed., *The Latin Poetry of English Poets* (London, 1974), pp. 63, 65. (Milton is discussed in Ch. 2.)

often well worth examination. It is not easy to come to definite conclusions on the various shades of likelihood, the distinction between what is probable and what is merely possible. One should try to avoid putting any stress on an interpretation that might be fanciful. But the accumulation of probable instances suggests that constructive allusion is indeed an important part of Alsop's poetic technique.

Two-thirds of the definite allusions are to Horace, the great majority to the *Carmina*. Much fewer, but still significant, are those to Virgil, and to Juvenal. The latter is interesting: the great satirist might well appeal to a modern lyric poet who often has a satirical point to make. Catullus, Ennius, and Lucan are clearly alluded to on a couple of occasions, Homer once, and there is a scattering of possible references to other authors. A wide selection of Horace's odes is represented, more than forty separate poems, if we include those allusions that I assess as possible rather than certain or probable. No single poem is overwhelmingly popular; two which provide the same phrases on more than one occasion are 3. 22 ('Montium custos . . . ') and 4. 2 ('Pindarum quisquis . . . '). They may have been favourites, or simply conveniently useful: the former for its relevance to medicine (practised by several of Alsop's close friends), the latter as an important discussion of the poet's art. A more unusual passage that Alsop appears to quote twice is Juvenal 6. 42–3, '. . . si moechorum notissimus olim/stulta maritali iam porrigit ora capistro' [if he who was once the most notorious of adulterers has now given himself to the yoke (or, literally, halter) of marriage].[55] It may have appealed because it summed up his own situation, or that of some of his friends (as discussed in Chapters 6 and 7).

---

[55] See Alsop 2. 6. 19; 3. 1. A47–8. It might have fitted the content of 2. 2, but is not actually quoted there.

4
Scholarship or Polite Literature

Alsop was writing in a period of vigorous literary activity, but also one of uncertainty over the activities that a scholar should attempt, and the methods that were appropriate. Bitter quarrels raged on this and other issues, in England and abroad, and Alsop was drawn into the debate. At one extreme stood a rigorous approach to scholarly problems; at the other, what might be called polite learning, or polite literature, an interest in past and present writing that concentrated on entertainment, instruction, and creativity. This attitude tended to foster Neo-Latin poetry, though restricting advances in scholarship. I here consider the way in which various aspects of polite literature appear in Alsop's work, and offer comparisons with other contemporaries.

Alsop's Aesop

Dean Aldrich commissioned Alsop's only scholarly publication, an edition of the fables of Aesop, *Fabularum Aesopicarum Delectus* (Oxford, 1698); this was to be the new year's book for 1698. These new year's books were an innovation of John Fell, Dean of Christ Church, resulting from his close involvement with the University Press; his successor, Henry Aldrich, continued the trend.[1] A text was chosen (often patristic under Fell, generally classical under Aldrich) for editing, with a Latin translation, by one of the young gentlemen of the House, generally a promising Student but occasionally an aristocrat. The result was distributed by the Dean as his new year present, and could also be offered for sale in the normal way (some books have variant title pages, one giving details of the bookseller). It was an opportunity for a young scholar to achieve a prestigious first publication. The choice of Aesop may have been partly dictated by the amusing similarity to Alsop's name. Or rather, Alsop may have been chosen as editor partly for that reason, for there were other good reasons for Aldrich to wish for a new edition of Aesop to appear from Christ Church. The book was part of the college's reply

---

[1] See H. Carter, *A History of the Oxford University Press* (Oxford, 1975); S. Morison, *John Fell* (New York and London, 1981).

to the criticisms that had been made of an earlier new year's book, Charles Boyle's *Phalaridis Epistolae* (Oxford, 1695), by the Cambridge scholar Richard Bentley.

The Phalaris controversy attracted great interest at the time, both in the academic world and among that considerable part of polite society that cultivated a reputation for learning by taking sides in academic disputes. The affair now retains its place in the history of scholarship as a result of Bentley's remarkable achievements: his opponents are seen as little more than his stepping-stones to immortality. But this view is the result of hindsight; 'many years elapsed before Tyrwhitt could describe the opponents of Bentley as "laid low, as by a thunderbolt" . . .'[2] Tyrwhitt's remark is in any case rather odd, if one expects a thunderbolt to act instantaneously, or at least with some show of urgency. In Alsop's lifetime, he and his Christ Church colleagues were generally considered to have held their own. Observers in society were less interested in the truth of the more detailed academic arguments than in the style, confidence, and wit of their presentation. Although Bentley was confident and full of scathing wit, his opponents could fully match him in these respects, if not in really substantial scholarship.

The origins and progress of the dispute have been analysed elsewhere, and I will not repeat the full story here.[3] Some points are particularly worth remembering, in order to assess Alsop's role fairly. To begin with, neither Bentley nor his opponents were seriously at fault. Both may be blamed for pursuing the argument, once accidentally initiated, with unseemly vigour. The misunderstanding between Boyle and Bentley stemmed from the behaviour of the bookseller, Bennett, whom Boyle had commissioned to arrange the collation of the Phalaris manuscript in Bentley's care as Royal Librarian: 'To Bentley, had the transaction been fairly stated, not a shadow of blame could be attached; and Boyle was censurable only for giving implicit credit to the representations of his agent.'[4] On the other hand, once the dispute had begun, Bentley deserves as much blame as anyone for its acrimonious nature. The magnificent learning that he displayed, and which has earned him such a place of honour in the scholarly pantheon, was accompanied by a sordid combativeness. Had he been a less ferocious character, he might have settled the dispute with less rancour, and

---

[2] J. E. Sandys, *A History of Classical Scholarship* (Cambridge, 1903–8), 2. 405.

[3] For a recent analysis see J. M. Levine, *The Battle of the Books* (Ithaca and London, 1991): full of relevant detail, but not always to be trusted implicitly (e.g. he is idiosyncratic in thinking that Cicero was a skeptic [*sic*], p. 17; that there was a Dean William Fell, p. 55; that William III was the father of the Duke of Gloucester, p. 343; that an Edward Burney wrote on music, p. 416). See also L. Lehnus, 'Callimaco redivivo tra Th. Stanley e R. Bentley', *Eikasmos* 2 (1991), pp. 285–309; C. O. Brink, *English Classical Scholarship: historical reflections on Bentley, Porson, and Housman* (Cambridge, 1986); R. J. White, *Bentley, a study in academic scarlet* (1965).

[4] J. H. Monk, *Life of Richard Bentley* (2nd edn., 1833), 1. 68.

without compromising either his honour or his devotion to the truth. His admiring biographer, Monk, is forced to conclude that 'his passions were not always under the control, nor his actions under the guidance, of Christian principles; that, in consequence, pride and ambition, the faults to which his nature was most exposed, were suffered to riot without restraint; and that hence proceeded the display of arrogance, selfishness, obstinacy, and oppression, by which it must be confessed that his career was disfigured'.[5]

Whatever the failings of his adversaries, they were provoked by 'Bentley's own singularly offensive character'; 'he argued so haughtily and violently that he created opposition in many readers who were genuine lovers of the classics'.[6] The force of Bentley's language was similarly provoked by the opposition that he received, but the result was still unattractive to most contemporary observers. Dodwell, an independent scholar who disagreed with Bentley's chronology, thought the second version of the *Dissertation* 'written in the same unpleasing style . . . or rather worse and more outrageous'.[7]

Alsop was one of the Christ Church Students who assisted Boyle against Bentley, but his chief contribution was the edition of Aesop rather than the explicit criticism of Bentley's *Dissertation*. The most active figure in the Christ Church camp was Francis Atterbury; if we are to believe a report, apparently from his own pen, he was responsible almost for the whole of it. A manuscript note[8] cites a letter from Atterbury to Trelawny, claiming to have written from the title-page to p. 60, pp. 90–112, 133–84, and 215–30, and 'almost all the examination of the dissertation upon the Fables of Aesop' (pp. 231–66). This leaves about eighty pages, and the index, unclaimed by Atterbury. The index, entitled 'A Short Account of Dr Bentley, by way of Index', is in fact an important part of the volume's sharp wit, as is clear from the opening entry, 'Dr Bentley's true story of the MS prov'd false by the testimonies of—Bennet, Gibson, King, Dr Bentley'. Atterbury was a vigorous controversialist, and it is at least plausible that he wrote more than two-thirds of the book. He may also have wished to exaggerate his own contribution to the joint effort. From the point of view of Alsop's *Aesop*, the important question is whether Atterbury's analysis of Aesop was accompanied by significant assistance in his younger colleague's edition.

The preface of that edition explicitly attacks Bentley, in its opening sentence: 'Scio extitisse nonnullos qui acerrime contenderent, has quae vulgo circum-feruntur Aesopi Fabulas, ab Aesopo illo Fabularum Philosopho non fuisse

---

[5] Monk, *Life* 2. 416–7.   [6] G. Highet, *The Classical Tradition* (Oxford, 1949), pp. 286, and 284.
[7] Levine, p. 78.
[8] Bodleian: printed book, shelfmark Radcliffe.e.100, a copy of *Dr Bentley's Dissertations on the Epistles of Phalaris, and the Fables of Aesop, Examin'd by the Hon Charles Boyle, Esq* (London, 1698). (Printed by T. Bennet, who had a personal axe to grind.)

conscriptas: quod nuperrime fecisse audio Richardum quendam Bentleium Virum in volvendis Lexicis satis diligentem.' [I know there have been some who argue most bitterly that the fables commonly ascribed to Aesop were not written by that Aesop, the philosopher of the fables; I hear that this has most recently been stated by a certain Richard Bentley, a man of fair diligence in turning the pages of dictionaries.] This is rude, but wittily so. It was described as 'a gentle touch': though it was controversial enough to cause trouble for Alsop with the university authorities, who were reluctant to allow publication.[9] By the standards of contemporary literary debate it was a mild attack, its effect coming from the pretence that Bentley was an obscure figure, of whom one had barely heard. To a scholar not known for his modesty, even at this early stage in his career, the slight was well chosen. Bentley would fume at the *quendam*, the bubble of his self-esteem having been pricked, and would receive no sympathy from the polite world. The diligent use of dictionaries (arguably an accurate description of a scholar's life) did not command high social status.

The preface continues by explaining a polite scholar's view: 'Mihi vero non tam Autoris nomen quam Libri materiam et utilitatem expendenti, exhibere sufficit Fabellas si non ab Aesopo, ad illius saltem mentem et normam compositas, quas proinde Aesopicas inscripsi.' [I have been content, indeed, since I do not consider the author's name as important as the book's subject matter and usefulness, to print tales that, if not Aesop's, are at least composed in accordance with his spirit and method, which I have therefore called Aesopian.] He dodges the question of authorship and date by proclaiming its irrelevance, and chooses a title accordingly, *Aesopicarum* not *Aesopi*. This approach is an important aspect of the Christ Church case. In Boyle's original preface, before Bentley's wrath had descended, the question is left open (though the book's title is more straightforward): 'Epistolas has in manus sumenti non tam utile erit inquirere quis scripserit, quam jucundum experiri lectu dignas.' [For a person who takes these letters into his hands, it will be less useful to ask who wrote them, than pleasant to find out that they are worth reading.][10] Sir William Temple, in his uncritical advocacy of the ancients, had been much less careful on this point than Boyle, a distinction Bentley chose to ignore.[11] To a truly inquisitive scholar, it would hardly be satisfactory to leave the matter unsolved; for a lover of polite literature it was mere pedantry, and an admission of doubt would be quite acceptable.

[9] See Ch. 5.   [10] C. Boyle, *Phalaridis Agrigentinorum Tyranni Epistolae* (Oxford, 1695), sig. a3[r].
[11] Cf. Levine, p. 52.

Elegant versions and sharp satire

The main labour in Alsop's *Aesop* was not devoted to the text, but to the preparation of Latin verse translations for those numerous fables which were not otherwise translated. He explains his method in the preface: more respectable ancient versions will be left as they stand, but 'Ignoscet mihi lector si in Avieni et Tanaquilli Fabri versionibus, quae interdum curta essent supplere, quaeque caudam traherent, amputare, minime dubitaverim. In transferendis Fabulis quas hi Autores praeterierant, partem aliquam juventutis meae collocasse, cum senex Socrates idem fecerit, laudi duco. Quis cujusque versionis Autor fuerit, nisi quod valde metuo ex stylo satis innotescat, ex Indice cognosci potest.' [The reader will forgive me if, in the versions by Avienus and Tanaquillus Faber,[12] I have not hesitated from time to time to fill out what was abbreviated, and to cut short what dragged its tail. I am proud to have spent part of my youth in translating fables passed over by these authors, since the aged Socrates did the same. The authorship of each version, if it is not (as I fear it is) quite clear from the style, can be ascertained from the index.] The modesty about his style is attractive, and the size of the task can be seen by the frequency of unattributed translations in the index, each poem not otherwise marked being the editor's. About two-fifths (65) of the 158 Greek fables are accompanied by his Latin. He also translates three of the eight Arabic items, and one of the ten Hebrew, demonstrating the quality of Oriental teaching at Westminster and Christ Church: he may indeed have had help with those languages.

Atterbury and others might perhaps have contributed elsewhere. The analogy with Boyle's reply to Bentley would suggest a corporate effort. On the other hand, Alsop was a better Latinist than Boyle, was no aristocrat, and was engaged in a different type of enterprise, without the need for learned arguments. Others from Christ Church, particularly George Smalridge, were poets of comparable ability and distinction to Alsop (at this stage in his career); if the task proved too lengthy, they could have taken a share. Atterbury's work on Aesop for Boyle's reply does not prove that he took a hand here; though a competent versifier, as they all were, he was less devoted than Alsop to poetry. It would have been quite feasible, if hard work, for Alsop to have written them all in a fairly short time, completing a poem each day for two months or so.

The final fable (p. 128 [no. 237]) is a Parthian shot over his shoulder at Bentley, the arrow poisoned with inventive wit. It is entitled *Canis in praesepi* [the dog in the manger]; dogs feature regularly in the Aesopian canon, and the inattentive reader may be slow to spot that this is a modern imitation. It is worth quoting in full:

[12] The modern French scholar Tanneguy Le Fèvre, father of Mme Dacier.

> Bos post laboris taedia reversus domum,
> Pro more stabulum ingreditur, ut famem levet;
> Praesepe sed prius occupaverat Canis,
> Ringensque frendensque arcet a faeno bovem:
> Hunc ille morosum atque inhospitum vocat,
> Et fastuosum mentis ingenium exprobrat:
> Canis hisce graviter percitus conviciis,
> Tune, inquit, audes me vocare inhospitum?
> Me nempe summis quem ferunt praeconiis
> Gentes tibi ignotae? Exteri si quid sciant,
> Humanitate supero quemlibet Canem.
> Hunc intumentem rursus ita bos excipit;
> Haec Singularis an tua est Humanitas,
> Mihi id roganti denegare pabulum,
> Gustare tu quod ipse nec vis, nec potes?

> An ox, after wearisome labours, returns home and enters his stall, as usual, to satisfy his hunger; but a dog has already taken over his manger, and keeps the ox from the hay, snarling and gnashing his teeth. The ox calls him peevish and inhospitable, blaming his proud spirit; the dog is furious at these insults, saying 'do you dare to call me inhospitable—me, whom races unknown to you celebrate with great pomp? If foreigners know anything, I surpass all dogs in humanity.' As he swells with pride the ox addresses him again, 'Is this your remarkable humanity, to deny me food when I ask for it, which you yourself do not wish to, and cannot, taste?'

There is a clear allusion to the slight that sparked the quarrel, Boyle's remark towards the end of his 1695 preface (sig. a4^v) about the manuscript 'cujus mihi copiam ulteriorem Bibliothecarius pro singulari sua humanitate negavit' [of which the Librarian,[13] by his remarkable humanity, denied me further use]. The selfishness applies to the manuscript, which Bentley did not himself wish to use; it applies to the literature of Phalaris and Aesop, which Bentley despises, and will not let others enjoy. He cannot make proper use of it, since its charm and its moral lessons are not for the turner of dictionaries. There are other clever touches in the poem. The emphasis on the dog's pride is apt (and also absurd: whoever heard of a real dog with humanity?); that pride depends on the high opinion of foreigners, something of which Bentley, with his international scholarly correspondence, was indeed proud. The ox may be intended to remind us of the bull of Phalaris (of which an elegant image, designed by Aldrich, formed Boyle's frontispiece).

A dog was to bring Bentley into public ridicule on another occasion: 'A

---

[13] Bentley, as Royal Librarian. Boyle was not the only scholar he disobliged; 'the books lie in inexpressible disorder and confusion' (Bodleian, ms. Ballard 13, fo. 41: cited by Levine, p. 66 n.). Cf. Hearne, *Coll.* 1. 263, where we find the critic of Boyle's tardiness himself failing to return a ms. (a good example of Bentley behaving badly?).

young student of Magdalene College, Cambridge, having cut off the ear of a setting-dog belonging to Dr B——; the Dr demanded so much money for satisfaction, that the student thought proper to acquaint his tutor . . . and the following verses were spoken at a Tripos there, before the whole University:

> (Dr) . . . sportsmen, you must know,
> Value not only use but show;
> In both which always I excell'd,
> Far finer ne'er appear'd in field:
> Or where's the man throughout the nation
> Sells dogs of better education?
> (Tutor) Few, I confess, Sir, have been longer
> Than you a puppy-pupil-munger:
> But, Doctor, come—Let's have no more;
> The lad, I do assure you, 's poor:
> I'll offer fair enough, I think,
> Five shillings for your man to drink.
> (Dr) Five shillings!—paltry satisfaction!
> I'll hear no more—but bring my Action;
> I'll send this moment, Sir, and get
> From London an Exchequer-Writ . . .'[14]

The Master of Trinity, a notoriously tenacious opponent in his frequent law cases, could be laughed at for his selfish obstinacy; that Cambridge audience may well have remembered Alsop's dog in the manger.

His *Aesop* seems to have been well received, though Bentley himself was, unsurprisingly, scornful: 'A nameless Critick in Town told Mr Hartley, that he could find an errour in every ten lines throughout Aesop. I believe 'tis Dr Bentley; for I'me perswaded that nobody else would be soe eager of spying faults in such an ingenious performance.'[15] Bentley commented, on Alsop and John Freind, that 'if they can but make a tolerable copy of verses with two or three small faults in it, they must presently set up to be authors; to bring the nation into Contempt abroad, and themselves into it at home.'[16] There is no evidence that Alsop received contempt at home, except from a small circle of Bentley's partisan supporters; one foreign admirer of Bentley did express such contempt, without actually troubling to examine the *Aesop* in question.[17] Such attacks were regular features of literary life, and Bentley himself was the target of many.[18] Political

---

[14] Bodleian, ms. Ballard 29. 90 [fo. 137–8].
[15] W. Denison to A. Charlett, 12 February 1697/8: Bodleian, ms. Ballard 21. 85 [fo. 139].
[16] Bentley, *Dissertation* (in 1727 edn., p. xxxv); quoted in Sutherland and Mitchell, *Oxford*, pp. 526–7.
[17] Graevius, Latin letter to Bentley: C. Wordsworth, ed., *The Correspondence of Richard Bentley* (1842), p. 174.
[18] E.g., in addition to the Phalaris dispute, J. Ker, *Quaternae Epistolae* (1713): searching out examples of Bentley's impure Latin; R. Johnson, *Aristarchus anti-Bentleianus* (1717).

differences often exacerbated academic quarrels (as in the case of Oxford Tories against the Whiggish Bentley). This could operate to Bentley's disadvantage within Cambridge; he wrote in 1716 that 'the fury of the whole disaffected and Jacobite party here against me and Mr Waterland [Master of Magdalene] is unexpressible . . . [without help] the King's present of books [will] continue rotting in their baggs.'[19]

It is therefore unsurprising that Alsop's publication attracted some criticism; he was entering a field in which few made their mark to universal applause, since both poetry and scholarship were potentially controversial. A look at the translations themselves shows them to be a very respectable achievement for a young scholar. Most are reasonably short (from about 5 to 20 lines), in keeping with the bare narrative of the Greek. *Aquila & Scarabaeus* (p. 72 [no. 128]) is rather more substantial, with 45 lines, while *Lupus & Vulpes* (p. 97 [no. 167]) has 41: this latter fable being translated from the Hebrew. The eagle of the former, Jupiter's bird, makes an appearance as the hero of Alsop's dedicatory poem to Viscount Scudamore (reprinted by Bernard as ode 1. 5). Closer still is *Luscinia & Accipiter* (p. 17 [no. 28]):

> Dum querula opacam Luscinia super arborem
> Dulci canoros voce modulatur sonos . . .
>
> While a querulous nightingale sings her tuneful songs with a sweet voice
> on a shady tree:

which is very close indeed to 1. 5. 15–16:

> . . . et opaca in fronde Lusciniam videns
> Placidos canora voce modulatur sonos . . .
>
> seeing a nightingale on a shady leaf he sang to her his quiet sounds with
> tuneful voice.

The sweet singer is changed to the lark (who symbolises Alsop himself, in his search for a patron), but the nightingale is intent on similar complaints (line 17). The detail that Alsop creates, and then adopts for his own fable, is not dependent on the Greek. There, the nightingale merely 'κατὰ τὸ εἰωθὸς ᾖδεν' [sang as normal].

The nightingale pleads with the hawk to be spared, on the ground that she is a lesser meal, unworthy of him:

> . . . contra Accipiter; at me flectere
> Tuae illa linguae nec valebit suavitas.
> Me scilicet longe alitum stultissimum

[19] Bentley to S. Clarke: Wordsworth, *Correspondence*, pp. 526–7.

> Jure poteris vocare; si praedam meis
> Certam unguibus dimitterem, incertam sequens.
>
> the hawk replied: this eloquence of yours will not be able to turn me from
> my course; you could rightly call me the stupidest of birds by far, if I
> discarded a certain prey from my talons, in seeking an uncertain one.

The reply in the Greek is simpler, with no mention of the nightingale's suave tongue: 'ἀλλ' ἔγωγε ἄφρων ἂν εἴην, εἰ τὴν ἐν χερσὶν ἑτοίμην τροφὴν ἀφεὶς [sic], τὰ μὴ φαινόμενά πω διώκοιμι' [but I would be an idiot if, having discarded food ready in my hands, I were to pursue what was not visible]. The last one and a half lines are close enough, but ἄφρων is expanded to *longe alitum stultissimum*, ἂν εἴην to *me scilicet . . . jure poteris vocare*. It would certainly have been possible to render the Greek more succinctly. It need not be desirable, and Alsop's copious additions greatly enhance the literary charm of the stories, without losing their moral points. In this instance, the emphasis on the stupidity of a creature that abandons a good thing in its grasp is reminiscent of the *Canis in praesepi* fable. A general motive for expansion may be the championing of Aesop as a fine writer, an important aspect of the case for the 'ancients' in the controversy. If Phalaris and Aesop are not only spurious but also feeble, there can be no reason to read them; if they may be spurious, but are at least good, then a polite scholar may ignore their date and enjoy what he can learn from them. On this Boyle and Bentley differed; the dog in the manger would keep others away from what he cannot appreciate. *Luscinia & Accipiter* could be seen to have a similar moral: the stupidity of scorning what one has, in the search for uncertain alternatives, reminds us of the scholar's rejection of Aesop and Phalaris. The improvement of Aesop, in Latin verse that can stand comparison with Phaedrus and others, is a useful weapon.

James, 3rd Viscount Scudamore of Sligo (1684–1716), to whom *Aesop* is dedicated, was a young nobleman at Christ Church. He had succeeded to the title in July 1697. Having first matriculated at Gloucester Hall, he migrated in August 1697, remaining at Christ Church for little more than a year (his caution money being returned in November 1698).[20] He was a Tory, sitting in the English Commons.[21] The dedicatory fable is an attractive plea for patronage, combining praise of the young eagle's firmness and virtue with ridicule of alternative patrons, who are too absorbed in their own concerns, their own foolish songs, to listen to the lark. The use of fables to make such points is a

---

[20] Christ Church archives; his tutor seems to have been Robert Freind.
[21] MP for Hereford (city, 1705–15; county, 1715–6); James Brydges, Alsop's patron (see Ch. 7) was also a Hereford MP, 1698–1714. Scudamore married, in 1706, a daughter of the 4th Baron Digby of Geashill; Alsop's friend Dolben later married into the same family (see Ch. 7). Cf. G. E. C., *Peerage*; *History of Parliament*.

common literary phenomenon:[22] one may compare, in Latin, Pitcairne's Jacobite approach (discussed in Chapter 6). The vernacular offers a positive flood of fables from this period, many from 1698 itself, and other editions and imitations of Aesop, in various tongues, could easily be had; one may note particularly Roger L'Estrange, *Fables of Aesop* (1692), F. Barlow, *Aesop's Fables . . . in English, French and Latin* (1687, revised from 1666), and W. D. See, *Aesop's Fables* (14th edition by 1698). Apart from the interest of the Phalaris quarrel, readers of Alsop's version will have had plenty of opportunity to familiarise themselves with the genre. One may speculate, though with little certainty, as to how these particular fables might have been interpreted, by author or audience. *Luscinia & Accipiter*, for example, may have encouraged Alsop to realise the futility of music and rhetoric in the face of brutal power. Aesop does not spell out his morals, so there is room for each to draw his own.

The painter and the historian

Comparable to the Scudamore dedication, but interestingly different, is the iambic poem (reprinted by Bernard as 1. 6) written for Sir Godfrey Kneller (1646–1723). The most famous painter of the age, knighted in 1691, and created a baronet in 1715, he was notoriously vain, and it is possible that a hint of satire accompanies Alsop's praise. The comparison with the minor historian Velleius Paterculus, known for his support of Tiberius, may undermine Kneller's greatness. Kneller firmly supported the Whigs and the Hanoverian succession, and was thus at odds with Alsop's politics. They met in 1701, when Kneller came to Christ Church to draw Dr Wallis (see Chapter 6). He then declared that James II's son was legitimate, scorning the story that the baby was introduced in a warming pan; this he repeated before a large company at Aldrich's table, including Alsop, John Pelling, and Dr Hudson the librarian. David Gregory noted that 'the declaration of . . . Kneller upon this subject is the more to be regarded, because he is intirely in K. William's interest . . . and . . . owns all sort of aversion to K. James' memory and his party.'[23]

Hudson had edited Velleius in 1693;[24] this was reprinted in 1711, also in

[22] See, e.g., A. Patterson, *Fables of Power* (Durham and London, 1991): no bibliography, however, and the odd eccentricity (e.g. p. 149: Gay's *Beggar's Opera*, 1628 [*sic*] as an attack on Thomas [*sic*] Walpole's government); S. N. Zwicker, *Politics and Language in Dryden's Poetry* (Princeton, 1984); E. Hodnett, *Aesop in England* (Charlottesville, VA, 1979).
[23] Gregory's journal, Christ Church ms. 346; W. G. Hiscock, *David Gregory, Isaac Newton and their circle* (Oxford, 1937), p. 11.
[24] There is a variant title-page: one issue (for presentation as a new year's book) without booksellers' names, the other 'Prostant venales apud Joh. Crosley, Geor. West, Hen. Clements, & Joh. Howel'. The former has a letter *Lectori*, recording Arthur Charlett's encouragement and Dodwell's help (sig. *3ᵛ).

Oxford, for sale by the bookseller John Wilmot (who advertises some of his other classical offerings at the foot of the title-page). The reprint is dedicated to Kneller, with Alsop's verses (but not his name). The preface explains how the unnamed editor was encouraged by learned men to issue the book, 'Quum rara admodum essent exemplaria Velleii, anno MDCXII [sic] Oxoniae excusi' [since copies of the Velleius printed at Oxford in 1692/[3] are very rare]. It is not clear why Alsop wrote this particular dedication: probably to oblige the editor. He may have been amused and inspired by other poets' flattery of Kneller. One might compare Thomas Tickell's *To Sir Godfrey Kneller at his country seat*:

> . . . To court thy pencil, early at thy gates
> Ambition knocks, and fleeting Beauty waits . . .
> . . . Hast thou forgot that mighty Bourbon fear'd
> He still was mortal, till thy draught appear'd . . .[25]

Pedestrian praise of Kneller also appears occasionally in university collections: e.g. William Ince (Christ Church) in 1700, N. Benny (Queens', Cambridge) in 1702, and an alcaic ode by James Dalrymple (Queen's, Oxford) in 1708. Although Kneller is by far the most popular addressee, other artists did receive public praise in Latin verse. Isaac Hawkins Browne celebrated Highmore;[26] Alsop's medical friend Noel Broxholme honoured the sculptor Rysbrack.[27] Like Tickell, Alsop notes two classes of customer for the artist:

> . . . sive magnanimos duces
> Regesque pingis, seu decora virginum
> Describis ora . . .

> whether you paint great-hearted leaders and kings, or mark out the attractive faces of maidens (1. 6. 5–7);

similarly we note the portrait of Louis XIV, commissioned by Charles II:

> Pingente Velleio, Vinicii indolem
> Nec lector odit improbatve Tiberium:
> Pingente Knellero, nec horremus trucem
> Frontem Ludovici, aridasve Lyces genas.

> When Velleius paints the picture for him, the reader does not hate the nature of Vinicius, nor blame Tiberius; when Kneller paints, we do not shudder at the savage brow of Louis, or Lyce's dry cheeks (1. 6. 12–15).

The comparison with Velleius is subtle. Vinicius was Velleius' own dedicatee, consul in AD 30 and 45, executed in 46; Tiberius chose him as husband for his adopted granddaughter, Julia, the daughter of Germanicus (at whose untimely

---

[25] In R. Dodsley, *Collection* (1782 edn.), 1. 39–41.
[26] *Poems* (1768), p. 130; reprinted in Popham, *Selecta Poemata* (1779 edn.), p. 293. See Ch. 8.
[27] British Library, ms. Add. 51441 (unbound papers), fo. 108.

death, if we are to believe Tacitus, the emperor's grief was feigned). Vinicius was feeble rather than vicious;[28] Tiberius' reputation is much worse. Thus it is a doubtful compliment to say that the historian can make these people seem acceptable: that requires skilful economy with the truth, a technique that one can admire, but must beware of. Kneller can make the tyrant Louis seem attractive, but he is still a tyrant. The same might be said of his more regular patrons (especially William III; it is less likely that Alsop would think ill of Anne). Female beauty, as portrayed by Kneller, can conceal a horrible reality (as do the paints women apply to their own faces), a point emphasised by the allusion to Horace's Lyce, over whose deterioration into disreputable old age he gloats at *Carmina* 4. 13. Both Velleius and Kneller, manipulators of oily words and wonderful oils, are in some respects to be seen as frauds, clever deceivers of anyone so foolish as to be convinced. This is not to deny that admiration for them (as for masters of any creative medium) can be genuine. The ostensible purpose of Alsop's poem is purely laudatory, but he is himself a subtle artist, and can operate on more than one level of meaning.

The chief metre of the Aesop translations[29] is the iambic trimeter, also used in the poems to Scudamore and Kneller. Alsop's use of the metre is generally accomplished, though the results are much less elegant than his sapphics. As in other metres, he allows himself a range of freedoms. He is happy to use anapaests in the fifth foot (seven times in 1. 5, five in 1. 6); this is found, rarely, in Horace (e.g. *Epod.* 2. 35), but became common in Seneca.[30] More unusually, he can admit a dactyl in the fifth foot (1. 6. 16, 21), which seems a reversion to the greater freedom of the comic senarius, as found in Plautus and Terence. The Roman comedians were particularly familiar to anyone educated at Westminster, as a result of the Latin plays performed there. These free senarii are also used in the fables of Phaedrus, many of which appear in the *Aesop* edition. His style may well have been formed by a conscious desire to blend in with Phaedrus, or there may be an unconscious influence resulting from close familiarity with his work. For fables, Phaedrus is a more natural model than Horace.

He also freely divides his resolutions:[31] i.e., when the legitimate variations of the verse are deployed, as when the basic iambic foot is changed into a tribrach (with the long syllable resolved into two shorts), he allows a word-break to separate those two shorts, while classical authors tend to treat them as a pair. When these broken resolutions occur too frequently (as in the rather awkward final line of 1. 6), the poetry can suffer: the natural rhythm becomes harder for the reader to follow. Another slightly dubious feature of his iambics is the

---

[28] Tacitus *Ann.* 6. 15, 45 (cf. 4. 1, 'Germanici mortem inter prospera ducebat'); Cassius Dio 60. 25, 27.
[29] N.b. translations in hexameters: p. 48 [no. 82], p. 59 [no. 104], p. 60 [no. 107], p. 74 [no. 130], p. 78 [no. 139]. Other metres are also possible for fables: e.g. Avienus' elegiacs, p. 89 [no. 157].
[30] See D. S. Raven, *Latin Metre* (1965), p. 52.   [31] E.g. 1. 5. 15, 31; 1. 6. 15, 16, 18, 21 (twice).

occasional lack of a main caesura.[32] It is blemishes of this sort that Bentley will have sneered at; they are a sign of Alsop's free approach, and need not detract too much from the overall charm of the poetry. The large amount of iambic verse written rapidly for the demands of a specific occasion, the *Aesop* edition, did not endear the metre permanently to Alsop. He realised that the lyric ode offered much greater scope for his Muse. It was in lyric forms that he attempted large scale panegyric, of Ezechiel Spanheim (2. 27) and, if it is really his, of the University of Frankfurt-on-the-Oder, in the *Carmen Saeculare* of 1706 (4. 12).

Hearne describes the Encaenia ceremony held in commemoration of the German university; degrees were awarded, and George Smalridge of Christ Church pronounced a 'Noble Encomium' upon Mr Grabe, who was made DD, and given 'a Ring, signifying that the University of Oxford and Francfurt were now joyn'd together and became two Sisters, and that they might be more firmly united together as well in Learning as in Religion, he [Smalridge] kiss'd Mr Grabe. As soon as this part of the Solemnity was ended verses and Speeches were spoke by several Young Students, and Musick perform'd as usual upon such extraordinary occasions.'[33] Among the poems on the Encaenia programme are two sapphic odes that may possibly be Alsop's, the long *Carmen Saeculare*, recited by W. Harvey and A. Meredith, and the shorter 'Concentus secundus' (i.e. 4. 11, beginning 'Carminum praeses . . .'), which was set to music, and has no name beside it.[34] They both appear in the British Library manuscript, but without explicit attribution to him. The music for 4. 11 was probably by Aldrich; both words and music were used, with some variations, on other occasions.[35] I rather doubt that both the odes are Alsop's, although it is not impossible. He was sufficiently senior by 1706 for his work (if not his name) to figure so prominently. Equally, one or both may well be by another hand (perhaps Aldrich's), or a collaborative composition.

Possibly the interest in Prussia roused by the Encaenia led indirectly to Alsop's praise of Baron Spanheim (1629–1710), the distinguished scholar and diplomat.[36] Spanheim sent a copy of his new book to Oxford, with a Latin inscription thanking the university for giving him an honorary degree (taken in absence).[37] The book was the first volume of a new edition of his great

---

[32] E.g. 1. 5. 8, 1. 6. 12, 20: all with a *semiternaria*.

[33] *Coll.* 1. 235 (26 April 1706); cf. 1. 263–4 (King of Prussia's letter), 267–8 (Orator's answer 'hardly Latin, 'twas done anew by another').

[34] *Academiae Francofurtanae ad Viadrum Encaenia Secularia* (Oxford, 1706).

[35] See T. A. Trowles, 'The Musical Ode in Britain, *c.* 1670–1800' (unpublished D.Phil. thesis, Oxford, 1992), 2. 13–15.

[36] For his life, see V. Loewe, *Ein Diplomat und Gelehrter Ezechiel Spanheim* (Berlin, 1924). In 1690 Spanheim composed an interesting *Relation de la Cour de France*, ed. E. Bourgeois (Paris and Lyon, 1900).

[37] Hearne, *Coll.* 1. 269 (5 July 1706); cf. 1. 265 (21 June 1706: letter from Spanheim to Delaune about the Encaenia).

numismatic treatise, *Dissertationes de praestantia et usu numismatum* (London, 1706), first published in Rome in 1664 (under the eccentric encouragement of Queen Christina), and now presented as a massive and magisterial folio, illustrating the use of coins and medals for the study of all aspects of ancient history. The subject aroused much interest, influencing, for example, Addison's *Dialogues upon the Usefulness of Ancient Medals*. Spanheim had long been a diplomat in the service of the Palatinate, and from the 1680s of Frederick William of Brandenburg, the 'Great Elector'. From 1701 until his death he represented Prussia in London, and his great diplomatic prestige was indicated by the pomp of his formal entry into the city.[38] He would, under normal procedure, have been recalled in 1707, when his English counterpart left Prussia; but Anne chose to keep him: 'aegre licet virum tam egregium, aulae simul ac literati orbis ornamentum, e regnis nostris exire patiamur' [we would not wish to let so distinguished a man, an ornament of both the court and the world of letters, leave our kingdom].[39]

His scholarship was wide-ranging, including works on Aristophanes, Josephus, and Julian. He admired Bentley, and made efforts to assist him.[40] He could also attract criticism, for assembling a mass of ill-digested information.[41] The coins seem to have had a genuine appeal for Alsop; most of the examples he uses in the ode do occur in Spanheim's book. He may or may not have known him personally; the ode is more formal than his intimate letters to close friends. A possible link is Spanheim's interest in science, indicated by a legacy to the Royal Society (cf. Alsop's friends, discussed in Chapter 6).[42]

Frivolity and godliness in English

Alsop's serious devotion to Latin poetry led to work that was often humorous, but rarely trivial: polite literature at its best. An educated man could also turn his hand to lighter things, and Alsop wrote a number of pieces in English. They are not devoid of wit, and show a facility at the jauntier contemporary verse forms. Four light-hearted love poems were published by Dodsley,[43] of which the third,

---

[38] Loewe, p. 150.

[39] Loewe, p. 154; whoever wrote Anne's Latin seems to have understood Ciceronian clausulae.

[40] Monk, *Life of Bentley*, p. 24; Wordsworth, *Correspondence*, 1. 240, 260, 375.

[41] Cf. Wyttenbach, quoted in J. E. Sandys, *History of Classical Scholarship* (1908), 2. 402; Gibbon, *Decline and Fall*, ch. 24, n. 1 (but praise elsewhere). His mistake about Ovid: J. Masson, *P. Ovidii Nasonis Vita* (Amsterdam, 1708), pp. 3–11.

[42] R. K. Bluhm, 'Remarks on the Royal Society's Finances', *Notes and Records of the Royal Society of London* 13 (1958), p. 86.

[43] 4. 1, 2, 3, 4. R. Dodsley, ed., *Collection of Poems* (1748, often reprinted: in 1782 ed., vol. 6, pp. 256–68); cf. J. A. Tierney, ed., *Correspondence of Robert Dodsley, 1733–64* (Cambridge, 1988), p. 296: 'English pieces of Tony Alsop, quite unknown'.

The Fable of Ixion, is the most substantial. It is interesting to see the editor of Aesop using the genre in this very un-Aesopian way, no doubt influenced by the wide bounds of the vernacular genre. The story is retold in a lively manner, cleverly interspersed with details of Strephon's chaster passion for Chlorinda (these pastoral lovers being common to the set of four poems). The rhymes can be highly amusing, if sometimes stilted. It begins with aplomb:

> Ixion, as the poets tell us,
> Was one of those pragmatic fellows . . .

and continues in a similarly irreverent vein, making contemporary references to lighten the mythology. Thus Juno governs the clouds:

> . . . by nod or summons,
> As Walpole does the House of Commons.
> This cloud which came to her stark-naked,
> She dress'd as fine as hands could make it. (lines 54–7)

> [she brought:] . . . A quilted petticoat beside,
> With whalebone hoop six fathom wide;
> With these she deck'd the cloud, d'ye see?
> As like herself, as like could be:
> So like, that could not I or you know
> Which was the cloud, and which was Juno.
> Thus dress'd she sent it to the villain,
> To let him act his wicked will on . . . (lines 66–73)

The moral is that Chlorinda's seeming complaisance vanishes, when put to the test:

> And when he plum'd, and grew most proud,
> All was a vapour, all a cloud. (lines 96–7)

Whether this reflected Alsop's own wooing of the delectable, frivolous and highly dangerous Mrs Astrey, one can only guess; his other English poems are to John Dolben (4. 5, 6), and the wedding song uses the name Strephon again; this may suggest that Dolben, not Alsop, is the hero of the Chlorinda poems.[44] Although their genre is conventional, Alsop's English poems are somewhat better than the average standard of eighteenth-century light verse. Even so, there is no question that Alsop is but a minor poet in his native language, and a far finer one in Latin.

He did not publish any sermons, as more ambitious clergymen generally did, but reports of his preaching do survive. He preached in 1711, at St Mary's in Oxford, on St Thomas (15 April) and on the sale of Joseph by his brethren (28 December).[45] One remark in the latter might possibly be given a Jacobite, as

---

[44] See Ch. 7 for both Astrey and Dolben.   [45] Bodleian, ms. Rawl. D. 1348, fo. 99 and 137.

well as a safe, interpretation: 'Hence we learn that tho' God may suffer the innocent to be oppressed for a time, yet he will at last gloriously deliver you . . .'. An Oxford Tory might see himself as oppressed (though less so in 1711 than before or after), and look for divine deliverance on earth.

Hearne records a discussion which suggests that he was a controversial, but generally respected, preacher: 'Being last night with Dr Mill, Mr Pearce, who was then with him too, was pleas'd to run down Mr Alsop of Xt Churche's sermon . . . affirming that there was neither style, sense or judgement shewn in it. Dr Mill concurred with him, and from thence proceeded to call him the greatest Blockhead that ever lived. Upon which knowing Mr Alsop had the universal character of being a man of singular modesty, wit, and good learning, I spoke up for him, and told them that the sermon bore an extraordinary character in the university . . .'[46]

Alsop's religious energies could also be directed towards Latin verse, as is demonstrated by his paraphrases of the *Te Deum* (1. 1) and *Epinicion Deborae* (3. 5). These are very accomplished contributions to the long Neo-Latin tradition of religious paraphrase. *Epinicion Deborae* is based on the song of Deborah (*Judges* 5), at times rather loosely imitating the Bible, leaving out much and adding considerably to the poetic effect. The most dramatic points are retained and embellished. In many passages Alsop's ode is identical, or similar, to a fuller version by Dr John Burton (1696–1771), a keen writer of paraphrases; Burton uses 38 stanzas (nearly twice as many), following the story more closely.[47] Although Alsop might possibly have borrowed from Burton, it is more likely that the younger man adapted Alsop's work. There is vigour in the descriptions, triumph and pathos in the fall of Sisera. Alsop's natural style fits well with the repetition of the original, as in lines 65–8 (identical in Burton, lines 129–32):

> Heroa cerno sub pedibus tuis
> Lapsum, volutum; sub pedibus tuis
>   Lapsus, volutus, stratus Heros
>   Purpureo vomit ore vitam.

> Authorised Version, *Judges* 5. 27: 'At her feet he bowed, he fell, he lay down: at her feet he bowed, he fell: where he bowed, there he fell down dead.'

The version of *Te Deum* is closer to his model,[48] but still manages to add dramatic emotion and poetic elegance (especially in lines 37–40, and at the end of the poem).

---

[46] *Coll.* 1. 57 (17 October 1705).
[47] E. Popham, ed., *Selecta Poemata Anglorum Latina* (2nd edn., London, 1779), pp. 28–34.
[48] On which see, e.g., A. E. Burn, *The Hymn 'Te Deum' and its author* (1926); F. L. Cross, E. A. Livingstone, eds., *The Oxford Dictionary of the Christian Church* (2nd edn., Oxford, 1974).

Some other Latin contemporaries, and Alsop's hexameters and elegiacs

A number of poets gained a reputation from Latin verse in this period, evidence of the status of polite literature in society, and the interest taken in original Latin. None proved, in the end, quite as important as Alsop—certainly not in his preferred medium, the ode. Many wrote accomplished hexameter poems, chief among them Joseph Addison. Though Addison is remembered for his essays, he made his mark as a Latin poet. His most important poems are descriptive or mock-heroic.[49] His youthful commitment to Neo-Latin is underlined by his editing of an anthology of mainly recent British work, *Musarum Anglicanarum Analecta* (1699), an expansion of an anonymous edition of 1692. Samuel Johnson notoriously expressed a low opinion of Addison's Latin compositions (in the *Lives of the Poets*); it is the genre as a whole that Johnson scorns, for clothing trivial thoughts in sonorous language. The same strictures could well be applied to some of Johnson's own more pompous moments. Addison is a skilful and entertaining Latin poet, if not a great one.

George Smalridge's *Auctio Davisiana*[50] was popular enough to provide the motto to *Spectator* 389 (27 May 1712), the only Neo-Latin work so honoured; the quotation is attributed to Horace, a mistake that perhaps indicates the poem's popularity.[51] Another much-read piece was Edward Holdsworth's *Muscipula* (1709), a humorous satire that elicited a more pointed reply, *Hoglandiae Descriptio*.[52] Thomas Hill's *Nundinae Sturbrigienses* (1709) is another humorous vignette of contemporary life, centred on Stourbridge fair. Curll's publication of these pieces suggests their marketability.[53] A substantial amount of Latin prose and poetry by Matthew Prior survives (much of it in the form of academic exercises, or biblical paraphrase).[54] His *Carmen Seculare* was turned into Latin by Thomas Dibben, who produced a very substantial set of hexameters.[55]

Many poems that were successful separately or in anthologies had originally been composed for public recitation at one of the universities. It is to this genre of hexameter poetry that Alsop's pieces, *Givetta Ardens* (3. 8) and *Hircocervus* (3. 9) belong. Both of Alsop's extended hexameter poems are lively and amusing, though in different ways. *Hircocervus* is devoted to domestic satire, while *Givetta Ardens* returns to the subject of war (as seen in 1. 2 and 3. 6). Humour and the horror of war are combined; we can laugh at a Catholic monk, at a drunken

[49] Bradner, pp. 222–3; R. P. Bond, *English Burlesque Poetry, 1700–50* (Cambridge, MA, 1932); U. Broich, *The 18th century Mock-heroic poem* (Cambridge, 1990).
[50] Bradner, p. 215.   [51] See D. F. Bond, ed., *The Spectator* (Oxford, 1965) 3. 459.
[52] By T. Richards, possibly with some help from Alsop in correcting: Hearne, *Coll.* 2. 445.
[53] Bradner, p. 228.
[54] See H. B. Wright, M. K. Spears, eds., *The Literary Works of Prior* (2nd edn., Oxford, 1971), 2. 723–70 (works), 1044–60 (notes).   [55] Published with Prior's *Poems* (in 1725 edn., 1. 151–70).

Dutchman, and at a Swiss who commits suicide on the burning of his beloved beard; an explosion also tears a Frenchman apart, as the fire rages, destroying all before it and terrorising civilians. There is domestic humour as well, with the various speakers bickering about the reliability of newsletters (a subject Alsop was to return to: see Chapter 5). *Hircocervus* is rather closer to the Horatian pattern for satire, with varied examples of incongruity, several taken from literature (when comedy affects a tragic pose, the result is absurd). These familiar themes are nevertheless adapted to amuse a specifically Oxonian audience: we end with a view of the monstrosities in the Ashmolean museum.

Similar themes occur in some of the sets of elegiacs that have been attributed to Alsop. These attributions are not too reliable; very large numbers of poets could produce witty verses as college exercises, with some of the best being preserved, copied, and recited. The Lent verses published in 1723 are all anonymous. It is very dangerous to make attributions on stylistic grounds, while the generally fluid anonymity of the genre, in which rumour or error might easily reassign the authorship of one piece among hundreds in circulation, renders manuscript notes potentially misleading. Some of the poems are very good: but I hesitate to use that as a reason to make them Alsop's. A drunken Dutchman crops up in one of the epigrams (4. 19), which is a brilliant summary of the effects of alcohol (no doubt from bitter experience); the feeling of the whirling room may never have been better immortalised. The theatre, and incongruous situations, also provide subjects for wry satirical comments. The starving playwright convinced of his genius is a stock character, but one well handled in 4. 15; in a later part of that poem (or group of poems) Horace himself is accused of hypocrisy, a sign that he was not held in excessive awe. The picture of the sleepless beggar in the city (4. 14), on the other hand, is full of pathos, and possibly even anger at society's unfairness, provoked by the Juvenalian theme (taken from satire 3, later the model for Johnson's *London*). The continual, horrific self-punishment of Ixion (4. 16) reminds us of the much lighter treatment of the same myth in the English poem, 4. 3.

Perhaps the most interesting of the Lent verses, and one to which Alsop has a fair claim, is the counter-attack aimed at a Whig critic of the Oxford almanacks (4. 25). 'The almanacks for 1702 and the two preceding years provoked a pamphlet accusing Dean Aldrich of Jacobite and papist sympathies.'[56] There may have been something in the criticisms (there were certainly Jacobites there, including Alsop), and the designs were deliberately obscure. Since Aldrich designed them personally, the reputation of the almanacks mattered to him

---

[56] H. M. Petter, *The Oxford Almanacks* (Oxford, 1974), p. 7: finding the pamphlet 'ludicrous'; [Anon.], *Hieroglyphica Sacra Oxoniensia: being an Explanation of the Christ Church Almanacks since the commencement of this century* (London, 1702).

and to the college. The pamphlet asks 'whether the gentlemen of C[hrist] C[hurch] Principles and Morals, are fit persons to be intrusted with the Education of the Nobility and Gentry of England?': this affected Alsop's livelihood as a Tutor, and might well provoke a response. The almanack is defended not on the ground of loyalty, but because the carping critic sees things which are unproven, only one among a thousand possible interpretations. This is somewhat disingenuous; a cryptic Jacobite meaning is not far-fetched, and for many years the almanacks continued to be controversial.[57] Alsop's non-lyric poetry (of which the two large hexameter poems are the most important part) shows him to be the equal of any contemporary practitioner, a flexible devotee of polite literature in the public forms that were expected of him, as well as those he preferred for private use. Very different from the formal elegance of this type of poetry, and less well known, was the work of Joshua Barnes, discussed below; though a highly significant writer, he did not even rate a mention in Bradner's index.

The epic eccentricity of Joshua Barnes

While Bentley represented one aspect of scholarship, there were other approaches to it, apart from that of Boyle. There could not be a greater contrast between Bentley and his fellow Cantabrigian Joshua Barnes, a prolific classical scholar, and an equally prolific Neo-Latin poet.[58] As devoted to learning as Bentley (though very much less proficient), he did not see an opposition between scholarship and creative literature.

Barnes was admitted to Emmanuel College, Cambridge, in 1671, at the age of 17, and matriculated a year later; very soon after his matriculation, on 28 March 1673, he presented to the master and fellows a manuscript volume of his Greek poetry, entitled *Metaphraseis*, demonstrating that he was already a master of the fluent Biblical paraphrase that had been practised by James Duport; he acknowledges his debt to Duport by taking as his mottoes quotations from Duport's paraphrase of the Psalms. Bound up with this presentation volume (Emmanuel ms. 79) is another book, dedicated to Duport himself, containing his *Palizoos Homeros*. At the end of each of the books he fills the gap with a selection, as he puts it, from his epigrams: 'Ad implendam hanc lacunam

[57] E.g. 1712 (High Church triumph?); 1733 (Laud and Charles I blasphemously compared to John the Baptist and Christ?): Petter, pp. 47, 59. Aldrich, however, tended to copy figures from existing engravings (four separate sources identified by Petter for 1702; in 1694, just Poussin's *Dance to the Music of Time*): all need not be cryptic.
[58] See Levine, pp. 149–68 (on his scholarship, the difficulties he encountered, etc.): less good on his poetry, seemingly unaware that his unfinished epic survives and is in Latin, p. 154.

quaedam ex epigrammatis meis subjiciam . . .'. He prefaces the *Metaphraseis* with a Latin distich:

> Biblia Materiam, verborum flumen Homerus
> Contulit; Hunc Docti, ast Illa fovete Pii.

> The Bible provided my subject, Homer my torrent of words: learned men should cultivate the latter, but pious men the former.

His precocious literary career had commenced during his schooldays at Christ's Hospital; and this mixture of scholarship, religion and vigorous versification—truly a torrent of words—was to characterise the rest of Barnes' life.

The amazing fluency, in both extended pieces and extempore epigrams, that he had achieved by 1673 no doubt helped to impress the college authorities. He had some influential patrons, as is indicated by a letter to him from Edmund Calamy, dated 4 July 1672:[59]

> Joshua: Having this opportunity of sending a few lines to you . . . I am loath to let it slip, though my many urgent occasions will not permit me to inlarge. For the first place I would press you to thankfulness. God hath raised up many friends to maintain you first at Schoole now at University. When other young men . . . are cast out into the wide world to shift for themselves, you have a comfortable and competent allowance. Now to whom much is given much is expected both from God and man . . . take heed of spending too much time in visits either in your own college or abroad. Love not those ceremonies which the necessity of the times oblige you to observe, & think it no shame if others should discern that you comply with them as your burden . . . keep to your book and pen 12 hours a day, and let the other 12 be for sleep, meals and other divertisements: strive to be eminent in what you take in hand that your Tutor and the fellows may take notice of you. Spend more time in the rational part of learning than in the languages. Especially lay a good foundation in logic. I am called off. Let me hear of your proficiency . . . Your loving friend, Edmund Calamy.

It is likely that he followed Calamy's advice, and strove eagerly to make a good impression. He was rewarded with a fellowship in 1678, and, in 1695, became Regius Professor of Greek, which he remained until his death in 1712. He retained his youthful interest in composition: Emmanuel ms. 178 is a collection from the 1690s of his earlier and current work; he did not abandon pieces he had written long ago, but carefully revised them. Thus his revised version of *Palizoos Homerus* 'ut recentior sic contra Censuram munitior mihi apparet; sed quid vana spe laetor? Omnia sunt infirma, omnia vellicantibus obnoxia' [since it is newly revised, it seems to me to be better fortified against criticism; but why should I rejoice in vain hope? Everything is unsafe, all is at the

---

[59] Currently kept loose with Emmanuel ms. 175.

mercy of cavillers]: he attacks also the 'mordaces Criticorum turmas' [the carping hosts of critics]. It seems that Barnes was sensitive to criticism; Bentley is said to have given him the very backhanded compliment, on the subject of his scholarly editions, that he knew as much Greek as an Athenian cobbler. Similarly, in pouring out poetry in a continuous rapid stream, he made himself an easy target for malicious critics. He probably had as many admirers as detractors. His sensitivity, however, to his detractors is illustrated by the anecdote, quoted in the *DNB*, about the circumstances of his death: that a club of fellow critics meeting in a tavern made him give a public apology to a rival editor of Anacreon's poems, one William Baxter, with whom he had argued—he died a fortnight later, his death supposedly hastened by this embarrassment.

Whether or not we accept this particular anecdote, there is plenty of evidence that he felt he had not received the recognition he deserved. He died relatively poor, in receipt of the charity that he had himself freely bestowed in the past. The major cause of his financial difficulties was probably the failure to recoup investments from his major publication projects, not only classical: Euripides, 1694; Anacreon, 1705; Homer, 1710, but also his work in English history, a life of Edward III, published in 1688. He celebrates this achievement in an untitled Latin hexameter poem in Emmanuel ms. 171, and addresses the 'purpurei patres', noblemen and bishops:

> Vos facite, Angliacae ne jam praeconia famae
> Dentibus Invidiae nimium lacerentur acerbae:
> Ne nimis hoc verum, quod vatibus atque poetis
> Excidat omnis honos Patria; nec sera queratur
> Posteritas, quod dum vobis lux alma manebat,
> Laudibus ille suis, Liber aut Emptore careret.

> Now it's up to you to make sure that this publication of English glory is not torn to pieces by the teeth of bitter envy: let it not be all too true, that prophets and poets lack all honour in their own country; let not posterity complain that, while you had this kindly light amongst you, he lacked your praise, or his book lacked a purchaser.

He expresses his pessimism dramatically in an ode dated 1696: 'Frustra Pierias Deas/Frustra Maeonidem Patrem/Scenam & Cecropiam colo:/Si jacta Messis nulla penset semina.' [In vain do I cultivate the Muses, in vain cultivate Homer and the Attic stage, if there is no harvest to compensate for the seed that I sow.] A similar theme is developed in a short poem in ms. 178, nine parallel Greek and Latin hexameters (he very often wrote in both languages side by side, claiming that Greek was even easier for him than either Latin or English), *Peri ton Philomouson*, on patrons: 'sed ne me variis extinctum floribus ornes,/nec surdo extructos lapides impone sepulchro./At vivum foveas, si quid mea carmina curas.' [do not cover me with varied flowers when I am dead, nor place a stone monument on my deaf sepulchre: but support me while I am alive, if you think anything of my poetry].

It may have been fear that not enough people would care which prevented him from finishing his greatest original work, a Latin epic on the Black Prince, the *Franciad*; this was planned to be in twelve books, a perfect union of his interests in poetry and in English history. Two manuscripts of the unfinished work survive in Emmanuel, nos. 78 and 175. The first of these, no. 78, contains books one to six, neatly written out, as if for a presentation copy, and the seventh book, added later in a different ink, and with the lines much closer together; there are also a few additions and alterations earlier in the text: it was Barnes' normal practice to write on one side of the paper only, and to use the blank sides later for improvements to the text, or sometimes for completely new poems. The other manuscript, no. 178, was a less neat copy, and it contains considerably more notes and alterations, on the facing pages and in the margins; it also originally ceased with book six, and has book seven, and also a further, eighth book added in a larger, messier version of his hand. There is also a title for book nine, but no verse: the ms. contains notes for books nine and ten, and then there is a gap, before Barnes fills up the end of the volume with unrelated notes for a treatise on Greek accents, and miscellaneous commonplaces. In this, but not the former, manuscript, Barnes numbers the lines, and if we add up his figures for the eight completed books (discounting the numerous lines added by his alterations) we come to a total of 5,865 hexameters, a very substantial body of poetry.

The poem turns the story into a very competent Virgilian epic, with many powerful passages: the intention is clearly to provide England with a historical epic to rival Homer and Virgil, something we still do not have. The flavour of the poem can be illustrated by a short speech of the Black Prince (book 3, lines 460–468): the influence of Virgil is clear, but the imitation is creative:

> Haec oritur tandem nobis lux aequa labori
> Praeterito, o socii: siquid sudavimus olim
> Per mare et externas operoso milite terras,
> Perque tuas, Mars saeve, vices; jam cernitur hora
> Cernitur illa dies, qui digno munere cunctos
> Expleat et tanto pretium pro sanguine solvat.
> Ergo agite et dextris caeli captate paratis
> Praemia; se sistunt hostes; jam promite vires,
> Et fugient; dum nos victoria laeta sequatur.

> At last the day has come, my friends, for which we have laboured; if ever we have sweated, on sea and in hard campaigning on foreign soil, and suffered the vicissitudes of savage Mars: now the time is at hand, that day is at hand, which will reward all as they deserve, and pay out the price of so

much blood. Come, then, and use your ready hands to snatch the prize. The enemy wavers; now put forth your strength, and they will flee, until joyful victory shall follow us.

Although Barnes is undoubtedly an eccentric figure, he deserves attention as a poet. His verses gained him something of a contemporary reputation; Hearne was impressed by him, and records a comment (perhaps again backhanded) that Barnes was a better poet than critic.[60]

Atterbury and Pope

Francis Atterbury (1662–1732), the most active of the Christ Church party, was an important figure in Alsop's career. By the time of *Aesop* and Boyle's reply to Bentley he was already prominent in public life; he was a royal chaplain, holder of the prestigious and desirable lectureship at St Bride's (allowing him to reside in London, but retain his studentship). He had gained a reputation with *A Letter to a Convocation Man* (1696/7), 'cleverly aimed to fit in with the mood of the ordinary clergy'.[61] Most of the lower clergy were Tories, angry at their poverty and political impotence, and at the success of Whigs and dissenters. Atterbury demanded that Convocation, where their views could be expressed, should be allowed to debate and act, rather than be silenced. This church controversy continued into Anne's reign. A major crisis came in 1709–10, with the trial, light punishment, and subsequent triumphal progress of Henry Sacheverell, that most fiery of Oxford Tories. The affair acted as a rallying point for Tory feeling, and led to the downfall of the Whig government.[62] One may chart the development of his character in the bold, somewhat macabre Latin poems that Sacheverell wrote for the university collections of 1690 and 1695. Atterbury was not then quite as extreme as Sacheverell, and was alarmed at his behaviour; nevertheless he assisted in his defence, and profited from the ensuing Tory victory. He was elected Prolocutor of the lower house of Convocation, to the dismay of moderate bishops, who thought him 'not only a disturber of the peace of the Church but indeed the principal enemy of our order and authority'.[63]

The chief political aim of Atterbury's party was the passing of the Occasional Conformity bill. This had been introduced, and debated with great heat, in

---

[60] Hearne, *Coll.* I. 269–74, 280; cf. Levine, pp. 154–5.
[61] G. V. Bennett, *The Tory Crisis in Church and State, 1688–1730* (Oxford, 1975), p. 48.
[62] See G. Holmes, *The Trial of Dr Sacheverell* (1973); A. T. Scudi, *The Sacheverell Affair* (New York, 1939); for earlier items, F. Madan, *Bibliography of Dr. H. Sacheverell* (Oxford, 1884). Contemporary allusions to him are innumerable, taking many forms: a nice example being a church bell cast in 1710 to ring out with his loud eloquence, as its Latin inscription declares (seen at Charsfield church, Suffolk).
[63] Bennett, p. 127. See Ch. 3 on Alsop's involvement.

1702, 1703, and 1704. It was finally passed in 1711, by the victorious Tories, but repealed in 1718, a few years after the Whigs regained power. It was aimed at those dissenters who, by occasionally conforming to the Church of England, evaded their legal disabilities. Many Whigs were dissenters, and their discomfiture would relieve the frustrations of Tory parochial clergy.[64] Alsop was concerned with these issues, and could write ironically on church politics to his friend, and Atterbury's, Henry Brydges (2. 7: discussed in Chapter 7). Atterbury himself was promoted, against strong opposition: first, in 1711, to the deanery of Christ Church, where he antagonised the canons, and then in 1713 to the bishopric of Rochester. In 1714 his prospects altered, with the collapse of the Tories in the face of George I's accession. He had not previously been a Jacobite, but in 1716 he accepted the leadership of the Jacobites in England: 'he became involved in Jacobitism only when he despaired that the Tory party would ever be able to rise again . . . to restore the Church to its ancient status and authority.'[65] Alsop, by contrast, had been a Jacobite since the 1690s.

A series of ill-formed conspiracies (collectively called 'The Atterbury Plot'), in which plans changed repeatedly to reflect new circumstances, culminated in Atterbury's arrest in 1722. There was little evidence available, but Walpole's determination eventually secured a bill in Parliament that condemned him. The bill passed in May 1723, and in June he went into exile. He continued to serve the Pretender until 1727, when he resigned, convinced of the failure of his brand of protestant Jacobitism, given the indifference shown by duplicitous Catholic courts.[66] Anglicanism was very often combined with Jacobite loyalties (as in Alsop's case), but the enthusiasm proved difficult to sustain. Alsop and his circle remained closely connected to Atterbury (John Freind's involvement in the plot is discussed in Chapter 6). In him we find politics, religion and literary disputes all intertwined.

Atterbury had demonstrated his interest in modern Latin literature in the 1680s, a decade before the Phalaris controversy arose. He translated Dryden's *Absalom and Achitophel* (1681) into Latin in 1682 (with some assistance, according to Wood, from a fellow Student); nor was that the only attempt to capitalise on the poem's celebrity by producing a Latin version, for one William Coward of Merton College issued his rival piece in the same year. Both were published in Oxford, Atterbury's to be sold by Crosley, Coward's by Davis. Coward's was a slapdash and unsuccessful venture: but it is still striking evidence of Neo-Latin's position that two booksellers would act in this way. Atterbury takes as his motto Horace, *Ars Poetica* 365: 'Haec placuit semel: haec iterum repetita placebit'

---

[64] Bennett, pp. 13–4, 79–80 (the 1704 'Tack', an attempt to link the bill to essential finance), 176–9 (Schism Act against non-conformist education: passed, 1714; repealed, 1718).
[65] Bennett, pp. 206–7.
[66] Bennett, pp. 223–41 (plot); 258–75 (trial); 276–94 (as Jacobite minister).

[these things pleased once, and they will please again when repeated]. He alters Horace's *decies* [ten times] to *iterum*: it would not do to encourage another nine Cowards. The translation is handled well, for example in the famous opening lines:

> Nondum mystarum pia fraus eluserat orbem,
> Nondum uni conjux porrexerat ora capistro . . .
>
> In pious times, ere priestcraft did begin,
> Before polygamy was made a sin . . .

The repetition of *Nondum* is effective; the *fraus* makes explicit the condemnation of priestly wiles (a point on which Dryden had to exercise at least some restraint), its epithet *pia* making a neat oxymoron. The sufferings of the monogamous husband are indicated by the use of *capistrum*.[67]

Two years later Atterbury edited an important anthology, printed in London for two Cambridge booksellers, R. Green and F. Hicks: 'ΑΝΘΟΛΟΓΙΑ *seu selecta quaedam Poemata Italorum qui Latine scripserunt* (London, 1684). The Greek title reminds us of the literal meaning of an anthology, a gathering of the flower of literature (like the Latin *florilegium*, often used of collections of useful poetic passages). The flowers Atterbury picked are numerous, and range from the delicate to the grandly impressive.

The preface asserts that most of the poets are already well known; it explains the arrangement of the anthology, and discusses the qualities of the authors. The poems are arranged in four sections: eclogues; *didascalicῶν* [*sic*; i.e., didactic]; odes; and miscellaneous (*varii argumenti, sylvae*). He begins with Sannazaro, 'cui parem, apud Italos, in bucolicis; aut proxime subsequentem invenire qui velit, frustra est. Nam adeo candidus, tener, simplex, venustus est' [anyone acts in vain, who wishes to find his equal, or even a close second, among the Italians in pastoral poetry. For he is so candid, tender, simple, and elegant]. The words that he chooses to praise Sannazaro, especially *tener* and *venustus* [elegant or witty: inspired by Venus], suggest a Catullan view of poetry. This is suitable for the pastoral genre: although Catullus himself was not a pastoral poet, the chief ancient models for Renaissance pastorals, Virgil's *Eclogues*, are imbued with his neoteric (newer, or modernising) spirit (and themselves draw on Hellenistic predecessors, as Catullus does). The most Catullan of the authors chosen by Atterbury is Flaminio, who begins the section of odes. Most of these are in hendecasyllables (Catullus' favourite metre), or epodic forms, rather than the stanzas of Horace's *Carmina*. In the whole section, with more than forty poems, there are only three sapphic and four alcaic odes. The preface brings out the Catullan qualities of Flaminio: 'Catulli enim, ut mihi videtur, non tam imitator,

[67] Cf. Ch. 3, on Juvenal's and Alsop's uses of the word.

quam aemulus prope dici meruit' [For in my opinion he deserves to be called not so much the imitator as virtually the rival of Catullus].

The arrangement of the volume can occasionally be confusing: the numbering breaks down in places, and the categories of poetry are loose. For the most part the editing is sensible, and he does include some of the most important Renaissance works. Heading the second section is Fracastoro's *Syphilis* (pp. 40–77), that greatest and most readable of medical didactic poems, with much of the character of epic narrative. This work attracted considerable interest: it was translated into English, for example by Nahum Tate, the poet laureate.

Atterbury's statement, in the preface, that the poets are already well known may perhaps be misleading. A few in England had no doubt read widely in the existing collections of Continental verse, of which the most important were the *Delitiae* anthologies of the early seventeenth century, or in the published poems of individual authors; Continental work can also appear in manuscript miscellanies. More recent was the anthology of William Dillingham, *Poemata varii argumenti* (1678)—discussed in Chapter 2—which may have inspired Atterbury to produce a more thorough and improved selection, concentrating on the Italian Renaissance. Even Atterbury cannot resist the inclusion of four non-Italian works: one by Daniel Heinsius (*Thyrsis*), one by Hugo Grotius (*Myrtilus*), and two by George Buchanan (*Desiderium Ptolemaei . . .* and *Desiderium Lutetiae*), all four placed at the end of the first section, numbered as eclogues VIII-XI.

Knowledge of modern Latin writing will have varied widely. A passing acquaintance with Mantuan, and the knowledge of other poets' names, was the norm for a reasonably educated man.[68] Those Continental works that were printed in England are likely to have been quite well known: e.g. C. Quillet, *Callipaedia*, a lively didactic poem influenced by the *Georgics*, was printed in London in 1709 by the Bowyer press, later used by Bernard for Alsop's odes.[69] Marco Girolamo Vida, author of the treatise *De Arte Poetica* (longer than Horace's ancient model, more elegant than Scaliger's prose), received regular attention, with editions appearing in England in 1701, 1722, 1723, 1725, and 1733.[70] The Vida edition of 1722 included Alsop's friends John Dolben and Charles Aldrich among its subscribers, as well as the learned physician Dr Mead.

One result of the continued interest in such works in the early eighteenth century was a revised edition, in 1740, of Atterbury's anthology. This was edited by Atterbury's friend, Alexander Pope: a striking, and not often remembered, aspect of his literary career. That Pope, the famous translator (or imitator) of Homer and scourge of dunces, should make the effort to prepare this revision

[68] See M. L. Clarke, *Classical Education in Britain, 1500–1900* (Cambridge, 1959), especially n. 10, pp. 6–7.
[69] Quillet was translated by another laureate, Nicholas Rowe.
[70] An example used in J. W. Binns, 'Latin Labours Lost', *Times Higher Education Supplement* (27 Oct. 1989): an eloquent summary of the relevance of Neo-Latin studies.

demonstrates the place of Neo-Latin in the mainstream of British intellectual culture. The title-page does not mention Atterbury's name, although Pope will have been aware of his responsibility for the anonymous original of 1684; the Greek title, ΆΝΘΟΛΟΓΙΑ, is dropped, the subtitle being elevated (with the minor omission of *quaedam*) to provide a more immediately informative Latin title.[71]

There are considerable changes to the body of the work, indicating that Pope took the task of revision seriously. Among the more significant additions are the three books of Vida's *De Arte Poetica*, placed in the third section (of a revised scheme, now in six parts), together with the same poet's descriptions of silk-worms (*Bombycum Libri*) and chess (*Scacchia Ludus*), both of which Atterbury had printed, though in different sections. The latter had originally been placed at the start of the miscellaneous works in part 4 (pp. 191–209); to bring it together with other didactic[72] writings of Vida seems a sensible rationalisation. Pope does not do this with complete consistency, but the arrangement is generally more logical, and thought has clearly been devoted to it. The reasons for the addition of particular works are not always clear. In the case of Vida, we have seen that he had been frequently reprinted in recent years, and Pope may have thought it odd to leave out the chief work of such a prominent author; on the other hand, one might have thought that all those English editions rendered yet another less necessary. The market wanted Vida, it seems, and by including *De Arte Poetica* Pope added to the usefulness of the anthology, as a collection of the poems an interested Englishman would wish to possess.

Not all of the Vida poems do occur together in Pope, since the distinctions of genre prevent it: he adds three of his eclogues (*Daphnis, Corydon, Nice*) to the first section. While the opening five eclogues of Sannazaro remain, the rest of that section is radically altered. As well as Vida's, he adds three more eclogues by Giovanni Baptista Amalteo[73] to the two that Atterbury printed, and drops all four of the non-Italians. The removal of these interlopers might seem a natural decision, if he intended to make the contents entirely consistent with the book's title. It is therefore surprising to see that Pope later includes two different poems

[71] *Selecta Poemata Italorum qui Latine scripserunt, cura cuiusdam Anonymi Anno 1684 congesta, iterum in lucem data, una cum aliorum Italorum operibus, Accurante A. Pope* (London, 1740: 2 vols., printed for the booksellers J. & P. Knapton).
[72] The definition of didactic literature can be unclear: such descriptive poetry falls into this grey area, but can arguably be classed alongside more obviously didactic pieces. Pope praises Vida's *De Arte Poetica*: *Essay on Criticism* 704–8 (and the game of Ombre in *The Rape of the Lock* may have been influenced by Vida's *Scacchia Ludus*).
[73] Rather less famous than some other names in the anthology, Amalteo (1525–73) was a precocious talent (*Carmina*: Venice, 1550); a later eclogue, *Doris*, not included here, was written for Mary I and Philip II. His works appeared with those of his brothers, *Trium fratrum Amaltheorum Carmina* (Venice, 1627). Cf. A. Perosa, J. Sparrow, *Renaissance Latin Verse* (London, 1979), p. 317.

by Buchanan, who can by no means be described as Italian (though his extensive sojourn in France and Portugal made him as much a European as a Scottish author). This is the major change that Pope makes to the section of odes (now renumbered as part 5). Buchanan's *In Neaeram* and *Calendae Maiae* fit in there well enough, apart from the question of nationality, but the collection would have been substantial and varied without them.

Pope omits Atterbury's preface, and does not replace it with any of his own, preferring to let the poems, in their new arrangement, speak for themselves. The second of Atterbury's sections, *didascalicôn*, is effectively divided into three (parts 2 and 3, in vol. 1, and 4, in vol. 2). The new part 2 consists of only two poems, both by Fracastoro: *Syphilis*, as before, although with the beginnings of books 2 and 3 now clearly marked, and an additional shorter work, *Alcon, sive de cura canum Venaticorum* (pp. 96–101). One may imagine that an English country gentleman, devoted to his hounds, or indeed a hunting parson, might find the subject of hunting-dogs more interesting than a doctor's (albeit lively) speculations on the transatlantic origins of a deadly disease. As in the case of most didactic poetry, its interest does not stem so much from a need for practical information as from the fascination of seeing that subject in verse. Pope shows himself to be alive to the possibilities of attracting a wider audience, offering Fracastoro for squires as well as cultivated physicians.

Pope's third section contains four works: the three Vida didactics already noted, and Aonio Paleario, *De Animorum Immortalitate* in three books (pp. 211–70), another major addition to Atterbury's selection. This subject, too, would have interested many of Pope's contemporaries, since philosophical debate between deists and Christians was increasingly bitter. As a Roman Catholic, Pope may have wished to bring forward a neutral viewpoint (in the universally acceptable, and more elegant, medium of Latin verse) to join the numerous justifications of Anglican faith. Paleario was a good choice for this, being far from a doctrinaire Catholic: he had sympathised with Luther, whose position he defended a few years after his poem appeared, and was finally, in 1570, executed for heresy.[74] Fourteen years after Pope's anthology, an Englishman produced a successful Latin treatment of the same topic.[75]

The fourth part, entitled *Elegiae*, is greatly expanded from a group of ten elegiac pieces rather awkwardly placed at the end of Atterbury's didactic section. All those are retained: to four elegiac poems by Sannazaro he adds a further seven, and five new authors provide ten elegies. The new subjects are varied, and likely to appeal: Francesco Maria Molza *Ad Venerem*, Pontano *Ad Bacchum*, Politian *De Ovidii Exilio et Morte*, and so on. The Politian would have been poignantly applicable to the exiled Atterbury (though he could not have known

[74] Perosa and Sparrow, p. 309.   [75] Isaac Hawkins Browne, *De Animi Immortalitate*: discussed in Ch. 8.

that in 1684), and indeed to all Jacobites; that may have been one of Pope's motivations for including it, along with a typical selection of less emotive works. As a Roman Catholic, Pope will have found Molza's *Ad Henricum Britanniae Regem, Uxoris Repudiatae nomine* [To King Henry VIII, in the name of his rejected wife] especially emotive; Molza uses the Ovidian epistle as a powerful weapon against the tyrant whose scandalous behaviour led to the breach with Rome.[76] If this choice is full of meaning for the anthologist (and at least part of his audience), most other poems seem to be selected for their variety and literary quality. Pope's twenty-seven elegiac poems, arranged as a distinct section in themselves, improve on Atterbury's slightly half-hearted offering, and illustrate the way in which Italians exploited the capabilities of the elegiac form.

Politian is also prominent in the new part 6, *Sylvae*. To *Rusticus*, printed by Atterbury, Pope adds his other three hexameter treatises on literature, *Nutricia*, *Manto*, and *Ambra*[77] (vol. 2, pp. 105–80). While the single poem is welcome, and can readily stand in an anthology, it is much more satisfactory for serious reading of Politian to have the full set available. As elegant introductions to Virgil and Homer, these poems might appeal to Pope himself and to readers of his Homer. Like Vida's *De Arte Poetica*, they also reflect an interest in literary criticism: purchasers of Pope's *Selecta Poemata Italorum* had all the material they needed to think about the creation of Renaissance and modern poetry, as well as to enjoy the results. Other notable additions to the sixth part are fifteen further poems of Fracastoro, the first eight of them quite substantial sets of hexameters; there are also five more poems by Baldassare Castiglione, to add to his *Cleopatra* from the 1684 volume.[78] Three elegiac pieces are omitted from this section, two by Pietro Bembo: in compensation, his *Benacus* is added. Pope is therefore not merely piling on further material in a haphazard manner, but considering what might improve on or complement Atterbury's selections, quite prepared to jettison and rearrange whenever necessary. He was in 1740 towards the end of his career (he died in 1744); the fourth book of the *Dunciad* (1742) was still to come, and the editing of *Selecta Poemata Italorum* may have stimulated his thoughts on scholarship and polite literature. Bentley appears as the critic Aristarchus in the fourth book (lines 201–74):

> Thy mighty scholiast, whose unwearied pains
> Made Horace dull, and humbled Milton's strains. (lines 211–2)

Later in the same passage, Aristarchus parades the pedantic details of Bentley's scholarship:

---

[76] This poem is also printed by Perosa and Sparrow, pp. 261–4.
[77] The title comes from the name of Lorenzo's villa; delivered as an introduction to a lecture course on Homer. Cf. Perosa and Sparrow, p. 136.
[78] Pope translated *Cleopatra*: N. Ault, J. Butt, eds., *Minor Poems* (Twickenham edn., vol. 6) pp. 66–8.

'Tis true, on words still is our whole debate,
Disputes of *me* or *te*, of *aut* or *at*,
To sound or sink in *cano*, O or A,
Or give up Cicero to C or K.
Let Freind affect to speak as Terence spoke,
And Alsop never but like Horace joke:
For me, what Virgil, Pliny may deny,
Manilius or Solinus shall supply . . . (lines 219–26)

Pope may be poking a little fun at Robert Freind and Alsop, for such is his nature, but there is no doubt that he treats them more affectionately than the pedants. Spence reports him saying that 'these two lines . . . have more of satire than compliment in them, though I find they are generally mistaken for the latter only. It goes on Horace's old method of telling a friend some less fault while you are commending him, and which, indeed, is the best time of doing so. I scarce meet with anybody that understands delicacy.'[79] This should not be interpreted as meaning that Pope was lukewarm towards Alsop: when he had real attacks to make, he did not try to be delicate. In any case Alsop was no longer alive to be offended.

Pope's attitude to scholarship is ambiguous; while the notes of the *Dunciad* are part of the satire, those on Homer are serious and full. He received help on scholarly points,[80] one unacknowledged helper being John Jortin, an accomplished Neo-Latin poet.[81] Thomas Parnell, whose help did obtain recognition, and whose own poems were edited by Pope, had translated the *Rape of the Lock* into Latin verse.[82] Modern Latin poetry, for Pope and his circle, goes hand in hand with other forms of creativity. The battle of the books had helped to create the circumstances in which Pope's satire could flourish, and he is to be found on the side of polite literature. Atterbury had been delighted by Swift's *Battle of the Books* (written in 1697, early in the dispute, but published in 1704)—in which we find the royal librarian 'renowned for humanity', an echo of Boyle's notorious phrase.[83] Nearly forty years later his friend Pope is still concerned with various aspects of the issue, not least of them the editing of *Selecta Poemata Italorum*, with which he could give a practical demonstration of useful, un-Bentleian learning.

[79] J. Spence (ed. J. M. Osborn), *Anecdotes . . . collected from the conversation of Mr Pope* (Oxford, 1966) 1. 150 [no. 336]. [80] See Levine, p. 197, etc.
[81] Author of *Lusus Poetici* (1722: reprinted with additions, 1724, 1748); see Bradner, pp. 240–1, etc.
[82] Levine, p. 202. [83] Levine, pp. 112, 117.

5
Revenge and Laughter

Although Alsop's contemporary reputation rested largely on the circulation of his poetry in manuscript form, a few of his poems did appear in print during his lifetime. Perhaps the most interesting of these publications is the pair of odes satirising Arthur Charlett, Master of University College, Oxford. The attack takes the form of a pair of imaginary verse letters, one written by Charlett to a friend, Percival, and the other Percival's reply. The ostensible reason for the exchange of letters is Percival's unnerving experience at the hands of highwaymen; but there are many other subjects raised, as the poet develops his sharply observed parody of a rambling pair of correspondents. The scene is set in the middle of the night, but despite the inappropriateness of the hour, 'Acer ad notos calamus labores/Sponte recurrit.' [. . . my keen pen runs back of its own accord to its familiar labours. (1. 9. 3–4)] The function of the poems is to excite laughter; but perhaps they also allow the poet to revenge himself upon his laughable victims. Their effectiveness as literature rests on an appreciation of their historical context; and, in turn, the poetry can illuminate various complicated strands of history. In particular, it is the complex character of Arthur Charlett that provided Alsop with both the motive and the means for satire; and therefore this chapter concentrates on an investigation of that character, and of the reactions of Alsop and other contemporaries to it.

Publication of Alsop's satirical attack on Arthur Charlett

Alsop's poems were issued in broadsheet form in 1706. They were reprinted in 1711 by Edmund Smith,[1] presumably a sign that they had achieved some success or notoriety; Benjamin Loveling was later to appropriate other Alsop odes in a similar fashion. In Bernard's 1752 edition of Alsop's odes, the Charlett poems are numbered 1. 9 and 1. 10. The 1706 pamphlet is now rare, but a copy survives in the Bodleian (octavo St. Amand 405), pasted into the back of a copy of the *Musarum Anglicanarum Analecta* (Oxford, 1692). The pamphlet has one sheet

[1] E. Smith, *Works* (1711; repr. 1719, etc.), pp. 88–91.

only, and is set out with 1. 9 (headed *Charlettus Percivallo suo*) on the left, and 1. 10 (headed *Percivallus Charletto suo*) on the right, with its postscript beneath. The poems are printed with no significant difference from Bernard's version. The publication is entirely anonymous: neither Alsop's name nor the printer's appears. The only other information is:

> Vaeneunt Londini Anno MDCCVI
> Pr[etium], 2d. [For sale at London, 1706, price twopence]

We do not know how many copies were sold, but the pamphlet was clearly intended to appeal to at least the more educated part of the London public, rather than being simply a parochial Oxford exercise.

Manuscript copies of the odes also exist, and provide a little further information about the supposed date of composition; at the end of the first ode, which he entitles *Ode Epistolaris*, the anonymous copyist adds:

> Dabam Oxonii Kalend: April: 1705
> Arthurus Charlett.

And at the end of the reply (*Ode Responsoria*):

> Dabam Londini Kalend: Gra'c: (?)
> ——Percival.

The word written 'Gra'c' or 'Gra's' is certainly *Graecis*, making the phrase 'on the Greek Kalends', i.e. on a non-existent date. The phrase is apparently a whimsical expression of the Emperor Augustus (Suetonius, *Augustus* 87), and has achieved a wide currency in English. The other date offered, 1 April, may also be selected for humorous effect.[2] Nevertheless, April 1705 or thereabouts would be a plausible time for the poems' composition. Later in the same manuscript volume[3] appears some further evidence of great interest: the English translations of the two odes. That of 1. 9 (*An Epistolary Ode from Dr Ch—t to Mr P—val of Xt.Ch.*) has only a sign at its end; but 1. 10 (*Mr P—val's Answer*) has a similar sign, and also the name A. Evans, which appears to indicate that both translations are his work, since they are very much a pair.

'A. Evans'

This is almost certainly the clergyman and minor poet Abel Evans (1674–1737).[4] He was born on 26 February 1673/4, and went up to St John's, Oxford at the

---

[2] April Fool's Day is probably intended: the phrase was current in Alsop's time (cf. *OED*, s.v. 'April', 3, quoting Congreve, 1687: 'April-Fools').
[3] Bodleian, ms. Lat. misc. e. 19 (fo. 153–4 for the Latin, 174–5 for the English).
[4] His birth-date is given as 1679 in the *Dictionary of National Biography* (*DNB*: where the entry on Alsop is similarly in error).

age of 17, where he matriculated on 2 July 1692. He obtained a clerical living comparatively early, becoming vicar of Kirtlington, Oxfordshire (a village very close to Oxford) in 1700: this is twelve years before Alsop obtained a living, and (though many were quicker than Alsop) very rapid progress. He no doubt kept his Oxford connections, at least until he moved to the vicarage of Gt Staughton, Hunts., in 1723; thus he was in a position to be aware of the subject matter of Alsop's Charlett odes. From 1724 until his death in 1737 he was rector of Cheam, in Surrey.

He was briefly chaplain to St John's, but was ejected because of a speech in Hall in which he publicly attacked the President, Delaune, and other members of the college. The favour of the Duchess of Marlborough, however, apparently gained him reinstatement. This episode seems strikingly similar to Alsop's attack on Canon Gastrell in a public speech (discussed below) and suggests that Evans was of a similarly lively and potentially belligerent nature. He is described as 'a loose, ranting gentleman'. All this makes him a highly suitable candidate for turning the attack on Charlett into English verse. His reputation was as a satirist, more than as a priest. After his reinstatement at St John's he apparently 'reformed his course of life'.[5] He did this not by abstaining from satire, but by attacking his low-church former friends. In 1710 appeared *The Apparition*, including attacks on Tindal and White Kennett, and in 1713 *Vertumnus*, an epistle to J. Bobart (friend of the antiquarian Lhwyd and other Oxford figures). He was also a friend of Pope, who mentions him as a poet at *Dunciad* 2. 116, along with Young and Swift. Thomas Hearne's typically unflattering judgements on his character are distorted by party prejudice, stemming from Evans' early days as a low-churchman.

The style of the translations of the odes is typical of many early eighteenth century satirists; but it is certainly not implausible to attribute them to Evans, and the attribution in the manuscript to him may therefore be provisionally accepted. His character and connections make him very much the sort of person who would have appreciated satire on Charlett, and have been able to add to his English versions details omitted in the Latin. Alsop's name is not linked by the copyist to either the Latin or English version, although he does give attributions, where he knows them, for some of the other poems in the volume.[6] Alsop's name does occur on fo. 153 directly before the Latin versions, in a record of an inscription in the Peckwater Quadrangle at Christ Church set up by James, Earl of Salisbury (see Chapter 3). But since it may merely be a coincidence that the copyist has placed these items together, it would be rash to assume from this that he knew the poems following were Alsop's.

[5] Details of his career in *DNB*.
[6] E.g. fo. 156: ——Clutton AB, ChCh; fo. 177: ——Blunt, SJC schol. 1709.

The Relationship between the English and Latin versions

The English is not merely a translation of the Latin: it expands on it in some places, in others it adds incidents completely foreign to the Latin, and also leaves out some that the Latin includes. It is therefore certainly a poem in its own right, not a slavish reworking of the Latin for non-Latinists, and could in theory even have preceded it. On the other hand, there are several factors that suggest that the Latin did come first. The English, though not actually in sapphics, is in a metre that is not particularly common in English, except for imitations of Latin sapphics, for which it is quite normal. The short last line of each stanza echoes the adonic at the end of a sapphic stanza. Furthermore, while it is easy to see the point of translating Alsop's witty Latin into a lively English version, both to increase its circulation and to add to the amusement of those already familiar with the Latin, it is less easy to see why Alsop should have translated a fairly ephemeral English poem into Latin. There is no evidence that Alsop was fond of translation.

Many, though not all, of the differences found in the English are clearly for the sake of rhyme. The presence of differences that cannot be explained in this way suggests that Evans was familiar with the events described, independently of Alsop's Latin. Nevertheless, this does not prevent the English from being, for the most part, a translation of the Latin, and this seems more plausible than the reverse. If we do accept April 1705 as their date of composition, it appears that publication followed fairly soon afterwards. This makes it at least possible, though not necessary, that they were originally intended for publication. It is equally possible, however, that Alsop merely intended them to raise a laugh among a few friends, and was later persuaded that a wider public would also find them amusing.

And they are clearly intended to amuse. This is particularly obvious in the lively English versions: but no less central to the point of the Latin. What the English lacks, but the Latin possesses, is the dignity and elegance that Alsop never (or hardly ever) abandons in his Latin writing. But this superb handling of the language should not deceive us into thinking that these are solemn poems. Their superficially serious presentation alerts us to the fact that the author is mocking the letter writers. It is a common technique of parodists to present ludicrous subject matter in a serious form. In fact, as we shall see, this is a parody of the highest quality: very acute observation of the foibles of the subject, combined with a literary style that, while not reducing the effect of the content, is in itself delightful.

Parody may take a number of forms. It need not always hold up the subject to ridicule. Alsop seems to do so; it may be argued whether the ridicule is mild or severe, but it is present as an element in the author's intention. Indeed it may well be the leading element. The actual subjects discussed in the poems are generally neither significant, nor particularly amusing. This tendency is more marked in the Latin than the English; the reader is likely to gain considerable amusement from reading the latter, taking it as a straightforward humorous poem. The Latin is more subtle, less concerned to raise a laugh from its contents: and therefore much more reliant for its effect upon the element of ridicule.

The supposed addressee, William Percival

The supposed addressee (and supposed author of the reply, 1. 10) is noted by Bernard as: 'Aedis Christi alumnus' [member of Christ Church]. He is certainly William Percival (*c.* 1674–1734), son of George Percival, a gentleman of Ireland (according to the college matriculation books). Charlett is a more significant figure than Percival, and it is his correspondence which is ridiculed. It is an interesting question why Percival was chosen as a 'partner' for Charlett in the odes. He is certainly not the only one of Charlett's numerous correspondents who might have been chosen.[7] His recent contretemps with the highwayman, combined with his being a fellow member of Alsop's college, no doubt influenced the choice.

He matriculated, aged 15, on 26 March 1689, and was thus a close contemporary of Alsop: younger, but a year ahead in college. He became BA in 1692/3, MA in 1695, BD and DD in 1714/5. His ecclesiastical preferment was rapid: he was prebendary of Killaloe (1701), archdeacon of Cashel (1703–25), dean of Emly (1714–34), and prebendary of Christ Church, Dublin (1720–34). He was thus already a beneficed minister of the Church of Ireland at the time of the poems. The Latin suggests that he is resident in London (lines 25–8 ask about London news), although Evans perhaps implies that he is in Ireland, with his greater interest in Irish affairs, and requests for news of Dublin, Armagh and Tuam (30: quoted below).

Percival's surviving works include two polemical pamphlets, *A letter to Dr. Synge* . . . and *A reply to a vindication* (Dublin, 1710 and 1711), and a sermon, preached in Ireland, but published in London (1713). Most interesting is a verse broadsheet, *A Description in answer to the Journal* (Dublin, 1722), which is a personal attack on Dean Swift, from a disgruntled fellow member of the chapter. The previous dean's generosity is praised:

> . . . In short he Liv'd, and that's what few can
> Justly report of Sw——t our new Dean.

---

[7] Hearne suggests that Percival was chosen as another notorious news-lover, which seems likely (*Coll.* 11. 106).

> He sometimes to a chapter goes,
> With sawcy strut and turn'd up nose;
> Leans on his Cushion, then he'll bid ye
> *Hearken*, to what all knows already . . .

Swift's meanness in entertainment is attacked, then:

> . . . But let's proceed from these poor tricks
> O'th *Kitchen* to his Politicks.
> On plot and schemes, he'll read long lectures,
> To country curates and their rectors;
> They stare and think he knows as well
> All depths of state as *Machiavel*,
> It must be so since from him flows
> Whate'er the *Earl of Oxford* knows:
> He swears the project of the Peace
> Was laid by him in Anna's days;
> The *South Sea*[8] ne're could have miscarried,
> As he contriv'd, but *Others* Marr'd it . . .

Percival was clearly a character who relished controversy, and was witty enough to engage in it himself. This may well be why Alsop chose him from Charlett's host of correspondents as the most suitable target for his wit.

Percival surfaces again in another satirical poem (4. 8) that may very well be Alsop's; together with 4. 9, a rather similar piece, it is one of the most risqué, if not obscene, poems among his works (and possible works) in Part II of this book. Addressed to Sir Thomas Vesey, a Christ Church contemporary, and later an Irish bishop,[9] 4. 8 considers his keen sexual appetite in shocking and hilarious detail. Percival is suggested as a more moderate model; in fact, Percival's extreme caution in his marital relations is equally funny, his weekly fumblings hardly a fit source of inspiration. No doubt, if he knew of it, Percival would not have found this ode to his taste. He is still a figure of fun, although a new aspect of his life, too intimate even for the broadsheet of 1706, is now exposed.

A bizarre counter-attack

In the first edition of Edward Popham's anthology, *Selecta Poemata Anglorum Latina*,[10] is reprinted what purports to be a reply to Alsop's odes by a friend of

---

[8] For literary involvement in the bubble, see the Ch. on Blunt in H. H. Erskine-Hill, *The Social Milieu of Alexander Pope* (New Haven, 1975).

[9] Matriculated in 1689; fellow of Oriel, 1695; ordained, 1700; Bishop of Killaloe, 1713; of Ossory, 1714; died 1730.

[10] Vol. 2 (1774), p. 103; omitted from the abridged 1779 edition: see Ch. 8.

Percival. It is a strange piece: a personal attack on Alsop (which suggests that Alsop's fairly mild satire on Percival was much resented). It makes the author look a lot sillier than Alsop, his target. The attacks are unsubstantiated by evidence or argument (except the feeble assertion, stanza 1, that one cannot use a 'tender' metre for satire), and not in very good taste. And while Alsop is equated with Archilochus in line 2, he is twice threatened with the fate of Archilochus' enemy, Lycambes (stanzas 6 and 13), and encouraged to 'go and hang himself'. It is particularly hard to take the third stanza seriously, with its heavy echoes of Horace, *Carm.* 3. 20:

> Flebis: audacem nemore excitasti
> Improbus fulvae catulum leaenae:
> Acer a tergo tibi *Percivallus*
>   Imminet ultor.

> You'll regret it! You have foolishly roused a lioness' brave cub, and swift Percival lies in wait behind you to take his revenge.

Whether Percival would really be flattered by this allusion, and the implied comparison with the bitchy behaviour of a Horatian lover, one might very well doubt. And it appears that he would be fully capable of defending himself; given Percival's own belligerence, there seems little cause to blame anyone for attacking Percival.

Popham attributes the counter-attack to one 'J. U—' of King's, giving the date 1737; this will not be the date of composition (which was presumably not long after the original insult), but the date of publication in Popham's probable source, the *Gentleman's Magazine*, 7. 631 (October 1737), which refers to Smith's publication of Alsop's pair of odes.[11]

'J. U— of King's College' is most likely to be James Upton (1670–1749), although we cannot be so sure of this attribution as we can with Evans'. Upton matriculated at King's in 1693/4; thus he was several years behind Alsop at University, although of about the same age. He became BA in 1697/8, and MA in 1701, having already been elected a fellow in 1696. He took orders (deacon 1697, priest 1701), but his career was primarily as a schoolmaster. He had been an Eton scholar at King's, and he returned to Eton to teach soon after taking his MA. He was vicar of Brimpton, Berkshire, from 1701 to 1711, and of Monksilver (1712), then of Plympton, Devon, until his death in 1749. From 1704 onwards he was mainly resident in the West Country, as master of Ilminster school (1704–11), and Taunton Grammar School (1739–49), which he made the largest (with 200 or more boys) and most respected of English provincial schools.

He was 'an eminent grammarian and classical author'.[12] His main produc-

---

[11] The counter-attack is also found in British Library ms. Add. 30162, fo. 58ᵛ–59ʳ.
[12] J. and J. A. Venn, *Alumni Cantabrigienses* (Cambridge, 1922).

tions are editions of texts: Aristotle's *Poetics*, 1696 (a re-editing of Gaulston's 1623 text); *Dionysius of Halicarnassus*, 1702; Ascham's *Scholemaster*, 1711; and a selection of Greek authors for schools, 1726. There is no record of him as a polemical Latin poet; but such would not be inconsistent with his talents. Certainly, as a distinguished schoolmaster, one would expect him to be a competent composer of Latin verse. Nor is there any record of a link with Percival. He did have Oxford connections later in his life, through his son John (1707–60), who went to Merton College in 1724. Popham's version of the name, 'Joh.', suggests that the son rather than the father wrote the poem: this is quite possible (although the father is much better known as a writer); alternatively Popham may have confused the two (as does Foster, *Alumni Oxonienses*). The father, not the son, was at King's. There is no reason, however, for him not to have been a friend of Percival's; presumably that was his motive for attacking Alsop.

The Character of Arthur Charlett: 'The Oxford Intellegencer'

There is no dearth of information available for the student of Charlett. He was concerned with so many things that even in this mass of material there are gaps; in particular, little is known about his relations with Alsop, and nothing at all about his reactions to these two poems, which he can hardly fail to have seen. Nevertheless, it is possible to amass enough small pieces of information to engage in some reasonable speculation about what they thought of each other (and hence, why Alsop decided to write these odes).

Charlett lived from 1655 to 1722 (and was thus about 50 when the odes were written, while Alsop was about 35). He matriculated at Trinity College, Oxford, on 13 January 1668/9, proceeded to his BA in 1673, to his MA in 1676, and in 1680 was elected a fellow of Trinity. In 1683 he was junior proctor of the University, and in December 1684 became BD. In 1688/9 he was appointed tutor to Lord Guilford, a man of Jacobite family (whom Alsop mentions at 1. 9. 27, as discussed below); according to the *DNB* he was advised at this time by the non-juror Hickes (a significant character in his career, as will be seen) to 'keep college constantly', as such frugality was popular with his patrons. On 7 July 1692 he accepted the mastership of University College, Oxford, a significant promotion. In November 1697, through the influence of Archbishop Tenison, he was appointed to the rectory of Hambledon, Buckinghamshire (where he often resided thereafter); but he remained the head of University College until his death.

The main traits of his character satirised by Alsop are sufficiently well known to have been included in the *DNB* article. He was 'vain and given to gossip' (according to Hearne), and 'commonly called the Gazeteer or

Oxford Intellegencer . . . '. He delighted in extensive correspondence, and in meddling (which is said to have cost him his chances of a bishopric). Charlett's correspondence was truly vast; most of the letters he received have been preserved (as the Ballard mss. in the Bodleian). They may fruitfully be compared to William Wake's equally vast correspondence (Christ Church, Wake mss.); Wake's number and variety of correspondents is a useful reminder that Charlett was by no means unique, even if he was unusual, in the range of his letter-writing. Were one to run the risk of a dangerous generalisation, however, one might note that Wake's letters (or rather, those sent to him: his own are usually lost) have more continued seriousness than Charlett's; the bulk of them stem from his period as a senior churchman, bishop and archbishop, and are on clerical matters, e.g. requests for assistance or patronage, and so on. In particular, no gossipy letters from his Christ Church acquaintances, such as Alsop or John Dolben, survive: although we have good reason to assume (from Alsop 3. 2. 24, 4. 6. 6) that Wake was on convivial terms with both. This does not, of course, prove that Wake never gossiped; it would equally be a travesty to suggest that Charlett always gossiped. A very large proportion of his surviving correspondence is on entirely serious scholarly and antiquarian matters. There is, however, a very much higher proportion of gossip in Charlett's correspondence than in Wake's.

But Charlett's gossip was by no means idle. Although he was interested in people, whether or not they were of any political significance, he was particularly interested in watching the political climate of his University. A good example of the combination of fussiness with inquisitiveness may be taken from a letter of his to Wake (dated Hambledon, nr. Henley-upon-Thames, 10 March, 1719/20):

> My Lord,
>   The Ways and Wether on Saturday Morning, being equally discouraging, I thought it safest, (after so [long?] a Disuse of a horse, being also not well Mounted,) to indulge my self the use of a light chariot . . . [he then discusses his position as an observer:] . . . I who ought, by so constant and long a residence, and many particular opportunities, not very common, to understand the Desires and Wants of the University, do heartily and sincerely rejoyce, (as much as I did grieve at some former proceedings) . . .[13]

Charlett's period of nearly continuous residence dates from his arrival at Trinity College in 1669, fifty years before the above letter. He began to make an impact on the University in the mid-1680s; certainly from 1692 (thirteen years before Alsop's poems) he can be considered one of the leading, or at least most prominent, Oxford figures. This he achieved without being especially rich, or especially learned, or especially pious (though by no means deficient, either, in

---

[13] Christ Church, Wake mss., vol. 16, no. 73.

any of these qualities). He was indeed the head of a college: but University was a small college, and his impact was much greater than one would expect from a Master of University. The best explanation for a man of only moderate wealth, learning, piety and position making such a disproportionate mark, is his assiduous activity. He was busy with other things as well as news-gathering; but it is not surprising that his interest in news would strike others as peculiarly ludicrous, and provide a means of ridiculing him to those who, perhaps, disapproved also of his other activities. His news-gathering consisted in obtaining news from a multitude of informants, and in return retailing it to his many correspondents. This was not, at least in 1705–6, an organised 'news service': but it was nevertheless effective. Those to whom he retailed news included (among a host of less important people) such politicians as Bromley and such churchmen as Wake. From them and other contacts, he was in turn in a peculiarly good position to keep Oxford informed of goings-on in London.

There is no doubt that this informal information network was in existence soon after Charlett became Master of University. By 1695 we find him discussing controversies in politics and religion with Lancaster of Queen's (Hearne's 'old smooth-boots'), who can denounce an opponent with vivid rhetoric: 'You may call the Doctrine impious, the reasoning Scandalous, and the Language Billingsgate, (where the author had most of his breading) without being in danger of a Reprimande from Court.'[14] He also receives information from one Thomas Hinton (whom both Alsop and Evans mention) on a sermon denouncing Locke (and the behaviour of the audience: 'the Eyes of the congregation were as much fixed upon Mr Tyrrell [a Whig] this year, as they were upon the Scotchmen the last.').[15] In 1707, after Alsop's poems appeared, he actually published a newssheet, called *Mercurius Oxoniensis*. Before Alsop's poems, in 1703, he had been publicly lampooned by the traditional jester at the Act, the 'Terrae Filius', in the merciless fashion usual on such occasions;[16] it may well be that this attack had something to do with Alsop's writing of the poems, although there seems little doubt that Charlett would have been prominent enough without it.

'Abraham Froth' in Spectator No. 43

Charlett received further public ridicule a few years after Alsop's poems; this time (as with Alsop's poems) in front of a London audience, unlike the audience of 1703, that had been restricted to Oxford. Hearne noted in his diary for 22 April 1711: 'Memorandum that there is a daily paper comes out called the

[14] Bodleian, Ballard mss. [hereafter cited as *Ballard*], 21 fo. 62.   [15] *Ballard* 38, fo. 4.
[16] Bodleian, ms. Rawl. D. 697, fo. 1.

Spectator, written, as is supposed, by the same hand that writes the *Tattler*, viz. Captain *Steel*. In one of the last of these papers [no. 43] is a letter written from *Oxon*. at four a Clock [*sic*] in the morning and subscribed *Abraham Froth*. It ridicules our Hebdomadal meetings. The said *Abraham Froth* is designed for *Dr. Arthur Charlett*, an empty, frothy Man, and indeed the latter personates him incomparably well, being written, as he uses to do, upon a great variety of things, and yet about Nothing of Moment . . .' [other characters, 'cronys' of Charlett's, are meant for Clarke and Gardiner of All Souls', and Lancaster of Queen's, all frequent correspondents of his; Hearne ends by noting:] '. . . men that are indifferent commend it [i.e. *Spectator* no. 43] highly, as it deserves.'

It would be interesting to speculate whether the picture of Froth in the *Spectator* is materially influenced by Alsop's earlier work. It is worth quoting at length Steele's attack on Charlett's character. The essay begins:

> There are crowds of men, whose great misfortune it is that they were not bound to Mechanick Arts or Trades: it being absolutely necessary for them to be led by some continual Task or Employment. These are such as we commonly call Dull Fellows; Persons, who for want of something to do, out of a certain vacancy of Thought, rather than Curiosity, are ever meddling with things for which they are unfit. I cannot give you a Notion of them better than by presenting you with a letter from a Gentleman, who belongs to a society of this Order of Men, residing at *Oxford*.

The ensuing letter from 'Abraham Froth' is dated from Oxford, 13 April 1711, [*Spectator* 43 came out on Thursday, 19 April], *Four a clock in the Morning*. This initial joke parallels that in Alsop's 1. 9, and may have been inspired by it, although Steele could equally well have been independently aware of Charlett's habits. The letter emphasises the seriousness of some clubs, in response to *Mr Spectator*'s attacks on the concept of clubs. The example given is the 'Hebdomadal meeting'—the official executive body of the University, consisting of the Heads of Houses: 'We think it our Duty . . . to take care the Constitution receives no harm . . . To censure Doctrines, or Facts, Persons or Things, which we don't like; To settle the Nation at home, and to carry on the war abroad, where and in what manner we see fit: if other people are not of our Opinion, we can't help that. 'Twere better they were. Moreover, we now and then condescend to direct, in some measure, the little Affairs of our own University . . .'.

This is a different picture to Alsop's; Alsop ridicules Charlett for his obsession with trivial news and speculation, not for interfering in national politics. Charlett's real meddling, as noted above, although inspired by national considerations, was entirely at a local level, and generally intended to save Oxford from hostile outside interference. Steele's satire, however, dates from the time when Oxford

Tories were most likely to think that they had national influence: although the High-Church party was mortified to discover that it did not, in fact, control the government.[17] Steele exaggerates this situation to good effect: 'I must let you know, good Sir, that we look upon a certain Northern Prince's March, in conjunction with Infidels [i.e. Charles XII with the Turks after Poltava] to be palpably against our Good Will and Liking . . . What the Neutrality Army is to do, or what the Army in *Flanders*, and what two or three other Princes, is not yet fully determined among us; and we wait impatiently for the Coming of the next *Dyer's*, who, you must know, is our *Aristotle* in Politicks. And 'tis indeed but fit there should be some Dernier Resort, the absolute Decider of all Controversies . . .'. The letter ends: '. . . I have much more to say to you, but my Two good Friends and Neighbours, *Dominic* and *Slyboots*, are just come in, and the Coffee's ready.'[18]

The ending, and the mention of Dyer's newsletter as a source of information, parallel Alsop's ode. This may, of course, be coincidence also, but it somewhat strengthens the view that Steele was aware of, and partly drew upon, Alsop's work. Steele's picture, however, is not based on Alsop's; Alsop's Charlett is a lone news-gatherer, Steele's the head of a club of armchair statesmen. Both, though, eagerly await the notoriously unreliable Dyer (and, Steele emphasises, treat him as gospel).

Steele's summing up notes that such 'dull fellows prove very good Men of Business. Business relieves them from their own Natural Heaviness, by furnishing them with what to do . . .'. They are not, he claims, interested in useful solutions, but 'the Turn of their Minds tends only to Novelty'. This is a travesty of Charlett's character, which, although incurably busy, was not always facile or 'dull'; Alsop captures his traits better than Steele, concentrating on the letter-writing, news-gathering and vanity. Steele is creating a Theophrastan 'character' of the 'Dull Fellow', and attempting to fit Charlett into his model: he is interested in Charlett only in passing, as an example of the type, while Alsop satirises him as an individual. The two approaches are radically different, although it is certainly possible, and perhaps even likely, that Steele drew some inspiration from Alsop, both in minor points (the midnight scribbling, Dyer, the interrupted ending) and in the general picture of Charlett as a vain and fussy buffoon. The vanity of Alsop's Charlett is different from, but may have partly suggested, the armchair politics of Froth and his companions. Alsop's Charlett seeks news from Percival on a rapid series of subjects:

> Scribe securus, quid agit Senatus,
> Quid caput stertit grave Lambethanum,

[17] Cf. G. V. Bennett, *The Tory Crisis in Church and State* (Oxford, 1975), pp. 118–38 (ch. 7: 'High Church Zenith, 1710–1711').   [18] D. F. Bond, ed., *The Spectator* (Oxford, 1965) 1. 180–5.

> Quid comes Guilford, quid habent novorum
>   Dawksque Dyerque.
>
> Write safely to tell me what Parliament does, how that weighty head
> snores in Lambeth Palace, what Lord Guilford is up to, what news Dawks
> and Dyer have. (1. 9. 25–8)

Ichabod Dawks (1661–1730) began his newsletter in August 1696; it was printed from type designed to imitate handwriting; the prospectus announced that 'This letter will be done upon good writing paper, and blank space left that any gentleman may write his own private business. It does undoubtedly exceed the best of the written news, contains double the quantity, with abundance more ease and pleasure, and will be useful to improve the younger sort in writing a curious hand.'[19] He is a figure of fairly mild fun in the *Tatler* of 30 May 1710: '. . . honest Ichabod is as extraordinary a man as any of our fraternity, and as particular,—his style of dialect between the familiarity of talking and writing . . .'.

Dyer's newsletter was similar, although handwritten. Under William, Dyer's reports had a Jacobite flavour, for which he received a number of threats of punishment, and occasional periods of imprisonment.[20] These newsletters, posted regularly, provided a systematic news service for country gentlemen. The *Tatler* of 21 May 1709 ridicules the prodigies they reported: 'I remember Mr Dyer, who is justly looked upon by all fox-hunters in the nation as the greatest statesman our country has produced, was particularly famous for dealing in whales, insomuch that in five months' time . . . he brought three into the mouth of the Thames, besides two porpoises and a sturgeon. The judicious and wary Mr Ichabod Dawks hath all along been the rival of this great writer, and got himself a reputation from plagues and famines, by which in those days he destroyed as great multitudes as he had lately done by the sword. In every dearth of news, Grand Cairo was sure to be unpeopled.' The two were thus notoriously inaccurate, but very popular, sources of news; intended, however, for ignorant country squires, rather than men of Charlett's standing—so his eagerness for them is humorous.

Charlett's interest in Lambeth refers to Thomas Tenison (1636–1715; Archbishop of Canterbury, 1695). He was a trusted adviser of William III, but he lost favour under Anne, who preferred the advice of Sharp and the other Tory clerics. He voted against the occasional conformity bill, and was a leading supporter of the Hanoverian succession, urging the Electress Sophia to come

---

[19] H. R. Fox Bourne, *English Newspapers* (1887) 1. 58. See also S. Morison, *Ichabod Dawks and his News-Letter* . . . (Cambridge, 1931); H. L. Snyder, 'Newsletters in England, 1689–1715, with special reference to John Dyer', in D. H. Bond, W. R. McLeod, eds., *Newsletters to Newspapers: 18th century Journalism* (Morgantown, WVa, 1977); H. Love, *Scribal Publication in 17th century England* (Oxford, 1993), pp. 11–12.
[20] Hearne, 3 December 1705: *Coll.* 1. 113.

to England. He suffered from gout; but it was royal disfavour more than disease which kept him from court, and he was active, just before his death, in securing George I's accession: he lived to crown him on 20 October 1714. For political reasons, one can see how he would be unpopular with Charlett (a moderate Tory), and anathema to Alsop (an extreme Tory). Personally, too, he would be distasteful to the hospitable Charlett, and the even livelier Alsop. James II is said to have called him 'that dull man' (cf. Alsop's *stertit*?), and the epithet was repeated by others, e.g. Swift: 'a very dull man who had a horror of anything like levity in the clergy, especially of whist', or 'hot and heavy, like a tailor's goose' (*DNB*). It is thus unsurprising to find Tenison humorously depicted as a serious old fool, snoring away in Lambeth Palace. It is notable that Evans does not translate this stanza closely, but replaces it with Irish affairs:

> To me thou mayst securely write.
> Are Dublin, Armagh, Tuam right?
> And is your Church, like ours, out quite
> of Danger? (29–32)

The 'Church in Danger' is a political slogan of the age, used by the Tories to attack the government. The issue came to a head with the Sacheverell trial (1709–10), but was almost as topical in 1705. Sacheverell first delivered his infamous 'perils among false brethren' sermon in Oxford on 23 December 1705; so the phrase would be current in Oxford while Evans was writing. By asserting that the church is out of danger, Charlett is adopting a moderate, even Whig, standpoint. The Irish church, as a minority establishment in a Catholic land, was even more in danger. J. U[pton], meanwhile, does pick up on Alsop's attack on Tenison: 'senties tandem grave *Lambethana*/fulmen ab arce' [you will feel, in the end, a heavy thunderbolt from Lambeth Palace (27–8)], echoing Alsop's epithet, but transferring it to the *fulmen*. As usual, his criticism is confined to empty threats of revenge.

Alsop's *Guilford* is Francis North, 2nd baron Guilford, son of the more famous 1st baron. The 2nd baron, born in 1673, was educated at Winchester, and Trinity, Oxford (matriculated in February 1688/9; MA in 1690). During his brief stay at Oxford, as noted above, his tutor was Charlett. He was active as a Tory peer: his name appears on 78 protests in the House of Lords journal, more than half of the total for the period. He was dismissed from the Privy Council on George I's accession. Swift, admittedly a partisan source, calls him 'a mighty silly fellow'.[21] But if others agreed, Alsop might wish the reader to remember his silliness. He is a suitable example of a dull political informant; Charlett had many

---

[21] G. E. C., *Peerage*.

such, so that the Tory leader, Bromley, could write '. . . but I need not write News to you, who have what occurs from better Correspondents.'[22]

Apart from the doings of the great, Alsop's Charlett is interested in more local gossip; the first such piece of news is the sudden death of Rixon, a rather obscure painter. Fortunately, as Percival says, he can easily be replaced by Thomas Wildgoose (1. 9. 31–2; 1. 10. 21–4).[23] Percival's shallow and selfish outlook is shown by his easy acceptance of consolation for Rixon's death; the existence of another qualified practitioner does not normally mitigate one's own distress at a friend's demise. On the other hand, if Rixon was only a workman, rather than a friend, Charlett's and Percival's initial grief seems rather excessive. It is perhaps suggested that the two of them are free with insincere demonstrations of feeling, which one may contrast with the finer sentiments of Alsop's own friendships.

Disreputable companions

Much of Alsop's satire of Charlett's behaviour centres on the low company that he keeps, and upon which he relies for much of his information. Even in the middle of the night, he is being visited by 'meus, quondam tuus, e popinis/ Jenny' [my Jenny, once yours too, from the kitchens (1. 9. 29–30)]. Jenny (a man, as is clear in the Latin) kept an Oxford coffee house, sometimes a resort for controversial academic gossip. It is possible that something more controversial is hinted at. There were rumours of Charlett's homosexuality; a fellow of his college was expelled in 1698 for spreading them. And Alsop is certainly capable of dropping hints on the subject (as he does in his ode 2. 4: see Chapter 7). Percival's reply to this part of Charlett's letter may set the reader's mind running along similar lines: Jenny is the closest of friends, 'Qui tibi totus vacat, et vacabit,/ nec vetat uxor.' [Who is wholly at your service, and will be so: nor does his wife forbid him. (1. 10. 35–6)] So in Evans' *Answer*:

> Jenny with Thee whole weeks dos spend
> I hear, nor dos his wife pretend
>   To chide him. (34–6)

Whatever the precise nature of the friendship, Alsop is emphasising its closeness: and Jenny is hardly a fitting friend for the head of a college.

[22] 7 October 1701: *Ballard* 38, fo. 133.
[23] Wildgoose (d. 1719) was a painter of miscellaneous subjects, active in Oxford, where he was buried. He repainted the 'old heads' in the Bodleian in 1715 (cf. E. Waterhouse, *Dictionary of British 18th century painters* (1981); Hearne, *Coll.* 3. 401, etc.). He was earlier involved in litigation with the University, which Hearne describes.

Other informants are no better. A certain Pricket is described as a *nuntius* (1. 9. 38). He was probably ill-educated; his writing is very difficult to read, and his spelling unusual (even for a period when much variation was tolerated). A letter of his to Charlett, dated 'Oxon ffebr. 15th 1702' reports miscellaneous news, including a disturbance at St Peter's-in-the-East: '. . . four or five boyes atop of the Church and finding their sum great stones roled ym a Long ye Leads which maid avery great noyes in the Church in Soe much yt all yt wear their thought vereley yt ye Church was falling . . . [and so rushed out, losing hats, gowns, etc.] . . . thankes be to god nobody was kil'd but agreat maney hurt but not mortall . . .' [*sic!*].[24]

Pricket seems to have delivered messages for Charlett; '. . . all of them, even John Pricket, one of Dr Charlett's Lacqueys, were admitted to kiss her Majesty's hand . . .'.[25] Hearne frequently uses pejorative expressions like 'lacquey' for his opponents; but in this case it is probably accurate. Charlett talks only with 'such as are as ignorant as himself, and particularly with one William Sherwin, formerly a Barber, and now one of the Yeoman Beadles, a Pert, forward, conceited, unskillfull Person, John Prickett (the Pragmatical Butler of the College) and one Clarke, a Scrivener . . . These three persons . . . are his Oracles . . .'.[26]

Percival sends his good wishes to Pricket and Sherwin, 'pueroque Davo/ Mitto salutem.' [. . . and my regards to the boy Davus (1. 10. 31–2)]: '. . . Dr. Charlett has turn'd off his famous Boy (call'd Davus in the verses upon him and Mr. Percival wch I have inserted at ye End of the last vol.) for several Pranks wch he had plaid, and particularly for one that was put in the Review and Observator viz. his getting drunk one night at New College, and lighting his Master home with a Silver Tankard instead of a Dark Lantern.'[27]

Hearne's copy of the poems seems to have been lost; but this is important evidence of their reception (and also date, putting the broadsheet in the first months of 1706). The boy's name may have been Davy or David; alternatively, it is possible that the name is chosen without reference to his actual name, because of its classical allusions. Davus is the name of the slave at Horace, *Serm.* 2. 7, who, 'Libertate Decembri' (line 4), tells his master a few home truths, and at the end of the poem is threatened: 'ocius hinc te/ni rapis, accedes opera agro nona Sabino.' [. . . unless you run off pretty damn quick, you'll find yourself doing hard farm labour.] Charlett's mischievous young servant is thus neatly paralleled by Horace's. Davus criticises his master for inconsistency and insincerity in his

---

[24] *Ballard* 38, fo. 15.
[25] Hearne, *Coll.* 2. 384 (2 May 1710); Lancaster, 'old smooth-boots', takes a Whiggish address to the Queen from the University.
[26] *Coll.* 2. 182; Pricket as messenger, *Ballard* 24, fo. 98.
[27] Hearne, 3 April 1706: *Coll.* 1. 215.

statements: 'Romae rus optas . . .' (line 28) [when at Rome you want the country . . .] Charlett might well be criticised for more serious inconsistencies. Davus also criticises Horace for adultery and exaggerated connoisseurship; the latter, at least, may be intended to be recognised in Charlett, with his pretensions to being a patron of learning; gluttony, also, may be visible in Charlett the generous host.

Davus is a stock slave name in comedy; a slave called Davus appears at Persius 5. 161ff. This scene, typical of new comedy, is imitated from the Prologue of Menander's *Eunuchus*. Persius has in fact followed the Greek so closely as to replace the original names, Davus and Chaerestratus, rather than using those adopted by Terence, Parmeno and Phaedria. Note that the conversation is about (in the words of Jahn's 1932 edition of Persius) what to do, 'amore Chrysidis meretricis derelicto' [a whore's love lost]. Such a conversation would not be appropriate for one of Charlett's dignity—and thus it is likely that Alsop wishes us to remember it. Westminster-educated youths were of course very familiar with Terence, whose plays were frequently acted. The link with Menander was also well known at the time.[28]

It seems probable that both of these allusions, to Horace and to Persius/ Terence/Menander, are intended by Alsop. If this is so, by skilful use of classical allusions he manages to convey to the reader a startling variety of uncomplimentary ideas about Charlett. And no harm is done if the reader fails to pick up all possible allusions, and merely remembers that Davus is a classical slave's name. Hearne's comments suggest that the boy may have been notorious, even before Alsop's poems. Thus any allusion to him might be recognised, and might remind the reader of gossip or newspaper stories.

Evans has a nice macaronic stanza, alluding directly to Alsop's Latin:

> To Promus [i.e. butler] Pricket, valet Davy
> And to the Tonsor who dos shave ye,
> *Mitto salutem*, that's God save ye,
>   Or *Idem*. (*Answer* 37–40)

And Evans tells us more details than Alsop knew (or, at any rate, felt inclined to include) about the seamier side of Charlett's Oxford: 'And light-foot Sherwin seiz'd a Punk [i.e. whore]/ with Pricket' (47–8), to which Percival replies, '. . . The Nymph I do suppose You'l Cart,[29]/So Bestial!' (*Answer* 31–2). 'Bestial'

---

[28] E.g.: Juvencius' note on Chaerestratus, in his edition of Persius (Paris, 1700), p. 77: 'Adolescens quidem, malis amoribus implicatus, ex fabula Menandri, loquens hic inauditur; ut in Terentio, apud quem vocatur idem adolescens Phaedria.' For further references, cf. A. Koerte, ed., *Menander* (Leipzig, 3rd edn., 1959), 2. 304 (index s.v. Δᾶος).
[29] A common punishment for loose women: cf. *OED*, citing Butler and Pope.

rhymes nicely with the ironic 'Vestal' (of an innkeeper's daughter) in the previous stanza.

The Trimmer

Gossip about servants' drunkenness and their master's 'empty, frothy' letter-writing may possibly be enough to inspire literary attacks. But it seems likely that more deep-seated *animus* might be needed; and indeed from other aspects of Charlett's busy activity enmities might certainly arise. Politically, Charlett might be described as a 'court Tory'. This attitude he shared with many other moderate Heads of Houses (especially Lancaster, who was Vice-Chancellor 1706–9). During Whig ministries, this meant that he made every effort to avoid giving offence, and deplored the occasional Jacobite excesses of the rash younger members of the University. This naturally brought him into conflict with more extreme Tories, while his Toryism made him still suspect to the government. This uncomfortable position is most noticeable in the period after George I's accession; the chief aim of moderate Heads of Houses at this time was to avoid a visitation, and thus preserve the Tory status quo, at all costs. That this was a sensible, and also a reasonably sincere, policy need not be doubted. This did not make him a government supporter: he was attacked by the government, as pro-Vice-Chancellor, for failing to denounce the riots of 1715; he blocked the loyal address of 1717, and in 1721 we find him, with Gardiner and other moderates, at loggerheads with the King. In 1717 he was dismissed from the royal chaplaincy which he had obtained under William III.[30]

However firm his Toryism was fundamentally, he could, and did, arouse deep suspicion in other Tories by appearing to compromise their principles. He was 'always sensitive to the political breeze'.[31] Although the above-mentioned incidents are all well after Alsop's poems, he was also politically active before. In March 1701 he took the lead in getting Bromley elected as MP for the University.[32] In 1703 he supported Whitelock's candidacy (who, with Bromley, went on to lead the attack on Occasional Conformists). One position that might possibly have made him suspect to the extreme Tory is his refusal to vilify Bishop Nicolson of Carlisle (and help refuse him a DD) for his opposition to Atterbury in Convocation (1702); but such neutrality was also the official position of Christ Church and Magdalen, whatever the private sentiments of their more extreme members. He is later (1710, after Alsop's poems) accused by the Earl of Abingdon of shifting to the low-church interest. But by 1705 his interventions in

[30] W. R. Ward, *Georgian Oxford* (Oxford, 1958), pp. 56, 63, 124, etc.   [31] Ward, p. 42.
[32] Ward, p. 20; *Ballard* 21, fo. 166–8; 30, fo. 54.

politics were not sufficiently serious to make him hated by the extreme Tories, even if a tendency to 'trimming' might be discernible.

'A good deal of caution . . .'

If he was not yet an enemy of the extreme Tories as a whole, Charlett had nevertheless by 1705 managed to antagonise a number of Tory individuals, among whom was very probably Alsop. He did so as a result of his ceaseless activity, seen as 'meddling' by those whom he disobliged; but this activity was by no means entirely harmful and was certainly not intended to be so. Hearne grudgingly admits that he was 'a great Encourager of good Letters'.[33] He did so, not by financial sponsorship so much as by ceaseless enthusiasm. After Fell's death, he and Henry Aldrich were the twin pillars of the University Press, and if Aldrich's was the more learned and versatile talent, Charlett's was at least equally practical.[34]

In 1694 Charlett was appointed to the Delegacy of the Press. His peculiar contribution was in salesmanship; his ceaseless letter-writing and hospitality kept the friends of the Press (like his political friends) informed, and he was assiduous in circulating lists of publications, and only less busy than Aldrich in thinking of worthy subjects for new works for the press to print. Like Aldrich, although to a lesser extent, he adopted Fell's practice of commissioning and buying press books for new year's presents (e.g. Hudson's *Velleius Paterculus* of 1693, for which Hudson got £10). It is a significant testimony to his effectiveness that he, alone of early eighteenth-century delegates, made a mark as a salesman; after 1722 all attempt at direct sale to the public was abandoned.

So Charlett's involvement with the press was highly fruitful. But he managed to cause considerable offence (and also to exceed the strict limits of his duty) as a result of his fear of offending the government, or even the government's supporters. The reasons for this are not hard to see, and fit with his political methods described above. He seems, however, to have carried caution unnecessarily far, and to have imposed it on his colleagues, to the extent that his motives became suspect even to those who might concede the value of caution in certain circumstances. Early eighteenth-century governments were indeed offended by seditious libels on the monarch or actual members of the government, and it would have been most unwise to allow the University's official press to be involved in any such publication (as the majority would have agreed). The offence, however, given by a fairly minor attack on a noted supporter, but not member, of the government would hardly be so great. This is especially so,

---

[33] Hearne, *Coll.* 5. 55.   [34] H. Carter, *History of Oxford University Press* (Oxford, 1975).

when the dispute is entirely an academic one, and no reflection is made on the government's policies.

The issue is complicated, and it is best to examine in detail the evidence for Charlett's behaviour. George Smalridge, who, though a Christ Church man, was noted for his moderation, and distanced himself from Atterbury's more forceful group within the college, wrote in 1698:

> Our V[ice]-Ch[ancellor] has shown a good deal of caution in doing any thing that might offend the Govt. or any one that is in favour of it. He suppressed for some time the Aesop published by Mr. Alsop, because in the preface of it there was a gentle touch upon Dr. Bentley.[35] He has at last given leave to the vent of it on condition that his *Imprimatur* be not printed with it. He put a stop to a Discourse of Mr. John Keill's, a Scotchman of Baliol, because notice was taken in it of an astronomical mistake of Dr. Bentley's; but after expostulating with him, he at last granted that it come out, even with his *Imprimatur,* on its being approved by our Mathematical Professors. An 'Anglo-Saxon Pentateuchon', i.e. the five books of Moses, and Joshua and Judges in Saxon is suppressed by him, because dedicated to Dr. Hickes, a Non-juror, though there is no other compliment paid to him, but that he is skilled in Saxon and has promoted the study of it.[36]

The Vice-Chancellor of 1698 was W. Paynter, not Charlett (preceded in 1697 by J. Meare). But both Meare and Paynter were generally admitted to have little independent spirit, and there is good reason to think that their obstruction of the publications mentioned by Smalridge was inspired by Charlett's advice. Charlett was much more closely connected with the press than they were; he is known to have been a forceful character, and they are known to have been the contrary. There is also direct evidence for a belief in Charlett's involvement: 'Now the V-Ch has confessed, he was put upon this by Dr. Charlett'.[37]

Thwaites' *Heptateuchus* (1698), one of the suppressed books, was 'a scholarly performance', according to the modern editor of the text.[38] The only possible objection to it was the praise of a non-juror, not for non-juring, but for past academic achievement. Charlett is particularly open to criticism in this case (whether we consider his caution expedient or not) because of his own personal obligations to the non-juror concerned (discussed below). Keill's problems, like Alsop's, stemmed from a passing criticism of Richard Bentley. Dr Bentley was by no means noted as a mathematical expert. There can be no doubt that Keill was right to expostulate. Keill was a friend of Alsop's, it seems a very close friend; he was also a friend, and scientific colleague, of Alsop's friends, David Gregory and

---

[35] This part of Alsop's career, including his opposition to Bentley during the Phalaris controversy, is covered in Ch. 4.   [36] Nichols, *Illustrations* 3 (1818), p. 261.
[37] Bodleian, ms. Rawl. letters, 108, fo. 245 (E. Thwaites to Hickes).
[38] S. J. Crawford, *The Old English version of the Heptateuch* (1922).

John Freind (see Chapter 6). So it is reasonable to assume that Alsop will have resented his friend's troubles with the press; it is still more likely that he will have been annoyed at his own.

Keill's criticism of Bentley runs as follows:

> I know Dr *Bently* in his last Lecture for the *Confutation of Atheism*, asserts that tho the *axis* had been perpendicular, yet take the whole year about we should have had the same measure of heat we have now. But I am not surprised to find an error of this nature asserted by one who as it appears is not very well skilled in *Astronomy*; for, in the same Lecture, he confidently saies, that *'tis matter of fact and experience that the Moon alwaies shews the same face to us, not once wheeling about her own Centre*, whereas 'tis evident to any one who thinks, that the Moon shews the same face to us for this very reason, because she does turn once, in the time of her period, about her own Centre. But it were to be wished, that great Criticks would confine their Labours to their Lexicons, and not venture to guess in those parts of Learning which are capable of demonstration, for this is our present case . . .[39]

The last sentence is a cutting rebuke, alluding to the preface of Alsop's *Aesop*.[40] Since Bentley's version of classical scholarship relied heavily on 'demonstration' of facts, rather than on elegantly formed but subjective opinions, this rebuke adds a further twist to the controversy: a natural philosopher may support the polite literature of his friends, and scorn the misapplication of scientific method. The issue is more serious than a simple point of mathematics, and one can see how the cautious Charlett would have been worried by Keill's intervention in the quarrel.

'This malicious, invidious Prevaricator'

Hearne (the author of the above remark) is not an unbiased witness. His relations with Charlett are, however, of great interest, and shed light on what Alsop's relations may have been (indeed, as he and Alsop were friends, Alsop was probably aware of Hearne's views, and the reasons for them). Hearne was not a continual opponent of Charlett; although he is notorious for an inability to concede many virtues to his enemies, he manages to speak well of Charlett on occasion—which says much for Charlett's powers of conciliation:

> Altho' Dr. Charlett hath not been pleas'd to speak to me ever since the Publication of the Life of King Aelfred . . . yet yesterday being at the

---

[39] J. Keill, *An Examination of Dr. Burnet's Theory of the Earth* (Oxford, 1698), p. 70.
[40] See Ch. 4.

Bodleian library with two Gentlemen Strangers, he was pleas'd . . . to ask me some Questions . . . and to talk with me near half an Hour with much civility; which I take very kindly, and shall with this sort of usage be ready to forget and forgive all his former Injuries to me.[41]

These 'former injuries' consist largely of interference in publications, similar to the cases of Thwaites, Keill and Alsop discussed above. The root cause of Charlett's suspicion is Hearne's non-juring, and the reason, again, his desire to avoid the appearance of countenancing anything at which he feared the government would take offence. This attitude was particularly noticeable in Charlett's relations with non-jurors, and, as in Hearne's case, could combine injuries with incivility; although it is striking to find Charlett polite towards a man whose presence, especially in an official capacity, he clearly thought dangerous to the University. Again he risked, by his very affability, being seen as 'playing a double part', since injuries are resented particularly when they are unexpected. Hearne's description of an invitation to dine with Charlett is instructive:

[a literary discussion commences] . . . this malicious, invidious Prevaricator, Dr. Charlett, will not allow any thing of the Non-Jurors to be well done, tho' indeed, it is of no moment what his opinion be, he being one of the worst Judges of Learning in the world . . . [Charlett criticises Aldrich as] a Despiser of Antiquities . . . I told the Master [Charlett] that the Dean [Aldrich] was a truly learned Man, and that he must, therefore, be a Lover of Antiquity, Learning being nothing else but Antiquity. He was only for polite Learning, says the Master. Why, said I, that is Antiquity. From this Discourse I gathered that the Master was one of those inveterate, malicious Enemies that were against my Edition of Roper's Life of Sir Thomas More, tho' he be not willing to own it . . . After all, I look upon this Invitation to Dinner as a premeditated Design to insult and affront me, upon no other account that I know of, but because I will not give up my Conscience and act contrary to my understanding.[42]

Without a full account of that eventful evening, we cannot be sure that Hearne's final assertion is correct: indeed, it seems more plausible that, in his annoyance, he exaggerates, and that Charlett had intended to persuade or conciliate, rather than to humiliate. It is interesting to find Charlett critical of Aldrich; if Hearne were not himself a leading Antiquary, one might take Charlett's criticisms more seriously. The most important point, however, is Charlett's violent fear of association with non-jurors. This is illustrated by an earlier incident recorded by Hearne: [a visitor comments on a preface by Hickes; Charlett shows no interest whatsoever, despite] 'having some small interest with Dr. Hickes, for whom however he cares no farther than he perceives 'twill be for

[41] Coll. 3. 274.   [42] Coll. 6. 46–7 (24 April 1717).

his own interest, and in all probability he would have all the Non-Jurors punished with the utmost Severity, it being his Business now to act and talk for the Whiggs on purpose that he may get Preferment, which however he will hardly obtain, notwithstanding his project of setting up Statues, etc.'[43]

This ingratitude to Hickes, stemming from fear of association with non-jurors, was believed (by some, at least) to have done Charlett's reputation harm. We may consult, as well as Hearne, sources favourable to Charlett: '. . . If you can bear hearing one false step Dr. Charlett made, I will tell it you, otherwise it shall remain a secret as hitherto it has done with regard to me.'[44]

It is probable, but not certain, that the story recounted below is the 'false step' Brome here refers to; it is in any case certainly a mistake, stemming from the traits of Charlett's character with which we are concerned:

> . . . But behold the fluctuation of Humane Affairs. Ld. Somers was raised by Dean Hickes; he was one of the Counsel to the seven bishops by the Dean's recommendation: that advanced him after the Revolution, and engaged him in a firm friendship for the Dean: and at the very instant when Dr. C——t was suppressing the Dedication [to Hickes] thereby to make court with Ld. Somers, there were in my house Saxon Charters lent the Dean by Somers, and one of the Books with the Dedication got loose before ye seisure was sent him by the Dean; and so were others to Lambeth etc, Ld. Oxford then Mr Harley etc. So that the Grandees had the book with its Dedication, whilst at Oxford they were thus busie to suppress it. And I verily believe this very proceeding of Dr. Ch. was a Bar to his future preferments. The Dean's kindness for him abated, but he had so much humanity as to do nothing to his prejudice; tho' I suppose he might not endeavor to promote him, which 'twas in his power to have done. Ld. Oxford, who without doubt knew of this matter (for it made a terrible noise) might resent it; for he loved the Dean entirely, and has told me he thought him the greatest man in the world . . . [45]

It seems that Charlett underestimated the influence of one non-juror, at least, and offended where he hoped to please. Even if he had pleased the ministers, his betrayal of Hickes would have shown an unappealing side of his character. Whether or not this incident was the reason, Charlett failed to receive the bishopric for which he hoped, and occasionally intrigued, and remained merely Master of University for thirty years.

[43] *Coll.* 2. 290 (20 October 1709). Charlett had disagreed with the fellows of University College over the position of a statue of Queen Anne; they wanted it inside the college, next to that of James II (a potential embarrassment), while he insisted it should go outside.
[44] W. Brome to T. Rawlins, 4 August 1735: *Ballard* 19, fo. 38.
[45] Brome to Rawlins, 25 October 1735: *Ballard* 19, fo. 48.

'Our general benefactor'[46]

Charlett had many admirers, and it would be a mistake to conclude a discussion of his character without stressing this. Thus Brome to Rawlins, a couple of weeks before the last letter quoted above:

> . . . and with great concern I have, when twas *too late*, reflected on myself for not thinking of recommending my *Tutor* and Dr Charlett; for whom I could have gott as good as a Preb[end] of Worc[ester]. Dr Charlett was as good a Natured man as ever lived [;] was as generous a man; was as publick a spirited man; and had he had an equal fortune would have done wonders for the reputation of the University: he was most orthodox in his Principles. These excellent qualities plunged a person of his narrow circumstances into great difficulties and distresses; out of which to extricate himself, wanting a firm resolution, he made this false step, which instead of tending to his advantage and advancement was perhaps the greatest obstacle—& must be well known to Ld. Somers Ld. Oxford & others. [And the same to the same, a few months earlier:] . . . 'twas pity he [Charlett] was so straightened in circumstances, he would have done wonders if he had had a large fortune. His was an active life, and might disoblige some, which did him ill offices (perhaps) with Lord Oxford, who was always ready to encourage such persons . . . [47]

It is interesting to find such stress put on Charlett's financial problems. He was of some independent means, but not as rich as many supposed. It appears, in fact, that he obtained the mastership of University at least in part because of his private fortune: he was seen as 'a potential benefactor (whose benefactions remained potential)'.[48] He was also popular for his affability and scholarship: but these alone may not have been enough to give him the post. But it was not always possible to persuade the best candidates to accept the mastership, since its salary was not very large. Charlett's income, in addition to his private means, is recorded by Hearne, 'when Dr Hudson was Burser' in 1699, as '£110. 10s. 4d., not reckoning his Lodgings, a Load of Hay and other perquisites'.[49] This was, indeed, a respectable income for a clergyman; but most senior clerics would expect more (many attractive rectories were more valuable). Thus one can understand Charlett's frustration at his lack of further preferment: £110 p.a. is too little for a would-be philanthropist. We must add to it his private means, and from 1707 Hambledon rectory: he was clearly well off, even if he had to curtail his acts of generosity.

Charlett's political influence is remarkable, when we consider the modest position normally held by a Master of University, one of the smallest colleges. Others, indeed, gained prominence in the university despite belonging to a

[46] Gibson, in preface to Camden's *Britannia* (1695).
[47] 10 October and 16 July 1735: *Ballard* 19, fo. 47; fo. 33.   [48] Ward, p. 5.   [49] *Coll.* 1. 300.

small foundation.[50] But one needed a powerful character to make one's voice heard by the large colleges, and bully Vice-Chancellors. Charlett's forcefulness was usually amiable. His character contained something of the buffoon, but also much that excited admiration. Rawlinson called him 'that worthy patron of all learning, and no inconsiderable judge of it', and 'that generous universal correspondent'.[51] Charlett, as a correspondent, is a sympathetic as well as a ludicrous figure. A number of people in Alsop's circle corresponded with him: Clarke, who told Charlett of Alsop's troubles, Dr Arbuthnot, John Keill, and David Gregory.[52] The correspondence illustrates Charlett's friendliness, his influential position in Oxford politics, and his delight in news. His critics ridicule him with reason; but his character also had an appealing side.

Edward Lhwyd and Charlett

As an example of the impression that Charlett made on a lively, but neutral contemporary, it is interesting to read the views of the naturalist and antiquarian Lhwyd (1660–1709). As early as 1689, when Charlett was still at Trinity, Edward Lhwyd suspected him of some dubious intrigue. Later, Lhwyd hopes that Charlett's influence might be used on his behalf; and he gives the following picture of Charlett's character:

> One Dr Charlet . . . tells me he designs to wait on you . . . He is a person of a very public spirit, and of the greatest sway and interest I think of any here: and mindes nothing more than the reputation of the University, the satisfaction of the public, and the encouragement of such young men as he finds deserving. I have often wished you acquainted with him (tho. he is more a man of *Parts*, and genteel converse, than learning) that so we might secure his favour and helping hand on emergent occasions. He has that influence, that he can persuade the University to print any book etc. provided it be well approved; tho. of never so singular a subject . . .

So early in his mastership, then, Charlett is a leading force in the University. And Lhwyd's assessment of his learning is valuable, mid-way between the admiration of Brome and Rawlinson, and the hostility of Hearne and Steele. A few years later, about the time of Alsop's poems, Lhwyd is again disenchanted with Charlett: '. . . Our Sr Charls Cotterel and noise-monger A.C. [Charlett] has [*sic*] divided the [University Press] catalogue now into three parts . . . in

---

[50] Of the Oxford colleges, University and Lincoln usually had the fewest senior members resident: Sutherland and Mitchell, *Oxford*, pp. 39–40.   [51] *Ballard* 2, fo. 6 and 10.
[52] *Ballard* 20 and 24, passim.

which last [part] he inserts anything (whether ever likely to be printed) if he thinks it will meet with a publike applause . . .'[53]

Charlett is still concerned for 'ye satisfaction of ye public', but he goes too far in an attempt to satisfy people, and ends up an unsatisfactory 'noise-monger'; this seems to be a similar picture to the one that Alsop paints, full of bluster and lacking in substance. But Lhwyd's own character was quite impulsive, and he was not always so critical; so it is possible that he would have agreed with Brome's more sympathetic summing up: '. . . setting aside some humane fraylties, [Charlett] was a most worthy person, and considering circumstances, was as great an encourager and patron of learning and virtue as any of his age . . .'.[54]

One example of Charlett's patronage appears at Alsop 1. 10. 17–20; in Evans' English (here fairly close to the Latin):

> Wou'd you the Place exactly know,
> Which conscious was of all my woe;
> Consult Ben Cole, who works so slow
>   Map-making. (*Answer* 17–20)

Benjamin Cole was a surveyor, engraver and map-maker based in Oxford, flourishing *c*. 1695–1720. He had published *Wells Atlas* (1700), *Twenty miles round Oxford* (1705), later adding *Twenty miles round Cambridge* (1710), and other works.[55] Alsop seems to be making a mild criticism of the slow progress of a project sponsored by Charlett. The recent publication of his *Twenty miles round Oxford* (ten years after his first plan of Oxford, hence *lente*) would probably have brought him into Alsop's mind when he was composing the poem. The scene of the robbery is thus placed within 20 miles of Oxford (presumably on the London road).

Cole does not seem to have been educated at the University: he was 'town' rather than 'gown', although under Charlett's patronage. He is recorded as receiving the status of *privilegiatus* from the University on 10 October 1690, aged 24, where he is described as a *Bibliophola* [bookseller], the son of a Maximilian Cole.[56] His maps were probably worth the wait: '. . . if *Coles*

[53] Lhwyd, *Letters*, ed. R. T. Gunther (Oxford, 1945): 15 August 1689; December 1693 [?]; 28 July 1705.
[54] *Ballard* 19, fo. 174.
[55] Cf. P. Eden, ed., *Dictionary of Land Surveyors and Local Cartographers . . . 1550–1850* (1975); R. V. Tooley, *Dictionary of Mapmakers, part 2* (Map collectors series, 28, 1966). The most detailed (but still brief) account of him is at E. G. R. Taylor, *The Mathematical Practitioners of Tudor and Stuart England* (1954) p. 291.
[56] Foster, *Alumni Oxonienses*. He is not, however, included in H. R. Plomer, *Dictionary of Printers and Booksellers, 1668–1725* (1922): surveying and cartography were probably his main activities, rather than traditional printing and bookselling. He, or his son (of the same name), is probably responsible for the compiling and printing of *Constitution of the Free-masons* (London, *c*. 1728–9, and another edition with B. Creake, 1731).

Mapp be what I mean, it is a scarce and valluable thing, mention'd by T: Hearne in one of his Books . . .'.[57]

'The Rogue Alsop'

We have seen that Alsop had a reasonable motive for attacking Charlett in verse; Charlett's growing public notoriety no doubt brought back memories of the troubles Alsop had had in 1698, as well as any more recent irritations. The satire certainly has a number of barbs, and aims to hurt its victim. But the tone may not be entirely malicious; a sense of fun, rather than revenge, may be the main motive. A number of reasons may be adduced in support of this idea. Firstly (and most tentatively), there is Charlett's later forgiveness of Alsop, as indicated by the interest that Charlett took in his plight in 1717; it seems unlikely that Clarke would have written to a well-known foe of Alsop in such a sympathetic tone (see Chapter 7). But after a gap of eleven years, even a bitter insult may be forgiven (especially when the culprit is plunged into adversity). Stronger evidence appears in a letter from Brome to Rawlins:

> . . . My friend Mr Urry told me in it [a censor's speech, now lost, delivered at Christ Church] he [Alsop] lashed Gastrell (afterwards the worthy Bp of Chester) in a severe manner . . . In Mr Lloyds [i.e. Lhwyd's] Archaeologia the copy of verses in J. Keill's name are Alsops; which Keill knew nothing of, till he saw them in Print; which raised his Caledonian Blood to a high ferment; and had no other revenge than to call him the Rogue Alsop . . .[58]

Here are two examples of Alsop's wit in operation. The lashing of the moderate canon Gastrell shows that he is capable of aggression. The *Archaeologia* verses are more in the nature of a practical joke. Keill was annoyed at Alsop's audacity, but no doubt soon forgave him and joined in the laughter: at least, they seem to have continued firm friends. The *Archaeologia* verses appear among a set of fair copies in William Parry's calligraphic hand, with the subscription, in another hand, 'Authore Antonio Alsop [DD deleted] BD.'[59] The joke at Keill's expense is fairly mild: in a reasonably conventional set of verses praising Lhwyd, Keill is made to stress his own rusticity, and thus approval of archaeological subject matter:

> . . . Scotia me genuit, rigidi terra aspera Fergi,
> Terra antiqua, potens armis, tamen ubere gleba
> Haud nimium felix; placidis sed amica Camoenis;
> Utcunque Aoniae mihi non risere sorores.

[57] T. Ward to (?) Rawlins, 'Warwick, ffebr. ye 20th 1728': *Ballard* 38, fo. 87.
[58] 27 September 1740: *Ballard* 19, fo. 162.   [59] *Ballard* 29. 22 [fo. 55].

Rusticitas mihi prisca placet, salebrosaque vocum
Fragmina, quae patriis in montibus audiit olim
Cum proavis atavus, quique hos genuere parentes . . .

Scotland bore me, the rough land of strict Fergus, an ancient land, powerful in war, though not too well provided with fertile soil; but it is friendly to the Muses. For all that, they have not smiled upon me: I prefer old-fashioned rusticity, and ragged fragments of words, which my distant ancestors, and their ancestors, heard on our native hills. (3. 11. 8–14)

For an urbane person like Keill, it must have been mortifying (unless he could laugh at himself) to appear in print as a supporter of rustic ballad-writers, to whom classical elegance was a mystery. Thus Alsop's wit is well applied: a seemingly normal set of congratulatory verses in fact ridicules their supposed author. The abnormal (for Alsop) number of trite classical allusions may also be part of the fun. Alsop's attacks, even in print, need not be malicious; against Keill, it is almost certainly in the nature of a practical joke among friends. Against Charlett and Gastrell, there is likely to have been a little more *animus*. But we should not forget that light-hearted exploitation of any potential for amusement is likely to be a significant motive. The Charlett odes contain telling observation of foibles, and good-humoured ridicule. They are intended to amuse the reader at the subject's expense, but probably not to inflict too serious a wound. Laughter, for Alsop, is generally more important than revenge.

The Tallard Broadsheet

Similar to the Charlett odes in date and mode of publication, but rather different in content, is a broadsheet of 1708, with a Latin poem that purports to be a letter from the imprisoned French Marshal Tallard (captured at Blenheim, 1704) to his colleague the Duke of Vendôme, recently defeated at Oudenarde (11 July 1708, N.S.). The poem is attributed to Alsop in the British Library manuscript,[60] which seems extremely plausible: the language and style of humour are both firmly Alsopian. There is much of interest in this ode, including hints of Jacobitism; since the words are placed in a Frenchman's mouth, it is possible to praise the Jacobite leaders fighting against Britain. Opponents would not be too shocked, seeing it as part of Tallard's character; sympathisers could notice and appreciate the sentiments. There are several levels of satire, ridiculing the French, and also loyal English propagandists such as Tom D'Urfey (1653–1723), who is the butt of one of Alsop's most inspired Horatian allusions:

[60] 11409. h. 30; also (unattributed) Bodleian, ms. Lat. misc. e. 19, fo. 172.

Multa Durfeii levat aura Musam
Dum super nubes et in alta surgens
Marlburum caelo et mediis micantem
          Inserit astris.

A lot of wind raises D'Urfey's Muse above the clouds: he rushes on high to place Marlborough in heaven, and make him twinkle amongst the stars.[61]

The poem is humorous, in his liveliest vein, but also potentially serious. It suggests that he followed and reacted to contemporary events (whether through Dawks, Charlett, or some better source), and retained the patriotism that fuels earlier military pieces,[62] as well as developing his pose of amused detachment. As in the case of the Charlett odes, there is just enough of reality about the supposed circumstances to make the letter pointed as well as amusing. Tallard was allowed to correspond freely during his internment at Nottingham, although his letters were routinely opened by the secret service. This fact was well known, since intercepted letters were used against William Greg, who had been tried for treason in January 1707/8.[63] There was thus a politically sensitive side to the issue, which may have attracted Alsop's interest to Tallard's letters. The poem was written and printed (whether on Alsop's instructions or not) fairly soon after the battle, which indicates its topicality and potential appeal to a metropolitan audience. Laughter was still the principal aim, though other motives lay under the surface.

---

[61] 3. 4. 37–40. Cf. Hor., *Carm.* 4. 2. 25–8. D'Urfey's pretensions are satirised by Pope: 'Verses occasion'd by an '&c' at the end of Mr D'Urfy's name', in N. Ault, J. Butt, eds., *Minor Poems* (Twickenham edn., vol. 6), pp. 85–90.   [62] See 1. 2; 3. 6; 3. 8.
[63] I. S. Leadam, *History of England, 1702–60* (London, 1909), p. 131.

6
Newtonian Jacobites

Alsop was a close friend, at various stages in his life, of several of the leading scientific figures of the age. David Gregory, John Freind, and John Keill were all exponents of the Newtonian natural philosophy which was in the process of revolutionising scientific thought in Europe; the first two (and possibly also the third) were also committed to Jacobitism, and therefore to an old-fashioned political philosophy, one rejecting the progressive Whiggish notions that under-pinned the Glorious Revolution, and looking back to the Stuart certainties of a previous age. This combination of attitudes may seem paradoxical; but it has always been the case that respected scientists, as individuals, are capable of holding views on religion and politics that other scientists find inexplicable. Support for Newton often has been associated, rather crudely, with Whig politics.[1] An examination of Alsop's poems to these three Newtonians reveals a complex relationship between science, literature and personal beliefs; the author's lively approach ensures that humour and sex are also prominent ingre-dients in the mixture.

A Jacobite epithalamium for Gregory

David Gregory (1661–1708) was a Scottish mathematician and astronomer, one of the most important of Newton's followers. He was born in Aberdeen, but moved to Edinburgh to teach mathematics. He delivered his inaugural (Latin) lecture as an Edinburgh professor in 1683, at the age of 22. In Edinburgh he became a close friend of Dr Archibald Pitcairne, the physician and Latin poet who was, after the Revolution, a leading Jacobite. Gregory himself, as an Episcopalian, refused to subscribe to the Confession of Faith, and was in some danger of losing his post at the hands of the Revolution commissioners.[2] In 1691 he came to London, in the hope of obtaining the Savilian Professorship

---

[1] E.g., M. Jacob, *The Newtonians and the English Revolution, 1689–1720* (Ithaca, NY, and Hassocks, 1976). But cf. A. Guerrini, 'The Tory Newtonians', *Journal of British Studies* 25 (1986), pp. 288–311.
[2] A. G. Stewart, *The Academic Gregories* (Edinburgh, 1901), pp. 53, 58.

of Astronomy at Oxford, then vacant. This he eventually did, through the influence of Newton and Flamsteed. His rival was the atheist Halley; Gregory's religion, to which Anglicans would be much more sympathetic than the Scottish authorities had been, probably swayed the balance. Newton's letter of recommendation, dated 28 July 1691, is warm in his praise, though based as much on reputation as on personal knowledge:

> Being desired by Mr David Gregory Mathematick Professor of the Colledge in Edinburgh to certifie my knowledge of him, and having known him by his printed Mathematical performances, and by discoursing with travellers from Scotland, and of late by conversing with him, I do account him one of the most able and judicious mathematicians of his age now living. He is very well skilled in analysis and Geometry both new and old. He has been conversant in the best writers about Astronomy and understands that Science very well. He is not only acquainted with books, but his invention in mathematical things is also good. He has performed his duty at Edinburgh with credit as I hear and advanced the mathematicks. He is reputed the greatest mathematician in Scotland, and that deservedly, so as my knowledge reaches, for I esteem him an ornament to his country, and upon these accounts recommendable to the Electors of the Astronomy professor into the place at Oxford now vacant.[3]

On receiving the professorship he joined Balliol College, and was rapidly made FRS; he seems to have developed strong links with Christ Church, numbering Aldrich and Smalridge, as well as Alsop, among his friends. His son David (1696–1767) was eventually, in 1756, to become Dean of Christ Church. He could also count upon the support of his 'great ally', Arthur Charlett.[4] But Thomas Hearne was less approving, particularly of his self-confessedly poor Greek, calling him 'Dr Gregory the Scotch man who understands just as much of Antiquity as he does of Greek. And yet some are so wise as to hearken to him both in this and other matters, and to take him as an oracle.'[5] This weakness does not harm his work in modern, Newtonian mathematics; but he was obliged to seek Dr Hudson's help with Euclid, and natural philosophy was not then wholly divorced from classical studies. In 1695, the year of Alsop's ode to him, he published *Catoptricae et Dioptricae Elementa* (bearing Aldrich's *imprimatur*). He was appointed tutor in 1699 to the young Duke of Gloucester, son of Princess (later Queen) Anne; he held the post all too briefly, since the boy died in the following year. He dedicated his *Astronomiae, Physicae et Geometricae Elementa* (1702) to Anne's husband, Prince George of Denmark; astronomy was relevant to him, as Admiral, a point that Gregory stresses in his preface: 'cum hinc omnino pendeant Artis Nauticae . . . studia a quibus petenda sunt et

---

[3] Bodleian, ms. Rawl. D. 742, fo. 7 (different draft in *Corresp.* 3. 154–5, ed. H. W. Turnbull, 1961).
[4] Stewart, *Academic Gregories*, pp. 64, 74.   [5] 14 May 1707: *Reliquiae*, p. 59.

ornamenta et praesidia Reipublicae . . .' [since hence depends the whole study of navigation, from which we must seek both the ornament and the defence of the state]. A rather hostile and unfair modern summary of his career emphasises his significance, both as a scholar and in Oxford society: 'Intellectually the most eminent—though personally the most obnoxious—of the group around Newton was David Gregory . . . flattering, toadying, acting as a focus for an active group of disciples centred on Christ Church, and keeping a gossipy and highly revealing private diary'.[6]

Gregory was married in 1695 to Elizabeth Oliphant, of Langtoun in Scotland. The bride's family had many branches, and this was not the most prominent. Some, such as the Oliphants of Gask, were certainly Jacobite.[7] Gregory wrote from Edinburgh, on 29 September 1695, to Charlett:

> Reverend Sir,
> I receaved your most kind letter whil I was in the North, and am affrayed that I shall be forced to accept of the allowance of time that you was pleased to name for my return to Oxon. The Equippage Sir that I have lately gott by being married is one excuse which I know will weigh with you, and I must beg your assistance and interest with the Vice-Chancellour to the same effect. This change of life is what cannot again happen, and if I once wer at Oxford the occasions of being from it will be more rare than formerly. I expect to part hence next week; for being now forced to travel in Coach (because of my company) I am not so much master of my time as to part when I will . . .

He continues with the news from Scotland (no doubt remembering Charlett's fondness for such information); it being the vacation, there is little to tell. The 'great affair' is the oath administered to the clergy. 'Nothing less than dragoons can displace them [recusants] in those malignant Northern places. But heir in the city the Episcopal meeting houses are shutt, and indeed the Magistrates of this Town bid as fair to be Canonized in the Church that has no use for a Calendar, as any ever did. The only commendable piece of government that I have observed since I came from the North, is that this day sailed from Leith Road, half a dozen ships to Bourdeaux, to fetch Claret, of which we continue very well provided.'[8] French claret was the preferred Tory drink, the political link with Portugal being reflected on Whig tables. Britain was at war with France, and Gregory is enthusiastic about trade with the enemy. This remark is not an open admission of Jacobitism. Gregory must have been aware of Charlett's moderate Tory views, his abhorrence of non-jurors and Jacobites and

[6] A. Thackray, *Atoms and Powers* (Cambridge, MA, 1970), p. 45.
[7] T. L. Kington, *Jacobite Lairds of Gask* (1870).
[8] Bodleian, ms. Ballard 24. 23 [fo. 38]. Cf. Guerrini, p. 302.

concern to avoid offending the government; to remain on good terms, he had to tread carefully.

Evidence for his real feelings comes from Alsop's poem, copied into Gregory's journal[9] under the year 1696, but presumably written in the previous year, on the occasion of the marriage. Bernard's edition omits two passages (lines 33–6 and 49–64); the first is mildly risqué, the second openly Jacobite. The journal is the source for the full text of the ode: one may assume that he would preserve an accurate copy of the poem as it was presented to him. Two alternative versions, one politically and morally safe, the other unrestrained in both respects, probably circulated in manuscript. The British Library manuscript offers the extra stanzas, either from the journal itself or another copy. Alsop may have made the necessary cuts himself. The abbreviated version is effective and thought-provoking in its own right, but it does end rather abruptly, and is thus less satisfactory from a purely aesthetic standpoint; for many contemporary readers, other considerations were of greater weight.

Gregory died in 1708. His wife arranged for a monument in St Mary's, Oxford, the University Church. Charlett was closely involved; the Latin inscription was composed by Robert Freind, who wrote to him from Westminster School on 26 June 1711: 'I am desir'd by Mrs Gregory to give you the trouble of delivering the inclos'd to the Stonecutter if you approve of it. More might have been said of the worthy Dr, but according to the model that was given me, this is as much as the stone will admit of. His arms are in Dr Morisons book, but I have sent you an impression from a seal both of his and hers. She has left it to Dr Stratford to agree for the price of the monument, and will pay what he directs her. I endeavour'd to wait upon you when I was last at Oxford, to thanke you for a kind present that you intended me tho' by some mischance or other it never came to my hands. Young Gregory and Smith do very well here.' On the same sheet is a note in Charlett's hand, dated from Hambledon, 3 July 1711, to a Mr Townsend: 'By this from Dr Freind, you may see Mrs Gregory's intentions, according to which you are to act. All I doubt not will be well done and to content.'[10] The monument is still visible, and praises his achievements: '. . . aetatem illi heu brevem natura concessit, si[b]i[11] ipse longam prorogavit scriptor illustris . . .' [alas, nature allowed him a brief lifetime, but he himself lengthened it by being an illustrious writer].

There is no Horatian parallel for Alsop's epithalamium. Catullus may have provided some general inspiration. He mentions Catullus (line 28), and perhaps recalls Catullus' epithalamia, poems 61 and 62; but he does not imitate him, and

[9] Christ Church, ms. 346, pp. 187–8; W. G. Hiscock, *David Gregory, Isaac Newton and their circle* (Oxford 1937), p. 4.   [10] Bodleian, ms. Ballard 35. 94 [fo. 158–9].
[11] The stone clearly reads *sitni*, presumably a mistake.

the ode's effect does not depend upon any Catullan link. Martial 4. 13 is another possibility.[12] He may also have known Statius, *Silvae* 1. 2, an extended hexameter poem on the marriage of a fellow poet, L. Arruntius Stella, to Violentilla; that poem offers wit (e.g. lines 16–45, on Stella's reluctance to marry) as well as copious mythological allusion. Innumerable epithalamia, like Statius', suggest that marriage brings increase, and is in tune with cosmic regeneration: an idea highly relevant to Gregory the astronomer. The fourth of the *Fescennina* appended to Claudian's epithalamium *In nuptias Honorii et Mariae* offers a liveliness in sexual description that parallels Alsop; but many other bawdy poems in Catullus, Martial, or elsewhere could also have influenced him. The formal, public nature of Claudian's imperial epithalamium does make it the precursor of many Neo-Latin and vernacular poems that unite marriage and politics.[13]

The personal, sexually charged, epithalamium plays a significant part in Neo-Latin: of particular interest is Pontano's *Branchatus & Maritella*, and equally relevant is Joannes Secundus' well-known series of poems on kissing, the *Basia*. There was a flourishing tradition of vernacular marriage verse, a genre employed by Spenser, Donne, Jonson and many others. The political epithalamium was very common in seventeenth-century England. Royal weddings regularly produced torrents of poetry, and a crucial part in the poetic celebration was played by the Latin verses in the university collections. These included some lyric poems, as well as the more usual hexameters and elegiacs. There seems to be originality, in this otherwise well-worn genre, in Alsop's combination of a personal epithalamium and a subversive political message. His ode is very different from the conventional flattery found in official collections, although his formal opening, replete with vocatives and exclamations, may be a deliberate parody of that style:

> O qui meanti conscius aetheri
> Pictum decoris sideribus polum
>   Perpendis, et sagaci ocello
>   Aethereos penetras recessus!
> O Archimedis nobilis aemulum!
> O invidentis Wallisii parem!
>   Quo sospite exultat Nutonus,
>   Saviliique superbit umbra . . .

You understand the wandering heavens, weigh up the pole, painted with beautiful stars, and with your clever eye penetrate the depths of space. You are a rival of noble Archimedes, the equal of envious Wallis; Newton rejoices in your safety, and the shade of Savile is proud.[14]

---

[12] *Macte esto*, in Martial's line 2, may have influenced Alsop 2. 16. 10–11.
[13] See V. Tufte, *The Poetry of Marriage* (Los Angeles, 1970); J. D. Garrison, *Dryden and the Tradition of Panegyric* (Berkeley, 1975).   [14] 1. 11. 1–8.

My translation does not attempt to reflect all the Latin's excesses.

John Wallis (1616–1703) was a distinguished mathematician and cryptographer; he was appointed by Cromwell, in 1649, as Savilian Professor of Geometry. He was confirmed in his post on the Restoration, having 'discovered nothing to the rebels which much concerned the public safety . . . though . . . he could have discovered a great deal'; he was 'the greatest of Newton's predecessors' (according to *DNB*), whose achievement one might expect Gregory to envy, rather than vice versa. But he was given to making extravagant claims: that he had invented a flooring technique that was already in use in the university,[15] and that he could prove the illegitimacy of 'James III', a suggestion that might well infuriate Jacobites. He was a Fellow of Exeter, a Whiggish college; he dedicated his works (1693–9) to King William. When Sir Godfrey Kneller came to draw Dr Wallis, in 1701, he did so in Gregory's house;[16] despite their political differences, their rivalry remained friendly. Both their professorships had been founded in 1619 by Sir Henry Savile (1549–1622), an extremely learned man who might indeed have been pleased that his benefaction had produced good results.

Although produced early in his career, this is one of Alsop's most ambitious works, joining with striking effect the jocular, the erotic, and the serious. The changes of tone are not illogical: he moves smoothly from jocular augury of happiness to erotic description of it, and when he turns to politics, the abrupt change is intended to shock:

> Dum Mars per orbem saevit, et undique
> Commissa fervent proelia; dum micat
>   Districtus ensis, et ruinae
>   Terribilis nitet apparatus;
> Tu coniugali mollior in toro
> Spectas tumultus . . .

> While war rages over the globe, and battles are everywhere fiercely joined, while the unsheathed sword glitters, and the terrible machinery of ruin shines forth, you look out from the softness of your marriage-bed upon the confusion.[17]

There is a pointed contrast between chaos outside, and Gregory reclining on the breast of his new wife. The war that raged was the nine years war, at its height in 1695; it was to end with the peace of Rijswijck in 1697. The coalition that fought the nine years war against Louis XIV was determined to restrict the French king's ambition; the conflict was soon to erupt again, as the war of the Spanish succession, and William III's campaigns are precursors to the more

[15] W. H. Quarrell, M. Mare, *London in 1710* (1934), p. 68.
[16] Gregory's journal: Hiscock, *David Gregory*, p. 11.   [17] I. ii. 41–6.

famous ones of Marlborough. The alliance which William held together, based on Britain, Holland, and the Empire, was under great strain; German princes had continually to be bribed, and Dutch citizen-soldiers cajoled, into doing any fighting. In the face of these difficulties, William managed to avert catastrophe, but could not produce victory. He usually faced defeat at the hands of superior forces, as at Landen in 1693, in spite of stubborn and not unskilful generalship. With the war far from successful, the death of Queen Mary on 27 December 1694 was a grave political blow to William, as well as a personal tragedy. In the ensuing crisis, James II had another reasonable opportunity to regain his throne. These genuine (and seemingly well-founded) hopes in the Jacobite camp lie behind Alsop's optimism; an excited ending arises out of the grim scene of war:

> En! tempus instat, en! veniet dies,
> Cum rursus in Coelum caput efferet
>   Nomen Stuartorum . . .

> Look—the time is at hand, look, the day will come, when the name of Stuart will again raise its head to heaven.[18]

The poet has effectively prepared for this joyful prophecy, not only by mentioning the astronomer's predictive powers, but also by introducing as a classical parallel (lines 17–20) the return of Apollo to Delos. As the god returned, the reader thinks, so will the king return. Emotions veer from joy to pessimism, and then to a final joy which is more complete, because it transcends the personal happiness of a married couple in national and dynastic resurgence.

The king did not return. William survived on his precarious throne for various reasons. The French did not support James with an invasion attempt, as they had as recently as 1692–3; Princess Anne, and thus her supporter Marlborough, remained loyal. A serious Jacobite plot to assassinate William was discovered and suppressed in February of 1695/6, and in its aftermath his popularity rose. William had also achieved in 1695 his first major success of the war, the capture of Namur: it was a 'magnificent victory . . . perhaps the strongest place in Europe was taken in the face of an army of 100,000 men which had not dared to come to the relief of the fortress.'[19] The loyal Latin poet William Hogg celebrated the event in an extended hexameter work, *Ad . . . Gulielmum III post victam Namuram ΠΡΟΣΦΩΝΗΤΙΚΟΝ*,[20] with much emphasis on Jacobite plotting at that chaotic time: 'rumoribus omnem/ Quando Jacobitae falsis fremuere per urbem' [when Jacobites were raging

---

[18] I. II. 57–9.
[19] S. B. Baxter, *William III* (1966), p. 330; cf. G. N. Clark, *The Later Stuarts* (1934), pp. 165–6, 177–8.
[20] This forms the main part of W. Hogg, *Victoria . . . Regis Gulielmi Tertii, Qui Urbem & Arcem Namurae, a Gallis occupatam, fortiter obsedit, & feliciter recuperavit, expulso Gallorum praesidio* (London, 1695).

madly through the whole city bearing false rumours (p. 7)]. The knowledge that success for his own side might be imminent lends fervour to Alsop's ode.

Alsop avoids any serious treatment of Newtonian astronomy; instead, he makes much poetic use of astrology. The pseudo-science was influential in the seventeenth century, and not always separated, even in the minds of astronomers, from more modern methods of studying the stars, and motives for doing so. There is an obvious poetic incentive to use astrology, regardless of whether or not they genuinely believed in its value.

Pitcairne's Latinate Jacobitism

Gregory's friendship with Archibald Pitcairne (1652–1713) may have influenced his politics. It certainly provides an interesting link between Alsop's Jacobite circle in England and the most important Jacobite literary figure in contemporary Scotland. Pitcairne's poetical works were published posthumously, in R. Freebairn, ed., *Selecta Poemata* (Edinburgh, 1727), with some poems there attributed to other Scottish writers. Pitcairne's group may be compared to Alsop's: there is no doubt of the leading Latin poet in each group, but the contribution of others, if only or chiefly as recipients and admirers, was essential to the functioning of such an uncommercial enterprise.

Pitcairne was a physician and natural philosopher of considerable reputation; he had been, briefly, a professor at Leiden, before returning to practise in Edinburgh. He had studied in Montpellier, and received an MD from Rheims in 1680. In his year at Leiden (1692–3) he had taught both Mead and Boerhaave, making an impact on two figures who were to be of great importance, and spreading his Newtonian approach to the subject. A treatise from that period, *Oratio qua ostenditur Medicinam ab omni Philosophorum secta esse liberam* [On proving the Profession of Physic free from the Tyranny of any sect of philosphers], has pride of place in editions of his works,[21] as a manifesto of novelty. This approach was profoundly influential, applying the new methods of mathematics to the problems of medicine.[22] He could afford to scorn such witty anonymous criticisms as [E. Eizat] *Apollo Mathematicus* (1695): 'But whatever be in this, that Mathematicks are necessary for a Physician, I am sure Physick is very necessary for some Mathematicians, and that a good swinging Dose too' (p. 11). Later in the eighteenth century, though his work was still highly respected, his obsessive

---

[21] E.g., *Dissertationes Medicae* (Rotterdam, 1701); *Works* in English translation (London, 1715); *Opera Omnia Medica* (new edition: Leiden, 1737); etc.
[22] Cf. T. M. Brown, *The Mechanical Philosophy and the Animal Oeconomy* (New York, 1981); A. Cunningham, 'Sydenham versus Newton: the Edinburgh fever dispute of the 1690s between Andrew Brown and Archibald Pitcairne', *Medical History*, supplement 1 (1981), pp. 71–98.

reliance on mathematics was judged to be misplaced,[23] but most progressive contemporaries were full of admiration. In the preface to *Selecta Poemata*, Freebairn calls him 'Medicus celeberrimus . . . stupendi plane ingenii vir . . . neque suae modo, quam nobilissimis suis inventis ditavit et auxit, sed omnium quotquot sunt elegantiorum Artium, insigne decus ac ornamentum. Dissertationes ejus medicae . . . omnium fere manibus jam teruntur . . .' [a most celebrated physician, a man of quite amazing intellect, a great ornament not only to his own profession, which he has enriched and augmented with his most noble discoveries, but to all the elegant arts. His medical treatises are continually in almost everyone's hands . . . (p. ix)]. In an epigram on his death, R. Calder exclaims 'Ecce Mathematicum, Vatem, Medicumque, Sophumque . . .' [Look, a mathematician, poet, doctor and wise man (p. 98)].

Pitcairne himself expresses his admiration for Newton, in six neat elegiac lines comparing him favourably with Pythagoras of Samos:

> . . . At Samius magno tantum superatur ab Anglo,
>   Est quanto major terra Britanna Samo.

> But the Samian is surpassed by the great Englishman by as much as the size of Britain exceeds that of Samos. (p. 13)

Samos is not a large island. The clever comparison is typical of the Renaissance epigram, a tradition in which Pitcairne is at home. The emphasis on Britain's physical magnitude may be intended to suggest the expansion of the bounds of knowledge resulting from modern Newtonian ideas, breaking out of the learned but parochial sphere of the Greeks. Newton is mentioned again in an ode to Robert Gray, a Scot who has gone to London to practise medicine, in which he laments the death of David Gregory, 'decus illud aevi/ Scotici' [that glory of the age for Scotland]:

> . . . Ille Neutonum incolumem lubenti
> Narrat Euclidi, Siculoque Divo,
> Miraque augusti docet almus Angli
>   Coepta stupentes.

> He announces that Newton is well to a pleased Euclid and to the divine Sicilian (Archimedes), and kindly tells an astonished audience of that noble Englishman's wonderful undertakings. (p. 47)

There is respect for Greek antecedents, but Newton is far superior to them. This poem indicates that the friendship between Gregory and Pitcairne persisted

---

[23] C. Webster, *An Account of the Life and Writings of the Celebrated Dr Archibald Pitcairne* (Edinburgh, 1781). For a summary of Pitcairne's significance, cf. B. Lenman, *The Jacobite Risings in Britain, 1689–1746* (London, 1980), pp. 223–5; for comparable figures, see B. Lenman, 'Physicians & Politics in the Jacobite era' in J. Black, E. Cruickshanks, eds., *The Jacobite Challenge* (Edinburgh, 1988). pp. 74–91.

throughout Gregory's life, even after Gregory, like Gray, had departed for the South. He retained close links with other progressive scientists, often visiting London to see them: these associates included Cheyne, Mead, and both of the other Newtonians discussed in this chapter, Keill and Freind.

The majority of Pitcairne's poems are relatively short: epigrams in elegiacs or odes of no more than half a dozen stanzas. There are some longer pieces too, including a very long sapphic ode of 37 stanzas in which he adopts the persona of Walter Danniston, a recently deceased poet,[24] to conjure up their great predecessor, Buchanan. The use of alternative personae is one puzzling aspect of his work. Some of his poems are difficult to understand; this may be deliberate, a way of keeping a private joke within his circle. Alsop tends to be more accessible, even when there are also subtleties that might easily be missed. Pitcairne can become bogged down in rather turgid mythological allusion, a fate that Alsop's lightness of touch avoids.

The Jacobite sentiments in Pitcairne's poetry are frequent and barely concealed at all. It is striking that they could be published openly, if posthumously, in Scotland at the beginning of 1727, and be reissued with a London title-page two years later.[25] The fact that the poems are in Latin perhaps helped to cloak the sedition. So also does the stress on dates of Stuart significance, not all of them purely Jacobite; the Gunpowder plot, the execution of Charles I, and the Restoration are all quite legitimate subjects, of more emotional power for Tories than Whigs, but analysed in countless sermons and student exercises by adherents of all parties. Among these less inflammatory dates we find the expressions of Jacobitism, not hidden by any cryptic timidity, but somewhat camouflaged by their surroundings. A Whig who read the book carefully could not fail to be horrified, but a casual glance need not reveal everything.

There are some passages that are clear enough. He is disgusted at the rule of the mob, by which he means the overthrow of the divine right of kings as a result of the Revolution, and the imminent danger of Hanoverian rule:

> . . . Namque novos cives mutataque regna videbis,
>   Passaque Teutonicas sceptra Britanna manus,
> Legatosque Deum populo mandata ferentes;
>   Nam vulgus nunc est maxima cura Deum.

> You will see new citizens and a changed kingdom, the British sceptre grasped by German hands, and God's representatives taking their authority from the people; for now God cares chiefly for the mob. (p. 8)

In deploring the state of Scotland, he observes that 'Omnia vulgus erat, scelerisque licentia vulgo' [the mob was all, the mob had freedom for crime (p. 5)].

---

[24] Bradner, p. 246; several of Pitcairne's other poems are quoted and his work compared to Alsop's, pp. 193–5, 245–9.   [25] Bradner, p. 366.

His reworking of Phaedrus 1. 2, the fable of King Log (a familiar fable in Royalist and Jacobite poetry), reminds us that the people can regret their rash revolutions:

> . . . Ah! sors nulla diu potest placere
> Ventoso populo! sed ipsa tandem
> Libertas gravis . . .
>
> Ah, no lot can please a fickle populace for long; even liberty itself is at length hard to bear. (p. 22)

But when he considers the state of affairs, and in particular the likelihood of a Stuart restoration, he can be optimistic. He issues a Horatian invitation to a modest celebration, ending thus:

> . . . Sunt mihi mensae pateris onustae,
> Et coronatum stat, amice, vinum;
> Te leves risus, sale cum pudico,
>   Opperiuntur.
> Pone mordaces super orbe curas
> Brittonum; hostiles trepidant catervae
> Et nivis ritu, superante Solis
>   Igne, liquescunt.
>
> I have tables laden with bowls, and a garlanded wine-jar stands ready, my friend; light laughter, not indelicate wit, awaits you. Put aside your fellow Britons' biting worries about the world; the enemy hordes are fearful, and dissolve like snow before the sun's fire. (p. 16)

He alludes to Horace, *Carm*. 3. 8. 17, 'mitte civilis super urbe curas' [put aside political worries about the city],[26] encouraging us to remember lines 19–20, 'Medus infestus sibi luctuosis/dissidet armis' [the hated Persians are at war with each other]. The poem is not explicitly Jacobite, since the hostile hordes could be Britain's external enemies, soon to be defeated again in Flanders. The internal conflict among those hordes, as implied by the Horatian allusion, fits the Whigs better than the French; there can be a combination of both ideas. The sun god is an appropriate conqueror of the sun king, if we take the enemies as foreign; if domestic, we recall that Apollo is patron of both poetry and medicine (as both Alsop and Pitcairne frequently point out), and he may use the summer sun to suggest the Pretender.

One summer day is a special cause for celebration: 'Pitcarnius rogat Tho. Kincadium ut ad se veniat Decima Junii, quae sacra est Divae Margaritae Scotorum Reginae' [Pitcairne asks Thomas Kincaid to come to him on 10 June, which is sacred to St Margaret, Queen of Scotland. (title, p. 41)] This is

---

[26] Cf. also Hor., *Carm*. 1. 18. 4, 'mordaces . . . sollicitudines'; 2. 11. 18, 'curas edaces' (both on the effects of wine).

an innocent reason, on the surface. But the real significance of that date is as the Pretender's birthday:

> . . . Namque graecandum est, decimaque Juni
> Vina libandum Carolo et Nepoti,
> Quem suis misit decus adfuturum
>   Diva Britannis.

> For we must feast like Greeks on the 10th of June and pour out wine to toast Charles and his grandson,[27] whom the saint has sent to be a future glory for the Britons. (p. 42)

Graecandum makes a stirring gerundive, and is an unusual word; *pergraecor* [to play the Greek, i.e. revel] appears in Plautine comedy. A love of frivolous parties may not be the only Greek quality they need: Greeks were also renowned for cleverness and deceit, essential ingredients for Jacobite success.

His attitude to Queen Anne, like that of many Jacobites, is moderate; she is a Stuart, and reigns well, although she ought not to keep the rightful heirs away from the throne any longer than is necessary. She can suppress the Whiggish hydra that did not depart after William's death, but returned, as dangerous as ever (*Ad Annam*, 1711: p. 72). Ten lines of elegiacs, *Ad Carolum II*, sum up his thinking:

> Carole, si pratis iterum reddare paternis,
>   Quem mox custodem jusseris esse gregis?
> Cui calamos tradas cum pastoralibus armis,
>   Prataque Teutonico nuper adempta lupo?
> An fratri rursus? vel, quae praesentior, Annae?
>   An puero, fratrem quem vocat Anna suum?
> At frater nimium prisci virtute Catonis
>   Gaudet, et ad Superos non revocandus abest.
> Anna igitur calamos et pastoralia sumet,
>   Quae reddet fratri, si sapit Anna, suo.

> Charles, if you were to return to your ancestral meadows, whom would you appoint as guardian of your flock? To whom would you give your pipe and rustic tools, and the meadows recently seized by the German wolf? Back to your brother? Or to Anne, the more recent incumbent? Or to the boy whom Anne calls her brother? But your brother rejoices too much in the virtue of ancient Cato, and is not to be recalled from heaven. Anne therefore will take up the pipe and rustic things, which she will pass on to her own brother, if she is wise. (pp. 20–1)

The pastoral setting provides a traditional metaphor for the kingdom, particularly useful for supporters of absolutism, since the sheep rely wholly on the

---

[27] The Pretender, born 10 June 1688, grandson of the martyred Charles I; or, if *nepos* means 'nephew' here, the Pretender and Charles II are toasted.

benevolent shepherd; the Bible can join with pagan eclogues as a model. The king as shepherd is a familiar motif on Jacobite medals. The sheep are not mentioned here, but are implied not only by the shepherd's pipe (*calamus* could also be a legislator's pen) and crook, but by the 'grim Wolf with privy paw',[28] in the form of the prospective Hanoverian successors. They have not actually taken over as yet, so Pitcairne is rather premature; he adds to the poem's vividness by anticipating that horror. Nor are the Dutch, whose rapacity has already been experienced, so different from the Germans. The most controversial assumption in the poem is that Anne will recognise the Pretender as her half-brother and heir; this was central to Jacobite hopes of peaceful victory, and was not far-fetched, although eventually proved mistaken. She was not unsympathetic towards him in the earlier part of her reign, although his abortive expedition of 1708 hardened her attitude against him; but she was angry at Hanoverian attempts to secure their spoils prematurely, and a Jacobite might reasonably continue to cherish some optimism. The stoic virtue and sacrifice of James II makes the younger Cato a noble parallel (if one equally doomed to failure). His son need not be tainted by Catonian failure. The comparison occurs in another poem, *Ad Jacobum*——(a title that does not thrust Jacobitism upon the reader):

> Ergo magna tui tellurem liquit imago,
>   Illa tui, qua non sanctior ulla fuit:
> Te mox adspiciet contentus Rege STUARTO
>   Virtuti similis Semideusque Cato . . .

> Thus your great image, than which none was more sacred, has left the earth; soon the demi-god Cato, alike in virtue, will look upon you, and be happy with a Stuart king. (p. 19)

A more savage epigram on his burial is allowed an unambiguous title by the editor, *In Jacobum II Britanniae Regem*, and one can supply with ease the missing letters in the traitor's name:

> Barbarus exclusit tumulo te Nasus avito,
>   Perfidia fidens, Marl——oe, tua.
> Urbs caret exuviis; at Barberinus inultos
>   Jacobi manes fecit in urbe coli.

> The barbarian Nassau kept you from your ancestral tomb, relying on Marlborough's perfidy. The city lacks funeral splendour, but Barberini has made James' unavenged shade worshipped in the city. (p. 41)

The Renaissance wordplay is made more obvious by a note: 'Quod non fecere Barbari, fecere Barberini' [what the barbarians did not do, the Barberini did], quoting a well-known satirical attack on the depredations of that family in

---

[28] Milton, *Lycidas* 128.

Rome. *Nasus* is an unusually brief and contemptuous Latin form for William III (generally *Nassovius*, or similar); it allows a cruel pun on *nasus* [nose]. Marlborough's behaviour in joining William, and then flirting ineffectually with Jacobitism to insure his position, was no more perfidious than the norm. He did owe more than most to James, whom he had defended against Monmouth, and his prominence made him a natural target for a frustrated Jacobite's scorn. The dismemberment of James' body, with relics deposited in various locations, was a rather sordid affair; the Jacobites and their French hosts have themselves inflicted even greater indignities than the hated William.

There is more to Pitcairne's poetry than Jacobitism, even though he is a poet passionately devoted to politics and like-minded companionship. Other passions are near the surface:

> . . . Sancta Venus, quantos solvam tibi tutus honores!
>   Quam te non ficta relligione colam! . . .
> Mirentur Mahometem Arabes, mirentur et Indi,
>   Alteriusque alios numinis urat amor;
> Ast ego furtivae Veneris praeconia dicam,
>   Illi sacra libens tempus in omne feram . . .

> Holy Venus, how much will I honour you in safety; how will I worship you, with no feigned religion! Let the Arabs and the Indians wonder at Mahomet, let the love of another divinity burn up other people: I shall spread the creed of furtive Venus, I shall gladly sacrifice to her for ever. (p. 11)

The juxtaposition of secret lust and a believer's public profession of faith is a mischievous idea. By mentioning modern as well as classical religion, he leaves the immoral but safely canonised literary world of Propertius or Ovid for a more contemporary scene. He is careful not to be openly blasphemous by rejecting Christianity for his new amorous cult. After Mahomet, *alterius* is unspecified, but Christ is the most natural alternative. Even if he was not an atheist, Pitcairne was inclined to be irreverent, and he certainly had little respect for the stern Presbyterianism of the established Church of Scotland. To him are attributed two English works of a disreputable nature, *The Assembly, or Scotch Reformation: a comedy* and *Babell: a Satirical Poem on the Proceedings of the General Assembly in the Year MDCXCII*, that circulated in manuscript to anti-clerical chuckles. *Babell* is a romp in the style of Butler's *Hudibras*. In the 'Appollagie for the Author' we find 'defend his verse' rhymed with 'come kiss his —'; the 1380 lines of the poem proper allow a little welcome metrical variety. The clergy are not treated with respect: 'This said, he sat down on his bum/Which made a noise like to a drum.'[29]

---

[29] G. Kinloch, ed., *Babell* (Edinburgh, 1830): lines 1000–1. N.b. speeches in heroic couplets, lines 703–46, 847–72. 'The calumny of Atheism . . . is absurd and false', p. vi.

The Assembly was printed in London in 1722; its modern editor usefully sum-marises Pitcairne's career and the play's place in Scottish literature.[30] Two young men, Frank and Will, use the absurdities of the Assembly to woo their girls, and comment on the times; thus Will to Frank: 'Gad! That's a pack of Jacobitish Williamites the strangest Monsters in the Kingdom, with Jacobite Hearts and Williamite Hands, Jacobite Heads and Williamite Tongues . . . Gad! they'll drink his Health, if they should be hang'd for it, in contempt of the Govern-ment: They never made a farther Plot to Restore their King than writ a mystical Letter, speak some ambiguous Words without either Sense or Meaning; are shipt up, gives Caution, takes an Oath, Escapes—and all this suffering for their King . . . .'[31]

The sympathy for Jacobitism is obvious, but half-hearted supporters, many of them nobles, are mocked. The epilogue ends with the prayer,

> Let the just Heav'ns, our King in Peace Restore,
> And Villains never wrong us any more.[32]

This could be taken by a Williamite as referring to the Protestant king, away in the wars; but a Jacobite interpretation is clearly intended by the author. Pitcairne himself was briefly imprisoned for seditious correspondence (1699–1700), then let off with a reprimand by relatively tolerant authorities, as he 'offered the explanation that he was intoxicated when he wrote the letter'.[33] This is not so dissimilar to the behaviour that he had ridiculed in *The Assembly* (quoted above): but caution in avoiding punishment was a sign of good sense.

After his death, his library (of 1,906 volumes) was acquired for Peter the Great's Academy of Sciences, on the initiative of Thomas Ruddiman and the Tsar's Scottish physician, Andrew Erskine. Individual Latin poems had been imitated by Prior and translated by Dryden, but it was in their original learned language that his works were best known. An important recent study of literary Jacobitism does not discuss Latin in detail, but acknowledges its influence.[34] There is no doubt that he was a remarkable man, arguably the leading Scottish figure in both science and literature in his age; he is closely allied to Alsop's scientific friends in beliefs and character, and without him the followers of Newton would have been a less colourful band.

A seditious Newtonian in England

The natural philosopher to whom Alsop was closest, on the evidence of the ten odes addressed to him, was John Freind (*c.* 1677–1728). He was the son of a

[30] T. Tobin, ed., *The Assembly* (Lafayette, Ind., 1972). Cf. Guerrini, p. 296.
[31] Tobin, pp. 78–9.   [32] Tobin, p. 98.   [33] Tobin, p. 15.
[34] M. G. H. Pittock, *Poetry and Jacobite Politics in 18th century Britain and Ireland* (Cambridge, 1994).

clergyman, the rector of Brackley in Northamptonshire; he became a King's Scholar at Westminster in 1691, and then in 1694 a Westminster Student at Christ Church. He had as tutors there his own elder brother, Robert, and George Smalridge. He seems to have been aged 17 on matriculation. He took his BA in 1698, MA in 1701; he followed those with the medical degrees, becoming MB in 1703, and MD in 1707. He was active in college teaching between 1698 and 1704, and vacated his studentship in 1708.[35] He played an important part in Oxford's scientific life in these years. Chemistry courses had recently been instituted in the Ashmolean's basement, together with an exhibition of what Hearne called 'Knick Knack or Gim-Cracks'.[36] Freind gave nine lectures there in 1704; these were published as *Praelectiones Chymicae* (1709), and translated into English by 'J. M.' as *Chymical Lectures* (1712). Freind was a member of the progressive Newtonian group that included Gregory and Keill.[37] His scientific standing was recognised by the award of FRS in 1711/2, and FRCP in 1716.

He wrote and published his lectures in Latin, as was quite normal. His earlier classical studies had received encouragement from Dean Aldrich; together with Peter Foulkes, he edited the new year's book for 1696, orations by Aeschines and Demosthenes. It has been suggested that this pairing is intended to be an elaborate allegory of contemporary politics;[38] there may have been some intention to tease their opponents with subversive ideas, but it is difficult to believe the suggestion that Tories would have identified themselves thoroughly with Aeschines, allowing Demosthenes to be spokesman for the Whig Revolution. Demosthenes was too great a figure to be abandoned so lightly, as the inspiration for Cicero's *Philippics*,[39] and thus the archetypal campaigner against the sort of tyranny that William III represented. The two editors are keen to praise both orators in their preface, but Demosthenes' fame is deservedly the greater: 'Itaque nemo est orator, qui se Demosthenis similem esse nolit' [and so there is no orator who does not wish to be like Demosthenes (sig. b1ᵛ)]; the contest itself, rather than allegorical interpretation of it, attracts them: 'Quid enim aut tam visendum, aut audiendum fuit, quam summorum Oratorum, in gravissima causa, accurata et inimicitiis incensa contentio?' [what is so worth seeing or hearing than a struggle between consummate orators, speaking on a most serious occasion, and fired by personal enmity? (b4ʳ)]. Their fulsome dedicatory letter to Thomas Sprat, Bishop of Rochester and Dean of Westminster, explains that he unites the *sonitus* [sonorousness] of Aeschines with the *vis* [force] of

---

[35] Christ Church archives; G. F. R. Barker, A. H. Stenning, *Record of Old Westminsters* (1928); *pace DNB* on age of matriculation.   [36] *Coll.* 10. 209.   [37] Sutherland and Mitchell, *Oxford*, pp. 649, 663, 704.
[38] R. J. J. Martin, 'Explaining John Freind's *History of Physick*', *Studies in History & Philosophy of Science* 19 (1988), pp. 399–418. These arguments, p. 401; Martin's later remarks on the *History* are interesting and plausible.   [39] It is Cicero who is depicted on the frontispiece, to emphasise the connection.

Demosthenes. Loyalty to Sprat and Westminster School is obvious; one would not expect loyalty to King James to be explicit, but if we are to say it is there at all, there should be some hint of it, and I can see none.

Nor can I accept Martin's assertion that Freind's other classical publication of 1696, an edition of Ovid's *Metamorphoses*, was 'a declaration of fealty to the Stuarts'. To offer a revised extract from the Delphin edition of Ovid, read also by the exiled Stuart prince, need not be a Jacobite act; to attempt to better the Delphin could just as easily be a snub to the Stuarts, a declaration that the education they provided was inadequate. It is probably not a declaration of any sort, except of a very young scholar's existence. The dedicatee is Henry Ewer, a young gentleman-commoner of Christ Church. The production was commercially motivated (unlike the other volume, a new year's book for Aldrich to distribute): printed in Oxford, but at the expense of the London booksellers Swall and Child. Freind's note to the reader (pp. 10–11) ends by drawing our attention to the new index, which 'sumptu suo curavit Bibliopola' [the bookseller arranged at his own cost]: this runs for 170 pages (pp. 477–647), and must have been thought worth the money. As for his relationship to the Delphin editor, Freind tells us that he keeps much but tinkers on nearly every page; he is sceptical of the Delphin approach, as well as grudgingly respectful: 'Fusa illa et plena interpretatio, qua se tantopere commendare videntur Poetae in Delphini usum editi, quemcunque in juventutis gratiam prae se fructum ferat, opus certe fuit et taedii et periculi plenum' [The copious and full commentary with which the poets edited for the Dauphin's use seem to recommend themselves, whatever fruit it may bear in the gratitude of youth, is certainly a labour full of boredom and danger]. It is an *opus periculi plenum*[40] to see Jacobitism in every work by a Jacobite; *taedii plenum*, perhaps, to dwell on a modern interpretation of the young Freind, but the issue seems important. Too much zeal in speculation can detract from the crucial significance of real Jacobite literature for the study of the period. If Freind had firm political opinions at this early stage, they will have echoed the prevailing Toryism, but it is rash to use these early publications as evidence of his extreme views. Later, his Jacobitism is clear. These books do illustrate his classical expertise. He contributed verses to the university collections of 1695, 1700 and 1702, and it is probable that he continued to gain pleasure from writing Latin poetry in later life.[41]

In 1705 he went to Spain, as physician to Peterborough's army, and also visited Italy. On his return he published *An Account of the Earl of Peterborow's Conduct in Spain* (1707), which brought him into prominence in Tory literary

---

[40] Freind's phrase probably alludes to Hor., *Carm.* 2. 1. 6, 'periculosae plenum opus aleae'.
[41] Thus Alsop implies (2. 11. 33–6); cf. Bradner, p. 233.

circles. He defended the erratic earl's behaviour, portraying him as a Tory hero, and as a worthy rival to Marlborough, the government's favourite.[42] Charles Mordaunt, 3rd Earl of Peterborough, had several possible links to Freind, in addition to a shared Toryism; he was a fellow Old Westminster, twice Lord Lieutenant of Northamptonshire, and married a doctor's daughter. Few would now consider him much of a military genius, but for a time he did seem to be a successful leader; contemporary opinions owed much to political bias, and Freind's arguments were welcomed by his party. He dined with the Tory leaders, Harley and St John, and wrote for the *Examiner*.[43] In 1712, he accompanied the Duke of Ormonde, Tory replacement for Marlborough and later a Jacobite leader, to the theatre of war in Flanders.

His political connections were strengthened by marriage to Anne Morice, daughter of Thomas Morice, paymaster of the forces in Portugal; her cousin, Sir Nicholas Morice, was a High Tory with strong inclinations towards Jacobitism. He opposed the 'godly bill to root out the best established Church in the world', and was to remain a steadfast opponent of Walpole, refusing 'to stoop and submit, cap in hand, to a man whom I fear not and value much less . . .';[44] these views on Church and State were widely shared in Alsop's circle. Sir Nicholas Morice sat in Parliament for Newport, Cornwall, from 1702 to 1726, and had much interest in the neighbouring borough of Launceston. He was no doubt largely responsible for Freind's own entry into Parliament, representing Launceston from 1722 to March 1723/4, and again from March 1725 to 1727. He was unseated on petition, but returned at a by-election. He appears to have made some mark in 1722: 'I am told that Dr John Freind spoke very well . . .'; and in January 1725/6, 'Dr Freind speeched it yesterday in the House . . . There were some things which seemed to reflect upon Walpole's management of elections . . . his creatures Pelham and Lord Tyrconnel fired upon Dr Freind. But Dr Freind's side carried it.'[45]

Freind also became deeply involved in Jacobite plotting. He corresponded with the Stuart court after 1714. The Pretender wrote to Lord Strafford on 30 March 1722, 'I think you have done very well to let Dr Freind into the secret . . . He is a most worthy man and out of good will to me would have quitted both his practice and his country to have attended me if I would have allowed

[42] G. M. Trevelyan, *England under Queen Anne* (1930), 2. 76, 324. He did not go unchallenged, for both style and substance: see the sarcastic *Remarks upon Dr Freind's Account . . .* ([Anon.], London, 1708): 'Account . . . is but a *Grub-Street* epithet, and consequently avoided by all polite Authors' (p. 2); 'Inuendo's and Sly Insinuations' (p. 11); 'bare-faced Untruth' (p. 18); '[evidence] which you may expect at Doomsday in the Afternoon' (p. 113), etc.
[43] E. Cruickshanks, in R. Sedgwick, ed., *History of Parliament: Commons 1715–54* (1970), 2. 53–4.
[44] Letters of 10 March 1718/9, 4 October 1724: *History of Parliament* 2. 278.
[45] *HMC Portland* 7. 339 and 422; cf. 377, on his ejection; W. Munk, *Roll of the Royal College of Physicians of London* (London, 1878) 2. 48–56; *History of Parliament*.

him . . .'.[46] Walpole believed that he was to have been made a Secretary of State, had the Pretender succeeded. He may have been entrusted with the 'military chest' for the Atterbury plot, in which he was almost certainly involved. He was arrested on 12 March 1722/3, on the evidence of an English nurse whom he had engaged on the Pretender's behalf, and sent to the Tower. There he was held without trial until June, habeas corpus having been suspended; there was insufficient evidence against him, and so he escaped Atterbury's fate. He might have remained longer in the Tower had not Dr Mead (so it was said) refused to treat Walpole while Freind was incarcerated.[47]

He was a most successful physician. In 1724 he had been summoned to attend Princess Caroline's children; when she became Queen in 1727, Freind was chosen as her doctor. He then distanced himself from politics, appearing to abandon his Jacobitism, and declining to stand at the general election. Some were offended at this behaviour; when he died in 1728, the waspish Stratford commented: '. . . He has not left his equal in his own profession. . . . Had he excused himself from being physician in waiting . . . but offered readily to attend when called . . . he might have had as much power and not much less money, and no one could have made the least exception to it.'[48] But Atterbury, more closely concerned, was more charitable: 'I dare say he died in the same political opinions [i.e., Jacobite] in which I left him. He is lamented by men of all parties at home, and of all countries abroad.'[49]

His brother Robert probably wrote the inscription for his monument in Westminster Abbey (cited by Munk): '. . . quanta prius apud omnes Medicinae fama, tanta apud Regiam Familiam gratia floruit . . . societatis et convictuum amans, amicitiarum (etiam suo alicubi periculo) tenacissimus . . . Juvenis adhuc scriptis coepit inclarescere, et assiduo tum Latini tum Patrii sermonis usu orationem perpolivit: quam vero in umbraculis excoluerat facundiam, eam in solem atque aciem Senator protulit . . .' [he enjoyed universal renown, and then in equal measure the favour of the Royal family, as a physician; he loved society and companionship, being firmly loyal to his friends, even at some risk to himself; in his youth he began to shine as an author, and he continuously improved his style in both Latin and English; the eloquence that he had developed in relative obscurity he brought forward to general notice as an MP]. The reference to his tenacious loyalty hints at his support for Atterbury, and consequent imprisonment.

His practice of medicine had been lucrative, and enabled him to purchase an estate at Hitcham in Berkshire as early as 1700. He gave mundane, but sensible, advice to many patients, such as Judge Henry Watkins: 'I am sorry you cou'd not

[46] Stuart mss., 46/149: quoted in *History of Parliament*.   [47] Munk, *Roll* 2. 52, n.
[48] *HMC Portland* 7. 467.   [49] Nichols, *Anecdotes* 5. 101: quoted in *History of Parliament*.

bear us company last Thursday; it wou'd have bin some diversion to you and not
the worse for your health . . . I dare say that with the assistance of a little more
plain Claret than you now drink, you wou'd in a little while find yourself quite
recover'd'; '. . . but supposing it shou'd be warm weather, all the difference will
be that You must drink your waters so much the earlier: and I dont see but you
may very well stay out the time You propose . . .'.[50] Thus doctors make their
fortunes.

His medical scholarship was considerable, and he published some important
and controversial works. Pieces appeared in *Philosophical Transactions* for Septem-
ber 1699 and March/April 1701;[51] his *Emmenologia* (1703) was 'a masterly essay
. . . elegant and learned'.[52] It benefited from Pitcairne's Newtonian approach to
the study of the human body. There was a Latin letter of 1705, addressed to
Keill, on the fever in Portugal: 'among the best Preservatives he mentions Malt
and Oat Beer'.[53] His edition of Hippocrates, *De Morbis Popularibus*, 1st and 3rd
books (1717), provoked an acrimonious dispute with Dr Woodward. To Mead
was dedicated *De Quibusdam Variolarum Generibus* (1723). In the enforced leisure
of the Tower he planned his *History of Physick* (part 1, 1725; part 2, 1726). A
pamphlet purports to defend this work, with heavy irony: '. . . for he reads
every thing himself, as he pretends . . . But it seems Galen was not worth Dr
Freind's reading; for if he had, he might there have found Oribasius' account in
so many words . . . Freind has nothing to value himself on his reading . . .'.[54]

Another pamphlet, published after his death, defends his scholarly achieve-
ments, and also notes his literary skill: 'I should have before observed, that Dr
Freind was (as well as his friend Dr Hannes) an excellent poet. This his exercises
will testify, as may be seen in the University Books'.[55] That Latin verses in
university collections are given as proof of his talent suggests that such produc-
tions were taken seriously, and that Freind gained a reputation for polite learning
as well as for Newtonian science. His chief later publications, *Hippocrates* and the
History, are more concerned with the past than the present; but he believed in
the relevance of ancient knowledge for the modern physician.

Distinguished medical contemporaries often combined their scientific studies
with literature: Arbuthnot, Garth and Blackmore are notable examples in the

---

[50] Christ Church, ms. 353/11–12 (letters of 29 May and 18 June [1721]).
[51] 'Hydrocephalus', 1699; 'Spasmi Rarioris Historia', 1701. The latter begins with elegant thanks for the
former's kind reception, 'ut vereri debeam ne id mihi jure succenseas, si Patrocinium Tuum, ad quod me ita
ingenue provocasti, tanquam non invitatus defugerem . . .' [so that I should fear your justified disapproval, if
I were to decline the patronage that you so openly offered me, on the ground that I had not been
invited . . . (p. 799)].   [52] Munk, *Roll*, 2. 49–50.   [53] Hearne, *Reliquiae*, p. 13.
[54] [Dr W. Cockburn?] *An answer to what Dr Freind has written . . . concerning several mistakes which he pretends
to have found.* On Freind's dispute with Woodward, cf. J. M. Levine, *Dr Woodward's Shield* (Berkeley and Los
Angeles, 1977), pp. 9–17.
[55] Dr Rouse, *Memoirs of . . . John Freind MD and of the physical controversies wherein he was engaged* (1731).

vernacular, Hannes and Pitcairne in Latin. The wealth of the most successful physicians allowed them to pursue other activities. Dr Mead was a collector and patron of letters, Dr Radcliffe a great benefactor to Oxford University. In this exalted company Freind's varied interests are not exceptional; but he was well regarded in several fields, and above the general level of his profession.[56]

It was common for doctors, particularly those with reputations outside the medical world, to receive poems of praise. A poet in Popham's anthology thus celebrates Dr Mead: 'Seu tu patronus nobilis artium/ Audis, benignus sive salutifer/ Morbos levare . . .' [whether you are called a noble patron of the arts, or a kind saviour from disease].[57] Radcliffe was honoured with a whole collection, the Oxford *Exequiae* of 1715, as well as individual tributes. Michael Maittaire wrote in praise of Freind and Mead, as well as R. Hale and J. Hollins, MD.[58] There are additional poems to Freind in the British Library Alsop manuscript; one is attributed to Wigan (p. 105), and there is a single unattributed stanza (p. 111) on his engraved portrait:

> Cui suas artes sua dona laetus
> Et lyram et venae salientis ictum
> Scire concessit, celerem et medendi
>   Delius artem.

> To him Apollo happily granted the arts in his gift: knowledge of the lyre and the cutting of a leaping vein, and the swift art of healing.

Wigan, the volume's editor, had printed this below the frontispiece of Freind's *Opera Omnia Medica* (1733); it may perhaps be by Alsop, or by another member of his circle, though Wigan must be the most likely candidate. It may be compared to three short poems printed by Bernard, 1. 7, 1. 8 and 1. 12. Freind is a suitable recipient for a fine old edition of Caesar: 'quot enim Britannos/ Caesar immisit, totidem retentat/ Freindus ab Orco.' [for Freind has saved from Hell as many Britons as Caesar sent thither.][59] This is a nicely exaggerated compliment, suitable for a friendly dedication. It reminds us how different Freind is to the traditional burlesque doctor, more renowned for finishing off his patients than saving them. Apollo tells Alsop that Freind is the right man, 'vulsa/Cynthius aure' [Apollo grabbed my ear];[60] on the surface, this is but a hackneyed literary device. There is an allusion to Virgil, *Eclogue* 6, lines 3–4: 'cum canerem reges et proelia, Cynthius aurem/vellit, et admonuit' [when I was

---

[56] On non-medical activities of doctors, see Lord Moynihan, *Truants* (Cambridge, 1936). Blackmore's *King Arthur*, as much as his medical skill, gained him a knighthood and the post of physician to William III in 1697; Radcliffe boasted of having no medical books in his library: H. J. Cook, *The Decline of the Old Medical Regime in Stuart London* (Ithaca and London, 1986), pp. 54, 215.
[57] Popham, *Selecta Poemata* (1774) 2. 201, lines 5–7.
[58] Maittaire, *Senilia* (1742), pp. 71–7, 108; see also Bradner, p. 230.   [59] 1. 7. 6–8.
[60] 1. 7. 3–4. Cf. 1. 12 (Apollo), 2. 15 (Sappho).

going to sing of kings and battles, Apollo grabbed my ear and warned me off].
This is highly relevant to Freind's situation, since his defence of Peterborough's
actions in Spain made him an author of partisan military history, like Caesar
himself. The reader may remember lines 6–7 of the same *Eclogue*:

> . . . namque super tibi erunt qui dicere laudes,
> Vare, tuas cupiant et tristia condere bella.

> For you will have others, Varus, who will want to praise you and write
> about sad wars.

Thus will Freind celebrate Peterborough. And we will also remember that Virgil
did eventually turn to war, on finding an epic subject; similarly, a worthy hero
might tempt Alsop on to a grander stage. A Jacobite victory could find its Virgil.
One need not make all of these connections to gain something from the
allusion; if it is recognised at all, it adds significantly to the power of an otherwise
rather slight poem.

Alsop regularly praises the medical skill with which Freind can save British
lives. He can also turn this idea to humorous effect, by choosing an embarrassing
ailment such as 'wind', or flatulence; Freind's skill is needed to relieve the pain in
a patient's belly: 'aperta/Fac ruat porta, et melius Britannis/Navibus afflet.'
[make the wind rush from an open gate, and let it blow more usefully on the
British navy.][61]

Ode 2. 1 is an extended encomium of Freind's various abilities. He is praised
as a physician, and as a historian of medicine, both Greek and Arabic; a dusty
volume of Arab lore does not merely hold an antiquarian interest, but can be
'aptum/Usui' [fit for use] (lines 38–9). His writings and speeches in Parliament
both set the standard for others:

> O rudi natum dare scriptitantum
> Coetui leges! tua perlegendo
> Scripta, seu discant studia aemulari, aut
>   Parcere chartae.
> O potens forti eloquio movere
> Curiam! fidus patriae, utilisque
> Consili suasor, nec hiante contra
>   Ore potentum
> Territus! . . .

> You were born to give laws to the rough crowd of scribblers; by reading
> through your writings, they can learn whether to emulate your studies, or
> save their paper. You have the power to move Parliament by the strength
> of your eloquence. You are a patriot, an advocate of good counsel: nor are
> you frightened by the gaping mouths of powerful opponents.[62]

---

[61] 2. 25. 14–16.   [62] 2. 1. 49–57.

He is, in an effective coinage, a 'Medico-Senator' (line 61), both physician and parliamentarian. Accordingly, at the end of the ode, he can 'medentum/ Spernere vulgus' [scorn the medical mob]; the idea seems less arrogant as a result of the allusion to Horace, *Carm.* 2. 16. 39–40: 'malignum/spernere vulgus' [scorn the malignant mob]. Horace's justified dislike of the profane crowd gives a classical note to Freind's equally justified defiance of his many political and medical opponents.

Jacobitism may well be implicitly present in this ode; it is the cause for which Freind must struggle against his enemies. It is also behind Alsop's triumphant welcome to Freind on his release from prison. The poem is, unusually for Alsop, a sustained allusion to a single ancient model (Horace, *Carm.* 1. 22); some parts are very close to the model, with clever alterations, and others are more loosely parallel. The wickedness of the Hanoverian government is powerfully described:

> Pone me invisae prope limen aulae,
> Et domos justis dominis negatas,
> Quod latus regni nebulo malusque
>   Arbiter urget;

> Place me near the threshold of the hated court, and palaces denied to their rightful masters, because a scoundrel and an evil minister oppresses the kingdom.[63]

The last two lines of the stanza are a splendid alteration of the Horatian original, 'quod latus mundi nebulae malusque/ Iuppiter urget'. Only three words are altered. *Mundi* [world] can easily become the smaller world of Great Britain. The slight change from *nebulae* [clouds] to *nebulo* [scoundrel] is quite brilliant, immediately giving a savage bite to a previously innocuous word; the god Jupiter can become the malevolent demi-god, Walpole.

Another of the poems from the British Library manuscript displays a similarly full-blooded Jacobitism; addressed to John Dolben, a different Jacobite companion (discussed in Chapter 7), it too laments that 'Jam, nefas, duro premit opprimitque/ Sub jugo infaustos Britonas Tyrannus' [But now a tyrant (o sacrilege!) oppresses the unhappy Britons, pressing them down beneath his harsh yoke].[64] It is likely that several more members, if not all, of Alsop's circle were Jacobites. The poet could not always express his feelings openly, even in work for private circulation; but these few instances are enough to make his convictions clear. We have in David Gregory and John Freind a fascinating pair of Jacobite figures from the poet's circle, both eminent practitioners of Newtonian natural philosophy; Freind's career also embraced medicine and politics, and provided Alsop with the material for a wide variety of poems.

---

[63] 3. 3. 17–20.   [64] 3. 1. 13–14.

John Keill, the merry mathematician

John Keill [or Keil][65] (1671–1721) was another Scotsman; he had come to England with Gregory in 1691, after studying at Edinburgh. He obtained a Scottish exhibition at Balliol, and was incorporated MA in 1694. He lectured in natural philosophy at Hart Hall, teaching the new, experimental methods. His *Examination of Dr Burnet's Theory of the Earth* (1698) caused some controversy, as discussed in Chapter 5. In 1699 he became deputy to the Sedleian Professor, Millington, and seems to have joined Christ Church. His lectures were published in 1701, as *Introductio ad Veram Physicam*; other editions followed in 1705, 1715, and 1741, with an English translation in 1736. He contributed frequently to *Philosophical Transactions*. On Gregory's death in 1708, he hoped to succeed him in his professorship; on that occasion he was disappointed, but he was elected to the post in May 1712. In the mean time he sought government employment through the influence of various supporters. He was made Treasurer to the fund for Palatine refugees in 1709; he conducted them to New England, returning in 1711.[66] Stratford commented, on 30 September 1711, that Atterbury 'told J. Keill he would not be quiet till somewhat was done for him, but John does not think there is any occasion for the Dean's application . . . when your Lordship [Edward Harley] has been so kind as to declare you would be his friend . . .'.[67]

After obtaining the professorship he still sought additional income; Stratford wrote on 22 November 1712: 'When will your Lordship send J. Keill to us? I hear he stays in expectation of the decipherer's place. Is he likely to succeed?'[68] Eventually he did, although at a lower salary than his predecessor; he held that post, for £100 per annum, until May 1716, declining an offer of employment from the Venetian Republic in order to do so. Like Gregory, he counted Arthur Charlett among his supporters; he wrote to Charlett with gratitude on 18 July 1713, saying that he 'always had a great value for your friendship, you having through the course of your life given great encouragement to those you thought could be serviceable to the encrease of learning', and going on to discuss verses by Halley which 'Dr Bentley has made bold to emend and alter in several places without asking his leave[.] I am of opinion the emendations are not near so good as the original [;] some of them are intolerable . . .'.[69] He clearly took an

---

[65] Bernard has 'Keil', as do some other sources; 'Keill' is more common.
[66] *DNB*; W. A. Shaw, 'The English Government and the Relief of Protestant Refugees', *English Historical Review* 9 (1894), pp. 662–83.
[67] *HMC Portland* 7. 62 (he does seem to have been intimate with Stratford and Harley, as well as Atterbury and his circle: 7. 151, 174).   [68] *HMC Portland* 7. 114.
[69] Bodleian, ms. Ballard 24. 16 [fo. 25–6]; with an impression of Keill's seal, a cupid on a globe, with the motto 'omnia vincit [amor]', alluding to Virgil, *Ecl.* 10. 69. The choice of seal reflects his amorous nature.

intelligent interest in Latin verse. Alsop could play a trick on him, by putting his name to the verses for Lhwyd's *Archaeologia* (as discussed in Chapter 5).

His friendship for Alsop was close, and based on a similarity of temperaments. Clarke, writing to Charlett on 3 June 1718, looks forward to Alsop's 'comeing back to be merry in prose with his friend John Keil.'[70] He was indeed a merry man, and excessive conviviality was thought to have killed him at the age of 49. Hearne noted in his diary for 1 September 1721 that

> Yesterday Morning . . . died John Keill, MD, and Savilian Professor of Astronomy . . . at his house in Holywell . . . [he had previously had a fall] but that which immediately contributed to his Death (as is said) was drinking late on Saturday Night at his own House, where he entertained with Wine and Punch the Vice-Chancellor, Sir William Gifford, and some others . . . This Dr Keill . . . was an ingenious man, and an excellent Mathematician . . . He was a Man of very little or no Religion, and lived a very debauched life, till such time as he married Moll Clements, who, tho' of mean Education, yet proved a very good Wife to him, as he also proved a good Husband . . . [he overdid it again on the next day:] Mr Humphrey Lloyd of Jesus Coll. (a great Sportsman) told a Friend of mine that Dr Keil was so drunk that he never [did] see one drunker in his Life.'[71]

An eighteenth-century sportsman had many opportunities to sample and observe the various degrees of inebriation, so we may treat Mr Lloyd's testimony with respect. Keill's drunkenness was probably shared by his distinguished guests, but if he could outdo the sportsmen at their own liquid recreations he was a stronger drinker than the average professor. Though he was unsteady on his feet from time to time, this periodic intoxication did not affect his scholarly standing.

Belligerence in dispute

Keill took an active part in the later stages of the dispute over calculus between the rival camps of Newton and Leibniz, the chief controversy within European science at the time.[72] There was plenty of acrimony on both sides, with Leibniz's Continental supporters continuing the rather pointless debate after his death, led by Johann Bernoulli, despite the efforts of Newton's correspondent Pierre Varignon to mediate between them. Varignon pretended to be impartial, but was distinctly cool towards Keill. Newton himself had been closely concerned in Keill's early contributions to the debate, but by 1719 he seems to have lost patience with the matter, and discouraged his

---

[70] Bodleian, ms. Ballard 20. 77 [fo. 120].   [71] *Reliquiae*, pp. 237–8.
[72] A. R. Hall, L. Tilling, eds., *The Correspondence of Isaac Newton, vol. 7, 1718–27* (Cambridge, 1977): the dispute and Keill's involvement, pp. xxx–xxxv; for the earlier part of the dispute, see vol. 6.

supporter from further belligerence; Keill's later interventions, therefore, were on his own initiative, and show his character in an interesting light.

Bernoulli attacks Keill's morals in the 1719 *Acta Eruditorum*, referring to him as 'Homo quidem, natione Scotus, qui ut apud suos impuris inclaruit moribus, ita apud exteros jam passim notus odio plus quam Vatiniano . . .' [a certain Scotsman, who is outstanding among his countrymen for the impurity of his morals, and now notoriously hated abroad]. This is a violent piece of invective, surpassing the normal level of the *ad hominem* arguments that were characteristic of the period. It is also interesting to see classical allusion used so freely in the invective of a natural philosopher; he would expect his cultured international readership not only to understand his Latin, but also to know about *odium Vatinianum* (the phrase is taken from Catullus 14. 3). Publius Vatinius was a disreputable opponent of Cicero, whose villainous character and deformed appearance are mercilessly lashed: he is called a *struma* [scrofulous tumour].[73] He was laughed at as well as hated, and indeed could use his cleverness to avoid the 'inimicorum . . . et in primis Ciceronis urbanitatem' [the wit of his enemies, and chiefly of Cicero].[74] Bernoulli seems to have forgotten this aspect of his character. To him, anyway, Keill is compared; or possibly to another horrid creature of the same name who flourished at the court of Nero, an ugly buffoon responsible for the most scandalous of accusations, and responsible for a new kind of drinking-cup.[75] I do not suppose such rhetoric is often to be seen in *Nature* or the *New Scientist*.

Rémond de Monmort commented unfavourably on Bernoulli's behaviour: 'Les disputes litteraires ne doivent point aller jusques la. J'en suis fache pour M. Bernoulli, qui n'a pas eté en droit de faire un pareil reproche a M. Keill . . .' [literary disputes should certainly not go to these extremes. I am ashamed for Mr Bernoulli, who was in the wrong to make such an attack on Mr Keill].[76] Keill himself was understandably upset, and his printed response was read at a meeting of the Royal Society on 26 May 1720, together with 'A letter of Dr Keill dated at Oxford the 21 May 1720 . . . wherein he makes a complaint against Mr Bernoulli a Fellow of this Society for affronting him with scurrilous language in the Lipsic Acta of the year 1719. And desires that this honourable Society would take such course to shew their Dislike of such foul proceedings, as has been customary when any of their members has been so abused by another.' It seems that the Society eventually allowed the matter to drop.[77] Bernoulli had earlier, in a Latin letter dated 21 December 1719, N.S., complained to Newton that he had been omitted from the Society's list of members, 'meo nomine quod miror

[73] Cic., *Ad Att.* 2. 9. 2; Cic., *In P. Vatinium testem interrogatio* (during the trial of Sestius: mostly abuse, rather than questioning).   [74] Seneca, *De Constantia Sapientis* 17. 3.   [75] Juvenal 5. 46.
[76] Letter to Brook Taylor of 11 June 1719, N.S., quoted in Newton, *Corresp.* 7. 13–14.
[77] Royal Society Journal Book, quoted in Newton, *Corresp.* 7. 13.

prorsus exulante' [with my name thrown out, to my amazement], in the three years 1717–9; he was restored in 1720, and Newton assured him he had not been expelled.[78] He had not, despite his expostulations, been entirely open in his participation, continuing to deny authorship of a 'scandalous Libel' (in *Charta Volans*, 1713) that Leibniz himself had revealed as Bernoulli's. One may wonder whether someone at the Society had quietly left him off the list, in the vain hope that he would not protest.

The belligerence which Keill displayed towards his opponents is well illustrated by a fairly short letter (eleven lines of text in the printed edition) to Newton, dated 24 June 1719, in which he twice uses the word 'Rogue', apparently a favourite expression of his: 'I sent some time agoe to Dr Halley my Answer to Mr Bernoulli and the Lipsick Rogues . . . I believe Johnson at the Hague has played the Rogue with me . . .'; this Johnson edited the *Journal Literaire de la Haye*, but in fact it was Newton himself who had caused the delay of which Keill complains. The Leipzig rogues were more to blame, 'de nova calumniandi methodo . . . qua in Indicibus suis probra et convitia in alios fundunt' [for a new method of calumny, in which they heap insults and accusations upon other men in their indexes].[79] Keill was free with accusations of roguery; we may recall that he used the same word to refer to Alsop over the *Archaeologia* verses (discussed in Chapter 5). He asks that Newton should direct his reply to Keill's brother James, who practised medicine at Northampton. James had been ill since 1716, and died in July 1719; presumably John was staying with him to offer comfort and physic, or to check on the very large legacy that he stood to inherit. His brother's illness will have been a cause of concern at the time of his marriage, although Alsop does not refer to it in his light-hearted ode.

Brook Taylor wrote to Keill on 26 April 1719, giving the answer of Nikolaus Bernoulli of Padua, nephew of Johann, to an aggressive challenge that Keill had made: 'J'accepte la promesse de M. Keil qui est de me donner 5 pistolles pour chaque mensonge dont je le pourrai convaincre. Si donc M. Keil tient sa parole je gagnerai au moins 20 pistolles . . .' [I accept the promise of Mr Keill to give me 5 pistols (of money) for every lie that I can prove him to have made; if, therefore, Mr Keill keeps his word I will win at least 20 pistols].[80] Taylor, unlike Newton, remained an enthusiastic supporter of Keill's belligerent attitude. The controversy rumbled on, with insults flying in all directions; on 26 August 1721 Taylor ends a letter to Keill with an assurance of continued loyalty, despite the attempts of the Bernoulli clan to drive a wedge between them: 'I had almost

[78] Newton, *Corresp.* 7. 75–9 [no. 1332].
[79] Newton, *Corresp.* 7. 48–9 [no. 1321]; the attack on the Leipzig indexes there quoted from the subtitle to Keill's *Epistola* (1720). Similar tactics had been used in the Phalaris dispute (discussed in Ch. 4).
[80] Newton, *Corresp.* 7. 37–8 [no. 1316].

forgot to tell you, that his accusing me of charging you with partiality is a mere calumny.'[81] Nor was Taylor happy about Bernoullian accusations of plagiarism. While there was friction between other Newtonians and their Continental opponents, it was Keill who annoyed them most. James Stirling wrote to Newton from Venice, on 17 August 1719, N.S., adding a long postscript: 'Mr Nicholus Bernoulli, as he hath been accused by Dr Keill of an ill will towards you, wrote you a letter some time ago to clear himself . . . I find more modesty in him as to your affairs than could be expected from a young man, Nephew to one who is now become head of Mr Leibnitz's party. And among the many conferences I've had with him, I declare never to have heard a disrespectfull word from him of any of our country but Dr Keill.'[82]

Abraham de Moivre wrote to Varignon, a fortnight after Keill's death, that 'la Mort de M. Keil . . . leve un grand obstacle à la paix' [the death of Mr Keill removes a great obstacle to peace].[83] Keill had not been the only recalcitrant party, as Varignon found when he tried to bring about an amicable conclusion; he had achieved nothing by the time of his death in December 1722, and thereafter the controversy merely fizzled out through lack of interest in further argument. Keill's own role had been significant. He took seriously the need to defend Newton and himself against unfounded criticism. By doing so in an abrasive way, he exacerbated the conflict; but with Bernoulli as an opponent this would have been difficult to avoid. When Alsop wrote to him, he certainly had a high profile in the international scientific community. The dispute does not appear in the ode, but Alsop will have been aware of it; the aspects of Keill's character that Alsop does explore are quite consistent with that of the belligerent Newtonian.

More astronomy and sex

Keill had varied experience of high and low life, in taverns as much as learned societies. His marriage to Moll Clements provided the stimulus for Alsop's poem to him, and also amused Canon Stratford:

> The adventure I am going to tell you is so extraordinary that I would not deny you the diversion of hearing it. Your old acquaintance John Keill is married to a pretty woman, but to one whose quality and fortune are alike. She was a servant, niece to Harry Clements, her father was a book binder, the widow her mother . . . earns by washing what she has not from the parish . . . But John talks like a philosopher; he has been married

---

[81] Newton, *Corresp.* 7. 151 [no. 1367].   [82] Newton, *Corresp.* 7. 54 [no. 1324].
[83] Quoted by Varignon, to J. Bernoulli, 21 October 1721, N.S.: Newton, *Corresp.* 7. 168 [no. 1374].

five months, and says he likes his wife better now than he did before he married her, that she is that which is agreeable to him, that she is one who will live just as he would have her, and that he has more ease in his mind now than he had in his former life, and in this last point he is certainly right.[84]

His decision to marry a girl of low social standing, formerly his mistress, was fairly honourable, if unconventional. When he had money, he was generous to her, as Stratford notes: 'John Keill had 200 £. from Lord Carnarvon [Chandos] for his dedication, and he has laid out good part of it on his lately betrothed. He has bought her a gold watch, a white satin gown . . . [etc.]. Had she been an honest woman when he married her, I am afraid he would not have done so much for her.'[85] The dedication was that of *Introductio ad Veram Astronomiam* (1718), the major publication of his later years; while the Duke of Chandos received the honour of the Latin edition, the Duchess' name graced the English translation that appeared in 1721. He had also produced mathematical textbooks, *Euclidis Elementorum libri . . .* and *Trigonometris Elementa* (1715). The typical cynicism of his last remark reflects Stratford's moral views, and also hints at the niggardly behaviour of some more respectable husbands, who saw matrimony as a source of profit rather than an occasion for largesse. Keill's behaviour did attract notice; on 10 November 1721, discussing one Bowles of Oriel, Stratford is reminded of him: 'Upon changing sides . . . [Bowles] has changed manners and taken up those of the Whigs, and keeps a wench here pretty publicly. That is somewhat new in this place, nor do I remember any instance of it before but in J. Keill, and he was forced to cover her with the name of a wife.'[86] Professors and heads of houses were able to escape the celibacy that was imposed on other college fellows, whose illicit liaisons needed to be reasonably discreet; as a professor, Keill's position was easier than that of many others, who would be correspondingly envious of the relationship he could flaunt, and then make legitmate without resigning his academic career.

In the last years of his life, if not earlier, Keill was a wealthy man: 'dying worth a great deal of Money (which came to him chiefly by his late brother, who practised Physick at Northampton).'[87] He had the 'wonderful luck' to save a substantial sum, £2,000 or more, from the South Sea catastrophe, but he then lost it in the failure of Middleton's bank.[88] His brother's legacy presumably meant that he could afford such a loss.

Alsop's ode to him, numbered 2. 2 by Bernard, dates from shortly after his marriage, during Alsop's exile: some time in early 1718 is most likely. The poem

---

[84] *HMC Portland* 7. 229 (6 November 1717). Keill's former moral standards are reflected in 4. 9 (either by Alsop or another member of their circle), where he is the ideal person to procure a whore.
[85] *HMC Portland* 7. 244.   [86] *HMC Portland* 7. 307.   [87] Hearne, *Reliquiae* pp. 237–8.
[88] *HMC Portland* 7. 280, 287–8.

seems to have been popular; there are several surviving manuscript copies,[89] and it appeared in print in Benjamin Loveling's *Latin and English Poems* (1738, reprinted 1741), pp. 105–8, under the title 'A.A. ad J.K., M.D., Epithalamium'. Such piracy is a sure sign of admiration, and reflects a shrewd assessment of the poem's value. The Latin text appeared in the *Gentleman's Magazine* for June 1739 (vol. 9, p. 324), with an English translation the following month (p. 378); a longer and looser translation was published in 1751, in *The Student* (vol. 2, p. 29). It is possible that Alsop himself had a hand in this version (if it was composed in his lifetime); certainly its author knew enough about him to elaborate skilfully on the Latin, but notes in a manuscript might have provided this information. Interest in the poem spread well outside the immediate circles of Alsop and Keill. Its lively, light-hearted approach to the subject of sex helps to explain this appeal.

The poem broaches its subject directly, without the politeness that had been offered to Gregory. The news of Keill's marriage is attributed in the opening lines to John Freind, emphasising the links between the three of them:

> Keile, ni mendax mihi falsa mittit
> Freindus, ex moecho fieri maritus
> Cogeris, partesque agit usitatas
>   Pellicis uxor.

> Keill, unless deceitful Freind sends me false information, you have been compelled to become a husband instead of a libertine, and your wife carries out the functions with which she was familiar as your whore.

The version in *The Student* expands on this considerably, without mentioning Freind's name (which an audience outside their circle might find irrelevant):

> Dear John, if you are not bely'd,
> You've changed your course of life;
> You, that so many nymphs have try'd,
> To take, good Gods, a wife!

> Of all the wondrous female scum
> What jade, the devil take her,
> Could thus bewitch thee to become
> Cuckold, from cuckold-maker?

This is a neat addition to the Latin, suggesting one of the chief dangers of matrimony for a loose-living man, that he must always fear for his honour, and can expect to be a laughing-stock if he falls victim to the tricks he once practised. Alsop goes on to praise marriage, comparing his own favourably to

---

[89] One of them, Nottingham University Library, Pw V 143, appears to have been sent to a member of the Harley family (probably the Earl of Oxford) while Alsop was still in exile (though one cannot tell how close the copyist was to Alsop's circle).

Keill's; while the poet has many joys apart from sex, 'quod tu ingrediare castra,/ Quae fuit causa ante Helenam duelli,/Unica causa est.' [there is only one reason why you engage in this conflict, which caused wars before Helen's time];

> *My* motives sure no man can blame,
> So many charms I wed;
> *Thee*, something I forbear to name
> Drew to the nuptial bed.[90]

The English conveys the point of the Latin without copying the classical allusion. The passage of Horace to which Alsop alludes makes perfectly explicit what he only implies; thus he can be humorously risqué without quite over-stepping the bounds of propriety, leaving the reader to supply the obscenity from a respectable ancient source.[91] The Horatian context, concerning laws against adultery, is also appropriate to Keill's former behaviour, and might add to the amusement of a reader who recalled it. Given Moll Clements' social status and previous relationship with Keill, the crudeness of Keill's supposed motivation is reasonable enough. Nor need the poem offend her, since she would not be able to read Latin.

There follows praise of Keill as a mathematician and astronomer, and a witty explanation of how the stars can be of use in his marriage. As in Gregory's epithalamium, astrology is a central feature; but here it is needed to prevent Keill from becoming a cuckold:

> Si tuos audax thalamos adulter
> Scandere optabit, vetet ars et aether
> Improbos ausus; et inermis esto, et
>   Incolumis frons.
>
> Nay, should some bold invader dare/ to whisper in your spouse's ear,/ the dire attempt your art forewarns,/ and guards your forehead safe from horns.[92]

Alsop makes the astrologer better informed than does Thomas More, who denies that the stars will reveal a wife's infidelities.[93] *The Student* adds some delightful touches:

> . . . And if your wife should go astray,
> Don't blame her inclination.
> But Mars and Venus you will say

[90] 2. 2. 18–20; *The Student*.
[91] Hor., *Serm.* 1. 3. 107–8: 'nam fuit ante Helenam cunnus taeterrima belli/causa'; I leave it in decent obscurity.
[92] 2. 2. 29–32; *Gentleman's Magazine*. Cf. 4. 8. 29–32, where astronomy is needed for successful conception (in a humorous sexual context).
[93] More, Epigram 43: F. J. Nichols, *Anthology of Neo-Latin Poetry* (New Haven, 1979), p. 462.

> Favour'd this new alliance,
> And, whoring in an honest way,
> To horns you bid defiance . . .
> . . . No rakes, by wanton glance allur'd,
> Will e'er attempt thy bed;
> Thy wondrous knowledge hath secured
> Thy astronomic head.

Particularly neat is the assurance that '. . . sure as you found your wife a maid/ she will continue pure . . .'; whoever wrote this translation will have been aware that, while Moll was a maid in one sense, a maidservant, she was far from conspicuous for the maidenly virtue that would ensure her continued purity. By implication, a good deal of skill would be needed to ward off those fateful horns. Thus the translation adds an extra layer of irony to the poem.

Keill is now in a position to enjoy sex whenever he wants, day and night, without resorting to uncomfortable expedients: 'Non opus sylvae, aut recubare subter/Tegmine foeni' [You need not seek or hedge or grove/or thickets, out of shame/or on the hay-cock, bed of love/caress the sun-burnt dame].[94] The allusion to the opening line of Virgil's *Eclogues* is intended to raise a smile, but is also given a subtle and appropriate twist by the alteration from Virgil's famous *sub tegmine fagi* [under a beech tree] to . . . *foeni*, tumbling in the hay being a typical form of English rural jollity, perhaps a little undignified for a professor. Loveling misses this characteristic piece of Alsop's wit by printing *fagi*, creating a more obvious allusion (though in the other version it is still very clear), but a more ordinary one.

The poet continues by assuring Keill that he will now be a more welcome guest, because a less dangerous one: 'Gratior posthac eris hospes, ex quo/Nata fors matri, dominaeque serva/Casta redibit' [Where e'er you go, a thousand cares/are by this means allay'd: /No mother for her daughter fears/no mistress for her maid].[95] The translation omits a nice cynical touch, the word *fors* [perhaps], a subversive little monosyllable that is enough to suggest that, even now, Keill might not be able to restrain himself from further sexual adventures that are liable to cause distress and embarrassment to his hosts.

The last three stanzas of the ode turn in a different, and rather surprising, direction, one that has more to do with Alsop's own situation than Keill's. He hopes that Keill and his new wife will be happy; but, if she dies, he should swiftly take another. This rather callous-seeming suggestion must precede the death of Alsop's own wife (after which it gains a tragic dimension; he did not take his own advice to remarry). The view that wives are expendable and easily

---

[94] 2. 2. 35–6; *The Student*.
[95] 2. 2. 38–40; *The Student* (changing the order slightly: the tenth stanza of the Latin is translated between the two parts of the ninth).

replaced is probably not put forward as the poet's own, but as satire of Keill's attitude. For him, sex is all that matters, and he must ensure a reliable supply. As well as allowing more fun at Keill's expense, this change of direction gives Alsop an opportunity for humorous reflection on his own troubles. He has earlier celebrated the delightfulness of his own marriage, but this happiness stands out against a darker background. The alternative wife that he recommends (should Keill need one) is none other than Elizabeth Astrey, his own former mistress, whose prosecution of him for breach of promise has driven him into exile (as discussed in Chapter 7). If he can marry her off to someone else, then she will no longer be able to claim her damages. The Latin does not give her name, though she is clearly intended; the version in *The Student* makes a clever pun on it, calling her after Astraea,[96] the goddess of justice, a most appropriate parallel for the litigious Mrs Astrey:

> *Astraea* with refulgent grace,
> For aught I know, a maid,
> May meet thy strenuous embrace.
> Troth, she's an able jade.

Again, as in the case of Keill's current wife, the suggestion that she might be 'a maid' is ridiculous, and would raise a good laugh among all who knew of her. She is well fattened (*bene pasta*), no doubt both literally and, metaphorically, with Alsop's money. Some manuscripts offer an alternative reading, *bene pota*, printed by the *Gentleman's Magazine*; in that translation, 'There is, you know, a boozing lass/strong for a burden as an ass'. A witty note[97] attributes the reading to Gruter, an interesting piece of evidence for contemporary familiarity with his *Delitiae* anthologies of the early seventeenth century; a modern poet is thus humorously assimilated into the international Neo-Latin tradition.

The epithalamia that Alsop wrote, more than twenty years apart, for these two astronomers make a fascinating pair. They reflect his enduring series of friendships with men at the forefront of natural philosophy, and also his poetic concerns, in using astrology to make some effective and amusing points. Both are personal, but in different ways. The first combines personal feelings with politics, while the second has a distinctly satirical air, combined with genuine affection for the target of his jibes. Both are full of eroticism, but the description of the pleasures that Gregory has in store is more straightforward than the subtle mixture of veiled insult and innuendo that befits an experienced rake. His own character has striking parallels with that of Keill, particularly in the case of sexual entanglements, and he is not afraid to use this similarity to good effect in creating vigorous poetry.

---

[96] Pope called Aphra Behn 'Astraea': *Imitation of Horace, Epistle 2. 1*, line 290. The use of the name for Alsop's opponent seems even more apt.
[97] 'Gruterus legit bene pota': found in several copies, e.g. Bodleian, ms. Rawl. lett. 31, fo. 142.

7
Scandal, Exile and Retirement

The chief crisis in Alsop's life was brought on by his marriage, on 31 December 1716, to Mrs Margery Bernard, the widow of the previous incumbent at Brightwell.[1] The marriage itself, though brief, appears to have been very happy; so, at least, Alsop frequently says in his odes, both before and after his wife's death. But the marriage proved unwise, since it brought about a crisis in his rather complicated private life, soon to become a subject for the malicious gossip of Canon Stratford:

> We have nothing to entertain you with from this place but the news of a marriage which makes some noise here. Mr Alsop, who was engaged by twelve years' courtship to a woman here, has left his old mistress to wear willow, and married his predecessor's widow. I am afraid there is enough under his hand to occasion a prosecution in Doctors Commons. He was so unhappy too as to assure his old mistress under his hand, since last All Hallows day, that he would make good all his promises to her and marry her. When he was asked why he renewed his promise so lately when he had other designs, he said he was not then sure of the widow, and he had a mind to have two strings to his bow. It occasions much talk here, and it is said a little volume of love letters will be published. I am the more concerned on the account of the good Bishop of Rochester [Atterbury], this rogue having been his chief minister. C. Aldrich, Nicols of Westminster, and Bagshaw that was chaplain here, were the persons summoned to attend this honourable marriage.[2]

Stratford's pretended sympathy for Atterbury's embarrassment is typical of his biting sarcasm; far from being sympathetic, he gloats over Alsop's distress as he reports further developments:

> . . . I suppose you have heard that Alsop's mistress has recovered two thousand pounds damages. A pretty mulct, if you take too into the computation the load of infamy in this world and guilt in the next. Do you think

---

[1] Parish register, St Agatha's, Brightwell: Berkshire Record Office, D/P 25 1/2. The service was performed by Francis Bagshaw; her maiden name was Winlowe, and her first husband had been rector 1702–15.
[2] *HMC Portland* 7. 214 (6 Jan. 1716/7: incorrectly assigned to 1715/6 in *HMC*).

your friend the Bishop of Rochester will help him to pay his fines? Bob
Freind ought to have some pity on him, it was almost his own case.[3]

On the same day as Stratford wrote this letter to Harley, Thomas Hearne was
confiding a rather more detailed version of events to his diary, and suggesting
that Alsop was not wholly in the wrong:

> . . . one Mrs Astrey commences a suit against him, as having made a contract
> of Marriage with her. The Matter hath been tryed at London . . . The said
> Mrs Astrey is Daughter in Law to Dr Smith, late Principal of Hart-Hall.
> Some merry Letters of Mr Alsop's were produced. She is a very light body,
> even, as some say, a meer Whore, and the witnesses were suborned, and 'tis
> looked upon by honest Men as a Party Business, carryed on chiefly by one
> Dr Lasher, a notorious Whigg, who is uncle to the Girle. Which Dr Lasher
> hath been also a very loose Man. Yet it must not be denyed but that Mr
> Alsop is to be blamed for having had, even in an innocent way, any thing to
> do with her.[4]

The scandal develops

One may well be forgiven for doubting that Alsop's relationship with this 'very
light body' had been at all innocent. The lively references to sex in his poems
indicate that he was far from strait-laced. On the other hand, his guilt is clearly
lessened if he is not to be seen as having corrupted and betrayed a blushing
maiden.[5] And a new dimension is added by Hearne's view of the political aspect
to the trial; Alsop's poor behaviour may have been seized upon as an excuse to
punish and humiliate the Oxford Jacobites as a whole. There can be no doubt
that Oxford Whigs would have enjoyed the discomfiture of a political oppo-
nent, although it is less certain that they would have gone to such lengths to
create it. Over the next few days, Hearne added further information about the
unfairness of the trial:

> Dr Pearson, Principal of Edmund Hall, told me last night . . . that the
> Original of the Proceedings against Mr Alsop was purely Malice, and that
> no wise Man believed any thing of a real, serious Contract of Marriage, but
> the contrary . . . The Jury against Mr Alsop were most of them, I hear,
> Presbyterians. The Judge was Lord Chief Justice Parker, a notorious Whigg.[6]

---

[3] *HMC Portland* 7. 224 (18 July 1717); on Robert Freind's case, ibid. pp. 101, 119, 122.
[4] *Coll.* 6. 73 (18 July 1717), = *Reliquiae* pp. 186–7.
[5] See Ch. 6. Mrs Elizabeth Astrey (or Atkins: ms. n. in British Library 11409. h. 30; or Allestree: ms. n. in
Nottingham University Library, Pw V 151/8) was certainly not a youthful innocent: she died in October
1728, aged about 50, at her mother's house in New Inn Hall Lane (Hearne, *Coll.* 10. 55); see also note at
Nichols, *Corresp.* 2. 42.   [6] *Coll.* 6. 73–4 (19, 20 July 1717).

Alsop could not pay the enormous sum of £2,000 in damages,[7] and negotiations ensued between the parties in an attempt to settle the dispute for a lesser sum. They met with little success: he 'offered £700 to compound the matter, and it has been rejected with scorn.' He was supported with advice and good wishes (but not the £2,000) by his ecclesiastical patrons, and eminent lawyers suggested various delaying tactics, such as 'loading the living [Brightwell] with his debts . . . that he may have bread from his prebend,' or, to keep his stipend as prebendary safe from creditors, obtaining leave of absence, so that the Cathedral Treasurer could truthfully say, 'There is nothing due to him.'[8] Lord Harcourt, according to Stratford, 'was here lately upon no other account but to endeavour if he could by threats or wheedles to bring the lady . . . to a composition, but he was forced to return *re infecta* [with the thing unaccomplished]. This I think was the proper work of an attorney, and somewhat beneath one who had been in the high station [Lord Chancellor] he once filled.'[9] Nor was he a mere cynical observer of Alsop's important but ineffective allies; Hearne was 'well informed that Dr Stratford, Canon of Xt Church, had the chief hand in hindering Mrs Astrey from accommodating Matters with Mr Alsop.'[10] If so, this indication of biased interference suggests that his earlier reports to Harley are less than sincere, and that Hearne's account is the more reliable.

Although delaying tactics might be used to encourage opponents to negotiate, if those opponents refused to accept any compromise, there remained only one practical option (apart from payment of the damages) to avoid the debtor's prison. Thus, about the end of September 1717, he decided to go into exile in Holland, out of reach of the English courts: 'Alsop is indeed distracted with a multiplicity of little affairs; too many of which he has crowded into too little room, and scarce knows how to make his way through them all before the time when he must abscond . . . he must therefore spend all his remaining time between London and Brightwell.'[11]

His departure was seen by Stratford as a victory for his enemies: 'Alsop is at last certainly gone to Rotterdam, which I take to be the completion of his ruin.'[12] But Atterbury was more optimistic: 'Alsop is safe, and his prosecutors are at a loss how to proceed; and begin, as I hear, to be uneasy that they did not hearken to a composition upon easy terms.'[13] There was a stalemate. Alsop was cut off from his home and friends (though not his wife), while his erstwhile mistress was prevented from reaping the harvest of litigation. The situation might not, indeed, continue indefinitely, since Alsop's supplies of money from

---

[7] Cf. £2,000 damages in the case of Knox Ward: celebrated in verse, British Library, ms. Add. 30162, fo. 38.
[8] Atterbury to Trelawny: Nichols, *Corresp.* 2. 42.   [9] *HMC Portland* 7. 224–5 (26 August [1717]).
[10] *Coll.* 6. 96 (6 October 1717).
[11] Atterbury to Trelawny: Nichols, *Corresp.* 2. 44 (23 September 1717).
[12] *HMC Portland* 7. 244 (15 October 1717).   [13] Nichols, *Corresp.* 2. 47 (8 November 1717).

bankers or well-wishers could dry up; but there was every likelihood that he would be able to stay safely abroad long enough to exhaust Mrs Astrey's patience.

Then, some time in the spring of 1718, he was struck by tragedy. His wife died, and he was distraught. The strain of being in a foreign country, and with uncertain prospects of return, added to his grief. A letter from George Clarke to Arthur Charlett provides a *terminus ante quem* for his bereavement, and discusses the situation:

> Poor Mr Alsop has suffered much, for a short satisfaction: will the losse of his wife make his mistresse more, or lesse tractable? Now his Expence is lessen'd, he may live abroad the longer, upon the Mony he has taken up, upon his preferments; and, consequently, there are more accidents for her never being paid the Monstrous fine wch was layd upon him: I wish this, or any other considerations may make her hearken to reason . . .[14]

The negotiations did eventually resume, and in the autumn of 1719 she agreed to a compromise settlement. The financial arrangements are described by Clarke, who had heard from Trelawny 'that Mr Alsop's affair was all ended, and he had a full discharge from the Woman: it seems Mr Broxholm your travelling Physician, gave him 300£ towards paying his Composition, wch came to somewhat above 1000£, and he received 350£ or thereabouts from the Church of Winchester, wch his brethren might have divided in his absence, if they had thought fitt.'[15] Thus he did not escape without having to pay a very substantial sum, slightly more than half of the original damages; but it was a reasonably satisfactory outcome, and the assistance of friends and colleagues greatly softened the blow. As well as Broxholme's money, he could rely on the patronage of some distinguished figures. Harcourt, Atterbury and Trelawny might have little political influence under George I, but Alsop had also obtained the powerful protection of the Duke of Chandos.

Henry Brydges [or Bridges], son of the 8th Baron Chandos, had been a younger contemporary of Alsop's at Westminster and Christ Church, and was the recipient of several jocular odes in later life. This friendship brought Alsop into the circle of a truly grand family. Henry's elder brother, James, also an Oxford contemporary of Alsop's, became the 9th Baron in 1714. He had previously been a Tory politician, MP for Hereford from 1698 to 1714, and Paymaster from 1705 to 1713, during which time he was able to amass vast and 'irregular' profits, enough to build a magnificent palace at Canons. He preserved his position under the Georges by joining the Whigs, being rewarded initially by the titles of Viscount Wilton and Earl of Carnarvon, and in 1719 by being

[14] Bodleian, *Ballard* 20. 77 [fo. 120].   [15] Bodleian, *Ballard* 20. 85 [fo. 135] (21 January 1719/20).

created Duke of Chandos. The splendour of Canons was notorious. His house-hold included an orchestra, under the direction of J. C. Pepusch, and with Handel as resident composer in 1717–19. Alsop's own musical interests may have been an additional recommendation to the duke; they had been members of the same musical club (see Chapter 3). In any case, there can have been few patrons more useful in shielding Alsop from any lingering resentment on the part of his Whiggish enemies. In the years following 1719, the newly-created duke was too great a man for lesser Whigs to cross.[16]

Alsop is full of gratitude for Chandos' help, in a poem addressed to his brother:

> Sit manus felix ea, sit perenni
> Copia exundans, mihi quae penates
> Visere antiquos dedit, et malignam
>   Temnere sortem.
> Non dehinc caecis tuguri latebris
> Abditus lucem fugiam; nec urbes
> Exteras quaeram profugus, metuque
>   Carceris exul.
> Testium fraudes, rigidique frontem
> Judicis non ulterius timebo;
> Peierent illi licet, ille flectat
>   Jura retrorsum.

> May that hand be fortunate, and overflowing with a continual stream of riches, since it has allowed me to revisit my old home, and despise malevolent fate. No more shall I flee the light, hidden in the dark corners of a hut; nor shall I seek out foreign cities as a fugitive, and an exile driven by fear of imprisonment. I shall no longer fear the deceit of suborned witnesses, or the judge's stern face; let them perjure themselves, or that man twist the laws.[17]

It is possible that Alsop is exaggerating the importance of Chandos' actual assistance, as would be natural when complimenting Henry. Or, although Clarke did not list the duke as a benefactor, he may have opened his purse; this would be consistent with Bernard's note on line 10 of the poem.[18] The danger of further trouble would be averted by patronage, and the resulting confidence may have been as welcome as more tangible help from other friends. The greater the political motivation behind the original prosecution, the greater the benefit of Chandos' influence. Alsop's previous experiences with a corrupt legal system are vividly recalled.

---

[16] On Chandos generally see: *DNB*, Grove, G. E. C. *Peerage*, etc.; war profits for Canons: B. Williams, *Whig Supremacy* (1960 edn.), p. 338.   [17] 2. 13. 17–28.
[18] Dextera: Ducis Chandoisensis, cuius erga Alsopum eximia erat munificentia [The hand of the Duke of Chandos, whose munificence towards Alsop was outstanding].

The poem also emphasises the horrors of exile, perhaps with some exaggeration. Alsop did not return from Holland immediately his problems were solved. Instead, he remained for a while in Rotterdam, fulfilling a promise he had made to the English merchants to officiate at their Anglican church. But the last months before the settlement were anxious ones, and it appears that he had made alternative plans to emigrate to America, a desperate solution. Atterbury told Trelawny in September that 'there is a treaty now on foot with his creditors, which may probably succeed very soon and, if it does, he will then be here openly, and throw up all thoughts of his Carolina-journey; upon which, otherwise, I take him to be fully bent.'[19] An ode to his friend John Nicol, second master of Westminster, mentions these plans with resignation rather than enthusiasm:

> Quin sita hinc longe loca, pristinoque
> Saeculo ignotum paro me per orbem
> Devehi, aversis dubius ferarve, an
>   Auspicibus, Diis.

> So I am preparing myself to be taken to a place far distant, and through a world unknown to past ages, uncertain whether I go with the omens against me, or in my favour.[20]

It was Nicol with whom, according to Atterbury, Alsop planned a secret meeting 'at a seaport town in Essex.' This poem was written earlier, about four months after his wife's death; so he contemplated emigration for the latter part of 1718 and most of 1719, despite his expectation that America would prove hot and quite devoid of culture.

Deplorable Dutchmen

America might well be a cultural and physical desert; but Alsop is no more complimentary about Holland, his actual place of exile. When he writes from exile to John Freind, he compares his situation to Ovid's experiences among Getic barbarians; Ovid could at least have the pleasure of writing to his wife. The Dutch are no more civilised. Alsop complains of the 'furor ponti, populusve ponto/saevior' [the fury of the sea, or a people more savage than the sea].[21] He has not received any truly inhumane treatment (if he had, we would hear of it); he simply found his hosts uncongenial.

Another poem to Freind suggests a particular reason for his dislike of Holland. The country is dominated by commerce, and he finds that he has

---

[19] Nichols, *Corresp.* 2. 91 (7 September 1719).   [20] 2. 9. 29–32.   [21] 2. 11. 18–19.

nothing in common with its citizens. Their obsession is humorously treated, but not without a note of bitterness. He recounts a visit (probably real) to the stock exchange, where he overhears a conversation between a father and his sons. That part is almost certainly imagined: apart from the outrageous nature of the father's advice, there is no reason to think that Alsop could understand sufficient Dutch. He makes the speech both plausible and horrific, using an imaginary episode to criticise the culture of a nation. The natural way in which he introduces the episode, describing his wanderings and consequent need for liquid refreshment, allows him to weave together fact and fiction with a novelist's skill:

> Inde me spissae, haud bene curiosus,
> Infero bursae: nihil hic negoti,
> Nil agens rerum, ut medius catervae, huc
>   Trudor et illuc.
> Multus hic sermo est, quid ubique mercis;
> Quid novi apportent tabulae; quid anceps
> Italus, Teuto quid agat, quaterno
>   Foedere fretus.
> Hic lare in parvo, properans Falerni
> Poculis siccum relevare guttur,
> Talibus patrem pueros monentem
>   Audio dictis.
> Ite vos, inquit, mea stirps, propago
> Aemula; accendat sacra vos cupido,
> Dia spes auri; nec opum reclamet
>   Quis satur, ohe!
> Per nefas, per fas ruite, o Batavi,
> Patrio ritu quid iniquum et aequum
> Viderint Angli; facitote vos quo-
>   cunque modo rem.
> Sic pater: plaudit patre digna pubes,
> Et lubens dicto obsequitur. Crumenae
> Jam timens me proripio, domumque
>   Sospite tandem
> Aere, sed fessus, redeo . . .

Thence, out of ill-advised curiosity, I take myself to the busy exchange; I have no business here, nothing to do, as I am pushed to and fro in the middle of the crowd. There is much discussion here: how trade is every-where, what novelties the news-sheets bring, what the unreliable Italian is up to, or the German, relying on his Quadruple Alliance. Here, in a small room, as I rush to refresh my dry throat with some cups of wine, I hear a father giving this advice to his sons. 'Go ye, my offspring,' he said, 'my emulous brood: let sacred covetousness, the divine hope for gold, fire you up—and let no one cry that he has enough of wealth. Hurry on by foul means and fair, Dutchmen, in your ancestral manner, whatever the

> English see as reasonable or unreasonable; just make sure you get a profit in any way you can.' Thus spoke the father: his children, worthy of such a father, applaud and gladly do as he told them. Now I am worried for my purse, and I tear myself away, and finally, tired but with my coins still safe, I return home.[22]

The Dutchman's tirade is one of Alsop's most effective pieces of virtuoso writing, combining a rapid succession of blunt imperatives with sophisticated use of classical allusions. The reader is reminded of Virgil's famous suspicion of lucre: 'quid non mortalia pectora cogis,/auri sacra fames?' [what do you not make people do, accursed hunger for gold?];[23] an allusion to Lucan[24] turns criticism into encouragement, while encouraging the reader to remember the origins of the phrase and draw the inevitable conclusions. Similarly, an exclamation is chosen from Horace,[25] where it is the language of vulgar abuse, of slaves and watermen; the implication is that, despite his rhetoric, the Dutchman is fundamentally crude in manners as well as morals. The use of pompous epic vocabulary (*stirps, propago*) elsewhere in the speech helps to emphasise the vulgarity by contrasting with it. We laugh at the inappropriateness of Virgilian vocabulary on such a burgher's lips. Earlier on, the description of the wine shop may also be intended to recall Horace,[26] and to remind us that, while Horace's poor man is safe from the snares of wealth, the Dutch who surround Alsop, even in such low places, are most definitely not.

Although the passage is dense with clever allusions, it can still be enjoyed by a reader who ignores them. The humour of the situation, working up to the farcical climax in which the poet runs away to save his purse, is obvious, but so too is the savagely satirical attack on a materialistic attitude to life. This satire is as appropriate to our age as to Alsop's: one might imagine oneself overhearing such sentiments from a sharp-suited individual brandishing a mobile phone in a bar on Wall Street or London's Docklands. While the message is of universal application, Alsop provides it with a detailed contemporary setting. Political news, closely linked to the events of 1718, interests the merchants. The unreliable Italian is probably Victor Amadeus II, Duke of Savoy (1666–1732), who 'would have won the approval of Machiavelli.'[27] An alternative is Cardinal Alberoni, who controlled Spanish policy as the chief minister of Elizabeth Farnese, second wife of Philip V. The German is probably the Emperor, who joined with Britain and France in August 1718 to curb the ambitions of the turbulent Elizabeth Farnese. The Dutch were to be the fourth member of the 'Quadruple Alliance', but they never formally joined. Thus, their merchants are

---

[22] 2. 12. 33–57.
[23] *Aeneid* 3. 56–7; Alsop's *cupido* recalls Virgil's *tam dira cupido, Aeneid* 6. 373 and 721.
[24] 5. 312–3, 'per omne/fasque nefasque rues?'.   [25] *Serm.* 1. 5. 12–13, 'ohe,/iam satis est!'.
[26] *Carm.* 3. 29. 14, 'parvo sub lare'.   [27] G. M. Trevelyan, *England under Queen Anne* (1930), 1. 304.

likely to have watched the situation closely, since their own position was uncertain. A complicated transfer was proposed, by which Savoy was to exchange Sicily for Sardinia, and Farnese gain the reversion of Parma and Tuscany for her son. She refused. Her invasion fleet was destroyed by the British at Cape Passaro.[28] The Emperor, as Alsop's phrase suggests, did rely on the Alliance to defend his interests, and the whole crisis will have been closely followed by traders and speculators. In a few lines Alsop indicates these concerns; his satire is both timeless and closely linked to these few turbulent months.

There are other reasons for Holland to be distrusted by a Jacobite; not only is it a republic, but it produced the Jacobites' chief villain, William III. Alsop suggests this in passing, but gives more emphasis to the depressing materialism to be found in 'proterva/ Regibus tellus, vacuasque lucri ex-/osa Camoenas.' [A land rebellious towards kings, and hating unprofitable poetry.] He adds further detail about this 'halecum patria' [fish-pickle country]:

> Crassus hic aer, et hebes virum gens
> Barbaro squallens habitu, efferisque
> Moribus; durum genus, hospitique in-
>   hospita turba.
>
> The air here is heavy, and there is a dull race of men, barbarously dressed, and with savage manners; a hard race, and a crowd that is inhospitable to visitors.[29]

There is a rather convoluted classical allusion, amusing if disentangled, to two ancient insults;[30] and while Juvenal had altered Horace's slur on the Boeotians to call the Abderites mutton-heads (*vervecum*), Alsop can offer a further alteration to fit the odoriferous cuisine of his hosts, at the same time as alerting the perceptive reader to his place in a long tradition of literary invective. The Billingsgate atmosphere is appropriate: the Amsterdam fish market 'was also a favorite spot for tourists who marveled at the versatility in profanity of the fishwives.'[31]

One may well ask whether Alsop's attitude was unfair. He was embittered by the circumstances of his exile, and thus predisposed to find fault with the place where he found himself. He did rather grudgingly acknowledge the elegance of Dutch architecture, and their glorious humanistic heritage (as exemplified by a statue of Erasmus); but these positive aspects of the country are used to stress his own listlessness, and to add to the shock of the ensuing drama in the exchange. Other contemporary visitors sometimes found that Holland did not live up to their expectations. Ludwig Holberg, later to be Denmark's greatest author (in Latin as well as Danish), was no embittered exile, but an eager young man walking across

---

[28] B. Williams, *Whig Supremacy* (2nd edn., 1960), p. 173.   [29] 2. 12. 9–12; above, lines 6–8, 13.
[30] Juvenal 10. 50, itself alluding to Horace, *Epist.* 2. 1. 244.
[31] J. J. Murray, *Amsterdam in the age of Rembrandt* (1972), p. 8; other unfavourable views, pp. 16–17.

Europe. Travelling a few years earlier than Alsop, he made very similar observations: 'Nitidi sunt in parvis, sordidi vero in magnis . . . opibus immensis pauperem vitam agunt' [they are spotless in small things, but sordid in great ones . . . with huge wealth, they adopt a pauper's lifestyle]; most interestingly, Holberg also found that commerce drove out culture: 'tanquam in secessu vivebam . . . cum solus colitur Mercurius, nulla Minervae ratione habita, tristem ibi vitam agit literatus' [I lived as if in retirement . . . when the god of industry alone is worshipped, and no account made of Athena, a man of letters has a sad life there].[32] Alsop does not mention any compensating pleasures of life in the English community abroad: they would fit ill with the poetic image of a lonely exile who can only find solace in his books and correspondence. But he did not rush to leave as soon as he could, being prepared to remain for a while in the reasonably congenial society of his temporary congregation. If, by the end of his stay, he had still detested it as much as his poems imply, it is unlikely that he would have allowed any sort of informal agreement to prolong the suffering. Literary hostility to Holland was not unusual in late seventeenth-century England;[33] the Dutch had been tenacious enemies, capable of inflicting embarrassing naval defeats. The tradition of anti-Dutch literature may have helped to form Alsop's attitudes, although personal experience was needed to spark off his explosive poetry of exile.

John Nicol, the helpful schoolmaster

Three friends are mentioned together in Alsop's exile poetry: Nicol, Broxholme and Hinton. Alsop accuses Freind (whether seriously or in merely playful pique) of preventing them from writing to him.[34] The first two provided him with real assistance in his difficulties; his relationship with the third is more difficult to define.

Noel Broxholme, MD (1689?–1748), the 'travelling physician' who gave Alsop money towards his damages, had been educated at Westminster and Trinity, Cambridge, before migrating to Christ Church in 1705 as a Canoneer Student, under the tutelage of Thomas Terry. He studied medicine with Dr Mead at St Thomas' Hospital, from 1709, and was awarded a Radcliffe Travelling Fellowship in 1715. In that year he contributed Latin verses to the *Exequiae* for Radcliffe, Oxford's official tribute to its great medical benefactor; he also wrote Latin poetry on other occasions, and must have been an important part of Alsop's poetic circle, even though no surviving ode is addressed to him.[35]

---

[32] L. Holberg, *Epistola ad virum perillustrem* (part 1, 1727), pp. 151 and 190.
[33] Also found earlier, e.g. Owen Felltham's lively pamphlet, *A Brief Character of the Low Countries under the States* (printed 1652; circulated in ms. from 1630s; often reprinted). [34] 2. 11. 49–50.
[35] Cf. Bradner, pp. 230, 245, 293; British Library ms., 11409. h. 30, p. 103.

Initially, he combined medical studies with teaching at Christ Church, where he was praelector (1709–10) and tutor (1710–11); he was warned to exhibit letters of (holy) orders on 24 December 1717, and forfeited his studentship a year later upon failing to do so (see Christ Church archives). He later became a distinguished physician: MD in 1723, FRCP in 1724/5, and Harveian Orator in 1731. According to Dr Stukeley (quoted in *DNB*), he was 'a man of wit and gayety. . . lov'd poetry, [and] was a good classic;' but little inclined to practise. He married in 1730, and committed suicide in 1748.

John Nicol (*c.* 1685–1765) was a close friend of Alsop, one of the few people who attended his wedding, and the man whom he arranged to meet at the end of his exile. The Nicol family [also spelt Nicoll, or Nichol(s)], like the Dolbens and Freinds, was from Northamptonshire. Like many of Alsop's circle, he proceeded from Westminster to Christ Church, where he matriculated in 1704. His tutor was Peter Foulkes, a contributor of Latin verses to university collections (and collaborator with Freind: see Chapter 6). He took his BA in 1708, and his MA in 1710/11; in 1717 he received an official warning to take holy orders (according to the college archives), and his studentship eventually lapsed in 1722, the year after he accepted the rectory of Hannington in Hampshire. This living was given either by Alsop's patron, Trelawny, who died on 19 July 1721, or by his successor Trimnel; in 1728 Trimnel gave him Meonstoke in the same county.[36] He had acted as a college tutor in 1713, and in 1714 became second master, under Robert Freind, at Westminster. In 1733 he succeeded Freind as headmaster, and took a DD by diploma; he remained in the post until 1753. From 1751 until his death on 1 September 1765 he was a canon of Christ Church. Thus his career broadly followed that of Robert Freind (second master, 1699–1711; headmaster, 1711–33; canon 1737).[37]

There are two odes addressed to Nicol in Bernard's edition (2. 3 and 2. 9). One may add to them a hexameter poem that is very likely to be Alsop's (3. 10). It appeared without attribution in the *Gentleman's Magazine* of April 1735, and if it was actually written on the date given there, Lady Day 1735, then it cannot be his; but that is probably just the date on which the poem was sent in to the magazine. If *hypodidascalus* in the title means 'second master', then it must precede Nicol's promotion to headmaster. Several manuscripts offer attributions to Alsop; the verses are in a lively style that is consistent with his authorship.[38]

[36] Foster, *Alumni Oxonienses*; Le Neve, *Fasti*; *Victoria County History, Hampshire*, 4. 231 and 3. 257.
[37] G. F. R. Barker, A. H. Stenning, *Record of Old Westminsters* (1928); J. Sargeaunt, *Annals of Westminster School* (1898).
[38] Cf. 'S. W. S.' in *Notes and Queries* 16 (Feb. 1850), p. 249. Alsopian words and phrases include *quare age* (line 24); *occo* (34; cf. 2. 1. 12); *pubes* (1; cf. 2. 3. 3); one might note a general similarity to 2. 14. 21–8, 2. 3. 3–4 and 7–8.

The poem is an extended comparison between wifely attributes and the gram-matical terms that a schoolmaster would use, with some amusingly risqué jokes.

There is a similar tone of affectionate satire in ode 2. 3, which must post-date Nicol's appointment as second master, 'Prime post Freindum domitor juventae' [chief trainer of youth, after Freind]; the predictable mention of his power over frightened pupils is tempered with friendly respect. The scene is set in the country, either at Alverstoke in 1714, or at Brightwell in 1715 (or after Alsop's return from exile: but an earlier date is more likely, given the references to Broxholme's travels and Hinton's court connections). Broxholme has apparently returned from Scotland for the sake of his stomach, and Alsop wonders whether he is off visiting Paris, or keenly studying to be Mead's *instititor* (a word with connotations, in Horace, of dubious sexual behaviour).[39] Freind is treated with no greater respect, being described as a *medicaster*, a humorously insulting term on the model of *poetaster*. Edward Hinton is gently satirised for his involvement with the court: 'An statum regni et venientis acta/Ordinat aevi?' [Is he arranging the state of the kingdom and the acts of the next age?].[40] But he too may have departed for the country.

Hints of homosexuality

There appears to be satire of Hinton in 2. 3, and the same is true of 2. 4, directly addressed to him. Alsop can be uncomplimentary to his addressees, frequently aiming jocular insults at Freind, in particular, for some perceived neglect of their friendship. But it is a rather different matter to allow more serious charges to creep in, to be picked up by a reader who is alert to the poet's pointed vocabulary. This need not be wholly malicious; but Alsop's Hinton is an ambiguous figure.

Little biographical information on Edward Hinton (*c.* 1672–1745?) is avail-able. His father was from Witney in Oxfordshire; he matriculated at Magdalen Hall in 1687/8, aged 16, and migrated at some point to Christ Church, where he obtained his BA in February 1691/2, and MA in 1694. He was rector of Lillingston Dayrell, Buckinghamshire (1708), a living in the gift of Peter Dayrell, lord of the manor; and from 1712 of Sheering in Essex, of which the advowson had been purchased in 1699 by Christ Church.[41] There he resided until 1745. He should not be confused with Thomas Hinton, chaplain of Corpus Christi and an informant of Charlett (mentioned at Alsop 1. 9. 37).

---

[39] 2. 3. 9–16; cf. Horace, *Carm.* 3. 6. 30, *Epod.* 17. 20.   [40] 2. 3. 23–4.
[41] Foster, *Alumni Oxonienses*; *Victoria County History, Buckinghamshire* (1969) 4. 189; *Victoria County History, Essex* (1983) 8. 247, 268.

Edward Hinton had some powerful patrons, who attempted with little success to find him preferment in London. Canon Stratford wrote on 31 October 1713, 'We have now another public trial of interest with the Bishop of Rochester [Atterbury]; he recommends Mr Hinton for chaplain to the new Speaker; our Dean [Smalridge] recommends Dr Pelling. The commissioners of the public accounts join . . . in recommending Mr Hinton. The Duke of Ormond and Mr Secretary Bromley use their interest for Dr Pelling. We are apt to think we have the better end of the staff, and that we shall show the bishop we can beat him any where . . .'; and again on 23 February 1713/4: 'Your great neighbour [Lord Chancellor Harcourt] . . . interposed with great warmth, to oppose Dr Pelling and to recommend Mr Hinton . . . And out of mere despite for J. P.'s success he did a very extravagant thing in giving the schoolmaster's place at Ewelme to one Newcome . . . It is certainly not in the Chancellor's gift . . . The man to whom it is given is very infamous . . . The place instead of a school will be a bawdy house—perhaps his Lordship may call in . . .'.[42] Earlier, in 1711, Harcourt had considered Hinton for the 'great living' at Reading. He continued to appear in High Tory circles, if only as a rather unsuccessful hanger-on, in later years; in 1725/6 he is mentioned as an associate of Bolingbroke.[43] This desire for association with the powerful (or potentially powerful) is the cause of Alsop's mild satire of Hinton the would-be courtier. He knows the workings of Harley's mind (2. 4. 22): this is likely to be Robert Harley, Earl of Oxford (1661–1724), but probably from the period after his fall from power (alternatively, his son Edward). There may be a hope that he will return, with a Stuart restoration. And it may have been a contact that Hinton boasted about a little too much.

When Alsop addresses Hinton, he calls him *mollis* [soft], and an *assecla* [hanger-on]. These expressions are far from innocent. The latter is probably an allusion to a passage in Juvenal where the *assecla* assists his patron in a homosexual context; a few lines earlier we find *mollis* used as a technical term for a homosexual.[44] There is a pun on the contemporary slang 'Molly' (derived from 'Mary', not the Latin), very frequently used for homosexuals. It is possible to read the stanza without taking note of the allusion and its implications (and thus it could remain uncensored by Bernard), but the hint of homosexuality is there for those who will appreciate it, and the poem becomes much more meaningful if one does.

This is an interesting addition to the literature of homosexuality in the period. 'Though buggery remained a capital offence, it was no secret that London harboured sodomites' clubs and brothels ('molly houses'), and well-

---

[42] *HMC Portland* 7. 170; 7. 181–2.   [43] *HMC Portland* 7. 35; 7. 431.
[44] Juvenal 9. 48–9 and 38; cf. Cic., *Att.* 6. 3. 6.

connected male homosexual activity ran little risk of prosecution.'[45] A person like Hinton, with court connections, would find some tolerance among aristocrats (more, at any rate, than among country gentry); but even 'aristocrats . . . had normally to be circumspect. William III's affection for one or two of his courtiers very nearly had grave political consequences.'[46] Lord Hervey (1696–1743) was an exception. The relative openness of his affair with Stephen Fox led to a pamphlet attack on his 'unnatural, reigning vice'; Hervey fought a duel with the pamphlet's author.[47] It was not always easy to raise the subject in print, although John Dunton's *The He-Strumpets* (1707) was much reprinted.[48] The issue was certainly one with which Alsop's readers will have been familiar, and therefore a good opportunity for a witty insinuation; but one can only speculate as to whether there was much substance behind the hints, in the case of Hinton or indeed of Freind, whose hanger-on he is accused of being.

Hinton is 'expers/Fraudis' [without guile] at 2. 11. 49–50: perhaps ironically. In 2. 4, he is full of guile. It is not necessarily a compliment to be praised for skill in business, and it appears that Hinton is as devious as a peasant. A certain amount of deviousness has its uses, and Alsop elsewhere (e.g. 2. 8, 2. 26) presents himself as more worldly-wise than the person he presumes to advise. The Hinton poem is not chiefly devoted to satire of the addressee, although that aspect is of particular interest. The main focus is on Alsop's own delight in rustic life, a delight that Hinton probably shared. Alsop boasts of his skill in cultivating the hop (humorously juxtaposed with Hinton's inside knowledge of politics); what he needs is Hinton's keen commercial sense, in order to make a good bargain for his crop. Without him, there is little chance of avoiding the cheats. Rustic life is celebrated, but not romanticised, in this poem.

Remembering his love

A romantic view of life in the country appears in the ode to Freind on his wife's death (1. 4, *In obitum uxoris*). There is some effective, but not unconventional,

[45] R. Porter, *English Society in the 18th century* (1982), p. 116; see also P.-G. Boucé, *Sexuality in 18th century Britain* (Manchester, 1982).
[46] R. Trumbach, 'London's Sodomites: Homosexual behaviour and Western culture in the 18th century', *Journal of Social History* 11 (1977), pp. 1–33 (quote: p. 20); cf. N. A. Robb, *William of Orange* (1966), 2. 399; R. A. Day, *Told in Letters* (Ann Arbor, 1966) on a homosexual novel set at William's court, *Love Letters* (1723).
[47] A. L. Rowse, *Homosexuals in History* (1977), pp. 77–8; J. R. Dubro, 'The third sex: Lord Hervey and his coterie', *18th century life* 2 (1976), pp. 89–95.
[48] P. Wagner, *Eros Revived* (1988), p. 36; on interest in sodomy trials, *c.* 1720–30, including a scandal involving clergymen at Wadham College: pp. 121–2. There is little mention of homosexuality in D. Foxon, *Libertine literature in England, 1660–1745* (1964).

rhetoric. Turtle-doves are common enough extras for an amatory tableau. Alsop
does use them cleverly; he alters and expands a particular Virgilian image,
making the bird's moaning tragic.[49] The tricks of the bird-catcher that have
deprived the dove of his mate may be intended to suggest the sharp practice used
by Alsop's enemies, indirectly responsible for his bereavement.

The most moving part of the poem is not the series of anguished exclama-
tions, but the delicately remembered picture of their life together in the country,
walking through the fields, plucking apples from the trees, or sitting quietly at
home:

> Aestuat pectus memor anteacti
> Gaudii, cum tu comes implicansque
> Dexterae laevam, per aperta ruris
>   Ferre solebas
> Leniter gressus, vel odora mecum
> Visere hortorum spatia, hinc et inde
> Vellicans quae mi placuere, dante
>   Te quia, poma.
> Tu mihi (sed non acus otiosa
> Interim) attentam dederas legenti,
> Quam placens, aurem, docilis sacrorum, et
>   Laeta doceri.

My breast heaves as it recalls our past joy, when you held my right hand in
your left, and used to walk gently by my side through the open country-
side, or visit perfumed gardens with me, plucking apples here and there,
which pleased me because it was you who gave them to me. How pleased
I was when you listened carefully to my reading (though in the mean time
your needle was not idle), able and happy to be taught scripture.[50]

There is some unusual vocabulary and syntax here (such as the oddly abbreviated
and inverted *dante/Te quia*), but it does not detract from the poignant effect.
Indeed it may add to it, suggesting that the poet is wrestling with the language as
he compresses the complexity of his feelings into a few brief stanzas. The
contrast with the surrounding material is an important part of the effect, since
he ends as he began, with highly allusive rhetorical flourishes. If only he were as
fine a poet as Orpheus, he would not hesitate to retrieve her from the under-
world. We know it is a vain hope; but the allusion is not without point, or
merely a way of stressing futility. As well as the Orpheus of Virgil's *Georgics* and
other familiar passages, we are called to remember Horace.[51] Thus Alsop does
not need to repeat Horace's ending: 'durum; sed levius fit patientia/quidquid
corrigere est nefas' [it is hard; but whatever we cannot help is made easier by

---

[49] I. 4. 22–4; alluding to Virgil, *Ecl.* 1. 59, 'nec gemere aeria cessabit turtur ab ulmo'.
[50] I. 4. 33–44.   [51] *Carm.* 1. 24. 13, 'quid si Threicio blandius Orpheo . . .'.

patience]. The moral might have sounded mawkish or insincere if he had stated it explicitly, as a consolatory end to the ode; but by subtle use of allusion he can add another layer of meaning, and introduce a note of resigned consolation that fits his own case perfectly.

John Dolben, baronet and priest

The most important of Alsop's friends in later life, during the period of retirement at Brightwell and Winchester that followed his return from exile, was John Dolben (1684–1756). He was the addressee of ten odes (a number equalled only by Freind). He was the grandson of the John Dolben who was Archbishop of York (1683–6), and was born in his grandfather's house at Bishopsthorpe, Yorkshire, on 12 February 1683/4. The Archbishop had two sons, the elder, Gilbert, being our Dolben's father. The two brothers married two sisters, the daughters of Tanfield Mulso, lord of the manors of Finedon and Burton Latimer, in Northamptonshire. On Tanfield Mulso's death in 1673, the sisters split the inheritance; but Gilbert and his wife Anne later bought the other share from their siblings, who suffered from numerous financial embarrassments due to the imprudence of John, a gamester and politician. This John, uncle of our Dolben, was instrumental in the impeachment of Sacheverell in 1709–10; he died of fever in May 1710.

Gilbert, our Dolben's father, was a lawyer and Member of Parliament, created a baronet in 1704; his associations were wide, including Ireland, where he was a judge 1701–20, and the three widely separated boroughs that he represented at various times (Ripon, 1685–7; Peterborough 1689–98, 1700–10; Yarmouth, Isle of Wight, 1710–14). He was a 'High Tory member of a High Tory house', a supporter of Sir Justinian Isham (for many years member for Northampton borough or county), to whom he wrote on 17 July 1698: '. . . I am heartily glad you are prevailed upon to sacrifice your particular interest at Northampton to the General Interest of the Kingdom by accepting the Election of the County in order to hinder an ill man from being our representative'.[52] This Toryism of Gilbert's continued the tradition of his father, the Archbishop, who had fought for Charles I (suffering wounds at Marston Moor and York), and served as clerk of the closet to Charles II. During the Commonwealth, deprived of his Christ Church studentship, he had preserved, with Fell, the Anglican rites (an act commemorated in a picture by Lely, of which there is a copy in Christ Church Hall, and another in Finedon church).

[52] Isham Longden archive, Northamptonshire Record Office, no. 1586; quoted in E. G. Forrester, *Northamptonshire County Elections and Electioneering, 1695–1832* (1941), p. 21.

Politically, Gilbert's brother John abandoned the family tradition of High Toryism, by joining Godolphin. But he had obtained his place in parliament (for Liskeard, Cornwall, 1707–10) by the patronage of Bishop Trelawny, the patron of Alsop, and a fellow Christ Church man. His colourful career was a subject for ballads, e.g. *The Old Pack* (*c.* March 1710), comparing the House to a pack of hounds, and here mentioning a trip to the West Indies, and losses in the 'Oak Royal' lottery:

> . . . There's blasphemy Jack that was shipped by Oak Royal
> The republican whelp of a sire that was loyal;
> With gaol-birds and whores to plantations he crossed
> Till the sharper retrieved what the bubble had lost;
> Now in hopes of a place, he still yelps and impeaches,
> Though your pert forward cur oft himself overreaches . . .[53]

The following humorous epitaph on him was current shortly after his death:

> Under this marble lies the dust
> Of Dolben John the chaste and just.
> Reader, walk softly, I beseech thee:
> If he awake he will impeach thee.[54]

Members of the Dolben family had been educated at Westminster and Christ Church since the Archbishop's father, William (who died in 1631 before he could take up the bishopric for which he had been nominated). Alsop's friend was thus the fourth generation of the family to receive the same education. Dolben contributed a poem in five alcaic stanzas, the second shortest of the five Latin lyrics in the collection (of which three are alcaic, and two asclepiadic), to the Westminster school volume of 1700; there are in addition 23 poems in Latin elegiacs or hexameters, 8 Greek and 4 Hebrew poems. The young Dolben's work is very competent (as are the other poems in the collection), and, given the difficulty of finding new things to say about royal deaths, not uninventive. The poem begins with an apostrophe to Windsor:

> Vinsora moles condita Regibus
> Et chara semper Regibus unice,
> Frustra salutares et undas
> Esse tibi memorant, et auras.

> Windsor, founded by kings and always uniquely dear to them, it is in vain that they say you have healthy waters and breezes.

He then addresses the dead prince, and exclaims:

[53] G. F. Lord, *Anthology of Poems on Affairs of State* (1975), p. 720.
[54] See *DNB*; also 'Gleanings about Dolbens', Northamptonshire Record Office, D (F) 1.

. . . quae violentia,
  Quae tanta febris te redonat
    Diis proavis, patrioque caelo!

what violence, what great fever returns you to your divine ancestors, and
your home in heaven.

This last line is conventional, but none the less reasonably effective. Britain and
Denmark (the Duke was the child of Princess Anne, later Queen, and Prince
George of Denmark) are described as trees; Germany and France could boast no
equal to the young prince; but now, you lay on earth your 'altum caput' [high
head (metaphorically high, not literally, one must presume)]. The poem ends
with the Horatian reflection that death comes equally to *plebs* and *duces* (cf.
Horace, *Carm.* 2. 14. 11–12). The whole is perhaps slightly awkward, the
connections between the sentiments being abrupt; but it is a credit to the
teaching at Westminster. Even if Dolben did not write Latin verse in later life,
this early training would make it easy for him to appreciate Alsop's work.
According to Alsop's 2. 15. 10–12, he seems to have been a keen reader of his
friend's poems, which, in itself, would act as a stimulus to Alsop to write to him.

After studying at Westminster, Dolben matriculated at Christ Church in
1702, and received not a Westminster studentship but a Canoneer studentship.
He matriculated as a gentleman-commoner; his tutor was John Freind, through
whom Alsop and Dolben probably met. In January 1704/5, Dolben took his BA
degree (only two years after his matriculation: such rapidity was not uncommon
for the more wealthy students). He remained on the books of Christ Church
until 6 December 1708, when his caution money was returned, but he was
probably not in residence for more than a part of this period. In 1707 he took his
MA, and was also at the Inner Temple in London; possibly, though not neces-
sarily, as a result of his family's legal connections, his father's uncle William
(1627–94) and his father both being judges. But Dolben chose the church as a
career, and was presented by his father to the vicarage of Finedon in 1714, and in
March 1718/9 to the rectory of nearby Burton Latimer, also in his father's gift.
At this time he also received preferment from Nathaniel Crewe, Bishop of
Durham, who presented him to the 6th stall at Durham in 1718, and to the
more valuable 11th ('Golden') stall in 1719.

Dolben's patron, Lord Crewe

The Crewes were also a Northamptonshire family, with their seat at Steane; the
bishop's father was created baron of Steane in 1661, and the bishop was born
there in 1633. Apparently, he had the same wet nurse as his great rival, Henry

Compton, born ten miles away in the previous year. Even as an infant he is supposed to have had a 'very delicate ear for music';[55] he later became a good performer on the fiddle and the theorbo lute. He attended Lincoln College, Oxford, where he gained a fellowship in 1656 and, in 1659, the post of sub-rector. In 1663 he made a favourable impression on the king, but also an unfavourable impression on many in the University (his successful 'trimming' being resented). Two years later he was presented for ordination by Dr Dolben, the future archbishop. He remained at court after Dolben (on Clarendon's dismissal) lost his influence. At Oxford, he had been a member of the Musical Club which met in Broad Street (later patronised by the visiting Holberg), and had the reputation of being a good judge and performer of music, although Wood states with characteristic spirit that he always played out of tune.[56] In 1668 he was unanimously elected rector of Lincoln, and in 1671 was made bishop of Oxford.

He owed his rapid preferment to his friendship with James, Duke of York (later James II), at whose marriage he officiated in 1673, and whose children he baptised. Dolben and Compton were his main rivals for the valuable bishopric of Durham, which became vacant at the beginning of 1672; he eventually obtained it in August 1674. In 1677, on Sheldon's death, he was the Duke of York's candidate for the primacy: but Danby supported Compton, and in the end Sancroft, a compromise candidate, was successful. In 1683, Crewe was offered the archbishopric of York, but rejected it (it went, as we have seen, to Dolben); its revenues were less than those of Durham.[57] One of Crewe's protégés at this time was Jonathan Trelawny, whom he consecrated at Bristol in 1685.

Under James II, Crewe was the leading churchman who attended the Commission for Ecclesiastical Affairs (Sancroft was a member, but stayed away); their first business was to suspend Compton from the bishopric of London and to appoint Crewe as one of the commissioners in his place. The Vice-Chancellor of Cambridge, Peachell, was deprived of his office for refusing to grant a degree to a Roman Catholic; similarly, Crewe gave no assistance to the fellows of Magdalen in their campaign to reject James' Catholic nominee. But his loyalty to James was strained and he ceased to attend the privy council when a Catholic was admitted.

A fellow Bishop, about this time, thought him 'the weak, vain man of Durham'; a disappointed applicant called him 'levis iste ac versipellis episcopus' [that light and turncoat bishop].[58] He was certainly a gentleman and a courtier; Whiting is keen to defend his record as a churchman, but cannot pretend that

[55] C. E. Whiting, *Nathaniel Lord Crewe, Bishop of Durham (1674–1721), and his Diocese* (London, 1940), p. 7.
[56] Whiting, p. 27; Wood, *Life & Times*, I. 274.
[57] Whiting, pp. 42–6, 94, 125; on values of sees, B. Williams, *Whig Supremacy* (1960 ed.), map 1.
[58] Whiting, pp. 166, 149.

his loyalty to his patron, James, did not put him in a most awkward position. It was a position from which he only recovered with difficulty at the restoration, by rapid 'trimming'; even under Anne, he was not at first trusted with the Lieutenancy of his County Palatine, which he had enjoyed under Charles and James. 'Oh falseness!', wrote Wood, 'he that ran with the humour of King James now forsakes him to cringe to the Prince of Orange in hopes to keep his bishopric'.[59] His dean at Durham, Granville, was more heroic, and soon followed James into permanent exile, after failing to rouse the county in his defence. With reluctance, Crewe took the oath to William and Mary; in an anonymous French newsletter, he is 'cet évêque qui s'accommode à tout' [this bishop who accommodates himself to everything].[60]

In his last years, the time when Alsop's Dolben will have known him, he was still active, and regularly visited Durham; he took some interest in Tory politics. He stood at George I's right hand on 20 October 1714, Crewe's third coronation (the others being James' and Anne's), and seems to have been on reasonable terms with him, joking about burying his successor (his enemy Burnet, who had been promised Durham, died in 1715). Like that other Oxford trimmer, Arthur Charlett, he remained deeply suspicious of non-jurors; he sympathised, perhaps, with Jacobites but took no part in their plots.[61] He died in 1721; Dolben was one of the five trustees appointed in his will, which seems to indicate that Crewe held him in esteem. Each trustee was bequeathed a set of twelve silver plates.

We cannot be sure why he patronised Dolben; and it must be remembered that Dolben was only one of many who received Crewe's patronage. Dolben was a gentleman, something Crewe appreciated, and a man from Northamptonshire. He was a Tory, and a lover of music. He was the grandson of the man who had first presented Crewe for ordination; and there is no particular reason to believe, *pace* the anonymous *Examination* of Crewe's life, that the two fell out later, despite their rivalry for preferment. Any or all of these reasons may have made Crewe friendly to Dolben, and Dolben as grateful and affectionate towards Crewe as we find him in Alsop's poetry.[62]

Marriage, music and children

In 1720, now assured of a large income from his preferments, as well as whatever he might receive from his father, Dolben married. His bride was the Hon. Elizabeth Digby, eldest daughter of William, 5th baron Digby of Geashill (in Ireland); she was about 30, he 36. Digby was a Tory member for Warwick,

---

[59] *Life and Times*, 3. 298.   [60] Whiting, p. 215: quoting *HMC 7th report, Denbigh mss.*, p. 207.
[61] Whiting, pp. 303–4, 324.   [62] See 2. 21. 1–4, 3. 1. B43–60.

1689–98, and had High Tory and non-juring links, although he himself had refused to sit in James II's Irish parliament of 1689, and had been attainted by it. In 1698 he inherited the estate of Sherborne, Dorset, and retired from Parliament.[63] Their wedding anthem survives, with the ms. note: 'This anthem was composed for the wedding of Dr. [B.D. & D.D., 1717] Do[lben] with the Hon. Mrs. Elizabeth Digby 1720 when Dr. Croft, Mr. Hug[hes,] Mr. Freeman and Mr. Baker came to Finedon to Perform That and a song [com]posed by Dr. Croft on the same occasion: the Words by Mr. A. Alsop.'[64]

Alsop's ode 2. 5 centres on Dolben's interest in music, linking him with Croft; it also celebrates Alsop's love of the country, and encourages Dolben to take more notice of the *musica ruris*: the grunting of pigs can have its charms. The serious musician is thus gently teased as well as celebrated. Nearly every one of his other poems to Dolben alludes to music in some way. Clearly, Alsop considered it one of the most important aspects of Dolben's life. We do not know when Dolben acquired this interest; but at Oxford, and Christ Church in particular, he would have had ample opportunity to develop it. Dean Aldrich, head of the College during Dolben's residence there, was an enthusiastic musician and composer (as well as architect, logician, drinker, smoker, etc.). He held weekly musical meetings in Christ Church, and composed church music, as well as humorous catches, of which the 'Smoking catch' and 'Hark the bonny Christ Church bells' became famous.[65]

Music, indeed, was widely popular in this period, in all classes of society. Thus 'the gentry sang to the lute and danced to the accompaniment of stringed instruments';[66] this sort of domestic music-making is described by Alsop, with Dolben's lute in the classical guise of the lyre struck by a plectrum. Church music was also important to Dolben (as it was to Aldrich). Alsop describes his singing at the Chapel Royal; at Finedon, he took care to ensure a high level of music in church, and in 1717 donated a fine organ, which still survives. This organ was probably built by Christopher Schrider, a son-in-law of 'Father Smith' (Bernard Schmidt); both were very distinguished organ builders, 'Father Smith' having built the organ of St Paul's, and his son-in-law later working at St Martin-in-the-Fields and Westminster Abbey. The organ was opened by

[63] G. E. C., *Peerage*; H. H. Erskine-Hill, *The Social Milieu of Alexander Pope* (1975) has a useful section on the Digby family. Pope was a friend of the 5th baron's son, Robert, and praised Sherborne. Scudamore, dedicatee of Alsop's *Aesop*, had married the 4th baron's daughter (see Ch. 4).
[64] Northamptonshire Record Office, D (F) 11. *Pace* G. E. C., who has them married at Sherborne. The song by Croft and Alsop also survives in ms. at the Royal College of Music (no. 995) [= Alsop 4. 5], in the hand (according to B. Crosby, letter of 28 April 1982 to N. R. O.) of Cuthbert Brass, a chorister at Durham. This 'Cuddy Brass' is mentioned in a letter to Dolben from Thomas Sharp, a fellow prebendary (N. R. O., D (F) 86).
[65] *Pleasant Musical Companion* (1726); Sir John Hawkins, *A General History of the Science and Practice of Music* (1776); cf. Grove.   [66] G. N. Clark, *The Later Stuarts* (1934), p. 386.

William Croft, organist at the Chapel Royal; included in *A Collection of Anthems, as now perform'd in the Cathedral Church, Durham* (1749) is a piece 'compos'd for and perform'd at the opening of a new Organ at Finedon in Northamptonshire May 17th 1717, by Dr. Croft'. The first organist appointed by Dolben was James Kent, born in 1700, who was a chorister at the Chapel Royal under Croft; he remained at Finedon from 1717 until 1731.

Dolben's life before his marriage will have been closely associated with the court, as Sub-Dean in the Chapel Royal, from which he was dismissed in 1718. He shared Alsop's Jacobitism, and was not sorry to leave (see 3. 1). The evidence of Alsop's poems suggests that he was, or at least seemed to his friends to be, a novice in love; he certainly married at an age that could no longer be called young, although Alsop himself had been ten years older still when he married. At one point, about 1717, he was wooing a certain Miss Meadowes;[67] but otherwise we know nothing of his premarital adventures.[68]

He seems to have enjoyed a very happy married life, if we are to believe Alsop, spending most of his time at Finedon, of which he became master on his father's death in 1722, when he also inherited the baronetcy. His duties at Durham were not onerous: prebendaries were expected to reside for 21 days in a year, and these three weeks were largely spent in entertainments.[69] For this, Dolben received the very substantial income, about £300 per annum, of the 'Golden' stall. The rest of his time, at Finedon, Dolben no doubt enjoyed the company of his wife and children, and his hobby of music. He had eight children, of whom four survived into adulthood: three girls and a boy. His first four children were born in Alsop's lifetime, and there is much in Alsop's poems about them. His light-hearted English poem to Dolben (4. 6) reflects the preoccupations of the Latin odes:

> . . . How should I joy to see the lady
> That makes three sweet ones call you dady!

We see the children as heirs, and as images of their parents:

> Resembling either parent's face
> The Digby and the Dolben race;
> To read in every line and feature
> *Avi avorum* wrought by nature.[70]

At the end of 2. 24, Alsop imagines the delight that the father will feel at his son's first musical efforts:

[67] 3. 1. A52.
[68] See 2. 14. 13–28; his marital sex life is examined with humour at 3. 2: milder than, but not wholly dissimilar to, the scandalous advice to Vesey, 4. 8 (cf. also 4. 9 and 3. 10).   [69] Whiting, p. 70.
[70] 4. 6. 54–5, 60–3. They are 'pretty heirs apparent' (56; cf. 2. 20. 9–12, etc.), and 'little representers' of their parents' features (58; cf. 2. 15. 30; 2. 20. 2; 2. 21. 29–30).

> . . . cum jam puer, ore formans
> Syllabas, lingua titubante profert
>   Sol la mi fa sol?

> when the boy can now form syllables, and stutter out his 'Doe, a deer, a
> female deer . . .'.

The use of the notes of the scale in this final adonic is a brilliantly bold touch. (I
fear that I mar the sobriety of my translations by alluding to *The Sound of Music*:
the temptation was irresistible.)

The earlier part of the poem provides a comparison with home life very
different from that of the singing Dolbens. He has been rereading a parody of
the ballad *Chevy Chase* by Philip, Duke of Wharton (1698–1731), only son of
Thomas, Marquis of Wharton (the leading Whig politician). From his youth,
Philip was an unsteady, if occasionally brilliant character. He married (March
1714/5) against his father's wishes; he soon deserted his wife, although he
succeeded to the marquisate and a large income in April of that year. In
1716, leaving his tutor, he paid a visit to the Pretender, and to the court of
James II's widow; but on his return to England he 'acted in direct opposition to
the Jacobite sentiments he had so recently displayed'. In January 1717/8 he was
created a duke, the ministry wishing to 'secure his talents to the Whig party'. His
quietest and least disreputable years were 1718 and 1719; he appears to have
returned to his wife and lived in the country. After his introduction to the Lords
in December 1719, he turned to violent opposition. In February 1720/1 his
attacks angered Stanhope (a Secretary of State, and 'the greatest of the existing
ministers') so much as to cause him to break a blood vessel in replying; Stanhope
died the next day. In 1723, he opposed the bill against Atterbury, with an
impressive speech. But after 1725, ruined financially, he left the country, and
became again an open Jacobite; most of his last years were spent in Spain, 'an
everlasting talker and tippler'.[71] The ballad that Wharton parodies is a famous
one:

> Chiviae campos, procerumque in armis
> Grande par, quis non Britonum recenset?
> Quae Withringtonum reticebit aetas
>   Crure minorem?

> What Briton does not recall Chevy Chase, and that great pair of armed
> leaders? What age will cease to celebrate Witherington, and his missing
> leg?[72]

The original ballad is set in the time of Henry II. The two noblemen are the

---

[71] *DNB*; B. Williams, *Whig Supremacy* (1960 edn.), p. 178. On his character, cf. Pope, *Moral Essays, Epistle* 1.
178–209.   [72] 2. 24. 5–8.

Northumbrian Lord Percy and the Scottish Earl Douglas; Witherington is one of the more bizarre characters:

> Then stept a gallant squire forth
> Witherington was his name.
> Who said, I would not have it told
> To Henry our great king for shame,
> That e'er my captain fought on foot,
> And I stood looking on:
> You are two Earls, said Witherington,
> And I a squire alone;
> I'll do the best, that do I may,
> Whilst I have power to stand . . .

Later, as the battle becomes more bloody, nearly everyone on both sides falls:

> For With'rington I needs must wail,
> As one in doleful dumps;
> For when his legs were smitten off,
> He fought still on the stumps.[73]

The appearance of Witherington as a memorable character in the ballad is sufficient to explain his mention here. But it is possible that Alsop also expects the reader to think of the contemporary Lord Widdrington, one of the Jacobite leaders in 1715, given that Dolben shared Alsop's Jacobite sympathies. The rising led by Widdrington took place in roughly the same region as 'Chevy Chase'; one of his fellow leaders was Thomas Forster, a relation of Dolben's patron Lord Crewe (in 1700, Crewe married Forster's aunt—he was 67, she 27—and she died on 16 October 1715, apparently killed by the shock of hearing that a warrant had been issued for her nephew's arrest). There was considerable sympathy in Durham for the Jacobites: a large crowd assembled to pay respect to the body of the executed Earl of Derwentwater. But any allusion to the '15 in this poem is well hidden.

The praise of 'Chevy Chase' may recall not only the ballad's enduring appeal, as part of the rustic pose adopted in 2. 5 and 2. 6, but also the discussion of its merits, a few years before Alsop's poem, by Addison (*Spectator* 70 and 74). Addison claimed to see some of the virtues of classical epic in the ballad, and praised 'the essential and inherent perfection of simplicity of thought', as opposed to the 'Gothick' extravagances of much seventeenth-century writing.[74]

---

[73] Hence *crure minorem*; cf. Hor., *Carm.* 3. 5. 42: 'capitis minor'. English text from one of the many printed versions of the ballad: *The Famous and Memorable History of Chevy-Chase*, anon., no date, pp. 16ff. (Cf. British Library, ms. Add. 30162, fo. 15–26: parallel English and Latin versions.)

[74] *Cambridge History of English Literature*, 10. 219; D. F. Bond, ed., *Spectator* (Oxford, 1965) 1. 298–303, 315–22 (cf. no. 85, pp. 360–4, comparing another ballad with Horace).

The new version of the ballad is as full of exuberance as the original, though the conflict is different:

> En novi heroes, nova lis! nec alter
> Deficit vates: Comitem Ducemque
> Cumbrici cantant pueri, additosque
>   Haustibus haustus.
> Quis struem illius spoliumque noctis
> Narret? hic fusos calices, vitrique
> Fragmina; hinc vulgi procerumque mixtim
>   Corpora, fundo
> Strata, non siccae monumenta pugnae?

> Here are new heroes, and a new conflict! Nor do we lack a new bard:
> Cumbrian boys sing of the Earl and the Duke, and gulp taken on top of
> gulp. Who can tell of the destruction and spoils of that night? Here are
> scattered wineglasses, and fragments of glass; and here are the bodies of
> commoners and peers all mixed together, laid low on the ground, the
> evidence of a thoroughly sozzled fight.[75]

The Earl is Anthony Grey, styled Earl of Harold (1695/6–1723), the son of Henry Grey, Duke of Kent, who had been created Earl of Harold in 1706. He was a Tory under Anne, but took office with the Whigs under George I, 'ratting with great judgement'. Anthony Grey was styled Earl of Harold from 1706 until his death: 'he is said to have been choked with an ear of barley, which he had inadvertently put into his mouth'.[76] He was summoned to the Lords in his father's lifetime (November 1718), under another of his father's titles, Baron Lucas of Crudwell. He married in 1718, and was a lord of the bedchamber, 1720–23. Though much less flamboyant than Wharton, he appears in many ways to have been a similar character.

Wharton's *Drinking Match*, as the name implies, substitutes cups for the weapons of 'Chevy Chase'. Wharton and Harold drink each other under the table, and their companions follow suit. The poem was published in *Whartoniana* (1727); Alsop, who died in 1726, must have known of it in manuscript, in which form it no doubt circulated widely. It also appears in *The Poetical Works of Philip late Duke of Wharton, and others . . .* (London, 2 vols., no date [1731/2?]). Wharton's other poems do not show great merit, though they are lively enough; they rather resemble Alsop's English verses, with a mixture of amorous pastoral and Swiftian banter. In the *Drinking Match*, the struggle is furious:

> And many a gallant Gentleman
> Lay spewing on the ground . . .

[75] 2. 24. 9–17.   [76] G. E. C., *Peerage*.

Full lustily and long they swill'd,
Many a tedious hour,
Till like a vessel over-fill'd
It run upon the floor. (stanzas 13 and 21)

There is no mention in Wharton's poem of broken glass: Alsop adds that detail (lines 14–15), making the scene even more like a battlefield than Wharton does. He revels in the boisterous humour of the ballads; but he rejects it by contrast with the idyllic life that Dolben has created at Finedon, an idyll that he is honoured to join, as a close friend of the family.

Alsop did not live to learn of Dolben's personal tragedy; his poems to him are full of hope for the future. The year 1730 saw the death of Dolben's wife and four of his children (one at Finedon, and three, with Elizabeth, at Aix-en-Provence); there is a memorial to them in the Cathedral at Aix.[77] We know little of Dolben's last years; he continued to take part in the Durham chapter, and in 1750 he refaced the rectory of Burton Latimer. He also retained contact with Oxford, although with a different College: he became Visitor of Balliol College in 1728. He died on 25 November 1756, asking in his will that his 'body be open'd by some skillful physician or surgeon in hopes that some Discoveries may be made in order to prevent my dear children or grandchildren being subject to be distress'd by the same sore Distempers with which I have been Afflicted'.[78] He was succeeded by his only surviving son, William, who in 1748 had married Judith English.

Robert Eyre and colleagues at Winchester

It was a considerate act on the part of the Winchester chapter to refrain from confiscating Alsop's income during his absence. The bishop's influence, or Christian charity, may have swayed them. Or, in the short time that he spent there before his exile, Alsop may have made himself a popular figure. He was able to spend much of his time at Winchester after his return, cementing his friendships and enjoying some convivial company—perhaps to excess, given the unfortunate accident that resulted in his death.

Death was never far from this English Arcadia. Disease and the threat of death, rather uneasily combined with his usual humour, dominate the only poem that Alsop addresses to a friend at Winchester. Robert Eyre, DD (c. 1656–1722) had occupied the sixth prebendal stall since 1701; Alsop was a relative

---

[77] H. I. Longden, *Northamptonshire and Rutland Clergy from 1500* (Northampton, 1938–52); cf. *Gentleman's Magazine* 1. 26 (Jan. 1731).
[78] Quoted at J. L. H. Bailey, *Finedon otherwise Thingdon* (Finedon, 1975), p. 34.

newcomer in the fourth (1715–26).[79] He had matriculated and become a probationer Fellow at New College in 1676; he took his BD and DD in 1697; in 1703, shortly after becoming a canon, he became rector of Martyr Worthy in Hampshire; he was also a Fellow of Wykeham's College in Winchester, where he had been educated.[80] He was an older colleague, therefore, well-established but ailing, when Alsop wrote this ode in late 1720 or 1721.

The poem must pre-date the death of John Wickart [or Wichart] in January 1721/2; probably by some months, since it would be in poor taste to joke about him on his deathbed. Wickart had been Dean of Winchester since 1692, and was thus an even more senior figure than Eyre. He had corresponded with William Wake, encouraging his research and recommending to him one Mr Carto, a Jersey clergyman.[81] The first illness that Alsop mentions is Wickart's shortness of breath. This turned out to be fatal: 'qui ex Asthmate efflavit animam' [he breathed out his life as a result of asthma].[82]

The following stanza records the inconvenience suffered by Charles Woodroffe, DCL, 'parte postica . . . dolentem' [suffering from a pain in his posterior].[83] This complaint offers some scope for humour. Alsop sympathises, because he has suffered there himself; but he tells Woodroffe to cheer up, since it is believed that it won't kill him. There is probably a jocular reference to a piece of popular wisdom, to the effect that long life is promised to those afflicted by this relatively minor ailment. Woodroffe may have been an old friend from Oxford days; he was a fellow member of the musical club there. He occupied the tenth prebendal stall from 1706 to 1727, and died at the age of 54 on 13 February 1726/7; he was therefore closer to Alsop's own age than the other two colleagues mentioned in the ode.[84]

Eyre himself died at the age of 66 on 15 October 1722; when Alsop wrote to him, according to Bernard's note, 'carcinomate afficiebatur, quo postea confectus est' [he was afflicted by a cancer, from which he later died]. Alsop refers to the illness:

> Eximi saltem meruit peric'lo
> Os tibi, os dulci eloquio et placendi
> Artibus pollens; sacra seu tueri
>   Dogmata vindex
> Strenuus, seu vis salibus jocisque
> Ludere. Heu! frustra: superante morbo,

[79] LeNeve, *Fasti.*
[80] Foster, *Alumni Oxonienses.* Shortly before his death, he also obtained the living of Fawley, Hampshire (March 1721/2).
[81] Christ Church, Wake mss., 17. 133 (16 June 1700), 24. 6 (14 Sept. 1720).
[82] Note in Bodleian, ms. Don. e. 53.
[83] 2. 16. 9; 'haemorroide laborantem' [pained by piles] according to Bodleian, ms. Don. e. 53.
[84] LeNeve, *Fasti*; monument, north aisle, Winchester Cathedral.

> Nec jocus linguae, tibi nec loquela
>   Profuit hilum.

At least your mouth deserved to be kept out of danger, that mouth so effective at pleasing with its sweet eloquence, whether you vigorously defend sacred doctrines, or prefer to play with wit and jokes. Alas, it was not to be: as the disease gains hold, no joke or sermon can do your tongue any good at all.[85]

The archaic word *hilum* at the end of the stanza (and the poem, in the version printed by Bernard) gains dramatic effect by its strangeness. If there is humour here, it is overlaid with pathos and a real sense of man's inability to counter impending disaster.

The stress on Eyre's eloquence was appropriate for the disease from which he suffered, as well as for his character; similar sentiments form part of the long and elegant memorial inscription, possibly by Alsop himself, in the 'Venerable Chapel' of the Cathedral's south transept. He is praised for handling the finances of Cathedral and College, and described with affection: '. . . acerrimo fuit et expolito ingenio/eleganti et recondita eruditione,/nec nimia levitate indecorus/ in colloquendo comis et festivus/in concionando gravis et ornatus/in promo- vendis amicorum commodis indefesse benevolus/in pauperibus sublevandis inexhauste liberalis . . .' [he had a very keen and polished mind, possessed polite and abstruse learning, was pleasant and lively in conversation, without unseemly frivolity, and when preaching serious and elegant; tirelessly concerned for his friends' comfort, he was inexhaustibly generous in relieving the poor . . .]. One of his sermons had been published, many years before;[86] he was an obscure figure outside Winchester.

The tone of this poem, because of its rather awkward subject matter, tends to veer between the portentous and the light-hearted. In the printed version, it ends on a portentous note. A final stanza was left out by Bernard. There is no obvious reason for this omission, but several possible causes. The stanza contains Greek, and this mixing of languages is rather unusual. While Latinised spellings of Greek words are common in classical verse, Greek script is generally confined to some prose works, such as Cicero's letters. There are examples in Juvenal and Martial, and it is found from time to time in British Neo-Latin.[87] In fact, the use of Greek is the best feature of the stanza; the addition of a Latin *-que* to a Greek word is a witty touch. Humour, even if muted, is a natural part of Alsop's character, and the poem benefits from the inclusion of this final joke. The

---

[85] 2. 16. 13–20.

[86] *A Discourse Concerning the Nature and Satisfaction of a Good and Inoffensive Conscience* (1693).

[87] Juvenal 6. 195, 9. 37; Martial 9. 12. 15, probably imitating Lucilius (at Cic., *De Fin.* 1. 3; A. Gellius 18. 8, etc.); also Ausonius. Elsewhere in Alsop, 3. 3. 16 (obviously omitted by Bernard for Jacobitism). Alsop is perhaps imitated in a (mis-accented) reference to Achilles at Popham, *Selecta Poemata* (1779 edn.), p. 285.

author may not have wished Eyre himself to see it, since it might have offended him to see his imminent death joked about, even under the cover of a classical parallel; Alsop may also have wished to make the poem more sombre in revising it after the deaths of Eyre and Wickart in 1722.

From politics to parties

Alsop had one close friend engaged in the law, Joseph Taylor (?1679–1759), to whom he addressed four odes. Taylor was a successful London lawyer, clerk of Bridewell and Bethlehem hospitals from 1707 to 1759. He probably met Alsop through Atterbury, who was preacher at Bridewell (and later a prominent client); Stratford calls him 'Taylor the solicitor, clerk of Bridewell, our Dean's [Atterbury's] creature'.[88] He was counsel for the Earl of Oxford on his impeachment in 1715, and probably also acted for Viscount Bolingbroke: 'Par tamen dispar procerum tueri/Ausus' [You act boldly, however, for an unequal pair of nobles].[89] These were the two leading Tory politicians, although both discredited; Bolingbroke's influence revived after 1726, with his articles for *The Craftsman* and return to political intrigue.

Taylor himself entered politics, but unlike Freind he only succeeded in becoming an MP after Alsop's death. He had been legal adviser to Edward Gibbon, the historian's grandfather, and it was in the Gibbon family interest that he contested Petersfield, Hampshire, in 1722. On that occasion he abandoned the contest before the poll; he succeeded in January 1727, was unseated on petition, but re-elected at the general election in the same year. He then held the seat until 1734, when the Gibbons replaced him with the historian's father. It was not a particularly impressive career, but his first attempt to enter Parliament provided the occasion for one of Alsop's finest odes.

The poet offers humorous advice for the election campaign; his greater knowledge of rustic society allows him to give that advice to an inexperienced canvasser. There can be no doubt that Taylor is well fitted for the job, if he can contrive to get elected:

> Sed per immensum oceanum, et liquores
> Mille, sulcanda est via; multa fumi
> Nubila erumpent, fluitansque rivo
>   Alla perenni.

[88] *HMC Portland* 7. 87; for the best notice of Taylor, see R. Sedgwick, ed., *History of Parliament: House of Commons 1715–54* (1970).

[89] 2. 17. 5–6; Bernard's note identifies them as Oxford and Bolingbroke. The former spent two years in the Tower, while the latter fled to France, until Walpole scornfully allowed his return in 1723: *dispar* because the position of one is strengthened by Taylor, the other's restored (lines 7–8).

Quo salutandi titulo modoque
Ordines nosti procerum; ambiendus
Quo sit aut sartor laniusve ritu,
    Forte docendus.
Dexteram dextrae, sed onustam, inani
Junge (res magni); neque fastuosus
Temne nudato capite ante tectos
    Stare colonos.
Disce responsum rude, disce scomma
Perpeti, et plebem stupide insolentem,
Forsque narrantem graviora veris
    Crimina de te.

But you must cleave your way through a great ocean of liquor; many clouds of smoke must pour out, and a perpetual river of ale must flow. You already know how, and by what titles, to address the higher ranks of society; but perhaps you need to be told how a tailor or a butcher should be canvassed. Shake hands: but with yours full, and theirs empty (a most important point); and do not be too proud to stand bare-headed before farmers in their hats. Learn to put up with a rude reply, and a jest, and the common people being stupidly insolent, and telling stories about you that might even be worse than the truth.[90]

Taylor himself is not immune from a little sly satire: we are left to wonder what unflattering truths there might be for his opponents to exaggerate and the boorish gossip of the electors to dwell upon. The description of the passing of bribes from loaded hand to empty is brilliantly concise; the detail of the hats sums up the way in which the normal forms of deference are reversed in the topsy-turvy world of the election, one of the many indignities that the candidate must learn to accept.

As a lively satire on the unreformed parliamentary system, this ode deserves a place in the literature of politics alongside such more famous examples as Dickens' 'Eatanswill', in chapter 13 of *Pickwick Papers*, to which it is fully equal in verve. The other three poems addressed to Taylor are shorter and less immediately impressive than the *tour de force* of 2. 26; nevertheless they contain much of interest. 2. 17 and 2. 22 are both compaints that Taylor is ignoring the poet. They are probably not too serious, more excuses for poetry than genuine expressions of anger. There may have been some feeling behind them, and he does show irritation at friends' behaviour elsewhere.[91] The odes are the same length, and there is some repetition of material, but with interesting variations. The similar subject matter is presented in a different order: 2. 17 begins with his complaint, while 2. 22 saves it for the fourth stanza. In both poems he alludes to Ennius' famous line on Fabius' delaying tactics. The reference is much fuller in

[90] 2. 26. 5–20.   [91] See 2. 6; 2. 11. 45–56; 2. 23.

2. 22, and there is a satirical tinge to it: the lawyer's actions are not really quite as heroic as the great general's.[92]

In 2. 17, we come across that familiar obstacle, the servant who denies that his master is at home; in 2. 22, the situation is even worse, since Alsop cannot exchange a word with the busy Taylor, despite their being under the same roof. The final stanza of 2. 17 offers some witty good wishes:

> Quid favens Bacchus (Venerem tacebo)
> Dulce largiri poterit, tibi opto;
> Deditos rixae, loculique largi,
>   Opto clientes.
>
> I wish that you may have everything sweet that it is in Bacchus' power to supply (I shall keep quiet about Venus'); and I wish you may have clients who are devoted to quarrelling, and have fat purses.

While most people desire peace, the lawyer needs continual conflicts, and rich clients to take part in them. This is a cynical, but devastatingly accurate, summary of a lawyer's motivation, and contrasts amusingly with the more idealistic image that had appeared earlier in the poem, when Alsop is praising the services that Taylor has been able to perform for his noble employers.

Ode 2. 19 is a reworking of a common Horatian theme, the invitation to enjoy a party in a simple rural setting. The opening alludes to Horace, *Carm.* 4. 11, but substitutes October ale, a thoroughly English beverage, for the original wine. Other significant allusions also have a constructive purpose, encouraging the reader to examine the relationship between Alsop and Horace; it is not merely a parody or a tired imitation of an ancient cliché. Modernity is not only represented by the ale; a host can also offer 'Vasculum Bacchi, quod amica, clam quaes-/tore, ratis fert' [a little bottle of brandy that a friendly ship brings over without the excise-officers noticing].[93] Smuggling was an accepted part of life: 'Everyone, from Walpole to Parson Woodforde, bought up contraband, Walpole using an Admiralty barge to run his smuggled wine up the Thames'.[94] Here it is mentioned with humour: the diminutive *vasculum*, the epithet *amica*, and the rather farcical *quaestor* raise a smile. There is the *frisson* of danger (for the smugglers, if not the drinkers) to add excitement.

---

[92] 2. 17. 8; 2. 22. 10–12.   [93] 2. 19. 7–8.
[94] R. Porter, *English Society in the 18th century* (1982), p. 115; Woodforde's diary, 29 March 1777, cited by G. M. Trevelyan, *English Social History* (1944), p. 387.

How to get on in the Church

We have seen how grateful Alsop was for the assistance of the Duke of Chandos, but it was not only gratitude to the family that made him write poetry to Henry Brydges. It is to Brydges that Alsop chose to comment on the current state of the Anglican Church, and he could also tease him with something of the mixture of respect and satire that he used with other close friends. Brydges was at Westminster in 1688, and matriculated at Christ Church in 1691; he was the 3rd praelector there in 1696; from 1699 to 1717 he held the rectory of Broadwell with Adlestrop, Gloucestershire, but tended still to reside in Oxford. He was also a chaplain to Queen Anne, and in 1701 to the factory at Aleppo; his father had been ambassador to Turkey (1680–86), and his maternal grandfather was a Turkey merchant.[95]

In 1720 he was made Archdeacon of Rochester by Atterbury. Lewis Atterbury had hopes of it, but his brother explained: 'the person, to whom I told you I had gone very far towards engaging myself for the Archdeaconry, was Dr Brydges, the Duke of Chandos' brother, and him I am this day going to collate to it'; he was in fact collated only ten days after the death of his predecessor, Thomas Sprat junior.[96] Sir William Drake gave him the rectory of Agmondesham [Amersham], Buckinghamshire, in 1721; finally, in 1722, he became a Canon of St Paul's.[97]

He may have been ambitious for further preferment. Stratford wrote, with heavy irony, on 24 September 1721: 'No doubt that See [Durham] will be supplied as well as Hereford has been. My godfather was positive that Duke Chandos by proper methods would prevail for his brother. I was humbly of opinion that the usual methods would not be allowed to take place in that case. I proved to be in the right . . . No doubt Ruffe [Atterbury] will put in for Durham, as he did for Winchester, but I cannot think he will prevail.' The search for livings and prebends would go on from year to year; on 14 June 1713 Stratford had observed that Brydges 'solicits very earnestly for the canonry . . . This looks like our Dean's [Atterbury's] project'[98] Brydges' long-standing friendship with Atterbury would tend to prejudice Stratford against him.

He died at Bath on 9 May 1728, aged 54, 'universally beloved and sincerely lamented; he had been a good-natured, cheerful man, of lively, firm and orthodox piety'.[99] He published two sermons. The first, *A Sermon Preach'd Before the Queen . . . January 31. 1708/9. Being the Anniversary of the Martyrdom of King Charles I* (1709), is a typical example of Tory doctrine on the execution: 'this

[95] Foster, *Alumni Oxonienses*; Christ Church archives; G. E. C., *Peerage*; *Victoria County History, Gloucestershire* (1965) 6. 14–15.   [96] Nichols, *Corresp.* 2. 100; Le Neve, *Fasti.*
[97] Foster; *Victoria County History, Buckinghamshire* (1969) 3. 154; on Drake, G. E. C., *Baronetage* 2. 107–8.
[98] *HMC Portland* 7. 304; 7. 141.   [99] Nichols, *Corresp.* 1. 397 n.

presumptuous Mockery of Justice, this solemn Violence upon Majesty, is the masterpiece of Wickedness, and the peculiar Reproach of this Day and Nation' (p. 10). Of greater interest is *A Speech to the Clergy of the Diocese of Rochester at the Archidiaconal Visitation . . .* (1721). He makes a violent attack on the government's policy of toleration for occasional conformists, a policy supported by Whig bishops, but detested by most clergymen. 'I do not yet doubt, but by. . . a steady Prosecution of those Advantages which the Laws have still continued to us, we shall be able to bear down the Discouragements we often meet with . . . It is astonishing to observe how far a resolute Obstinacy in those who unhappily differ from us, has been able to support as weak a Cause, and Persons of as mean Qualifications to recommend it, as perhaps ever disturbed a Christian church. And methinks we might learn Wisdom from our Enemies . . .' (pp. 6–7). Thus he stiffens the sinews of the parish priests. He thinks that it is 'high time to change a false Moderation into a true Zeal for the House of God. The Indulgence, that was at first sought and granted as a Favour to Consciences truly scrupulous, is now insisted upon by those who were never designed to be comprehended in it . . .' (pp. 7–8); and he opposes 'the wicked Policy of blending Creeds . . . disguising truth for fear it should give Offence, and throwing down Walls and Bulwarks, that the Enemy might not take umbrage at them . . .' (p. 11).

All this is vigorous rhetoric, and while it might inspire a Kentish audience it was not calculated to appeal to the moderate Whigs who held most of the power in the Church. The speech was delivered on 31 May 1721, and printed a couple of months later.[100] Alsop's ode 2. 7 presumably came shortly after that. It is a brilliant piece of satire, disguised as advice, and comparable in quality to 2. 26; but while the satire of electioneering is easily identified and combines a sharp view of corruption with broad humour, 2. 7 depends upon sustained and quite bitter sarcasm:

> . . . quis te malesuadus egit
> Impetus durum fidei exoletae
>   Dogma tueri?
> Plurimos nescis procerum patrumque
> Stare te contra?
>
> what ill-advised impulse led you to defend the stern principles of an abolished faith? Do you not know that most of the lords and bishops are your opponents?[101]

You must face the opposition of 'gens animosa, Fratrum/Ordo Polonum' [the vigorous race of the order of Polish brethren]; these are the Socinians, a sect founded in Poland by Faustus Socinus, and an influence on Locke, Newton and

[100] 24 July, according to a ms. n. in the Cambridge University Library copy.   [101] 2. 7. 10–14.

others both within and outside the Church of England.[102] Pope alleges that it flourished under William III (*Essay on Criticism*, 544–9):

> The following licence of a foreign reign
> Did all the dregs of bold Socinus drain;
> Then unbelieving priests reform'd the nation,
> And taught more pleasant methods of salvation;
> Where Heaven's free subjects might their rights dispute,
> Lest God himself should seem too absolute.

Poland was also associated with Whiggism because of its elected monarchy, far removed from Tory belief in Divine Right; the point is made by Dryden (*The Medall* 1–21), and in a Jacobite poem, *The Duumvirate*:

> The Kingdoms antient Laws they quite forsake,
> And of old England a new Poland make.[103]

This being so, Brydges is urged to learn the doctrines that now bring advancement:

> . . . Cultus sit ubique norma
>   Libera et exlex;
> Sit fides, sit mens sua cuique, nullo
> Sub duce aut ductu: imperiosa cleri
> Ferre quis possit juga, quis sacerdo-
>   tale capistrum?
> Quare age, et sit pro licito licenter
> Velle; sit recti sibi quisque judex;
> Tros fuat quisquam Tyriusve, nullum ex-
>   amen inito.
>
> You should espouse a form of worship that is free of rules and strict beliefs; let each man have his own faith and opinions, with no leader or guide. Who can bear the clergy's imperious yoke, or priestly control? So act in this way, and let there be free choice; let everyone be his own judge of righteousness; let there be no enquiry into who is Trojan or Tyrian.[104]

The allusion to Virgil reminds us that free association between the Trojans and Dido's Carthaginians was not a success. Liberty may seem superficially attractive; Alsop presents these arguments with a straight face, expecting the reader to see their underlying hollowness. 'This is the state of Liberty, that some Men seem to contend so violently for now: a state, to which God condemned a disobedient People more than once, when they trifled with Him and their Religion' (Brydges' *Speech*, pp. 12–13).

---

[102] 2. 7. 15–16; H. J. McLachlan, *Socinianism in 17th century England* (Oxford, 1951).
[103] Bodleian, Carte mss. 208, 62, fo. 397ᵛ.   [104] 2. 7. 19–28.

If he does follow the course of expediency, he can expect a bishop's mitre; the suggestion is ironic, but there may also be a warning that, if he does persevere in his principles (as Alsop naturally expects), he should abandon hopes of rising higher. He had declared his determination in the preface to the *Speech*: 'may [it] stand as a Reproach against me, should any Worldly Motives ever prevail upon me (as I trust . . . they never will) to act contrary in any respect to what I have here laid down'. In the political climate of 1721 (and far more so after 1723), Atterbury's friendship would be a distinct liability; a Tory who spoke his mind would get little from the Whigs, and certainly not a bishopric.

Alsop can congratulate Brydges on his success in obtaining Agmondesham (2. 8) and the Archdeaconry (2. 14); will he wish to be known by a lengthy title, 'An magis gaudes, velut ante, amicis/Dicier Harry?' [Or do you prefer, as before, that your friends call you Harry?].[105] The combination of an archaic infinitive and a modern colloquialism in an adonic line is delightfully audacious; it is also a witty way of stressing that one should not let acquired grandeur stiffen friendship into formality. The rest of the ode turns to Dolben's need for advice in love: a lively, light-hearted piece.

Advice is also proffered in 2. 8, when his noble ancestry may be an obstacle to getting the best out of a country living. An agent may have handled his business, and cheated him, in the past. Now Alsop suggests that he should call in a more competent friend, either the poet himself, or Charles Aldrich, or John Pelling. It may be that these two, though good friends, were not ideal candidates for the job; Alsop, knowing their failings, might be laughing as he puts them forward. Pelling, rector of St Anne's, Westminster and formerly tutor and senior censor at Christ Church, had not always been a pillar of respectability. In 1695 he was suspended for six months from his studentship and confined to the library for beating a porter.[106]

Aldrich, the late Dean's nephew, had too many domestic troubles in his Henley parsonage to dispense advice. His wife and mother were argumentative drunkards, his sister 'with a big belly, the father . . . not yet owned'. This information is provided with exaggerated relish by Stratford, not indeed an impartial source, since he had a long-running and bitter dispute with Aldrich, whom he despised as Atterbury's 'creature and tool too, to as infamous a degree as so poor a wretch could be'. Again, on 9 May 1723: 'I hear my old friend Charles Aldrich has taken care to convince his new friends, by his late sermon, that he has contracted no political malignity by his former intimacies with the Bishop of R. [Atterbury]. But there was no occasion for poor Charles to lay in so fresh a stock of merit. His former qualifications gave him a good title to some dignity, if perjury, matricide, incest and the last degree of stupidity may be

[105] 2. 14. 7–8. [106] Christ Church archives.

thought to deserve any thing. I wonder who cooked up Charles's sermon. He could not, I believe, so much as transcribe it himself. I wonder how he read it. He must have had recourse to his old crony Alsop.'[107] One may add that Charles Aldrich, like Pelling, was a regular contributor of Latin verse to the Oxford collections; he is unlikely to have been the imbecile Stratford depicts, but he was not remarkable for his organisation either. His name appears pompously hyphen-ated, straddling the caesura as *Aldrico-Carolum*.[108] It would be a characteristic touch of Alsopian wit if he did not quite live up to his billing. Even gently mocked, he was a good companion still, yet another example of the way in which Alsop's rural retirement was fertile in friendship and in poetry.

---

[107] *HMC Portland* 7. 175, 352, 359; for their dispute see 85–110, etc.   [108] 2. 8. 27.

8
After Alsop

The middle of the eighteenth century was still a fruitful period for Latin verse, and several of Alsop's contemporaries and successors deserve to be read. Many of Benjamin Loveling's witty odes were rather too exciting for the public attention of past critics, though they might raise more than a smile in private.[1] In the same volume as his elegant obscenities we find translations from Habakkuk and from Stephen Duck:

> Tho' Stephen's Muse in Humble Metre flows,
> And warbles Numbers near ally'd to Prose,
> Thy genius gives a Lustre to his Rhimes,
> And such a Bard may live to Future Times.
> So modern B–sh–ps by Translation thrive,
> And Drones receive the Labours of the Hive.[2]

The amusement of turning a notoriously rustic contemporary into Latin appealed to Loveling and his readers; the comparison with the bishops hints at the sharp satire to be found elsewhere in the volume (e.g. the venal *Patriot*, p. 165).

Christopher Smart became well known at Cambridge for his witty Latin Tripos verses; he translated some very substantial works of Pope, an exercise that Pope himself encouraged,[3] distrusting the impermanence of English (a sign that Waller's views, quoted in Chapter 1, still held good). He turned his hand to Milton's *L'Allegro*;[4] some Latin doggerel translations from *Hudibras* appeared in *The Student*, as did his much more elegant sapphics to Samuel Saunders.[5] He also used *The Student* to publish a poem of Alsop's, with a vigorous translation (possibly his own, though more probably by one of Alsop's contemporaries: see 2. 2, discussed in Chapter 6). More Latin poems appeared in another periodical, *The Universal Visiter*. Among Continental Neo-Latin authors, he

---

[1] Bradner, pp. 237–8.
[2] From 'To the Author of the following Poems', [Loveling], *Latin and English Poems* (1741 edn.), p. iii.
[3] B. Rizzo, R. Mahony, *Annotated Letters of Christopher Smart* (Carbondale and Edwardsville, IL, 1991), pp. 1–3; K. Williamson, ed., *Poetical Works; 4, miscellaneous poems, English & Latin* (Oxford, 1987): *St Cecilia*, pp. 32–6, *De Arte Critica*, pp. 66–88.   [4] Williamson, *Works*, pp. 103–7.
[5] Williamson, *Works*, pp. 6–10 (*Hudibras*), 139 (Saunders).

was certainly familiar with Sannazaro and DuFresnoy.[6] As a translator of Horace, and as a writer of Latin, he reflects the bilingual culture of his age.

Nicholas Hardinge, educated at Eton and King's College, Cambridge, made a career in Parliament (as clerk, then MP from 1748 until his death in 1758), and wrote varied Latin poetry, mostly in Horatian lyrics, that was published posthumously in 1780.[7] His work included Biblical paraphrases (one, like Loveling, from Habakkuk), praise of Walpole's country seat, and miscellaneous occasional poetry of considerable interest, though less vivid and vigorous than Alsop's. John Jortin and John Burton also produced some fine lyric verses.[8] Michael Maittaire was a distinguished scholar as well as a poet, the editor of many classical texts and the owner of an enormous library. His original Latin verse, entitled *Senilia* (1742),[9] was printed for him by Bowyer, and the list of subscribers offers an indication of the popularity of Neo-Latin in society (or the author's snobbery); the list includes some foreigners, and many Englishmen (generally for one or two copies, rather than the forty-two ordered by Horace Walpole). Maittaire addresses odes to William Stratford, the castrato Farinelli, and several physicians: Freind, Hale, Hollins, and Mead (the latter in both Latin and Greek, on Kneller's portait). He has a wider circle than Alsop, but fewer of his poems are sent to real friends (and his decision to publish them reflects their less intimate nature). None of these poets is a real rival to Alsop; their Latin is still as interesting as most vernacular writing of the age. Some more famous figures are examined in the following pages.

William King of St Mary Hall, Principal Jacobite

The most important literary and intellectual figure among the Oxford Jacobites was a prolific Latin poet; William King[10] was for many years (from 1719 until his death in 1763) Principal of St Mary Hall, one of the smaller foundations (it still stands, though without its independence, having been absorbed into Oriel College). His prominent place in university life derived from his own force of character, not the size of his college. In that respect he resembles Arthur Charlett (discussed in Chapter 5); in other respects, the two are poles apart, since King abhorred the cautious moderation to which Charlett devoted his career.

The Jacobite tradition had long flourished in Oxford, as we have seen in previous chapters. One entertaining example of its more extreme form can be

[6] Williamson, *Works*, pp. 363 (translation from Sannazaro), 95 (quote from DuFresnoy).
[7] Also a 2nd edn., 1818; Bradner, pp. 238-9.
[8] Bradner, p. 240 (Jortin); p. 249 (Burton: quoting his praise of Cowley's *Sex Libri Plantarum*).
[9] Bradner, pp. 236-7.
[10] Bradner, pp. 258-65; D. Greenwood, *William King, Tory and Jacobite* (Oxford, 1969).

found in an anonymous epitaph on 'Oliverius Angliae Secundus, Gulielmus iste dictus Tertius' [that second Cromwell, the so-called William III], preserved among the Wake papers (though the archbishop would not have shared its fanaticism): William was 'trium patris Regnorum fur improbus/. . . diabolo-datus, Atheus, Parricida,/Romani pontificis Socius et Amicus,/Mas-stuprator, Sodomita, Misogynos,/. . . Juvenis De-Wittos rabidae Plebis manibus,/Pseudo-rexque tandem Britanniarum factus/Janizariis suis Glencoanum gentem/. . . trucidavit./. . . Tiberius, Nero, Heliogabalus/et quemadmodum alter Molock/ sola caede, pace non bello, expiandus/. . . Subditos contra Regem/Liberos contra Patrem/Exercitum contra Imperatorem/Servos contra Dominum/Post-habito Divino omni humanoque jure/In Anglia concitavit,/ In Gallia concitare voluit . . .' [the wicked thief of his father's (i.e. father-in-law's) three kingdoms, devil-sent, atheist, parricide, the ally and friend of the Roman Pope, a mastur-bator, sodomite, and woman-hater; as a youth he murdered the De Witts at the hands of the raging mob, and at length, being made pseudo-king of the British Isles, he murdered the race of Glencoe with his Janissaries; he was a Tiberius, a Nero, an Elagabalus, and a sort of new Moloch, only to be satisfied by slaughter, in peace rather than war; abandoning all divine and human law, in England he roused subjects against their king, children against their father, an army against its general, and servants against their master, and he wished to do the same in France . . .].[11] The comparison of William's troops with the ruthless guards of the Turkish sultan is topical (given the recent threat to Vienna) and clever, for the Janissaries were taken from Christian families, and forced to betray their origins. Other ideas are more risible, especially the notion that he was in league with the Pope (though Papal foreign policy might periodically require alliance with Protestants, it looks strange for a supporter of James II and the Pretender to imply that the Pope is evil).

King's Jacobitism is more elegant, but no less impassioned. He was able to print most of his hexameter satires, because they are not explicitly seditious; but the underlying position was quite clear to contemporary readers. He could camouflage his more dangerous material, to some extent, with the generalised abuse of moral decay that is expected of the satirist; thus, in the preface to his *Opera* (printed but not issued, 1754),[12] he can despair 'quum video mores civium nostrorum omnium, praeter perpaucos majoribus suis et vetere Britannia dignos, adeo esse corruptos ac depravatos . . . leves ac nummarios homines . . . [when I see that the manners of all our citizens, except a very few who are worthy of their ancestors and Britain's past, are so corrupted and depraved . . . that men are fickle and money-grubbing . . .]. These words are of relevance to the Jacobite, but might be accepted by a moralist of any party.

---

[11] Christ Church, Wake Mss. 18. 514.   [12] See Bradner, p. 264, n. 44.

The reaction to the first of these satires, as later dissected by King, offers a good example of the place of Neo-Latin in eighteenth-century society. He remarks, with some truth, that 'nothing is more common than to hear a little pedant . . . criticise the works of an elegant scholar, and magisterially affirm that such and such expressions are not classical.' We are still on the battlefield between scholarship and polite literature (as discussed in Chapter 4), and King vigorously defends the latter camp: 'In the year 1738 I published *Miltonis Epistola ad Pollionem*. As this was a political satire, and nothing in the same manner had been published before in this country,[13] it was universally read by those who either understood, or pretended to understand the language, and was frequently extolled or condemned according to the prejudice of party: there was not a courtier, or a creature of the prime minister's, who did not set himself up as a profound critic . . .'.[14] He proceeds to tell how he swiftly found classical parallels (from the index of the critic's own editions)[15] for the disputed phrases. Criticism of modern Latin is politically motivated, and a controversial Latin work is read in London society, as a new English work would be. This early success encouraged King to produce further satires, of which *Templum Libertatis* (1742–3) is the most substantial, its two books each running to over 600 lines.

King's finest hour was in 1749, when he delivered his *Redeat* speech in Oxford, to an audience assembled for the opening of the Radcliffe Camera. It was clear that the repeated *Redeat* [let it (or, him) return] applied to the Pretender, as well as to the abstract virtues for which it ostensibly called. The rhetoric was simple enough to be understood even by those who 'pretended to understand the language'. The speech was probably the most prominent usage of Latin, and most public expression of Jacobitism, in the years when Bernard was preparing his edition of Alsop (as noted in Chapter 3). King remained belligerently involved in Oxford politics in the 1750s.[16] His enthusiasm did wane, and in his last years, with the accession of George III, he could look back from a less partisan standpoint. He ridicules the non-juror, who 'would be content to see the nation involved in general ruin, and the extirpation of three or four millions of our people, if by that means the House of Stuart might be restored.'[17] His own disillusionment is traced to the clandestine visit of the Young Pretender in 1750; the Prince's ignorance, callousness, arrogance, and refusal to abandon his mistress, lost him many friends. King observes that 'the most odious part of

---

[13] There had been other satires, but few so aggressively political in recent years; cf. Bradner, pp. 253–6.
[14] *Political and Literary Anecdotes of his own Times* (2nd edn., London, 1819), pp. 150–1.
[15] This critic, who was not gratuitously pedantic, but asked by others to give an opinion, was Michael Maittaire.
[16] Especially the 1754 election: see W. R. Ward, *Georgian Oxford* (Oxford, 1958); R. J. Robson, *The Oxfordshire Election of 1754* (Oxford, 1949).   [17] *Anecdotes*, p. 193.

his character is his love of money . . . the certain index of a base and little mind.'[18] There seems an echo of this private disappointment in the 1754 preface, quoted above: the Prince, like his Whig opponents, is *levis* and *nummarius*.

Gray and Browne

Thomas Gray is one of the most famous English poets of the eighteenth century, famous particularly for his *Elegy written in a Country Churchyard* and *Ode on a distant prospect of Eton College*; the ending of the latter is a familiar quotation, applicable to countless generations of students:

> Thought would destroy their paradise.
> No more; where ignorance is bliss,
> 'Tis folly to be wise.

This poem was written in 1742, a few months after the death of his close friend, Richard West, to whom he had addressed much of his previous poetry, in both Latin and English. His Latin lyric poetry contains three major odes, two of them sent to West (using humorous variations on the Latin version of his name, Favonius, that had been current in their small group of friends); the sapphic ode of 1738, 'Barbaras aedes aditure mecum . . .',[19] expresses horror at the prospect of becoming a lawyer, while an alcaic ode, 'Mater rosarum . . .' was sent from Rome in 1740. Letters to West included other lyric fragments. The third major piece, on the Grande Chartreuse, was also written on his travels, and set down in the album of that monastery, as well as his own commonplace book. He was then aged 24, and was chiefly a Latin rather than an English poet.

It was to West that he sent from Florence, in April 1741, 'the beginning not of an Epic Poem, but of a Metaphysic One. Poems and Metaphysics (say you, with your spectacles on) are inconsistent things. A metaphysical poem is a contradiction in terms. It is true, but I will go on. It is Latin too to increase the absurdity.'[20] This does not seem very promising: but one should not take the self-depreciatory tone, typical of the sophisticated poses assumed by these friends, as evidence that the project was not serious. The work was entitled *De Principiis Cogitandi*; the philosophy that he aimed to present in Latin hexameters is that of John Locke, himself an occasional writer of Latin verse, whose *Essay concerning Human Understanding* was first published in 1690. His reputation was comparable to that of Newton in natural philosophy. Locke is invoked as 'O decus Angliacae certe o lux altera gentis' (line 7) [certainly the glory and new

---

[18] *Anecdotes*, pp. 201–2.   [19] Wittily alluding to Horace, *Carm*. 2. 6 (and perhaps Catullus 11).
[20] P. Toynbee, L. Whibley, eds., *The Correspondence of Thomas Gray* (Oxford, 1935), 1. 183.

illumination of the English people]: his name is not given in the text, but appears in the margin of Gray's commonplace book.

West himself was a competent writer of Latin. His poem of 1736, in the Oxford *Gratulatio* on the marriage of Frederick, Prince of Wales, is if anything rather more accomplished than Gray's offering to the equivalent Cambridge volume. It is called *Merlinus, Ecloga*, and conjures up the national prophet to offer some Virgilian encouragement. 'As for my poor little Eclogue,' West wrote to Gray, 'it has been condemned and beheaded by our Westminster judges;[21] an exordium of about sixteen lines absolutely cut off, and its other limbs quartered in a most barbarous manner.'[22] The *disjecta membra* still put up a good showing.

After the shock of West's death, the poem was not abandoned, but slowly allowed to die. In 1744 Gray could joke about its state: 'Master Tommy Lucretius (since you are so good as to enquire after the Child) is but a puleing Chitt yet, not a bit grown to speak of, I believe, poor Thing! it has got the Worms, that will carry it off at last.'[23] As late as 1747 he sent Horatio Walpole the fragment of the fourth book (begun in 1742), called the second in his commonplace book; this fragment is only 29 lines long, and forms a heartfelt elegy to West. After this personal tribute, thought as a philosophical subject seems to have lost its appeal; as he wrote in English, 'Thought would destroy their paradise'.

The 207 lines of the (presumably completed) first book are largely devoted to the five senses, vividly and charmingly described, and to the ways in which ideas approach the soul (a term used in the commonplace book's margin). It is a pity that we have no more of it; the lack does not indicate a malaise in Neo-Latin didactic, so much as a reluctance in Gray to finish anything. In the letter that offered book 4, he spoke in equally self-mocking terms of other projects, such as his unfinished English play: 'Agrippina can stay very well, she thanks you; and be damned at Leisure.'[24] Despite ample opportunities and varied interests, Gray never wrote anything very substantial in any language; despite a lifetime at Cambridge, and eventually the Professorship of Modern History, he produced no work of scholarship. He often started things (including Latin verses on beetles), but did not persevere.

Of Gray's other poetry, his biographer A. L. Lytton Sells thinks the Ovidian epistle *Sophonisba Masinissae* is the most impressive, more inventive than any of his English works.[25] Barry Baldwin,[26] on the other hand, is concerned to point

---

[21] Christ Church was dominated by former Westminster pupils; Gray and West were from Eton.
[22] *Corresp.* 1. 43 (24 May 1736).   [23] *Corresp.* 1. 225.   [24] *Corresp.* 1. 265.
[25] A. L. Lytton Sells, *Thomas Gray* (London, 1980), p. 164.
[26] B. Baldwin, 'On some Latin and Greek poems by Thomas Gray', *International Journal of the Classical Tradition* 1 (1994), pp. 71–88.

out classical borrowings, and to criticise other commentators for not noticing them. He makes fun of Hagstrum's fanciful interpretation[27] of *De Principiis Cogitandi* 1. 64–84; his own 'proper scrutiny' shows 'lashings of Lucretius'. I find most of his 'parallels' unconvincing and feeble, evidence of a general similarity of tone and style, rather than of substantial borrowing; hence his comments on the 'sheer accumulation of classical tags' are quite unjustified, if one takes a 'tag' to be a familiar and readily identifiable phrase.[28] It can be valuable to identify possible sources for the words of Neo-Latin poets, but the technique has its limits. When one cannot prove that conscious borrowing has occurred, the connection is purely speculative, and (unless one can show a reason for its significance) of only moderate interest. All these poets were familiar with the classics; having been taught with the use of graduses or other aids to versification, they could unconsciously echo ancient phrases. This does not make them unoriginal. In the case of Gray, one can cite innumerable parallels for the more memorable phrases of his English verse.[29] When he is most successful, as so often in Augustan verse, it is not originality but elegance that satisfies the reader; in Pope's famous words, 'What oft was thought, but ne'er so well expressed'.[30] Gray is a supremely elegant man of letters, in whose art and life little was achieved, but some of that little achievement had the precious brilliance of gem-stones.

If Gray tended to be difficult and dilatory, Isaac Hawkins Browne was more colourful. According to Dr Johnson, Browne was a delightful conversationalist; he also said that Browne 'drank freely for thirty years, and that he wrote his poem *De Animi Immortalitate* in some of the last of these years. I [Boswell] listened to this with the eagerness of one who, conscious of being himself fond of wine, is glad to hear that a man of so much genius and good thinking as Browne had the same propensity.'[31] Gray, whom Johnson had never met, he called '. . . dull every where. He was dull in a new way, and that made people think him great'; Gray meanwhile thought Johnson's style 'turgid and vicious'.[32]

One of Gray's early letters contains a humorous Greek hexameter on tobacco; he may have remembered Raphael Thorius' *Hymnus Tabaci* (1625), which regularly appeared in later anthologies.[33] Browne's *Pipe of Tobacco* is one of

[27] In J. Downey, B. Jones, eds., *Fearful Joy* (Montreal and London, 1974).
[28] This discussion, p. 75; his 'parallels' elsewhere are equally thin; when he discusses the *dubia* (p. 89), I feel he confuses Ambrose Philips (parodied in Browne's *Pipe of Tobacco*: discussed below) with John Philips (*Splendid Shilling*).   [29] See, e.g., R. Lonsdale, ed., *Poems* (London, 1969).
[30] *Essay on Criticism*, line 298.
[31] *Tour of Hebrides*: 5 Sept. 1773 (cited in *DNB*). Browne could also, like Addison, be low until revived by drink; as an MP (1744–54) he never spoke, usually voting for the government.
[32] Boswell, *Life* (ed. Hill and Powell, Oxford, 1934–64) 2. 327: cited by Lytton Sells, p. 246; he concludes that Gray was naturally indolent, and capable of extravagant dislikes.
[33] Bradner, p. 73; Baldwin, 'Gray' p. 79–80; *Corresp.* I. 7 (17 Nov. 1734).

the most successful of eighteenth century parodies; it was reprinted in Dodsley's *Collection*, and continued to form the standard by which such well-known later efforts as the *Rejected Addresses* were judged.[34] The imitations of six well-known English writers catch their style neatly, laughing both at the usual targets of their satire, and at their own characteristic mannerisms. Thus, in imitation of Alexander Pope:[35]

> Blest leaf! whose aromatick gales dispense
> To templars modesty, to parsons sense . . .
> Poison that cures, a vapour that affords
> Content, more solid than the smile of lords . . .
> Inspir'd by thee, dull cits adjust the scale
> Of Europe's peace, when other statesmen fail.
> By thee protected, and thy sister, beer,
> Poets rejoice, nor think the bailiff near.
> Nor less the critick owns thy genial aid,
> While supperless he plies the piddling trade . . . (no. 5, lines 1–2, 5–6, 9–14)

He is even more direct in imitating the brutality of Swift:

> Let all be plac'd in manner due,
> A pot wherein to spit or spue,
> And London Journal, and Free Briton,
> Of use to light a pipe or ★ ★ . . . (no. 6, lines 3–6)

This sort of thing had been done before, most memorably in Henry Carey's attack on the childish verses written for aristocratic children by Ambrose Philips, from which we take the phrase '*Namby-Pamby*':

> As an actor does his part,
> So the nurses get by heart
> Namby-Pamby's little rhymes,
> Little jingle, little chimes,
> To repeat to little miss,
> Piddling ponds of pissy-piss . . . (lines 31–6)

Ambrose Philips is one of Browne's six poets (although that parody was originally supplied by his 'ingenious friend', John Hoadly, son of the famous Whig bishop, and published in several newspapers in 1735, with improvements by Browne),[36] and the *Pipe of Tobacco* parody is rather more subtle than Carey's,

---

[34] H. F. B. Brett-Smith, ed., *A Pipe of Tobacco* (Oxford, 1923), p. 1. Curll took four of the parodies, and coupled them with John Philips' Latin and English ode to Henry St John, Lord Bolingbroke (later Browne's intellectual opponent): *Of Smoking* (1736).

[35] Pope thought the parody 'just and well taken': Spence, quoted at Brett-Smith, p. 15.

[36] Brett-Smith, p. 8.

keeping closer to the language that Philips might actually use, and suggesting his
poverty of thought by the repetition of one of Philips' own couplets:[37]

> Happy thrice, and thrice agen,
> Happiest he of happy men. (no. 2, lines 11–12, repeated 21–2)

Browne was interested in fine art as well as literature, and was aware of the time-
honoured didactic connection between the two. He addressed an elegant
sapphic ode to the artist Joseph Highmore:

> . . . Tuque cognatae cape dona Musae,
> Spiritus nostras regit unus artes . . . (lines 17–18; p. 131 in 1768 edn.)

> Accept the gifts of a related Muse, since a single spirit rules our arts.

And to Highmore he dedicated his English epistle *On Design and Beauty* (pp. 96–
108). The esteem was mutual, for Highmore not only painted Browne, but he
also translated his major Latin work into English prose, 'made soon after the
Publication of the Original, before any other translation had appeared, and
intended to be so close and literal as even to preserve (in some degree) the
Latin Phraseology'.[38] Browne was a versatile poet, showing his mastery of a
light, witty technique in other poems: especially amusing are *A Letter from a
Captain in Country Quarters*, and *To some ladies, who said the Author loved Chicken*.
This was standard fare for an Augustan drawing-room; but his most significant
work is in Latin.

Isaac Hawkins Browne's Latin didactic poem, *De Animi Immortalitate* (1754),
was influenced by trends in both vernacular and Neo-Latin literature. Alexander
Pope's *Essay on Man* (1733) helped to raise the profile of deistic philosophy
among the readers of polite literature. On the other side of the debate, Cardinal
Melchior de Polignac's *Anti-Lucretius* (1747) was published, translated, and read
in England: there were two London editions (1748, 1751) shortly before Brow-
ne's poem appeared, and a translation shortly after, in 1757.[39] Browne's poem is
much shorter than Polignac's, being complete in two books of under 400 lines
each, and places the emphasis on variety and readability, rather than detailed
argument. The subject was one of serious contemporary debate, but could be
treated in a lighter way to attract a less specialised audience. It is quite likely that
Browne was aware of the tradition of Renaissance Latin didactic poetry, though
without being unduly influenced by it. The most relevant Renaissance work is

[37] Brett-Smith, p. 10.
[38] J. H[ighmore], *Essays, Moral, Religious, and Miscellaneous. To which is added a Prose Translation of Mr Browne's Latin Poem, De Animi Immortalitate* (London, 1766), 2. 108 (the translation, pp. 109–73).
[39] Bradner, p. 277. George Canning, father of the statesman, published yet another translation (London, 1766). William King of St Mary Hall met Polignac, found him 'a fine gentleman, as well as an elegant and polite scholar', and discussed a published portion of the *Anti-Lucretius*: King's *Anecdotes* (2nd edn., London, 1819), pp. 9–11.

Aonio Paleario's *De Animorum Immortalitate* (in three books), included in Pope's *Selecta Poemata Italorum* (discussed in Chapter 4).[40]

Browne's *De Animi Immortalitate* was translated into English by Soame Jenyns (1704–87), himself an accomplished poet in a number of prevalent genres: his *Modern Fine Lady* is a nice example of the social satire that had amused the readers of Pope, Lady Mary Wortley Montagu, and other sophisticated authors. In 1757, three years after Browne's poem first appeared, Jenyns published *A Free Enquiry into the Nature and Origin of Evil*; he was already a commissioner of trade and MP for Cambridge, both positions that he would retain until 1780. He was a public figure of some importance, concerned with theological issues as well as lighter literature, and it is significant that he chose to devote his attention to Browne. Gray thought his poetry respectable: 'Mr Soame Jenyns now and then can write a good line or two' (high praise for him); the *Free Enquiry* went down less well: 'I have read the little wicked book about Evil, that settled Mr Dodsley's conscience in that point, and find nothing in it but absurdity . . .'.[41] Jenyns' 'elegant' translation was printed by Isaac Hawkins Browne, junior, after the Latin text of his father's poem, making it clear that this was his preferred version:[42] the poem had been popular enough to inspire several rival translations.

William Hay, MP, was one of those who rushed out a version in 1754: 'The Original is a noble work: it shines in the Language and Beauties of Horace, Virgil, and Lucretius: may be read as long: and be, like its subject, immortal. The Author has as happy a Talent for English Verse: and could best have done himself Justice in a Translation. But One, fired with all the Beauties of the Original, could scarce condescend to such a Task . . .'; he takes the task seriously, with quite a long preface (pp. v–viii) on the theory behind his translation: 'If I am asked, why I chose Rhyme? my Answer is, because an English Ear loves the Gingle . . .'. Interest was still there in the following decade, and J. Cranwell looks forward to a new edition of the Latin, while offering his translation (Cambridge, 1765).

Thirty years later came John Lettice, another former fellow of Cranwell's college, Sidney Sussex, dedicating his labours to the poet's son, by now an MP, as his father and two of his father's earlier translators had been; Lettice provided a very thorough edition, with translation, parallel text, commentary, and annotations (Cambridge, 1795). The 'advertisement' emphasises his desire to be read by his 'elegant countrywomen': 'For I am ambitious of having many readers of that Sex, being entirely persuaded, that were the groveling principles of Materialism, and of the Mortality of the Soul, once to become as prevalent among the Ladies of this Country, as they have been for some time among the Female Citizens of a

---

[40] Cf. also Scipione Capece, *De principiis rerum* (1546): not included by Atterbury or Pope.
[41] *Corresp.* 1. 298; 2. 499. Johnson also strongly disapproved.
[42] It is also the version printed in Dodsley, *Collection* 6. 74–104 (in 1782 edn.).

neighbouring people, there would want little else, at this alarming Crisis, than that Universal Depravation, which such a circumstance would certainly, and quickly, produce, to shake the Constitution and Government of Great Britain to their very foundations . . .'—and more in the same rhetorical vein. He is indeed a wordy commentator, taking 77 pages to paraphrase what he has just translated, before beginning the detailed annotations. Amid the rhetoric is a serious point. The French Revolution has made the poem more relevant than ever, a vital (and accessible) intellectual bulwark against the horror of female citizens gloating beneath the guillotine.

His poem's success had led Browne, in his last years, to begin a more polemical work of Latin didactic poetry; of this, his son published 165 hexameters, calling it simply *Fragmentum*. The target was again the philosophy of Pope's mentor, the former Jacobite Henry St John, Viscount Bolingbroke. The fragment was first translated, then completed, by the eccentric physician, Sir William Browne (not, as far as I know, a relation), founder of the Cambridge prize medals for verse composition.[43] He dedicated his translation, 'this second *Religio Medici* from the same name and county', to the physicians at Bath. At the end he added this couplet:

> Auctorem huc terris ostendunt fata, nec ultra
> Esse sinunt: finem fidus meditatur amicus.

He translated it as follows:

> Thus far the author's fate allows: the end
> Is undertaken by his faithful friend.

The promise was fulfilled the following year, 1769, with 171 more lines of Latin (197 in English), dedicated to Isaac Hawkins Browne, junior.[44]

In his *De Animi Immortalitate*, Browne looks for evidence to support his case from various features and foibles of the human condition; in doing so he was influenced not only by didactic predecessors, but also by the related genre of satire. Modern reworkings of ancient satire were a feature of the English 'Augustan Age': Pope produced highly politicised imitations of Horace's *Sermones*, Samuel Johnson's *London* (1738) had modernised Juvenal, and to that had most recently been added his *Vanity of Human Wishes* (1749), based on Juvenal's

---

[43] Bradner, p. 278.

[44] *Fragmentum Isaaci Hawkins Browne, sive Anti-Bolingbrokius liber primus, Translated . . .* (London, 1768); *Fragmentum Isaaci Hawkins Browne completum, Anti-Bolingbrokius liber secundus* (London, 1769): both published by W. Owen, who had also issued one of the (anonymous) translations of 1754. Cambridge University Library, Nn.12.33³, is a presentation copy 'To his Nursing Mother Cambridge from Sir W. Browne'; in line 164 of book 2, (Nn.12.33⁴) he has noticed that *bubones* will not scan at the end of a hexameter, and has recast the line to begin with that word.

tenth satire. There may be echoes of this in Browne's plan, and in phrases of Jenyns' translation, for example,

> Each weak attempt the same sad lesson brings,
> Alas, what vanity in human things!

which translates 'heu! quantum in Rebus inane!' (1. 28). He can take a close look at the behaviour of his own countrymen:

> Nonne videmus uti convictus criminis, ipso
> Limine sub mortis, culpam tamen abneget omnem;
> Mendax, ut sibi constet honos atque integra fama?
> Nempe animis haec insevit Natura Futuri
> Indicia, obscurasque notas; hinc solicita est mens,
> De se posteritas quid sentiat; at nihil ad nos
> Postera vox, erimus si nil nisi pulvis et umbra;
> Sera venit, cineres nec tangit fama quietos. (1. 143–50)

This Jenyns translates as follows:

> For fame the wretch beneath the gallows lies,
> Disowning every crime for which he dies;
> Of life profuse, tenacious of a name,
> Fearless of death, and yet afraid of shame.
> Nature has wove into the human mind
> This anxious care for names we leave behind,
> T' extend our narrow views beyond the tomb,
> And give an earnest of a life to come:
> For, if when dead, we are but dust or clay,
> Why think of what posterity shall say?
> Her praise, or censure cannot us concern,
> Nor ever penetrate the silent urn. (lines 170–81)

We note that there is no mention of this wretch consigning himself to Hell by failing to repent: Browne does not press the details of Christian, still less of Anglican, doctrine (although dedicating his work to the Archbishop of Canterbury, and praising John Hough, Bishop of Worcester, in his second book). Bacon and Newton are obvious candidates for praise,[45] Hough less so; yet the nonagenarian cleric is

> Ille, decus mitrae, Libertatisque satelles,
> Dum tanti tempus propugnatoris egebat
> Houghius; . . . (2. 284–6)
> The Mitre's glory, Freedom's constant friend,
> In times which ask'd a champion to defend. (300–1, in Jenyns' translation).

---

[45] Named at 1. 112, 116.

Hough's heroism had been shown in 1687, when he had been ejected by James II from the presidency of Magdalen College, Oxford;[46] the college's resistance to the king's plan to turn it into a Roman Catholic seminary was a crucial prelude to the Glorious Revolution. Though Magdalen was generally Tory (and was to produce Dr Sacheverell, the fieriest Tory of them all), this was too much to bear; even after Hough's reinstatement, the college refused to join the rest of the university in welcoming the birth of James' son, later known as the Old Pretender. If the stress on Hough's battles for liberty indicates Browne's political stance, so also does the dedication. The Archbishop of Canterbury in 1754 was Thomas Herring—a distinctly fishy prelate, for anyone of Jacobite sympathies. He had earned the primacy by his behaviour during the Jacobite invasion of 1745, when as Archbishop of York he rallied support, and raised cash, for the government: 'His rousing speech . . . captured the patriotic imagination as nothing previously had. It was to remain long in the collective mind of patriotic Protestantism and did something to enhance the Yorkshireman's perception of his special place in English history.'[47] Many loyal Whigs, like the king himself, were not Anglican, and a broadly Christian outlook is appropriate for Browne, as an admirer of Herring. Nor is Browne parochial; he ridicules some philosophical systems, particularly Stoicism in book 2, but he is also happy to collect evidence from far afield, including oriental religions. Here he describes the burning of Indian widows:

> Nec minus uxores fama celebrantur Eoae:
> Non illae lacrymis, non foemineo ululatu
> Fata virum plorant; verum, (mirabile dictu!)
> Conscenduntque rogum, flammaque vorantur eadem.
> Nimirum credunt veterum sic posse maritum
> Ire ipsas comites, taedamque novare sub umbris. (1. 177–82)

In Soame Jenyns' translation (lines 211–8):

> Nor is less fam'd the oriental wife
> For stedfast virtue, and contempt of life:
> These heroines mourn not with loud female cries
> Their husbands lost, or with o'erflowing eyes;
> But, strange to tell! their funeral piles ascend,
> And in the same sad flames their sorrows end;
> In hopes with them beneath the shades to rove,
> And there renew their interrupted love.

---

[46] Hay's translation reminds the reader of this, with the note 'Bp of Worcester, turned out of Magdalen College by James II' (p. 35); Jenyns leaves him to remember the details by himself. On Hough and William Digby (whose relationship to Dolben is discussed in Ch. 7), cf. H. H. Erskine-Hill, *The Social Milieu of Alexander Pope* (New Haven and London, 1975), Ch. 5 (esp. pp. 140–1, 148–9).

[47] P. Langford, *A Polite and Commercial People* (Oxford, 1989), pp. 202–3.

The subject had been treated by classical writers, and Browne may be remembering, in particular, Propertius 3. 13. 15–22, though without direct allusion. The Virgilian phrases are clear in Browne's Latin; he takes *foemineo ululatu* from *Aen.* 4. 667 (n.b. *fama* in the previous line), and the whole passage is reminiscent of Dido, who did renew her marriage in the underworld. Her story is not quite the same as that of the Indians (in both Propertius and the eighteenth century): they follow their first husbands immediately, while Dido waited, and was driven to suicide by Aeneas' desertion. There is thus a neat tension between the Indian situation and the epic story, which Browne can recall to our minds by allusion, without needing to spell out the relevance of the example. When classical allusion can be used in this creative way, it is a sign of sophistication in the poet, not of mere slavish imitation and lazy borrowing.

The use of Indian material is also interesting (since it seems probable that Browne is not simply remembering Propertius and other ancient sources). The practice of suttee, widow-burning, was outlawed by the British in 1829, and controversial from the 1780s onwards.[48] In the early 1750s, India was a rather unusual interest: British power was thin and in danger of getting thinner (the French had taken Madras in 1746, restoring it in 1748 with the peace of Aix-la-Chapelle).[49] A likely source is Alexander Hamilton, *A New Account of the East Indies* (Edinburgh, 1727; reprinted London, 1744): he records odd variations on the horrible event, such as the escape of one widow, rescued by a European, and another, strong in limb and will, dragging an unfaithful former lover to join her in the flames.[50] Browne treats suttee with amused detachment, as a custom that illustrates his point, not adopting the patronising outrage of later colonialists.

Apart from Gray and Browne, there are other notable didactic poets from eighteenth-century Britain. At the beginning of the century, the descriptive poem, a related genre, was highly popular; Addison made a name for himself by writing in Latin about barometers, puppet-shows and bowling-greens.[51] An obscure Irishman, Demetrius McEncroe, wrote a fine botanical poem, *Connubia Florum* (1727), praised by Atterbury and influencing Erasmus Darwin.[52] In the 1790s we can find splendidly poetic expositions of the systems of Descartes, Plato, and Newton from the pen of Robert Percy Smith.[53] Scientific and philosophical subjects are regular topics for brief sets of elegiac verses, offering an amusing, if trivial, angle on their themes. The more pessimistic Gray, while offering his fragmentary fourth book, thought that 'Literature (to take it in its

---

[48] The first usage of the word 'suttee' noted in *OED* is from 1786; Jenyns, though he does not use it, may possibly hint at it with 'stedfast virtue': Sanskrit *sati* = 'virtuous wife'.
[49] Cf. J. P. Lawford, *Britain's Army in India* (London, 1978), pp. 68–85.
[50] Quoted, with other examples, in H. Yule, A. C. Burrell, *Hobson-Jobson* (London, 1886), pp. 669–70.
[51] Cf. Thomas Bisse, *Microscopium*, etc.: Bradner, pp. 224–5.   [52] Bradner, p. 275.
[53] Bradner, pp. 304–8. Mentioned also in Ch. 10.

most comprehensive sense . . .) seems indeed drawing apace to its Dissolution; and remarkably since the beginning of the war [of the Austrian Succession] . . .'[54] But reports of its death were exaggerated.

Samuel Johnson's unsatisfactory achievement

It is unfair to blame Samuel Johnson for failing to be a great Latin poet. Nevertheless, that is what I propose to do. As a critic, he was fully prepared to comment on the failings of others, and he deserves the critical attention of posterity. He was not a great Latin poet. It is questionable whether he was a very good one. The small scale of his work, and its variable quality, make it difficult to judge what he might have produced, if circumstances and his own inclination had allowed it. Gray's small production was the result of indolence and a private income; Johnson produced far more, driven both by greater devotion to scholarship and by the need to make his living as a prominent literary figure. The vast majority of Johnson's work was in prose; he had the talent to be a major poet in both Latin and English, but in neither language did he devote sufficient energy to the task. Commercial pressures are a partial explanation: he could not afford to concentrate on writing large amounts of poetry unless he could be sure of selling it. It was also a matter of temperament. Johnson is a fascinating example of the conflict between the competing impulses of scholarship and polite literature. He tended towards scholarship, tempered by creativity. One cannot imagine Bentley (for all his skill as a theologian) exploring moral themes in a work like Johnson's *Rasselas*. Nor can one see Alsop commencing, or Gray persevering with, such a labour as the *Dictionary*.

Some recent work, especially that of Jonathan Clark, has stressed the importance to Johnson of non-juring and Jacobite feelings, and the central place of the classical tradition in his writings.[55] There is also a new edition of his Latin and Greek poetry, with text, translation, and extravagant commentary by Barry Baldwin.[56] It remains to be seen whether or not this attention will spark off

---

[54] *Corresp.* 1. 265.

[55] See J. C. D. Clark, *Samuel Johnson* (Cambridge, 1994); R. DeMaria (jun.), *The Life of Samuel Johnson: a critical biography* (Oxford and Cambridge, MA, 1993). Clark makes good use of Greenwood's *William King* to support his argument. DeMaria frequently quotes in Greek, nearly all of it wrong in some respect: examples on pp. 47, 125, 165, 199, 228, 231, 259, 300, 324; my confidence in the rest of the book is not absolute, but he does have much of interest.

[56] B. Baldwin, *The Latin & Greek Poems of Samuel Johnson* (London, 1995). His dust-jacket promises a 'substantial introduction', which turns out to be pp. 1–8, tripping along via Joyce, Rimbaud, and P. G. Wodehouse; commentary follows each poem, pp. 9–268. He has some fascinating material: because Johnsonians will (or ought to) make much use of his work, I record my occasional disagreements.

further detailed examination of his Latin. As an aspect of Johnson's career, it is
crucial. As literature in its own right, it is rather less impressive than much other
Neo-Latin, particularly that of Alsop. Baldwin is enthusiastically erratic; he does
not offer an overall assessment of Johnson as a Latin poet. It is not easy to say
what is distinctly Johnsonian about a minor set of elegiacs; hence, stylistic
criteria for assessing the *dubia* are not helpful.[57] He piles on information about
classical parallels, sometimes sensible, sometimes not too close to the mark.[58] He
offers faint praise and periodic criticism to an American MA thesis of the
1950s,[59] without consistently surpassing its sophistication. He points out faults
in the printing and layout of previous editions, while adding his own.[60] More
seriously, he frequently misleads on matters of metre.[61]

The classics were central to Johnson's literary life, the source of his learning
and the inspiration for English poetry: as is noted above, his two substantial
English poems, *London* and *The Vanity of Human Wishes*, are both imitations of
Juvenal, that acerbic observer of a corrupted society. The imitations are notably
successful as English poetry, and have offered much scope for comparisons with
Juvenal. Since Johnson is engaging in free imitation, not translation, there are
naturally many differences; their significance, if any, cannot always be
fathomed.[62] Discussion of Johnson's supposed innovations may rest on ques-
tionable assumptions about Juvenal's position, not necessarily shared by either
the ancient or the modern poet. DeMaria takes it for granted that Juvenal is a
Stoic;[63] if rejection of Stoicism is a part of Johnson's message, he is more likely to
be thinking of modern examples (such as Addison's *Cato*). No doubt he would

[57] E.g., p. 172: 'a recognisable classical allusion in the Johnsonian manner' (i.e., the manner of virtually all
Neo-Latin).
[58] E.g., p. 51, 'it is hard not to believe that Johnson is here influenced by Quintilian'; p. 56, 'I seem to hear
tinkles from Ovid', etc.
[59] E. V. Mohr, *Dr Johnson's Latin Poems* (Columbia M.A. dissertation, 1952); 'the concept of literary
criticism is almost touchingly naive' (Baldwin, p. viii). At least Baldwin gives us Mr Spock (p. 132).
[60] There are problems with the Greek, p. 47, with wild apostrophes, one dignified with a circumflex
accent; elegiacs are printed without indentation, pp. 164–6, 214.
[61] 'Habeo dedi quod alteri . . .' (p. 96): not 'trochaic septenarii' but iambic dimeters; the translation from
Euripides (pp. 122–4) he calls, vaguely, a 'medley of lyrical lines': I take it to be anapaestic dimeters (i.e. four
feet per line), rounded off with a monometer; 'O qui benignus crimina ignoscis, pater . . .' (p. 142): not
'iambic dimeters' but iambic trimeters; 'Nunquam jugera messibus onusta, aut . . .' (p. 225: hendecasyllable)
does not scan (it needs a consonant after *messibus*).
[62] E.g. unconvincing remarks on 'differences' in diction in *London*, DeMaria pp. 51–2; I do not see why
'oblique case and weak syntactical position prevent it [*virtutibus*] from achieving [Johnson's] abstract sense';
he cites E. A. & L. D. Bloom, 'Johnson's *London* and its Juvenalian texts', *Huntington Library Quarterly* 34
(1970), pp. 1–23.
[63] E.g. 'Johnson rejects Juvenal's Stoicism', pp. 137, 139. The quotation from Juvenal on p. 135 omits the
most important word. The suggestion of a shift from the 'more obviously political third satire', p. 130,
seems to misunderstand what political poetry might mean for Juvenal, and conflate it with Johnson's very
different circumstances.

remember what Juvenal has to say about fraudulent homosexual Stoics in the
second satire. In *The Vanity of Human Wishes*, the extended space given to the
scholar seems important, with clear personal feeling behind the famous lines
(159–60):

> There mark what ills the scholar's life assail,
> Toil, envy, want, the patron, and the jail.

As well as expanding the space, he changes the emphasis. The case of Laud, the
learned man who manages to escape obscurity, is a closer parallel to Juvenal's
examples, Cicero and Demosthenes. The most striking aspect of Juvenal's Cicero
is his laughably poor poetry, *ridenda poemata* (10. 124). This has no echo in
Johnson, despite the popularity of attacks on poor poetry, Pope's recent *Dunciad*
being an obvious model. No doubt it would not fit Laud, or any other suitable
modern figure. Nevertheless, an observant eighteenth-century reader would
note its absence, and wonder whether Johnson was frightened of similar ridicule.
There are potential dangers in the imitation of a razor-sharp original.

Among Johnson's early projects was a proposal (of 1734) to publish the poems
of Politian, with a history of Neo-Latin in Italy.[64] This was abandoned, for lack of
encouragement (although Pope's anthology, discussed in Chapter 4, did appear a
few years later). The books he had taken up to Pembroke College, Oxford,
included several volumes of modern Latin, among them Buchanan, Vida, both
Scaligers, the contemporary Frenchman Landesius (André Deslandes), and the
seventeenth-century Frenchman Quilletus (Claude Quillet).[65] Quillet's *Callipae-
dia* is called by DeMaria, inappropriately, a 'student's book'. It is an elegant
didactic poem, on pregnancy and eugenics (of more interest to doctors and
parents than the average student, but worth reading for its literary qualities); a
Jacobite might appreciate and reapply to his own age the attack on English
revolutionary licence in book 4, written shortly after the execution of Charles I.

The writing of dictionaries, like their obsessive perusal, could be seen as a
dry, ungentlemanly labour.[66] Johnson enlivened his with carefully selected
quotations.[67] He commemorated its revision (1772; for the fourth edition,
1773) with one of his best Latin poems, in 54 hexameters, choosing for his title
the famous Greek phrase, *Gnothi Seauton* [know yourself].[68] His knowledge of

---

[64] Cf. Clark, pp. 19–20.   [65] DeMaria, p. 16.
[66] Clark, p. 14, quotes 'turning over voluminous dictionaries' (though he does not say so, perhaps recalling Alsop's *Aesop*: see Ch. 4).
[67] On non-jurors cited in Johnson's *Dictionary*: Clark, p. 131 (n.b. also Bowyer as a non-juring printer, p. 155); A. Reddick, *The Making of Johnson's Dictionary* (Cambridge, 1990).
[68] Baldwin, *Johnson*, pp. 75–86. He alludes to the younger Scaliger, line 2 (cf. Baldwin, p. 82). This poem has been discussed by several scholars, who are cited (and castigated for failing to spot classical parallels) by Baldwin.

himself leads him to wry thoughts on the limits of his intellectual capacity, and to melancholia. Another significant hexameter poem (36 lines: 'Sanguine dum tumido . . .'), addressed to Dr Thomas Lawrence, begins with physical afflictions, and moves on to reflect on attitudes to natural philosophy.[69] His relationship to Dr Lawrence, a learned physician, makes an interesting comparison with the members of Alsop's circle. Johnson is more serious and inward-looking, more concerned with his own symptoms;[70] Alsop occasionally refers to the symptoms of others (e.g. 2. 16). Of Johnson's various elegiac poems, perhaps the most interesting is the nostalgic piece on Stowe Mill, which seems to rely on complicated classical allusions.[71] *Geographia Metrica*, in 36 hexameters, versifies dull information (not unlike Gray's beetles): the poem merely plays with numbers, and is scarcely similar to the Renaissance marine eclogues to which Baldwin compares it. The contrast between vast and tiny areas (Asia, 10,250,000 square miles; Lucca, 280) may have amused him.[72] If he had channelled this scientific precision into didactic poetry, rather than frigid exercises, something better might have come of it.

Johnson's Latin poetry includes a small number of odes; the odes written on Skye have regularly been praised, while other poems have received less attention.[73] The sapphic ode *In Theatro*,[74] an amusing piece of self-mockery, suggests the awkwardness of an aged scholar among the entertainments of society. He had used the alcaic metre to seek patronage from Edward Cave, publisher of the *Gentleman's Magazine*, which he celebrates for its combination of the serious and the witty (*Ad Urbanum*).[75] The sapphic ode from Skye ('Permeo terras . . .')[76] is chiefly devoted to Mrs Thrale, on whom Johnson's thoughts centre. Its alcaic companion ('Ponti profundis . . .')[77] has more philosophical content, attacking the Stoics, and showing how God controls the turbulent waves of the mind. This final stanza suggests mental anguish: the combination of pain and fervent rather

---

[69] Baldwin, *Johnson*, pp. 86–91. Commenting on line 9 (p. 90), he fails to note a clear allusion to Horace, *Carm.* 1. 1. 3, 'Sunt quos curriculo' (with an indicative verb, *pace* his suggested emendation). The fanatical sportsman is the first of several characters Horace declines to imitate; Johnson similarly puts forward a choice between the blinkered and the enquiring mind.

[70] Other poems to Lawrence include five alcaic stanzas ('Fateris ergo . . .': Baldwin, *Johnson*, pp. 117–19), advising him with (perhaps heavy-handed) humour, and anapaests on his symptoms ('Nunc mihi facilis . . .': Baldwin, pp. 129–32; also in T. Kaminski's pamphlet, *Five Latin Poems*: Samuel Johnson Society, Chicago, 1991).

[71] Baldwin, *Johnson*, pp. 157–62; might he allude to more than one myth about Nisus (*pace* Baldwin's rejection of the Yale edition's 'aberration')?

[72] Baldwin, *Johnson*, pp. 152–7; 'One epigram (an elegiac couplet, in fact, not pure hexameters) and a single extended metrical *tour de force* hardly constitute a trend.' I take the 'epigram' to be on the speed of sound ('Quot vox missa . . .': p. 151); this is in 'pure' hexameters, not elegiacs, *pace* Baldwin [!], and its second line is similarly numeric.

[73] E.g. Bradner, pp. 250–2. Baldwin, *Johnson*, p. 98, cites other admirers, and wishes to redress the balance by stressing 'generally overlooked qualities' elsewhere.   [74] Baldwin, *Johnson*, pp. 71–5.

[75] Baldwin, *Johnson*, pp. 37–41.   [76] Baldwin, *Johnson*, pp. 103–6.   [77] Baldwin, *Johnson*, pp. 97–102.

than confident Christian faith help to make this one of Johnson's most powerful poems. Baldwin finds line 18, 'Rex summe, solus tu regis arbiter' [highest king, you alone rule as judge . . .], 'very feeble', because repetitious. One might equally find the repetition solemn and moving (and offering the chance for alliteration and chiasmus: R, S/ S, R); in any case, the second half of the line is needed to provide a subject and verb for line 17, so can hardly be called superfluous padding.

A poem written by Johnson on this home of romantic Jacobitism, the island of Flora Macdonald and the Pretender's escape, might reasonably be supposed to hint at the past. There is nothing explicit, unless one were to take 'Rex summe' as a nod towards a king over the water, as well as in heaven (a rather far-fetched notion, given the obvious religious reference: yet such cryptic hints can continuously lurk in the background). The second stanza emphasises present peacefulness. The stress on this point, and the way it is put, serve to remind one that things were not always thus. He uses the language of exile (*exulat*, line 5); the subject of that verb, *cura*, can mean not only 'care, trouble' but also 'the person for whom one cares'.[78] He contrasts *credo* [I believe] in line 5 with *certe* [for sure] in line 6. The verb *credo* may suggest political (or religious) convictions, as well as an opinion on a matter of fact. There is certainly peace now. One might remember, in the context of Hanoverian behaviour in the Highlands, the celebrated remark in Tacitus that conquerors devastate, and then call it peace.[79] In lines 7–8, *ira* [anger] and *maeror* [sadness] no longer lie in ambush (*insidias*). The idea of abstract qualities pouncing upon their victims is Horatian,[80] and one cannot be certain that Johnson is thinking of the real ambushes set for the Pretender. The Johnson of 1773 would still remember the political emotions of youth, and subdued, melancholy political reminiscence may be one of the strands in this enigmatic ode.

Johnson translated nearly a hundred epigrams from the Greek Anthology during sleepless nights towards the end of his life. Apart from their association with Johnson, most are not of great interest. Among the more impressive are a pair that offer a contrast between a pessimistic and optimistic outlook on life.[81] In turning these into Latin, Johnson could examine the two sides of his own character. He also selected Theocritus' epitaph for Hipponax, producing a fair Latin rendering in the metre of the limping iambic (or scazon), that Hipponax

---

[78] Cf. Virgil, *Aen.* 1. 678: 'puer . . . mea maxima cura', of Ascanius, Aeneas' son, about to lead the restoration of the exiles' fortunes; cf. also *Aen.* 10. 132; what better model for the Young Pretender?
[79] Tacitus, *Agricola* 30: 'libertatis extremos recessus' and 'sinus' (possible echoes in Johnson's lines 1 and 4), 'ubi solitudinem faciunt, pacem appellant'. Baldwin cites *Agricola* 10 (to illustrate 'profundis', and seas off Scotland), p. 100.   [80] Cf. *Carm.* 2. 16. 21–4 (with personified *Cura*).
[81] Baldwin, *Johnson*, pp. 231–4 (translating 9. 359–60).

had invented for his fierce satire, and which Theocritus uses in homage to him.[82] This too might act as a wry comment on Johnson's own life and poetry; he will not welcome scoundrels, but will provide a safe seat on which the good can snooze. The choice of *marmor* [marble monument] for the tomb may not be significant; it is a natural expression, and works well at the end of the line (where the limp adds emphasis). Possibly it recalls his early political satire, *Marmor Norfolciense*,[83] a work in the spirit, if not the metre, of Hipponax, where Jacobite comments are thinly disguised as Whig antiquarianism. In his last month of life, he also turned to translation from Latin into English (of Horace, *Carm.* 4. 7), summing up 'that Roman finality from which his religion offered deliverance.'[84] Most of his Latin poetry was deeply personal, written on a small scale for a small audience; in that he resembles Alsop, but the flashes of brilliance are fewer. One regrets the lack of any attempt at something truly great.

The discreet charm of Vincent Bourne

One of the most popular of eighteenth-century Latinists was Vincent Bourne, admired by Cowper and Lamb.[85] He was an accomplished writer of epigrams, the master of the witty theme verses that were a central part of education. As well as those elegiacs, he attempted some short poems in other metres, including the occasional ode. His chief lyric effort is the sapphic ode *Anus Saecularis*, in 11 stanzas, turned by Cowper into 10 English stanzas, *Ode on the Death of a Lady, who lived one hundred years, and died on her birthday,* 1728, with short and punchy trochaic lines to bring home the message. That message Storey takes to be 'a rather soured comment on life . . . . a tempered world-weariness . . . in what amounts to a fine balance between profundity and near-colloquialism. . . . he combines admiration with a strong sense of his own inadequacies, and human frailty in general.'[86] The central portion of the poem is pretty pessimistic:

[82] Baldwin, *Johnson*, p. 254 (translating 13. 3). I assume that Baldwin takes it to be in ordinary, non-limping iambics, thus quite missing the point of both Greek and Latin; all he says is that 'three poems are iambic' (p. 202): the other two are ordinary, pp. 252, 260. The scazon is used in Latin by Catullus (e.g. poem 8, quite a well-known piece) and Martial, and numerous Neo-Latin authors.

[83] Baldwin, *Johnson*, pp. 63–8 (in pseudo-medieval metre: Leonine hexameters, in fact, as Baldwin almost observes, p. 67). Cf. Clark, pp. 159–60.

[84] Clark, p. 254; but n.b., Horace's last judgement (by Minos, rather than Christ) comes after the passage he quotes. Clark's ending is perhaps a trifle unfair: 'By comparison with Johnson's apologia, that of his protégé was a vain boast' (p. 255); Boswell cited Horace, *Carm.* 4. 9. 25 ('Vixere fortes . . .'), which makes the point that the unrecorded, however heroic, will be forgotten. Boswell is still read, and has been the most essential factor in perpetuating the fame of his hero.

[85] Bradner, pp. 266–73; M. Storey, in J. W. Binns, ed., *The Latin Poetry of English Poets* (London, 1974), pp. 121–49.

[86] Storey, pp. 143–5; he quotes lines 1–12, 41–4. He prints 'woman kind' for 'human kind' in Cowper's fifth line (a feminist slip?).

> Occulit mors insidias, ubi vix
> Vix opinari est, rapidaeve febris
> Vim repentinam, aut male pertinacis
>   Semina morbi.
> Sin brevem posset superare vita
> Terminum, quicquid superest, vacivum
> Illud ignavis superest, et imbe-
>   cillibus annis.
> Detrahunt multum minuuntque sorti
> Morbidi questus gemitusque anheli;
> Ad parem crescunt numerum diesque
>   Atque dolores.
> Siquis haec vitet (quotus ille quisque est!)
> Et gradu pergendo laborioso
> Ad tuum, fortasse tuum, moretur
>   Reptilis aevum:
> At videt, moestum tibi saepe visum, in-
> jurias, vim, furta, dolos, et inso-
> lentiam, quo semper eunt, eodem
>   Ire tenore.[87]

Cowper's version runs as follows:

> Seeds of merciless disease
> Lurk in all that we enjoy;
> Some that waste us by degrees,
> Some that suddenly destroy.
>
> And, if life o'erleap the bourn
> Common to the sons of men,
> What remains, but that we mourn,
> Dream, and dote, and drivel then?
>
> Fast as moons can wax and wane
> Sorrow comes; and while we groan,
> Pant with anguish, and complain,
> Half our years are fled and gone.
>
> If a few (to few 'tis given),
> Lingering on this earthly stage,
> Creep and halt with steps uneven
> To the period of an age,
>
> Wherefore live they, but to see
> Cunning, arrogance, and force,
> Sights lamented much by thee,
> Holding their accustom'd course!

[87] Lines 13–32. In 1734 edn., p. 90; Mitford's edn., 1840, p. 120.

Bourne's Latin is bold. In the first stanza quoted, there is the repeated *vix*, followed by further alliteration in *-ve* and *vim*, then *male pertinacis*: the allusion to Horace[88] is shockingly tasteless. He takes a famous phrase about the amorous games of the young, and applies it to insidious disease. The shock is probably deliberate, the bad taste purposeful. We think back to the rest of Horace's ode, contrasting a frozen world with the opportunities of youth, 'donec virenti canities abest/morosa' [whilst green youth lacks glum white hair (lines 17–18)]. There is nothing to be proud of in reaching one's century, if one hasn't scored freely on the way.

In the next stanza we see a drivelling old imbecile; there is more alliteration (two prominent words beginning with 'v', three words with 'v' in the middle: *vacivum* being a striking word, from the language of Plautine comedy). Cowper's alliterative line catches the tone of contempt. Like Alsop, Bourne is free with the metre; with 'pergendo laborioso' we lack the usual caesura (and also shorten a final 'o': see Chapter 3 for discussion of these points). The last stanza I quote is particularly bold, with words run over the ends of both the first and second lines; his list of five evils, emphasised by this bizarre use of the metre, is far more powerful than Cowper's three, well chosen though they are. The next two stanzas, condensed by Cowper to one, offer a depressing, almost nihilist picture of a world in which nothing changes. Cowper's shortened version sounds trite and proverbial: '. . . Earth produces nothing new' (for 'Nil inest rebus novitatis').[89] Bourne's additional stanza allows him to have more than a simple cliché, and to stress yet again the feeble foolishness of man ('nugarum et ineptiarum', line 38). He does not seem to have much respect for the old woman, or himself, or indeed the reader. I am not entirely sure that, in Storey's words, 'he manages to steer clear of anything that we get from the "grave-yard school"': we are in similar territory to Gray's *Ode on a distant prospect of Eton College* (if not quite the *Elegy* itself). Compare the penultimate stanza of the Eton *Ode*, written eight years after Bourne's:

> Lo! in the vale of years beneath
> A grisly troop are seen,
> The painful family of Death,
> More hideous than their Queen:
> This racks the joints, this fires the veins,
> That every labouring sinew strains,
> These in the deeper vitals rage:
> Lo! Poverty, to fill the band,
> That numbs the soul with icy hand,
> And slow-consuming Age.[90]

---

[88] *Carm.* 1. 9. 24, 'male pertinaci'.   [89] Cf. *Ecclesiastes* 1: 9, 'there is no new thing under the sun', etc.
[90] Lines 81–90; cf. R. Lonsdale, ed., *Poems* (London, 1969), p. 62, with parallels from Dryden, Garth, Pope, etc. Other 'graveyard' thoughts in Latin: cf. Jortin, quoted by Bradner, p. 240.

While the sight of youth brings these thoughts to Gray, Bourne gets the same idea, less surprisingly, from age. Gray may have remembered Bourne's Latin, among other possible sources. Bourne's ode is not cosy, but cold-hearted, cynical, and quite subtle. To gain anything positive from it at all, one has to remember Horace's advice, in the poem to which he alludes, 'quid sit futurum cras fuge quaerere' [stop asking what might happen tomorrow],[91] and get on with one's life. His elegiac poems rarely sustain such sophistication. This school-master's bourgeois wit is ambiguously charming; a reticent paw occasionally extends itself to scratch.[92] *Fanaticus* depicts a preacher in wildly satirical hex-ameters, revelling in the almost macaronic quality of some rare or new words (e.g., 'Stattacitus, multumque screans . . .' [rapid (?) and howling], line 2).[93] Hogarth's harsh art he celebrates in Catullan hendecasyllables.[94] The 'Harlot's Progress' is described in suitable language:

> . . . Ut tentat pretio rudem puellam
> Corruptrix anus, impudens, obesa;
> Ut se vix reprimit libidinosus
> Scortator, veneri paratus omni: . . .
>
> how the shameless, fat, corrupting old bawd tempts a country girl with money; how the lustful whoremonger can scarcely restrain himself, ready for every vice. (lines 7–10)

The ending of the poem sounds Catullan, in vocabulary (*cachinno*), and with repetition, a superlative, and a near oxymoron (laughter can be rigid, if from a stiff person, but the idea is bold):

> Censura utilior tua aequiorque
> Omni vel satirarum acerbitate,
> Omni vel rigidissimo cachinno.
>
> your judgement is more useful and fairer than any bitter satire, or any inflexible laughter. (lines 24–6)

Thus we are reminded of Hogarth's underlying moral message. Another sapphic ode, in 9 stanzas, deals with a Catullan theme; *Ode Nuptialis* is a blander work than *Anus Saecularis*, pleasantly moral and only slightly risqué, developing (in alternating choruses) the traditional marriage metaphor of the vine wedded to the elm-tree.[95] There are some nice repetitions, and the poem ends with an appropriate one-word adonic ('Connubialem'). If Bourne had attempted more

---

[91] *Carm.* 1. 9. 13: a variation on the 'carpe diem' theme (cf. *Carm.* 1. 11. 8).
[92] Storey discusses his cat poem rather fancifully, pp. 129–30: and is duly scratched in review by J. Diggle, *Times Higher Education Supplement* (13 Sep. 1974); Storey does have other interesting examples of Bourne's technique: 'constant refusal to strive for effect' (p. 146).
[93] *Carmina Comitialia* (1721), p. 85; Mitford's edn., 1840, p. 149.
[94] In 1734 edn., p. 146; Mitford's edn., 1840, p. 190.
[95] In 1743 edn., p. 202; Mitford's edn., 1840, p. 213. Cf. Catullus 62, especially lines 49–58.

lyric poetry, the results might have been very fine. What he did write, though modest in scope, is full of clever touches.

Popham's anthology

Towards the end of the eighteenth century, Neo-Latin culture was still suffi-ciently vigorous to produce a new and very full anthology. Edward Popham's *Selecta Poematum Anglorum Latina* (a title perhaps deliberately reminiscent of Pope) appeared at Bath in three volumes, the first two in 1774, the third in 1776.[96] The fashionable world might combine elegant Latin with their flirta-tions, gambling, dancing, novel-reading, and immersion in supposedly salu-brious springs. A much altered second edition, in one volume, was printed by Dodsley (London, 1779). The final poem in both editions is Browne's *De Animi Immortalitate*; the many other poems, covering over 500 pages (even in the shorter version), represent most of the genres of eighteenth-century poetry, from both obscure and famous authors. There are Biblical paraphrases, poems on contemporary and scientific subjects, and some translations of English verse. Popham finds a lively and unusual alcaic ode on a chemical theme, dated 1714, by one R. Sedgwick, MB, of Catharine Hall, Cambridge. Its last two stanzas enquire into a girl's loss of appetite (from too many test tubes, perhaps):

> Quae causa tantae, Chymica, nauseae?
> Quid? Num calorem Lesbia non habet?
>   Natura molli num puellae
>   Pectora frigidiora fecit?
> At intumescunt sanguine mammulae:
> Salitque venis purpureus liquor:
>   At ipse flagro, et palpitantem
>   Urit amor meliore flamma.

> What causes such nausea, Chemistry? What? Surely Lesbia doesn't lack heat? Surely nature hasn't given a cold heart to a soft girl? But her little breasts are swelling with blood, and red liquid leaps in her veins; but I myself am on fire, and love burns me, palpitating, with a finer flame.[97]

Samuel Johnson is represented by his version of Pope's *Messiah*.[98] Gray's original odes, and *Gaurus Mons*, also make their appearance.[99] But it might be appropriate to end this chapter, that has surveyed a wide range of glittering

---

[96] Bradner, pp. 292–6.   [97] Vol. 2 (1774), p. 79.
[98] Vol. 3 (1776), p. 16; 1779 edn., p. 304. Cf. Baldwin, pp. 26–33.
[99] Vol. 3 (1776), pp. 168, 194; 1779 edn., pp. 447, 462.

material (some of it not wholly solid), with a Latin sapphic version of Gray's *Ode on the Death of a Favourite Cat, Drowned in a Tub of Gold Fishes*:

> Quae placet cordi, placet aut vaganti
> Lumini, praedam fugias; nocebit
> Tacta; non omnis licita est, nec omne,
>   Quod nitet, Aurum.[100]

> Not all that tempts your wandering eyes
> And heedless hearts is lawful prize;
> Nor all that glisters gold.

---

[100] 'E. B. G.', in Popham, *Selecta Poemata* (London, 1779), p. 98.

9
A Multitude of Muses

The writing of Neo-Latin was by no means confined to the major poets discussed in previous chapters. Large numbers also composed occasional verse; their poetic talents may have been less remarkable, but their social standing was often higher. Their work, in general, survives only through the medium of the university collection, a fascinating literary genre, and one of the utmost importance for the history of British universities and of British Neo-Latin culture.

The genre of the commemorative collection

For a period of about two hundred years, from the middle of the sixteenth century to the middle of the eighteenth, the two English universities regularly produced official or semi-official collections of poetry in commemoration of major public events (whether of national or more local significance).[1] There were also occasional collections published by schools, individual colleges (mostly in the early seventeenth century), or the universities in Scotland and Ireland. There is a book from Woodstock School, *Votivum Carolo Secundo* (1660); another from Westminster, *Duci Glocestriae . . .* (1700), included a contribution by Alsop's friend John Dolben (discussed in Chapter 7). Edinburgh University and School both issued volumes in 1661. The Scottish collections tended to be smaller than the English, but otherwise comparable. Thus, for example, *ΕἸΣΟΔΙΑ Musarum Edinensium* (Edinburgh, 1633) contains seven Latin hexameter poems, seven in elegiacs, three in Greek, and two in English, by fourteen authors, some writing quite long pieces. By the eighteenth century, the field was largely left to the English, although from time to time we find works such as

---

[1] On the origins of the genre, see Binns, *Intellectual Culture*, pp. 34–45; Bradner, pp. 99–102, 206–7; on the bibliography of Cambridge volumes, H. Forster, 'The rise and fall of the Cambridge Muses (1603–1763)', *Transactions of the Cambridge Bibliographical Society* 8 (1982), pp. 141–172; J. C. T. Oates, 'Cambridge books of congratulatory verses (1603–40) and their binders', *Transactions of the Cambridge Bibliographical Society* 1 (1949–53), pp. 395–421; on Oxford English poets of the 1630s, R. A. Anselment, 'The Oxford University poets and Caroline Panegyric', *John Donne Journal* 3 (1984), pp. 181–201 (for Anselment, 'Latin and Greek remain understandably daunting', p. 181). For further English comparisons, see D. Kay, *Melodious Tears: English Funeral Elegy from Spenser to Milton* (Oxford, 1990): but very little on Latin, 'that is another subject', p. 6.

Lachrymae in obitum J. Smithaei (Edinburgh, 1736), or *Gratulationes in Regis et Reginae Nuptias* (Dublin, 1761).[2] The collections were read in the metropolis, but rarely published there; one does not find comparable corporate efforts from the Inns of Court, for example, where individuals or small groups, rather than a whole academic community, might engage in literature.

A large number of poets would contribute to each of the Oxford and Cambridge volumes: often about a hundred, and sometimes considerably more. All sections of the university were represented: heads of houses, fellows of all ages, and, among the students, both prominent aristocrats and obscure young scholars. The collections were an important (perhaps even the most important) way for the university to demonstrate its genius and public spirit, for the colleges to compete for pre-eminence, and for individuals to establish a reputation for polite learning (and possibly obtain some patronage as a result). And so,

> Whenever Princes grace the nuptial State,
> Or fall a victim to impartial Fate;
> The poet strikes his diff'rent-sounding Lyre,
> As joy or grief the various Notes inspire . . .[3]

The tone of the poems did indeed differ according to the subject matter; but also, within each volume, there is a surprising variety of differing sounds. In this Chapter I sample some of them, in both Latin and English.[4]

There is evidence of rivalry between Oxford and Cambridge collections, suggesting that they were taken seriously as proofs of status. A Cambridge poet, in 1658, suggested Oxford was lapsing into senility:

> Oxonium infantem jactat novisse sororem:
>   At nos bis pueros novimus esse senes.
> Oxonio linguam, et senio sibi lumen ademptum,
>   Restituit medica Granta benigna manu . . .

> Oxford boasts that she knew her sister as an infant; but we know that the old fall into second childhood. Kind Cambridge has restored to Oxford, with her medicinal hand, the eloquence and light that had been removed through old age.[5]

---

[2] Note also Bernard's Harvard collection of 1761 (discussed in Ch. 3).

[3] J. Hoo (Magdalen), in *Pietas* (Oxford, 1738).

[4] I quote from a disproportionate number of Oxford English poems, in the hope that they may be of interest to the reader, and as a counterpart to Forster's 'Cambridge Muses'; I have prepared a list of the Oxford English poets: D. K. Money, 'A Diff'rent-Sounding Lyre: Oxford Commemorative Verse in English, 1613–1834', *Bodleian Library Record* 16 (1997), pp. 42–92 (list, pp. 58–92, preceded by a discussion taken partly from this Chapter). Further bibliographical and archive material will, I hope, appear in *Bodleian Library Record* and in a volume of conference proceedings (*Print for Free . . .*), ed. J. R. Raven (forthcoming).

[5] 'S. S. J. C. M. D. M. A.' (i.e. probably S. S. of Jesus College, MD and MA) in *Luctus et Gratulatio* (Cambridge, 1658).

This is part of a tradition of humorous attacks; from the early eighteenth century, the rival epigrams of Trapp and Browne are well known (and help to perpetuate the myth that Cambridge was thoroughly Hanoverian).[6] The rivalry raises its head in two sets of Cambridge verses from 1669; Oxford might boast of greater speed in producing its tributes, but their rivals attempt to turn the tables:

> Haud prius a Gallis Reginae, Oxonia, nosti
>   Interitum, spargis quam tua Threna foras:
> Sic Galli occipiunt nimio, quasi fulmina, cursu;
>   Lente accensa quibus fax superesse queat:
> Praecedant alii citius properando feretrum;
>   Ut deceat, tardo nos pede consequimur.

> No sooner did you hear from the French of the Queen's death, Oxford, than you scattered your laments abroad. Thus do the French hurry on with excessive speed, like thunderbolts; torches that are lit at leisure can outlast them. Let others rush to go before the hearse; as is more fitting, we follow at a slow pace.[7]

Another poem, 'Tardae Cantabrigiensium Lacrymae' [the slow tears of the Cambridge poets], expands on this point for 26 lines:

> . . . Namque dolet vere qui tacet atque stupet . . .
> Masculus est noster luctus gemitusque virilis,
>   Non oculos nostros, pectora flere putes . . .
>   . . . Qui natat in lacrymis, est levis ille dolor . . .
> Quin age: quae prior in luctu, nunc nemo rogabit;
>   Continuus falsae decidet imber aquae . . .

> For the true mourner is silent and amazed; our grief is masculine, our groans are those of men; you would think our hearts wept, not our eyes; it is a light sort of grief that swims in tears; come then, now no one will ask who was first in grief; a continual rain of insincere tears will fall . . .[8]

The most obvious feature of this literary genre is the sheer number of poets celebrating any individual event; this could lead to repetition and dullness, but it could also be seen as an advantage. The first of the Oxford poets to write in English, indeed, emphasises the honour resulting from the presence of so many contributions:

> One Homer was enough to blazon forth
> In a full loftie stile Ulisses praise,
> Caesar had Lucan to enroule his worth,

---

[6] Nichols, *Anecdotes* 3. 330; famous enough to be in the *Oxford Dictionary of Quotations* (2nd edn., 1953), pp. 87, 548.   [7] S. Hern, BA (Clare Hall), in *Threni Cantabrigienses* (Cambridge, 1669).
[8] J. Edwards, BD (St John's), ibid.

Unto the memory of endlesse daies:
Of thy deeds *Bodley*, from thine own pure spring
A thousand Homers and Sweet Lucans sing . . .[9]

The ancients are models; but the moderns have the strength of numbers, and no inferiority is acknowledged. 'A thousand' may be an exaggeration, but it is not an absurd one: I count more than 240 Oxford poets lamenting Bodley in print,[10] and unpublished tributes may have swelled that total still further.

Some mercenary Muses

Nearly all the poets, whether young students or senior academic figures, composed their own poems. Young aristocrats did sometimes receive help from tutors, or commission whole poems to be written on their behalf.[11] Of particular interest, in the context of the present study, is evidence that Alsop was involved in such a transaction; he is said to have received £3. 4s. 6d. for the poem in the collection of 1700 under the name of Sir Bourchier Wrey.[12] That poem is fairly conventional, although it compares well with the general standard of the collection. There is a witty stanza on the effect of the young prince's death, at an age when he was too young for serious courtship:

Te turba plorant aemula virgines,
Olim parantes illecebras tibi;
    Curamque formae jam relinquunt,
        Atque minus cupiunt placere.

The virgins lament you, a crowd of rivals; once they prepared their snares for you, now they cease to care about their appearance, and have less desire to please.[13]

Wrey's tutor was probably not Alsop (the archives suggest G. Bull), but he will have had a reputation as the better poet. The sum involved is reasonably large, perhaps a month's income for an average tutor, and is enough to tempt an author who has already made his name to forego the public credit of another contribution. It was fairly common practice for rich and lazy students to have others perform their everyday exercises: 'I shall furnish a Gentleman or two with an empty set of distichs'; '. . . 'twas usual . . . to make the exercises of idle scholars, either for money or something worth it from the buttery book.'[14]

[9] P. Prideaux (Exeter), in *Justa Funebria* (Oxford, 1613).
[10] In *Justa Funebria* and Merton College's *Bodleiomnema* (1613).
[11] Cf. Forster, p. 153 (n. 9), mentioning, from Oxford, Lord Stormont's verses of 1751.
[12] E. G. W. Bill, *Education at Christ Church, Oxford, 1600–1800* (Oxford, 1988), p. 230, citing *HMC, 11th report*, app. vii (1888), 155.   [13] 4. 10. 29–32; cf. 1. 6. 7–8.
[14] Bill, p. 230, citing British Library, ms. Add. 36707, fo. 36; Wood, *Athenae* 4. 853.

These college 'themes' were taken much less seriously than work for the printed university collections, but idle habits could easily spread from one to the other. Alsop's friend Noel Broxholme received £2. 2s. for an ode printed under the name of Edward Harley, and also wrote prize verses for the speaker's son, Thomas Bromley.[15] Many of the Encaenia verses were recited by young aristocrats, but written by college fellows.[16] The Encaenia books differ from the full collections in having far fewer poems, and those poems are rarely the unaided work of those whose names appear. In the full collections, one can generally trust the names that are recorded; but one must remember the possibility that aristocrats enjoyed outside assistance. Humbler scholars might sometimes find that their poems were judged insufficiently competent for the collections; Tickell briefly makes fun of them in *Spectator* 619: 'To the Gentleman of Oxford, who desires me to insert a copy of *Latin Verses* which were denied a Place in the University Book. Answer: *Nonumque prematur in annum*.'[17]

The eccentricity of using English; and some sophisticated Latin

The vast majority of the poems were in Latin; paradoxically, English first appears in substantial numbers in deference to a Frenchwoman, Queen Henrietta Maria. The first of these large groups of English poems opens with an explanation (from an anonymous pen, probably either the Vice-Chancellor's or that of the volume's editor) addressed to the Queen:

> Our Mother tongue is Latine, yet since You . . .
> Did with our Prince our English Language wed . . .
> Wee here translate some of our joyes, and sing
> This part to You, the other to the King.[18]

(He does not mean that an exact translation is to be provided: although some of the English poets also write in Latin, they produce quite separate pieces in each language.) Only a single poet, Frederick Tonstall of Exeter College, takes the more obvious route to the Queen's ear, and writes in French. Later, we find other ingenious excuses for addressing the Queen in English:

> . . . to you
> In every language praise and blessing's due.

[15] Bill, p. 230, citing *HMC Portland, 15th report*, app. iv. (1897), 516; cf. introduction to *HMC Portland 7*. xviii (Harley), ix-x, 110–13 (Bromley).

[16] Bodleian ms. Don. e. 53 often lists both reciters and authors, for verses from the 1733 Encaenia.

[17] D. F. Bond, ed., *The Spectator* (Oxford, 1965), 5. 116 (12 November 1714); the dismissive quotation is from Hor., *Ars Poet*. 388 [let it be suppressed until the ninth year]. Shortly afterwards *The Spectator* did print a Latin translation from Addison's *Cato* (Bond, 5. 146–7: no. 628, 3 Dec. 1714).

[18] Anon., in *Solis Britannici Perigaeum* (Oxford, 1633); on Henrietta Maria, cf. Anselment, p. 182.

> Ile like my native best though, when 'tis said
> That English brought Your Majesty to bed.[19]

It is particularly important to remember, when considering these collections, that English is a minority language in a literary genre dominated by a vigorous use of Neo-Latin. Students of modern English literature are not, in general, used to considering the vernacular in this light. Many official volumes have no English at all; only a semi-official production, such as the small book for Sir Bevill Grenvill in 1643, could be entirely in English. In these university collections, Latin outnumbers English overall by a ratio of about ten to one; even at the end of the tradition, English remains in the minority, its highest proportion being 40 per cent in the first of the two Oxford volumes of 1761 (Cambridge's highest is 35 per cent in 1751). And with the decline in original Latin, the tradition itself declined: there was insufficient enthusiasm to sustain it in any new guise as a largely vernacular genre.[20] (One may compare a similar, but far smaller, volume of tributes from 1834: only now is English in the majority, with 63 per cent.)[21]

This dominance of Latin means that those who wrote in English made a positive choice to flout convention by doing so. Few will have been unable to compose a Latin poem: the writing of Latin verses was a fundamental part of school and college education. In this sense, the seemingly strange remark quoted above, that Latin was the Oxford scholar's mother tongue, is not so strange after all. And those who could not write Latin might easily have remained silent, or hired some assistance. To obtain a high profile, Latin was virtually essential: until 1727 (for Oxford) or 1733 (Cambridge), English was generally banished, when admitted at all, to a separate section at the end of the book. This practice underlined the vernacular's inferiority to the learned languages. This is not, however, to say that the English poems would remain unread, or that only obscure men chose English.

Sometimes, a position at the very end could be seen as a place of honour. Joseph Trapp's poem of 1708 is the only English poem of the volume (and, indeed, of the whole period 1690–1715, which produced seven collections);[22] placed at the end, it is a surprise for the reader, and a bold statement by Trapp, as Professor of Poetry, of his poetic individuality. In Chapter 3, I discuss Alsop's

---

[19] M. Bate (St Edmund Hall), in *Horti Carolini Rosa Altera* (Oxford, 1640).

[20] One may speculate (as does Forster, p. 143) that the tradition died because there was nothing to celebrate under George III. But royal births had been eagerly welcomed in the past, and might still have provided an excuse, if the poetic enthusiasm had survived (on the decline of Neo-Latin, see Ch. 10).

[21] *Congratulatory Addresses . . . at the Installation of his Grace the Duke of Wellington* (Oxford, 1834).

[22] The improvement in the size and physical appearance of the volumes probably led to the loss of the less dignified vernacular after 1669 (with the exception of 1688–9, when political confusion apparently loosened standards); cf. Forster, p. 149.

contribution to the same book, and his relationship with his noble pupil, Lord
Salisbury. It may be worth returning to them, as an example of the subtle
considerations sometimes associated with the genre.

There is striking symmetry in the arrangement of Alsop's and Salisbury's
pieces. Salisbury's poem is printed second, preceded only by William Lancaster,
the Vice-Chancellor; the Vice-Chancellor's verses always began a collection,
and were generally followed by those of other dignitaries, whether heads of
houses or young noblemen. Salisbury's status as the most important pupil in the
entire university is indicated by the place given to his words. The poem by
Savage (Salisbury's other tutor) comes after the heads of houses, a place of
moderate distinction. Alsop's is the very last Latin poem, followed only by the
English poem of Joseph Trapp. It seems likely that Alsop's position is also
intended to be one of honour, rounding off the learned languages and neatly
balancing the prominence given to Salisbury.

Savage's piece is much more straightforward than Alsop's. He concentrates on
sympathising with the Queen: '. . . Nam tibi notus amor, qui mutuus arsit
utrique' [for you know the mutual love that burned in both (line 15)]. Neither
Salisbury nor other subjects appear. Salisbury is somewhat more adventurous; he
sees Anne's nervousness at facing problems alone:

> Quis mihi civiles pectus firmabit ad ausus?
>   Ecquis foemineas extera ad arma manus?
>
> Who will strengthen my spirit against revolt, or my female hands to face
> strife abroad? (lines 15–16)

But the precocious peer bids her stiffen the upper lip:

> Da plebi miserae vanos urgere dolores,
>   Et longum flecti nescia, fata queri.
> Tu major: Te regna manent, manet, Anna, senatus;
>   *Austriacusque* tuam vendicat orbis opem . . .
>   . . . Egregios emitte duces ad certa trophaea,
>   Sola regas populum, sola tuere lares.
> Abreptum frustra quereris, qui tractet habenas
>   Consortem; imperio sufficis una tuo.
>
> Let the unhappy common people lament in vain, and carry on complain-
> ing about fate that cannot be altered. You are above that; you still have
> your kingdoms, Anne, and your Parliament, and the Austrian defends
> your great position in the world. Send out distinguished generals to
> inevitable victory, rule the people alone, watch over your house alone.
> In vain do you complain that the husband who could manage the reins is
> snatched from you; you are capable of power on your own. (lines 21–4,
> 31–4)

The overall message of consolation is repeated by other poets, but this particular youth is able to be forthright, since such advice from a future legislator is less presumptious than from a future curate. It may well be that his pen was guided by a more experienced poet; but whoever was behind it, the Latin forms a fitting public statement that Salisbury is not to be ignored.

Salisbury does not mention Marlborough; he is no doubt one of the many sent out to inevitable victory, while *Austriacus* (his colleague Eugene, or the Emperor) is given priority. This may not be accidental. Many Tories were uncomfortable with the eminence won by Marlborough at Blenheim, Ramillies and Oudenarde, and wished to stress the achievements of rival commanders, including the erratic Earl of Peterborough (defended by Dr John Freind). Others in both universities are delighted to sing in praise of Marlborough. The Vice-Chancellor of Cambridge addresses him at the start, and finishes the book thus:

> Euge Liber, variam varius qui tendis in Aulam;
>   Gratus eris Lacrymans, gratior ibis Ovans.
> Quin propera, ne non numeret tot pagina versus
>   Quot nova dat Titulos laurea *Marlburio.*

> Go on, book, in your varied way to a varied court; you will be welcome for your tears, and more welcome for your triumphant celebrations. So hurry, lest your pages should fail to number as many verses as the titles that his new victories give to Marlborough.[23]

Prince George, the ostensible subject of the book, is all but forgotten.

It is not unusual for private patrons to be addressed, using the public commemoration as a vehicle for individual flattery. In the Cambridge volume for the peace of Utrecht, an event Oxford did not dignify with a full collection, a number of politicians and negotiators are chosen for such attention; the final poem, a very long ode in Latin alcaics,[24] is devoted to Matthew Prior, in his role of diplomat rather than poet. John Robinson, Bishop of Bristol and plenipotentiary, is thrice selected; Harley, Ormonde, and Harcourt all make an appearance as Tory heroes;[25] a philosopher, Mr Paul of Jesus, spares a thought for William Harrison, who died of fever while working on the treaty.

The Oxford book celebrating that peace, though on a much smaller scale, contains much of interest. As one might expect, there is lavish praise of Ormonde, as well as Harley, Robinson, and Bromley, the Speaker (whose son was among those selected to recite verses, in his case a hexameter poem on the procession to St Paul's). The freedom of the academic press is another topical

[23] J. Covel (Christ's), in *Epicedium Cantabrigiense* (Cambridge, 1708).
[24] C. Anstey (St John's), in *Gratulatio . . . de Pace* (Cambridge, 1713).
[25] Again, contradicting the myth that Cambridge was predominantly Whig.

issue that attracts comment. The son of a Barbados landowner, with a work entitled *Commercium ad mare australe*,[26] demonstrates his excitement at the opportunities for South Sea trade, where Britons can now succeed at the expense of proud and brutal Spaniards, and show their superiority to Dutch merchants. He sees his homeland, not England but Barbados, as the geographical centre of a new maritime empire:

> Tu quoque luxurians nativo nectare tellus,
> Chara mihi patria, exultes; tu debita jungas
> Gaudia; te posthac supremo in limite Regni
> Non distare querar; non terminus ultimus Annae
> Sceptri eris: Angliacum nunc ipsum respicis Austrum,
> Teque orbis mediam video, Imperiique Britanni.

> You also should rejoice, dear land of my birth, abounding in your native nectar, you should join in the rejoicing that is due; after this I shall not complain that you are on the farthest edge of the kingdom; you will not be the final outpost of Anne's power: now you can look back at an English South Sea, and I can look upon you as the mid-point of the world, and of the British Empire.[27]

This is a powerful poetic statement of a colonial vision. Similar sentiments were prominent among Victorian and twentieth-century imperialists; in the early eighteenth century, they can best be expressed in elegant Latin, to an audience that remembered Virgil's promise of Empire without end, and might feel themselves to be worthy successors of Augustan Rome.[28]

Another poem in the same book addresses the most vital aspect of this new and profitable peace, an aspect rarely dwelt upon by contemporary English poets:[29] slavery. The title (*Assiento, sive commercium Hispanicum*) refers to the treaty agreement with Spain that opened up the large markets of Spanish America. The poem explains the morality of the trade, by stressing the beastliness of the negroes in Africa: the obscure heroes of their dark internal wars are ironically described, and any of their captives who might escape cannibalism and human sacrifice are lucky enough to be sold. The slave is indeed lucky in his place of exile (*exilio felix*); in any case, he would otherwise have died horribly. The Spaniards need labour to develop rich lands; without it, Columbus' discoveries would be useless. We then turn to a pastoral picture of a British colony, echoing the opening of Virgil's first

---

[26] Not to be confused with the satire of the same name (1720), on the bubble speculation, attributed to H. Randolph (praised by Bradner, pp. 255–7).

[27] J. Alleyn (Magdalen), in *Comitia . . . Annae Pacificae* (Oxford, 1713).

[28] *Aen.* 1. 279, 'Imperium sine fine dedi.'

[29] Cf. H. H. Erskine-Hill, 'Pope and Slavery', in *Alexander Pope: World and Word* (forthcoming).

Eclogue (in which the leisure of the fortunate is contrasted with the eviction of the unfortunate):

> . . . Platani sub tegmine fusus
> Spumantes potat succos, citreique liquorem
> Angliacus dominus; dum pictis Turba flabellis
> Dulces alliciunt auras, stratumque coactis
> Oblectant Zephyris, mulcentque sapore reclinem.

> The English master, lying in the shade of a plane tree, drinks foaming juices and lemonade, while a crowd (of slaves) attract sweet breezes with painted fans, pleasing him as he reclines with the freshness of artificial zephyrs, and soothing him with sweet-tasting drinks.[30]

This idealised image of exploitation without cruelty (for that is left to the Africans) would have intrigued and attracted contemporary readers, unused to such literary material. Only towards the end of the eighteenth century did the abolition of slavery become a subject for debate (inflamed by Thomas Clarkson, who began in the 1780s with a Latin essay).[31] It is difficult, today, to look at earlier attitudes in an unprejudiced light, given the demands of 'political correctness'; one can merely observe that this Latin treatment of the issue is original poetry, on a theme of immense historical importance.

When they lamented their benefactor George I, and welcomed George II (a mixture of emotions that frequently recurs in the collections), the Cambridge poets could also find room for other ideas. Samuel Hadderton, the librarian, dreams about the beauties of his city, a dream helpfully adorned with footnotes, detailing the churches, and prison, one would pass on the left and right, and preparing us for rapture at the gift of £1000 from the Duke of Chandos, £500 from his bride, and so on for five pages of elegiacs, a page of hexameters, and then two further pages of elegiacs. His muse is eccentric; nevertheless, the variety of purposes that lie behind the elegant tributes of the commemorative volumes is remarkable. The poets are free with their flattery, but the results are by no means formulaic. Each has a point to get over, and a talent (whether modest or spectacular) to display. Panegyric can be deftly handled: it can even (as perhaps in Salisbury's case) have subtle overtones of criticism. To be represented in the collections, with an assurance of free distribution to the houses of the great, and of sale to other interested and critical readers, was something few could despise.

---

[30] J. Maynard (St John's), in *Comitia . . . Annae Pacificae* (Oxford, 1713).
[31] The topic for the prize essay of 1785 ('Anne licet invitos in servitutem dare?'), was chosen by the Vice-Chancellor, Peter Peckard (Magdalene), who had himself spoken against slavery. The topic takes the form of an old-fashioned Latin disputation theme. The circumstances of the essay: Clarkson, *History . . .* (London, 1808), 1. 206–7; a modern biography: E. G. Wilson, *Thomas Clarkson* (London and Basingstoke, 1989).

What makes a poet?

Few of the men who wrote poems for these collections, whether in Latin or English, would have considered themselves primarily as poets. The writing of original verse may have taken up a substantial portion of their lives at school and in college, but it was not their only occupation. As a result, many of them express some modesty about their poetic talents. Sometimes one is tempted to agree: but modesty can be used by a vigorous writer as a sophisticated literary device, as well as by a feeble one as no more than a bumbling excuse for mediocrity. Sir John Williams, welcoming Catherine of Braganza in 1662, expresses this modesty on behalf of the academic poets:

> . . . Muses are Country Girls, and Poets lay
> Their Scene with Clownes, in rude Arcadia.
> No Sirens they to captivate and warme
> The sences; sing they may, but cannot Charme.
> Such strangers to all Courtship, should they trye,
> They'd spoil an honour to a Curtesy.
> 'Mongst those that here doe their allegiance, many
> Masters of Art may be, not Ceremony.
> The Rhetorick which we hac[k]nys magnify
> Is but Book motion; and rude Pedantry.
> No Colledges for Inns-of-Court were meant;
> Those are th'Academy's of Complement,
> Scholars to Gallant transubstantiate;
> They're Princes there, and Vers'd in mimick state.
> Oxford and Temple different arts professe;
> We only learn to speak; they to Caresse.
> This Distance is confess'd 'twixt one and th'other,
> As that which is their Mistresse, is our Mother . . .[32]

But Williams, himself a baronet, would not necessarily feel any social inferiority to the young gentlemen of the Inns of Court in London; instead, he uses the pretence of modesty as a cloak for a humorous attack on the fashionable fops who think that London can offer an education that is comparable or superior to that provided at the universities. He stresses their differences: but the solid rhetoric of Oxford is better than London's caressing flattery.

Williams associates learning with honest rusticity; others make a clear distinction between the two, and assume confidently that learning and poetry are inextricably linked:

> While Crouds officious to declare their Joy
> In rustick Layes their uncouth Rhimes employ

---

[32] From *Domiduca Oxoniensis* (Oxford, 1662).

> Shall those Bright Seats, where Phaebus ever reigns,
> Sullen refuse their more Harmonious Strains . . .[33]

But more common than such arrogance, or Williams' false modesty, is a genuine-sounding admission of inexperience, and a modest request that the addressee should accept

> . . . These artless numbers, that unstudied flow
> From the rude lip of ill-dissembling Woe.
> Ne'er yet I bow'd before the tuneful Nine
> To bless my Verse, and smooth the polish'd Line,
> Happy if now these trivial strains declare
> A Head unskillful, but a Heart sincere . . .
> . . . These weighty Themes to abler pens belong
> Too high alas! for my untutor'd Song.
> From the slow Cherwells low sequester'd Vale,
> I bring domestic sorrows humbler Tale . . .[34]

This aristocratic author even uses his choice of river to emphasise modesty: Oxford is more commonly associated in verse with the noble Isis (i.e., Thames), and its lowly tributary is a relatively unusual alternative.

Modesty about the university poets' skill can be turned to humorous effect; in 1640, for example, after a long series of royal births seems to have exhausted the possibilities for novel tributes,

> O How the Poets feare your Births! as They
> That Nothing have except their feares to Pay.
> And now their stocke of wit being spent and gone,
> As wasted Youth, they put Religion on . . .[35]

And another writer considers that the addressees, as well as the poets, may be feeling the strain:

> Great Queene, You are not yet deliver'd, Wee
> From throwes, and labours shall not thinke you free,
> Till you have pass'd ours: which I dare maintaine
> (Ill verse is such a torment) the worse pain . . .[36]

In general, the poems are most effective as literature when they attempt something more than a simple expression of grief or joy. Very often, it is some satirical aside that enlivens a piece; and, when it is compatible with the poems' primary purpose of commemoration, this satire can be deployed on a more extended

---

[33] G. Costard (Wadham), in *Epithalamia Oxoniensia* (Oxford, 1734).
[34] Hon. Allen Bathurst (New), in *Epicedia* (Oxford, 1751).
[35] T. Hervey (Christ Church), in *Horti Carolini Rosa Altera* (Oxford, 1640).
[36] M. Bate (St Edmund Hall), ibid.

scale. The death of Viscount Bayning in 1638 called forth a set of laments from Christ Church. There is some vigorous criticism of funereal hypocrisy:

> Hence from This Tomb, you that have only chose
> To Mourn for Ribbands, and the sadder Cloths,
> That Buy your Grief from the Shop; and desperat lye
> For a new Cloak till the next Lord shall Dye;
> You that shed only wine, and think when all
> The Banquet's past, there's no more Funerall:
> You that sell Teares, and only Weepe for Gaine,
> I dare not say you Mourn, but fill the Traine . . .[37]

This description of the insincere mourner shedding other people's wine, instead of his own tears, is a powerful and poetic image; one might compare it to the brutally direct final stanza of one of Horace's greatest odes on death (a passage that a seventeenth-century Oxonian would undoubtedly recognise), in which the ungrateful heir '. . . mero/tinget pavimentum . . .' [will stain the floor with wine].[38] The satire here is not irrelevant to the aim of providing a suitable memorial for Bayning, for the author emphasises the need to avoid such sham grief. But poor hangers-on are not the only targets; elsewhere in the collection, idle aristocrats are attacked, for the dead man, it is claimed, was

> . . . Not like our Silken Heires, who only bound
> Their knowledge in the Sphear of Hawke or Hound,
> And, there confin'd, limit their scant discourse,
> Know more the *Vaulting* then the *Muses* Horse:
> Who if They rescue Time from Cards or Dice
> To Lance or Sharpes, or some such manly Prize,
> Advance their Lineage, raise their Stock, if They
> But more severely loose the Precious Day . . .[39]

As for our hero, according to another poet:

> . . . Whil'st others studied how to loose their time,
> Thinking that *Logick* would their Birth beslime,
> As if it were Gentile not to Dispute;
> It was his chief ambition to confute . . .[40]

Thus, it is by comparison with the sloth of others that Bayning's own qualities are made to shine. Unlike other aristocrats, he threw himself whole-heartedly into the proper business of academic life, and not merely into trivial entertainments. Without the satire of his noble contemporaries, the poems would be less effective as encomia, as well as less interesting as literature.

---

[37] W. Towers (Christ Church), in *Death Repeal'd* (Oxford, 1638).   [38] Horace, *Carm.* 2. 14. 26–7.
[39] F. Powell (Christ Church), in *Death Repeal'd* (Oxford, 1638).   [40] R. West (Christ Church), ibid.

Violence, embarrassment, and hypocrisy

At times of real political crisis, this tendency towards forcefulness of expression was stimulated by a great increase in the hatred felt (especially by Oxford poets) for their master's enemies. While they may have disliked the sort of hypocrites and wastrels who surrounded Bayning, such people can be treated with a mixture of amused contempt and exaggerated outrage. When the threat is not idleness but treason, more urgent passions are inevitably roused. This process can be observed in some of the other volumes from the period leading up to the civil war (and, even more so, in the belligerent writings of the war itself, when the King's headquarters were established in Oxford, and all resident members of the university were firmly and literally in the royalist camp).

Yet another royal birth, in 1636, is a cause for optimism about British expansion, and a signal for rumbles of opposition (the author hopes) to be overwhelmed by expressions of loyalty:

> . . . Perchance for the fift issue there may be
> Another part (for why not five, if three?)
> O' the world disclos'd after *America*,
> And nought from yours be *Terr' Incognita*:
> Let none repine at Caesars generall Taxe
> At this blest Birth-day (when a Soveraigne lacks
> Who can be close, and loyall?) . . .[41]

The Oxonians were later to prove, by melting down their plate for the King, that their loyalty prevented them from being 'close' with their money. This poem was written during the long-running crisis over Charles' claim for ship money from inland counties. The comparison of Charles' unpopular methods of taxation with the efficient, universal, and irresistible administration of Imperial Rome is a clever device. The reader will remember, as well as 'a decree from Caesar Augustus, that all the world should be taxed', Jesus' refusal to condemn Roman taxation. The question was one of great relevance for convinced opponents of Charles I: 'Is it lawful to give tribute unto Caesar, or not? . . . And they brought unto him a penny. And he saith unto them, Whose is this image and superscription? They say unto him, Caesar's. Then said he unto them, Render therefore unto Caesar the things which are Caesar's . . .'.[42] The allusion is enough to remind the contemporary reader whose image and superscription is on the money in his own purse.

---

[41] J. Robinson (Christ Church), in *Coronae Carolinae Quadratura* (Oxford, 1636). Part of this passage quoted, without much discussion, by Anselment, p. 193.
[42] *Luke* 2: 1 (decree . . .); *Matthew* 22: 17–21, = *Mark* 12: 14–17 (render . . .).

As war approaches, poets begin to express violent sentiments, although still hoping that peace may be preserved:

> . . . thence we
> May vanquish treason with your piety.
> And may bestrow the Pavements where he treads
> With loyall Subjects hearts, or Rebells heads.[43]

The printer, whose verses commonly closed a volume at this period, notes the fine line between peaceful and warlike proofs of loyalty:

> The Schollers now, like Volunteers, professe
> As Loyall Service in this learned Presse,
> As those that drinke Your Twelve-pence: They would Fight
> Should You command, as willingly as Write . . .

They compete in their eagerness to write;

> . . . May there be only such contentions; let
> My *Founts*, to give You Ioy, for ever sweat.
> But unto such as doe oppose Your Throne
> May every Letter be a *Killing* one.[44]

And once the war has begun in earnest, some authors are quite unrestrained:

> Go Burne some Rebell Towne; for such alone
> Are Bonfires suiting to the Ioyes we owne.
> And bid the falling Ashes sprinkled lye
> On Traitors heads: let them Repent and Dye . . .[45]

Others, however, retain more humour, and can laugh at the close involvement of the university in military affairs, as well as finding a new twist for an assertion of modesty:

> What? Scholars digge; ambitious clergy! hence,
> Good works were thought to be your bane long since.
> Digg, sweat for verses now, till some are made
> So blunt as if writ not with Penne, but Spade . . .[46]

The Glorious Revolution caused, if anything, even more embarrassment to the writers of commemorative verse than the civil war and the Restoration. In Oxford's case, at least, a reasonable time elapsed between the last volume

[43] 'I. T.' (Balliol), in *Horti Carolini Rosa Altera* (Oxford, 1640); cf. Anselment, p. 193. He is borrowing from Thomas Carew (whose posthumous *Poems* appeared in 1640), 'Strew all the pavements, where he treads/ With loyall hearts, or Rebels heads': *A New Years gift to the King*, lines 31–2 (ed. R. Dunlap (Oxford, 1949), p. 90). [44] L. Lichfield (printer), in *Horti Carolini Rosa Altera* (Oxford, 1640).
[45] W. Barker (New), in *Musarum Oxoniensium 'EΠIBATHPIA* (Oxford, 1643).
[46] R. Steevenson (St John's), ibid.

praising Charles I (1643) and their tribute to the victorious Oliver Cromwell (1654), and between the Cromwellian volume and the Restoration. Cambridge, which had welcomed Richard Cromwell in 1658, was forced to make a more abrupt change of tune. But both universities were equally caught out by the rapid succession between the birth of the Prince of Wales (the Old Pretender) and the loss of his father's throne. No sooner had they lauded James II and his offspring, than they were required to reverse their sentiments and welcome William and Mary. Naturally, attempts were made in the latter volume to atone for, and to explain away, the mistakes of the former:

> In dull commanded Strains the Royal Boy
> We lately greeted with dissembled Joy,
> In such low notes our rugged Numbers flow'd,
> At once our Loyalty and Minds we shew'd . . .[47]

Or, again, in the ode that follows:

> . . . But sing, O sing with more auspicious Layes,
>   Then when I urg'd thee on to praise
> A spurious Hero, whose ignoble rise
> No Muse could praise, no Verse immortalize . . .[48]

Neither of these individuals had actually written in praise of the Prince of Wales, so they could revile him with a reasonably good conscience. More complicated was the position of Henry Downs of New College, the only Oxford poet contributing in English to both volumes; his poem of 1689 is very much longer, perhaps as a deliberate act of atonement. But, if one considers the books as a whole, he is far from alone; I count at least 27 Oxonian 'Vicars of Bray', men whose published opinions underwent a sudden and expedient change between 1688 and 1689. The list includes the Vice-Chancellor and two other heads of houses, who no doubt felt it necessary to safeguard the university's political position under the both the old and the new regime. Members of these three colleges (New, St John's, Wadham) make up more than half of the total of turncoats, so it seems likely that the heads' action influenced some of their juniors.

   This suspicious behaviour was noted and remembered by those in London who might seek to embarrass Oxford and Cambridge Jacobites. Some of the poems from both universities on the Prince of Wales were mischievously reprinted, in *State Amusements, Serious and Hypocritical . . . to which is added a True List of the Members of Both Universities that Amused his Majesty . . .with some Select Copies of Amusing Verses, taken out of those two Famous Volumes, intitul'd, Strenae Natalitiae . . .* (London, 1711). This was not the only occasion on which

---

[47] F. Knapp (St John's), in *Vota Oxoniensia* (Oxford, 1689).   [48] E. Nicholas (Merton), ibid.

university verses had been satirised in London (a sign of the attention that they received outside a strictly academic audience). On the other hand, it was thought acceptable in the universities to reprint some of the best pieces of 1685 or 1688, in spite of their praise of James II.[49]

The verses on the death of William III, and accession of Queen Anne, led to the Latin riposte, *Satyra in Poetastros O—C—enses* (London, 1702). In his preface, the anonymous author is keen to avoid the accusation that he satirises the occasion for the verses, 'ne . . . Invidus aliquis me Malevolentiae se suspectum subsusurrasset . . .' [lest any hostile person might whisper that he has suspected me of ill-will (towards the dead king)]. The poets, 'nimia gloriae siti impulsi' [driven by too great a thirst for glory], are not up to the task of praising so great a prince as he deserves. I take this to be the genuine belief of a Williamite, rather than heavy-handed irony, but one can never be quite sure; the author will have been well aware of the number of Jacobites in the universities, writing insincere tributes to William, and (if he was a partisan Whig) the thought might reasonably infuriate him. His satire begins with the indignation that befits the genre:

> Non merito irascar cum tot prurigine Famae
> Quos neque Melpomene, neque Clio, aut ulla Sororum
> Donavit Citharave, Lyrave, aut Pectine dulci,
> Principis Invicti conentur dicere laudes?

> Am I not right to be angry, when so many whom not one of the Muses has blessed with any poetical talent itch for fame, and try to praise that undefeated prince?

These poets do not have any regard for truth: they will credit their hero with triumphs at which he was not even present (p. 2). The poet, he sarcastically suggests, knows all the details:

> Vidisti (nam certe aderas) quot miserit Orco
> Pugnaces animas, dederis quot naula Charonti . . .

> You have seen (for, of course, you were there) how many soldiers' souls he sent to Hell,[50] how many times you have given Charon his passage-money . . . (p. 3)

He becomes most irritated at the progressive deification of the king; first the classical gods are introduced, and he joins their number ('Ridiculum', p. 3), then:

> (Qui modo Divus erat subito est factus Deus, et qui
> Par modo erat Superis, minor at Jove, Jupiter idem

---

[49] Thus in Addison's *Musarum Anglicanarum Analecta* (1699), by no means a crypto-Jacobite production, we find congratulations from 1685 (anonymous: 2. 202–10) and 1688 (V. Corbet: 2. 99–101; G. Dixon: 2. 102–4).   [50] Cf. Homer, *Iliad* 1. 3.

> Fiet, si Vati placeat. Quis sanus haberi
> Vult ipse, et tamen hos neget insanire Poetas?)
>
> Who was just now 'divine' is suddenly made God, and he who was just
> now equal to the divinities, but less than Jove, can become Jove himself if
> the poet wishes. Who can want to be thought sane, and yet deny that
> these poets are mad? (p. 4)

The dubious flexibility of the mythological pantheon, as used by Christian poets, is a fair target for attack. The university poets do indeed regularly deify monarchs,[51] following classical precedents, and there is great potential for awkwardness in the mixture of Christian and pagan theology. Yet this problem arises in vast numbers of works outside the university collections, in both Neo-Latin and vernacular literature; the satirist is criticising a widespread poetic convention, not a failing exclusive to his poetasters. He continues by recalling how a typical poet lists the king's virtues, and stresses his own grief; this is fine, but if we wait a moment, we will soon see him falling into the same trap, calling him sacred, and declaring that:

> Morti Hunc surreptum saltem vel oportuit Unum.
> Quis teneat risum? . . .
>
> 'This one man, at least, ought to have been snatched from death!' Who
> could restrain himself from laughter? (p. 6)

For death is universal, and it is simply absurd to suggest that its rules should be bent for a human king, however great. He laughs at those Cambridge poets who saw portents in a star (pp. 10–11). He is on better ground when he criticises those for whom this is merely a financial transaction (pp. 14–16), when a master sends his servant to negotiate a fee with a literary hack. Commercialism was not confined to the universities. This aspect, nevertheless, could reasonably bring the books into some contempt, though the quality of the poems would be improved, if those attributed to some noblemen were actually from more experienced pens. Overall, the *Satira in Poetastros* does not convince one that the university poets are particularly bad; some faults are exposed in vigorous language, but they apply to mediocre poetry in general.

And members of each university tended to cast a critical eye over the productions of their rival sister. 'What wretched stuff are the Cambridge verses', exclaimed Canon Stratford (one of our Vicars of Bray) in a letter of 23 June 1713 to his distinguished young friend Edward Harley.[52] Dean Hickes, similarly, had written to Arthur Charlett on 29 January 1708/9: 'The Oxford book of verses exceeds that of Cambridge in the excellency of poetry, as much

---

[51] Cf. Alsop 1. 2. 1–8, 38, 65 (on Mary; but he avoids it in 1. 3).   [52] *HMC Portland* 7. 146.

as in the number of languages . . .'.[53] The poetry that he considered excellent
may have included Trapp's solitary piece of English, but nearly all the rest will
have been Latin.

The inclusion of esoteric and oriental languages is an interesting aspect of
the tradition. Latin was not difficult or alien to a member of the seventeenth-
or eighteenth-century universities, nor to any reasonably well-educated Lon-
don reader. Greek, though more difficult, could expect a respectable audience;
the same, to a lesser degree, might be said of Hebrew, since most theological
students will have made at least some effort to acquire the sacred tongue.[54]
The Oxford volume of 1708, praised by Hickes, had two Hebrew pieces, two
Anglo-Saxon, and one Coptic. Only a tiny minority (of which Hickes was
one) knew Anglo-Saxon, Coptic still fewer. Cambridge, in 1702, had boasted
Hebrew, Arabic, Turkish, and Persian. Thomas Hyde, of Queen's College,
Bodley's Librarian and Professor of Arabic, was responsible for much of
Oxford's variety. He contributed to every volume from 1662 to 1702 in
Arabic, Turkish, Persian, or Malay (sometimes in two or three of them).
The chief purpose of such works (since translations were hardly ever provided)
was to impress with unusual learning, rather than to be widely understood.
But outlandish tongues were always peripheral to the collections; the core was
invariably Latin. Greek was significant, but minor: both universities usually
averaged about five Greek pieces in each volume (though more than ten, or
less than three, sometimes occur). At Cambridge, Joshua Barnes and James
Duport (the former discussed in Chapter 4, the latter mentioned in Chapter 2)
were prominent users of Greek. Philip Bouquet, Professor of Hebrew at
Cambridge, regularly wrote in both Hebrew and Latin (also Greek, in
1713), the languages effectively complementing each other; in Hebrew, he
can compare Louis XIV, at the peace, to the suppliant Queen of Sheba, and
the victorious Anne to King Solomon (in an amusing reversal of sexual
stereotypes). Some of his Latin poetry shows a similar eye for the unconven-
tional image.[55]

Counting the multitude

The numbers of poets involved in this tradition of Neo-Latin verse are very large
indeed. In the last hundred years or so of the volumes, from the Commonwealth
to the first years of George III (including Alsop's lifetime, and a generation either

[53] Bodleian, Ballard Mss., 12, fo. 110.
[54] See D. K. Money, J. Olszowy, 'Hebrew Commemorative Poetry in Cambridge, 1564–1763', *Transactions
of the Cambridge Bibliographical Society* 10 (1995), pp. 549–76; D. Patterson, 'Hebrew Studies', in Sutherland
and Mitchell, *Oxford*, pp. 535–50.   [55] Money and Olszowy, pp. 557–64.

side of it), there are about three thousand poems from each university (even counting a group of epigrams as a single poem).[56] Most poets write only once, quite a few write twice, and a small number are regular contributors over several years; thus Britain can boast of well over four thousand Latin poets (at a conservative estimate) in that period. If one also considers the previous hundred years, many more need to be added: the genre was particularly vigorous in both the early and late seventeenth century. Those who saw their Latin verse published might number in the region of ten thousand poets: a veritable multitude of Muses.

When calling these men poets, I do not mean that they all devoted their lives to Latin poetry, or necessarily cared very deeply about it. For many, it will have remained a life-long interest. Others, though more concerned with non-literary pursuits, will still have been affected by the experience of publication; for most of them, it was the only occasion on which their name was ever attached to any elegant or learned production (or indeed any book at all). They cannot easily have forgotten that fact, however little importance they may have attached to it. Even if they chose not to read or purchase Neo-Latin books, they were aware of the existence of such literature, and their own former participation.

It may be objected that my definition of a Latin poet is too loose to be meaningful, and that there were not really ten thousand Englishmen worthy of such a name. In applying the term only to those appearing in print, I have in fact been ignoring far larger numbers of occasional (and more serious) poets whose manuscript works either still survive or may be presumed to have once existed, whether in the form of school or college exercises, or as the adult amusement of leisure hours. Were they, too, counted as poets, we would be talking not of ten thousand, but of many hundreds of thousands, if not a million or two, who have attained a high degree of competence in the writing of Neo-Latin, and derived much satisfaction from it. An example of such manuscript material is the group of poems from Merchant Taylors' School collected by John James.[57] These exercises consist of independent poems in both Latin and English (one language does not translate the other), which are eminently lively, and suggest a real creative enthusiasm among their young authors. Again, one might argue that they ought not seriously to be classed as poets. But it is such widespread amateur

---

[56] There are some statistics (approximately, but not wholly, accurate) in D. K. Money, 'British Latin Verse . . .' (unpublished Ph.D. thesis, Cambridge, 1992), pp. 19–29. The figures will be revised as part of an ongoing database project, D. K. Money, *Biographical Register of British Latin Poets* (work in progress). Forster lists the Cambridge volumes, and has details of Cambridge poets writing in English.

[57] Cambridge University Library, Ms. Add. 2615, fo. 30–73. See D. K. Money, 'Neo-Latin Literature in Cambridge', in R. C. Alston, ed., *Order and Connexion* (Woodbridge, 1997), pp. 77–95 (these mss., pp. 85–8).

activity, more than the publications of a few great authors, that lends vitality to a literary culture.

A few individual poets did publish quite large amounts of Latin verse in the volumes.[58] Among users of English, two seventeenth-century Christ Church authors stand out: William Cartwright and Jasper Mayne.[59] Even without them, the college would have outdistanced all its seventeenth-century rivals; but the situation later became more evenly balanced. In Latin, by contrast (and on a much larger scale), Christ Church never did lose its dominant position: it is still offering far more than any other college in the 1760s. At Cambridge, while Trinity is usually the largest college, others can periodically equal or surpass its contribution.

It is difficult to assess the overall nature of their poetic achievement. Individually, many of the poems are charming; some, for example that of the would-be arsonist of rebel towns (quoted above), are far from charming, but nevertheless vividly express their authors' opinions. Collectively, they form a substantial body of literature, and a major contribution of the universities to national cultural life. The fact that so many of those who came to enjoy positions of influence in church and state, whether as bishops and ministers or as parsons and squires, had themselves offered poetry for publication should not be ignored by historians. It must have helped to influence their attitudes in later life, and to establish them as men of culture and members of a long and distinguished tradition.

[58] John Laughton (Trinity, Cambridge) contributed over a thousand lines to ten volumes: Money and Olszowy, p. 557.
[59] Cf. Anselment, pp. 184–5; n.b. also D. Flynn, 'Jasper Mayne's translations of Donne's Latin epigrams', *John Donne Journal* 3 (1984), pp. 121–30.

10
Purity and Emptiness

The history of British Latin verse since the late eighteenth century is one of general decline, gradual in the nineteenth and early twentieth centuries, rapid in the last few decades. This is the overall trend; many significant exceptions do need to be noted. The decline, at least in the nineteenth century, is not in the amount of verse written. More was written in schools and universities than ever before, and it achieved higher standards of technical excellence, when judged by fidelity to classical models. Less of it was published, and deservedly so, for mere purity of diction does not imply much literary merit. An ever increasing proportion of Latin poetry ceased to say anything original. In the place of originality came exercises in translation from English poetry. Such translations are almost inevitably of less interest than the original writings that they adapt; they demonstrate the translator's skill and feeling for poetry, but are devoid of real literary purpose. The skill displayed is still impressive. Naturally, the enthusiasm of students varied; a fascinating study could be made of the references to composition, whether as a painful task or a pleasant recreation, in Victorian novels of school and college life (from *Tom Brown's Schooldays* onwards). Hardly any of today's Classics students could do as well, nor have they been offered the chance to spend an equivalent time on this rewarding but initially difficult discipline. Impressive though they are as exercises, and important as a historical phenomenon, these pieces rarely have the same startling impact as the best work of the eighteenth century.

Exercises cause unhealthiness

The reasons for decline are not wholly certain, but various plausible suggestions may be brought forward. One of the most interesting is that the end of Jacobitism as a serious emotional force (with the accession of George III, a genuinely British Hanoverian) removed a major motive for using Latin. There was no longer such a call for sophisticated, subversive Latin literature. Jacobites have loomed large in this book, primarily because of Alsop and his circle. Even discounting them, one would see that many of the chief figures in original Latin literature harboured seditious thoughts: Archibald Pitcairne and William King are particularly strong cases (see Chapters 6 and 8). Other Latinists were Whig, and one cannot claim Jacobite domination of the medium; nevertheless, Jacobites were disproportionately active in Latin, and could readily express ambiguous sentiments to an educated, receptive audience.

Another feature of the early years of George III is the ending of the university commemorative tradition; again, it is not quite clear why this occurred (see Chapter 9). Once this outlet for poetic expression by large numbers of ordinary students and scholars was removed, energies might naturally be turned away from original composition. Equally, emphasis on translation could stultify originality, and make further collections impracticable. The two developments do seem related. More rigorous approaches to classical education are very probably also to blame. The search for purity leads to emptiness. A copy of verses was valued more for avoidance of errors than for poetic vigour. This is the opposite of the normal eighteenth-century attitude; then, an occasional false quantity might easily slip past (for no author's memory was perfect), new words might be introduced, and Renaissance liberties were freely taken. What mattered was not perfection but poetry, except for the most pedantic of critics (who tended to use pedantry as a convenient weapon in literary wars begun from other motives). The imitation of the ancients was less important than the cultural enrichment of the present. Translation could not claim such literary value, but could train a young mind in elegant precision; imperfections were no longer defensible.

The natural result of these changes was the marginalisation of original Latin poetry in British society. In the eighteenth century, Neo-Latin was still central to intellectual culture. In the nineteenth, it became peripheral, something more associated with schoolmasters and eccentrics than vital new literature. Translation was culturally central, practised with pleasure by thousands of Victorians, both eminent and forgotten. Its practitioners were not really Latin poets (even in the limited sense used of occasional versifiers in Chapter 9), for they tended not to see Latin as a vehicle for public statements or private self-expression, unless they had no feelings too personal to be clothed in other men's ideas.

The Age of Landor

The most important single figure of the nineteenth century (and the end of the eighteenth) is Landor; his Latin work has received some critical attention, which I shall not attempt to duplicate here.[1] His career began, primarily, in Latin; his

---

[1] See A. Kelly, 'The Latin poetry of Walter Savage Landor', in J. W. Binns, ed., *The Latin Poetry of English Poets* (London, 1974), pp. 150–93; Bradner, pp. 315–25; I understand that Landor will be re-examined by T. Bicknell (dissertation, University of York: work in progress).

'Latine scribendi defensio' [defence of writing in Latin], published with his *Poems* in 1795, is a powerful piece of argument, and reveals his own reading of Neo-Latin literature. It is significant that he felt obliged to defend his use of the language. Earlier in the century, no defence would have been necessary, because few would have thought it odd to be writing in Latin. Lettice's edition of Isaac Hawkins Browne, dating from the same year (see Chapter 8), indicates that some still saw the relevance of modern Latin. An ever increasing majority was less easily convinced. As a result, such defences are regularly found in the prefaces of later anthologies and graduses, and reflect a general decline.

Landor's use of Latin for political poetry links him with the ages of Alsop and William King, as do his personal Latin poems. Landor was not a practical politician; as will be seen below, a number of serious parliamentary figures were accomplished Latin poets, though without Landor's prolific intensity. George Canning had been one of the best Oxford poets of his generation; his prize poem on Mohametan pilgrimages (1789) is praised by Bradner (p. 308). The Classics lay behind some of his more celebrated English productions, for example, the satirical sapphics from the *Anti-Jacobin*, 'The Friend of Humanity and the Needy Knife-grinder',[2] written in collaboration with John Hookham Frere, another significant politician and diplomat of the Napoleonic wars. The personal side of Landor's Latin is echoed in Coleridge's private notebooks, with a vast collection of material in several languages, including some wild macaronic neologisms, records of Neo-Latin inscriptions, and some original Latin verse.[3] He writes in hendecasyllables to complain about Wordsworth's attitude to seeing himself praised in print: Coleridge will not allow the tyranny of another's false modesty to silence his own Muse. The same metre is used to an unnamed male friend, who is urged to write 'si tibi igniculus vetusti amoris/. . . manet' [if a little spark of your old affection remains].[4]

The collections of school and university verse published in the nineteenth century did often include original poetry, though translation later predominates. An Etonian of the Napoleonic wars, John Patteson (later a distinguished judge), wrote in 1808 of the succour that Britain could offer to the exiled Bourbons:

> . . . Dabit Anglia quicquid
> Fas dare, et amotum solio miserata, tyranni
> Ridebit secura minas; licet undique gentes
> Sponte in vincla ruant: socias licet Austria vires

[2] Repr. in (e.g.) R. Lonsdale, ed., *The New Oxford Book of 18th century Verse* (Oxford, 1984), no. 544, pp. 824–5; cf. other attempts at sapphics in English, by Southey (no. 523, pp. 823–4), and Thomas Morris (no. 327, pp. 498–500: an amusing transferral of Hor., *Carm.* 2. 16 to Canada).
[3] Cf. K. Coburn, ed., *The Notebooks of Samuel Taylor Coleridge* (London, 1957–): with corrections of J. Diggle, 'Greek & Latin in Coleridge's notebooks' (forthcoming, perhaps *Notes & Queries*?).
[4] Coburn, no. 2750 and no. 1283 (with Diggle's discussion).

Submittat Corso, et, quod dudum parturit aegris
Victa odiis, pariet dolitura America bellum.

England will give whatever is right, sympathising with an exile, and will
laugh from safety at the tyrant's threats, even though on all sides peoples
rush of their own accord into slavery, even though Austria may submit to
alliance with the Corsican; and treacherous America, defeated by sick
hatreds, will bring forth the war that she has long been carrying in her
womb.[5]

This is a powerful description of the crisis that Britain faced. Russia had just
joined Napoleon's side, with the meeting of the two emperors in 1807; Austria
was to assert its independence of action, unsuccessfully, in 1809; war with
America finally did erupt in 1812.

Latin verse was important to Lord Wellesley,[6] both at the beginning and end
of his life. Richard Wellesley, the elder brother of the Duke of Wellington and
Governor-General of India, was both a statesman and a poet, with some flair for
Horatian lyrics, among other Latin metres. He wrote much at Eton and Oxford,
but was still writing Latin after his retirement from public affairs, when he
arranged the publication of his *Primitiae et Reliquiae* (London, 1840). The Latin
verse of other major politicians and literary figures appeared in the *Musae
Etonenses*; Gladstone wrote on Canning's death in 1827, and the same year
saw a poem by Arthur Hallam, whose death was to form the subject of
Tennyson's great *In Memoriam* (Tennyson's brother Frederick was another con-
tributor). Edward Creasy, historian of *Decisive Battles*, wrote a fine alcaic ode, on
mountain scenery, in 1830. Edward Stanley, later 14th Earl of Derby and prime
minister, wrote hexameters in 1815 and 1816 on medicine and gardening.[7]
Derby translated the *Iliad* into English, an enduring sign of his devotion to
the Classics.

Among those who wrote a substantial quantity of Latin in the nineteenth
century, several further names should be mentioned. William Herbert[8] was an
accomplished writer of odes; he also used hexameters for a noteworthy attack on
slavery (cf. Chapter 9); also significant are his friend William Frere (brother of
Canning's collaborator, and Master of Downing College, Cambridge),[9] and
Charles Wordsworth.[10] Charles Stuart Calverley[11] is typical of many later
Neo-Latin authors, in that his initial vigour, displayed in original prize poems,
was soon diverted to the exercise of translation (both from English into Latin,

[5] *Musae Etonenses* (Eton, Cambridge and London, 1862), p. 137.   [6] Bradner, pp. 302–4.
[7] Bradner mentions Gladstone and Creasy, p. 329. See *Musae Etonenses* (Eton, Cambridge and London,
1869), pp. 24–6 and 32–4 (Stanley), 92–3 and 96–7 (Gladstone), 94–5 (Hallam), 98–9 (Creasy), 77–8 and
120–3 (F. Tennyson: the latter in Greek sapphics).   [8] Bradner, pp. 309–14.
[9] Bradner, p. 309: comparing Frere unfavourably with Herbert.   [10] Bradner, pp. 325–7.
[11] Bradner, pp. 327–8.

and Latin into English). His best work, and perhaps also his worst, is in a burlesque vein, and in English. His English poem on 'Beer', replete with Horatian echoes, can be thoroughly recommended. One other minor master of the Horatian ode, as well as of evocative translations into English, was the eccentric Eton master William Johnson Cory. Cory is not discussed by Bradner;[12] H. A. J. Munro, perhaps rather idiosyncratically, thought Cory produced 'the best and most Horatian Sapphics and Alcaics that have been written since Horace ceased to write'.[13] Prize poems and other university verses varied in their literary seriousness. Some were of the highest quality, treating their topics as an opportunity for real didactic poetry. The philosophical poems of Robert Percy Smith, explaining modern systems in a manner that might seem to rival Lucretius, were particularly admired by Landor himself.[14]

Alongside more serious literary genres, miscellaneous forms of humour continued to flourish, among them macaronic verses, with their wild mixture of words from different languages. Such burlesque poems are often very witty, and their effect relies upon the reader's familiarity with Latin metre. They can thus be considered a part of British Neo-Latin culture, albeit a minor and frivolous one. One amusing example describes a dissenters' convention, attended by those who have a grudge against the ecclesiastical establishment:

> All, in a word, qui se oppressos most heavily credunt
> Legibus injustis, test-oathibus atque profanis;
> While high-church homines in ease et luxury vivunt;
> Et placeas, postas, mercedes, munia graspant.[15]

The Latin hexameter is perfectly preserved, while the vocabulary is as much English as Latin. The English is sometimes left in its original state ('most heavily', 'luxury'), sometimes given a classical ending ('placeas', = 'place' [i.e. sinecure] + as: best scanned as two rather than three syllables, to preserve the English pronounciation, and differentiate it from the Latin word *placeas* [you might please]). Between these burlesques and the weightiest philosophy, there was a wide spectrum of poetry, and also some prose. Landor's long lifetime saw a great deal of varied Latin writing; but his own was by some distance the most deeply committed to the continuation of the tradition. Later nineteenth-century productions look very thin by comparison.

---

[12] Cory's *Key to Lucretilis* (Eton, 1871) appears in Bradner's 'Supplemental List', *The Library* 5th ser. 22 (1967), pp. 93–101. Some elegant odes by Cory in J. Sparrow, ed., *Poems in Latin* (1941). Cf. F. J. Lelièvre, *Cory's Lucretilis* (Cambridge, 1964).
[13] Cited by N. A. Bonavia-Hunt, *Horace the Minstrel* (Kineton, 1969), p. 77. Bonavia-Hunt disagrees with Munro, and so do I.   [14] Bradner, pp. 304–8, 325; Kelly, p. 156. (Mentioned in Ch. 8.)
[15] Anon., *Epistula Macaronica* (1790).

Entertaining diversions

Many modern scholars and schoolmasters have produced small quantities of original verse, usually in a light and occasional vein, and larger amounts of translation. Teachers, more often than pupils, now thought that their versions, whether originally written for private amusement, or as fair copies used in class, deserved a wider audience. W. R. Hardie, Professor at Edinburgh, published a heavier volume:[16] it consists mainly of translations, but there are a few original poems, including two quite substantial sets of hexameters (together numbering nearly 600 lines), in praise of the University of St Andrews, and of George Buchanan. In the nineteenth century, Herbert Kynaston had written much rather parochial verse centred upon St Paul's School.[17]

A little more entertaining, if very much less serious, is the little book by Henry Broadbent, fittingly entitled *Leviora* [lighter things] (Eton, 1924). It is all translation, with everything on a tiny and frivolous scale; it is redeemed from dullness by the enterprising choice of items for translation, including the details of small personal advertisements in *The Times*:

> Psittacus en venit pulcher, prope Amazona natus;
> Sibilat et loquitur belle, feritate remota;
> Suavior haud comes esse potest; emere at licet octo
> Cum cavea aureolis; pignus neque deerit ementi.
> Lautus ego; at domus est vicensima tertia, Pago
> Qua Saltatorum vicus se tendit in Amplo,
> Africus et nomen (sexta haec pars) dat regioni.

> 'Parrot, handsome Amazon: clever talker, whistler; tame; ideal pet; good companion; guarantee; £8. 10s, with cage. Smart, 23 Dancer Rd., Fulham, S. W. 6.' (pp. 2–3)

From the advertisement he omits nothing of significance, including the name and full address (*in Amplo* for Fulham is clever, though I doubt one would get it without the crib); he seems to have knocked the price down by ten shillings, which is rather an insult to the parrot's pride. He proves that one really can put anything into verse; it is the incongruity of form and content, and the challenge of finding Latin words for the paraphernalia of modern life, that provide the fun. Otherwise, the activity seems quite pointless, and one wearies of the joke after a few pages.

Better humour is to be found in the work of A. D. Godley,[18] author of the brilliant macaronic declension of the 'motor bus' (. . . the noise and hideous hum/*indicat motorem bum*, etc.). One of the most amusing of sustained parodies is his *Q. Horati Flacci Carminum Liber Quintus* (Oxford, 1920), in collaboration with

---

[16] *Silvulae Academicae* (London, 1912).   [17] Bradner, p. 341.   [18] Bradner, p. 344.

Rudyard Kipling and Charles Graves, who supplied English versions of the fifteen new odes 'discovered' as a fifth book of Horace.

Playing the game

The educational and moral value of verse composition was vigorously defended. In the 1840s, an Eton master had asked the rhetorical question: 'If you do not write good longs and shorts, how can you ever be a man of taste? If you are not a man of taste, how can you ever be of use in the world?'.[19] This attitude became more difficult to justify, but less extravagant claims could be made: without writing verses, one would have no ear for poetry or correct pronounciation. 'The practice of Latin verse composition has been an object of scorn to so many writers for so many years past . . .', laments the preface to A. C. Ainger and H. G. Wintle's much reprinted *Gradus* (1890; 17th impression, 1963); yet it does force pupils 'from the very first to think for themselves'. A longer defence is offered by Sir Robert Tate, educated at Shrewsbury, and public orator at Trinity College, Dublin, then a reactionary institution in its curriculum as well as its politics: 'probably the only seat of learning in existence which makes the writing of verses a compulsory part of every examination for Honours in Greek and Latin.'[20] He quotes humorous verses by Hubert de Burgh to illustrate the perils of an untrained ear; de Burgh laughs at 'a young lady' who can rhyme 'lanes' with 'Aristophanes', 'tides' with 'Euripides', 'gates' with 'Socrates', 'affright us' with 'Tacitus', and so on. Such is the march of modernity, against which Tate and others fight gallant, if perhaps misguided, rearguard actions.

As an example of translation's occasional power, when applied to English of some real historical significance, we may examine the central section from Tate's version of Sir Henry Newbolt's *Vitai Lampada*:

> Versa acies retro cedit; qua pandit harenas
>   Africa desertas terra cruore madet.
> Dux jacet exanimis, sine fulmine machina torpet,
>   Fumus et immixto pulvere cuncta tegit.
> Nomen inane fides; patriae trans aequora longe
>   Litora; mors tumida saevit ut amnis aqua.
> Sed revocat fractas pueri vox illa cohortes:
>   'Eia age! perstandum est qua decet arte viros!'[21]
>
> The sand of the desert is sodden red,—
> Red with the wreck of a square that broke;—

[19] M. L. Clarke, *Classical Education in Britain, 1500–1900* (Cambridge, 1959), p. 56: citing L. Stephen, *Life of Sir J. F. Stephen* (1895), p. 81.   [20] Sir R. W. Tate, *Carmina Dublinensia* (Dublin and London, 1946).
[21] Tate, p. 25. His response to criticism of the translation, p. xx.

> The Gatling's jammed and the Colonel dead,
> And the regiment blind with dust and smoke.
> The river of death has brimmed its banks,
> And England's far, and Honour a name,
> But the voice of a schoolboy rallies the ranks:
> 'Play up! play up! and play the game!'

Newbolt's poem epitomises the heroism shown in numerous small Imperial conflicts, as viewed from the safety of an English armchair. The picture is romanticised, but not triumphalist. It does not portray the British as victorious; rather, they are desperately defending themselves, and they win (if they do win at all) by perseverance in the face of fast and hostile bowling. The differences between war and cricket would have been apparent to the reader. That a parallel should be drawn is intentionally shocking. The young voice that urges his older and more experienced subordinates to fight on may or may not be successful; if one finds oneself in such a dreadful situation, it is better to try to live than to collapse without even trying. Retreat means only death: readers of Tate or Newbolt would remember that 'mors et fugacem persequitur virum,/nec parcit imbellis iuventae/poplitibus timidove tergo.' [death also pursues the fugitive, nor does it spare the knees or timid back of unwarlike youths.][22] This is what happens when a square breaks: an ordered defence, in which most will survive, becomes a mass of fugitives, of which most will be cut down. Playing the game is not a romantic ideal, it is a necessity of survival.

The military tactics envisaged by Newbolt are not essentially different from those of the Napoleonic wars;[23] once the machine-gun is out of action, simple courage is required to redeem the failures of technology. These tactics were suited to battles in Sudan, or fighting Zulus (who broke one British force, but were defeated by a large and disciplined square); they were useless against the rifles of the Boers, very shortly after Newbolt's early poetry appeared, and not of great use on the frontier of India, where many of Newbolt's young cricketers fell.[24] The Boers lost in the end, and so did the Kaiser. The Great War did indeed see appalling casualties. A large and skilful European enemy could never be subdued without them. Young men's enthusiasm for the game became blunted; yet the endurance of Newbolt's poem remained.

---

[22] Horace, *Carm.* 3. 2. 14–16. Other poems of Newbolt have Latin titles, e.g. 'Laudabunt alii' (from Hor., *Carm.* 1. 7. 1), 'Vae victis' (from Livy).   [23] He regularly wrote on Nelson's navy, as well as Drake's.
[24] See, e.g., 'Clifton Chapel': especially the last stanza, with the 'frontier-grave', and the Latin inscription that ends the poem, . . . *Sed miles, sed pro patria*, a nice example of Latin incorporated into an English rhythm (scan as accentual iambic tetrameter); cf. Tennyson's Catullan 'Frater ave atque vale'.

The translation is as effective in Latin as the original in English; all the essentials are there, though the order of the parts within some couplets is reversed. The Latin has a more measured tone, perhaps more sombrely tragic than the frantic, rhetorical approach of the English (red, —/red . . . wreck . . . broke, etc.). This applies particularly to the refrain. Although it is poignant to imagine the young officer using the English version, it still sounds ridiculously inappropriate to the circumstances. *Perstandum est* [one must endure] has nothing foolish about it, nothing applicable only to a game. While abandoning the word 'game', Tate has added the word 'men' (*viros*), uttered by a boy's voice. Thus we see the fragility of a boy who leads men, without his rallying-cry being invalidated. His version of the refrain can be switched from cricket to war, and never appears absurd.

Though the translation had been written earlier, Tate allowed it to be republished in Dublin directly after the Second World War (a war in which the neutral Irish government had at times behaved poorly: I do not suppose that Tate concurred in their official condolences on the demise of Hitler). The general situation of Newbolt's beleaguered regiment can be transferred to a nation, in the 1940s, standing up against evil at immense cost: as Britain and the rest of the Empire did. Individual Irishmen had been a vital part of the heroism celebrated by Newbolt (making up a disproportionate share of the British army throughout the nineteenth century); their sacrifice was remembered by some, if officially scorned. The printing of the translation can be seen as a defiant gesture, not only against the declining status of Latin composition, but also against the political priorities of contemporary Dublin. These thoughts may not consciously have occurred to Tate or his readers. Newbolt's is one poem reprinted among many. If Latin is merely a vehicle for pure and empty exercises, it hardly matters what is translated. Some may have cared, however, and if we are now to appreciate the use of Latin as a recent historical phenomenon, it is at least worth considering whether there can be more to it than virtuosic vacuity.

'The Ram'

An excellent example of the glaring weaknesses of twentieth-century Latin composition (from an aesthetic, rather than technical, viewpoint), and of some of its minor strengths, can be seen in the life and publications of A. B. Ramsay, teacher at Eton, and (from 1925 to 1947) Master of Magdalene College, Cambridge. The recent *History* of the college gives a very negative picture of his stultifying influence on the establishment, and bias towards Etonian

classicists.[25] Remembered with affection (or derision) as 'the Ram', he treated
undergraduates as schoolboys; particularly notorious were his 'saying lessons', in
which he required them to recite from memory large passages of Demosthenes
(or other classical authors) while standing on a particular spot of carpet, chosen
to ensure that the blinding light of the sun periodically tested their deport-
ment.[26] Many of Ramsay's distinguished guests witnessed these recitations:
Kipling thought them ludicrous, but Stanley Baldwin (prime minister, 1923,
1924–9, and 1935–7) thoroughly approved.[27] Ramsay was largely responsible for
William Empson's long exile from British academic life, insisting upon his
expulsion in 1929 for possession (when a junior fellow, not a student) of 'engines
of love' (i.e., contraceptives).[28]

Ramsay's work is treated sympathetically by Bradner (pp. 341–3), an assess-
ment based on the first two of the four uniform volumes that Ramsay
published at Cambridge, all of them combining work in Latin and English.[29]
A good deal of Ramsay's verse, in both languages, is cloyingly sentimental, and
obsessed with the parochial worlds of Eton and Magdalene. A typical example
is *October*,[30] where the whole of creation is summed up in a few small courts
and gardens:

> . . . And Magdalene in the morning
> Is why the world was made.
> For Magdalene in October
> Is glorious to behold . . .
> All sombre things and sober
> Are not for me this morn,
> For Magdalene in October
> Is why a man was born.

I suspect that 'sober' was chosen largely for the rhyme, although the avoidance
of sobriety is indeed appropriate. The poem is best recited in a light-headed
mood, returning to college as the dawn sunshine reveals its beauty, and before
the onset of the inevitable hangover—not that Ramsay would have behaved
riotously:

[25] R. Hyam, in R. Hyam, ed., *A History of Magdalene College, Cambridge, 1428–1988* (Cambridge, 1994), pp.
232–7. His skill at Latin verse is briefly mentioned, p. 235, though there is no discussion of his books, or
suggestion that Hyam has read them.
[26] Mentioned by Hyam, p. 236; a full and hilarious account by C. Ray, 'The Saying Lesson', *Magdalene
College Magazine and Record* new series 35 (1990–1), pp. 43–5.
[27] Sir R. Melville, letter in *Magdalene College Magazine and Record* new series 37 (1992–3), p. 50.
[28] Hyam, pp. 245–6; full details in R. Luckett & R. Hyam, 'Empson & the engines of love', *Magdalene
College Magazine and Record* new series 35 (1990–1), pp. 33–40.
[29] *Inter Lilia* (1920), *Ros Rosarum* (1925), *Frondes Salicis* (1935), *Flos Malvae* (1946).
[30] *Flos Malvae*, p. 51.

> Bacchicum iactant alii liquorem;
> Dona Pomonae Cererisque ducunt;
> Zinziver zytho vel acerba miscent
>   Hordea lymphis.
>
> Others boast of Bacchic liquor; they take the gifts of Pomona or Ceres;
> they mix ginger with ale, or bitter barley with water.[31]

Instead, he worships tea with his morning and evening prayers. The stanza is quite lively in parts (especially the alliteration of *zinziver zytho*, more evocative than ginger-ale deserves), even if the message is insipid.

Ramsay was certainly prolific, and he treated Latin as a medium equal to English; but he lacks the weight of a major poet. Some of his short pieces do have a real poetic quality (though most do not). It is unfortunate that he never attempted more substantial writing, since a major topic, rather than school routines, might have brought out the best in his talent. He can make something worthwhile out of an event such as the arrival of a touring cricket team from India:

> Terribili densae serpunt ibi tigride silvae;
>   Turrigero spissae stant elephante viae.
> Ipsa suos frustra mirabilis India captat.
>   Huc veniunt, nostrae dedita turba pilae.
> Huc veniunt lusum; magni cupiuntur honores;
>   Pax alitur ludis et fit amica fides.
>
> Thick woods there creep with fierce tigers, the roads are lined with howdah'd elephants. India's marvels fail to attract its own people. They come here, devoted to our game of cricket. They come here to play; great honour is at stake; sport nourishes peace, and leads to loyal friendship.[32]

Cricket is arguably the most worthwhile legacy of the British Empire; the Empire abandoned in the eighteenth century has adopted its trivialised form, and to the Empire of the twentieth century has been bequeathed this cultural jewel in its full brilliance. Ramsay makes his point lightly (and one does not suppose that all India is as exotic as he suggests), yet the fostering of peace between races that have good reason for mutual hostility is a real achievement, deserving of celebration.[33] As in Newbolt's poem, the playing fields can serve a serious purpose.

---

[31] 'Tea', lines 1–4: *Flos Malvae*, p. 8.   [32] 'The Indian Team', lines 7–12: *Frondes Salicis*, p. 20.
[33] This was the first Indian touring team to play a Test match (Lord's, 25–8 June 1932); England won by 158 runs, but the Indians had shown themselves to be worthy opponents by reducing England to 19 for 3 on the first morning. The captain of the tour (though, wisely, not of the Test team) was the Maharajah of Porbander, reputedly the only first-class cricketer to have more Rolls Royces than runs: M. Bose, *History of Indian Cricket* (London, 1990), p. 69.

The Great War inspired some of Ramsay's more moving poetry, with genuine feeling for the shattered lives of hundreds of brave Etonians, remembered amidst their closed society, but forgotten in the crass euphoria of victory.[34] Latin is usually thought of, in the context of war poets, merely as the source of the infamous phrase, 'dulce et decorum est pro patria mori' (Hor., *Carm.* 3. 2. 13); it is less often observed that the rest of Horace's stanza (quoted above with reference to Newbolt) undermines any sense of jingoism that might ignorantly be attached to the line, making further heavy-handed irony quite ridiculous. Ramsay shows a sensitive awareness of this fact in his asclepiadic ode, 'Dulce et Decorum'. Using a different metre (Horace's 'Roman odes', 3. 1–6, are all alcaic), Ramsay develops Horace's phrase into a message of Christian resignation that, while very different to the pagan original, still respects its value:

> . . . Nunc opponere fortiter
> His invicta malis pectora discimus,
> Sistentes lacrimas si placuit Deo
>   Dilectissima quaeque
>   Dulci pro patria mori.

> We now learn to keep our hearts unbowed by these disasters, stopping our tears, if it is God's will that all we loved the most should die for our sweet fatherland.[35]

Ramsay is fully concerned with the modern world (even if, for him, that world is an enclosed one); he can also deal with the latest discoveries of science in a humorous way:

> O parva summo stella micans polo,
> Quae corda caeca nuper origine
>   Humana turbabas, ab ipsis
>   Astrologis meliora docti
> Nunc scimus omnes corpore quo tua
> Natura constet, cassitero calens
>   Fumante ventosisque nitri
>   Nubibus hydrogenaque vivo.

> O little star, twinkling in the heavens, who used to trouble human hearts with the mystery of your origin, we have been taught better by the star-gazers, and now all know what you are made of: you are hot with smoking metal, and wind-blown nitrogen clouds, and active hydrogen.[36]

---

[34] 'Armistice', *Inter Lilia*, p. 93: quoted by Bradner, p. 343.
[35] *Inter Lilia*, p. 96 (lines 20–4); cf. Hor., *Carm.* 3. 2. 13–16.
[36] 'Twinkle, twinkle, little star; now we all know what you are': *Frondes Salicis*, p. 3.

The present and the future

The current position of Latin verse composition in universities is not strong, although it is studied in some places by small numbers of students. Cambridge still awards prizes for original verse by undergraduates; they are not awarded every year, for lack of suitable entries. The Oxford Chancellor's prize is now given only for translation into Latin. Original verse and translations continue to be written, as an entertaining diversion, by a few more senior figures. H. H. Huxley and F. J. Lelièvre have published several slim and elegant books (largely of translations) in recent years. Latin prose continues to be used for the speeches of university orators, and in the prefaces of some texts; original verse is occasionally inserted by more enterprising writers of prose.[37] Several orators have published their speeches: James Diggle is the best and most recent example, with several passages of verse of varying length and metre.[38] There are certainly good things to be found in twentieth-century Latin, only some of which I have been able to mention; but there has also been much that is rather superficial and unworthy of scholarly attention, and translation has continued to act as a blight on the health of more adventurous literature.

If Latin is to be taken seriously again as a modern British literary language, it needs more than translations and trivia. What is needed is a substantial, original work of Latin poetry. I should perhaps add that I have myself done something towards this (with about 800 hexameters so far completed, as part of a larger project). I have no narcissistic urge to intrude a sample of my own poetry into the present volume; I mention it only to show that I try to practise what I preach. It is genuinely feasible and fun to write in Latin verse today, and I urge students of the tradition to consider participating in it.

Conclusion to Part I

Though this tenth chapter approaches its end, the book is far from over; indeed, these ten chapters could be seen as a preamble (or at least a complement) to the book's real substance, albeit rather a long and discursive one. The text of Alsop's poems is yet to be read and studied widely; I present, in Part II, what I hope will be a reasonable and convenient working version of it. Further research will almost certainly reveal mistakes and omissions, but the essence should remain of

[37] Cf. M. L. West, preface to *Iambi et Elegi Graeci* (Oxford, 1971; further verses in 2nd edn., 1989); earlier, A. E. Housman's *Manilius* (1903).
[38] J. Diggle, *Cambridge Orations, 1982–93: a selection* (Cambridge, 1994). He salutes Ted Hughes in 7 alcaic stanzas, p. 24: rather more elegant than the poet laureate's own verse (not that that is saying a great deal). Cf. also Diggle's 'Mars', in *Bimillenario Virgiliano* (Valle d'Aosta, 1981), pp. 31–5.

value. Let him be called the English Horace, as long as his own poetic individuality is not compromised. He cared for Horace, but he cared far more for England. Alsop's place in the literary canon is not established. Should he continue to be excluded, as no more than a name (and that only known to a few)? Or should he be accepted as one of the more interesting figures of the eighteenth century, whom no student of the period, or of the history of Latin literature, can afford to ignore? I have argued for his significance. Each reader will come to an independent conclusion; as long as his distinctive art receives a fair hearing, I doubt that he would be too concerned with our verdict. He might shrug his shoulders at the vicissitudes of fortune, and order another divinely intoxicating round of drinks. There is something to be said for imitation, in literature as in life.

PART II
The Poems of Anthony Alsop

Introductory Notes

The arrangement of the text

Books 1 (miscellaneous odes) and 2 (epistolary odes) are taken from Bernard's edition, 1752, using his numbering (I have added a number, [27], to the final ode in book 2). In general, his arrangement within each book is arbitrary; there seems little advantage (and considerable chance for confusion) in disturbing it.

Additional poems are arranged by myself in two books, as follows: Book 3 contains Latin poems, in both lyric metres (1–7) and hexameters (8–11), that may be assigned to Alsop with reasonable certainty. Book 4 is in two distinct parts; firstly, English poems (1–7: all almost certainly Alsop's); secondly, additional Latin poems (8–25) of more doubtful attribution.

Doubtful and spurious attributions

The degree of doubt attached to the poems in book 4 varies; in some cases, I may be being over-cautious in not assigning them to book 3. The distinction between the books is not clear-cut; nevertheless, I feel it is worth making (even tentatively and somewhat artificially), in order to allow a clear statement that books 1–3 are the core of Alsop's work, and that the poems in book 4, whether his or not, are less important for the study of his achievement. Much of the elegiac poetry in book 4 is not, in any case, of the highest quality, and it lacks the distinctive personality so characteristic of his odes.

Most of my additional poems are noted by L. Bradner, 'Some notes on Anthony Alsop's *Odarum Libri Duo*', *Bodleian Library Record* 9 (1976), pp. 231–4. Two attributions suggested there I consider quite unlikely (and therefore omit from my text); one, the 'Prologus Westmonasteriensis' in the British Library ms., could be by any of the Westminster poets (who mostly proceeded to Christ Church or Trinity, Cambridge), and the fact that Alsop went to the school merely makes him one of many candidates. More seriously, the poem seems to refer to the Duke of Newcastle's visit to Cambridge in 1755, which would make the attribution to Alsop quite impossible. The other, to 'Mr C.' on the breeching of his son, refers to Penn Assheton Curzon in the ms. title; I take this to be the MP (d. 1797), father of Earl Howe, who matriculated at Brasenose in 1774, aged 17; again, the date precludes Alsop's authorship. Neither of these is attributed to Alsop in the manuscript.

Poems not included

The Aesop translations are omitted partly for practical reasons, as they would unacceptably swell the length of the book. There are other considerations: there may be some doubt that Alsop was wholly responsible for them all; as translations, they are probably of less interest than original works. The original poem 'Canis in praesepi' is quoted in full in Chapter 4. Bernard's dedicatory poem to the Duke of Newcastle is not included (I rather doubt that Alsop would have approved of such toadying to a Whig); it is discussed and quoted from in Chapter 3. See also notes on elegiac attributions, preceding 4. 13 and following 4. 25.

Note on transcription policy

In general, the text of books 1–2 is left as printed by Bernard. Accents have been removed from the Latin. In a few cases (e.g. Orcus, Camoena) capitalisation has been standardised. Punctuation has occasionally been clarified (with a note on any cases of difficulty). In the case of mss., spelling, capitalisation, and punctuation vary widely (and are often inconsistent within a ms.); numerous minor differences have not been noted.

Note on the commentary

The commentary is deliberately kept to a minimum; the more important odes are discussed in some detail in the preceding chapters. In each case, I give a reference to the relevant chapter. For page references to my earlier discussions, the reader should consult the index of passages cited from Alsop's poems. A note after each poem lists the printed or manuscript sources, together with an estimate of the poem's date (estimates of uncertain dates are based on internal evidence: e.g. people or events alluded to in the poem). Commentary notes appear at the foot of the page (divided by a short rule, when they cover more than one poem on the same page). The numbers at the beginning of each note refer to the line numbers of the Latin; line numbers are also given in the translations (in brackets: i.e. '(9)' means that the following translates the stanza beginning at line 9 of the Latin). The notes are not intended to provide a full list of textual variants; in general, only those that I consider significant are noted. More detail might possibly have been desirable, but would also have added to the size and complexity of the book, and therefore delayed its publication. Nor have I followed Harold Love's valuable advice for the editing of scribally published texts: for which see his *Scribal Publication in 17th century England* (Oxford, 1993). In the case of an author not yet accepted into the mainstream canon, I judged it important to offer a readable working edition to accompany the chapters in Part I; as long as one remembers that such an edition has its limitations, it should prove serviceable enough. I generally refrain from expressing an opinion on the merits of variant readings, unless they significantly alter the sense. Although Bernard's edition is later than many surviving mss., few mss. can be closely associated with Alsop's circle.

Sources cited in abbreviated form

Bern. = Bernard's edition, 1752
BL(a) = the British Library ms., i.e. the ms. addenda and new poems in 11409. h. 30
BL(b) = British Library, ms. Add. 30162
[other British Library items, cited less often, are given in full: BL ms. Add. . . . = British Library, Additional manuscript no. . . .]
D = Bodleian, ms. Don. e. 53
E = Bodleian, ms. Eng. poet. f. 13
L = Bodleian, ms. Lat. misc. c. 14
Nott. = Nottingham University Library, Portland collection

See the note on *Text* after each poem for other sources abbreviated in the commentary below (e.g., *G.M.* for *Gentleman's Magazine*).

Book 1
Miscellaneous Odes

1.1 TE DEUM

Te Deum laeto celebramus hymno;
Te Deum, Te nos Dominum fatemur;
Te Patrem aeternum veneratur omnis,
    Qua patet, orbis.
5 Voce Te laeta chorus Angelorum,
Te vocant alti spatia ampla caeli,
Quaeque circumstant solium supremi
    Agmina regis.
Te Cherubini sine fine clamant;
10 Et Seraphini sine fine clamant,
Sancte! dicentes, iterumque Sancte!
    Sancte! potentum
Rex Deusque exercituum timende!
Gloria immensum tua complet orbem;
15 Vasta Majestas tua complet alti
    Atria caeli.
Hinc Tibi laudes dat Apostolorum
Turba; respondent socii Prophetae;
Martyrum claudit celebrationem
20   Splendidus ordo.
Quotquot in sacros ubicunque coetus
Junxerit cultus fideique norma,
Te Deum unitis animis et uno
    Ore fatentur:
25 Te Patrem immensae dominationis;
Unicum agnoscunt et honore plenum
Filium, Patri aequiparem, coaevum, ae-
    queque potentem:

Translation: [paraphrase of the] 'Te Deum'

We celebrate you, o God, in a happy hymn; we confess that you are our God and master; the whole wide world worships you as its eternal father. The chorus of angels, and the broad spaces of high heaven, and the hosts that surround the throne of the supreme king, call upon you with happy voices. (9) The cherubim sing of you endlessly; the seraphim sing of you endlessly, saying 'Holy, holy, holy, king and fearful God of powerful hosts; your glory fills the huge world, your vast majesty fills the halls of high heaven'. (17) The crowd of apostles praises you from here; the prophets join in reply; the splendid order of martyrs closes the celebration. (21) All who are anywhere linked in ritual and orthodox faith by holy gatherings confess with united hearts and one voice that you are God, the father of a huge dominion; they acknowledge your only son, full of honour, his father's equal, equally ancient, and equally powerful. (29) They praise the spirit, as master and God, the giver of grace and heavenly life. Everlasting glory, o Christ, invests you as king; you are born as the eternal son of the eternal father; nor did you refuse to enter

5 *G.M.* reads *juncta* for *laeta*.   9–12 The triple *Sanctus* is separated, and made vocative; but the repetition in 9–10 restores the hieratic effect. Only this and the penultimate stanza are not end-stopped.   13 Probably alluding to Hor., *Carm.* 3. 1. 5, 'regum timendorum'. *G.M.* reads *tremende* for *timende*.   19 *G.M.* reads *Martyres claudunt*; Bern. has the genitive, *Martyrum*, with *ordo* (probably an improvement), but leaves the verb in the plural; I alter it to the singular, to fit *ordo* (though, loosely, the plural might be acceptable).   26 Probably alluding to Hor., *Carm.* 4. 14. 2, 'plenis honorum muneribus'.   27 *Aequiparem* and *coaevum*: words from late Latin.

Spiritum laudant Dominum Deumque
30   Gratiae et vitae aetheriae datorem.
     Christe, Te nunquam peritura vestit
          Gloria Regem:
     Ortus aeterno es Patre sempiternus
     Filius: nec Te piguit subire,
35   Unde homo humanum genus expiares,
          Virginis alvum.
     Tu simul morti caput ac dedisti
     Mortis atque Orci domitor, repente
     Ostium caeli resonabat, intro-
40   ite, fideles.
     Gloria cinctus solio in supremo
     Assides dextrae Patris; et sedebis,
     Ultimum donec sua cuique reddas
          Ante tribunal.
45   Adjuva, Judex hominum futurus,
     Adjuva servos Tibi supplicantes,
     Quos tuus sanguis, pretium ter amplum,
          Morte redemit.
     Fac tui servi numerentur usque
50   Caelites inter pariter beati:
     Protege et semper rege quot tuus grex
          Rite vocantur.
     Tolle in aeternum altius altiusque
     Gloria ornatos: hodie in diesque
55   Diceris magnus; coleris colerisque
          Omne per aevum.
     Fac diem hunc recto pede transeamus
     Labis immunes: miserere nobis,
     O Deus, nobis miserere. Amoris
60   Aetherei lux
     Surgat in cunctos Tibi qui fideles;
     Surgat in me qui Tibi fido: noli
     O Deus, noli exitio, Deus mi,
          Tradere servum.

the virgin's womb, whence as a man you could expiate the human race. (37) When you gave yourself to death, and also conquered death, suddenly the gate of heaven resounded, 'come in, all ye faithful'. You sit at the right hand of the father on the highest throne, surrounded by glory; and you will sit there, until you give to each his fate at the last judgement. (45) Help us, man's future judge, help your servants who beseech you, whom your blood (a thrice-sufficient payment) has redeemed from death. Grant that your servants may always be numbered alongside the happy company of heaven; protect and rule forever all those who are called your flock. Raise them higher and higher for all time, adorned with glory; you are called great today, and every day; you are worshipped and will be worshipped for all time. (57) Grant that we may pass through this day uprightly and without sin; have pity on us, o God, have pity on us. Let the light of eternal love rise up in all who are faithful to you; let it rise in me, who am faithful to you; do not, o God, do not hand me over, my God, as a slave to death.

Text: Bern.; *Gentleman's Magazine* 5. 609 (October 1735); BL(b), fo. 52ᵛ-53ᵛ. *Date*: unknown.

31–2 Alluding to Hor., *Epist.* 1. 18. 22, 'gloria quem supra vires et vestit et unguit'.   35 G.M. reads *scelus* for *genus*.   38 G.M. reads *reclusum* for *repente*.   37–40 The stress on the initial submission, and then the moment of victory, is a particularly dramatic innovation of Alsop's.   41 G.M. reads *Gloriae . . . radio perenni*.   43 G.M. reads *reddes*.   45–8 A crucial moment, turning from praise to prayer, is emphasised by repetition.   46 G.M. reads *tibi qui ministrant*.   47 *Ter amplum*: cf. Hor., *Carm.* 2. 14. 7.   52 Alluding to Hor., *Carm.* 1. 32. 16, 'rite vocanti'.   55 The first *coleris* is in the present tense, the second in the future. (G.M. places the '-que' at the start of line 56.)   58–9 G.M. reads *nostri* for *nobis*.   61–4 The striking end alters the message significantly; at the beginning of the stanza he expands on 'misericordia', and uses repetition again; at the very end he returns to humble pleading, under the shadow of destruction, and highly charged with emotion.

1.2 IN OBITUM REGINAE MARIAE

O Umbra Divis mista volentibus!
Matura sacris heu! nimium choris,
    Quae patrio donata caelo
        Inter avos atavosque regnas!
5 O! quae receptum in sidera Carolum
Utrumque spectas! o! cui brachiis
    Occurrit expansis Elisa
        Et capiti nova serta nectit!
Spectare ab alto si vacat aethere
10 Terras relictas; si lachrymabiles
    Luctus triumphos, et sepulchri
        Cernere non vacuos honores:
Videbis Isin nunc tua funera
Plorare, et umbrae carmina nobili
15   Donata consecrare, partem
        Funerei haud minimam triumphi:
Videbis atras ut decoret vias
Pullatus ordo Virginum, amabili
    Decora luctu turba, telae
20   Immemores simul et choreae:
Videbis aegro murmure conqueri
Durum relicta cuspide militem;
    Tuumque jam primum propinquo
        Nassaidem trepidare fato.
25 Hic inter omnes impavidus stetit
Mortis tumultus; undique militum
    Turmas ruentes, ultimosque
        Audierat gemitus cadentum.
Illum nec armis fusus Hibernicis
30 Senilis Heros; nec tua funera,
    Graftone, nobilesque rapti
        Talmasii quatiunt ruinae.
Tu prima magni pectora Conjugis,
Maria, frangis; jam refugit metu

Translation: 'On the death of Queen Mary'

  O shade mixed with welcoming gods, you have gone, alas, far too early to join the sacred choirs; you have been given to your native heaven, and rule among your ancestors; you gaze upon each King Charles, both of them received among the stars; Queen Elizabeth runs to you with open arms and twines new garlands for your head. (9) If you have time to look down from heaven on the lands you have left behind, and can see grief's sad triumphs and the honours (that are not empty) paid to your tomb, you will see that Thames now weeps at your funeral, and consecrates songs to your noble shade—which form not the least part of the funereal pomp. (17) You will see how a sombrely dressed train of maidens adorns the black roads, elegant in their loving grief, and forgetful of both loom and dance; you will see a tough soldier lamenting with a sick murmur, his weapons abandoned; and now for the first time you will see your Nassau tremble at the nearness of his fate. (25) He stood fearless amongst all death's tumults; he had heard on all sides the noise of regiments in rout, and the last groans of the fallen. (29) Nor did that aged hero, killed by Irish arms, nor your death, Grafton, nor the noble fall of Tollemache shake him. (33) You are the first, Mary, to break the heart of your great husband; now the shattered hero recoils in fear, and an unaccustomed paleness trem-

2 *Matura*: 'young', cf. Virg., *Aen.* 7. 53 (of Lavinia).   6 *Cui* scanned as two shorts: unusual but classical (cf. Martial 1. 105. 22, 12. 49. 3; Juv. 3. 49 [unless a spondaic 5th foot]; Ausonius, *Ephem.* 1. 15 [in sapphics]).   11–12 Alluding to Hor., *Carm.* 2. 20. 23–4, 'sepulchri/ mitte supervacuos honores'. Should the reader, remembering Horace, conclude that they are empty now?   13 1695 reads *in* for *nunc* (allowing a short fifth sylla- ble).   18–19 *Amabili luctu*: a nice oxymoron (cf. Hor., *Carm.* 3. 4. 5–6).   30 The Duke of Schomberg (1615–90), killed at the Boyne.   31 Henry Fitzroy, 1st Duke of Grafton (1663–90), an illegitimate son of Charles II; distinguished in the naval battle of Beachy Head, in June 1690, and died at Cork in October.   32 Lt.-Gen. Thomas Talmash (or Tollemache) (1651?–94); distinguished in Ireland and Flanders; William's senior general, after Marlborough's dismissal; mortally wounded while commanding the attack on Brest, 1694, of which the French received ample warning (from Marlborough, among others).

35   Perculsus Heros, et madenti
         Insolitus tremit ore pallor.
     Tu leniebas consilio Ducis
     Duros labores; Tu, Dea, gaudium
         Quae semper illi, quae Britannis
40   Una dabas, dabis una luctum.
     Eheu! genarum purpureum decus,
     Eheu! nitentis fulgura luminis,
         Formaeque flores heu! caducos
         Corripuit maculosa pestis.
45   Quis jam levabit, quis miserabiles
     Luctus egeni? quis viduae feret
         Solatium? quis dulce reddet
         Auxilium fragili senectae?
     Absente quis nunc incolumes Duce
50   Praestabit Anglos? imperium maris
         Quis asseret? quis tradet igni
         Celtiacas iterum carinas?
     En! flamma ferventi aequore volvitur
     Contraria: en! puppes avido Thetis
55   Mergit barathro, semiustos
         Dum liquidus lavat ignis artus.
     En! acta nigro sulphuris impetu
     Surgunt in altum corpora fumea:
         En! specto nubes inter altas
60   Attonitos volitare Gallos.
     Frustra at Mariae tempora laureae
     Cingunt Coronae; frustra agit Anglia
         Victrix triumphos: Gallicanis
         Saevior heu! Libitina telis
65   Divam subegit. Non populi preces
     Te, chara, servant; non miserae graves
         Gentis querelae: non repellit
         Fulmineum tua laurus ictum.
     Frustra auget undas navita fletibus,
70   Damnatque Parcas et sua sidera,
         Armatque classes: heu! sepultam

bles on his damp face. (37) You used to lighten by your counsel his hard tasks as leader; you, goddess, who used alone to give joy to him, and to Britons, will now alone give grief. Alas, the rosy loveliness of your cheeks, the thunderbolts of your shining eyes, and the, alas, fading bloom of your beauty have been snatched by a foul disease. (45) Who now will relieve the miserable griefs of the pauper? Who will bring solace to the widow? Who will give sweet help to fragile old age? Who, when their leader is absent, will now keep the English safe? Who will assert their power on the sea? (51) Who will again set fire to the French fleet? Look—the flame is whirled back on the boiling sea; look—Thetis submerges their ships in the greedy deep, while liquid fire washes half-burned limbs. Look—driven by the force of black sulphur smoky bodies rise high into the air; look—I see astonished Frenchmen flying among the high clouds. (61) But laurel crowns surround Mary's brows in vain; in vain does victorious England celebrate her triumphs: Death, more savage, alas, than French weapons, has defeated our goddess. The people's prayers do not save you, dear though you are to them, nor the heavy complaints of your unhappy family; nor does your laurel repel the thunderbolt's stroke. (69) In vain does the sailor add his tears to the sea, and curse the Fates and the stars by which he steers, and arm his fleets; alas, no ship will bring back our buried mistress. (73) So, with our goddess dead, there remains one hope;

35–6 Probably alluding to Hor., *Epod.* 7. 15–6, 'tacent et albus ora pallor inficit/ mentesque perculsae stupent'. *Epode* 7 is a bitter attack on civil war: for a Jacobite, William's actions wickedly renewed civil war, and Alsop stresses the carnage he causes.   37 Cf. Hor., *Carm.* 3. 4. 41, 'lene consilium'.   40 An elegant chiasmus.   41 Probably alluding to Hor., *Epod.* 5. 7, 'hoc inane purpurae decus'.   44 Possibly alluding to Hor., *Carm.* 4. 5. 22, 'maculosum . . . nefas'; if so, a Jacobite might apply Horace's opening to James II: 'Divis orte bonis . . . abes iam nimium diu'.   49–50 Possibly alluding to Hor., *Epist.* 1. 16. 16, 'incolumem . . . praestant'.   55–6 Cf. 3. 8. 85, 'semiustosque artus'.   60 Cf. 3. 8. 151 (more flying Frenchmen).   61–2 Possibly alluding to Hor., *Carm.* 2. 14. 13–5 (repeated *frustra*); if so, an appropriate reminder of one of Horace's greatest odes on death (cf. n. on 72).   68 Probably alluding to Hor., *Carm.* 3. 16. 11, 'ictu fulmineo'.   69–72 A humorous conceit followed by a cliché: real grief has vanished.

Nulla ratis Dominam reducet.
Quin interempta restat adhuc Dea
Spes una; restat Nassaides, suae
75   Custos Britanniae, superque
      Celtiacas metuendus oras.
I, magne Princeps, Borbonias tuo
Expelle naves victor ab aequore;
    Et Gallicae agnoscant triremes
80   Supplicibus tua signa velis.

there remains Nassau, the guardian of his Britain, a man feared on the shores of France. Go, great prince, and as victor expel the Bourbon ships from your sea; and let the French galleys acknowledge your flags by dipping their sails.

Text: Bern.; *Pietas Universitatis Oxoniensis* (Oxford, 1695); *Musarum Anglicanarum Analecta* (1699) 2. 275–8. *Date*: early 1695.

1.3 IN OBITUM GEORGII PRINCIPIS DANIAE

Translation: 'On the death of George, Prince of Denmark'

Cur non, ut olim, Diva sciens lyrae,
Audis vocantem? Flebile cur fugis
    Movere plectrum, luctuosi
      Carminis officium recusans?
5 Nam nec jocosum fas tibi perpetim
Sperare pensum; nec vacuum ciet
    Testudo luctum; nec dolentem
      Destituit sua fama Musam.
Non sic Mariam passa silentio
10 Perire; non Glovernus ubi occidit,
    Obmutuit torpens Camoena:
      Quidni et in hunc facilis laborem
Se tradat ultro? Surgite, vos, quibus
Feliciorem Cynthius indolem
15   Indulsit, augustosque manes
      Non humili memorate cantu.
Vos, Regiae Arces, Tuque, Domus meae
Nutrix juventae, jure mihi aedibus
    Praelata cunctis, quas benignus

Why, goddess of lyric poetry, do you not now hear me calling upon you, as you did in the past? Why do you flee from plucking the tearful lyre, and refuse the duty of grief-stricken song? For it is not right that you should always hope for a playful task; nor is it empty sorrow that the lyre will rouse; nor has her own voice abandoned the lamenting Muse. (9) You did not allow Mary to perish in such silence; nor, when Gloucester died, was the Muse numbly silent: why should she not give herself freely and readily to this labour also? Rise up, you goddesses to whom Apollo granted a happier nature, and remember his grand spirit in no humble song. (17) You royal towers, the house that nursed my youth, rightly preferred by me to all the other colleges that kind Thames washes with its noble waters—

72 Probably alluding to Hor., *Carm.* 2. 14. 24, 'ulla . . . dominum'.   73–4 Probably alluding to Hor., *Carm.* 4. 4. 70–2, 'spes . . . interempto'; if so, probably subversive, suggesting that William offers no real hope. (Cf. 3. 5. 78)   74–5 *Suae* is strained, for Dutch William, as a Jacobite would notice: conventional loyalty can have a subtly subversive undertone.

10 Anne's son, Gloucester, lamented in the 1700 *Exequiae*; Alsop may refer to his own work, under Sir Bourchier Wrey's name (4. 10: see Chapter 9), or to Oxford's combined efforts.   17 1708 reads *bonae* for *meae*.

20   Ingenuo lavat Isis amne,
    Wolsaea sedes! o citharae potens!
    O sueta centum vocibus eloqui!
            I, pange carmen; I, recentem
                Adde Ducis tumulo coronam.
25 Dic quo per hostes impete Georgius
    Incessit acer; dic ut ad arduos
            Contendit ausus, Suevonumque
                Arva rubro madefecit imbre.
    Dic ut phaselis Angliacis viam
30 Munivit immensum oceanum supra,
            Seu merce Eoa, seu redirent
                Borbonidum spoliis onusti:
    Ut conjugalis foedera vinculi
    Intaminatis splendida honoribus
35   Servavit, exemplum futuris
                Perpetuum faciens maritis.
    Haec usque decantanda memor tuae
    Committe pubi non sterilis parens:
            Laus Georgii praebebit omni
40   Materiem citharae perennem.
    Sic blanda faustum spondeat exitum
    Fortuna coeptis; sic tibi moenia
            Superba surgant, sospitante
                Aldrichii genio penates.
45 Sic te faventis Cecilii integra
    Virtus honestet; sic aveat Tuus
            Dici Trelaunus Wintonensis
                Grande decus columenque Mitrae.

seat of Wolsey, master of the lyre, accustomed to speak in a hundred voices—go on, and sing your song; go on, and add a new garland to the leader's tomb. (25) Tell how furiously George advanced through his enemies; tell how he fought with arduous daring, and made the Swedes' fields wet with bloody rain. Tell how he secured routes for English ships over the huge ocean, so that they might return weighed down with Eastern merchandise, or with spoils taken from the Bourbons. (33) Tell how he preserved the splendid bond of marriage with its honour intact, providing an everlasting example to future husbands. As a fertile parent, remember to repeat this lesson always to your young charges: praise of George will provide continuous subject matter for every lyre. (41) Thus may kind Fortune give a happy end to your undertakings; thus may your proud walls rise, with the genius of Aldrich preserving the household gods. Thus may the unblemished goodness of your patron Cecil bless you; thus may Trelawny, the great glory and support of the see of Winchester, rejoice to be called one of your own.

Text: Bern.; *Exequiae . . . Georgio Principi Daniae* (Oxford, 1708); BL(b), fo. 60; *Musarum Anglicanarum Analecta* 3 (1717), pp. 184–6. *Date*: 1708. This poem is discussed in Chapters 3 and 9.

21 Wolsey founded Cardinal College, taken over by Henry VIII as Christ Church; originally with 100 Students (*centum vocibus*, 22?), then 101.   27 Swedes, Denmark's enemies in the Great Northern War (1700–20); an unclassical form, metri gratia for *Suevorum*; 1708 reads *Sueonumque*.   30 1708 reads *super* for *supra*. 32 Possibly alluding to Virg., *Aen*. 1. 289; cf. Alsop 3. 5. 72–3; 3. 6. 20.   34 Alluding to Hor., *Carm*. 3. 2. 17–18, 'intaminatis . . . honoribus'. 1708 reads *splendide* for -*a*.   41–2 Possibly alluding to Hor., *Carm*. 4. 14. 37–8, 'fortuna . . . exitus'.   48 Alluding to Hor., *Carm*. 2. 17. 3–4.

I.4 IN OBITUM UXORIS

Arte quam certa genus omne morbos
Freindus it contra medicae cohortis
Primus! ut felix opifer maligno
    Debile corpus

5   De toro tollit! quibus auspicato
Fert opem aegrotis, levior Charontis
Cymba scit dudum, et Lachesis triumphos
    Fassa minores.

Profuit multis ubicunque Freindi
10 Dextera, (et prosit precor;) heu! Deorum
Ira, fatorumque vices! mihi nil
    Profuit uni.

Occidit longe mihi prae meipso
Chara, pars nostri melior: quis, o Dii!
15 Quis modus desiderio? quis aequet
    Luctus amorem?

O caput charum! o dolor! o voluptas
Unica! o nunquam reditura amantum
Gaudia! o totum mihi quod supersit
20   Flenda per aevum!

O mea, heu! jam non mea! te nec orto
Sole, nec cesso gemere ingruente
Vespere: at qualis residens opaca
    Turtur in ulmo

25 Triste flet nidi comitem, plicavit
Quem dolis auceps, levibusve telis
Fixit, hic ruptos queritur perenni
    Murmure amores.

Te sine, o conjux, neque dulcis aura,
30 Nec virens hortus, nec amica fessis
Umbra, ceu quondam, placitura: Te nil
    Dulce remota.

Aestuat pectus memor anteacti
Gaudii, cum tu comes implicansque
35 Dexterae laevam, per aperta ruris
    Ferre solebas

Leniter gressus, vel odora mecum
Visere hortorum spatia, hinc et inde
Vellicans quae mi placuere, dante

Translation: 'On the death of his wife'

How sure is the skill with which Freind, first in the regiment of doctors, fights every kind of disease! As a successful bringer of help, he raises a weak body from its sick-bed! Charon's lighter boat, and Fate that can admit fewer victories, have long known the good fortune with which he brings help to the sick. (9) Freind's hand has been of use to many everywhere (and may it so continue!); but—alas, for the anger of heaven, and the mutability of fate!—to me alone it has been of no use at all. (13) She has died, my better part, far dearer to me than my own self: what limit, ye gods, what end to my longing? What grief can equal my love? O dear head! Ah, the pain! My one pleasure is gone—our lovers' joys are never to return. I must mourn you for all the life that remains to me. (21) My own—ah, now no longer my own—I do not cease from groaning as the sun rises, nor as evening draws down: but I am like a turtle-dove in a shady elm, that sadly weeps for the companion of his nest, whom a hunter has tricked and caught in his thin nets, and complains in a continuous murmur that his loves have been broken. (29) Without you, my wife, the breeze is not sweet, nor is the garden green, nor is shade welcome relief for tiredness, as once it was: nothing is sweet now that you are removed. (33) My breast heaves as it recalls our past joy, when you held my right hand in your left, and used to stroll through the open countryside, or visit perfumed gardens with me, plucking apples here and there, which pleased me because it was you who gave them to me.

1 Ms. D reads *morbi* for *-os*.   14 Cf. Hor., *Carm.* 1. 3. 8 (and Nisbet & Hubbard's n., in their *Commentary* (Oxford, 1970), p. 48); n.b. English parallels, e.g. Milton, *Paradise Lost* 5. 95.   15–17 Alluding to Hor., *Carm.* 1. 24. 1–2, 'Quis desiderio . . . modus/ tam cari capitis'. Cf. n. on 54.   21 Cf. Virg., *Geo.* 4. 497.   22–4 Alluding to Virg., *Ecl.* 1. 59, 'nec gemere aeria cessabit turtur ab ulmo'.   26–7 Ms. D reads *levibusque* for *-ve*, *raptos* for *ruptos*.

40   Te quia, poma.
        Tu mihi (sed non acus otiosa
        Interim) attentam dederas legenti,
        Quam placens, aurem, docilis sacrorum, et
            Laeta doceri.
45   Quidquid adversum mihi sors secusve
        Obtulit, Tu mi per utrumque casum
        Aequa, seu durum relevare, fausto
            Sive potiri.
        Quam tibi mite ingenium indolesque
50   Casta; quam fervens pietatis ardor;
        Mutui quam nos in amore, quae non
            Chorda sonabit?
        O! Ego si par citharoedus essem
        Thracio vati, celerisque doctus
55   Pectinis; non Elysias timerem
            Ire sub umbras
        Cantor; immites animos Tyranni
        Flecterem arguto sonitu; nec ante
        Sisteret plectrum mihi quam referrent
60   Tartara sponsam.
        Inde Te ductor superas ad oras
        Redderem, o Dulcis; metuenda quanquam
        Styx iter volvat medium, et noveno
            Obstrepat amne.

(41) How pleased I was when you listened carefully to my reading (though in the mean time your needle was not idle), able and happy to be taught scripture. (45) Whatever my lot brought me, bad or otherwise, you were in either case able to relieve harsh fortune, or take hold of the good. How gentle was your spirit, how chaste your nature; how fervent your love of piety; what string will not recall how we were attuned in love? (53) If I were a lyric poet equal to the Thracian bard, learned in swift music, then I would not be afraid to go under the shades of Elysium as a singer; I would bend the tyrant's harsh soul with clear sounds; nor would my instrument cease its course before the underworld returned my wife. (61) Thence would I lead you back to the world above, my sweet, though fearful Styx whirled along before me, and roared with its nine-branched stream.

Text: Bern.; ms. D, fo. 42ᵛ–43ᵛ. *Date*: *c.* 1718. This poem is discussed in Ch. 7.

1.5 VICECOMITI DE SCUDAMORE, PRAEFIXA AESOPI FABULIS

Augusta pubes! o! perantiquae domus
Spes summa! surgens Scudamoreorum
                                    decus!
Accipe benignus, accipe Aesopi sales,
Quos Croesus olim, quos amabant Caesares:
5   Quos dum tibi audax defero, liceat mihi,
Aesopi ad instar, hanc referre fabulam.
        Alauda dum per arva, per segetes volat
Diuque secum animo volutat anxia,

Translation: 'To Viscount Scudamore, prefixed to Aesop's Fables'

Noble youth, last hope of a most ancient house, rising glory of the Scudamores, please be kind enough to accept this wit of Aesop's, which Croesus and the Caesars once loved. And, while I am so bold as to bring it to you, may I, in Aesop's manner, tell you the following fable? (7) A lark was flying over the fields and crops, for a long time wondering

43 Alluding to Hor., *Carm.* 4. 6. 43, 'docilis modorum'.   54 Alluding to Hor., *Carm.* 1. 24. 13. Cf. Alsop 3. 7.
1–4.   63 Possibly alluding to Virg., *Geo.* 4. 480, 'novies Styx interfusa'.

Cui molle carmen, cui daret liquidum melos,
10 Ad vada Caystri properat et amoena parat
Mulcere Olorem suavitate carminis.
At ille, cur me provocas cantu tuo,
Cui cantilena mortis est praenuntia?
Ergo avolans Alauda per silvas iter
15 Radit, et opaca in fronde Lusciniam videns
Placidos canora voce modulatur sonos:
Sed illa nimis intenta solitis quaestibus,
Ploransque sublatum nece immatura Ityn
Singultat eheu! flebilique murmure
20 Contristat omne nemus, et aeternum dolet.
Elusa rursum Alauda sese in aethera
Nisu frequenti tollit, et vaga nubium
Tractus pererrat: mox avem praenobilem
Hinc inde quaeritanti in aspectum venit
25 Generosus Aquilae filius, qui lumine
Defixus immoto igneum solis jubar
Ardescit intuendo, et expleri nequit.
Hunc conspicatum et sic locutum accepimus:
En ille nostro dignior modulamine!
30 Grandia juvat moliri, in audaces juvat
Assurgere modos, ingenique viribus
Certare summis, spiritumque effundere.
Spernant Olores, ludicrum spernat melos
Luscinia, numeros ille si modo respicit.
35 Haud Milvus, haud me eviscerabit unguibus
Vultur tremendis: me teget, me fortior
Defendet Ales, tela qui jam sustinet
Phoebi, Tonantis mox futurus armiger.

anxiously to whom he might give his gentle song and flowing music. He hurried to the river Cayster, and was preparing to soothe a swan with the pleasant sweetness of his song, when the swan interrupted him: 'why do you provoke me with your singing, when for me singing is the prelude to death?' (14) So the lark flew on through the woods, and seeing a nightingale on a shady leaf he sang to her his quiet and tuneful sounds; but she was too absorbed in her usual complaints, and wept with sobs for Itys, carried off to an early death, and saddened the whole grove with her sad murmur, for ever grieving. (21) The lark escaped again and struggled high up into the air, wandering through the clouds; soon, as he searched hither and thither for a most noble bird, there came into his sight the eagle's noble son, who burns by looking directly at the sun's fire, and cannot be made to flinch. (28) We heard that he saw him, and addressed him thus: 'Here is one more fully deserving our music! It is pleasing to take on great tasks, to rise to bold poetry, to compete with the mind's greatest strength, and pour out one's spirit. (33) Let swans and nightingales scorn a humorous song, if only he looks kindly on our poetry. No kite or vulture will tear me apart with its fearful claws: a stronger bird, who can now bear up against Phoebus' weapons, and will soon carry Jupiter's thunderbolts, will protect and defend me.'

Text: Bern.; dedicatory poem to Alsop's *Fabularum Aesopicarum Delectus* (Oxford, 1698). *Date*: 1698. This poem is discussed in Ch. 4.

22–3 Probably alluding to Hor., *Carm.* 4. 2. 27, 'nubium tractus' (Pindar as a swan).   25 For the myth of the eagle's offspring looking directly at the sun, see D. W. Thompson, *A Glossary of Greek Birds* (Oxford, 1895), p. 6. (Also entries for other bird myths in this poem, p. 10–14, 106–7.) Perhaps recalling Lucan, 9. 902–6.   27 Alluding to Virg., *Aen.* 1. 713, 'expleri mentem nequit, ardescitque tuendo'.

1.6 GOTHOFREDO KNELLER, BARONETTO, PRAEFIXA VELLEII PATERCULI OPERIBUS

Translation: 'To Sir Godfrey Kneller, bt., prefixed to the works of Velleius Paterculus'

Knellere, succorum o potens! o artifex
Praelate cunctis, quotquot aetas pristina
Praesensve peperit: Te nec antiqui stylus
Zeuxis, recentiorve Raphaelis manus
5 Superasse jactat: sive magnanimos duces
Regesque pingis, seu decora virginum
Describis ora, quas juventuti neces
Olim datura, ni favens adsit Venus!
Hunc tu libellum sume, tu Paterculi
10 Breves tabellas cape, ubi adest imaginum
Non indecorus ordo, nec vanus color.
Pingente Velleio, Vinicii indolem
Nec lector odit improbatve Tiberium:
Pingente Knellero, nec horremus trucem
15 Frontem Ludovici, aridasve Lyces genas.
Quare aequus aspice culta scriptoris opera,
Utcunque manca, non tamen pretii indiga,
Jucunda lectu, fructuosa legentibus.
Haec tradidisse scripta quam vellem tibi
20 Perfecta! at o! Paterculi laboribus
Quis ausit aliquid addere tuisve tabulis.

Kneller, master of paints, you are a greater craftsman than all others to whom past or present ages have given birth; neither the pencil of ancient Zeuxis, nor the more recent hand of Raphael can boast of having surpassed you, whether you paint great-hearted leaders and kings, or mark out the attractive faces of maidens, that will soon deal death among the young men, unless kind Venus lends a hand. (9) Take up this little book, and take the brief tableaux of Velleius Paterculus, where there is no inappropriate series of images, nor wasted colouring. When Velleius paints the picture for him, the reader does not hate the nature of Vinicius, nor blame Tiberius; when Kneller paints, we do not shudder at the savage brow of Louis, or Lyce's dry cheeks. (16) So look kindly upon the polished works of this author: though they are thin, they are not without value, being pleasant to read, and fruitful to their readers. How glad I would have been to give these writings to you in a perfected state; but who would dare to add anything to Velleius Paterculus' labours, or to your pictures.

Text: Bern.; liminary poem in Hudson's *Velleius Paterculus* (Oxford, 1711). *Date*: 1711. This poem is discussed in Ch. 4.

1.7 JOHANNI FREIND, M.D., PRAEFIXA CAESARIS COMMENTARIIS

Translation: 'To John Freind, M.D., prefixed to Caesar's commentaries'

Dum steti volvens animo et revolvens
Cui darem haec prisci monumenta praeli,

While I stood wondering over and over again to whom I should give this

---

1 *1711 omits the first 'o'.*   5 *1711 reads* jactet *for* -at.   15 Alluding to Hor., *Carm.* 4. 13, on Lyce's deterioration: *genas* (Horace's line 8), *aridas* (line 9), making explicit what Horace implies, that her cheeks are now dry.

2 Probably alluding to Cat. 1. 1, 'Cui dono'; Catullus dedicates his work to Nepos, in a poem that makes an important statement about his own poetic aims. This may suggest a similar programmatic aim for this poem, with Freind as dedicatee for Alsop's work (which the poet did not, in fact, collect): a contrast between Catullus and the self-effacing Alsop.

Adfuit tandem monuitque vulsa
　　Cynthius aure.
5　Ergone ignotus tibi noster, inquit,
　Freindus? huic dona: quot enim Britannos
　Caesar immisit, totidem retentat
　　Freindus ab Orco.

record of ancient battle, Apollo finally came and grabbed my ear: (5) 'So,' he said, 'do you not know my own Freind? Give it to him; for Freind has saved from Hell as many Britons as Caesar sent thither.'

Text: Bern.; Bodleian ms. Rawl. J. quarto 2, fo. 180 ('before an old edition of Caesar's commentaries printed in Venice, 1494, were these verses by Mr Alsop'). *Date*: unknown; perhaps c. 1707–8. This poem is discussed in Ch. 6.

1.8 PRAEFIXA FREINDI OPERIBUS

Estne qui fidus super astra tendat,
Estne Dircaeum superans olorem
Ales? hunc Coo properet parenti
　　Tradere librum.
5　Freindus hunc mittit tibi, dicat, auctor,
　Proximus post te genius: tuere
　Tu tui nati, tueatur orbis
　　Ille salutem.

Translation: 'Prefixed to Freind's works'
　Is there a bird that can fly faithfully above the stars, is there one that can surpass the swan of Dirce? Let such a bird rush to give this book to the Coan father. (5) 'Freind, the author,' let him say, 'the greatest genius after yourself, sends this to you: you look after your son's health, and he can look after the health of the world.'

Text: Bern.; J. Freind (ed. J. Wigan), *Opera Omnia Medica* (1733), p. 155. *Date*: probably *c*. 1718. This poem is mentioned in Ch. 6.

1.9 CHARLETTUS PERCIVALLO
SUO S.

Hora dum nondum sonuit secunda,
Nec puer nigras tepefecit undas;
Acer ad notos calamus labores
　　Sponte recurrit.

Translation: 'Charlett sends greetings to his friend, Percival'
　When the clock has not yet struck two, and the boy has not yet heated the dark water, my keen pen spontaneously returns to its familiar labours. What

---

3–4 Alluding to Virg., *Ecl.* 6. 3–4.

1 1733 reads *missus petat astra pennis*.　　　2 Alluding to Hor., *Carm.* 4. 2. 25. Humorous hyperbole in the suggestion that the swan can be surpassed: Horace's lines 1–4 stress that the fate of Icarus awaits Pindar's rivals. Cf. Alsop 3. 4. 37. 3 The Coan is probably Hippocrates (rather than Asclepius), subject of Freind's edition, 1717.　　　5 1733 reads *dicat, Tibi mittit Auctor*.

2 Cf. Lucr. 3. 829, 'nigras . . . undas'.

5	Quid prius nostris potiusve chartis
	Illinam? Cuinam vigil ante noctem
	Sole depulsam redeunte scriptor
	Mitto salutem?
	Tu meis chartis, bone Percivalle,
10	Unice dignus; tibi pectus implet
	Non minor nostro novitatis ardor:
	Tu quoque scriptor.
	Detulit rumor (mihi multa defert
	Rumor) in sylvis modo te dedisse
15	Furibus praedam, mediumque belli im-
	pune stetisse.
	Saucius num vivit adhuc caballus?
	Anne Iernais potiora gazis,
	An, tua vita tibi chariora,
20	Scripta supersunt?
	Cui legis nostras relegisque chartas?
	Cui meam laudas generositatem?
	Quem meis verbis, mea nescientem,
	Mane salutas?
25	Scribe securus, quid agit Senatus,
	Quid caput stertit grave Lambethanum,
	Quid comes Guilford, quid habent novorum
	Dawksque Dyerque.
	Me meus, quondam tuus, e popinis
30	Jenny jam visit, lachrymansque narrat,
	Dum molit fucos, subito peremptum
	Funere Rixon.
	Narrat (avertat Deus, inquit, omen)
	Hospitem notae periisse mitrae;
35	Narrat immersam prope limen urbis
	Flumine cymbam.
	Narrat—at portis meus Hinton astat,
	Nuntius Pricket redit, avocat me
	Sherwin, et scribendae alio requirunt
40	Mille tabellae.

should I write of first, or emphasise? To whom should I send greetings, awake in the small hours? (9) You alone, good Percival, are worthy of my letters; your heart is filled with no less keen a desire for news than mine; you too are a writer. Rumour has told me (as it tells me many things) that you have just recently given booty to thieves in the woods, and stood unharmed in the midst of the conflict. Is your wounded nag still alive? And are your writings, more dear to you than Irish treasure, more dear even than life itself, still surviving? (21) To whom do you read and reread my letters? To whom do you praise my generosity? Whom do you greet in the morning with my words (your hearer not knowing they are mine)? Write in safety about the doings of Parliament, about how the heavy head of Lambeth snores; about Lord Guilford, and the news that Dawks and Dyer have. (29) My Jenny (once yours) now visits me from the kitchens, and tells me, weeping, how Rixon was snatched by sudden death while he ground his dyes. He tells me (and may God, he said, avert the omen!) that the hostess of the famous Mitre has perished, and that a boat has sunk in the river by the edge of the city. He tells me—but my friend Hinton stands at the door, my messenger Pricket returns, Sherwin calls me off, and I have a thousand other letters to write!

5–6 Probably alluding to Hor., *Serm.* 1. 4. 36–8   15 Probably alluding to Hor., *Carm.* 2. 19. 27–8.
31 *Molit* may possibly have a sexual connotation (and pun on 'Molly'); see discussion of homosexual hints, Ch. 7, and cf. 4. 9. 27.

Imitation: attributed to 'A. EVANS'
Bodleian ms. Lat. misc. e. 19, fo. 174

An Epistolary Ode from Dr. Ch—t to Mr. P—val of Xt. Ch.

Betwixt the Hours of twelve and one,
When all Things else to Rest are gone,
With pleasing Itch I'm seiz'd (I own)
    Of writing;
5 Of writing only Letters tho',
To such ingenious Friends as you,
Dear Purcival, thyself no Foe
    To' Enditing.
For you, I'm sure, like me, delight
10 In charming news to spend the night;
Therefore these Lines belong of Right
    To you Sir.
Rumour relates to me this day,
(And what to me don't Rumour say?)
15 That you to Thieves became a Prey.
    Is't true Sir?
I hope your wounded Horse is safe
Yourself nor hurt, nor servant Ralph;
And did your Papers all escape
20   Capturam?
Your own dear works, which you do
                hold
More precious far than Irish Gold,
Nay, than your Life, I will be bold
    T' assure 'em.
25 Well—Do'st thou tell St. Patrick's
              Nation,
How I abhor all moderation,

How Civil am in Conversation
    With stranger.
To me thou mayst securely write.
30 Are Dublin, Armagh, Tuam right?
And is your Church, like ours, out quite
    Of Danger?
Ah, woefull Tale! which Jenny late
Brought panting to our College Gate,
35 (Jenny, with Thee once intimate
    As Brother.)
How Rixon, who no mischief meant,
As he stood grinding of his Paint,
Quick from this world by Fate was sent
40   To t'other.
Mine hostess at the Mitre, too
(What will not Pains and Agues do?)
Is Dead; fat Beconsale not so,
    But Sick yet.
45 A Barge was at the Folly sunk,
(Tis thought the Bargemen all were
            drunk)
And light-foot Sherwin seiz'd a Punk
    With Pricket.
Things he related many more;
50 But Hinton's knocking at my Door,
And letters I have half a Score
    Not writ yet.

(imitation, line 42: ms. 'Aches', unless a disyllable, seems incorrect)

Text: Bern; broadsheet, *Charlettus Percivallo suo* (London, 1706). *Date*: 1705 or early 1706. The references to proper names in this and the following ode (1. 10) are discussed at length in Ch. 5. (There are some rather unhelpful ms. notes in Trinity College, Cambridge, H. 5. 17.)

1.10 PERCIVALLUS CHARLETTO SUO S.

Qualis ambabus capiendus ulnis
Limen attingit tibi gratus hospes,
Quum sacras primum subit, aut relinquit,

Translation: 'Percival sends greetings to his friend, Charlett'

As when a welcome guest arrives, a man to be hugged closely on his first arrival in or departure from the sacred city of

Isidis arces;
5   Qualis exultat tibi pars mamillae
Laeva, quum cantu propiore stridant,
Missiles et jam moneant adesse
        Cornua chartas;
Tale per nostrum jecur et medullas
10   Gaudium fluxit, simul ac reclusis
Vinculis vidi bene literati
        Nomen amici.
Obvios fures, uti fama verax
Rettulit, sensi pavidus tremensque;
15   Sed fui, sumque, excipias timorem,
        Caetera sospes.
Scire si sylvam cupias pericli
Consciam, et tristes nemoris tenebras,
Consulas lente tabulas parantem,
20   Te duce, Colum.
Flebilis legi miseranda docti
Fata pictoris: sed et hoc iniqua
Damna consolor, superest perempto
        Rixone Wildgoose.
25   Quae tamen mitram mulier labantem
Fulciet? Munus vetulae parentis
Anna praestabit, nisi fors Ierni
        Hospita cycni.
Laetus accepi celeres vigere
30   Pricketi plantas; simul ambulanti
Plaudo Sherwino, pueroque Davo
        Mitto salutem.
Jenny, post Hinton, comitum tuorum
Primus, ante omnes mihi gratulandus;
35   Qui tibi totus vacat, et vacabit,
        Nec vetat uxor.
Haec ego lusi properante Musa,
Lesbiae Vatis numeros secutus:
Si novi quid sit, melius docebit
40   Sermo pedestris.
(P.S.:)
Coenitant mecum comites Iernae,
Multa qui de te memorant culullos
Inter; et pulli, vice literarum,
        Crus tibi mittunt.

Oxford, or as your heart leaps at the sound of a nearby horn, announcing that letters are about to be hurled at you, so did joy flow through all my inmost being, when I broke the seal and saw the name of my friend, the man of letters. (13) As the report truly stated, I met the thieves with fear and trembling; but I was, and am, if you set aside the fear, otherwise safe. If you wish to know the wood that saw my danger, the gloomy thickets of the forest, you should consult Cole, who slowly prepares his maps under your leadership. (21) I wept to read of the sad fate of that learned painter; but I can offer this consolation for the cruel loss, that while Rixon is dead, Wildgoose is still alive. But what woman will support the slipping Mitre? Anne will fill her aged parent's shoes, or perhaps the hostess of the Irish Swan. (29) I was happy to hear that Pricket's fast feet are flourishing; at the same time I praise Sherwin as he walks around, and send greetings to the boy Davy. Jenny, who is (after Hinton) the chief of your companions, deserves my congratulations above all; he always has time for you, and will do (without wifely prohibitions). This I have jotted down in a hurry, following the metre of Sappho; if there is any news, plain prose will tell it better. (P.S.) Irish companions dine with me, who say a lot about you in their cups, and send you a chicken-leg instead of a letter.

5–6 Probably alluding to Juv. 7. 159, 'laevae parte mamillae'; expecting the reader to recognise the allusion (otherwise, the phrase sounds odd). Charlett is more excitable than Juvenal's callow schoolboy. Pencilled n. in Trinity College, Cambridge, H. 5. 17: '*Strident* against the world and your copy, because it follows *Et moneant* (Bowyer).' (I disagree: but such comments are a sign of the learned printer's personal interest.)   13 *Uti* scanned as two shorts: unclassical, but Neo-Latin is more flexible.   16 Probably alluding to Hor., *Epist.* 1. 10. 50, 'cetera laetus'.   21 *Flebilis* tends to be used of bereaved women, making Percival seem ridiculous.   36 Trinity H. 5. 17: 'I like *Nec vetat* better than *Ni vetat*—the metre is the same either way; but the compliment heightened by *Nec vetat* (Bowyer).'

Imitation: attributed to 'A. EVANS'
Bodleian ms. Lat. misc. e. 19, fo. 175–6

Mr. P—val's Answer

Not Thou with greater Joy dost meet
Some foreign Scholar in High-Street,
Who comes to view the Muses Seat
    On Isis;
5 Nor dos thy Blood more nimbly flow,
When Post-Boy merry Horn dos blow,
As He the Pacquet brings, to shew
    Advices;
Than mine did, when enflam'd with
                  Joy,
10 Taking a letter from my Boy,
Thy learned Name subscrib'd I saw
    At Bottom.
What honest Fame reports, is right;
The Rogues did put me in a Fright,
15 And had it not been wrong to Fight,
    I'd shot 'em.
Wou'd you the Place exactly know,
Which conscious was of all my woe;
Consult Ben Cole, who works so slow
20   Map-making.
Tho' sudden Death has Rixon slain,
Still honest Wildgoose dos remain,
Which somewhat serves my Grief and
                  Pain
    To slacken.

25 But who'l the Mitre now support,
Like Her that's Dead? in any sort,
Is not her Daughter Nan fit for't
    That Vestal?
But what dos most revive my Heart,
30 Is Sherwin's playing of his Part;
The Nymph I do suppose You'l Cart,
    So Bestial!
To Jenny, pray, my Love commend;
Jenny with Thee whole weeks dos
                spend
35 I hear, nor dos his wife pretend
    To chide him.
To Promus Pricket, valet Davy
And to the Tonsor who dos shave ye,
Mitto salutem, that's God save ye,
40   Or Idem.
Thus, worthy S^r I've sent a Letter,
Like yours, wrought up in merry Metre,
Tho' once I thought plain Prose did
             better
    Delight you.
45 Some Irish Peers, who sup with me,
A Woodcok's Thigh have sent to Thee,
A Token of their Amity.
    Good bye t'ye.

Text, Date: as for 1. 9 (see Ch. 5).

1.11 DAVIDI GREGORY,
    ASTRONOMIAE PROFESSORI
    SAVILIANO

O qui meanti conscius aetheri
Pictum decoris sideribus polum
    Perpendis, et sagaci ocello
        Aethereos penetras recessus!
5 O Archimedis nobilis aemulum!
O invidentis Wallisii parem!

Translation: 'To David Gregory, Savilian Professor of Astronomy'
You understand the wandering heavens, weigh up the pole, painted with beautiful stars, and with your clever eye penetrate the depths of space. You are a rival of noble Archimedes, the equal of envious Wallis; Newton rejoices in your

Quo sospite exultat Nutonus,
    Saviliique superbit umbra:
Ecquid planetas inter amicius
10 Affulsit astrum? Quae bona Scotico
    Praetendit orbi nuptialem
      Stella facem, gelidasque castis
Accendit oras ignibus! En! tibi
Gratantur Arctoa aethera! Cernis ut
15   Tellus renidet percipitque
      Insolitas tepefacta flammas!
Nativa non sic gestit Apolline
Delos recepto, cum Dryopes fremunt
    Praesente jam Divo, integratque
20   Terra choros iterumque saltat.
Scimus benigno sidere prosperas
Lucere taedas; scimus ut omine
    Caelesti amores auspicatos
      Junxit Hymen; neque te fefellit
25 Perspectus aether: jam niveo in sinu
Sponsae recumbens ebibis oscula
    Mellita, quot nec basianti
      Lesbia praebuerat Catullo.
Jam blandi honorem frontis amabilem,
30 Jam purpuratae dulce decus genae,
    Nunc ora spectas, nunc ocellos
      Sideribus minus invidentes.
Mox qua mamillarum via lactea
Ducit, pererras improbula manu;
35   Ludisque passim, et suaveolentem
      Per Veneris spatiaris hortum.
Has dum revolvis delicias, graves
Falluntur horae; jam fugiunt retro
    Curae metusque, et plena nullae
40   Gaudia contemerant procellae.
Dum Mars per orbem saevit, et undique
Commissa fervent proelia; dum micat
    Districtus ensis, et ruinae
      Terribilis nitet apparatus;
45 Tu conjugali mollior in toro
Spectas tumultus, et miserabiles

safety, and the shade of Savile is proud. (9) What more friendly star has shone amid the planets? How good a star holds out the nuptial torch to Scotland, and burns those cold shores with chaste fires! Look, the Northern heavens are congratulating you! You see how the earth reflects them and feels the heat of unaccustomed flames! (17) His native Delos is not so eager when it receives Apollo, when the Dryopes are excited by the god's presence, and the land renews its dances and leaps up again. (21) We know that propitious marriage-torches shine under a kindly star; we know that the marriage-god has joined loves together with a good omen from above; nor has the heaven you see clearly deceived you: reclining on your wife's white breast you now drink more honeyed kisses than Lesbia ever offered to Catullus. (29) Now you look at her lovely face—the noble forehead, the blushing cheeks—and now her eyes that are less envious of the stars. Soon you wander with your wicked little hand where her breasts' milky way leads on; you play everywhere, and walk through Venus' sweet-smelling garden. (37) While you repeat these delights, time seems to stand still; now troubles and fears flee, and no storms disturb the fullness of your joy. (41) While war rages over the globe, and battles are everywhere fiercely joined, while the unsheathed sword glitters, and the terrible machinery of ruin shines forth, you look out from the softness of your marriage-bed upon the confusion, and the pitiable relics of a church on the point of collapse, and a doubtful reign. (49) You can see (not without tears springing to

---

7 *Nutonus* spelt thus metri gratia: *Newtonus* is normal Neo-Latin; Nott. reads *Neutonus*, unmetrically.   9 *Amicius*: adjective rather than (rare) adverb. Cf. Cat. 62. 26, 'iucundior ignis'.   12–14 Cf. Hor., *Carm*. 1. 26. 3–4, 'sub Arcto . . . gelidae . . . orae'.   14 *Aethera*: neuter plural, unclassical (in late antique, and Neo-Latin).   17–20 Alluding to Virg., *Aen*. 4. 143–6.   27–8 Cf. Cat. 5 & 7 (more Catullan kisses, Alsop 2. 18. 15–20).   29 BL(a): *blandae* (rightly?).   33 Another astronomical pun; cf. Ovid, *Met*. 1. 168–9; Cat. 55. 17.   35 *Suaveolentem*: cf. Cat. 61. 7; n.b. synizesis (or read as two words, with 'e' elided).

Ecclesiae jam jam ruentis
    Relliquias, dubiumque regnum.
Vides (obortis non sine lachrymis)
50 Tristes ruinas Caesareae Domus;
    Pulsosque principes avitis
        Sedibus, atque iterum exulantes.
At si qua vestris sideribus fides,
Si non poetae fallimur augures,
55   Nec vana jactamus protervis
        Carmina diripienda ventis;
En! tempus instat, en! veniet dies,
Cum rursus in Coelum caput efferet
    Nomen Stuartorum, et per omne
60   Imperio potietur aevum;
Dum stabit undis cincta Britannia;
Dum clara fulgent sydera per polum
    Versatilem, tuusque Phoebus
        Aethereos micat inter ignes.

your eyes) the sad ruins of our royal house, our princes thrust from their ancestral seats and again exiled. (53) But if we can trust your stars, if we poets are not unreliable prophets, and do not throw out empty songs to be torn apart by tempests, then look—the time is at hand, look, the day will come, when the name of Stuart will again raise its head to heaven, and possess power for all time—for as long as Britain stands surrounded by waves, for as long as stars shine clear through the turning pole, and your sun-god is bright among the fires of heaven.

Text: Bern. (lacks lines 33–6, 49–64); Christ Church ms. 346; BL(a); Nott. Pw V 141. *Date*: 1695. This poem is discussed in Ch. 6.

I.12 ODE VOTIVA

Phoebe, ter dixi, Pater o medentum,
Fautor et vatum, duo magna caeli
Dona te supplex peto; convalescam,
    Aptaque scribam.
5 Phoebus his;—Siquid tua vis valere
Vota, fac noster tibi Freindus adsit:
Ille scribendi mihi par scit artem,
    Ille medendi.

Translation: 'Votive ode'
    Phoebus, father of physicians and supporter of poets, I have invoked you thrice, and I beg you to grant two great heavenly gifts: may I have good health, and write well. (5) Phoebus thus replied: 'If you wish any of your prayers to succeed, make sure my own Freind is at hand: he knows the art of writing, and the art of healing, as well as I do.'

Text: Bern. *Date*: unknown; probably after 1717. This poem is mentioned in Chapter 6.

64 Probably alluding to Hor., *Carm.* 1. 12. 46–8; a fervently political poem of Horace is appropriate for Alsop's Jacobite enthusiasm.

2 Possibly alluding to [Virg.], *Culex* 12–13, 'Phoebus erit . . . carminis auctor,/ et . . . fautor'.   4 Writing comes after health, but is clearly important (perhaps more than religion or scholarship).   5 The reply is concisely introduced; cf. Virg., *Aen.* 2. 348. The chiasmic effect adds to the poem's neatness: *medendi, vatum* (1, 2)/ *scribendi, medendi* (7, 8).

Book 2
Epistolary Odes

2.1 JOHANNI FREIND

Freinde, quem Phoebus genio altiori
Splendide ornavit, docuitque corpus
Morbidum letho eripere, et fugacem
    Sistere vitam;
5 Freinde, quem proli metuensve sponso
Anxie implorat genitrix, et uxor;
Certa, tu quoque venias, salutem
    Ire sequacem:
Namque tu nosti, Dea quot reclusa
10 Pyxide emisit, superare morbos;
Dura nec filum, nisi te remoto,
    Atropos occat.
Non tamen servas placuit per artes
Surgere, et turpi obsequio aucupari
15 Lucra famamve; ingenuo sed actus
    Impete sursum
Tendis, insueto super astra quaerens
Tramite ascensum: probat omnis ausum
Turba Divorum, praeiensque Phoebus
20   Firmat euntem.
Ductor hinc audis Medicae cohortis;
Hinc tibi in morbos domitu malignos
Traditur grande imperium.—I, potenti
    Munere felix:
25 Perge per terras Opifer vocari;
Perge mortales stabilire vires,

Translation: 'To John Freind'

Freind, Phoebus has splendidly adorned you with a higher genius, and taught you to snatch a diseased body from death, and halt departing life; a mother or wife, fearful for child or husband, anxiously calls for your aid, certain that wherever you come, safety will follow. (9) For you know how to defeat all the ills that Pandora let out of her box; nor does harsh Fate cut the thread of life, except in your absence. (13) But you were not content to rise through menial skills, and hunt for wealth and fame by foul fawning; instead, driven by a noble impulse you rise upwards, seeking a new route above the stars: the whole crowd of gods approves your attempt, and Phoebus goes ahead to support your passage. (21) Hence you are spoken of as the leader of the medical regiment; hence you have been given great power against malignant diseases. (23) Go forward, happy in your potent gift; carry on, to be called a bringer of help throughout the nations; carry on, to secure the strength of mankind, as its most powerful guardian. (27) But, as you

1 Cf. 2. 8. 21.   2 Possibly alluding to Hor., *Carm.* 3. 11. 35, 'splendide mendax', a famous oxymoron. If so, a constructive allusion on two levels: humorously undermining the praise of Freind (cf. 2. 2. 1–2), and comparing him to Horace's heroic Hypermnestra. Freind, as a Jacobite MP (taking the oaths to George I), and when examined after his arrest, was obliged to be 'splendide mendax'.   3 Possibly alluding to Hor., *Carm.* 2. 14. 1, 'Eheu, fugaces . . .'.   4 Possibly alluding to Statius, *Silvae* 3. 4. 23–5.   5 1733 reads *Te* for *quem*.   13 Cf. Hor., *Epist.* 1. 19. 19.   17–18 Possibly alluding to Prop. 4. 1. 107–8.   19 *Praeire* with short 'ae' is classical: Virg., *Aen.* 5. 186; Ovid, *Fasti* 1. 81.   21 *Ductor* is usually military (hence *cohortis*); perhaps a pun on 'doctor'.

Praepotens custos! tamen hac laborum
     Mole plicatus
Ne piger cesset calamus, memento.
30 Evocat quoquo series negoti,
Scribe: quod Mauro faciat ruborem,
     Scribe. Medentum
Hoc rogant, palmam tibi porrigentes,
Ordines cuncti; duce te, priorum
35 Acta rimari, medicosque docti ex-
     quirere fontes.
Te duce, antiquas Arabum tabellas,
Pulvere excusso, rapiunt; quid aptum
Usui Rhazes, Mesuesve scripsit,
40   Volvere aventes.
Tu doces, primo repetens ab ortu,
Quem Pater Cous, Medicique ab illo
Tramitem Graii tenuere: Tu per
     Barbara vectus
45 Sec'la, quantillis gradibus, quibusque au-
     toribus, crescens fluitansve retro
Pharmaces ibat status, ordinemque et
     Tempora signas.
O rudi natum dare scriptitantum
50 Coetui leges! tua perlegendo
Scripta, seu discant studia aemulari, aut
     Parcere chartae.
O potens forti eloquio movere
Curiam! fidus patriae, utilisque
55 Consili suasor, nec hiante contra
     Ore potentum
Territus! Quam te variis refinxit
Dotibus coeli favor! excolendis
Artibus donans genium, et ferendis
60   Legibus aptum!
Quare age, oranti, Medico-Senator
Subveni late populo; vocarit
Civicum seu jus, Britonumque causa
     Strenuus adsis

are involved with this mass of labours, remember that your busy pen should not stop writing. Wherever your business calls you, write; write something that will make the Moor blush. (32) All classes of physicians ask this of you, offering you the palm; under your leadership, they have the learning to examine the deeds of their predecessors, and seek out the founts of medicine. (37) Under your leadership, they snatch up and dust off ancient Arab texts, eager to consider what useful things Rhazes or Mesues wrote. You teach the path that the Coan father and his Greek successors followed, from its earliest beginnings. (43) Travelling through barbarian centuries, you indicate their history: by what slow degrees, and with which authors, the state of medicine rose or fell back again. (49) You were born to give laws to the rough crowd of scribblers; by reading through your writings, they can learn whether to emulate your studies, or save their paper. (53) You have the power to move Parliament by the strength of your eloquence. You are a patriot, an advocate of good counsel: nor are you frightened by the gaping mouths of powerful opponents. How various are the gifts with which heaven's favour has blessed you, giving you a genius for promoting the arts, and for passing laws. (61) So then, both doctor and MP, give lavish help to a people that begs for it: if civil law and the Britons' cause call you, may you be a vigorous decision-maker; or if the sick voices of dying men rouse you, praying you to bring help, may you be kind, and

28 1733 reads *retentus* for *plicatus*.   31–2 The repetition is varied, as an effective rhetorical device (here, in 3rd and 4th lines of a stanza: at 25–6, in 1st and 2nd lines). *Mauro* reminds us of medieval Islamic science; one would not expect to see a Moor blush.   39 *Rhazes*: Persian physician (Ar-Razi); frequently cited by Freind, *History of Physick* I (1725), p. 278, etc. *Mesues*: the name of two Arabic physicians (Jahya ben Maseweih); Freind refers to the younger, 'Joh. Damascenus called Mesue' (p. 280).   41 Cf. 2. 27. 33; possibly alluding to Virg., *Geo.* 4. 286. 42 Hippocrates (or Asclepius); cf. 1. 8. 3.   45–6 Un-Horatian splitting of word (cf. 2. 4. 30–1, 2. 12. 13–14: see Ch. 3).   47 1733 reads *Artis undabat* for *Pharmaces ibat*.   49 *Scriptitantum*: a favourite, effective word; cf. 2. 7. 17, 2. 11. 53, 2. 15. 14.   51 1733 reads *vel* for *seu*.   52 Alluding to Juv. 1. 18, 'periturae parcere chartae'.   61 1733 reads *Medice ac Senator*.

65   Arbiter; seu te morientium aegrae
      Suscient voces, fer opem, precantes;
      Sis bonus, morbi quate vim, proculque
          Ire jubeto.
      Sic tibi fama super ire cunctos
70   Det potens artis Deus, insolentes
      Sub jugo errones premere, et medentum
          Spernere vulgus.

shake the disease's power, and bid it depart. (69) Thus may the god, master of such skill, grant that you may surpass all others in fame: that you may press insolent truants under your yoke, and scorn the medical mob.

Text: Bern.; the first liminary poem in J. Freind (ed. J. Wigan), *Opera Omnia Medica* (London, 1733). *Date*: *c.* 1722–6. This poem is discussed in Ch. 6.

2.2 JOHANNI KEIL

Keile, ni mendax mihi falsa mittit
Freindus, ex moecho fieri maritus
Cogeris, partesque agit usitatas
    Pellicis uxor.
5   Quidni ego laeter tibi gratulari
Conjugi conjux? Ego qui reliqui
Connubi causa patriam domumque ux-
    orius exul.
Dum sales spargunt lepidi sodales
10 Te super vel me, cuperem interesse
Magna pars risus: sed ab his acerba
    Lege remotus
Perfruor dulci alloquio, pudicae
Osculis sponsae, placidoque vultu;
15 Nec videt sponsum mage amantem
                    amatumve
    Aethereus sol.
Mille mi, praeter Paphia in palestra,
Gaudia: at, quod Tu ingrediare castra,
Quae fuit causa ante Helenam duelli,
20   Unica causa est.
Estne quis, cunctos quot amant Mathesin
Inter, o Ductor gregis, estne qui te

Translation: 'To John Keil' [or Keill]

Keill, unless lying Freind has sent me false news, you are compelled to change from a seducer to a husband, and your wife acts the part she learned as your whore. Why should I not happily congratulate you, as one husband to another, since I left my home and country for my marriage, as a husbandly exile. (9) While our witty friends joke about you or me, I would like to participate in the laughter; but far from them (because of a harsh law), I enjoy the sweet conversation, modest kisses, and calm face of my wife; nor does the sun in heaven look upon a more loving or beloved husband. (17) I have many joys, apart from those of the bedroom; but there is only one reason why you married, the same that caused wars before Helen's time. (21) Is there anyone among the lovers of Mathematics, whom you lead, who knows better than you, or can look with a keener eye on the motions of the stars? You will know in

72 Alluding to Hor., *Carm.* 2. 16. 39–40.

1 Nott. 142 reads *derisor nisi* for *ni mendax mihi*. G.M. reads *narrat* for *mittit*.   3 G.M. reads *usitatae* for -*as*. 7–8 Alluding to Hor., *Carm.* 1. 2. 19–20, 'ux-/ orius amnis'.   11 Cf. Virg., *Aen.* 2. 6, 'quorum pars magna fui'.   13 Probably alluding to Hor., *Epod.* 13. 18, 'dulcibus alloquiis'. A favourite phrase: cf. 2. 12. 62; 2. 23. 18; 2. 22. 16–17; with *eloquio*, 2. 16. 14.   13–14 Alluding to Hor., *Carm.* 3. 5. 41, 'pudicae coniugis osculum'. G.M. inserts *et* before *pudicae*.   19 Alluding to Hor., *Serm.* 1. 3. 107–8. G.M. reads *Helenae*.

Rectius novit, vel acutiori
　　Lustrat ocello
25　Siderum motus? Tibi siqua proles
Nascitur, quicquid minitentur astra,
Quid ferant laetum, docilis futuri
　　Ante videbis.
Si tuos audax thalamos adulter
30　Scandere optabit, vetet Ars et Aether
Improbos ausus; et inermis esto, et
　　Incolumis frons.
Quare age, et totis licitae diebus,
Noctibus totis, Veneri litato:
35　Non opus sylvae, aut recubare subter
　　Tegmine foeni.
Crede mi, quoquo venias locorum,
Gratior posthac eris hospes, ex quo
Nata fors matri, dominaeque serva
40　　Casta redibit.
Interim quicquid vetulae et puellae
Garriant, ne te jecur intus angat:
Sed domi sistens ede, lude, pota et
　　Temne quod ultra est.
45　Sis amans sponsae, et, mea si valent quid
Vota, sis felix: sed iniqua si fors
Dempserit primam, mora nulla, sponsam
　　Sume secundam.
Est, uti nosti, bene pasta virgo,
50　Cuilibet sat par oneri ferendo;
Ipse quam, sed mi meliora Divi,
　　Ducere rebar.
Hanc cape; et nostro ex loculo repente
Aera bis centum accipies, et ultra:
55　Sed pari nullum, nisi Te, procorum
　　Dote beabo.

advance if any children are being born to you, whatever the stars threaten, and what happiness they might bring. If a bold adulterer wishes to climb into your bedroom, your art and the heavens will forbid the wicked attempt, and your forehead can remain safely unarmed (without cuckold's horns). (33) Come then, devote each day and night to licit love; you do not need to lie in a wood or under the hay. Believe me, wherever you go, you will be a more welcome guest from now on, since perhaps a daughter may now return chastely to her mother, a servant to her mistress. (41) Meanwhile do not worry about the gossip of hags and girls, but sit at home eating, playing, drinking, and despising everything else. (45) May you be loving towards your wife, and (if my prayers have any power) may you be happy; but if unfair fate removes your first wife, do not delay, but take a second one. (49) There is, as you know, a well-fed maiden, who can carry any sort of burden, whom I thought of marrying (but heaven granted me something better). Take her, and you can have £200 or more straightaway from my purse; but I would give no one but you such a dowry.

33–4 Nott. 142 reads *Pergito totis placito* . . . / . . . *dare Te labori*.　　35–6 Alluding to Virg., *Ecl.* 1. 1.　　44 Probably alluding to Hor., *Carm.* 2. 16. 25–6, 'quod ultra est/ oderit curare'. Horace's *otium* is an appropriate parallel.　　47 Probably alluding to Hor., *Carm.* 2. 5. 13–16 ('dempserit', 14); the husband-hunting Lalage is most relevant to Alsop's situation.　　49 *G.M.* reads *ubi* . . . *pota* (some mss., including Nott. 143 and 144, have n. 'Gruterus legit . . .', discussed in Ch. 6); BL(b) reads *nota*.　　50 *G.M.* reads *sed* for *sat*.　　55–6 He does not wish to give an enforced dowry, by paying his damages (see Chs. 6 and 7).

Translation: *Gentleman's Magazine* 9. 378 (July 1739); cf. Bodleian, ms. Ballard 47, fo. 54

Doctori KEIL, e Coll. Baliol. Astronomiae Professori. Imitated.

Dear *Keil*, if bant'ring *Freind* says true,
You've just begun your life anew:
Till now a libertine in love,
A very husband must you prove.
5 Sweet spouse now acts, with equal art,
Each *quondam bona roba*'s part.
I gratulate with heart of glee,
To find you're in the noose with me.
For this, my country lost and home,
10 An exile I uxorious roam.
While all our *Oxford* wits infest
Both you and me with fleering jest,
I wish with them the mirth to share,
But banish'd I! decree severe.
15 My wife's sweet converse I enjoy,
And kisses too, which never cloy;
Nor has the sun, in all his round,
A man more lov'd, or loving found.
A thousand joys my soul engage,
20 That you with me the *Paphian* stage
Now tread: The cause the very same
Which threw all *Greece* into a flame.
O great Professor! isn't true,
Does any better know than you
25 The various beauties of the skies,
Or view the stars with keener eyes?
Whether they're well or ill inclin'd,
Appears to your presaging mind;
You know each aspect rough or mild,
30 Or if your wife shall prove with child;
Nay, should some bold invader dare
To whisper in your spouse's ear,

The dire attempt your art forewarns,
And guards your forehead safe from
                                    horns.
35 Go on (dear *Keil!*) with joy to prove
Whole days and nights of lawful love:
You're better off than heretofore,
Nor woods, nor haycocks haunt no
                                    more.
Believe me, whencesoe'er you come
40 At mine you're always at your home;
Since now you've lost your wonted
                                    taste,
Our maids and daughters may be chaste.
Ne'er mind what girls and beldams
                                    prate,
Nor let what's past your spleen create;
45 With ease and plenty blest, be wise,
And all beyond this mark despise.
Be happy, then, and love your spouse,
I truly wish, if heav'n allows.
But should fate call this first away,
50 A second take without delay:
There is, you know, a boozing lass,
Strong for a burden as an ass;
The gods have thrown me on a shelf,
Or else I thought her for myself.
55 Take her, and know I will disburse
Two hundred pounds from my own
                                    purse;
Or more with her 's at your devotion,
58 None else from me has such a portion.

Translation: *The Student, or Oxford and Cambridge Monthly Miscellany* 2. 29 (1751)

An Epistle from Mr. Alsop to Dr. Keil on his Marriage

Dear John, if you are not bely'd,
You've changed your course of life;
You that so many nymphs have try'd,
To take, good Gods, a wife!
5 Of all the numerous female scum
What jade, the devil take her,

Could thus bewitch thee to become
Cuckold, from cuckold-maker?

Since thou art in-for't now, old friend,
10 And fetter'd past retreating;
Give me, a husband, leave to send
To thee, a husband, greeting;

I who, hard fate! am forc'd to rove,
True to my nuptial vows,
15 And leave my country out of love,
An exile for my spouse.

But I, by heav'ns decree, remain
Blest on a foreign shore;
And hourly such delights obtain,
20 I need not wish for more.

Me a kind wife's embraces chear,
A lovely creature she;
Nor can the sun find out a pair
More hap'ly join'd than we.

25 Fain would I hear the jests that pass,
The mirth that's made on me;
Fain would partake the circling glass,
And vent my wit on thee.

My motives sure no man can blame,
30 So many charms I wed;
Thee something I forbear to name
Drew to the nuptial bed.

O Keil, in algebra and statics
Who has not heard thy fame,
35 Thou constant friend to mathematics,
Thou lover of that same.

No mortal can like thee decide
The motions of the sphere,
What planets at our birth preside,
40 What good or ill draws near.

You know the mighty pow'rs, the sway
They bear on human passion;
And if your wife should go astray,
Don't blame her inclination.

45 But Mars and Venus you will say
Favour'd this new alliance,
And, whoring in an honest way,
To horns you bid defiance.

Thy front requires no foreign aid,
50 In native brass secure;

Sure as you found your wife a maid,
She will continue pure.

No rakes, by wanton glance allur'd,
Will e'er attempt thy bed;
55 Thy wondrous knowledge hath secur'd
Thy astronomic head.

No man can now with justice blame
The heat of your complexion;
Quench then at home thy lawful flame,
60 'Tis conjugal affection.

Where e'er you go, a thousand cares
Are by this means allay'd;
No mother for her daughter fears,
No mistress for her maid.

65 You need not seek or hedge or grove
Or thickets out of shame,
Or on the hay-cock, bed of love!
Caress the sun-burnt dame.

Careless of what the world may say,
70 Indulge it with thy dear;
Revel it all the live-long day,
And damn the wits that sneer.

But should thy stars, exceeding cross,
Bereave this spouse of life,
75 Bear with philosophy thy loss,
And take a second wife.

Astrea with refulgent grace,
For ought I know a maid,
May meet thy strenuous embrace,
80 Troth she's an able jade:

I once had thought the girl to wed,
Struck with a fond desire,
Till heav'n had otherways decreed,
And cool'd the youthful fire.

85 Take her, and with her as I live
An ample portion take;
But 'tis, if anything I give,
Believe me, for thy sake.

Text: Bern.; Loveling's *Poems* (1738; in 1741 edn., pp. 105–8); *Gentleman's Magazine* 9. 324 (June 1739); ms. D, fo. 31–2; ms. E, fo. 37–8; BL(b), fo. 64–5; Bodleian, ms. Rawl. lett. 31, fo. 142; Trinity College, Cambridge, ms. 615 (= R. 3. 35, fo. 11–13); Nott. Pw V 142, Pw V 143, Pw V 144, and Pw V 151/8. *Date*: early 1718. This poem is discussed at length in Ch. 6.

2.3 JOHANNI NICOL

Verticis custos bone Prisciani;
Prime post Freindum domitor juventae;
Qui manu torques metuenda pubi
    Sceptra togatae:
5 Si tibi nugis vacat interesse
Rusticae Musae, properata sumas
Dona, quae virga procul otiosus
    Mittit amicus.
Noster, ut nosti, Scoticis ab oris
10 Consulens ventri rediit Noelus:
Quid tulit secum, quid agitve agetve
    Scire laboro.
An studet vitae variis necisque
Artibus, docto cupidus vocari
15 Institor Medo? an Parisina malit
    Visere tecta?
Improbus quo se medicaster ille
Contulit Freindus? didicitne tandem
Seriis nugis adhibere corda ob-
20   lita jocorum?
Ecquid Hintonus bene gnarus artis
Aulicae grandi meditatur ausu?
An statum regni et venientis acta
    Ordinat aevi?
25 An sui ruris satagit negoti,
Publicae curae satur, horreisque
Congerit messem, sapienter usus
    Munere Divum?
Hos tamen versus modo dictitanti
30 Detulit fama Oxonios adisse
Te lares, nactum breve tempus oti
    Atque caballum.
Inde mi mittas quot habes novorum;
Ocyus mittas: tibi nam perennes

Translation: 'To John Nicol'

   Good guardian of the heights of grammar, chief trainer of youth, after Freind; you wield a sceptre of which your gowned pupils must beware. If you have time to spare for the trifles of a rustic muse, take up these hurried gifts, sent by a friend at leisure and far from the rod. (9) Our Noel, as you know, concerned for his belly, has returned from Scotland; I am keen to know what he has brought with him, what he does or will do. Is he practising his various skills over life and death, desirous of being called learned Mead's rival? Or does he prefer to visit Parisian houses? (17) Where has that wretched quack Freind taken himself off to? Has he finally learned to bring a humourless heart to serious trifles? (21) And what is Hinton, familiar with court intrigue, boldly planning? Is he arranging the state of the kingdom and the acts of the next age? Or is he, sated with public concerns, busy in his own fields, gathering the harvest to his barns, and wisely using heaven's gifts? (29) But just as I was composing these verses, I heard a rumour that you had reached Oxford, having obtained a little leisure, and a nag. Do send me the news you have from there; send it quickly; for, though the least of her people, I always hold my academic mother in honour.

---

1 Priscian: late antique grammarian, suitable model for a teacher. (in 18, his brother John). *Domitor* is humorous in this context.   2 Robert Freind, headmaster of Westminster   5 Yale reads *magis* for *nugis*.   10 *Noelus*: Noel Broxholme; cf. 2. 11. 52.   12 Probably alluding to Hor., *Epist.* 1. 3. 2, 'scire laboro' (cf. Alsop 3. 4. 24). A humorous comparison between Broxholme and Horace's general (later the emperor Tiberius) may be intended.   13 Yale and ms. D read *novis . . . studeat* for *studet . . . variis*.   14 Possibly alluding to Hor., *Carm.* 1. 2. 43, 'patiens vocari'.   15 *Institor*: in Horace, associated with dubious sexual behaviour (*Carm.* 3. 6. 30; *Epod.* 17. 20); unexpected here: humour at Broxholme's expense. Alluding to his visit to Paris as Travelling Fellow (though 'Parisian houses' might also be brothels).   17 *Medicaster*: humorously insulting.   27–8 Alluding to Hor., *Carm.* 4. 9. 47–8, 'deorum/ muneribus sapienter uti'.   33 Ms. D reads *quid* for *quot*.

35   Usque persolvo minimus tuorum,
          Mater, honores.

Text: Bern.; ms. D, fo. 8; BL(b), fo. 48ᵛ–49ʳ; Trinity College, Cambridge, ms. 615 (= R. 3. 36, fo. 34); Yale, ms. Osborn c. 233, p. 6; Nott. Pw V 145/1 and 151/2. *Date*: *c.* 1715–16. This poem is discussed in Ch. 7.

2.4 EDUARDO HINTON

Rite si scirem, sit ubi locorum
Mollis Hintonus; dubiusne linguae
Fallat agrestes; an in urbe Freindo as-
          secla jocetur,
5   Scriberem. Sed tu, cate, nescio qua
Transigis noctesque diesque totos,
Utrum ego vivam valeamque, necne,
          Inscius ultro.
Interim de me cape quae sequuntur.
10   Urbe Londino amoveor lapillo
Quinquies sexto; jacet, occidentem
          Versus, amica
Frugibus tellus segetumque felix,
Qua virent herbae: tamen inter omnes
15   Celsior surgit Lupulus, feritque
          Vertice coelum.
Nullus optanti utilior colono
Nascitur fructus: licet hic abunde
Farris et pinguis genus omne frugis
20   Fundat agellus.
Non tibi notum melius quid intra
Volvat Harlaeus sapiens bonusque,
Quam mihi quid sit Lupulo ordinando
          Utile, quid non.
25   Novi ego, quae sit ratio eligendae
Uberis glebae; cinerem fimumque
Misceo; nec me latet inserendi
          Germinis hora.
Aura quae plantae favet officitque,
30   Calleo prorsus. Tamen has inani in-
dustria, ni tu simul interesses,

Translation: 'To Edward Hinton'

If I had a proper notion of where on earth soft Hinton might be, whether he deceives the peasants with his ambiguous speech, or jokes as Freind's hanger-on in town, then I would write. But, you clever rogue, you are passing your whole nights and days heaven knows where, without knowing if I am alive and well, or if I'm not. (9) Meanwhile, take note of what follows about me. I am at the the thirtieth milestone from London; there lies, towards the west, some fertile land, where crops and grass flourish; but, among all the rest, the hop rises highest, and hits the heavens. (17) There is no fruit more useful to the eager farmer, even if his field pours out every type of rich produce. (21) You know no better what the wise and good Harley is thinking of, than I know what is useful, and what isn't, for growing the hop. I have learned the way of choosing good soil; I mix up ashes and mud; nor am I unaware of the time to sow seeds. I am well informed about the breeze that helps the plant along. (30) But I am following these studies with pointless industry, unless you take a part in it too. For a clever purchaser imposes upon me, when I sell my goods; but you know all the tricks, and could match his guile with yours. (37) I will be happy that I have got a fair amount

---

3–4 Probably alluding to Juv. 9. 48–9.   10–11 Presumably at Brightwell (nearer 40 miles), rather than Nursling or Alverstoke (over 70).   22 Robert Harley, Earl of Oxford (1661–1724); or possibly his son Edward. 26 Possibly alluding to Virg., *Geo.* 1. 79–81.   27 Yale reads *miselo* [*sic*] for *Misceo* (clearly miscopied). 28 Ms. D reads *Graminis* for *Ger-*.   30–1 Un-Horatian word-break; cf. 2. 1. 45–6, 2. 12. 13–14.

Prosequor artes.
Nempe mi solers, ubi vendo merces,
Emptor imponit: cui tu, dolorum
35 Gnare, si rite obstiteris, rependens
    Astubus astus;
Arte nos illa satis ampla nacti
Lucra plaudemus, licet usque et usque
Stare promissis proceres recusent,
40   Nil dolituri.

of money by this skill, and even though the bigwigs carry on and on refusing to keep their promises, I won't be pained.

Text: Bern.; ms. D, fo. 23ᵛ–24ʳ; Trinity College, Cambridge, ms. 615 (= R. 3. 36, fo. 36); Yale, ms. Osborn c. 233, p. 7; Nott. Pw V 145/2 and 151/3; Bodleian, ms. Rawl. lett. 31. *Date*: probably after 1715 (but not during exile, 1718–20). This poem is discussed in Ch. 7.

2.5 JOHANNI DOLBEN

Musicae praeses et amice Musis,
O chori ductor, tibi servit omnis
Omnibus nervis fidicen, fidesque
    Ileque felis.
5 Te tuus Croftus docilis modorum
Parque Purcello genius remulcet.
Interim, quae sit, patienter audi,
    Musica ruris.
Sole nondum orto excubitor fidelis
10 Gallus assuetos vocat ad labores;
Et comes nidi bene cantilenam or-
    ditur ab ovo.
Sat tibi notum quid alauda mane,
Quid canat noctu Philomela; non te
15 Aut loquax picus latet, aut futuri
    Praescia cornix.
Fors tamen nescis ut agrestium auri
Perplacet late resonans flagellum,
Hordei terror; neque te caballi

Translation: 'To John Dolben'

Master of music, friend of the Muses, leader of the choir, every lyre-player serves you with all his strength, as does the lyre, and the catgut string. Your Croft, skilled in melody and a genius equal to Purcell, is soothing you. In the meantime, be patient and hear what the music of the country-side is like. (9) When the sun has not yet risen, the faithful cock calls men to their regular labours; and the companion of its nest begins fine singing from the egg. You know well enough what the lark sings in the morning, the nightingale at night; nor are you unaware of the talkative magpie, or the crow that can foretell the future. (17) Perhaps, however, you do not know how the resonant whip, the terror of the granary, pleases the peasants' ears; nor do horse-brasses delight you, or the merry

32 Yale reads *Prosequar* for *-or*.   34 *Cui*: disyllable; cf. 1. 2. 6. *Dolorum/ Gnare*: another double-edged compliment.   35 Ms. D reads *repedes* for *-ens*.   37 Ms. D reads *non* for *nos*.   40 Alternatively, 'I won't cheat you'; 'they [the *proceres*] won't cheat you'; or more loosely, '[they can act] with impunity': I am not quite sure what point is being made. Yale perhaps reads *dolituris* for *-i* (unclear).

3–4 Alsop amusingly turns from elevated Horatian words to the gory materials used in a modern fiddle.
5 Borrowing from Hor., *Carm.* 4. 6. 43, 'docilis modorum' (cf. 51; 1. 4. 43, etc.). Yale, ms. D read *sonorum*.
11–12 Alluding to Hor., *Ars Poet.* 147, 'nec gemino bellum Troianum orditur ab ovo'. (Horace's point is rather more obscure, referring to the bizarre beginning of Helen's life, wisely passed over by Homer.)   19 Ms. D reads *Heu! Boum* for *Hordei*.

20   Pendula collo
    Aera delectant, hilarisve acutum
    Sibilum aurigae. Tamen hoc ubique
    Rusticus gaudet sonitu, nec Hebro
        Invidet Orpheum.
25 Arte contendant quibus Ars magistra est:
    Est satis nostro modulo vel agni
    Scire balatum, aut querulum columbae
        Murmur amantis.
    Dulce sat vestrae citharae, fatemur,
30 Dant melos: nobis melius quid affert
    Musica, et gratis vicibus remiscet
        Utile dulci.
    Grunniunt porci? Boream ingruentem
    Certus expecto: anser anasve stridet?
35 Mi domi plaudo, et video cadentes
        Aridus imbres.
    Quin notis istis tibi certiora
    Signa promitto: valido boatu
    Ter canit post plaustra, Domum reduco,
40   Messor, aristas.
    Omen hoc laetus rapio, horreisque
    Congero messem: sapiens bonusque
    Unum ob hoc dicor, quia plena turgent
        Horrea frugum.
45 Si sapis, si vis sapere, huc adesdum
    Urbis atque aulae satur: hic remotus,
    Hic chori primus, canito, hordea inter,
        Farra forumque.
    Sin rudem nolis decorare pompam;
50 Mittito vel quod recinat coloni
    Guttur, aut saltem indocilis modorum
        Dictet agrestis.

waggoner's shrill whistle. Nevertheless, the rustic everywhere rejoices at these sounds, nor wishes that Orpheus had been saved from the river Hebrus. (25) Let those for whom art is a mistress strain at their art; it is enough for my little music to know a lamb's bleat, or the querulous murmur of a loving dove. I do admit that your lyre gives a sweet enough song; but music brings something better to me, and in pleasant succession mixes the sweet and the useful. (33) Are the pigs grunting? I am sure to expect a North wind blowing up. Are the geese or ducks quacking? I congratulate myself on staying at home, and being dry as I watch the falling rain. (37) And I can give you even more certain signs than these: the harvester cries loudly three times, 'Harvest home!' behind his wagons. I gladly take this as an omen, and gather in my harvest to the granaries; I am called wise and good for this one reason, that my granaries are swelling with corn. (45) If you are wise, if you want to be wise, come hither when you are tired of the town and court; here, far away, and the first in the choir, you should sing, among the granaries, of flour and markets. (49) But if you do not wish to adorn our rustic festival, you should send something that a farmer's throat can sing, or at least that a peasant, unskilled in melody, can repeat.

Text: Bern.; ms. D, fo. 7–8; Yale, ms. Osborn c. 233, p. 7; Nott. Pw V 148/1 and 151/4. *Date*: after 1712; probably *c.* 1715–16. This poem is discussed in Ch. 7.

22 Yale, ms. D read ', tamen' for '. Tamen'.   24 *Orpheum*: disyllable by synizesis. Orpheus' dismemberment is a familiar tale: e.g. Virg., *Geo.* 4. 520–7, Ovid *Met.* 11, and Milton, *Lycidas* 58–63.   25 A striking statement at the poem's centre: potentially frivolous topics do not lapse into silliness.   27 Yale reads *querum* for *querulum* (miscopying).   32 Alluding to Hor., *Ars Poet.* 343, 'omne tulit punctum qui miscuit utile dulci'.   34 Yale reads *strident* for *-et*.   38–9 Ms. D reads *permitto* for *pro-*, *reducens* for *-o*; Yale reads *reduce*.   42–4 A serious point, that wordly success leads to a good reputation, is presented in a light-hearted manner.   45–6 An Horatian invitation to leave the city.   48 Ms. D perhaps reads *Fana* for *Farra* (unclear).   51 See note on 5.

2.6 JOHANNI DOLBEN

Quid senis Coi calamus, quid illi
Proximus, turbae utilior medentum
Scripserit Freindus, neque nunc, nec unquam
    Scire licebit.

5 Horum ego possum sapere et valere
Inscius: nec quid tuus iste tutor
Scribat aut praescribat avebo, vita
    Sospite, scire.

Seu lego libri interiora, seu non,
10 Nil mea refert: sed amicum amico
Parvulum pignus renuentem amoris
    Quis ferat aeque?

Estne amicorum quis amantior te,
Chare Vir? sed te propere avolasse
15 Rumor est nostris laribus, lapillo haud
    Longius uno:

Nec tamen vidi. Merui quid, oro,
Tale? quid de te? fueratne tantum,
Quod maritali implicitus capistro
20   Servio sponsae?

An, quod agrestis satagam negoti,
Temnor? an cunctos ubicunque pagos
Despicis, qua non laquear sacelli
    Organon ornat?

25 Rectius rem fors tetigi; vocavit
Nympha, non ultra patiens morari,
Nobilis Nympha, et mihi praeferenda ut-
    cunque sodali.

Sis, precor, felix; sonet omne plectrum;
30 Blanda sit virgo; sit abunde amicorum,
Et joci, et risus; ego, sic volunt Dii,
    Rure latebo.

Translation: 'To John Dolben'

I cannot now know, nor will I ever be able to know, what the old Coan wrote, or what Freind, his nearest rival and the most useful of the medical crowd, has written. (5) I can certainly do well enough without this knowledge; nor shall I wish to know what that tutor of yours is scribbling or prescribing, as long as my health is secure. Whether I look inside the book and read it, or whether I don't, is of no concern to me. (10) But who could bear with equanimity a friend's refusal of a trifling pledge of friendship? (13) Do I have any friend more affectionate than yourself, my dear man? But there is a rumour that you flew past, no more than a mile from my house, without my seeing you. I ask you, why have I deserved such treatment? Why do I suffer it from you? Was it simply because, caught up in a marriage bond, I serve my wife? (21) Or, am I scorned because I am busy with rustic matters? Or, do you despise all country places where the sanctuary ceiling is not adorned by an organ? (25) Perhaps I have touched on the true reason: a nymph, not too fond of waiting, has summoned you; she is a noble nymph, and thoroughly preferable to myself as a companion. (29) May you be happy, I pray; may every lyre resound; may the maiden be kind; may you have an abundance of friends, jokes, and laughter; as for me, since heaven so wishes, I will lie hidden in the countryside.

Text: Bern.; BL(b), fo. 45ᵛ–46ʳ. *Date*: probably early 1717. This poem is mentioned in Ch. 7.

1 Hippocrates, edited by Freind (who has failed to send Alsop a copy).   19 Alluding to Juv. 6. 42–3. Cf. 3. 1. A47–8.   20 Love as *servitium* is a literary commonplace; a nice Neo-Latin example is J. Secundus, ode 5, 'Ad Hadrianum Goesium'.   27 Probably Dolben's future wife, the Hon. Elizabeth Digby.

2.7 HENRICO BRIDGES

Grande par patrum, duo clara Roffae
Lumina, aeterno decorare plausu
Quis vetat? cui non Hominum Deumque
    Dulce sonat vox,
5   Quae caput charum cineresque amici
Deflet, invito tibi qui reliquit
Rite collatum titulum, praeivitque,
    Egregius dux?
Plauderem dictis, o amice, si sic
10 Omnia: at quis te malesuadus egit
Impetus durum fidei exoletae
    Dogma tueri?
Plurimos nescis procerum patrumque
Stare te contra? nihil est, quod ingens
15 Arrius, quod gens animosa, Fratrum
    Ordo Polonum
Scriptitant contra? Sape tandem, et artes
Disce, queis magnus poteris bonusque
Dicier. Cultus sit ubique norma
20   Libera et exlex;
Sit fides, sit mens sua cuique, nullo
Sub duce aut ductu: imperiosa cleri
Ferre quis possit juga, quis sacerdo-
    tale capistrum?
25 Quare age, et sit pro licito licenter
Velle; sit recti sibi quisque judex;
Tros fuat quisquam Tyriusve, nullum ex-
    amen inito.
Hisce si ductus monitis priori
30 Disparem vitae ingrediare cursum,
Forte mox cinget prius immerentes
    Mitra capillos.

Translation: 'To Henry Bridges' [or Brydges]

Who would refuse to celebrate that great pair of fathers, the two clear lights of Rochester, with eternal applause? What man or god does not find sweet the voice that laments the dear departed friend, who left to you (though you were sad to take it) the post that has been properly conferred upon you, and who preceded you as an outstanding leader? (9) I would applaud your speech, my friend, if that were all that you had said. But what ill-advised impulse led you to defend the stern principles of an abolished faith? (13) Do you not know that most of the lords and bishops are your opponents? Is it of no account that great Arius, and that vigorous race, the order of the Polish brethren, write in opposition to you? Be wise at last, and learn those skills, by which you can become called 'great and good'. (19) You should espouse a form of worship that is free of rules and strict beliefs; let each man have his own faith and opinions, with no leader or guide. Who can bear the clergy's imperious yoke, or priestly control? (25) So act in this way, and let there be free choice; let everyone be his own judge of righteousness; let there be no enquiry into who is Trojan or Tyrian. (29) If, led by this advice, you proceed on a course that differs from your previous life, perhaps soon a bishop's mitre will

---

1 Probably alluding to Hor., *Serm.* 2. 3. 243, 'par nobile fratrum'; if so, the contrast with Horace's disreputable context is humorous. Thomas Sprat (1635–1713), Bishop of Rochester, and his son, Thomas, the Archdeacon (Bernard's n.). 3 *Hominum Deumque*: cf. Virg., *Aen.* 1. 229, 2. 745, etc.   5 Probably alluding to Hor., *Carm.* 1. 24. 2, 'tam cari capitis'; cf. 1. 4. 15–17.   9–10 Alluding to Juv. 10. 123–4, 'si sic/ omnia dixisset'. Brydges' defiance of authority is compared to Cicero's: Juvenal's rejection of such fatal heroism fits with Alsop's ironically assumed tone of moderation.   15 Ms. D reads *Arius*.   17 Ms. D reads *Scriptitent* for -*ant*.   20 Possibly alluding to Hor., *Ars Poet.* 222–4 (his only use of *exlex*).   24 Cf. 2. 6. 19.   27 Alluding to Virg., *Aen.* 1. 574, 'Tros Tyriusque mihi nullo discrimine agetur' (and 10. 108, 'Tros Rutulusve fuat'). Ms. D reads *fuit*.

surround your head (that previously did not deserve one).

Text: Bern.; ms. D, fo. 14; Nott. Pw V 149/3. *Date*: probably mid or late 1721. This poem is discussed in Ch. 7.

2.8 HENRICO BRIDGES

Dum salutantum tibi plaudit agmen,
Hinc tua ad coelum merita, inde Draki
Munera attollens; ego non minori
    Cor animumque
5 Gaudio effusus bona cuncta fari
Quam lubens vellem: sed inops loquelae
Aulicae, atque artis, vice gratulandi,
    Pauca monebo.
Quid sacerdotem deceat, quid omni ex
10 Parte sit pulchrum expediatque, vel non,
Plenius nulli meliusque, Amice,
    Quam tibi notum.
Num tamen recte tibi res agentur
Rusticae, fas sit dubitare. Quoquo
15 Iveris, gens et genus omne fallax,
    Crede, colonum est.
Bobus, et porcis, et agrestium armis
Tempus et curas adhibere, nostrae
Convenit sorti moduloque; sed te
20   Stemmate cretum
Magno, et ornatum genio altiori
Dedecet vulgi labor: at caveto
Cui loces, aut quo vade, lucra fundi.
    Si tibi fidas,
25 Pol eris delusus: age, ergo, amicum
Sume te paulo sapientiorem,
Me, vel Aldrico-Carolum, aut honestum
    Forte Pelingum.

Translation: 'To Henry Bridges'

While you are congratulated by a long line of people, one praising your deserts to the skies, another Drake's generosity, my heart and mind are no less overflowing with joy for you, and would gladly give you all good wishes. But since I am poorly equipped with the tricks of courtly eloquence, I will give you a little advice, instead of congratulations. (9) What a priest ought to do, what is in every way fine and expedient, and what is not, you already know, my friend, better than anyone else. (13) But one may more fully and reasonably doubt whether your rustic business is in order. Wherever you go, believe me, the whole race of farmers is duplicitous. (17) It is convenient for my station in life, and my poetry, to pass my time in worrying about oxen and pigs and agricultural implements; but the labour of the common people is an unfitting subject for you, born as you are from a noble family, and adorned with a higher genius. (22) But beware to whom you entrust, and on what security, the wealth of your farm. If you rely on your own ability, you will surely be deceived; come, then, and take on a friend who is a little more worldly-wise than yourself—me, or Charles Aldrich, or perhaps honest Pelling.

Text: Bern.; ms. D, fo. 14ᵛ–15ʳ; BL(b), fo. 43ᵛ–44ʳ; Nott. Pw V 149/4. *Date*: 1721. This poem is discussed in Ch. 7.

2 Sir William Drake, who appointed Brydges to Agmondesham.   7 Cf. 2. 3. 21–2.   10 Possibly alluding to Hor., *Epist*. 1. 2. 3, 'quid sit pulchrum . . . quid non'; cf. *Carm*. 2. 16. 27–8, 'ab omni/ parte'.   28 Nott. reads *Polinghum*. (See Ch. 7 for these names.)

2.9 JOHANNI NICOL

Translation: 'To John Nicol'

Chare Vir, crebri officii benignus;
Chare Vir, nostris vicibus dolere
Suetus, et totum quod adest levamen
    Ferre paratus
5 Semper. O nostris semel et secundo
Rebus adiutor, facilis favensque,
Quo soles vultu, cape luctuosae
    Munera Musae.
Ter quater Phoebe, docilis novari,
10 Dispari aspectu similique fulsit,
Saeva mi de quo secuere dulces
    Fata hymenaeos.
Nullus ex illo vacuum doloris
Me dies, sponsae immemoremve vidit;
15 Nulla nox somnos placidos, ut olim, in-
    dulsit ocellis.
Sive per terram vagus hospes erro;
Sive iter rado liquidum per aequor;
Quo feror cunque aut fugio, peremptae ux-
20   oris imago
It comes, tristis comes. O placenti
Umbra deludens specie! o amantis
Vana spes! cui tam prope sponsa fertur,
    Tam procul absens.
25 Hanc mihi postquam rapuit Tonantis
Ira, non ardens patriam videndi
Cura cor tangit, nec habent, quod olim,
    Dulce penates.
Quin sita hinc longe loca, pristinoque
30 Saeculo ignotum paro me per orbem
Devehi, aversis dubius ferarve, an
    Auspicibus, Diis.
Artium expertes eo per popellos
Artium ipse expers; ubi non canori
35 Quis sciens plectri, nec amata Phoebo
    Pieridum vox
Uspiam auditur; licet arva Divus
Recta equos flectens propiore torret
Numine, et flamma rutilus potenti

Dear man, you have been the source of frequent acts of kindness; dear man, you are accustomed to lament my vicissitudes, and always prepared to give all the relief that is at hand. You have helped my troubles again and again; so now accept this gift of my grief-stricken muse with your usual ease and goodwill. (9) The changeful moon has renewed itself three or four times, since the time when harsh fate cut short my sweet marriage. No day since then has seen me free from sorrow, or forgetful of my wife; no night has indulged my eyes, as before, with quiet sleep. (17) Whether I wander about as a stranger over the earth, or set a course over the watery sea, wherever I am carried or flee, the image of the face that has been taken from me is my companion, my sad companion. O shade that deludes me with a pleasant appearance! O lover's vain hope, when a wife, absent so far away, is brought so close! (25) After God's anger snatched her from me, I had no ardent wish to see my native country, nor is my house, as before, sweet to me. (29) So I am preparing myself to be taken to a place far distant, and through a world unknown to past ages, uncertain whether I go with the omens against me, or in my favour. (33) Myself without skills, I am going through unskilled peoples, where there is none learned in lyre-playing, nor is the voice of the Muses, which Apollo loves, ever heard, even though the sun-god may turn his horses and burn flat fields with a closer heat, and fill everything with his powerful flame. (41) If harsh fate denies me a return from there, may I take its

---

18 Cf. Virg., *Aen.* 5. 170, 'radit iter'.   25–8 This stanza is omitted in some mss.   31 Bern. reads *ferarne* for *-ve*: corrected in BL(a), etc.   38 *Recta* is not entirely clear: possibly 'straight' (of the sun's course). Bern. prints *Rectà* (not *Rectâ*).   39 *The Student*, Yale read *Lampade* for *Numine* (a copyist's or editor's simplification?).

40   Omnia complet.
          Unde si Parcae reditum negabunt
          Tetricae, adversi fruar aequus ira
          Fati, amicorum memor atque ab illis
                  Fors memorandus.
45   Qui color vitae mihi cunque, scribam,
          Et tibi scribam: mihi sin dierum
          Instet extremus, renuatque plures
                  Jupiter annos;
          Carmen hoc magni accipias amoris
50   Ultimum pignus: valeas, Amice;
          Et mihi quicquid Superi negarunt,
                  Dent tibi laetum.

anger with equanimity, remembering my friends, and perhaps remembered by them. (45) I shall write, whatever complexion my life turns out to have; and I shall write it to you—unless my final day comes on, and God refuses me any more years of life. Please accept this poem as the last pledge of my great affection; may you fare well, my friend, and whatever heaven denies me, may it grant you happiness.

Text: Bern.; *The Student* 1. 159 (1750); ms. D, fo. 43ᵛ–44ᵛ; BL(a): for lines 41–4; BL(b), fo. 65ᵛ–66ᵛ; Yale ms. Osborn c. 233, p. 8; Nott. Pw V 145/3, 146, 147, and 151/1; Trinity College, Cambridge ms. 615 (= R. 3. 36, fo. 32); Bodleian, ms. Rawl. lett. 31. *Date*: autumn 1718. This poem is discussed in Ch. 7.

2.10 JOHANNI DOLBEN

          Saepe tentanti citharam movere
          Obstitit Musis minus aequa tellus;
          Quae madet tellus, Helicone adempto,
                  Omnibus undis.
5   Non amans silvae philomela, non hic
          Cantibus gaudet merula: at perenni
          Rana conturbat strepitu paludes,
                  Belgica Syren.
          Ecquid hac speres patria profectum
10   Musicis dignum auriculis? quid exspes
          Proferet vates, hominum deumque ex-
                  ercitus ira?
          Crede, post raptam (Jove sic jubente)
          Conjugem, nec mi placuit canoro
15   Pulsum ebur plectro, nec amata quondam
                  Pieridum vox.
          Quin domi memet, stupide inquietus,
          Nil agens, totis teneo diebus,
          Negligens prorsus fugiam, feramve, in-

Translation: 'To John Dolben'

    I often tried to strike my lyre, but this land, too flat for music, stood in my way. This land is soaked by every wave, and the Muses' mountain is missing. (5) Neither the nightingale that loves the woods, nor the thrush here rejoices in song; but the frog, that Dutch Siren, disturbs the marshes with its continual din. (9) So is there anything you could hope for, sent from this nation, that might be worthy of the Muses' ears? What could a bard produce who is devoid of hope, the target of mankind's and heaven's anger? (13) Believe me, since my wife was taken from me (such being God's will), I have not been pleased by the playing of any tuneful instruments, nor by the Muses' voice, which I once loved. (17) And so, stuck

41–4 Bern. and some mss. (including Yale) omit this stanza.   45 Alluding to Hor., *Serm.* 2. 1. 60, 'quisquis erit vitae scribam color'.   51–2 Possibly recalling Hor., *Carm.* 2. 16. 31–2, 'et mihi forsan, tibi quod negarit,/ porriget hora.'

11–12 Possibly recalling Virg., *Aen.* 1. 3–4, 'iactatus . . . vi superum . . . iram'.   19 Bern. reads *feramne* for -*ve*: corrected BL(a).

20   commoda vitae.
        Si foras, oti satur et negoti,
        Quo ferant gressus, eo, nescio quid
        Triste pervolvo: similique et intra ex-
                traque penates
25   Maceror luctu. Tibi nil benigni
        Tale Dii! seu tu fidibus canoris
        Canticum misces, agilique chordas
                Pollice versas
        Artifex; seu tu, ingenuos amicos
30   Inter, indulges salibus jocisque
        Libere, discors sonus omnis absit
                Atque sodalis.
        Serio sin te dare vis amori
        Connubi tandem experiens, Deorum
35   Quicquid in caelo, precor: esto felix;
                Esto pudicae
        Sponsae amans, illi redamatus aeque,
        Jurgio et rixa procul; esto qualis
        Et fui, et jam nunc, sineret Deorum
40   Ira, fuissem.
        Multa sunt quae te super haec monerem,
        Multa quae optarem: sed acerba torquet
        Cura cor intra, et Genius coercet
                Belga Camoenam.

at home by myself, foolishly restless, but doing nothing, I pass all my days; I care not whether I fly from, or bear, the unpleasantnesses of life. (21) If I go out, I walk wherever my steps take me, tired of both idleness and activity, and thinking some sad thought or other; in and out of my house, I am tortured by the same grief. (25) May kind heaven bring you nothing like this! Whether you mix your song with tuneful lyres, and as a skilled performer pluck the strings, or whether among honest friends you freely indulge in jokes and wit, may every discordant sound be absent—and every discordant companion! (33) But if you wish to give yourself over to serious love, at last trying out marriage, I pray to all the gods in heaven that you may be happy; may you love a chaste wife, and be equally beloved by her, far from quarrels and strife; may you be as I myself was, and would still be, if divine anger had not intervened. (41) There are many further things of which I would advise you, many things I would wish for you; but bitter care twists my heart inside me, and the Dutch genius restrains my Muse.

Text: Bern.; BL(b), fo. 44–5. *Date*: late 1718, or 1719.

2.11 JOHANNI FREIND

Qualis infauste profugus beatos
Italum campos, et amica Musis
Arva, jam tandem propior sepulchro
        Naso reliquit;

Translation: 'To John Freind'
        Ovid, an unfortunate fugitive, left the happy plains of Italy, those fields friendly to the Muses, when he was already quite

26 Cf. Hor., *Carm.* 1. 12. 11, 'fidibus canoris'.   27–8 Possibly alluding to Ovid, *Am.* 2. 4. 27, 'agili percurrit pollice chordas'. The reader may remember Ovid's pentameter, 'tam doctas quis non possit amare manus?': relevant to Dolben's amatory prospects.   34–5 Alluding to Hor., *Epod.* 5. 1, 'At, o deorum quidquid in caelo regit'. Cf. also *Carm.* 2. 1. 25 (and Livy 23. 9).

1 Possibly alluding to Virg., *Aen.* 1. 2, the most famous use of *profugus*; cf. Ovid, *Trist.* 1. 3. 10, *Ep. ex P.* 2. 9. 6.

5 Sed nec antiquae Getico sub axe
   Artis oblitus, geniumve inertem
   Passus, illustris recreavit exul
        Carmine curas.
   Pontici plectri sonitum audierunt
10 Chara gens vati, Latii sodales;
   Carmen absentis repetebat absens
        Sponsa mariti.
   O! mihi si par dederint levamen
   Fata; si dulcis superaret uxor
15 Literis nostris adeunda; non me
        Exilii sors
   Dura, vel brumae glacialis horror,
   Non furor ponti, populusve ponto
   Saevior, tristem pavidumve, salva ux-
20   ore, ferirent.
   Forte tum surgens lyra delicatis
   Auribus dignos numeros referret;
   Temneres nec tu joculare carmen
        Vatis amici.
25 Obstat heu! nostris inimicus ausis
   Jupiter; Phoebi chorus omnis obstat:
   Et pares visi fidicen fidesque,
        Exul uterque.
   Dum tamen mitto tibi quale Musae
30 cunque conamen; sat erit superque
   Si queam his nugis residem movere in
        Cantica Freindum.
   Quare age, ad notum docilis canendi
   Verte te ludum; ex locuplete penu
35 Prome, quae nostrae faciant pudorem,
        Carmina, Musae.
   Qualis audito grue, stridulove
   Ansere, extemplo philomela guttur
   Solvit, et cantu potiore sylvas
40   Arvaque mulcet.

near to the grave; but he did not forget his old skill under the Getic sky, or allow his genius to be inactive—that illustrious exile relieved his troubles with song. (9) A people dear to the poet, his companions in Italy, heard the sound of lyre-playing from the Black Sea; a distant wife repeated the poetry of her far-off husband. (13) Oh, if only fate had given me similar relief, if my sweet wife survived to be addressed in my letters; then the lot of exile would not be hard for me, nor (if my wife were safe) would winter's icy horror, the fury of the sea, or a people more savage than the sea, afflict a sad and frightened man. (21) Perhaps then my lyre would rise to produce music worthy of a sophisticated audience; nor would you scorn the humorous song of your friend, the poet. (25) Alas, an unfriendly god stands in the way of my aims; the whole choir of Apollo opposes me; and the lyre-player and his lyre have seemed to suffer the same fate, both of them exiled. (29) Meanwhile, however, I do send you some sort of attempt at poetry; it will be fully enough if I can by these trifles urge a reluctant Freind into song himself. (33) Come then, and as a skilful singer turn yourself to that familiar amusement; bring from your rich purse poems that should make my Muse blush. (37) It would be like, after hearing a crane or screeching goose, a nightingale suddenly opening its throat, and soothing the woods and fields with a finer song. (41) Certainly I might better write and demand news from Charlett or

---

5 *Getico*: the place of Ovid's exile: *Ep. ex P.* 1. 1. 2, etc.   10 Like Alsop's (41–55), Ovid's *sodales* could be unreliable (e.g. *Ep. ex P.* 4. 3).   19–20 Alluding to Hor., *Carm.* 1. 2. 19–20, 'ux-/ orius'. Cf. Alsop 2. 2. 7–8. 23–4 Probably alluding to Hor., *Carm.* 2. 6. 24, 'vatis amici', and *Carm.* 4. 6. 43–4, 'carmen, docilis modorum/ vatis Horati.' Cf. *docilis*, 33.   26 Alluding to Virg., *Ecl.* 6. 66, 'Phoebi chorus . . . omnis'.   27 *Fides*: 'lyre', but perhaps a pun on 'faith' (which Alsop has kept, to his wife and to Jacobitism). Cf. 2. 2. 6–8; 2. 5. 3.   31 Possibly alluding to Virg., *Aen.* 6. 814–5, 'residesque movebit/ . . . in arma'.   34 Probably alluding to Persius, 3. 74, 'in locuplete penu' (which scans in a hexameter, but not Alsop's sapphic): possibly a deliberate mistake, giving a humorous example of his inferiority to Freind (or, perhaps more likely, a simple lapse of memory).

Nempe Charlettum melius, bonumve
Poscerem scriptor nova Percivallum;
Mitterent illi, mora nulla, quicquid
    Sciret uterque.
45 Centies tu nil repetita curas
Vota; nec solum calami labori
Parcis; at cunctos prohibes amico
    Scribere amicos.
Non nisi per te tacuisset expers
50 Fraudis Hintonus; ferulae negasset
Nec brevem Nicol requiem, nec aegris
    Otia Broxholme.
Scriptitent illi modo; tu, sceleste,
Aut tace, aut scribe, aut age quod lubebit:
55 Pendeas quamvis, ego nil morabor,
    De trabe collum.

good Percival; they would without delay write all they knew. (45) You do not care about my prayers, repeated a hundred times; and you do not only spare your own pen the effort, but prohibit all my friends from writing to their friend. (49) Guileless Hinton would not have been silent, unless it were your doing; nor would Nicol have denied his rod a brief rest, or Broxholme have failed to let the sick have some peace. Let them only write; you, wretched man, either be silent or write, or do whatever you want—you can go and hang yourself, I won't delay you.

Text: Bern.; BL(b), fo. 47ᵛ–48ʳ. *Date*: late 1718, or 1719. This poem is discussed in Ch. 7.

2.12 JOHANNI FREIND

Tu domi felix, Britonum Machaon,
Sublevas aegros, adimisque letho:
Nec tibi Musae, nec amica Musis
    Otia desunt.
5 Uda me tellus, pelagi propago,
Detinet fato profugum, proterva
Regibus tellus, vacuasque lucri ex-
    osa Camoenas.
Crassus hic aer, et hebes virum gens
10 Barbaro squallens habitu, efferisque
Moribus; durum genus, hospitique in-
    hospita turba.
Hac ego halecum in patria, hinc et inde, ig-
narus ignotusque, vagor: tamen nec
15 Impotens Matris furor, aut rejectae

Translation: 'To John Freind'

You are happy at home, and as the Britons' Machaon you raise up the sick, and save them from death. Nor do you lack the Muses, and leisure friendly to them. (5) As for me, a wet land, the spawn of the sea, holds me, a fate-driven fugitive; the land is rebellious towards kings, and hates unprofitable poetry. The air here is heavy, and there is a dull race of men, barbarously dressed, and with savage manners; a hard race, a crowd that is inhospitable to visitors. (13) In this fatherland of pickled fish, unknowing and unknown, I wander hither and thither. The impotent fury of her mother, however, or the

41–2 For Charlett and Percival, see 1. 9, 1. 10 (and Ch. 5).   47–8 Probably a joke, or an exaggerated response to a temporary dearth of letters. His enemies might have thought Alsop disgraced, but it is unlikely that everyone would have deserted him.   55 BL(a) suggests (wrongly) *Pendeat* for *-as*.

1 Machaon: Homeric doctor; cf. Virg., *Aen.* 2. 263; Prop. 2. 1. 59, etc.   2 Alluding to Hor., *Carm.* 3. 22. 3, 'adimisque leto'.   6 Alluding to Virg., *Aen.* 1. 2, 'fato profugus'.   9, 13 A double allusion, to Juv. 10. 50, 'vervecum in patria crassoque sub aere nasci', which in turn alludes to Hor., *Epist.* 2. 1. 244, 'Boeotum in crasso iurares aere natum'.

Ira Puellae,
Aut vafri Brooki insidiae expeditum
Territant curis: sed apertus erro,
Negligens quo pes ferat, aut viai
20   Ductus aquosae.
Nunc per extructas nitide plateas,
Nunc per hortorum spatia, ordinesque
Suaviter mistos, eo: nunc per amnes
    Arte recisos
25 Tendo, qua multus trahitur caballo
Linter, ignavis rate vel quadriga
Gratior, somnum capere, aut Lyaei
    Munera, malint.
Templa, quae cultu meliore digna,
30 Bustaque heroum video, forumque
Aere qua fuso erigitur, Batavum
    Gloria, Erasmus.
Inde me spissae, haud bene curiosus,
Infero bursae: nihil hic negoti,
35 Nil agens rerum, ut medius catervae, huc
    Trudor et illuc.
Multus hic sermo est, quid ubique mercis;
Quid novi apportent tabulae; quid anceps
Italus, Teuto quid agat, quaterno
40   Foedere fretus.
Hic lare in parvo, properans Falerni
Poculis siccum relevare guttur,
Talibus patrem pueros monentem
    Audio dictis.
45 Ite vos, inquit, mea stirps, propago
Aemula; accendat sacra vos cupido,
Dia spes auri; nec opum reclamet
    Quis satur, ohe!
Per nefas, per fas ruite, o Batavi:
50 Patrio ritu quid iniquum et aequum
Viderint Angli; facitote vos quo-
    cunque modo rem.
Sic pater: plaudit patre digna pubes,
Et lubens dicto obsequitur. Crumenae

rejected girl's anger, or the tricks of that rascal Brooke cannot frighten me in my troubles; instead, I wander about openly, not caring whither my feet or the flow of the canals take me. (21) I pass now through finely constructed squares, now through spacious gardens, laid out with pleasing variety; now I travel along artificial rivers, where many a barge is dragged by a nag, a form of transport which the lazy folk find preferable to boat or coach, whether they prefer to take some sleep or drink. (29) I see churches that deserve a better form of worship, and tombs of heroes, and the market place where the Dutchmen's glory, Erasmus, is set up in cast bronze. (33) Thence, out of ill-advised curiosity, I take myself to the busy exchange; I have no business here, nothing to do, as I am pushed to and fro in the middle of the crowd. (37) There is much discussion here: what trade there is everywhere, what novelties the news-sheets bring, what the unreliable Italian is up to, or the German, relying on his Quadruple Alliance. (41) Here, in a small room, as I rush to refresh my dry throat with some cups of wine, I hear a father giving this advice to his sons. (45) 'Go ye, my offspring,' he said, 'my emulous brood: let sacred covetousness, the divine hope for gold, fire you up—and let no one cry that he has enough of wealth. Hurry on by foul means and fair, Dutchmen, in your ancestral manner, whatever the English see as reasonable or unreasonable; just make sure you get a profit in any way you can.' (53) Thus spoke the father: his children, worthy of such a father, applaud

---

17 *Brooki*: not identified; from the context, an adviser or counsel to Alsop's opponents. 17–18 Possibly alluding to Ter., *Ph.* 823, 'cura sese expedivit'. Cf. Alsop 2. 19. 18.   19 *Viai*: archaic genitive, an un-Horatian touch.   35 Ms. D reads *coronae*, written over deleted *catervae*.   41 Probably alluding to Hor., *Carm.* 3. 29. 14, 'parvo sub lare'.   42 Possibly alluding to Ovid, *Fasti* 3. 304, 'relevant multo pectora sicca mero'.   45–6 Ms. D reads *Parentis . . . libido* for *propago . . . cupido*.   46–7 Alluding to Virg., *Aen.* 3. 56–7; cf. *Aen.* 6. 373, 721; Hor., *Carm.* 2. 16. 13–16, etc.   48 Alluding to Hor., *Serm.* 1. 5. 12–13, 'ohe/ iam satis est!'.   49 Alluding to Lucan, 5. 312–3, 'per omne/ fasque nefasque rues?'.   53 Ms. D reads *Proles* for *pubes*.

55 Jam timens me proripio, domumque
        Sospite tandem
    Aere, sed fessus, redeo: hic Maronis
    Dium opus posco, numerosve Flacci
    Dulcis, aut scripta Hippocratis revolvo, in-
60   terprete Freindo.
    Sic tuis absens videor potiri,
    Freinde perchare, alloquiis: sepultam
    Deme quod sponsam doleo, et dolebo,
        Mente sat aequus.

and gladly do as he told them. Now I am
worried for my purse, and I tear myself
away, and finally, tired but with my coins
still safe, I return home; here I ask for the
divine work of Virgil, and Horace's sweet
poetry, or I turn over the writings of
Hippocrates, with Freind to elucidate
him. (61) Thus I seem to possess your
conversation, my most dear Freind, while
I am absent from you; and, apart from the
fact that I lament, and will carry on
lamenting, my buried wife, I am easy
enough in my mind.

Text: Bern.; ms. D, fo 21ᵛ–22ᵛ. *Date*: late 1718, or 1719. This poem is discussed in Ch. 7.

2.13 HENRICO BRIDGES

Urbis insanae, nihilo Ipse forsan
Sanior, curam strepitumque liqui,
Nec sciens rerum, neque quaestuosam at-
        tentus ad artem.
5 Nil mea refert, pede quo stat Indi
    Auctio aut Afri; nec avens requiro
    Quas ferant merces, quibus aut in oris,
        Libs, Notus, Auster.
    Largiter quod mi satis est, benigna
10 Dextera effudit; bene nota famae
    Dextera, afflictis dare, sublevare,
        Tollere humo rem
    Sueta jam dudum; mihi praeter omnes,
    Sive quid cantu fidibusve possim,
15 Sive opus tentem numeris solutis,
        Non reticenda.
    Sit manus felix ea, sit perenni
    Copia exundans, mihi quae penates

Translation: 'To Henry Bridges'
    I have left the trouble and din of the
insane city, perhaps no saner myself,
knowing nothing of public affairs, nor
concerned with the art of making money.
It is of no account to me, on what footing
the price of India or Africa stock stands,
nor do I eagerly ask what merchandise
each different southerly wind blows
onward, or on what shores. (9) A kind
hand has generously poured out a sum
quite sufficient for me; that hand is
famous, and long accustomed to give to
the afflicted, to support them, to raise
their fortunes from the ground. (13) As
for me, above all, if I can achieve anything
in song or lyre-playing, or if I attempt any
work in prose, I should not be silent about
this kind hand. (17) May that hand be

62 Ms. D reads *praeclare* for *perchare*.   64 Probably alluding to Hor., *Carm.* 2. 3. 1–2, 'aequam . . . mentem'. We are again reminded that Horace differed from the Dutch. The ending is quiet and personal; there is a far greater cause for sorrow than the irritations of exile. (Cf. 2. 18, etc.).

1 Possibly alluding to Hor., *Serm.* 2. 3. 52, 'insanum, nihilo'; Horace's Chrysippus presents a picture of general insanity; cf. Juv. 3; Virg., *Geo.* 2. 502.   2 Alluding to Hor., *Carm.* 3. 29. 12, 'strepitumque Romae': urging Maecenas to leave the city; Horace's patron prepares us for the subject of patronage, 9–28.   8 Three southerly winds, needed for return from the South Atlantic; *Libs* is unusual (found in Ausonius).   15 Probably alluding to Hor., *Carm.* 4. 2. 11–12, 'numerisque fertur lege solutis' (of Pindar); but Alsop's *solutus* implies prose, as regularly.

Visere antiquos dedit, et malignam
20   Temnere sortem.
Non dehinc caecis tuguri latebris
Abditus lucem fugiam; nec urbes
Exteras quaeram profugus, metuque
      Carceris exul.
25 Testium fraudes, rigidique frontem
Judicis non ulterius timebo;
Peierent illi licet, ille flectat
      Jura retrorsum.
Sed metus expers, vacuusque curis,
30 Rus meum, et ruris lepidos sodales
Laetus invisam, et fruar haud pudendis
      Luxibus oti.
Nunc per aprici spatia ampla campi,
Flosculos inter pecudesque vadam;
35 Nunc libros volvam, nimis heu! nimisque
      Passus inertes.
Nunc tubi et fumi satur, hordeique
Nobili succo modice madescens,
Proximum fratri, mihi multum amato,
40   Te memorabo.

fortunate, and overflowing with a continual stream of riches, since it has allowed me to revisit my old home, and despise malevolent fate. (21) No more shall I flee the light, hidden in the dark corners of a hut; nor shall I seek out foreign cities as a fugitive, and an exile driven by fear of imprisonment. (25) I shall no longer fear the deceit of suborned witnesses, or the judge's stern brow; let them perjure themselves, or that man twist the laws. (29) But without fear and empty of troubles, I shall happily visit my countryside, and charming rural companions, and enjoy leisure, a luxury one need not be ashamed of. Now I shall go through the open spaces of the sunny plain, amidst flowers and flocks; now I shall turn the pages of books that I have, alas, left far too much unread. (37) Now, smoking my pipe, and moderately soused in that noble substance, beer, I shall think of you, next to your brother, whom I love so much.

Text: Bern. *Date*: *c.* 1720–6. This poem is discussed in Ch. 7.

2.14 HENRICO BRIDGES

Est tibi tandem metricis recusans
Legibus dici titulus; merenti
Debitum munus, meritum sed infra,
      Judice crasso.

Translation: 'To Henry Bridges'
    You can at last be called by a title that refuses to be fitted into verse; it is owed to your deserts, though, as any fool could judge, less than you deserve. (5) Shall I

19–20 Probably alluding to Hor., *Carm.* 2. 16. 39–40, 'malignum/ spernere vulgus' (cf. n. on 2. 1. 72). It may remind us that *vulgus* (in the form of a jury) caused his misfortunes.   21 Probably alluding to Virg., *Ecl.* 1. 69, 'tuguri': Meliboeus' exile is an appropriate parallel to Alsop's.   23 Cf. 2. 11. 1.   24 He fears imprisonment for debt, not having paid his damages.   27 I tentatively take *ille* as the malevolent judge, rather than Chandos (who might bend the laws back in Alsop's favour).   37 Cf. 2. 15. 1.

2 *Titulus*: Bernard's n., 'Archidiaconus Roffensis' [Archdeacon of Rochester]. One could make this fit into an Alsopian sapphic (e.g. 'Rite tu Roffae archidiaconus jam . . .'), but it would be inelegant, and Alsop uses it as an excuse to play with alternatives, parodying the multiple names of ancient deities. He may remember classical complaints about metrically impossible names, e.g. Hor., *Serm.* 1. 5. 87. See R. Kassel, 'Quod versu dicere non est', *Kleine Schriften* (Berlin, 1991), pp. 131–7 (late sapphic examples, p. 135) (= *Zeitschrift für Papyrologie und Epigraphik* 19 (1975), pp. 211–18; sapphics, p. 215).   4 Bernard prints *Crasso* (capital 'C').

5 Tene Roffensis vocitabo lumen
Praesulis, lumen vigil et fidele?
An magis gaudes, velut ante, amicis
   Dicier Harry?
Quo salutem optas tibi cunque mitti
10 Nomine, hoc mitto: neque tu rogatu
Arduus surda excipias ferentem
   Vota Camoenam.
Dolben, ut nosti, tibi mique charus,
Coelibis vitae satur, aulicamque
15 Nil morans pompam, fruitur paterno
   Cum lare sponsa.
Sit, precor, felix; sit ad omne dexter
Conjugis munus; Dominae domusque
Expleat vota, incolumique servet
20   Corpore famam.
Sed rudis tyro est; furiosiorque aut
Cautior justo, vereor, subibit
Castra, ni, quid sat fuerit, quid infra,
   Signet amicus.
25 His super, quae tu documenta nosti,
Si dabis, non aut sterilem queretur
Sponsus uxorem, nimis aut inertem
   Sponsa maritum.

call you the light of the prelate of Rochester, his watchful and faithful light? Or do you prefer, as before, that your friends call you Harry? (9) Under whatever name you want to be sent good wishes, I send you this. Do not be deaf to the prayers that poetry brings. (13) Dolben, your dear friend and mine, has had enough of a bachelor's life, as you know, and unable to put up with the pomp at court now enjoys a wife and his paternal home. (17) May he be fortunate, I pray; may he be skilful at every duty a husband has, fulfil the wishes of his wife and house, and preserve his reputation with his person intact. (21) But he is a clumsy novice; I fear that he will breach his wife's defences either more furiously or more cautiously than he should, unless some friend points out to him what is enough, and what is less than enough. (25) In addition to this, if you tell him what you know, neither will the husband complain of a barren wife, nor the wife of a too flaccid husband.

Text: Bern. *Date*: 1720. This poem is mentioned in Ch. 7.

2.15 JOHANNI DOLBEN

Dum tubum, ut mos est meus, ore versans
Februis penso quid agam Calendis,
Pone stat Sappho, monitisque miscet
   Blanda severis.
5 Ergo Musarum male temnis aras

Translation: 'To John Dolben'

While I was smoking my pipe, as is my habit, and thinking what I should do on the first of February, Sappho stood in front of me, and mixes kind words with severe advice: (5) 'Do you thus, an infrequent

15–16 Cf. Hor., *Epist.* 2. 2. 50–1, 'paterni/ et laris'.   17 Cf. Ovid, *Ep. ex P.* 4. 16. 24, 'dexter in omne'.
21 Cf. Lucan, 5. 363, 'tiro rudis'; Cic., *De Or.* 1. 50. 218, etc.   23 *Castra*: the language of *militia amoris*, as found in Prop., Tib., Ovid.

2 Alluding to Hor., *Carm.* 3. 8. 1, 'Martiis caelebs quid agam Kalendis'; Alsop too is single (though a widower, not a bachelor): a subtle reminder of his wife's death, not explicitly mentioned here. G.M. and Trinity H. 5. 17 have *Martiis*.
5–8 Ms. D omits this stanza.

Infrequens cultor? merui quid, Erro,
Ut tribus nostrum venerere numen
      Vix quater annis?
Tale nil certe meruit, teipso
10 Teste, Dolbenus, tua suetus olim
Scripta volvendo melius locandum in-
      sumere tempus.
Ille amicorum memor usque, quas tu
Scriptites, nugis iterum vacabit;
15 Rectius quanquam sapit, altioresque
      Ebibit artes.
Quare age, assumptis calamo et tabellis,
Molle si quicquam potes aut facetum,
Scribe festinus. Tua fors recline in
20   Pectus Elisae
Carmina interpres leget ille, amatus
Plurimum interpres: nimis invidendus
Tu, modo haud excors videare, Elisa
      Judice, Vates.
25 Tu stylo quantum potes expolito,
Dulce par, nostro admonitu, saluta:
Dignius frustra thema, chariusve,
      Musa requiret,
Seu libet pulchram memorare prolem,
30 Vividas jam jam effigies parentum;
Seu velis magnas animae utriusque
      Pingere dotes.
Pingito hunc curae implicitum sacrorum,
Nec tamen plectri immemorem aut
      Camoenae;
35 Hanc domus rebus nitide ordinandis
      Pinge studentem.
Pinge, si par est calamus labori,
Ut fides constans, ut amor perennis,
Ludat ut circum temerata nullis
40   Gratia rixis.
Pinge—sic fata in mediis reliquit
Vocibus Nympha attonitum, impotemque
Amplius quicquam addere, praeter unum hoc,
      Esto beatus!

worshipper, scorn the Muses' altars? What have I done, you truant, to deserve the fact that you have scarcely worshipped me four times in three years? (9) For sure, Dolben has not deserved such treatment, by your own account, since he was once accustomed to spend time, that might have been better invested elsewhere, in reading over your writings. He always remembers his friends, and will again be free to read the trifles that you dash off, although he knows better, and appreciates higher arts than yours. (17) So then, take up your pen and paper, and hurry to write anything gentle or witty that you can. He will perhaps read your poems leaning on Elisa's breast, and he is a much loved reader; you are too much to be envied, if only you do not seem to be an unspirited poet, in Elisa's judgement. (25) You should take my advice, and salute that sweet pair in as polished a style as you can; the Muse would look in vain for a more worthy theme, or one closer to your heart, whether you wish to mention their beautiful children, who are already lively images of their parents, or whether you wish to depict the great spiritual gifts they each enjoy. (33) You should depict him bound up with his ecclesiastical business, but not forgetful of music or poetry; depict her taking care that the household is splendidly organised. (37) Depict, if your pen is up to the job, how constant is their faith, how eternal their love, and how grace tempered by no quarrels plays around them. Depict . . .' (41) But with these words she suddenly stopped in the middle of her advice, and left me astonished, and unable to add anything more, except for this one wish: 'Be happy!'.

6 Alluding to Hor., *Carm.* 1. 34. 1, 'cultor et infrequens'. For *erro* (noun), cf. 2. 1. 71; 3. 1. A48.   11–12 Cf. Hor., *Ars Poet.* 443, 'insumebat'.   18 Alluding to Hor., *Serm.* 1. 10. 44–5, 'molle atque facetum/ Vergilio adnuerunt gaudentes rure Camenae'; Virgil's rustic Muses are appropriate for Alsop.   19 *G.M.* reads *recumbi* for *recline.*   21–2 *Interpres* perhaps suggests that Dolben translates the poems (while reading them aloud to Elisa).   26 Cf. 2. 7. 1; 2. 24. 5–6.   27–8 *G.M.* and Trinity H. 5. 17 read 'meliusque scriptor/ Thema requiras', ms. D the same (with '-ve' for '-que').   37 *G.M.* and ms. D read *sit* for *est.*   41 An abrupt conclusion to Sappho's speech (as Alsop awakes from a dream?): the description of happiness is not allowed to cloy.   42 *G.M.* reads 'impotentemque' (with elision over the line break).

Translation in *Gentleman's Magazine* 5. 384 (July 1735)

Render'd into plain English for the sake of many of our Readers.
To the Rev. Sir John Dolben, Bart.

Blowing my pipe, as custom taught,
One *Lenten* morn, and busying thought
   How best to spend the day,
Sappho soft whisp'ring stood behind,
5 Mingling with threats monition kind,
   And said, or seem'd to say;
Is it for this you cease to write!
For this the Muses' altars slight!
   What's by this coldness meant?
10 Thou truant bard, there scarce appears
Four offerings now in full three years
   Which you have thither sent.
Be your own judge, and tell me true,
Has *Dolben* this deserv'd from you?
15   *Dolben*, once highly priz'd,
When hours (he could have better
                 spent)
Were wasted, while with kind intent
   Your trifles he revis'd.
He ever mindful of his friend,
20 Would still thy humble lays attend,
   For these some leisure spare,
Tho' praeengag'd on highest themes,
Whence truth and virtue dart their
                 beams,
   And heav'n demands his care.
25 Therefore resume thy gayest pen,
Wake thy brisk genius once again,
   Dull indolence detest,
Perhaps by some unlook'd for chance
To him thy labours may advance;
30   Lodg'd on *Eliza's* breast;
There he'll interpret and rehearse
Most lov'd interpreter! each verse
   From criticizing free;

And if thy numbers shou'd appear
35 Harmonious to *Eliza's* ear,
   Who wou'd not envy thee?
Then in thy most exalted air
Salute the fond indulgent pair,
   As I thy song inspire,
40 You'll never fitter subjects find
To raise ideas in the mind,
   Nor worthier can desire.
Whether you paint their beauteous
                 race,
Those likenesses of parent grace,
45   In every virtue taught.
Or venture with sublimer art
The beauties of the soul t'impart,
   Let each extend thy thought.
Paint him devout with harp in hand
50 Attentive to th' divine command,
   Yet to the Muses kind;
Eliza soft'ning all his cares
By ordering family affairs
   With elegance refin'd;
55 Then, if your skill suffice, proclaim
Their mutual faith, their purest flame,
   (Those types of future joy
Which neither discord, noise or strife
Those bitter incidents of life,
60   Did ever yet annoy).
Lastly with liveliest colours paint—
This said—She disappear'd—I faint—
   But riseing on my knee,
My verse, with my inspirer, miss
65 Amaz'd—I can no more—but this—
   For ever happy be!

Text: Bern.; *Gentleman's Magazine* 5. 384 (July 1735); ms. D, fo. 17; BL(b), fo. 51ᵛ–52ʳ; Nott. Pw V 148/2. *Date*: *c.*
1723–4 (Trinity College, Cambridge H. 5. 17 suggests March 1724).

2.16 ROBERTO EYRE

Ergo fatali grave rursus agmen
Pyxide emisit Dea, per Swithini
Claustra diffundens, meliore digna
    Sorte, ruinam.
5 Flens, gemens legi breviore Wichart
Halitu affligi: meruit vir ille,
Siqua sit Ventae, placida et salubri
    Vescier aura.
Parte postica Carolum dolentem,
10 Haud mali ignarus, miseror: sed esto;
Macte; nam spondet dolor iste, sic fert
    Fama, salutem.
Eximi saltem meruit peric'lo
Os tibi, os dulci eloquio et placendi
15 Artibus pollens; sacra seu tueri
    Dogmata vindex
Strenuus, seu vis salibus jocisque
Ludere. Heu! frustra: superante morbo,
Nec jocus linguae, tibi nec loquela
20   Profuit hilum.
Sic Phrygum terror, Thetidis propago,
Hostium talo jaculum recepit,
Quamquam ἐυκνήμις fuerat πόδας-que
    ὠκὺς Ἀχιλλεύς.

Translation: 'To Robert Eyre'

So then, the goddess has again let a dire host of diseases out of her fatal box, and poured out ruin among St Swithin's cloisters, that deserved a better fate. (5) I wept and groaned as I read that Wichart was afflicted by shortness of breath; that man deserved, if anyone at Winchester does, to enjoy quiet and healthy air. (9) I am sorry to hear that Charles has a pain in his posterior, being a sufferer myself; but let it be—live on regardless; for, so rumour goes, this particular pain does not promise to be fatal. (13) At least your mouth deserved to be kept out of danger, that mouth so effective at pleasing with its sweet eloquence, whether you vigorously defend sacred doctrines, or prefer to play with wit and jokes. (18) Alas, it was not to be: as the disease gains hold, no joke or sermon can do your tongue any good at all. (21) Thus the terror of the Trojans, Thetis' child, received an enemy missile in his heel, although he had been called 'finely-armoured and swift-footed Achilles'.

Text: Bern. (lacks lines 21–4); BL(a); ms. D, fo. 15; Yale ms. Osborn c. 233, p. 8; Nott. Pw V 149/5 and 151/5; Bodleian ms. Rawl. lett. 31. *Date*: late 1720, or 1721. This poem is discussed in Ch. 7.

1 *Ergo* scanned as a trochee (unusual, but classical: found in Ovid, and very common in late antique writers). A solemn opening (cf., starting the 2nd stanza, Hor., *Carm.* 1. 24. 5). *Agmen*, of diseases, is a bold usage (cf. 2. 25. 10: wind).   2 St Swithin (d. 862), Bishop of Winchester.   5–12 Yale and ms. D transpose the 2nd and 3rd stanzas.   8 Archaic infinitive in adonic: cf. Hor., *Carm.* 4. 11. 8.   17 Cf. 2. 23. 19, 'salibus jocisque'.   18 Possibly alluding to Hor., *Carm.* 1. 12. 38, 'superante Poeno'.   20 Echoing an ancient commonplace; cf. Ovid, *Am.* 3. 9. 21, 'quid . . . profuit?', imitated by Milton, *Lycidas* 58–9. *Hilum* is archaic (frequent in Lucretius), its strangeness adding to the effect. Possibly recalling Cic., *Tusc.* 1. 6. 10, 'neque proficit hilum'.   21 Achilles; cf. Hor., *Carm.* 4. 6 (possibly recalled), and *Epod.* 13. 12–18.   23 ἐυκνήμις: Homeric epithet for Achaeans (*Il.* 1. 17, etc.); πόδας ὠκὺς Ἀχιλλεύς often (*Il.* 1. 58, etc.). Yale reads τε for -que (slightly lessening the humorous macaronic effect).

2.17 JOSEPHO TAYLOR

Si dies, si pars quota sit diei
cunque, noxve esset tibi litis expers,
Non fores, hospes vetus, impudenti ab
    Hospite tutus.
5 Par tamen dispar procerum tueri
Ausus, hoc solum tibi das negoti,
Alteri ut firmes catus, alterique
    Restituas rem.
Hinc domi non es; fuerisve, vel non,
10 Fortiter servus negat intus esse:
Cogor et gressus animo inquieto
    Ferre retrorsum.
Nulla sin restet mihi te videndi
Copia et fandi quod uterque nostrum
15 Audit; hoc saltem liceat salutem
    Mittere versu.
Quid favens Bacchus (Venerem tacebo)
Dulce largiri poterit, tibi opto;
Deditos rixae, loculique largi,
20   Opto clientes.

Translation: 'To Joseph Taylor'

If you had any day, or any part of a day (however small), or any night that was free from litigation, you would not be free, my old host, from an impudent guest. (5) You act boldly, however, to protect an unequal pair of nobles, and give yourself this one piece of business, endeavouring cleverly to secure one man's position, and to restore the other's. (9) So you are not at home: whether you were or not, your servant vigorously denied that you were inside, and I am compelled to walk back in an unhappy frame of mind. (13) But if there is no chance of my seeing you or engaging you in conversation, I can at least send my regards in this poem. (17) I wish that you may have everything sweet that it is in Bacchus' power to supply (I shall keep quiet about Venus'); and I wish you may have clients who are devoted to quarrelling, and have fat purses.

Text: Bern.; ms. D, fo. 32; Nott. Pw V 149/2. *Date*: c. 1715–24; probably c. 1723. This poem is discussed in Ch. 7.

2.18 JOHANNI DOLBEN

Chare, tu vinc'lo implicitus suavi,
Seu dies, seu nox redit, invidendus,
Gaudii nunquam vacuus saturve
    Transigis aevum.
5 Dulce quam vestris foret interesse
Lusibus! dum tu, comitante Elisa,

Translation: 'To John Dolben'

Dear friend, you are to be envied each day and each night, for being bound up in such delightful chains; you do not spend a moment that is empty of, or sated with, joy. (5) How sweet it would be to be present at your games, when you, in Elisa's

1–2 Cf. Tib. 2. 6. 54, 'pars quotacumque'.   3–4 Possibly recalling Hor., *Carm.* 3. 4. 33, 'Britannos hospitibus feros'. Ms. D reads *insolenti* for *impudenti*.   5 Bernard's n.: 'Comes Oxoniensis et Vicecomes de Bollingbroke' (Robert Harley and Henry St John).   8 Alluding to Ennius, *Ann.* (ed. Skutsch) 363, 'unus homo nobis cunctando restituit rem': a famous line (taken up by Cicero, Livy, and most notably Virgil); Alsop also uses it at 2. 22. 10–12.   14 Probably alluding to Virg., *Aen.* 1. 520, 'coram data copia fandi'.   17 Possibly alluding to Hor., *Carm.* 3. 11. 50, 'dum favet nox et Venus'. Bacchus and Venus together: *Carm.* 1. 18. 6 (cf. Alsop's amusing parenthesis).   19 The cynicism here is in humorous contrast to the idealism of 7–8. Cf. Hor., *Carm.* 3. 14. 26, 'litium et rixae cupidos'; *Serm.* 2. 3. 105, 'Musae deditos'.

1 *Suavi*: very unusual (and late) as trisyllable.   2 Nocturnal pleasures suggest a hint of Alsopian salaciousness behind an otherwise bland cliché. The next stanza could be read as voyeuristic (though he is no doubt not seriously suggesting that he should join them at night).

Seu velis, seu non, manifestus index
    Prodis amorem;
Sive furtivo intuitu pudentem
10 Nequiter spectas, placidisque verbis
Aut palam allectas Dominam, aut in aurem
    Lene susurras;
Sive, quo polles, modulamen addis,
Vocis et plectri sociare gnarus
15 Rite concentum; vicibusque crebris
    Eripis ardens
Osculum, causam pretiumque cantus;
Osculum, quo nec Dea dormienti
Latmio, nec Septimio imprimebat
20   Suavius Acme.
Sic dies, certus scio, dulce euntes
Ducis. O felix, et amore tali
Digne! Dii firment sua dona, et extra im-
    mitius Orci
25 Collocent longe imperium. Quid ultra
Poscimus caelum? sed et est quod ultra
Poscimus. Cursus quoties novenos
    Luna peregit,
Adsit obstetrix Dea, quale nomen
30 cunque sortita; et prope stans Elisae
Leniat partus, jubeatque dici
    Te, bone, patrem.
Qui tibi sensus inerunt videnti
Huc modo atque illuc tenerum Johannem
35 Per lares duci, decimoque Elisam
    Mense minorem?
Prole tu multa similique felix
Nomen extendas veniens in aevum!
Tu cluas, Gentis columen; nec ultra, Ex-
40   trema domus spes.
Haec vovet, quotquot numeras amicos

company, show your love quite clearly, whether you wish to or not—either when you give her a furtive glance, or openly entice her, or whisper in her ear. (13) Alternatively, you sometimes add music, at which you excel, being experienced at properly uniting the concord of voice and lyre; and in quick succession you ardently steal a kiss, the reason for your song, and its price—no lovelier kiss did the goddess give to the sleeper of Latmos, nor Acme to Septimius. (21) Thus, I know for sure, you pass your days pleasantly. O lucky man, worthy of such love! May the gods confirm their gifts, and keep you far from the harsh power of the underworld. What else can we ask heaven for? But there is one other thing we can ask. (27) When the moon has passed nine times through its cycle, let the goddess of childbirth be present, whatever name she goes by; and let her stand by Elisa to relieve her labour, and to make people call you, good sir, a father. (33) What will you feel, when you see a little John led hither and thither about the house, and a thinner Elisa, in the tenth month? (37) May you be lucky enough to extend your name into the coming age, with many children like yourself; may you hear yourself called 'the support of your family', and no longer 'the last hope of the house'! (41) This is the prayer of one who, of all your friends, yields to none in his affection, and who still weeps for his wife, who was snatched from me

---

11 The language of ancient and modern unmarried love (*Domina* here; *ardens* 16) is used for this passionate marriage. Cf. Ovid, *Met.* 3. 643, 'aure susurrat'.   14 Possibly alluding to Hor., *Carm.* 4. 9. 4, 'verba loquor socianda chordis'; cf. also Ovid, *Met.* 11. 5, etc.   18–19 The Moon (Luna/ Selene) and Endymion, from Mt Latmus in Caria; cf. Ovid, *Ars Am.* 3. 83, etc.   19–20 Alluding to Cat. 45 (especially lines 10–12). N.b. no caesura in 19 (appropriate for a Catullan allusion, though quite common elsewhere in Alsop). Cf. also J. Secundus' *Basia*; *imprimo* is used for a passionate kiss (and bite) at Hor., *Carm.* 1. 13. 12.   29–30 The various names for the goddess of childbirth included the Greek Eileithyia, the Latin Juno Lucina, and the 'diva triformis' (Diana/ Luna/ Hecate) of Hor., *Carm.* 3. 22.   31 Probably alluding to Hor., *Carm. Saec.* 13–14, 'partus/ lenis'. Horace is uncertain how to address the goddess: Alsop probably alludes to this also.   37 Possibly alluding to Hor., *Carm.* 4. 5. 23, 'simili prole puerperae'; cf. Valerius Flaccus 5. 384; Virg., *Aen.* 6. 784.   38 Possibly alluding to Hor., *Carm.* 3. 3. 45–6, 'nomen . . . extendat'.

Nemini cedens in amore, raptam
Flens adhuc sponsam, (tibi nil sit hujus!)
    Hoc miser uno.

(may nothing like that happen to you!),
and is sad in that one respect alone.

Text: Bern. *Date*: late 1721 or early 1722. This poem is discussed in detail in Ch. 3, and mentioned in Ch. 7.

2.19 JOSEPHO TAYLOR

Est mihi Octobres cadus ad Calendas
Natus, et pernae satis, et farinae;
Nec foco aut mensae locus, aut cubili
    Defuit aptus.
5 Siquid haec ultra petis, est in anno
Forte fortuna semel et secundo
Vasculum Bacchi, quod amica, clam quaes-
    tore, ratis fert.
Quare age, his mecum fruere, et relicta
10 Paululum lauta dape, ferculisque
Arte conditis, tenui salino as-
    suesce, et inempto
Luxui. Hic vitae bona multa disces
Rusticae: hic purae data nox quieti,
15 Et dies transit sine lite; nulli
    Mane clientes
Somnia abrumpent, hilarisve lusum
Vesperae; hic curis potes expeditus
Vivere; et, ni quod tua Phillis absit,
20   Caetera felix.

Translation: 'To Joseph Taylor'
    I have a cask of October ale, filled on the first of that month, and enough ham and bread; nor do I lack a suitable place for a hearth, table or bed. If you seek anything more than this, just by chance I have, once or twice a year, a little bottle of brandy that a friendly ship brings over without the excise-officers noticing. (9) Come then, enjoy these things with me, and leave for a little while your rich feasts, with skilfully concocted courses: accustom yourself instead to a plain salt cellar, and unbought luxury. Here you can learn many good things about rustic life; here is night given to pure quietness, and the days pass without litigation. (15) No clients will interrupt your sleep in the morning, or the games of your joyful evenings; here you can live free from troubles, and (except that your Phillis would be absent) be otherwise fortunate.

Text: Bern.; ms. D, fo. 32ᵛ–33ʳ; Nott. Pw V 149/1. *Date*: unknown; after 1712 (and probably after 1715); not during exile (1718–20).

42–3 Cf. 2. 10. 13–14, 'raptam . . . conjugem' (where he is thoroughly miserable: now, he is otherwise happy); also 2. 12. 64.

1 Alluding to Hor., *Carm.* 4. 11. 1–2, 'Est mihi . . . cadus'. Cf. 19. Ms. D reads *Octobris* for -*es*.   2 *Perna*: leg of ham (plain fare, outdoing Horace in homeliness).   4 Ms. D and BL(a) read *Deficit* for -*fuit*.   6 *Semel et secundo*: an unusual usage; cf. 2. 9. 5; 2. 23. 3.   7 *Vasculum*: humorous diminutive (cf. Juv. 9. 141, etc.).
11 Alluding to Hor., *Carm.* 2. 16. 13–14, 'vivitur parvo bene, cui paternum/ splendet in mensa tenui salinum': subtly changed (no longer respectably *paternum*). Cf. Horace's invitation, *Carm.* 3. 29. 9, 'fastidiosam desere copiam'.   12 Probably alluding to Hor., *Epod.* 2. 48, 'dapes inemptas'.   17 Ms. D reads *abrumpant* for -*ent*.
18 Probably alluding to Hor., *Carm.* 1. 22. 11, 'curis vagor expeditis' (-*us* in some of the editions Alsop might have used). Cf. Alsop 2. 12. 17–18.   19 Another allusion (cf. 1) to Hor., *Carm.* 4. 11 ('Phylli', line 3). Alsop offers no female company (cf. 14, quiet nights). Ms. D leaves the name blank.   20 Probably alluding to Hor., *Epist.* 1. 10. 50, 'cetera laetus'; also used by Alsop at 1. 10. 16; 3. 4. 44.

2.20 JOHANNI DOLBEN

Estne te quisquam magis aut placente
Conjuge, aut partu simili, beatus?
Estne me quisquam tibi qui salutem ar-
    dentius optat?
5 Dii tibi, quicquid voveant parentes
Dulcibus natis, tribuere: nec quid
Defuit dudum tibi, praeter unum hoc,
    Ut pater esses.
Fis pater tandem: sciat hoc capaci
10 Ventre Montanus; nec amoena speret
Arva Findoni sibi destinari,
    Sospitibus Diis.
Interim laetus cape prima sponsae
Dona, non fallax sobolis futurae
15 Pignus, extremum tibi quae propaget
    Nomen in aevum.
Quare age, et fauste tibi qui labores
Cesserint, urge, preme, tende pernox:
Sit tibi exemplar, sit in hoc choregus
20   Optimus Harry.
Ille quot gaudet genitor puellis,
Tu tot exulta maribus; futuros
Unde plus una vice forte nectent
    Fata Hymenaeos.
25 Sanguine ex illo generosa surget
Stirps, avis quondam atque atavis datura
Gaudium; plectri melioris ictu
    Saepe sonanda.
Haec ego Ventae, sacra qua Camoenis
30 Tecta Wichamus posuit, recudi:
Mi tamen praesens favet (ecce signum)
    Nulla sororum.

Translation: 'To John Dolben'

Is there anyone more happy than you, with your lovely wife, and children that resemble you? Is there anyone who wishes you well more ardently than I do? (5) The gods have given you whatever parents pray for in their sweet children; nor for a long time have you lacked anything, except to be a father. You are a father at last: let Montanus know that in his fat belly, and no longer hope (by God's grace) that Finedon's pleasant fields are destined to be his. (13) Meanwhile, happily take your wife's first gift, which is a reliable pledge of future offspring, which will preserve your name far into the future. (17) So then, throughout the night, urge on, press on, extend the labours which have yielded you fruit; let your example, and chorus-leader, in this respect be that best of men, Harry. (21) For each of the girls that he rejoices to have fathered, you should boast of a boy; and perhaps more than one marriage will be made between them in the future. (25) From that union a noble race will arise, which will give joy to its grandparents and great-grandparents; they should often be celebrated in better music than mine! (29) This I have hammered out at Winchester, where Wykeham set up a college sacred to the Muses; but none of those Muses (as you can see) is here to help me now.

Text: Bern. *Date*: spring/summer 1722.

1, 3 Repeated *estne*: cf. 1. 8. 1–2.   2 Cf. 2. 18. 37.   7 Cf. 2. 15. 43.   9–10 Possibly alluding to Juv. 11. 40–1, 'ventrem . . . capacem'. *Montanus*: Bernard's n.: 'Dolbeni consanguineus, qui villae Findonensis se heredem esse jactitaverat' [a relation who had boasted that he was the heir to Finedon]. A ms. n. (in Huntington Library, RB 316448) suggests that this is William Stratford, Canon of Christ Church (mentioned frequently in Chs. 6–7; certainly a relation, cf. *HMC Portland* 7. 351–2: Mrs Dolben, a female cousin of Stratford's, is arrested: 'You may be sure I am in some concern for so near a relation'; *HMC Portland* 5. 474: 'my cousin Stratford' to run an errand for Sir Gilbert Dolben). If not Stratford, possibly a Montagu of Boughton: a Whig family (thus politically unattractive to Alsop and Dolben) with a long connection to the estate. See J. L. H. Bailey, *Finedon otherwise Thingdon* (Finedon, 1975), pp. 18, 21, 43.   18 Salacious encouragement to procreate with vigour.   20 *Harry*: Brydges. Cf. 2. 14. 8.   30 *Recudo* is very rare; the re-hammering of his material fits with a certain degree of repetitiveness in the Dolben poems.

2.21 JOHANNI DOLBEN

Quid senis sancti cineres, diuque
Debitum coelo caput, usque defles?
Sat suae famae dederat, Dunelmo
    Cum dederat te.

5   Quare age, et fausto recreato pectus
Omine: assuescas titulo futuro,
Et pater dici incipias, domusque ex-
    structor avitae.

Rusticos, (nec me numero eximendum
10   Duco) qui farris satagunt negoti,
Taedet ingrato sterilique sulco im-
    mittere semen.

Sin ferax tellus onere intumescat
Pollicens messem, venientis anni
15   Spem, focus large struitur; renidet
    Pinguibus offis

Mensa; spumanti calice hordeusque
Effluit succus, bene nota famae
Alla; nec circum joca, nec canora
20   Cantica desunt.

Si tamen passu piget ire quo rus
Gaudet; I, fretus genio altiore,
I, modos tenta, quibus erubescat
    Pecten amici:

25   I, Deam trino titulo, triformem,
Invoca, numen gravidis benignum;
Sit prope obstetrix Dea, sit cubanti
    Lenis Elisae.

Tuque seu matri similis puella,
30   Seu puer patrem referens in auras
Prodit; esto audax, placidoque, ut ante, in-
    cumbe labori.

Sic eant faustae tibi res; Elisae
Sit redux anno redeunte partus;
35   Et recens natos fidicen salutem
    Annuus hymno!

Translation: 'To John Dolben'

Why do you carry on lamenting for the ashes of that revered old man, and his head that had long been owed to heaven? He did enough to ensure his own fame, when he gave you to Durham. (5) So then, freshen your heart with this good omen: accustom yourself to your future title, and begin to be called a father, and the founder of an ancestral house. (9) Rustics who busy themselves with crops (from whose number I do not exclude myself) become tired of sowing their seed in an ungrateful and barren furrow; but if the fertile earth swells and promises a good harvest, the hope of the coming year, then the hearth is piled up generously, the table shines with fat foodstuffs; the barley-juice—that famous ale—foams up in the tankard, nor is there any lack of jokes and singing. (21) If, however, you are unwilling to follow rural forms of celebration, then rely on your higher genius, and attempt music at which your friend's lyre would blush. (25) Go on, and invoke the three-formed goddess by her three titles, that goddess who is kind to pregnant women; may the goddess of childbirth be near, and be gentle to Elisa in her labour. (29) Whether a girl like her mother is brought into the open air, or a boy resembling his father, you should be bold, and set about your pleasant task as you did before. (33) Thus may you be fortunate; may Elisa give birth again as a year goes by; and may I each year welcome your offspring with a new poem.

Text: Bern. *Date*: late 1722 or early 1723.

1 Bernard's n.: 'Nathanael, Baro de Crew, Episcopus Dunelmensis'.　　2 Cf. Virg., *Aen.* 12. 795, 'deberi caelo'; Crewe died on 18 Sept. 1721, aged 88, having been Bishop of Durham for 47 years.　　9 Cf. Hor., *Carm.* 2. 2. 18–19, 'numero . . . eximit'.　　11–12 Cf. Virg., *Geo.* 1. 23, 'sulcis committas semina'; *sulcus* of female genitalia, *Geo.* 3. 135–6; Lucr. 4. 1272. These lines have a clear sexual undertone: the metaphor allows him to turn to rustic merry-making, 13–20.　　14–15 Cf. Ovid, *Met.* 15. 113, 'spemque . . . anni'.　　17 *Hordeus* appears to be an Alsopian neologism (from *hordeum*, barley). The *-que* is perhaps awkwardly placed (I tentatively retain Bernard's punctuation: a pause after *calice* would have both advantages and problems).　　19 *Alla*: apparently another neologism; cf. 2. 26. 8.　　25–30 Cf. 2. 18. 29–31, 37; 2. 15. 29–30.　　31–2 Cf. 2. 20. 17–18.

2.22 JOSEPHO TAYLOR

Tu sciens legum, dubiique recti
Arbiter, noctem satagis diemque;
Seu fovens litem, dirimensve, coram
    Judice lis est.
5 Mane circumstat numerus clientum
Dispari forma: quota te fatigat
Aut timens doti vidua aut mariti
    Indiga virgo?
Tu Scoto fundis spoliato avitis
10 Fers opem gnarus; Fabiique ritu,
Arte cunctandi sapienter usus,
    Restituis rem.
Mi tamen, quanquam trabibus sub isdem
Dormio, et vestris edo, poto, scribo
15 Aedibus, vix ejiciendus hospes,
    Mi neque dulci
Perfrui fas alloquio, nec ora
Suave ridentis datur intueri;
Nec, nisi hoc versu, licet addere ipsum
20   Vive valeque.

Translation: 'To Joseph Taylor'

You are learned in the law, and spend all your nights and days as an arbiter of doubtful problems; whether you promote litigation, or settle it, the matter is before the judge. (5) Each morning a disparate crowd of clients stands around you: how often does a widow fearful for her dowry, or a maiden deprived of a husband, weary you? (9) You skilfully bring help to the Scotsman whose ancestral estate has been misappropriated, and like Fabius use delaying tactics to restore his fortunes. (13) But as for me, although I sleep under the same roof, and eat, drink, and write in your house, as a guest who can scarcely be thrown out, I am not allowed to enjoy your sweet conversation, nor to see your smiling face, nor (except in this poem) can I even bid you farewell.

Text: Bern. *Date*: unknown; probably similar to 2. 17. This poem is discussed in Ch. 7.

2.23 JOHANNI FREIND

Estne mi quisquam comitum undecunque
Charior Freindo? tamen ecquis aeque
Immemor nostri? Semel et secundo
    Ora novavit
5 Luna: Tu Baccho interea et Vacunae
Te dicas totum; neque me sepultum
Rure, vel vultu recreas, vel una,
    Dure, tabella.

Translation: 'To John Freind'

Do I have a companion anywhere on earth who is dearer to me than Freind? But is there one who forgets me so much? Two months have passed, and you have devoted yourself wholly to drinking and gluttony; nor have you refreshed me, buried as I am in the countryside, with the sight of your face, or even (hard-hearted

4 Alluding to Hor., *Ars Poet.* 78, 'et adhuc sub iudice lis est'.
9 *Scoto*: Bernard's n.: 'ad supremum forum libellos appellationis proferenti' [(a Scottish client) bringing an appeal before the highest court]. Probably alluding to Hor., *Carm.* 1. 12. 43–4, 'avitus . . . fundus'.   10–12 Alluding to Ennius: cf. 2. 17. 8.   13 Probably alluding to Hor., *Carm.* 3. 2. 27–8, 'sub isdem/ sit trabibus'.   14 Possibly alluding to Hor., *Epist.* 2. 2. 214–5, 'lusisti satis, edisti satis atque bibisti:/tempus abire tibi est'. Alsop may wonder if he is a similarly unwelcome guest.   16–17 Cf. 2. 2. 13.   18 Cf. Hor., *Carm.* 1. 22. 23, 'dulce ridentis'.
20 Possibly alluding to Hor., *Serm.* 2. 5. 110, 'vive valeque'.

3 Cf. 2. 9. 5; 2. 19. 6.   4 *Vacuna*: Sabine pastoral goddess; possibly alluding to Hor., *Epist.* 1. 10. 49 (cf. line 50, probably alluded to at 1. 10. 16, 2. 19. 20, 3. 4. 44).   7–8 'To bury oneself in the country' is a colloquial English usage, new in Alsop's day (Alsop makes early literary use of it; cf. Defoe and Johnson, cited in *OED*: Johnson may have borrowed from Alsop).

Excitem quid ni Furias trecenas
10   Improbo diras capiti imprecatus?
Obstat huic auso veterum recordans
        Pectus amorum.

Dum dies tecum recolo anteactos,
(O dies laetos!) nova per medullam
15   Funditur flamma, atque animo recursat
        Mira voluptas.

Lusibus tecum ingenuis vacare
Det favens caelum; alloquio suavi
Det frui rursum, et salibus jocisque, ut
20   Saepe, potiri!

Sin velint Divi uberius beare
Par amicorum, venerandus adsit
Ille, quem vestit, melius merentem,
        Infula Roffae.
25   Serias inter bonus ille curas
Misceat risum, et faciles lepores,
Perpetim felix, patiensque dici
        Noster amicus!

man!) with a single letter. (9) Why should I not rouse up three hundred furies to put a curse on your wicked head? My heart remembers our old affection, and prevents me doing so. (13) When I recall past days spent with you (o happy days!), a new flame spreads through my inmost body, and amazing pleasure fills my soul. (17) May kind heaven allow me the time to spend in innocent amusements with you; may it allow me to enjoy your delightful conversation again, and as often before to take part in your wit and joking. (21) But if the gods wished further to bless this pair of friends, let that reverend gentleman be present, who is now invested with the priestly bands of Rochester (though he deserves still better things). (25) May that good man mix laughter and light-hearted jests with serious concerns: may he always be fortunate, and patient enough to let himself be called our friend.

Text: Bern. *Date*: after 1713; or, if Brydges is meant (see n. on 24), after 1720.

2.24 JOHANNI DOLBEN

Canticum, quod Dux animante Bacchi
Numine inflatus cecinit, relegi;
Canticum pulchrae sobolem parentis
        Non inhonestam.
5   Chiviae campos, procerumque in armis
Grande par, quis non Britonum recenset?
Quae Withringtonum reticebit aetas

Translation: 'To John Dolben'
      I have read over again the ballad that the Duke wrote, under the inspiration of the wine-god; it is a ballad not unworthy of its fine parentage. (5) What Briton does not recall Chevy Chase, and that great pair of armed leaders? What age will cease to celebrate Withrington, and his missing

11 Cf. Ovid, *Her.* 14. 49, 'obstitit ausis'.   15 Possibly alluding to Virg., *Aen.* 4. 3, 'animo . . . recursat'.
18 Cf. 2. 2. 13; 2. 18. 1; Stat., *Silv.* 4. 3. 125, 'favente caelo'.   19 *Rursum*: the archaic form, perhaps remembered from comedy, adds solemnity; it also allows him to elide *et*.   22 Cf. 2. 7. 1.   24 Possibly alluding to Virg., *Aen.* 2. 429–30, 'nec te tua plurima, Pantheu,/ labentem pietas nec Apollinis infula texit'; cf. also *Aen.* 10. 538. Very apt, if the poem dates from after Atterbury's fall; otherwise, an ironic coincidence. Atterbury hoped for further promotion; the Pretender (but no-one else) might have made him Primate. Alternatively, the reference may be to Henry Brydges (occupying a less exalted position at Rochester; see 2. 7, 14, 20, etc. for his ambitions and friendship).   27 Alluding to Hor., *Carm.* 1. 2. 43–4, 'patiens vocari/ Caesaris ultor'. The implied comparison with Augustus is flattering (though possibly a sly laugh at Atterbury's pride).

1 Bernard's n.: 'Whartonensis'.   3 Since Wharton is the *parens*, the feminine is surprising; it may suggest he is effeminate, or echo Hor., *Carm.* 1. 16. 1; or one might change it to *pulchri*.   6 Cf. 2. 7. 1; 2. 15. 26.

Crure minorem?
En novi heroes, nova lis! nec alter
10   Deficit vates: Comitem Ducemque
Cumbrici cantant pueri, additosque
      Haustibus haustus.
Quis struem illius spoliumque noctis
Narret? hic fusos calices, vitrique
15   Fragmina; hinc vulgi procerumque mixtim
      Corpora, fundo
Strata, non siccae monumenta pugnae?
Dii meis talem laribus tuisque
Arceant stragem! Sit amica nobis
20   Turba, culullis
Vespere humescens modicis, jocorum
Plena, nec plectri vacua. Oh beata
Findoni sedes, placidi et perennis
      Conscia cantus!
25   Tu choris sueta harmonicis, lyrisque
Arte pulsatis, resonare disces
Jam notas, quas, non sine Diis canorus,
      Exprimet infans.
Quae patri tum mens erit, ecstasisque
30   Gaudii, cum jam puer, ore formans
Syllabas, lingua titubante profert
      Sol la mi fa sol?

leg? (9) Here are new heroes, and a new conflict! Nor do we lack a new bard: Cumbrian boys sing of the Earl and the Duke, and gulp taken on top of gulp. (13) Who can tell of the destruction and spoils of that night? Here are scattered wine-glasses, and fragments of glass; and here are the bodies of commoners and peers all mixed together, laid low on the ground, the evidence of a thoroughly sozzled fight. (18) May the gods keep such chaos from my house and yours! May we have a crowd of fond friends, soaking up moderate amounts of liquor of an evening, full of jokes, and not with-out music: oh, the happy seat of Finedon, that knows quiet and everlasting song! (25) You are accustomed to harmonious choirs, and well-struck instruments: now you will learn the musical notes that your divinely inspired infant will produce. (29) What will his father feel, how great will be his ecstasy of joy, when the boy can now form syllables, and stutter out his 'Doe, a deer, a female deer . . .'?

Text: Bern.; BL(b), fo. 46ᵛ–47ʳ. *Date*: probably late 1723, or 1724. This poem is discussed in Ch. 7.

2.25 JOHANNI FREIND

Quam tibi mitto, potior salute:
Displicet fors hoc; quid enim medenti
Proderit quisquam, cui sana mens in
      Corpore sano?
5   Ne tamen desit tibi sospitandus
Aeger, en! coram stat, opemque poscit

Translation: 'To John Freind'

I have good health, and send it to you; this may displease you, for what good can anyone be to a doctor, if he has a sound mind in a sound body? (5) But lest you should lack a sick man to be healed, here is one standing before you

10 Bernard's n.: 'De Harold'.   11 Cumbria: northern England (strictly north-west, here north-east).
21 Growing moist by gradual absorption of alcohol: a nice image.   27–8 Alluding to Hor., *Carm.* 3. 4. 20, 'non sine dis animosus infans'. Dolben's child will not have Horace's magical protection, but will be more preco-cious.   29 *Ecstasis* is unclassical (from the Greek of the Gospels: in late antique and medieval Latin).
32 The musical notes are scanned (arbitrarily, but effectively) as an adonic.

3–4 Alluding to Juv. 10. 356: a famous tag wittily used; for a doctor, perfect health is a problem.   5 *Sospitandus*: archaic (mainly in religious language), its heaviness providing a humorous touch.

Paene mi memet propior, nec uno
    Nomine frater.
Ille contortus misere inquietum
10 Ventre fert agmen; gelidaque in alvo
Tot premit ventos, quot habet capaci
    Aeolus antro.
Tu Notum Eurumque expedias iniquo
Carcere; extrusus Boreas aperta
15 Fac ruat porta, et melius Britannis
    Navibus afflet.

and asking for your help, someone who is almost closer to me than myself, my brother in more than one sense. (9) He is twisted up by carrying about a troublesome army in his belly: he presses down as many winds in his cold innards as the wind-god has in his ample cave. (13) You should release the south and east winds from their harsh imprisonment; make the north wind rush from an open gate, and let it blow more usefully on the British navy.

Text: Bern. *Date*: unknown. This poem is discussed in Ch. 6.

2.26 JOSEPHO TAYLOR

Te senatorum numero inserendum
Sponte suffragor: quis enim loquendi
Artibus pollet magis, aptiorve est
    Condere leges?
5 Sed per immensum oceanum, et liquores
Mille, sulcanda est via; multa fumi
Nubila erumpent, fluitansque rivo
    Alla perenni.
Quo salutandi titulo modoque
10 Ordines nosti procerum; ambiendus
Quo sit aut sartor laniusve ritu,
    Forte docendus.
Dexteram dextrae, sed onustam, inani
Junge (res magni); neque fastuosus
15 Temne nudato capite ante tectos
    Stare colonos.
Disce responsum rude, disce scomma
Perpeti, et plebem stupide insolentem,

Translation: 'To Joseph Taylor'

I vote of my own accord that you should be elected to Parliament; for who is more eloquent, or more fit to legislate? (5) But you must cleave your way through a great ocean of liquor; many clouds of smoke must pour out, and a perpetual river of ale must flow. (9) You already know how, and by what titles, to address the higher ranks of society; but perhaps you need to be told how a tailor or a butcher should be canvassed. (13) Shake hands: but with yours full, and theirs empty (a most important point); and do not be too proud to stand bare-headed before farmers in their hats. (17) Learn to put up with a rude reply, and a jest, and the common people being stupidly insolent, and telling stories about you

8 It is unclear how the brother is so in more than one way; one of the senses may be 'a brother in the Church' (of a fellow cleric).   10 Probably alluding to Virg., *Aen.* 1. 82, 'velut agmine facto', of Aeolus' winds. 12–14 Alluding to Virg., *Aen.* 1. 52–4 'rex Aeolus antro . . . carcere'. 'Wind' in the belly was a common contemporary term (*OED*); it could also be empty talk, humorously treated as flatulence.

8 Cf. 2. 21. 19.   9 Possibly alluding to Hor., *Serm.* 1. 6. 101, 'salutandi plures'.   14 *Fastuosus*: very rare alternative for rare *fastosus* (metri gratia, and with the sonority of an additional syllable). Ms. D adds *est* after 'res magni'.   17 *Scomma*: late antique; taken from Greek.   18 Possibly alluding to Hor., *Carm.* 1. 3. 25, 'audax omnia perpeti'; if so, Horace's picture of horrible ambition adds to the humour. Also perhaps alluding to *Carm.* 3. 29. 50, 'ludum insolentem ludere pertinax'.

Forsque narrantem graviora veris
20   Crimina de te.
Quos tibi vinum potiorve pellex
Junxerit, fratres sapiens adopta;
Sed patrem ante omnes venerere Brownum,
        Brownigenasque.
25 Proderit multum jocus: et jocari
Scito te, cum das colaphum datumve
Sustines gnare, patuloque tollis
        Ore cachinnum.
Quid pudens virgo, quid et impudica
30 Expetit, notum tibi sat superque:
Hae tibi ad partes, facilis vocatu
        Turba, vocentur.
Basium si fors anus optet, ah, ne
Respuas: nam quot vetulae salaci
35 Gaudia impertis, tibi tot rependet
        Grata trineptis.
Haec ego, vestri studiosus usque
Commodi, raptim documenta mitto:
Quid senatorem decet, ornat, effert,
40   Post moniturus.

that might even be worse than the truth.
(21) Be wise enough to welcome as broth-
ers those whom wine, or some stronger
inducement, have joined to your side; but
above all others revere father Brown, and
all the little Browns. (25) Good humour
will help you greatly: and you should
know that you are joking, when you
give a box on the ear or expertly take
one back, and open your mouth in
hearty laughter. (29) You already know
full well what a chaste girl wants (and a
shameless one too); you should call them,
an easy crowd to attract, to join your
party. (33) If by chance an old hag wants
a kiss, ah, don't refuse her: for every joy
that you give the lustful old baggage, her
grateful young great-great-great-great-
granddaughter will repay you in full.
(37) I have dashed off this advice to
send you, being always concerned for
your interest; later, I will warn you about
what befits, graces, and elevates a good
MP.

Text: Bern.; Loveling, *Poems* (in 1741 edn., pp. 109–11); ms. D, fo. 33; BL(b), fo. 67; Nott. Pw V 148/3. *Date*: 1722. This poem is discussed in Ch. 7.

2.27 EZECHIELI SPANHEMO, IN LIBRUM EIUS DE USU NUMISMATUM ANTIQUORUM

Diva, vocalis citharae perita,
Vatibus dudum comes; o potentum
Nomina heroum decorare versu

Translation: 'To Ezechiel Spanheim, on his book about the use of ancient coins'
        Goddess, skilled in the music of the lyre, and the poets' traditional compa-nion, accustomed to celebrate the names

21 *Pellex*: literally, 'whore': a refinement of electioneering. Cf. 4. 9. 33.   22 Possibly alluding to Hor., *Epist.* 1. 6. 54–5, 'frater . . . adopta' (also on the indignity of courting popularity).   23–4 Either an influential family at Petersfield (or one that might humorously be presented as such), or dissenters (from 17th century 'Brownists'). Cf. (another?) Brown at 4. 9. 15. Ms. D and BL(b) read *Brownigerosque* for -*genasque*.   25–8 This stanza omitted in Nott.   26 Ms. D reads *tu* for *te*.   30 Cf. Cat. 7. 2, 'satis superque'.   33 Old ladies are still interested in kisses at Hor., *Carm.* 1. 25; 4. 13, etc.   36 *Trineptis*: a late, unpoetical word (cited from legal authors in *OLD*, Lewis & Short): very effective humorous exaggeration. Young ladies will presumably repay Taylor in kisses, and perhaps in electoral influence, for his attentions to their truly antique relatives.

1 Cf. 1. 3. 21–2; perhaps alluding to Stat., *Silv.* 2. 7. 6, 'vocalis citharae' (cf. line 53, 'carmen . . . exeris', perhaps echoed in Alsop's line 6).   3 Cf. Hor., *Epist.* 1. 6. 37–8; 2. 1. 266.

Sueta perenni;

5   Eja, age, auratum modulare plectrum;
Exeras vocem, Dea; tu, modorum
Gnara, mansurae properes Spanhemum
    Tradere famae.
Cura Musarum propior, Spanheme,
10 Unus argutae citharis catervae
Sufficis; Phoebi recinet per aevum
    Te chorus omnis.
Seu studens pacem stabilire regnis
Hospes intersis populo Britanno;
15 Temperes seu consilio Borussi
    Caesaris aulam;
Seu ducum heroumque velis priorum
Volvere annales, memor anteacti
Seculi, et priscis modo nascitura
20   Tempora jungens.
Literis quantum tribuere lumen
Gens Spanhemorum, memorat Geneva
Artibus clara, ingenuaeque nutrix
    Leyda juventae.
25 Stirpe tu docta melior propago
Emicas longe, et spatium per orbis
Ultimum gentes quid agunt, quid olim
    egere, requiris.
Tu novum gazis pretium decusque
30 Adjicis; tu restituis metallo
Quicquid exedit situs, aut vetusta
    Condidit aetas.
Tu doces, primo repetens ab ortu,
Temporis lapsi seriem, vicesque
35 Pendulas rerum: tua, docte scriptor,
    Pagina monstrat
Quos tulere urbes Siculae tyrannos;
Sparta quos bello peperit feroces;
Quosque Musarum studiis dicarunt

of heroes in everlasting verse, come and pluck your golden instrument; raise your voice, goddess, and as an expert musician hurry to ensure Spanheim's lasting fame. (9) You are the Muses' chief charge, Spanheim, and alone suffice to occupy the lyres of the shrill throng; the whole chorus of Apollo will sing of you for ever: whether you come as a guest among the British people, concerned to secure peace for our kingdoms; whether you advise the King of Prussia's court; or whether you choose to turn over the records of past leaders and heroes, remembering past ages, and making links between new and old. (21) Geneva, famous for the arts, and Leiden, the nurse of honest youth, both recall how much light the race of the Spanheims has given to letters. (25) You shine out as the still better offspring of a learned family, and ask what the nations do throughout the whole world, and what they did in the past. (29) You add a new value and honour to treasures; you restore to metal coins whatever their disuse or antiquity have obscured. You start from the very beginning, and tell us of the passing ages, and the precarious vicissitudes of fortune; your page, learned writer, shows what tyrants the Sicilian cities brought forth, what fierce warriors Sparta bore, and whom Athens contributed to poetry. (41) Why do we look with admiration on the pomp of Rhodes, the Pharos tower, pride of a prodigal people, or the secrets that are held in a page of mysical

7 Cf. Stat., *Silv.* 4. 2. 3, 'mansuro carmine'.   9 Cf. Stat., *Silv.* 3. 4. 50, 'propior iam cura deae'; Ovid, *Met.* 13. 578.   10 Possibly alluding to Hor., *Carm.* 4. 6. 25, 'argutae . . . Thaliae'; cf. Stat., *Silv.* 2. 3. 8, 'tenerae . . . catervae'.   11–12 Possibly alluding to Virg., *Ecl.* 6. 66, 'Phoebi chorus . . . omnis'.   14 Probably alluding to Hor., *Carm.* 1. 2. 46, 'intersis populo'.   15–16 Frederick III, Elector of Brandenburg, crowned King of Prussia on 18 Jan. 1701 (when Spanheim was created a baron). Mentioned again, 66.   22 The learned Spanheim family came from Geneva; Ezechiel accompanied his father Frederick to Leiden in 1642; his brother (also Frederick) was Professor of Theology at Heidelberg (1655) and Leiden (1670), and seems to have been considered for Oxford's Hebrew professorship in 1691 (see Bodleian, ms. Ballard 25. 15; ms. Eng. misc. e. 184).   25 Possibly an inverted reworking (though without direct allusion) of Hor., *Carm.* 3. 6. 46–8, turning pessimism into progress. 26 Cf. Ovid, *Fasti* 2. 684, 'spatium . . . orbis'.   33 Possibly alluding to Virg., *Geo.* 4. 286, 'primo repetens ab origine'.   34–5 Cf. Hor., *Epist.* 1. 18. 110, 'pendulus'.

40   Palladis arces.
          Quid Rhodi pompam, Phariasque turres,
          Prodigi fastum populi, intuemur,
          Mysticis vel quod tenet involutum
               Charta figuris?
45   Rite tu priscos melius reponis
          Ordine heroas; tibi, quot metallo
          Artifex cudit manus, innotescunt
               Gesta virorum.
          Quo duces traxit Cleopatra vultu,
50   Explicas; quali Juba fulsit ore;
          Quo genus dium Ptolemaei, et ingens
               Stemma Seleuci.
          Julium per te decus, et Lycurgi
          Fama per longum viget aucta seclum;
55   Stat suus Graiis honor, et Quirini
               Gloria genti.
          Quin erit quondam, tibi cum recentes
          Paginam ornabunt tituli; ducumque
          Gesta vultusque artifici micabunt
60   Aere recusi.
          Sculptiles Cressae Blenhemique campos
          Aemuli quondam juvenes videbunt;
          Serta victori incolumis Britanno
               Flandria nectet.
65   Cerne, ut heroum numerosus ordo
          Splendet: ante omnes Fredericus astat;
          Et, potens nutu dare jura regnis,
               Anna refulget.
          Inter haec sacrae monumenta famae,
70   Dulce te docti columen Lycei,
          Te decus secli memorabit ultro
               Sera vetustas.
          Te suis aetas hodierna scriptis
          Inserit; te per memores reponent
75   Posteri fastos, adimentque letho
               Munera vatum.

signs? (45) You do better, by placing the ancient heroes in their proper order; for you, each coin struck by a craftsman tells of men's deeds. You explain the look with which Cleopatra seduced generals, the blazing eye of Juba, the divine race of the Ptolemies, and the huge Seleucid family tree. (53) Through you the glory of Caesar and the fame of Lycurgus are increased, to live on through the centuries; the Greeks have their honour, and the Roman race their glory. (57) And there will be a time when new titles adorn your pages, and the faces of leaders skilfully struck on medals will shine out to indicate their deeds. Then will young men see depicted the battles of Crecy and Blenheim, and wish to imitate such achievements; Flanders, saved from conquest, will wreathe a victor's garland for Britain. (65) See how splendid are the full ranks of heroes; before them all stands King Frederick, and Queen Anne shines, with the power to rule kingdoms by her nod. (69) Among these records of ancient renown, you will be remembered in the distant future as the sweet support of a learned society, and the glory of our century. The present age sets you up among its own writers; posterity will place you in its records, and the tributes of poets will save you from oblivion.

Text: Bern. (unnumbered, at end). *Date*: unknown, perhaps *c*. 1706. This poem is mentioned in Ch. 4.

47 Cf. Prop. 4. 2. 62, 'artifices manus'. *Innotescunt* (short 'o'): unclassical scansion, probably a mistake.   65 Cf. 1. 1. 20, 'splendidus ordo'.   67 Possibly alluding to Hor., *Carm*. 3. 3. 44, 'dare iura Medis'.   70 Probably alluding to Hor., *Carm*. 2. 17. 4 (as certainly at Alsop 1. 3. 48).   74 Possibly alluding to Hor., *Carm*. 1. 1. 35, 'inseres': ambitions for fame provide a similar context.   75 Almost certainly borrowing from Hor., *Carm*. 3. 22. 3, 'adimisque leto', though without implying that Horace's context is relevant here.

Book 3
Additional Odes and Hexameter Poems

3.1 JOHANNI DOLBEN

Chare vir Musis et amate nymphis,
Chare prae Musis mihi praeque nymphis
Omnibus, cui posthabeo meum cor,
    Excipe sponsam;
5 Estne qui scit te melius chorumve
Ducere aut sacro eloquio intonare
Regibus coram, aetheriove Regi
    Ordier hymnum?
Anna cognatis Dea mista Divis
10 Anna, dum terrae invigilabat, aurem
Dulce cantanti applicuit benignam
    Dulce loquenti.
Jam, nefas, duro premit opprimitque
Sub jugo infaustos Britonas Tyrannus,
15 Musicae et Musae indocilis choraules
    Inter asellus.
Frustra ad hoc monstrum canis, heu nec ullis
Vocis aut plectri illecebris domandum,
Surda non illo magis aut veneno
20   Plenior aspis.
Quin erit, si non cupidi auguramur
Vana, erit cum tu titulo altiori or-
natus incedes, reducisque laeta
    Caesaris aurem
25 Voce mulcebis. Britonas Britannus
Rex reget tandem, resonate plectra!
Cuncta vox clamet ter io triumphe!
    Caesar adesdum,

Translation: 'To John Dolben'

You are dear to the Muses, beloved by the nymphs, and more dear to me than all the Muses and nymphs, indeed (apart from my wife) there is nothing, not even my own heart, dearer than yourself. (5) Is there anyone who knows better than you how to lead a choir, or to preach eloquently before kings, or to raise a hymn to the heavenly King? (9) Queen Anne, now a goddess joined to her divine relations in heaven, turned a kindly ear on your singing and sweet speech, while she watched over the land. (13) But now a tyrant (o sacrilege!) oppresses the unhappy Britons, pressing them down beneath his harsh yoke, a man quite untaught in music and poetry, like an ass among the choristers. (17) You sing in vain to this monster, who cannot be tamed, alas, by any charms of voice or strings: a viper is no more deaf, no more full of venom! (21) But there will come a time (if we are not led by our desires to make vain prophecies), when you will walk adorned by a higher title, and will soothe the ear of our restored King with a happy voice. A British King will at last rule the Britons: sound the strings! Let every voice cry out, 'Hip,

1 Cf. 2. 5. 1; 2. 6. 14; 2. 18. 1.   7 Dolben as Sub-Dean of the Chapel Royal.   9 Cf. 1. 2. 1.   11–12 Alluding to Hor., *Carm.* 1. 22. 23–4, 'dulce ridentem . . . dulce loquentem'. Another allusion to this poem, line 42.   13–14 Ms. D reads *durus . . . infausto*.   19–20 Cf. *Psalm* 58. 4, '[the wicked] are like the deaf adder that stoppeth her ear'; Alsop may recall this passage, with its hope for vengeance.   24–5 'James III', unlike George I, was at least born in England.   27 Alluding to Hor., *Carm.* 4. 2. 49–50, 'ter . . . io triumphe,/ . . . io triumphe'.   28 Cf. 2. 5. 45.

Firmet hoc caelum. Interea penates
30   Tu tuos optatus adi, sodales
Inter et nymphas cape dulcis oti et
        Gaudia ruris.

Sint joci et risus hilaresque amici,
Molle nec plectrum neque cantus absit,
35   Nec meae temnas rudis exulisque
        Dona Thaliae.

Teutonum stupra horribilemque casum
Conscii lecti cane, nec tacendi
Quos pater movit, juvenisque dignus
40   Patre, tumultus.

(version A)

Gaudia haec inter tibi dum tuisque
Integer vivis, bene derelictae
Despice aulai strepitus: et o si
        Molliculum cor
A45   Rite sentiret quid amare amarique
Esset, et mellis quid haberet uxor,
Non maritale abnueres protervus,
        Erro, capistrum.

Crede mi nolles placidum capistrum
A50   Regiis mutare opibus. Quid ultra,
Quid piger cessas? Venus hoc rogatque
        Dulcis Agella.

(version B)

Gaudia haec inter tibi dum tuisque
Integer vivis, bene derelictae
Despice aulai strepitus—sed audi
        Aethere ab alto
B45   Juppiter laevum intonuit! Dunelmus
Te pater, divum genus et deorum
Coetibus dignum, potiore demptis
        Ornat honore.

Si mihi Graiae Latiaeve Musae,
B50   Qualis aut Sapphus fuit aut Horati,

hip, hurrah!'—may our monarch come, and may heaven make this certain. (29) Meanwhile, you are wanted at home, and should go thither, and enjoy the pleasures of sweet rural relaxation among your companions and the nymphs. Let there be jokes and laughter, and merry friends, nor let soft music and singing be absent; nor should you scorn the gifts of my rough and exiled Muse. (37) Sing about the Germans' debaucheries, and the disgraceful things their beds have seen; and you should tell of the uproar caused by the father, and by a youth whom such a father deserves. (41) While you live honestly for yourself and your friends amidst these pleasures, you can despise the din of a court that is wisely left behind. (A43) And if your gentle little heart knew aright what it is to love and be loved, and how honey-sweet a wife can be, you would not be so churlish as to refuse, you truant, the bonds of matrimony. (A49) Believe me, you would not wish to change such quiet bonds for the wealth of kings. Why then are you any longer reluctant? Venus asks this, and so does sweet Miss Meadows.

(B43) But listen—there has been a favourable sign from heaven; the father of Durham, of holy race and worthy of joining the gods, is giving you an honour greater than the one that you have lost. (B49) If I had the power of the Greek or Latin Muse, such as Sappho or Horace had, that man would not lack the reward of everlasting poetry; his grandsons would read that he was strong, pure in his life and

---

37 Possibly alluding to Hor., *Carm.* 4. 5. 21, 'nullis polluitur casta domus stupris'; if so, 'James III' will improve the morality of people and court, like Augustus.   39 George I, and the Prince of Wales (later George II); on these amours, see P. Langford, *A Polite and Commercial People* (Oxford, 1989), pp. 15, 23.   42 Alluding to Hor., *Carm.* 1. 22. 1, 'Integer vitae'. Cf. 11–12, B54.   A47–8 Cf. 2. 6. 19; 2. 15. 6.   A50 Cf. Hor., *Carm.* 2. 12. 21–3; Alsop's claim is less far-fetched (and equally, or more, effective).   A51 Cf. Tibullus, 2. 2. 10, 'quid cessas?'. A52 Miss Meadowes (according to ms. n.); Dolben did not marry her.   B45 Possibly alluding to Virg., *Aen.* 2. 693, 'intonuit laevum'. *Laevum* [on the left] could imply either good or bad luck: e.g. good at Ovid, *Fasti* 4. 833, bad at Hor., *Carm.* 3. 27. 15. For Lord Crewe, Bishop of Durham, see Ch. 7.   B49 Cf. Hor., *Carm.* 2. 16. 38, 'Graiae Camenae'.   B50 *Sapphus*: Greek genitive

Vis foret, non perpetui careret
  Munere versus
Ille Vir; fortem legerent Nepotes,
Integrum vitae, fideique purae,
B55 Et supra Reges meritis amicum,
  Auspicibus Diis.
Sed pudens parvo tenuare plectro
Magna, suspendo citharam; nec ausus
Plura, tam sancto capiti ter aevum
B60   Nestoris opto.

in his faith, and a friend (with heaven's blessing) more worthy than kings. (B57) But I am ashamed to diminish great things with my poor lyre, and I hang it up; not daring to say more, I end by wishing that so revered a head should live three times as long as Nestor.

Text: BL(a), pp. 97–9; ms. D, fo. 16 (lacks version B). *Date*: version A, late 1717 or early 1718; version B, perhaps *c.* April 1718. This poem is discussed in Chs. 6 and 7.

3.2 JOHANNI DOLBEN

Ergo tu crebris patiens duelli
Firmiter perstas validisque pernox
Ictibus bellum renovas, et inde-
  fessus agendo es?
5 Non ita, ut pridem memini, ante pugnam
Fortis aut fidens animi, sed anceps
Spem metumque inter, cupiens timensque
  Castra subisti.
Quin cave o audax! aderunt futura
10 Praelia, et frustra maribus tacendi
Exitus, cum fors acie retusa
  Hasta redibit.
Quinquies denos Priamus superbus
Cuspide implevit thalamos, sed eheu!
15 Torpuit tandem, ceciditque telum im-
  belle sine ictu.
Quare age et ritu admonitus feroci
Parcius saevi jaculo, nec ultra
Urge opus, denum repetendo in annum
20 Quam fueris par.

Translation: 'To John Dolben'
  So are you standing firm in the conflict, renewing the war each night with strong and frequent blows, and remaining tireless in your activity? (5) You were not so brave and confident, as I remember, before the battle, but instead you assaulted her defences wavering between hope and fear, full of both desire and nervousness. (9) So then beware, bold man! There will be further battles, you will emerge defeated (in a way men should stay quiet about), when by chance your spear returns blunted. (13) Proud Priam used his spear to fill his halls with fifty sons, but alas, he became exhausted at last, and his unwarlike weapon fell without striking home. (17) Come on, therefore, take proper heed of my warning, and be more sparing with your savage spear; do not push it too far, by seeking again the sort of girl you

B54 Again alluding to Hor., *Carm.* 1. 22. 1.   B56 Cf. 2. 9. 32; 2. 20. 12; Virg., *Aen.* 4. 45.   B57–8 Cf. Hor., *Carm.* 3. 3. 72, 'magna modis tenuare parvis'.   B59 Possibly alluding to Hor., *Carm.* 1. 24. 2, 'tam cari capitis'.   B60 Possibly alluding to Hor., *Carm.* 2. 9. 13–14. Nestor was famous for longevity.

1–3 Warlike metaphors for sex (cont., 10–18: various words for spear, all with a sexual connotation): cf. Hor., *Carm.* 3. 26; 4. 1; Ausonius, *Cento Nuptialis* 101–30; J. Secundus, *Epithalamium* 75ff; etc.   3–4 Probably alluding to Ovid, *Met.* 9. 199, 'indefessus agendo'.   13 Priam had 50 sons, none of whom could save him in the end. 15–16 Alluding to Virg., *Aen.* 2. 544 (of Priam), 'telumque imbelle sine ictu'. Alsop turns Virgil's real spear into a metaphor for erotic impotence; Priam remains pathetic, and becomes ridiculous, a cautionary example.   19 Cf. 2. 20. 17–18.

Sin senescentis monita haec amici
Respuas, fretus viridi juventa,
Hoc super nostri meliorem utroque
    Consule Wakum.

could cope with ten years ago. (21) But if, trusting in your vigorous youth, you reject these words of advice from a friend who grows old, consult Wake on this subject, who is better than both of us.

Text: BL(a), p. 139. *Date*: unknown; almost certainly before 1720, probably before 1716: perhaps *c.* 1710–12.

3.3 JOHANNI FREIND

Integer vitae cerebrique sanus
Non eget Mauri titulis nec arte,
Nec venenatas jaculante nugas,
    Freinde, Camoena:
5 Seu catenatis foribus retentum
Carcer includat, vel ahena turris,
Sive monstrorum numero aestuantum
    Certet inermis.
Namque te pulsum Deus ex senatu
10 (Quippe agis causam intrepide disertus)
Sospitat contra fera viperinae
    Sibila linguae:
Quale portentum neque foeda Lerna
Protulit dignum Herculeis sagittis,
15 Nec duo Arthuri domuere, monstro-
    μαστιγες ambo.
Pone me invisae prope limen aulae,
Et domos justis dominis negatas,
Quod latus regni nebulo malusque
20   Arbiter urget;
Pone sub vultu nimium propinqui
Judicis, quo nec fora nequiorem
Prisca cognorunt, similemve noscet

Translation: 'To John Freind'

    A man who is pure in his life, and of sound brain, does not need Moorish titles or skill, nor, Freind, a Muse that hurls poisoned trifles: whether a prison holds him behind chained doors, or a castle keep, or whether he struggles unarmed against a surging host of monsters. (9) For God protects you, on your expulsion from Parliament (since you fearlessly argued for your cause) against the savage hissing of viperish tongues; such a portent was never produced by foul Lerna as a worthy target for Hercules' arrows, nor did the two Arthurs, both scourges of monsters, conquer such a creature. (17) Place me near the threshold of the hated court, and palaces denied to their rightful masters, because a scoundrel and an evil minister oppresses the kingdom; (21) place me under the eyes of a too partial judge, than whom the ancient law courts have known none more wicked, nor will posterity know his like; (25) send me again

21 Alsop was 14 years older than Dolben.   22 Possibly alluding to Virg., *Aen.* 5. 295, 'viridique iuventa'; 5. 430, 'fretusque iuventa'. If so, we may remember that Dares loses his fight, and Euryalus (though he wins his race) comes to a sad end in book 9: more cautionary tales?   24 Presumably William Wake, the archbishop.

1–4 Altered from H 1–4 to reflect Freind's situation.   5–7 Loosely parallel to H 5–6, 'sive . . . aestuosas/ sive'. 6 Probably alluding to Hor., *Carm.* 3. 16. 1, 'turris aenea'.   8 Cf. H 12, 'inermem'.   9 *Namque*: H 9 (but H continues differently). Freind is probably expelled by arrest; if on petition, the date must be 1724, not 1723.   13 Cf. H 13, 'quale portentum'. Lerna: home of the Hydra.   15 Perhaps King Arthur and Arthur Charlett (see Ch. 5), a humorous combination. Charlett's opposition to non-jurors may be meant.   16 The Greek unaccented in ms.; a false quantity (long 'ι'). Based on Ὁμηρομάστιξ: cf. R. Pfeiffer, *History of Classical Scholarship* (Oxford, 1968), p. 70.   17 *Pone* (repeated 21): H 17, 21: keeping a loose connection. Also 'propinqui', 21.   19–20 H 19–20: cleverly altered to apply to Walpole.

Sera vetustas:
25 Mitte me rursus per inhospitales
    Belgiae campos, loca dura Musis,
    Dulce scribentem memorabo Freindum,
        Dulce loquentem.

through the inhospitable plains of Holland, a hard place for literature, and I will still recall Freind's sweet writing and sweet conversation.

Text: BL(a), p. 135. *Date*: probably summer or autumn 1723 (or 1724: see n. on 9). This poem is discussed in Ch. 6; it is a sustained allusion to Hor., *Carm.* 1. 22 [= H in notes below].

3.4 CHARISSIMO SUO DUCI DE VENDOSME TALLARDUS

Translation: 'Tallard sends greetings to his dearest friend Vendôme'

Spes erat nuper mihi te videndi
Et duces tecum graviora passos;
Fallor, et votis minus annuerunt
    Invida fata.
5   Tu tamen charis, age, dic amicis
    Quis status rerum, quot iniqua lethi
    Abstulit sors, quis tulit indecoro
        Vincula collo.
    Quid parat magni dominator orbis;
10 An studet victo dare jura mundo
    Herculis ritu? fuerintne Gades
        Meta triumphis?
    Forte jam damnat solium Philippi,
    Sanguinem fusum, miserasque strages;
15 Vult et intactas, sibi quas ministrat,
        India gazas.
    Rectius novi; neque sic siletur
    Fulmen Europae, Britonumque terror;
    Victus an vincat Lodoicus idem est,
20   Concinet hymnos.
    Martis invicti quid agant alumni,

I recently hoped that I might see you, and those generals that have suffered grievously with you; I was wrong, and hard fate did not grant my prayers. (5) But tell your dear friends, then, yourself what is the state of affairs, how many have been snatched by death's unfair lottery, and who languishes in chains. (9) What is the master of the globe preparing to do: is he like Hercules aiming to give laws to a defeated world? Was Cadiz the limit to his triumphs? (13) Perhaps he now damns the throne of Philip, the blood spilt there, and sad destruction; and he wants to keep the wealth of the Indies, which he manages, untouched for himself. (17) I know better: the thunderbolt of Europe and terror of the Britons is not thus silent; whether he wins or loses, Louis is the same—he sings hymns. (21) I am eager to know what the unde-

27–8 H 23–4; perhaps humour in comparing Freind to the girl, Lalage.

1 He might expect the defeated Vendôme to join him in captivity (in fact, he remained in command).
2 Alluding to Virg., *Aen.* 1. 199, 'o passi graviora'; probably also to Hor., *Carm.* 1. 7. 30–1, 'peioraque passi/ mecum'.
4 Cf. Stat., *Theb.* 10. 384; Phaedrus 5. 6. 5; Lucan 1. 70.   7 Possibly alluding to Hor., *Carm.* 2. 16. 29, 'abstulit . . . mors'; cf. *Carm.* 2. 1. 22, 'indecoro'.   9 Ironic: Louis XIV's ambitions (his name, 19).   10 Probably alluding to Hor., *Carm.* 3. 3. 44, 'dare iura Medis'.   11 Alluding to Hor., *Carm.* 3. 14. 1–4. Louis' ambition may be compared to Augustus'; but he might, like Hercules, gain glory at the cost of disaster. Gibraltar was lost in 1704, making Cadiz the limit of Philip V's Spain.   16 The treasures of Spanish America should not be wasted on Louis' wars.   17 Probably alluding to Hor., *Epist.* 1. 6. 67, 'novisti rectius'; cf. *Carm.* 1. 12. 21, 'neque te silebo'.   20 Hypocritical piety and pomp are used to cover up reverses; cf. Vendôme's 'most dishonest report': G. M. Trevelyan, *England under Queen Anne* (1930), 2. 365.

Quid duces nostri—Britonum quid heros,
(Regius certe juvenis) quid ipse,
        Scire laboro.
25 Te ferunt caesa doluisse dextra
Prodigum vitae cupidumque lethi;
Dum timent magni vitio parentis
        Arma nepotes.
Narrat hos Phthio similes Achilli
30 Fama veloces pedibus, nec ulla
Parte capturos nisi vulneratis
        Calcibus ictum.
Hic triumphales celebrare pompas
Et Duci laetos properant honores;
35 Dum poetarum genus omne cingit
        Tempora lauro.
Multa Durfeii levat aura Musam
Dum super nubes et in alta surgens
Marlburum caelo et mediis micantem
40   Inserit astris.
Si super me quid rogitabis, audi:
Vivo jucundus valeoque, praeter
Dura quod sors te socium negarit,
        Caetera laetus.
45 Dolium nobis bene praeparatum
Dulce lenimen misero, quod almos
Sensit Octobres quater et benignis
        Claruit annis.
Hoc dedit vires triplicique lauro
50 Stat Britannorum redimitus heros;

feated war-god's pupils, what our leaders are doing—and how that hero of the Britons does (who is surely a royal youth)—and about yourself. (25) They say that you suffered the pain of a wound in the hand, taking rash risks and looking for death; meanwhile, infected by the vices of their great parent, his grandsons fear to fight. (29) Rumour reports that they ran fast, like Phthian Achilles, nor would they take a wound in any part, except the heel. (33) Here they hurry to celebrate their triumph and give happy honours to the Duke, while all the race of poets surrounds his brows with laurel. (37) A lot of wind raises D'Urfey's Muse above the clouds: he rushes on high to place Marlborough in heaven, and make him twinkle amongst the stars. (41) If you have any questions about me, listen: I live pleasantly and well, and, apart from the fact that hard fate has denied me your company, I am otherwise happy. (45) A well-kept barrel of beer is a sweet relief to one's sorrows, when it has seen four Octobers pass and grown finer with the years. This gave the strength that led to the British hero standing thrice crowned

22 Probably James, Duke of Berwick, illegitimate son of James II, nephew of Marlborough, and a prominent Marshal of France (victor at Almanza, 1707); alternatively the Pretender himself, present at Oudenarde on the French side (in which case doubts over his parentage—the warming-pan story—may be rejected by *certe*).   24 Probably alluding to Hor., *Epist.* 1. 3. 2, 'scire laboro'; cf. Alsop 2. 3. 12.   25 Rumours of a wound; or, with the army's right cut off (as happened at Oudenarde).   26 Possibly alluding to Hor., *Carm.* 1. 12. 37–8. Vendôme fought in the front ranks (Trevelyan, 2. 363–4).   27 Alluding to Hor., *Carm.* 1. 2. 23, 'vitio parentum'; cf. *Carm.* 3. 6. 45–8. The parent is probably Louis; his grandson, the Duke of Burgundy, was nominally in command, supervised by Vendôme.   29 Cf. Hor., *Carm.* 4. 6. 4; Alsop 2. 16. 23–4; Achilles' qualities are humorously distorted (he was fast, and vulnerable only in the heel, but did not flee).   34 Marlborough.   35 Cf. 1. 4. 1; Hor., *Carm.* 3. 25. 20; *Carm.* 3. 30. 16.   37 Alluding to Hor., *Carm.* 4. 2. 25, (of Pindar) 'multa Dircaeum levat aura cycnum'. The allusion continues in 38: *nubes* (Hor.: 'nubium tractus', 27). Tom D'Urfey, *French Pride Abated* (1708), on Oudenarde. 1708 broadsheet reads *Durfeiam*.   40 Cf. Hor., *Carm.* 3. 25. 6, 'stellis inserere'.   42–3 1708 broadsheet reads *Viro . . . vatsoque* (clearly misprints); *sors quod* for *quod sors*.   44 Alluding to Hor., *Epist.* 1. 10. 50; cf. Alsop 2. 19. 20.   45 Alluding to Hor., *Carm.* 2. 10. 14–15, 'bene praeparatum/ pectus'; humorously turning moral advice into praise of drink.   46 Alluding to Hor., *Carm.* 1. 32. 15, 'dulce lenimen'; another amusing reworking.   47 October ale; cf. 2. 19. 1.   49 Blenheim (1704), Ramillies (1706), Oudenarde (1708).

Robur hinc crescit solidum mihique   with laurel; hence grows the solidity and
    Musa poetae.   inspiration of my poetry.

Text: BL(a); broadsheet, *Charissimo suo Duci de Vendosme Tallardus* (London, 1708: 'printed for John Morphew, near Stationers-Hall'); Bodleian ms. Lat. misc. e. 19, fo. 173–4. *Date*: 1708 (purportedly 'Nottingham, primo Cal. August.'). This poem is discussed at the end of Ch. 5.

3.5 EPINICION DEBORAE

Humana plusquam praelia, martias
Ducente turmas numine, et agmina
    Disjecta non levi ruina
        Tanaaci super arva campi,
5 Magnam triumphis materiam dabunt
Magnam canenti—surge potens lyrae,
    Debora, surge, desidesque
        In numeros, age, tende chordas.
At o! tremendum quis genio Deum
10 Parique dicat carmine, cum super
    Montes Idumaeos tonantes
        Egit equos volucremque currum?
Quo bruta tellus atque adamantina
Soluta mundi fabrica, quo Sina
15   Concussa nutavit vagique
        Desuper intremuere montes!
Heu! quanta passi funera Shamgaro
Regnante! quantas horruimus vices,
    Cum mortis armorumque terror
20   Attonitas tremefecit urbes!
Heu! quanta clades undique luridos
Tristavit agros, hostis et insolens
    Impune Judaeas per oras
        Explicuit sua victor arma!
25 Cum sic jacebas, Patria, sic brevi
Lapsura, jam tum non sine numine
    Debora surrexi, labantis

Translation: 'The victory song of Deborah'
    Superhuman battles, with God leading the warring squadrons, and armies broken with great slaughter on the fields of Taanach, will provide a great subject for triumphs, and for the singer; rise up, Deborah, skilled in the lyre, and rouse its idle strings to song. (9) But, oh! who could speak of God in song that might match his fearful power, when he drove his thundering horses and swift chariot over the mountains of Edom? Then the dumb earth and the hard fabric of the world were dissolved, and Sinai was shaken, and the mountains moved and trembled overhead. (17) Alas, how many deaths we suffered under the rule of Shamgar; how many vicissitudes we trembled at, when the terror of death and warfare shook our astonished cities! Alas, how great a disaster saddened all the wan countryside, when the insolent foe marched victorious and unharmed through Judah! When you lay there, our fatherland, on the point of collapse, then it was that I, Deborah, arose, with God on my side, as the great glory and support of the tottering kingdom. (29) Then our

51–2 1708 broadsheet reads *et tremendis,/Spiritus Anglis.*

1 Alluding to Lucan 1. 1, 'Bella . . . plus quam civilia'.   3 Borrowing from Hor., *Carm.* 2. 19. 15, 'disiecta non leni ruina'; possibly one should read *leni* for *levi* (which breaks Horatian practice by allowing a short 5th syllable; as Alsop does elsewhere: cf. 7, where one might read *surgas*, etc.). Alsop may wish to gain variety with *levi*.
4 Taanach: Canaanite town.   5 *Dabunt*: from G.M.; ms. *donat* does not scan.   6–7 Probably alluding to Hor., *Carm.* 1. 6. 10.   11–13 Borrowing from Hor., *Carm.* 1. 34. 7–9, 'tonantis/ egit equos volucremque currum,/ quo bruta tellus'.   17 Shamgar: an earlier judge (*Judges* 3. 31).   22 G.M. reads *aut* for *et* (unmetrically).   24 Borrowing from Hor., *Carm.* 4. 9. 44, 'explicuit sua victor arma'.

Grande decus columenque regni.
Jam tum resurgens contudit hostium
30 Minas feroces Patria, femina
    Ducente victrices catervas
      Lapsa ferox reparare sceptra.
Ignava quae vos otia detinent
Cives? quis horror? quo fugis, impotens
35 Reubene, dum mater supremo
    Terra jacet peritura fato?
Vos Nepthalaei, vos Zebulonii
Heroes, o! queis laudibus efferam?
    Vos prodigos vitae, cruenta
40   Per medias rapit ira caedes.
Cerno minaci fulgure lucidam
Pompam Gradivi, ferrea ut agmina
    Horrent in armis, dum cruentus
      Ambiguo furor haesitavit
45 In bella passu! tum Baraci manus
Vasto phalangas diruit impetu
    Currusque ferratos, virosque
      Foeminiis agitavit armis.
Ter Rex Deorum concutit aegida
50 Dextra rubenti; ter polus intonat
    Armatus; hostes ipsa fundunt
      Astra, graves jaculata flammas.
Quantis ruinis strata cadavera
Campos tegebant, quanta fugacium
55   Vis hostium in ripis jacebat
      Ambiguo peritura fato.
Testis Megiddi flumen, et amnium
Princeps Kisonus, testis adhuc pater
    Kisonus unda decolori
60   Scuta virum galeasque volvens.
Jaela, multi femina nominis,
Dilecta coelo femina, Siseram
    Tu splendide fallax recepisti
      Hospitio minus hospitali;
65 Heroa cerno sub pedibus tuis

fatherland rose up again to confound the enemy's fierce threats, fierce enough to repair its fallen kingdom, with a woman leading its victorious troops. What lazy leisure holds you back, citizens? What horror? Where do you flee, helpless Reuben, while your mother country lies about to perish for ever? You heroes of Zebulun and Napthali, with what praises should I celebrate you? Blood-stained wrath carries you, careless of your own lives, through the midst of slaughter. (41) I see the bright pomp of war, with its menacing gleam—how the iron-clad columns bristle with weapons, while blood-stained fury strides about, unsure which way the fight will swing. Then Barak's huge attack destroyed phalanxes and iron chariots, and roused up men with women's weapons. Thrice the king of the gods struck his aegis, with a reddened hand; thrice the armoured heavens sounded; the stars themselves defeat the enemy, hurling deadly flames. (53) How many men were brought low, their scattered corpses covering the fields; how many fleeing enemies lay on the river banks, about to suffer an uncertain fate. The river of Megiddo and Kishon, prince of rivers, bear witness to this; father Kishon still bears witness, rolling men's shields and helmets down on his discoloured waves. Jael, woman of great fame, beloved of heaven, you gloriously deceived Sisera, receiving him with less than hospitable hospitality. (65) I see a hero fallen, collapsed under your feet; under your feet is that hero fallen, collapsed, and laid low, gasping out life from

28 Cf. 1. 3. 48. Alluding to Hor., *Carm.* 2. 17. 4.   31 Borrowing from Hor., *Carm.* 3. 3. 63, 'ducente victrices catervas'.   35–7 Tribes of Israel.   39–40 Borrowing from Hor., *Carm.* 3. 2. 11–12; an appropriate source, perhaps reminding the reader of the famous 'dulce et decorum est . . .' that follows.   46 Alluding to Hor., *Carm.* 4. 14. 30, 'ferrata vasto diruit impetu'.   50–2 Probably alluding to Hor., *Carm.* 1. 2. 2–3, 'rubente/ dextera . . . iaculatus'.   53 Probably alluding to Hor., *Carm.* 4. 14. 19, 'quantis . . . ruinis'.   58 *Testis*: omitted by *G.M.* and ms.; restored from Burton's almost identical version of the passage.   60 Cf. 3. 6. 4. Alluding to Virg., *Aen.* 1. 101, 'scuta virum galeasque . . . volvit.'   61 Alluding to Hor., *Carm.* 3. 9. 7, 'multi . . . nominis'.   63 Cf. 2. 12. 11–12. Alluding to Hor., *Carm.* 3. 11. 35, 'splendide mendax'.

Lapsum, volutum; sub pedibus tuis
    Lapsus, volutus, stratus heros
        Purpureo vomit ore vitam.
Afflicta longas increpuit moras
70 Dixitque mater, 'Sisera, Sisera
    Ah! quae triumphales moratur
        Praeda rotas? spoliisve currus
Gemunt onusti? quae mihi, quae tibi
Captiva virgo regia serviet?
75   Captiva quae vestis triumphos
        Sidonio decorabit ostro?'
Misella mater! quidlibet impotens
Sperare! Nequicquam. Occidis, occidis,
    O nate! communique mater
80   Occidit interitura fato.

his red lips. His vexed mother complained of the long delay, saying 'Sisera, Sisera, what booty is it that delays your triumphal chariot-wheels? Are your chariots groaning, weighed down with spoils? What captive royal maiden will serve me, and yourself? What captured garments will brighten your triumph with their Sidonian purple?' Poor mother! She is helpless, for all her hopes are vain. You are dying, o son, you are dying; and your mother dies too, and will share your fate.

Text: ms. D, fo. 67–8; *Gentleman's Magazine* 6. 47 (January 1736). *Date*: unknown. This poem is discussed in Chs. 3 and 4.

3.6 BRITANNIA

Dum Mosa torpet sanguine Gallico,
Humique fumant oppida diruta;
    Dum decolori Rhenus unda
        Scuta virum galeasque volvit:
5 Quid nos loquacem tendere barbiton?
Et bella mensis pingere ludicra?
    Quid inter armorum tumultus
        Pacificam renovare pompam?
En! tuta vastis classibus Albion
10 Circumfluenti cingitur aequore;
    Regnatque victrix inter undas,
        Et liquido dominatur orbi:
Spargens frequentem lata per aequora
Classis ruinam, praesidium suis
15   Affert Britannis, navigatque
        Attonito metuenda ponto:

Translation: 'Britannia'

    While the Meuse runs slowly with French blood, and towns smoke, sacked to the ground, while the Rhine rolls in its discoloured waves the shields and helmets of men, why should we tune the sounding lyre, and depict a mock war on our hall-tables, and renew our peaceful pomp amidst the tumult of arms? (9) Look! England is safe with her vast fleets, surrounded by sea; she reigns victorious amongst the waves, and dominates the watery world. Her fleet, often scattering ruin all over the wide seas, offers protection to her British people, and is to be feared as it sails on the astonished sea. (17) I bear witness to the waves that are

68 Alluding to Virg., *Aen.* 9. 349; cf. Hor., *Carm.* 3. 3. 12.   72–3 Cf. 1. 3. 32; 3. 6. 20.   73–4 Probably alluding to Hor., *Carm.* 1. 29. 5–6.   76 Probably alluding to Hor., *Epist.* 1. 10. 26.   77–8 Alluding to Hor., *Carm.* 1. 37. 10–11, 'quidlibet impotens/ sperare'; and to *Carm.* 4. 4. 70, 'occidit, occidit'. Thus Horace's words on two famous enemies of Rome (Cleopatra and Hasdrubal) are transferred to those of Israel. Cf. Cat. 3. 16, 'o miselle'; Burton retains the song's gloating tone, but Alsop adds an interesting note of sympathy (as does Horace).

4 Cf. 3. 5. 60 ; from Virg., *Aen.* 1. 101.   5 Alluding to Hor., *Carm.* 1. 1. 34.   6 I am not sure how *mensis* fits in: I take it tentatively from *mensa* (alternatively, 'of the month'?).

Testor perempti sanguine navitae
Undas rubentes, et laceras trabes:
    Testor Britannum Gallicanis
20   Oceanum spoliis onustum.
En! picta velis aequora conspicor:
En! saevientes in fera praelia
    Ruunt carinae, mutuaque
       Exitium meditantur ira:
25 En! mugienti fulmina machina
Exire, certi nuntia funeris;
    Ignesque et undae dissonantes
       Perniciem dubiam minari.
Jam dissipatos impiger ordines
30 Carterus urget, non timidus mori;
    Fugatque classem, multa luso
       Pollicitam meliora Regi:
Frustra. Imminentem non prohibet necem
Aptata laurus jam capiti Ducis;
35   Quin victor effundit cruorem
       Et mediis moritur triumphis:
Gens Angla semper pube potens sua
Heroas almis jactat adoreis
    Ubique claros, et paratos
40   Oppositas cohibere gentes:
Nec, si reposcat Parca malignior
Unum, potentes deficient viri,
    Virtute qui instaurent hiantem
       Et reparent simili ruinam.
45 Suis remoti finibus Albion
Fraenare Martis noverit impetum;
    Potensque duplas, sive pacis
       Sive gravis per acuta belli
Miscere laudes, arma vel obviis
50 Opponit armis, vel celer ingeni
    Intentat artes, bellicasque
       Alma regit sine Marte gentes:
Sed nec Camaenis deficit indoles
Apta excolendis, nec gravis obruit
55   Bellator artes: utriusque
       Fervet opus proprium Minervae:
Superba claris Anglia vatibus,
Insigniores queis neque Graecia
    Nec Roma jactat, neve cedit

red with the blood of dead sailors, and shattered spars; I bear witness to the British ocean, weighed down with spoils taken from the French. Look! I see the water flecked with sails; look! the maddened vessels rush into fierce battle, and plot destruction with mutual hate. (25) Look! balls shoot out as the cannons roar, a sure warning of death; the fires and crashing waves threaten calamity. Now tireless Carter, unafraid of death, urges on the scattered battle-lines; and he puts to flight the fleet that had promised much better to its gullible king—in vain. The laurel wreath that was prepared for the leader's head does not prevent death from hanging over him; nay, victorious, he pours out his blood, and dies in the midst of his triumph. (37) The English race, always powerful because of its young men, can everywhere honour famous heroes, who were ready to restrain hostile peoples. Nor, if harsher fate demanded one of them, will these powerful men fail, when they can shore up, and repair, gaping ruin with equal courage. (45) England knows how to halt the attack of war far from her shores, and is powerful enough to combine the double praises of peace or harsh war, either meeting enemy armaments with arms, or with swift intellect turning to the arts; and she rules gently over warlike peoples without the use of force. (53) Neither does she lack the ability to cultivate the Muses, nor does a stern warrior weigh down the arts: each aspect of Athena's work is vigorously performed. England can be proud of her famous poets, than whom neither Greece nor Rome can boast any more distinguished; nor does Oxford give way to noble Athens, since a gentle climate and the genius of the place have made her a fit

---

20 Cf. 1. 3. 32; alluding to Virg., *Aen.* 1. 289.
56 Cf. Virg., *Aen.* 1. 436.

30 Rear-Admiral Richard Carter; killed at Barfleur.

60   Ingenuis Rhedycina Athenis,
     Quam mite coelum, quam Genius loci
     Fecere Musis aptam habitantibus:
          O sola cunctas praeter urbes,
               Chara Tuo, Rhedycina, Phoebo!
65   Phoebus novenis grande sororibus
     Decus, tuetur praesidio suam
          Turbam poetarum, quibusque
               Praesidet, ipse colit Camaenas.
     Gens Angla tali prole superbiat,
70   Et Diva laetis plausibus infremat;
          Secura despectetque belli
               Et pelagi pariter ruinas:
     Haec ingruentes undique conspicit
     Martis procellas, bellaque non sua
75   Audit, tumultusque; et Camaenis
               Innocuis vacat inter arma:
     Sic orbe quondam fluctibus eripis,
     Et fata firmas pendula; qui tuo
          Tutos reponis nos periclo,
80   Atque paras requiem labore:
     I nunc phalanges prorue Gallicas,
     Et tinge fuso lilia sanguine;
          Ornetque devinctus catenis
               Egregium Lodoix triumphum.

dwelling for the Muses: o Oxford, you alone are dear to your Phoebus, beyond all other cities. (65) Phoebus, the great glory of the nine sisters, guards his crowd of poets; and he himself worships the Muses over whom he presides. The English race should be proud of such offspring, and her goddess should cheer with happy applause; she can look down from safety on the destruction wrought equally by war and the sea. She sees the storms of war everywhere growing, and hears of wars and tumults that are not her own; and she has time for harmless Muses amidst the warfare. (77) Thus, on the earth, you snatch our wavering fate from the waters, and secure it; you keep us safe from the danger you face, and prepare rest by labouring. Go now, and rout the French brigades, and stain their lilies with bloodshed; let Louis, bound with chains, adorn your illustrious triumph.

Text: *Theatri Oxoniensis Encaenia sive Comitia Philologica Julii 7, Anno 1693 celebrata* (Oxford, 1693), sig. G1ʳ–G2ʳ; Bodleian, ms. Mus. Sch. c. 121; Christ Church, ms. 619, fo. 20–6 (cf. T. A. Trowles, 'The Musical Ode . . .' (unpublished D.Phil. thesis, Oxford 1992), 2. 13); *Musarum Anglicanarum Analecta* (1699) 2. 140–4 (recited by Samuel Lennard). *Date*: 1693. This poem is discussed in Ch. 3.

3.7 IN OBITUM ORNATISSIMI VIRI JACOBI HARRINGTON, ARTIUM MAGISTRI ET AEDIS CHRISTI ALUMNI

Translation: 'On the death of that most accomplished gentleman, James Harrington, MA, member of Christ Church'

     Adsis canenti, Threiciae lyrae
     Vocale pecten, quo sibi redditam
          Ex Inferis, volente fato,
               Eurydicen revocavit Orpheus.
5   Hic o! disertus quid poterit dolor

May you be beside me as I sing, o eloquent Thracian lyre, with which Orpheus would have been able to recall Eurydice, returned to him from Hell, if fate had been willing. Show what this

60 *Rhedycina*: common Neo-Latin for Oxford.   77 Presumably turning to address William III.

Ostende, vires prome reconditas;
　　Luctuque feralique versu
　　　　Funeream comitare pompam.
En! en! ruinam non reparabilem,
10　Virique magni relliquias breves:
　　　　En! invidendum pertinacis
　　　　　　Heu! decus opprobriumque fati.
Non sic agentem vidimus in foro:
Cum docta fudit divitis eloqui
15　　　Fluenta, mirantisque amorem
　　　　　Judicis invidiamque movit.
Nodosa legum aenigmata solvere
Doctus; latentes sedulus excutit
　　　Fallacias verborum, et ipsi
20　　　　Justitiae sua jura dicit.
Nutricis ast o! quam memor Oxoni!
Huc omne mentis huc studium tulit;
　　　Huc reddit acceptos labores,
　　　　　Atque datas bene gratus artes.
25　Hunc dum loquentem turba forensium
Miratur, invite attonita et stupet:
　　　En! alter en! Seldenus (inquit)
　　　　　En! reserat nova jura Cookus:
Quin o! tacet jam lingua silentio
30　Damnata longo: non iterum audiet
　　　Judex perorantem, nec aure
　　　　　Excipiet sitiente vulgus.
Frustra irruentis pagina nobilis
Mortis ferocem spreverat impetum;
35　　　Assurgit ultrix, asseritque
　　　　　Imperium Libitina saevum.
Frustra perenni carmine Carolum
Deflevit ablatum; potuit novam
　　　Qui mortuis donare vitam,
40　　　　Heu! propriam retinere nescit.
Te nos peremptum carmine non pari,
Jacobe, flemus: Te sequitur prope
　　　Lugubris ordo: lachrymosus
　　　　　Dum gemina fluit Isis unda.
45　Sic olim ademptum Te tua fleverat
Ormonde; sic sic Oxonium gemit
　　　Cum nuper Ormondum revisit

skilful grief can do, bring out your hidden strength, and accompany the funeral pomp with grief and funereal poetry. (9) Behold a disaster that cannot be repaired; behold the small remains of a great man; and, behold, his glory was envied and detested by grasping fate. We did not see him acting thus in court, when he poured out the learned streams of his rich eloquence, and moved the affection and envy of an admiring judge. (17) He was learned in solving the knotty riddles of the law; he was keen to expose the hidden fallacies in words, and he gave laws to justice itself. But how mindful was he of Oxford, his nurse! Hither, hither did he bring all the effort of his mind; hither he gave grateful thanks for the labours Oxford had expended on him, and for the arts that he had here been given. (25) While the crowd of lawyers admires him speaking, and is astonished, against its will, look! (it says), there is a new Selden; look! a Cooke is opening up new laws. But now his tongue is condemned to a long silence; a judge will not hear him summing up again, nor will the people listen thirstily to him. (33) In vain did his noble writing scorn the fierce onset of death; fate rises up in vengeance and asserts her savage power. In vain did he weep in everlasting song for Charles, taken from us; he that could give new life to the dead, alas, could not retain his own. (41) We lament you, James, now you are snatched from us, in song that cannot equal your own; a sad procession follows close behind you, while tearful Thames flows with her double stream. (45) Thus once had your people wept for you, Ormonde, taken from them; thus, thus does Oxford groan when it revisits

6 ms. *promo* [?].　　　17 Alluding to Juv. 8. 50, 'qui iuris nodos et legum aenigmata solvat'.　　　27 John Selden (1584–1654); distinguished jurist, oriental scholar, etc.　　　28 John Cooke (1666–1710); a slightly older lawyer than Harrington.　　　46–7 James Butler, 2nd Duke of Ormonde, Chancellor of Oxford University (and, much later, Jacobite leader); taken prisoner at Landen, 1693, but exchanged (these topical events alluded to here).

Vulneribus male sauciatum.
At vivit o! (vivatque precor diu)
50 Ormondus auctis laetus adoreis.
Jacobe, Te fatum, Stygisque
Irremeabilis unda cinxit.

Ormonde, grievously wounded. But Ormonde lives happily (and may he live long, I pray), with his glory increased. You, James, are surrounded by fate and the uncrossable waves of the Styx.

Text: ms. L, pp. 109–10. *Date*: 1693. This poem is discussed in Ch. 3.

3.8 GIVETTA ARDENS

B   Dum Bellona furit, dubioque in cardine rerum
     Haerent suspensi Reges, passimque per urbes
     Nuncia fama ruit; cur non (quoniam hoc datur
                                                    oti,
     Colloquiisque vacat, cur non) sermone vicissim
5   Ludimus innocui, et labentes fallimus horas?
L   Recta mones; tamen unde novae argumenta
                                               loquelae
     Sumamus? (B) Tu, si quid habes, profer. (L)
                                               Novitatem,
     Polleo ego; nam hanc semper amavi, et plurima
                                                    legi
     Scripta viri insignis, qui alternis praela diebus
10   Exercet, variaque implet novitate popinas;
     Hunc multosque alios semper lego. (S) Totus in
                                                    illis.
L   Totus in his fateor; quis enim tam divite vena
     Eloquii praepollet, et aequat praelia scriptis?
     Ut meminisse juvat bellum exitiale Namurci,
15   Et fusas Turcarum acies ad maenia Budae,
     Rubros Hungariaeque agros, ubi turbidus Ister
     Veloci cursu flaventes torquet arenas;
     Ingentes etiam memini Rheno duce pugnas.
B   O lepidum caput, atque insulso sidere natum!
20   Siccine cuncta notas, ut Rheni molle fluentum
     Esse virum credas? (L) Tu, si quid rectius istis
     Noveris, imperti. (S) Mitte haec, et ad altera
                                               transi:

Translation: 'The burning of Givet'

(B) While war rages, and kings hang on the uncertain hinge of fate, and rumour rushes through cities everywhere, why do we not amuse ourselves in conversation, and beguile the fleeting hours; why not, since we have been granted this leisure for chatting? (L; 6) That is good advice; but where can we get new subjects for our talk? (B) If you have any, say so. (L) I am full of news; for I have always loved it, and I have read many writings of that distinguished gentleman, who uses the printing press every other day to fill inns with varied news; him, and many others, I always read. (S) I'm engrossed. (L; 12) So am I, I admit; for who mines so rich a vein of eloquence, and does such justice to battles with his writings? How pleasant it is to remember the deadly war over Namur, and the Turkish ranks routed at the walls of Buda, and the bloodied troops of Hungary, where the turbulent Danube churns up the yellow sands in its swift course! I also recall huge battles under the leadership of Rhine. (B; 19) What a witty man, born under a tasteless star! Is that how you note everything, to think that the Rhine's soft flood was a man? (L) If you know better, pray share it. (S) Stop that bickering, and pass to other things: look at the bandits

52 Alluding to Virg., *Aen.* 6. 425, 'irremeabilis undae'.

3 Cf. Hor., *Serm.* 1. 4. 138, 'datur oti'. Folger reads *volat* for *ruit*.   5 Folger reads *inocuo*.   7 The speaker's names seem confused: I insert (B) between two speeches by (L). Folger has 'C' [i.e. (S)] in place of (L), perhaps rightly.   11 Cf. Hor., *Serm.* 1. 9. 2, 'totus in illis'.   16 I adopt Folger's *Rubros . . . agros*, for repetitious *Rubras . . . acies*.   21–2 Alluding to Hor., *Epist.* 1. 6. 67–8, 'si quid novisti rectius istis,/ candidus imperti'. Cf. Alsop 3. 4. 17.

En Conjuratos in regia fata latrones.
L   Res horrenda. (B) At carnifici haec tractanda
                                        relinquo.
S   Tu quoque carnificem caveas. (L) Hunc fama
                                        recenset
26   Insignem pietate virum, et super omnia justum
     Servantemque aequi; at notum mihi nomine
                                        tantum.
L   Sitque ignotus adhuc moneo. (B) Quid in hisce
                                        moramur?
     Altera res agitur, jactatque per oppida rumor
30   Maenia Caletana, exardentemque Givettam.
L   Caletum novi; jampridem audita Givetta est:
     Singula scire velim, et rem totam ex ordine
                                        gestam.
B   Sit meus iste labor cupio; namque omnia ad
                                        unguem
     Nota mihi, memorique manent in mente
                                        reposta.
35   Hic firmo Lodoix fretus munimine valli,
     Foecundam posuit messem, cerealia dona,
     Hordea, frumentumque, et, equorum pabula,
                                        foenum,
     Terrae incrementum, bellique alimenta futuri.
     Sed frustra impletur flavo teres area culmo,
40   Et plena conferta gemunt granaria messe.
     Wilhelmi auspiciis Athlonius advolat Heros,
     Ultricemque jacit flammam, et spem ludit
                                        inanem.
L   Quis tamen ille Heros? anne e nostratibus unus,
     Strenuus aut Rhodani potator, an accola Rheni?
B   Quae regio in terris illius non plena laborum?
46   Siccine nota tibi, rerum sic lecta novarum
     Scripta? hic est miseris notus Ginckleus
                                        Hibernis,
     Quo ducente, rubros hostili sanguine campos
     Fugere attoniti Celtae; atque ultricibus armis
50   Contemptor Divum Ruthrus (insatiabile
                                        monstrum)
     Occidit: ille etiam clausos in maenibus hostes
     Fudit, cognomenque evicta ex urbe recepit.

who conspired against the king's life. (L) A horrible thing! (B) But I leave these things to be dealt with by the hangman. (S) Beware the hangman yourself! (L) Rumour has it that he's a hero remarkable for piety, and remarkably just and even-handed; but I know him only by name. (L) I advise you to keep it that way. (B) Why are we dawdling with this stuff? Another subject is discussed; a rumour is circulating, about the walls of Calais, and the burning of Givet. (L; 31) Calais I know about; I have heard long ago about Givet: I would like to know the details, and the whole story in its proper order. (B) I wish to have that task; for I know all the facts intimately, and they are lodged in my memory. Here Louis, relying on the rampart's firm defences, placed his rich harvest, his wheat and barley and corn, and his hay, food for his horses: the gifts of the land, and sustenance for the coming campaign. But in vain was the smooth threshing-floor filled with yellow straw, and did the full granaries groan with the collected harvest. The hero Athlone, under William's auspices, flies there and hurls the avenging flame, and mocks their empty hopes. (L; 43) But who is this hero? is he one of our people, or a strong drinker of Rhone-water, or one who dwells by the Rhine? (B) What region of the earth is not filled with his deeds? Is this how you know and read the news-sheets? This man is Ginkel, well known to the unhappy Irish, under whose leadership the stunned Celts fled the field that had been reddened with their hostile blood; and St Ruth, that despiser of religion and insatiable monster, fell to his avenging arms. He also defeated the enemy when they were shut behind their walls, and took his title from that conquered city. (S) It is right for me to speak of what I know, and tell the story

23–4 Plot to assassinate William III: cf. P. Hopkins, 'Sham Plots & Real Plots in the 1690s', in E. Cruickshanks, ed., *Ideology & Conspiracy* (Edinburgh, 1982), pp. 89–110. Gratitude for William's survival is the official reason for the poem (see Encaenia title), but the subject is passed over quickly. Williamites took it much more seriously. Defoe, in 1728, remembered 'a Plot, fit only to have had its Origin from Hell or *Rome*. A Plot, which would have put *Hottentots* and Barbarians out of Countenance.' (*Military Memoirs of Capt. Carleton*, ed. J. T. Boulton (London, 1970), pp. 61–2.   26 Borrowing from Virg., *Aen.* 1. 10.   33 Cf. 'ad unguem' at Hor., *Serm.* 1. 5. 32; *Ars Poet.* 294.   34 Cf. Virg., *Aen.* 1. 26, 'manet alta mente repostum'.   45 Borrowing from Virg., *Aen.* 1. 460.   50 French general, commanding James' forces, killed at Aughrim. He is condemned in strong Virgilian language: alluding to *Aen.* 7. 648 (of Mezentius).

S   Fas mihi nota loqui, seriemque evolvere rerum;
     Fas bella ordiri, quae cuncta miserrima vidi,
55   Et quorum pars magna fui. (L) Quis funera tanta
     Explicet, aut possit verbis aequare laborem?
S   Vidimus attonitis jaculantem maenibus ignem
     Militem, et ardentes immisto sulphure glandes:
     Vidimus ad summa exurgentes culmina flammas,
60   Dum simul ignis equos, et equorum pabula
                                torret;
     Una domus dominosque, bovesque boumque
                                labores,
     Pulverulenta rapit flamma, et furit aestus ad
                                auras.
     Plebs confusa ruit, fugiuntque per oppida cives,
     Vitantes ignem; mox corripit acrior ignis;
65   Undique terribiles flammae, exitiumque
                              coruscum,
     Splendentesque ruinae, et late fulgidus horror.
     Nota petunt miseri, sed vana, levamina cives,
     Amotas tegulas, sublataque culmina tectis,
     Avulsumque pavimentum, nudataque terrae
70   Viscera conspexi, ut violentum ponderis ictum
     Excipiat molli amplexu, gremioque recondat.
L   Sic Parthus bellum devitans opprimit hostes
     Incautos prudente fuga, et cedendo triumphat.
     Unde tamen jactat distantes machina flammas
75   Edoceas, et qui tantos vigor excitat ignes.
B   Ferrata imposito volat ardens sulphure concha,
     Longum syrma trahens, scindensque in nubibus
                              arcum,
     It furiale rubens. (L) Pavidum sic territat orbem
79   Stella minax, volitatque accenso crine cometes.
S   Sed nec stella magis fatali exaestuat igne.
B   Illa cadens tremulam vasto quatit impete terram,
     Ingentique boatu dirupta evomit ignes,
     Et quassa elidit solido fundamine tecta,
     Evertitque domos: nunc mortis mille figuras,
85   Semiustosque artus, et singultantia corda,
     Et gemitus morientum audires: cuspide miles
     Deposita tremit, et caecam penetrare cavernam
     Secretosque locos quaerit; quin protinus altas
     Machina perrumpit latebras, et terra dehiscens
90   Involvit trepidantem, avidoque absorbet hiatu.
S   Surgentem ad flammam paleae volvuntur inanes,

of events; it is right to begin with wars, all of which I have seen in their horror, and in which I played a major part. (L) Who can tell of so many deaths, or fit his words to the task? (S; 57) We saw a soldier hurling fire onto the astonished fort, and heated cannon-balls mixed with gunpowder; we saw the flames rising to the roof-tops, as the fire burnt up both horses and the horses' food at the same time. A single dust-shrouded flame snatched houses and their owners, both oxen and the results of their labours; and the fierce heat rose to the sky. People ran about in confusion, and citizens fled through the town, avoiding the fire. Soon the fire took keener hold; terrible flames were everywhere, with fast flickering death, and glittering ruins, and brightly-flashing horror spread wide. The unhappy citizens sought relief in their usual ways, but in vain; I saw roof-tiles removed, the tops of houses removed, the pavement torn up, and the naked bowels of the earth dug up, in order that earth might receive the cannon-ball's violent blow in its soft embrace, and hide it. (L; 72) Thus does a Parthian avoid battle, using prudent flight to defeat his rash enemies, and triumph by yielding. But tell us how a machine hurls far-reaching flames, and what power roused such great fires. (B) A burning iron shell flies, filled with gunpowder; leaving a long trail behind it, and cutting a parabola through the clouds, it rushes red and terrible! (L) Thus does a threatening star frighten a fearful world, and a comet fly with its streaming hair alight. (S) But even a star does not burn with more fatal fire. (B; 81) That shell falls, and shakes the trembling earth with its vast impact, and in bursting pours out its fires with a huge crash; it dashes shaken houses from their fixed foundations, and overturns homes: now death takes a thousand forms. There are half-burned limbs, and you could

---

55 Borrowing from Virg., *Aen.* 2. 6. A witty use of allusion: the implied comparison with Aeneas emphasises the pretentiousness of the remark. Cf. Alsop 2. 2. 11. Folger reads *talia fando* for *funera tanta*.   61 Cf. Virg., *Geo.* 1. 325, 'boumque labores'.   70–1 I take this to refer to the defensive effect of earthworks.
79 Comets twice in Virgil: *Geo.* 1. 488; *Aen.* 10. 272.   82 N.b. no main caesura (a mistake, or striving for effect?).   88 Folger reads *Sacratosque* for *Se-*.   89 Cf. Virg., *Aen.* 8. 243, 'terra dehiscens'.

Flaventesque rubent segetes, stipulaeque volantes
Ardent, et crepitant victricibus hordea flammis.
B   Saevus ubique furor, regnatque per oppida
                                                luctus
95   Tristia, virgineisque choris gravis incubat horror.
       Undique diffugiunt tremulae per compita
                                                nymphae,
       Pulchra cohors, nec jam versato mollia fuso
       Pensa trahunt, agilique manu subtemina ducunt.
       Territa quin refugit subita formidine virgo,
100   Inque proci gremio jam primum blanda
                                                recumbit.
L   Crudeles flammae saltem violare puellas
       Parcite; non istis meruerunt ignibus uri.
S   Vidi ego per vicos trepidum genus omne
                                                virorum,
       Hinc natum exanimem deflet pater, inde
                                                maritus
105   Languentem tenet uxorem; charique colonus
       Spem gregis amissam luget, vacuosque labores.
B   Ingenti mox templa ruunt collapsa ruina,
       Relliquiaeque crucesque ardent, et sacra supellex
       Ignati, fumantque novis altaria flammis
110   Eversa, et juxta pinguis jacet hostia Flamen.
S   Hinc Monachum vidi abdentem timida ora
                                                cucullo,
       Signantemque manu pectus, tremulisque libelli
       Exciderant pavitanti, et sancta rosaria, dextris.
L   Mira refert. (B) Haud vera refert. (L) Ficta,
                                                omnia ficta;
115   Nam certum est nil tale meos memorare libellos.
S   Mene putas curare tuos ignare libellos?
       Improbus iste Auctor nunquam vel nomine
                                                tantum
       Me notat, aut narrat, quae gessi, ingentia bella.
B   Parcius ingenuis obtrudas ista memento.
S   Sed vidi majora; ambabus Belga diotam
121   Dum tollit palmis (heu lamentabile fatum!)
       Excutitur patera, et fusus liquor amnis in ipsum.
L   Heu! quantus lacrymarum imber jam proluit
                                                ora:
       Maluit hic altas rapuisse incendia turres,
125   Regalesque domos, quam sic violare Falernum.
B   Ut servet calicem, proprium caput offeret igni.
S   Quin aliud, dictuque oritur mirabile, monstrum:
       Helvetius graditur dum circum compita miles,

hear sighing hearts, and the groans of the dying. A soldier trembles, his weapon laid aside, and seeks to get into a dark cave or hidden place; yet straightaway the cannon breaks through his deep hiding-place, and the earth gapes to bury the frightened man, and greedily consumes him. (S) Straw is whirled helplessly with the force of the flame, and yellow crops turn red; burning stalks fly about, and the barley crackles under the victorious flames. (B; 94) There is savage fury everywhere, and grief reigns through the sad town, and horror lies heavily upon the choirs of maidens. The trembling girls, a beautiful group, run everywhere through the crossroads; nor do they now pull on soft wool as the spindle turns, and draw out threads with their agile hands. A maiden flees in sudden terror, and now lies complaisant for the first time in her admirer's lap. (L) Cruel flames, at least refrain from violating girls! They did not deserve to be burnt by these flames. (S) I have seen all kinds of frightened men throughout the town's districts; here a father weeps for his dead son, there a husband holds his dying wife; a farmer laments the loss of the best hopes of his dear flock, and his wasted labours. (B; 107) Now the churches fall, with huge destruction, and relics and crosses burn, and Ignatius' sacred stuff; the overturned altars smoke with new flames, and a fat priest lies next to his sacrifice. (S) Here have I seen a monk hiding his timid face in his hood, and beating his breast; the prayer-books and sacred rosaries had fallen from his trembling hands. (L) He tells us of marvels. (B) He's made it up. (L) Lies, all lies! For it is certain that my little books did not say anything about that. (S) Fool, do you think I care for your little books? That wretched author never even mentioned my name, or told of my great warlike deeds. (B) Remember not to press them too much in decent company. (S; 120) But I have seen greater things; while a Dutchman raised a wine-jar with both

---

92–3 Cf. Virg., *Geo.* 1. 85, 'stipulam . . . flammis'.   94 Folger reads *Saevit* (corrected from *Saevus*), perhaps rightly.   96 Cf. 'compita' at Virg., *Geo.* 2. 382; also 4 times in Horace's hexameters.   98 Cf. the refrain in Cat. 64: *subtemina* may remind us of fate.   106 Alluding to Virg., *Ecl.* 1. 15, 'spem gregis'.   107 Folger reads *collapsa ruant mox templa ruina*.   122 Folger reads *omnis et ipsa*.

Torva tuens, fumosque leves eructat in auras;
130 En! accensa volat fax, et stridente favilla
Excutit ore tubum; furit atrox flamma per ora,
Caesariemque plicatam urit, barbamque
                                                   micantem.
Hic furibundus alit vesano in corde dolorem,
Solamenque recusat, et ultro trajicit ense
135 Pectora, nec poterat barbae superesse crematae.
B   O frontis perfrictae hominem! non te pudet
                                                   horum?
Non haec Ferdinandus habet, nec talia fingit
Pagina Mandevilli. (L) An Mandevillius ille est,
Qui varios hominum mores describit, et urbes?
140 Hunc ego perlegi, miratus saepe virorum
Ingentesque pedes, summoque in vertice
                                                   ocellum.
Certe hic nil fingit. (S) Nec ego; tamen invidus
                                                   ille
Rumpitur invidia. (L) Et rumpatur. Nonne
                                                   aliud quid
Vidisti? nam audire juvat; fas visa referre.
S   Dum gladium femori, atque aurata monilia collo
146 Accingit, pyrioque refertas pulvere thecas
Circum humeros jactat Gallus, victorque
                                                   pererrat;
Scintilla exiguo suscepta foramine thecae
Sulphureum accendit globulum; furit illicet ignis,
150 Horrendumque tonat; rapitur sublimis in auras
Fumantes, nigroque levis volat aethere Gallus.
Mox cadit in terram discerptus membra; revulsus
Hic humerus jacet, inde caput, sparsumque
                                                   cerebrum;
Exta suumque petunt vel adhuc spirantia
                                                   truncum.
155 Vidi—(B) Quin parce auriculis; Tibi copia fandi
Sat concessa diu. Dum tot spectacula fingit,
Res ipsa est dubia, et minuunt mendacia verum.
L   Quales ille locos, et quae miracula vidit?
Quin vos ite leves nugae, chartaeque novorum
160 Repletae, et rapiant numerosa volumina
                                                   flammae.
Tu mihi solus eris liber, et tibi talia gesta
Narranti, totis gaudebo vacare diebus.
S   Ast ego, quam vellem praesentia cuncta tueri!
Quam cupio spectare iterum galeasque nitentes,
165 Armaque sanguinea, et fulgentes aere catervas,

hands, the cup was struck from them (alas, sad fate!), and the liquor poured in a river over himself. (L) Ah, what a storm of tears washed his face; he would have preferred the fire to have snatched high towers and royal palaces, rather than have wine suffer in this way. (B) To save his cup, he will offer his own head to the fire. (S) And another monstrous thing happened, amazing to relate: while a Swiss soldier walked about the crossroads with a fierce look, sending thin smoke up to the sky, a firebrand flew and with crackling embers knocked his pipe from his mouth; the dreadful flame ran over his face, and burnt his braided hair and glowing beard. Madness nourished his grief, and he refused any solace; he pierced his own breast with a sword, unable to survive the cremation of his beard. (B; 136) You smooth-faced man, are you not ashamed of these stories? Ferdinand has nothing like that, nor do Mandeville's pages invent such things. (L) Is that the Mandeville who decribes the varied manners and cities of mankind? I have read him through, and often been amazed at the men with huge feet, and an eye on the top of their heads. For sure, he invents nothing. (S) Nor do I; but this fellow is bursting with envy. (L) Let him burst. Did you see anything else? For it would be pleasant to hear it; it is right to tell what one has seen. (S; 145) While a Frenchman put a sword by his thigh, and golden trinkets round his neck, and took boxes filled with gunpowder on his shoulders, wandering about like a victor, a spark found a small hole in a box, and ignited a cartridge; immediately the fire runs wild, and explodes in a horrendous crash; the Frenchman is snatched into the smoking air, and flies lightly in the black sky. Soon he falls to earth, torn limb from limb; here lies an arm, torn off, here his head and scattered brain; his still-breathing innards seek their torso. I have seen—(B) But spare our ears! You have had quite enough chance to speak. While he makes up so many amazing sights,

---

133 Folger reads *vesanum* for -o.   135 Folger reads *barbae poterat*.   142 Folger reads *improbus* for *invidus*.
145 Cf. Virg., *Aen*. 1. 654, 'colloque monile'; *Aen*. 7. 278.   147 Folger reads *vicosque* for *victorque*.
151 Folger reads *volat levis*.   152 Cf. Virg., *Geo*. 4. 522 (of Bacchantes).   155 The diminutive 5 times in
Horace's hexameters.   160 *Repletae*: first syllable long, rare but classical (Lucr. 1. 394; Martial 7. 20. 19).

Oppidaque eversa, atque undantem pulvere
                                                    fumum.
B   Pergite vos Juvenes, et nobilis excitat ardor
     Ingentes animos: ite et per bella ruentes
     Igneus impellat vigor, atque interrita virtus:
170 Atque huc detulerit varios ubi fama labores,
     Magnanimosque ausus, celebrabunt praelia
                                                    Musae,
     Et vestra hoc olim resonabit facta Theatrum.

the fact itself is in doubt, and lies diminish the truth. (L; 158) What places, and what wonders did he see? Go, you light trifles and news-papers, and may your numerous volumes catch fire. You alone will be my book, and I shall be glad to spend all my days listening to you telling such tales. (S) As for me, how I would like to have been there to see it all! How I wish to see again the shining helmets, the bloodied arms, and the regiments shining with brass, the towns overthrown, and the billowing powder-smoke. (B; 167) Go on, young men; let noble enthusiasm excite your hearts; go on, and let fiery vigour and fearless courage drive you headlong through wars. And when fame has brought notice of your various labours and great daring hither, the Muses will celebrate your battles, and this Theatre will resound with your deeds.

Text: *Examen Poeticum Duplex, sive Musarum Anglicanarum Delectus alter* (London, 1698), pp. 76–86; *Musarum Angli-canarum Analecta* (1699) 2. 91–8; BL ms. Add. 34744, fo. 65–6; Folger ms. V. a. 232, pp. 127–31. *Date*: 1696; the speakers' names are: Charles Bertie (B), Richard Stewart (S), and Stephen Lennard (L), all of Christ Church; Encaenia programme, without text of poem: *Comitia Habita in Universitati Oxoniensi Apr. 16, 1696 in die gratulationis publicae pro salute regis Gulielmi*. This poem is discussed in Ch. 4. The Folger ms. is from the commonplace book of Henry Newcome (1650–1713: St Edmund Hall; rector of Middleton, Lancs.); many of its variant readings (not generally noted below) do not scan, or are not Latin, suggesting that Newcome is copying from an unclear original, or very carelessly. He calls the speakers 'A', 'B', and 'C', which implies that he did not know their names (or did not care).

3.9 HIRCOCERVUS

Esse quid hoc dicam? certe haec nil tale tulerunt
Secula; nec memini veteres cecinisse poetas:
Hoc nusquam Flaccum sublimi prodere cantu
Mens jussit congesta: Maro surgente Camoena
5   Arma virumque canit, sed non canit
                                                    Hircocervum.
Sed quid me impellit non convenientia Musae
Dicere? quid sacri canonem diffringere Smeti?
Nempe fugit doctas metri vox barbara leges,

Translation: 'The goat-stag'

What should I say this is? For sure, past ages have never borne anything like it. Nor do I recall the ancient poets singing of it. The full brain of Horace never bade him tell of this in his sublime song; Virgil sang in swelling verse of arms and the man, but he did not sing of the goat-stag! (6) But what impels me to speak of things that are not suited to poetry? Why should I break the rule of sacred Smetius?

167 Folger reads *excitet* for -*at*, which may well be right. publice proferebatur'.

172 N. in *Examen Poeticum Duplex*: 'Ubi hoc poema

1 Alluding to Ovid, *Amores* 1. 2. 1, 'Esse quid hoc dicam?'.
7 H. Smetius, whose *Prosodia* was a standard aid to composition. Cf. 2. 14. 1–2, n.

5 An obvious allusion to Virg., *Aen*. 1. 1.

Aversata artes placidisque inimica Camoenis.
10 Prodigium hoc variae (ut quondam Cretense)
                                        recondunt
Ambages Labyrinthi et inextricabilis error:
Ducenti quis caeca reget vestigia filo?
Quis dubio expediet latitans aenigmate
                                        monstrum?
Monstrum horrendum, informe, ingens, cui
                                Lumen ademptum.
15 Plaudite io! praesto est quod quaerimus: en
                                        vetulum istum
Contracta quem fronte habituque atque indice
                                        barba
Philosophum reor esse, illi nam plurima in ore
Scoti squallet imago, et docto pulvere sordet:
At mihi quaerenti biferi incunabula monstri
20 Hic quassans caput, et protenso pollice; inepte,
Quod quaeris sola est in mente; et plurima
                                        narrat
Ficticiae de incompossibilitate Chimaerae.
Nil tamen hoc; ultra quaerendum est; undique
                                        lustro
Ipsum hominem, qui, utcunque severus
                                dogmate, mores
25 Non aeque rigidos colit; at tegit aspera mentem
Vestis molliculam: en! hic est, quem quaero,
                                        biformis
Philosophus, vultu, scriptis, et moribus, omni ex
Parte sibi discors; quamque explicat ipse
                                        Chimaera est.
Quin tu, qui multo incedis spectabilis auro,
30 Et, Tyrio indutus distinctam murice vestem,
Philosophi pannos rimosaque pallia rides,
Profer, Cotta, caput: nitido tu in tramite passus
Metiris curtos, tu flabrum imitante galero
Ora foves, motosque reponis in ordine crines,
35 Idque unum exoptas nitidus bellusque videri.
Bellus homo es fateor; sed cur tibi lintea desunt?
Cur nulla interula est, quin callosam hispida
                                        pellem
Vestis arat? subtus squallentes aurea celat
Panniculos tunica; et fragranti in vertice spirant
40 Pastilli, tamen intus oles teterrimus hircum.

Surely this barbarous word flees from the learned laws of metre, rejecting art and hostile to the quiet Muses. The varied turnings of the labyrinth, and inextricable confusion, conceal this prodigy (like the Cretan minotaur); who will direct my blind footsteps with a guiding thread? Who will explain this monster that hides in a doubtful enigma? It is a horrible, formless, huge monster, from which light has been taken away. (15) Give your applause! Here is what we want: an old man whom by his furrowed brow and the indication of his dress and beard I reckon to be a philosopher, for he has the look of a medieval schoolman, and is filthy with bookish dust. But when I ask him about the origins of this twofold monster, he shakes his head and stretches a finger, saying 'that is a foolish question, what you ask is a figment of your imagination'. And then he tells me much about the impossibility of the fictitious chimaera. (23) But he says nothing of this; so we must seek further afield. I look everywhere for that man who, though he is strict in his philosophy, does not have such rigid habits, but has a gentle mind beneath a rough exterior. And here he is, the man I seek, a philosopher with two sides to him: in appearance, writings, and behaviour, he is quite inconsistent—he is himself that chimaera that he explains. (29) So bring yourself forward, Cotta, since you walk conspicuously adorned in gold and, clothed in a garment decorated with valuable purple dye, you laugh at a philosopher's shirt and ragged cloak; you trip along on your elegant way, you fan your face with your cap, replace those hairs that have been disturbed, and desire only one thing, to seem elegant and foppish. I admit that you're a foppish fellow; but why do you lack linen? Why is there no undergarment, to stop rough cloth rubbing your thick skin? A golden gown hides filthy little smalls, and while your face is perfumed,

11 Alluding to Virg., *Aen.* 6. 27.   12 Alluding to Cat. 64. 113, 'regens tenui vestigia filo'.   14 The entire line taken from Virg., *Aen.* 3. 658.   17 Unusual scansion of *philosophus*, with initial long (repeated 27); unclassical, but found in late antique authors (it will not otherwise fit in a hexameter).   18 Cf. Hor., *Carm.* 2. 1. 22, 'pulvere sordidos'. *Scoti*: Duns Scotus.   22 *Incompossibilitate*: humorously fills up the centre of the line (hence no main caesura); a lively, unclassical, expression, perhaps used to reflect the speaker's recondite pomposity; see R. E. Latham, *Revised Medieval Latin Word-List* (London, 1965).   32 Cotta appears at Juv. 5. 109; 7. 95; cf. [Alsop] 4. 15. 17.   40 Alluding to Hor., *Serm.* 1. 2. 27, 'pastillos . . . olet . . . hircum'.

At quae se dubiis pictura ostentat ocellis,
Semiferum referens hominem, formosa superne
Pectus et ora gerens, et membra decora juventae;
Altera post tergum species; at parte suprema
45 Exit equus, Dominique nates sua cauda flagellat?
Hic equus et praeceptor erat Centaurus Achilli,
Idem equitare docet juvenem, portatque
                            equitantem.
Huic similes hunc qui toties cecinere Poetae,
Descriptas variare vices, operumque colorem
50 Assueti, absimilesque sibi procudere versus.
Saepe levis tragicos audet Comoedia bombos,
Semideumque aggressa obtrudit pagina
                            monstrum:
Saepe cothurnatus tragicam subit histrio scenam
Torva tuens, tumidoque inflatus carmine buccas
55 Evomit ampullas, spumoso et turgidus ore
Fulminat, ingentique boatu verberat auras.
Spectator, metuis ne obtusae protinus aures
Surdescant, tremulumve ruat clamore theatrum.
Quin tu pone metum: huic totus mox excidit
                            ardor,
60 Mox insulsa humili jactat dicteria versu
Innocue, et sonitu verborum tinnit inani.
Nil tragicum spirat, lepidis sed hiantia circum
Ora modis distorquet, at iracundus Achilles
Thersites evadit, et exit comicus Heros.
65 Fingere nec mirum est adeo sibi dissona vates,
Nam gemino ostentat Parnassus vertice
                            monstrum,
Et primus monstravit equinas Pegasus alas.
Talis qui tumide resonanti ebuccinat aula
Jurgia causidicus, multum de jure boatu
70 Eructans patulo, talis venerabilis aurei
Imperii labor et luctus, curaeque nitentes,
Anxia majestas atque ingens pompa malorum.
Tale est Imperium, Sceptrum, Regnumque,
                          Forumque, et
Omne quod exit in Um, seu Graecum sive
                          Latinum.
75 Dicite, (nam nostis) Parnassia Numina, Musae
Dicite, quo titulo mirum hoc, quo nomine,
                          gaudet?
Parvum animal dubiae juxta confinia lucis
Egressum, vitans pariter noctemque diemque:

underneath you smell foul, like a goat. (41) But what picture appears before our doubtful eyes, showing a half-wild man, with an attractive face and breast, and a youth's elegant limbs, visible in front, but a quite different appearance behind his back, where in the end he turns into a horse, and where his tail whips its owner's buttocks? (46) This Centaur was the horse and teacher of Achilles; the same creature taught the young man to ride, and bore him when he rode. And like this creature are those poets who have so often sung of him, accustomed to vary their descriptions and the colour of their works, and to bring forth verses unlike themselves. (51) Often light comedy dares to affect tragic pomposity, and the page forces a half-divine monster upon us; often a buskined actor comes on to the tragic stage with fierce looks, his cheeks puffed up with swelling song, and disgorges bombast; he thunders from a full and spitting mouth, assailing the air with great shouts. (57) You, in the audience, are afraid that you will be struck deaf, and that the trembling theatre will collapse at the noise. But you should put aside your fear: soon all his fury dies, soon he harmlessly throws out his witless sentiments in humble strains, and jingles with empty verbiage. He breathes out nothing that is tragic, but distorts his gaping mouth with clever couplets: the angry Achilles leaves as a Thersites, and off goes the comic hero. (65) Nor is it to be wondered at that a poet can be so inconsistent, for Parnassus shows us a monster on its twin peaks, and Pegasus first demonstrated that a horse can have wings. Such also is the lawyer who trumpets his case out in an echoing hall, bringing up much about what is right with a shout, his mouth gaping; such is the venerable labour and grief of a golden empire, its glittering cares, its troubled majesty and huge train of evils. Such is empire, sceptre, kingdom, forum, and everything else that ends in '-um', whether Greek

42 Cf. Hor., *Ars Poet.* 4, 'formosa superne'.   45 Cf. Hor., *Serm.* 2. 7. 49.   46–7 Cf. Hor., *Epod.* 13. 11, etc.   49 Probably alluding to Hor., *Ars Poet.* 86, 'vices operumque colores'.   54 Cf. Virg., *Aen.* 6. 467; Hor., *Serm.* 1. 1. 21.   55 Cf. Hor., *Ars Poet.* 97, 'ampullas'; *Serm.* 1. 10. 36, 'turgidus'.   56 Cf. Virg., *Aen.* 5. 377.   62 Probably alluding to Hor., *Epist.* 2. 1. 166.   63–4 Possibly alluding to Juv. 8. 271, 'Thersitae . . . Achilles'. Cf. [Alsop] 4. 13.

Lenta huic porrigitur parvos membrana per artus,
80   Et tenui protensa inducit bracchia penna,
Qua suspensum agili fertur per inane volatu:
Quin nulla tegitur (nativa veste volucrum)
Pluma; ast incerti generis circumvolat erro,
Aut implumis avis, vestita aut bestia pennis.
85   Digna quidem exultet quae per palatia Regum,
Perfidaque in caeci splendescat Caesaris aula,
Et lectos inter proceres det jura Senator.
Multus ibi huic similis sublimi insignis honore
Transfuga, qui variis dubius pro partibus astat,
90   Omnibus infidus, mores cum tempore mutat;
Susceptam linquit causam, repetitque relictam;
Inque vices sumptam ponit, positamque resumit;
Omnibus ex aequo fit amicus, et omnibus hostis.
Sic plebs inconstans nunc huc nunc flectitur
                                          illuc,
95   Bellua multorum capitum: mutabile partes
Scinditur in varias neutrum modo mas modo
                                          vulgus.

Sic dubii generis sorex nunc incolit undam,
Nunc terram amphibius repetit, saltatque per
                                          herbas.
Cum tamen haec subeunt generis discrimina
                                          mentem;
100 Dicite Grammatici (nam vos narrare soletis
Plurima de vocum consensu) dicite discors
Quid sibi vult Genus hoc Epicoenum? foemina
                                          dici
Nec mas rite potest; sed repraesentat utrumque
Ex aequo sexum: certe Genus Hermaphroditum.
105 En! hilari multum Rhedycinae nota, popelli
Plurima in ore, vagae notissima bellua famae;
Cornutum vocitamus: ubi sed cornua? nusquam
Apparent: anne ille igitur (limacis ad instar)
Cornua pro libitu emittit retrahitque vicissim?
110 An nos cum populo seducti vera putamus
Cornua, quae lepidi finxerunt scommata vulgi?
Quicquid id est sane ignoro; metuo tamen olim
Ne me etiam populus surgentem in cornua
                                          monstret,
Et nota evadam ridentis fabula vulgi.
115 Hinc multa occurrunt animo portenta, supellex
Ashmoleae veneranda domus (ubi marmore
                                          manco
Fictos Heroum vultus, et ludicra monstra,

or Latin. (75) Tell us, Muses, goddesses of Parnassus, since you know it, by what title, what name this wonder rejoices to be called? It is a small animal that goes out in the twilight, avoiding both night and day; it has a tough membrane over its small limbs, and its stretched arms act as wings, by which it is supported as it flies with agility through the air. But it is covered by no feathers, as birds are; instead, it flies around as a truant of uncertain race, either a featherless bird, or a beast with wings. (85) It can boast indeed that it passes through the palaces of kings, and shines treacherously in a blind monarch's hall, and in Parliament gives laws amongst his peers. There is many a fugitive like him, who enjoys the greatest of honours, but who sits on the fence between different parties, unfaithful to all, and changing his manners to fit the times. He leaves the cause he has undertaken, and returns to the one he previously abandoned; and again in turn puts down what he took up, and resumes what he set aside; he is a friend to all alike, and to all an enemy. (94) Thus an inconstant people is turned now hither, now thither, a many-headed monster; the changeable mob is split into various parties, now masculine and now neutered. Thus a shrew of doubtful race lives amphibiously, now in the water, and now returning to the land, and leaping over the grass. (99) But since we are faced with this difficult decision, tell us, grammarians (for you are used to telling us much about how words agree), tell us what this discordant, epicene kind of thing wants to be called. It is not right to call it either masculine or feminine; instead, it represents both sexes equally—it is certainly hermaphrodite! (105) Look, here is a monster that is well known to laughing Oxford, much talked about by people far and wide: we called it the horned beast. But where are the horns? None are visible. Does he therefore, like a snail, send out his horns whenever he wishes, and then draw them in again? (110)

---

81 Cf. Virg., *Aen.* 12. 906, 'per inane volutus'.   87 Cf. Virg., *Aen.* 5. 758, 'dat iura'; 8. 670, etc.; 10. 213, 'lecti proceres'.   96 *Neutrum . . . vulgus*: alluding to Lilly's grammar (see n. on 3. 10. 7.; p. 14 in 1709 edn.).   113 Probably alluding to Virg., *Aen.* 10. 725, 'surgentem in cornua'.

Et luscus Phariam stupet antiquarius urnam)
Materies miranda et nostris digna Camoenis:
120 Scilicet haec rerum mixta ex farragine constant
Carmina, conveniuntque suo sibi dissona
                                        monstro.

Or should we be led by the people, and take as real those horns that have been invented in jest? I have no idea what the answer is; but I am worried that the people might at some time point me out as growing horns, and that I might end up as a tale for crowds to laugh at. (115) Hence many more portents come into my mind, the venerable junk in the Ashmolean Museum (where a one-eyed antiquarian can wonder at the imaginary faces of heroes in worn marble, and at ridiculous monsters, and Egyptian jars): this is an amazing subject, and one worthy of my Muse. Indeed, these songs are made from a confused mixture of things, and are dissonant enough to resemble the very monster they describe.

Text: *Musarum Anglicanarum Analecta* (1699) 2. 174–9. *Date*: unknown, *c*. 1693–8. This poem is discussed briefly in Ch. 4. There are parts of it that I do not fully understand: probably jokes about Oxford figures.

3.10 AD HYPODIDASCALUM QUENDAM PLAGOSUM, ALTERUM ORBILIUM, UT UXOREM DUCERET EPISTOLA HORTATIVA

Translation: 'A letter to a certain caning schoolmaster, a new Orbilius, encouraging him to take a wife'

Tu, commissa diu fuerat cui mascula pubes,
Accipe foeminei sexus, non amplius, unam;
Nec tamen aut dubiam cape, communemve
                                        duorum
Syllaba acuta sonans erit indubitabile signum
5   Unde genus noscas, signacula caetera sunt haec;
Sit personalis, perfecta modo, atque figura,
Propria quae maribus, nulloque heteroclita
                                        membro.
Sit flexu facilis; casus formanda per omnes;
Junctura gaudens, et crescens in genetivo:
10   Tum subito, quot habet partes oratio, discet,
Nec virgam metuet, quantumcunque arrigis,
                                        altam.

You, to whom masculine youth has long been entrusted, take one (and no more) from the feminine sex. Do not take one that is doubtful or common in gender. A sharp-sounding tone will be an unmistakable sign to judge her type, and these are the other little signs: (6) let her be personable, perfect in mood and form, appropriate for the male, and variable in no part. She should be flexible, able to be formed in all cases, enjoying links, and rising in the genitive; (10) then suddenly she will learn all the parts of speech: she will not fear your long rod, however stiff it may be. She will have her reward in the present, and in

1 Var.: *olim* for *diu*; *proles* for *pubes*.   2 Var.: *generis* for *sexus*.   3 Var.: *ne* for *nec*; *dubium* for *-am*.   4 Var.: *indubitabilis index* for *-ile signum*.   5 Var.: *sint* for *sunt*.   7 Line omitted in ms. D., *G.M.* 1735. *Propria Quae maribus* alludes to William Lilly's versified grammatical rules: these words were esp. familiar, as they began a section of the rules, which was referred to thus for convenience, as in *Propria Quae Maribus, Quae Genus, As in Praesenti . . . Construed* (London, n.d.). See, e.g., *Brevissima Institutio* (Oxford, 1709), p. 12 (one of many edns. Alsop and Nicol may have used).   11 Var.: *metuat virgam* for *virgam metuet*; *erigis* for *arr-*.

Aes in praesenti dabitur, post paulo futurum
Plurali in numero, modo sit concordia rerum,
Debita syntaxis, metrique prosodia mater.

15 Hanccine declinas? cave ne caruisse gerundis
Dicaris, quando hanc habeas licet usque supinam.
Scis bene nemo caret genitu; excipiesne teipsum
Regula ab hac? quid enim? an non substantivus
                                                    es, atque
Per te stare potes? fer opem bonus adjectivae

20 Quae nec stare potest, nec significare remote.
Sin bene conjungas bene conjungenda, magister,
Tertia prodibit persona; velut caro carnis,
Incerti generis, Bos, Fur, Sus, atque Sacerdos;
Quare age, et ad partes hanc omni mane vocato;

25 Haec tibi, ne metuas, bene respondebit et apte
Ici ictum, genui genitum, peperi quoque
                                                    partum.
Si quod erit regimen dubitas, memor esto,
                                                    dativum
Dandi verba regunt, genetivum verba monendi:
Sed quarto abstineas, et parcius utere sexto.

30 Propositi officium peragat conjunctio felix;
Quin hinc mitte procul quae disjunctiva
                                                    vocantur.
Haec te grammaticae docet ars; hinc nomina
                                                    cernas
Derivata tuo de nomine, nec tibi casu
Manca sit, aut numero defecta, propago, nec
                                                    occans

35 Syncope de medio tollat, quod epenthesis infert.

the future it will be plural, as long as the things agree, and there is due syntax, and prosody, the mother of metre. (15) Do you decline her? Beware lest you are said to lack gerunds, even when you have her supine. You know well that no one lacks generative power; will you except yourself from that rule? What then? Are you not substantive, and able to stand by yourself? Be good, and help an adjective who cannot stand by herself, nor be significant on her own. (21) But if, master, you conjoin well the things that need conjugation, the third person will come out, as flesh of your flesh; the following are of uncertain gender: ox, thief, pig, and priest. Come then, and may you call her each morning to those principal parts; she will respond well to you, never fear: 'I have struck a blow, I have caused a conception, and I have brought forth a birth'. If you doubt what the rule should be, remember that verbs of giving take the dative, verbs of warning the genitive. (29) But you should abstain from the fourth case, and use the sixth sparingly. Let happy conjunction perform the duty of a proposal; send far away anything that could be called disjunctive. This the art of grammar teaches you; hence you might see names derived from your own, nor should your offspring lack a case, or be defective in number, nor should omission cut from your midst, what insertion brings in.

Text: Gentleman's Magazine 5. 216 (Apr. 1735) and 41. 280 (June 1771); BL(a), pp. 133–4; BL(b), fo. 49ᵛ–50ʳ; BL ms. Add. 37684, fo. 39ᵛ–40; Nott. Pw V 150; ms. D, fo. 30ᵛ–31ʳ; Bodleian, ms. Rawl. lett. 31, fo. 144; Cambridge University Library, ms. Add. 7908/5/3. *Date:* unknown, after 1714 (on Nicol's actual wedding, or merely a rumour of his interest in sex?). The entire poem, discussed in Ch. 7, consists of risqué puns on grammatical terms, some (but not all) of which are readily understood in translation. Orbilius is a humorously harsh model (from Hor., *Epist.* 2. 1. 70–1; in fact, Nicol seems to have been a relatively mild schoolmaster). The text of this poem contains more variant readings than most Alsop mss. (marked as 'var.' below: I do not wish to burden the reader with a full list of mss. in

12 Var.: *As* for *Aes. Aes* is a witty combination of Lilly's 'as in praesenti . . . es in praesenti' (on verb forms: p. 53 in 1709 edn.).   13 Var.: *concordare facit res* for *sit . . . rerum.*   16 Var.: *Tu cunque* or *ubicunque* or *liceatque* for *licet usque.*   17 Var.: *genito; Excipiasque* for *-o . . . esne.*   18 Var.: *et qui* for *atque.*   20 Var.: *remota* for *-e.*23 Line omitted in *G.M.* 1735, etc.; Nott. reads *sive* for *atque.* More allusions to Lilly: 'non crescens genitivo, ceu caro carnis' (cf. lines 9, 22); 'bos . . . sacerdos' (pp. 13, 18 in 1709 edn.).   24 Var.: *omni tu* for *hanc omni.* 25 Var.: *dubites* for *metuas.*   28 *G.M.* 1771 reads *Genitiva . . . momendi* for *-um . . . mon-.*   29 The accusative and ablative cases; var.: *rarius* for *parcius* (Cambridge reads *Casu et nunquam*).   31 Var.: *Sed procul ista abeat* for *Quin . . . procul.*   32 Var.: *cernes* for *-as.*   34 Var.: *vel* for *nec; olli* for *occans. G.M.* 1771 has absurd *Mancusit* for *Manca sit.*

each case), suggesting that it circulated in several versions (none with obviously superior authority). *G.M.* 1771: 'The following Grammatical Cento was addressed by Dr [*sic*] Alsop to Dr Nichols . . . I do not remember to have seen it in your Magazine . . . ; a correct copy of it may therefore amuse your Readers.' Whether this text, which contains most of the variants listed below, is in fact more correct than *G.M.* 1735 is highly debatable (in lines 27 and 34 it is clearly worse; elsewhere, either reading makes good sense; the sender of 1771 clearly did not know of 1735, though it may have been the source of 'incorrect' mss. he did know).

3.11 AD EDVARDUM LUIDIUM IN PRIMUM ARCHAEOLOGIAE BRITANNICAE VOLUMEN

(Verses in Lhwyd's *Archaeologia*, 1707, under Keill's name)

Quo Te, Magne Brito, rudis indocilisque
            modorum
Carmine ego celebrare, aut quali dicere versu
Aggrediar doctos, Musa renuente, labores?
Non ego Cecropias urbes, non arva beatus
5   Itala lustravi, nec Classica rura viator
Calcavi pedibus: pauci, quos aequus Apollo
Dilexit, tanto laeti se munere jactant.
Scotia me genuit, rigidi terra aspera Fergi,
Terra antiqua, potens armis, tamen ubere gleba
10   Haud nimium felix; placidis sed amica Camoenis;
Utcunque Aoniae mihi non risere Sorores.
Rusticitas mihi prisca placet, salebrosaque vocum
Fragmina, quae patriis in montibus audiit olim
Cum proavis atavus, quique hos genuere
            parentes.
15   Te tellus, Arctoa polus qua sidere pascit,
Grata recognoscet; gelidique sub aetheris Ursa
Incolumis tibi stabit honos, serique nepotes
Cantabunt memores Luidi per secula nomen.

Translation: 'To Edward Lhwyd, on the first volume of his *Archaeologia Britannica*'

With what song, great Briton, when I am rough and untutored in poetry, shall I celebrate you, or in what verses should I attempt to tell of your learned labours, when the Muse refuses to help? I have not been happy enough to see Athenian cities, or the fields of Italy, nor have I trod the classic countryside as a traveller; only a few, whom even-handed Apollo has loved, can boast happily of such a boon. (8) Scotland bore me, the rough land of strict Fergus, an ancient land, powerful in war, though not too well provided with fertile soil; but it is friendly to the Muses. For all that, they have not smiled upon me: I prefer old-fashioned rusticity, and ragged fragments of words, which my distant ancestors, and their ancestors, heard on our native hills. (15) This land, where the pole feeds northern stars, will gladly acknowledge you; under the bear, where the sky is cold, your honour will be safe, and our distant grandsons will remember and sing the name of Lhwyd through the ages.

Text: among liminary verses to E. Lhuyd [*sic*], *Archaeologia Britannica* (Oxford, 1707), sig. c2ᵛ ('Haec cecini Amicitiae ergo/ J. Keill Scoto-Britannus'); Bodleian, ms. Ballard 29. 22 [fo. 55]. *Date*: 1707. This poem is discussed in Ch. 5 (with evidence for Alsop's authorship).

1 Alluding to Hor., *Carm.* 4. 6. 43 (as at Alsop 1. 4. 43, etc.)   9 Alluding to Virg., *Aen*. 1. 531, 3. 164, 'terra antiqua, potens armis, atque ubere glebae'.   14 Cf. Virg., *Aen*. 1. 606, 10. 597, 'genuere parentes'. 16 Possibly alluding to Virg., *Aen*. 8. 28 'gelidique sub aetheris axe'.   18 Probably alluding to Virg., *Aen*. 6. 235, 'per saecula nomen'.

Book 4
English Poems and Doubtful Latin Poems

English poems

4.1 DIALOGUE TO CHLORINDA

S   Cease, Chlorinda, cease to chide me,
When my passion I relate;
Why should kindness be denied me?
Why should love be paid with hate?

5   If the fruit of all my wishes
Must be, to be treated so;
What could you do more than this is
To your most outrageous foe?

C   Simple Strephon, cease complaining,
10   Talk no more of foolish love;
Think not e'er my heart to reign in,
Think not all you say can move.

Did I take delight to fetter
Thrice ten thousand slaves a day,
15   Thrice ten thousand times your betters
Gladly would my rule obey.

S   Strive not, fairest, to unbind me;
Let me keep my pleasing chain:
Charms that first to love inclin'd me,
20   Will for ever love maintain.

Would you send my heart a roving?
First to love I must forbear.
Would you have me cease from loving?
24   You must cease from being fair.

C   Strephon, leave to talk thus idly;
Let me hear of love no more:
You mistake Chlorinda widely,
Thus to teize her o'er and o'er.

Seek not her who still forbids you;
30   To some other tell your moan:
Choose where'er your fancy leads you,
Let Chlorinda but alone.

S   If Chlorinda still denies me
That which none but she can give,
35   Let the whole wide world despise me,
'Tis for her alone I live.

Grant me yet this one poor favour,
With this one request comply;
Let us each go on forever,
40   I to ask, and you deny.

C   Since, my Strephon, you so kind are,
All pretensions to resign;
Trust Chlorinda—You may find her
Less severe than you divine.

45   Strephon struck with joy beholds her,
Would have spoke, but knew not how;
But he look'd such things as told her
More than all his speech could do.

Text: R. Dodsley, ed., *Collection of Poems* (1748; p. nos. from 1782 edn.) 6. 256–9. These poems are discussed in Ch. 4.

4.2 TO CHLORINDA

See, Strephon, what unhappy fate
Does on thy fruitless passion wait,
 Adding to flame fresh fuel:
Rather than thou should'st favour find,
5 The kindest soul on earth's unkind,
 And the best nature cruel.

The goodness, which Chlorinda shews,
From mildness and good breeding
          flows,
 But must not love be styl'd:
10 Or else 'tis such as mothers try,
When, wearied with incessant cry,
 They still a froward child:

She with a graceful mien and air,
Genteely civil, yet severe,
15 Bids thee all hopes give o'er.

Friendship she offers, pure and free;
And who, with such a friend as she,
 Could want, or wish for more?

The cur that swam along the flood,
20 His mouth well fill'd with morsel good,
 (Too good for common cur!)
By visionary hopes betray'd,
Gaping to catch a fleeting shade,
 Lost what he held before.

25 Mark, Strephon, and apply this tale,
Lest love and friendship both should fail;
 Where then would be thy hope?
Of hope, quoth Strephon, talk not,
          friend;
And for applying—know, the end
30 Of every cur's a rope.

Text: Dodsley, *Collection* 6. 259–60

4.3 THE FABLE OF IXION, TO CHLORINDA

Ixion, as the poets tell us,
Was one of those pragmatic fellows,
Who claim a right to kiss the hand
Of the best lady in the land;
5 Demonstrating, by dint of reason,
That impudence in love's no treason.
He let his fancy soar much higher;
And ventur'd boldly to aspire
To Juno's high and mighty grace,
10 And woo'd the goddess face to face.
What mortal e'er had whims so odd,
To think of cuckolding a God?
For she was both Jove's wife and sister,
And yet the rascal would have kiss'd her.
15 How he got up to heaven's high palace,
Not one of all the poets tell us;
It must be therefore understood
That he got up which way he could.
Nor is it, that I know, recorded,

20 How bows were made, and speeches
          worded;
So, leaving this to each one's guess,
I'll only tell you the success.
But first I stop awhile to shew
What happen'd lately here below.
25 Chlorinda, who beyond compare
Of all the fair ones is most fair;
Chlorinda, by the Gods design'd
To be the pattern of her kind,
With every charm of face and mind;
30 Glanc'd lightning from her eyes so blue,
And shot poor Strephon through and
          through.
He, over head and ears her lover,
Try'd all the ways he could to move her;
He sigh'd, and vow'd, and pray'd, and
          cry'd,
35 And did a thousand things beside:

She let him sigh, and pray, and cry on—
But now hear more about Ixion.
The Goddess, proud (as folks report
                       her),
Disdain'd that mortal wight should
                      court her,
40 And yet she chose the fool to flatter,
To make him fancy some great matter,
And hope in time he might get at her;
Grac'd him with now and then a smile,
But inly scorn'd him all the while;
45 Resolv'd at last a trick to shew him,
Seeming to yield, and so undo him.
Now which way, do you think, she took?
(For do't she would by hook or crook):
Why, thus I find it in my book.
50 She call'd a pretty painted cloud,
The brightest of the wand'ring crowd;
For she, you know, is queen o'th'air,
And all the clouds and vapours there
Governs at will, by nod or summons,
55 As Walpole does the house of commons.
This cloud which came to her
                 stark-naked,
She dress'd as fine as hands could make
                 it.
For her own wardrobe out she brought
Whate'er was dainty, wove or wrought;
60 A smock which Pallas spun and gave
                 her,
Once on a time to gain her favour;
A gown that ha'n't on earth its fellow,
Of finest blue, and lin'd with yellow,
Fit for a goddess to appear in,
65 And not a pin the worse for wearing;
A quilted petticoat beside,
With whalebone hoop six fathom wide;

With these she deck'd the cloud, d'ye
                 see?
As like herself, as like could be:
70 So like, that could not I or you know
Which was the cloud, and which was
                 Juno.
Thus dress'd she sent it to the villain,
To let him act his wicked will on:
Then laugh'd at the poor fool aloud,
75 Who for a goddess grasp'd a cloud.
This, you will say, was well done on her
T'expose the tempter of her honour—
But more of him you need not hear;
Only to Strephon lend an ear.
80 He never entertain'd one thought
With which a goddess could find fault;
His spotless love might be forgiven
By every saint in earth and heaven.
Juno herself, though nice and haughty,
85 Would not have judg'd his passion
                 naughty.
All this Chlorinda's self confess'd,
And own'd his flame was pure and
                 chaste,
Read what his teeming Muse brought
                 forth,
And prais'd it far beyond its worth:
90 Mildly receiv'd his fond address,
And only blam'd his love's excess:
Yet she, so good, so sweet, so smiling,
So full of truth, so unbeguiling,
One way or other still devis'd
95 To let him see he was despis'd:
And when he plum'd, and grew most
                 proud,
All was a vapour, all a cloud.

Text: Dodsley, *Collection* 6. 261–4. This poem is discussed in detail in Ch. 4; cf. also 4. 16

4.4 A TALE, TO CHLORINDA

Dame Venus, a daughter of Jove's,
And amongst all his daughters most fair,

Lost, it seems, to'ther day the two doves,
That wafted her car through the air.

5   The dame made a heavy sad rout,
     Ran about heav'n and earth to condole
         'em;
    And sought high and low to find out,
     Where the biddyes were stray'd, or who
                      stole 'em.

    To the god, who the stragglers should meet,
10   She promis'd most tempting fine pay,
    Six kisses than honey more sweet,
    And a seventh far sweeter than they.

    The proposal no sooner was made,
    But it put all the Gods in a flame;
15   For who would not give all he had
    To be kiss'd by so dainty a dame?

    To Cyprus, to Paphos, they run,
    Where the Goddess oft us'd to retire;
    Some rode round the world with the sun,
20   And search'd every country and shire.

    But with all their hard running and riding,
    Not a God of 'em claim'd the reward;
    For no one could tell tale or tiding,
    If the doves were alive or were starv'd.

25   At last the sly shooter of men,
    Young Cupid (I beg the God's pardon),
    Mamma, your blue birds I have seen
    In a certain terrestrial garden.

    Where, where, my dear child, quickly shew,
30   Quoth the dame, almost out of her wits:
    Do but go to Chlorinda's, says Cu,
    And you'll find 'em in the shape of pewits.

    Is it she that hath done me this wrong?
    Full well I know her, and her arts;
35   She has follow'd the thieving trade long,
    But I thought she dealt only in hearts.

    I shall soon make her know, so I shall —
    And with that to Jove's palace she run,
    And began like a bedlam to bawl,
40   I am cheated, I am robb'd, I'm undone.

    Chlorinda, whom none can approach
    Without losing his heart or his senses,
    Has stol'n the two doves from my coach,
    And now flaunts it at Venus' expences.

45   She has chang'd the poor things to pewits,
    And keeps 'em like ord'nary fowls:
    So, when she robs men of their wits,
    She turns 'em to asses or owls.

    I could tell you of many a hundred
50   Of figure, high station, and means,
    Whom she without mercy has plunder'd,
    Ever since she came into her teens.

    But her thefts upon earth I'd have borne,
    Or have let 'em all pass for mere fable;
55   But nothing will now serve her turn,
    But the doves out of Venus's stable.

    Is it fit, let your mightyship say,
    That I, like some pityful flirt,
    Should tarry within doors all day,
60   Or else trudge it afoot in the dirt?

    Is it fit that a mortal should trample
    On me, who am styl'd queen of beauty?
    O make her, great Jove, an example,
    And teach Nimble-fingers her duty.

65   Sir Jove, when he heard her thus rage,
    For all his great gravity, smil'd;
    And then, like a judge wise and sage,
    He began in terms sober and mild.

    Learn, daughter, to bridle your tongue,
70   Forbear to traduce with your prattle
    The fair, who has done you no wrong,
    And scorns to purloin goods and chattel.

    She needs neither gewgaw, nor trinket,
    To carry the world all before her;
75   Her deserts, I would have you to think it,
    Are enough to make all men adore her.

    Your doves are elop'd, I confess,
    And chuse with Chlorinda to dwell;
    But blame not the lady for this;
80   For sure 'tis no crime to excel.

    As for them, I applaud their high aims;
    Having serv'd from the time of their birth
    The fairest of heavenly dames,
    They would now serve the fairest on earth.

Text: Dodsley, *Collection* 6. 265–8.

4.5 DR DOLBEN'S WEDDING SONG

Come all ye Tuneful Sisters, bring
Each Warbling voice, each Vocal String;
   'Tis Strephon bids attend—
Strephon, the Joy of Ev'ry heart,
5   Strephon, adorn'd with ev'ry Art,
     To ev'ry art a friend.

Phoebus, thou God of health and Song,
Preside in the melodious throng
   And Grace the Genial Feast.

10 Let the sweet Female Treble Joyn
The Manly Bass, and both combine
   To charm each am'rous breast.

Hail to Elisa, Chast and fair,
Hail to the loving lovely pair,
15   Guard 'em ye pow'rs above;
In all life's long and Happy Scene
Let naught be heard, let naught be seen
   But Harmony and Love.

Text: Royal College of Music, ms. 995, fo. 119^v–131^v. *Date*: 1720.

4.6 EPISTLE TO THE REV. SIR JOHN DOLBEN

Sir John or Doctor, chuse you whether;
Or Friend, a better name than either:
Had it pleas'd dame or madam Fortune,
T' have thrown me in some place
                  opportune,
5   To see, and hear, and talk with you
And Wake sometimes an hour or two;
Or say it hours were six or seven,
(For Will can joke from morn till even)
No need had been to pump for metre,
10 To furnish out an idle letter;
For then, instead of diting poesy,
I might have prated *viva voce*.
Then haply had the way between 's
Been miles and way-bits under teens,
15 I might have view'd fair Finedon's tow'rs,
Its walks, and avenues, and bow'rs,
The sweet abode of you and yours;
The noble furniture have seen,
The living furniture I mean;
20 For what is all the costly traffick,
That comes from India, Spain, or Afric,
Compar'd to sprightly wit and beauty,
That always pleasant is and new t' you?
Then had I seen in ev'ry kind,
25 Such beauties both of face and mind,

As oft are read of in romances,
But, save at Finedon, hardly found
On English or un-English ground.
Then had I—but I cry you mercy,
30 For I must be content with hearsay,
Nor hope to see such sights as there are,
Unless I liv'd a great deal nearer.
But miles there are twenty and thirty,
Both woundy long and plaguy dirty,
35 Which I, the laziest thing alive,
Could hardly pass in days twice five.
Would Pegasus let me bestride him,
And teach me skill, when up, to ride
                  him;
Or had I wings well glu'd and corded,
40 Better than Icarus or Ford had,
Away I'd fly, nor stay to bait,
Until I knock'd at Finedon gate.
Then wo be to the beef and claret,
For by my faith I would not spare it;
45 Nor should I, once possession taken,
Contrive or care to save your bacon.
But what a sot am I to think,
Of such poor things as meat and drink
And not revolve within my mind
50 The fairest of the fairest kind!

Since to the fair with heart most
                    fervent,
I vow myself an humble servant.
How should I joy to see the lady
That makes three sweet ones call you
                    dady!
55 To see those pretty heirs apparent
Trip it along like fairies errant!
To view those little representers
Surpassing nicest skill of painters,
Resembling either parent's face,
60 The Digby and the Dolben race;
To read in ev'ry line and feature,
Avi avorum wrought by nature.
These images, dear sir, I find

65 So strongly painted in my mind,
That all the while I tell my story,
Methinks I see 'em full before me.
Thus distant half a hundred miles,
I see their little play and smiles,
70 While, as the absent lover's use is,
Fancy supplies what fate refuses.
You see, sir, how this long epistle,
Just like young master's bell and whistle,
Has nothing else to recommend it,
But jingling sound, and yet I send it;
75 For where no better can be had,
Respect is shewn, tho' fare be bad.
Thus having tir'd myself and you, sir,
I kiss your hands, and so adieu, Sir.

Text: Gentleman's Magazine 8. 427 (Aug. 1738); Pearch, ed., *Continuation of Dodsley's Collection* (1770) 2. 294. Bodleian, ms. Ballard 47, fo. 52. *Date*: 8 March 1725 (at Brightwell): 1724/5 or 1725/6?

4.7 FROST AND SNOW

Poor Snow's dissolv'd, and six foot deep he lies,
Tho' wrapt in wool, yet is he cold as Ice.
But Frost is Hail, and Snow's not mist we trust
For Snow-broth is Frosts due, now Snow is dust.
5 Yet Frost remember, that thy Thaw is nigh
And Frost and Snow in the same dyke shall lie;
Then passengers shall cry when this they're told,
Snow broke the Ice, Frost caught a deadly cold.

Text: Bodleian, ms. Ballard 19. 10 [fo. 23ᵛ]. *Date*: unknown. William Brome asked Alsop to write a humorous epitaph on a Mr Frost and Mr Snow; quoted in a letter to Rawlins, 5 Apr. 1735. John Snow's heir was William Frost (Ballard 19. 11 [fo. 26]); a Mr Snow is mentioned at Bodleian, ms. Tanner 30. 114. In line 4, n.b. *Due* punning on 'dew'.

Doubtful Latin poems

4.8 VESEY

O recens divae Idaliae Sacerdos,
O amans Bacchi Cererisque, Iernae
Quem vigor surae validus mariti in
    Munia firmat;
5 Si brevem conjux satiata lusu
Languido indulget requiem veretro,

Translation: 'Vesey'

New priest of Venus, lover of Bacchus and Ceres, the strong vigour of an Irish leg strengthens you for a husband's duties. If your wife, satiated with languid play, allows your equipment to have a brief rest, listen candidly to the advice of your

Caelibes quid te moneant amici,
    Candidus audi.
Mitte tam crebros iterare saltus
10 Passerum ritu, coitu diurno
Nil magis solvit latera et salacis
    Robora nervi.
Sit satis sponsam tacite rogantem
Nocte complecti semel ante somnum,
15 Nec nocet dulces iterum experiri
    Mane labores.
Nonne abortivis uterum resolvit
Saepius Thomae nimium arrigentis
Uxor, eludens male spem cubilis
20   Praecoce partu?
Rectius multo tibi Percivallus
Vester exemplum praeit; hic peric'li
Gnarus, assultu nimio extimescit
    Findere sponsam;
25 Ergo septenis semel in diebus
Conjugem concha patula supinam
Permolit segni nate, nec puellae
    Aequus ad ictus:
Quin catus caeli faciem vicesque
30 Cynthiae explorat, metuens coire,
Spondeant laetam nisi cum parenti
    Sydera prolem.
Hujus exemplo monitus duellum
Rarius tentes; satur est et ohe
35 Cunnus exclamat, superest furenti
    Nec locus hastae.
Sin moras inguen tumidum recuset,
Ne sit ancillae tibi amor pudori,
Quae tenello olim domino admovebit
40   Ubera nutrix.

bachelor friends. (9) Stop leaping on her so often, like sparrows do: nothing reduces the strength of your organ as much as daytime intercourse. Let it be enough to embrace your wife, when she quietly asks for it, once in the night, before going to sleep; and it does no harm to repeat that sweet labour in the morning. (17) Surely Thomas' wife is going to miscarry, sadly deceiving the hopes of her bed with a premature birth, if he becomes too erect any more often? (21) Your friend Percival offers you a much better example; he knows the danger, and fears to split his wife with too much leaping; therefore once a week he rubs her, buttocks slack, as she lies with an open c*nt, nor is he now fit for the struggle with a girl. (29) Still, he is clever at exploring the appearance and cycle of the moon, fearing to copulate unless the stars promise that the offspring will be as happy as their father. (33) Be advised by his example, and attempt the struggle less often; the c*nt exclaims that it's had quite enough, and there is no place left for your furious spear. But if your swelling pr*ck refuses to delay, do not be ashamed of loving a servant girl, who will look after her tender little master as a splendid nurse.

Text: BL(a), p. 137 (attribution to Alsop deleted). Date: unknown. This poem is discussed in Ch. 5.

18 ms. n.: 'D[omi]nus Thomas Vesey Bar[onet]tus nec non apud Iernos Episcopi' [*sic*: -us?].   27–8 Presumably a lively *puella* (a whore, or former girlfriend) is now too much for him.   34 Cf. 2. 12. 48, n.   38 Alluding to Hor., *Carm.* 2. 4. 1.

4.9 ODE TO AN UNKNOWN ADDRESSEE

O amans Veri Historicus, faceti
Hospes o Keili, cohibe querelas
Nec tibi aeternos moveat dolores
    Uxor adempta.
5 Illa Leightonam Tibi quae recenti
Conjugi avulsit Libitina, castae
Invidens taedae nimium frequenter
    Ludit amantes.
Flevit Hannesus semel et secundo
10 Nuptias, fato superante, raptas;
Interim vita fruitur, sepulchro
    Dives amico.
Flevit uxores (modo fama verax)
Bobbius binas tumulo repostas
15 Laetior Browno, nisi quod supersit
    Tertia sospes.
Tu tamen maerens nimis inquietus
Ingemis noctu, neque lux revortens
Eximit planctus, viduive fallit
20   Taedia lecti.
Parce quin saevo dare Te dolori,
Parce jam longis nimium querelis;
I, graves curas sapiens, ut olim,
    Pelle Falerno.
25 Sin torus cunni vacuus benignos
Abnegat somnos, age dic olenti
Keilus e lustro tibi permolendam
    Afferat Hentham.
Hic supinandae quoties puellae
30 Arrigit, quovis facilem Corinnam
Fornice exquirit tumidique placat
    Inguinis iram.
Si tamen Bacchus, potiorque pellex
Nesciant maestum recreare pectus
35 Conjuge abrepta, minuat superstes
    Dos tibi curas.

Translation

    Truth-loving historian, guest of witty Keill, restrain your complaints, and let not the loss of your wife cause eternal grief. (5) The same fate that tore Leighton from you, her new husband, has all too often deceived lovers, being envious of their chaste marriages. (9) Hannes has twice wept for the marriages snatched from him, defeated by fate; meanwhile he enjoys life, rich in the friendship of the tomb. (13) Bobby (if reports are true) has wept for two wives placed in the tomb, and would be happier than Brown, were the third not still living. (17) You, however, lament too much, groaning through sleepless nights; nor does the returning dawn stop your lamentation, or mitigate the tedium of a widower's bed. (21) Stop giving yourself over to savage grief; stop your wailing, which has now gone on for too long; go on, be wise enough to chase away serious cares, as before, with wine. (25) If the lack of c★nt on your bed prevents you from sleeping, tell Keill to fetch Henth [?] from the smelly whore-house for you to screw. Whenever that man is stiff enough to lay a girl on her back, he seeks out a willing moll from some brothel or other, and placates the anger of his swelling pr★ck. (33) But if the wine-god, or that more powerful inducement, a whore, cannot refresh your sad heart when your wife has been snatched away, then let her surviving dowry reduce your cares.

Text: Nott. Pw V 151/6. *Date*: unknown. Ms. entitled 'Alsop ad . . .' (the gap implying that the copyist did not know the addressee's name); this must make the attribution more uncertain. The mention of Keill's name links the poem to

---

2 For Keill, see 2. 2, and Ch. 6.   3 Cf. 2. 9. 5; 2. 19. 6; 2. 23. 3, 'semel et secundo'.   5 Presumably the addressee's late wife was a member of the Leighton family.   9 Hannes: probably related to the Christ Church poet (discussed at the end of Ch. 2).   13 Cf. 1. 10. 13, 'fama verax'.   14 *Bobbius* looks like a nickname ('Bobby').   28 *Hentham*: presumably an Oxford whore.   33 Cf. Hor., *Epist.* 1. 5. 27; Alsop 2. 26. 21 (the similar expression may be a further argument for his authorship).

Alsop's circle, but another member of the circle may have written it (perhaps addressing it to Alsop himself—though the name in line 5 makes that unlikely). It should be possible to identify the addressee, but I have not as yet been able to do so. (I suspect Edward Lhwyd may be a possible candidate: cf. 3. 11 and Ch. 5.)

4.10 IN OBITUM GULIELMI,
DUCIS GLOCESTRIAE
(from Oxford *Exequiae*, 1700; under
the name of Sir Bourchier Wrey)

Translation: 'On the death of William, Duke of Gloucester'

Labentis aevi dum peragit vices
Extremus ordo: dum renovat choros
    Romana pubes, Saeculares
        Dum redeunt Italis triumphi:
5 Te, Chare Princeps, murmure flebili
Lugent Britanni, Te lachrymabili
    Versu requirunt; instruitque
        Funeream Rhedycina Pompam.
Quam mallet o! (si sic voluit Deus)
10 Non indecoro carmine bellicos
    Ornasse victoris triumphos
        Et capiti imposuisse sertum!
Narrare vellet pube Britannica
Gentes subactas, signaque barbaris
15   Direpta Mauris, et tremendas
        Trans Ligerim Rhodanumque
                turmas.
His nempe gestis agmine parvulo
Praelusit olim ludicra bellicae
    Imago pompae, cuspidisque
20   Innocuae puerilis ictus.
Illic Namurci vidimus aemulas
Nutare turres, parvaque dirui
    Munimina; effictoque rivo
        Boyniacas trepidare lymphas.
25 Quin o! vetabat Parca malignior
Contendere ultra. Scuta trahunt humi
    Moesti sodales, et perosas
        Abjiciunt humeris pharetras.
Te turba plorant aemula virgines,
30 Olim parantes illecebras Tibi;
    Curamque formae jam relinquunt,
        Atque minus cupiunt placere.
At quis dolorem Matris et impetum
Non exprimendum pinget? ut anxium

While the last order of the passing century changes, while the Roman youth renews its choruses, while the jubilee celebrations return to Italy, the Britons mourn you, dear prince, with a tearful murmur, and lament your absence in tear-stained verse; and Oxford makes ready its funeral pomp. (9) How much would it prefer, if God had so wished, to have celebrated your warlike triumphs with fitting song, and placed a wreath on your head! It would wish to tell of the peoples conquered by British youth, and standards snatched from the barbarian Moors, and your squadrons spreading terror beyond the Loire and Rhone. (17) For sure, the mock image of warlike pomp, with a tiny army and the childish blow of a harmless spear, once rehearsed these deeds. There we saw towers wobbling, to rival Namur, and small fortifications destroyed; and the waters of the Boyne trembled, in a make-believe river. (25) But malevolent fate forbade you to enter any further contests. Your sad companions drag their shields on the ground, and throw their quivers, now hated, from their shoulders. The virgins lament you, a crowd of rivals; once they prepared their snares for you, now they cease to care about their appearance, and have less desire to please. (33) But who will depict the grief of your mother, and its inexpressible force? How dreadful care ate at her anxious breast! How horror agitated her

35   Exedit atrox cura pectus!
            Ut furiis agitavit horror!
        Haec mentis impos dilacerat genas
        Tunditque pectus; murmura lachrymis
            Immiscet, et singultat eheu!
40   Atque cupit comes ire nato.
        Quin pone tandem tristitiae modum,
        Dilecta Princeps; hic populus rogat
            Voto frequenti, publicoque
            Ore preces iterat Senatus:
45   En! spondet omen blandus Amor toro
        Laetum jugali, progeniem novam;
            Tu nasciturae parce proli,
            Atque fove Ascanium futurum.
        Hic ludibundus Matris ab ubere
50   Pendebit Infans, tangere mox Patris
            Audebit hastam: atque ore balbo
            Garriet Auriaci triumphos.
        Mox et virili robore firmior
        Fraterna pugnax instruet agmina;
55   Hunc forte miles non pudendus
            Trans gelidum comitabor Istrum.

with madness! Losing control of herself, she tears her cheeks and beats her breast; she mixes murmurs with tears, and sighs aloud, and wishes to perish along with her son. (41) Beloved princess, finally set a limit for your sorrow; this your people asks of you, in our frequent prayers, and Parliament repeats these prayers with its public voice. Look! soft love gives a happy omen to your marriage bed—a new off-spring; you should be kind to the child that is about to be born, and look after your future Ascanius. (49) This playful infant will hang from his mother's breast, and will soon dare to touch his father's spear; and he will chatter with stammering voice of the triumphs of the Prince of Orange. Soon, having attained the strength of manhood, he will draw up his brother's columns as a martial leader; perhaps I myself, no contemptible soldier, shall accompany him across the chill Danube.

Text: *Exequiae Desideratissimo Principi Gulielmo Glocestriae Duci ab Oxoniensi Academia solutae* (Oxford, 1700). Date: 1700. This poem (and its attribution to Alsop) is discussed in Ch. 9.

4.11 ODE (untitled: set to music at 1706 ENCAENIA)

Translation

Carminum praeses citharaeque Clio,
Sive percussis fidibus canendo,
Voce seu mavis, bene praeparatum
    Dic age Carmen.
5   Qualibet lato spatiare coelo,
    Qualibet currum vaga per Olympi
    Sidera inflectas, retege involuta
        Nubibus ora.
    Turturum fraenans Cytherea bigas,
10 Quam juvat myrto caput impedire,
    Gratias Tecum facilesque Divos

Clio, Muse of song and the lyre, whether you prefer to sing with instrumental accompaniment, or voice alone, come and sing your well-prepared song. Wherever you go in the wide heavens, wherever you drive your chariot through Heaven's wandering stars, reveal your cloud-covered face. (9) Reining in your chariot drawn by doves, Venus, fond of myrtle-garlands, bring the Graces with you, and the Loves, those gods of easy virtue. And you, Apollo, famous for

3 Cf. Hor., *Carm.* 3. 4. 3, 'seu voce . . . mavis'.

6 N.b. false quantity, *per* long before a vowel.

Transfer amores.
Tuque lethali celebris pharetra
Phoebe, Pythone edomito superbum
15 Pone nunc arcum, fidibusque nervos
    Adde canoros.
O dies felix, redeunte seclo,
Artium sedis memor institutae,
Cura quam Phoebi decorat Viadri
20   Accola pubes!
Dextera Pallas quatiens Olivam
Advenit; Pallas studiis juventae
Praesidet, gaudens sociare Musas
    Anglo-Borussas.
25 Hic amor longum maneat per aevum,
Hic et ad seros veniat nepotes;
Sorte communi rata sint utrique
    Otia genti.
Isidis donec vitreas ad undas
30 Excolis doctas, Rhedycina, Musas;
Nulla dilectum tibi Francofurtum
    Secla tacebunt.

your fatal quiver, set aside your proud bow, with which you subdued the Python, and add tuneful strings to your lyre. (17) O happy day, when the centenary of that seat of the arts returns, which the young men dwelling by the Oder adorn, under Phoebus' protection. Athena comes, waving an olive branch in her right hand; Athena presides over the studies of youth, rejoicing in the association of British and Prussian Muses. (25) Let this love last for a long age, let it continue as far as our distant descendants; let the leisure of both peoples be ratified as linked in a common lot. While you cultivate the learned Muses, Oxford, beside the glassy waters of the Thames, no century will fail to declare that Frankfurt is dear to you.

Text: Academiae Francofurtanae ad Viadrum Encaenia Secularia (Oxford, 1706); *Musarum Anglicanarum Analecta* 3 (1717), pp. 39–40; BL(a); cf. related versions, Christ Church mss. 618 and 621. *Date*: This version, 1706; performed several times in different versions, *c.* 1700–6 (see Trowles, thesis cited in note to 3. 6; discussed in Ch. 4); cf. n. on the Encaenia proceedings at Bodleian, ms. Rawl. J. fol. 22, fo. 67–9 (with a copy of printed text, fo. 70–91).

4.12 CARMEN SAECULARE (1706 ENCAENIA)

Translation

M Diva, quam magni cerebrum Tonantis
    Matris expertem peperit, ferocis
    Arbitram belli, simul et tuendis
        Artibus aptam;
5 Seu Deos inter, Superumque coetus
    Proximos Patri capias honores;
    Seu favens terris dare jura malis
        Cecropis Urbi;
    Huc age auratum, Dea, flecte currum,
10 Huc vocata adsis; placidoque vultu

(M) Goddess, whom the mighty Thunderer's brain bore without any mother, as an arbiter of fierce war, and at the same time as a fit protector of the arts, whether you take the nearest place of honour to your father amongst the gods assembled in heaven, or prefer to show favour to the earth by giving laws to Athens, come, goddess, and turn your golden chariot hither; come hither when you are called, and look kindly upon the

15–16 Cf. Hor., *Carm.* 1. 12. 11, 'fidibus canoris'.
10 Cf. Hor., *Carm.* 3. 22. 3; *Epod.* 5. 5.

29 Cf. Virg., *Aen.* 7. 759, 'vitrea . . . unda'.

Publicos ludos tibi jam parantem
    Respice pubem.
H Te juventuti facilem precatur,
    Te vocat Musis bene notus Isis;
15 Caeteros praeter fluvios amicus
    Vatibus Isis.
M Te suis poscunt studiis benignam,
    Te die festo memorant Borussi;
    Qua sacer Musas recreat perenni
20   Amne Viadrus.
H Tu probos mores animosque castos,
    Virgo, des pubi tibi supplicanti;
    Da tuae pubi ingenium, otiumque et
    Laudis abunde.
M Ut juvat festos celebrare ludos!
26 Quos prius nemo aut hodie superstes
    Vidit, aut posthac, referente Phaebo
    Saecla, videbit!
    Cerne festivi varium triumphi
30 Ordinem, cerne ut juvenes patresque
    Docta festinant cumulare multo Al-
    taria dono.
H Hic lyra doctus fidiumque chordis,
    Aptat argutam citharae Thaliam;
35 Ille sermones metrico solutos
    Compede fundit.
M Abditos alter penetrat recessus,
    Quidque Natura efficiat; quid infra,
    Quid supra terras agitet, sagaci
40   Mente revolvit.
H Orbis extremos, ope linearum,
    Terminos signat; datur intueri
    Moenia, atque urbes, fluviosque, et agros,
    Indice charta.
M Solis Errores docet hic, vagaeque
46 Tramitem Lunae; referatque gnarus
    Quid ferant laetum, grave quid minentur
    Sidera terris.
H Quid per immensi dubitamus ultra
50 Aequoris tractus volitare, notis
    Siderum ducti auspiciis, et acti
    Remige vento?

youths who are now preparing public games for you. (H; 13) The Thames, well known to the Muses, calls you, praying to you as a patron of youth; the Thames is more friendly to poets than any other river. (M) The Prussians ask for you, since you are kind to their studies, and remember you on this festival day, where the sacred Oder refreshes the Muses with its everlasting stream. (H; 21) Virgin goddess, give virtuous manners and chaste hearts to the young men who pray to you; give your young men intelligence, leisure, and an abundance of praise. (M) How pleasant it is to celebrate the festival games, which no one has seen before, and which no one alive today will live to see return again, as Phoebus brings round another centenary! Look at the varied order of the festival triumph; see how the young men and their elders hurry to pile learned altars with many gifts. (H; 33) One of them, learned in music, applies the tuneful Muse to the lyre; another pours out speech that is not restricted by the rules of metre. (M) Another penetrates hidden places, and ponders in his wise mind what Nature can do, both below ground and above it. (H) He marks with lines the extreme boundaries of the earth; he is able to see forts, and cities, rivers, and fields, set out on a map. (M; 45) This man teaches us about the sun's wanderings, and the path of the wayward moon; and he could tell knowledgeably of the happiness that the stars can bring to the earth, or the evil they can threaten. (H) Why are we doubtful about flying farther over the huge ocean, led by the stars that we understand, and driven by the pressure of the winds? Why should youth, that is quick to learn, cease

---

21 Cf. Hor., *Carm. Saec.* 45, 'probos mores'.   27 Cf. Hor., *Carm. Saec.* 22; *Carm.* 4. 6. 42 (as at 109 below).   31–2 Probably alluding to Virg., *Aen.* 11. 50, 'cumulatque altaria donis'.   34 Probably alluding to Hor., *Carm.* 4. 6. 25.   49–50 Cf. Hor., *Carm.* 4. 2. 27.

Castra quid cessat docilis juventus
Ficta metiri, et simulacra pugnae?
55   Ecquis arcebit novus Archimedes
        Moenibus hostem?

M   Artium fautrix, Dea, Te trecenae
Concinunt linguae; tibi dissitarum
Gentium voces properant amico
60   Plaudere cantu.

Te sonant Musae, Dea, leniori
Italae cantu; bona tu Minerva
Diceris; lingua vocat altiori
        Pallada Graius.

H   Dispari fervet studio juventus
66   Aemula, explorans animo sagaci
Quicquid humanos peperere in usus
        Arsque laborque.

M   Quaerit hic aegris medicum levamen,
70   Seu cutem undosus gravet intus Hydrops,
Seu Febris venas nimio calentes
        Torreat aestu.

H   Ille rixanti populo viritim
Jura distinguit, Titiumque lites
75   Inter et Caium dirimens, iniquum
        Signat et aequum.

M   Hic sacris rite invigilans, Deorum
Explicat cultum, et dubio quod olim
Praecinens versu monuit Sibylla,
80   Te duce, pandit.

H   Diva, si gratum tibi quid Britannae,
Dulce si quando cecinere Musae;

M   Rite si vestrum juvenes Borussi
        Numen adorant;

H   Respice Ormondum, Dea, praeter omnes
86   Isidi charum; fera seu movere
Bella, seu gaudet stabilire custos
        Otia Musis.

M   Principi praesens faveas Borusso,
90   Principis curae faveas Togatis;
Protegat Musas, peragatque faelix
        Munia belli.

H   Qua lavat Camus, lavat Isis arces,
Anna tutatur Britonum Camaenas;
95   Te bonam, Pallas, bona, Te benignam
        Sentiat Anna.

Illa per longas Superis amata
Floreat messes; stabilem reponat

to measure out imaginary camps, and battle-plans? Will a new Archimedes keep the enemy from our walls? (M; 57) Goddess, supporter of the arts, three hundred tongues sing hymns to you together; the voices of distant peoples rush to praise you in friendly song. The Muses sound your name, goddess, in Italy's softer music; you are called 'good Minerva'; the Greek calls you 'Pallas' in his higher tongue. (H; 65) Rival youths show their enthusiasm in different ways, carefully exploring whatever art and labour have made for man to use. (M) One seeks for medical relief for the sick, whether a patient suffers from dropsy inside his skin, or whether a fever burns his warm veins with excessive heat. (H) Another marks out laws individually for a quarrelling people, deciding cases between Titius and Caius, and indicates what is right and wrong. (M; 77) This one watches properly over sacred things, explains divine worship, and lays open the warnings that the Sibyl once ambiguously gave, under your guidance. (H) Goddess, if British Muses have ever sung anything that pleased or delighted you—(M) if Prussian youths correctly worship your divinity—(H) look down on Ormonde, goddess, who is dearer to Oxford than all others, whether he chooses to wage fierce war, or to act as our guardian, securing the Muses' leisure. (M) Be present and kind to the Prussian prince, be kind to the wearers of the gown, for whom that prince cares; may he protect the Muses, and perform his martial duties with good fortune. (H; 93) Anne defends the British Muses, where Cam and Thames flow past their strongholds; let good Anne feel that you, Pallas, are kind and good. Let her flourish for many years, beloved of heaven; let her return stable peace to the nations, and nourish the quiet arts of peace. (M; 101) May you raise the name of the Prussian king above the stars,

Gentibus pacem, placidasque pacis
100   Nutriat artes.
M   Prosperis, Diva, auspiciis Borussi
Caesaris nomen super astra tollas;
Da dies laetos, studiumque dextro
Omine firmes.
105 Te duce, insignes referat triumphos
Victor, et lauro caput implicetur;
Ni comas malit potiore ramo
Cingere Olivae.
H   Saeculo festos revehente ludos,
110 Diva, sis nostri memor; artiumque
Dicier nutrix cupias; decusque
Adde Camaenis.
M   Mutuum gentis studium utriusque
Proroges fauste veniens in aevum;
115 Militet junctis opibus juventus
Anglo-Borussa.
H   Excolant artes socias Camaenae
Isidem amplexu foveat Viadrus;
M   Tu vicem alternans foveas amicum,
120   Isi, Viadrum.

goddess, under your prosperous auspices; give him happy days, and confirm his enthusiasm with a good omen. Under your guidance, may he be victorious, and celebrate famous triumphs, and be crowned with laurel, unless he prefers to surround his head with a better plant, the olive branch. (H; 109) When the century passes and brings back these games, remember us, goddess; may you wish to be spoken of as the nurse of the arts; add glory to the Muses! (M) May you extend the mutual enthusiasm of each nation with good fortune into the coming age; let Anglo-Prussian youth join forces and fight alongside each other. (H) Let the Muses cultivate allied arts; let the Oder embrace and cherish the Thames. (M) And may you, Thames, in turn cherish your friend, the Oder.

Text: Academiae Francofurtanae ad Viadrum Encaenia Secularia (Oxford, 1706); *Musarum Anglicanarum Analecta* 3 (1717), pp. 32–5; BL(a). *Date*: 1706. The reciters were William Harvey (H) and Amos Meredith (M), both of Christ Church.

Elegiac poems

This group of poems, none very securely attributed to Alsop, nevertheless does offer a useful cross-section of the sort of small-scale academic poetry to which he almost certainly contributed (examples from Christ Church were published anonymously in *Carmina Quadragesimalia*, 1723). They fall into two closely related genres; theme verses (4. 13–16), commenting on a quotation taken from ancient poetry, that might also have formed the subject of a prose essay; and disputation verses (4. 17–25), taking one of the two sides in a philosophical debate (the question posed being followed by *affirmatur*, if the poet agrees, or *negatur* if he disagrees). The debates tended to be on serious topics (often reflecting recent scientific controversies); the poems looked at the same topics in a more light-hearted way, illustrating them with a neat example from modern life (e.g. 4. 21), technology (4. 23), academic politics (4. 25), or ancient mythology (4. 24; cf. 4. 16). Some of them are discussed briefly in Ch. 4.

Dates: unknown (except for 4. 25); most of them probably date from the 1690s.

109 Alluding to Hor., *Carm.* 4. 6. 42.

Note on other possible attributions of elegiac poems

C. Wordsworth, *Social Life in the English Universities* (Cambridge, 1874), p. 311, suggests that Alsop may also have written poems on pp. 33, 96, and 158 of *Carmina Quadragesimalia* (which Bradner found to agree with a copy at Yale). But more than one poem starts on these pages, and it is not certain, at least from Wordsworth, which is supposed to be Alsop's. These attributions therefore seem even less reliable than the rest. I include only 4. 25 from the printed *Carmina Quadragesimalia*: that attribution is supported by a ms., and the poem is the most interesting and historically significant of the Lent verses. Notes of possible attributions: BL printed book 1507/ 656 (cf. 11409. ee. 12: both copies of the 'Glasgow' edn., 1757); Yale University Library, Beinecke collection, Lmd. 81. C48. 7230 (missing at the time of writing).

Additional Note: After this book was submitted to the publishers, the missing copy has been found (I am grateful to Vincent Giroud of the Beinecke Library for information about its annotations). The Yale book was first annotated by Sir John Stoddart, who gave it to his son, William Wellwood Stoddart, in 1832; there are further notes by Falconer Madan, who attempted to collate Stoddart's attributions with a few other copies, using information given by W. H. Gunner, *Notes & Queries*, 2nd ser., 42 (1856), pp. 312–3 and 'B. N. C.', ibid. pp. 355–6. Gunner attributes nothing to Alsop; 'B. N. C.' has Madan's four poems [= my 4. 25–8], though listed by item no. rather than page no., and with the second, item 128 [presumably = pp. 96–7, my 4. 27.] given an asterisk, clearly an indication of further doubt (the author does not explain this clearly; nearly 30 items are thus marked, in addition to a separate list of attributions that conflict with Gunner; if the mark implies 'double authorship', the other possible author is not in his list). All this serves to increase the confusion, without much strengthening the attributions. Overall, there is considerable disagreement between the various annotated copies, none of which has much authority. Nevertheless, several copies do agree in suggesting Alsop as author of four poems; for this reason, in addition to 4. 25, which I print in full, I have added a brief note on the others (which I call 4. 26–8) to conclude Part II of this book.

4.13 '—QUEM TE DEUS ESSE/ JUSSIT, ET HUMANA QUA PARTE LOCATUS ES IN RE/ DISCE—'

Translation: 'Learn what God has ordered you to be, and in what part of human affairs you are placed'

Comice, quid posito meditaris praelia socco?
　Et tenui magnum carmine pangis opus?
Te puer Arcadicus, qui vocum in cortice ludit
　Te juvat; et saevo fracta fenestra joco.
5　Excutit invitos festiva tragoedia risus;
　Dissimili et cantu comica grande sonant.
Siccine Phoebaeas exornas carmine laurus?
　(Nam cingunt stupidum laurea serta
　　　　　　　　　　　　　　　caput.)
Incedis viridi redimitus tempora lauro,

Why are you abandoning your trade, comic poet, to think about battles, and tell of a great subject in thin song? You enjoy the Arcadian boy, who plays on the surface of language, and the practical joke of broken windows. A festive tragedy forces unwilling laughter, and high-flown comedy sounds discordant. (7) Is it thus that you adorn Phoebus' laurels with song? (For laurel wreaths surround a stupid

Title: Persius 3. 71–3. Cf. Alsop 3. 9. 51–2.

10   Vatibus ut possis splendidus esse jocus.
        Sic postes soliti sertis ornare Quirites;
            Marcebatque pari vertice frondis honos.
        Frustra inhibente procax delirat Pallade
                                              Musa;
            Et fieri vates cum nequis, esse velis.
15   Nobilium Gnatho consuetus vivere mensa,
            Colligis inde dapes, colligis inde sales.
        I, minus invita deprome poemata vena;
            Nec solum placeat Musa jocosa tibi:
        Sic capiti haerebit multa cum laude corona,
20   Sic addes lauro Tu decus, illa tibi.

head.) You walk crowned with green laurel, so that you can be a splendid figure of fun for poets. Thus were the Romans accustomed to adorn their doorposts with wreaths, and the honour of the leaves used to wither along with them. (13) In vain does the pert Muse run riot, against Athena's opposition; and when you cannot be a serious poet, you want to be one. A parasite, used to living at the table of noblemen, you collect a dinner here, and a witticism there. Go on, put out poems in a less unwelcome vein; and let not your humorous Muse please only yourself. Thus will a crown remain on your head, with great praise; thus will you add glory to the laurel, as it will to you.

Text: ms. L, p 95.

4.14 '—MAGNIS OPIBUS DORMITUR IN URBE'

        Esurit infoelix media dum pauper in urbe,
            Et videt hinc illinc, queis caret unus, opes:
        Hunc circum luctus; saevaeque cubilia curae
            Ponunt; sola quies sed procul acta fugit.
5   Cura vigil somnos languentibus arcet ocellis,
            Velle facit somnum cura, eademque fugat.
        Pallida securos pellunt jejunia somnos,
            Et formido famis saevior ipsa fame.
        Stat magni conducta domus secreta, licetque
10   Pauper ubique jacet, somnus ubique fugit.
        Hunc laedit pariter Boreas, et mollior Eurus;
            Sol ardore suo, et frigore adurit hyems.
        Non intrat Morpheus humilem ambitiosus
                                              ocellum,
            Sed pretio semper prostat emenda quies.
15   Non miror miseris quod mors neget esse
                                              levamen,
            Cum non ipsa datur mortis imago quies.

Translation: 'Only the rich can sleep in the city'
    While the unhappy pauper is hungry in the midst of the city, he sees wealth all around him, that he alone lacks; grief surrounds him, and savage cares lay a bed for him; only quiet flees far away. Waking care keeps sleep from his tired eyes; care makes him wish for sleep, and also prevents it. (7) Pallid hunger keeps sleep at bay, and fear of hunger itself is more terrible than hunger. A house hired at great cost stands in privacy; but though a pauper can lie everywhere, everywhere sleep flies away. (11) The north wind and softer east both harm him; the sun shrivels him with its heat, winter with cold. Money-grubbing Morpheus does not enter a lowly eye, but quiet is always on sale, at a price. I am not amazed that death denies her relief to these miserable people, when even death's image, quiet, is not granted

12 I am unsure of the sense of *pari vertice*.   15 *Gnatho*: a parasite in Ter., *Eun.*; ms. *gnatho*?   17 Cf. Hor., *Epist.* I. I. 12, 'depromere'.   19 Alluding to Hor., *Serm.* I. 10. 49, 'haerentem capiti cum multa laude coronam'; cf. Lucr. 6. 95.

Title: Juv. 3. 235.   4 Cf. Hor., *Epist.* I. 17. 6.

Per noctis latebras amnem subit urna Cleanthis,
    Et libros, tenebras sole fugante, petit:
Nunquam grata quies fessos solatur ocellos;
20   Urna tenet vigilem nocte, dieque libri.

Text: ms. L, p. 99.

them. (17) Through the hiding-places of the night the Stoic's urn of fate pours out into the flood, and as the sun puts darkness to flight he seeks books; never does welcome quiet relieve his tired eyes; the urn keeps him awake at night, as books do in daytime.

4.15 '—EGOMET MIHI IGNOSCO'

Flagrat amans Corydon figitque in Phyllida
                        vultus,
    Et charum tacito pectore vulnus alit:
Nunc molles oculi, nunc viva corallia labris
    Urunt, accensis nunc rosa picta genis:
5   Mille procus Veneres dilectae virginis ardet,
    At sibi vel maculas conscia Phyllis amat.

Dum Bavii rauco damnatur fabula circo,
    Alterna circum damnat et ille vice:
Dirupta graditur tunica; macroque superba
10   Vatis magnifice squallet in ore fames:
Sic (ait) esuriit quondam divinus Homerus,
    Dum meruit, grandi quas canit ore, dapes:
Securus famae spernit ludibria vulgi,
    Quam non dat veniam turba, dat ipse sibi.

15   Malthini exagitat Venusinus pocula vates,
    Inflanti caluit dum sua Musa mero:
Cottarum turpes versu perstringit amores,
    Dum tepet in proprio Lydia pulchra sinu:
Mordaci damnat Romanos carmine mores
20   Flaccus, dum satyra dignior ipse sua est.

Translation: 'I forgive myself'
    Love-sick Corydon burns and stares at Phyllis, and nourishes the dear wound in his silent heart; now her soft eyes, now the living corals on her lips burn him up, and now the rose painted on her glowing cheeks. The swain burns for the thousand beauties of his beloved maiden; but knowing Phyllis loves even the blemishes on herself.

    (7) While Bavius' play is condemned by a jeering theatre, he too condemns the theatre in his turn; he goes around with a torn coat, and proud hunger can be seen bravely marking the poet's pinched face. Thus (he says) the divine Homer once starved, while he deserved the feasts that he sang about with his noble voice. Sure of his fame, he scorns the mob's follies; the pardon that the crowd denies him, he gives to himself.

    (15) Horace shakes the cups of Malthinus, while his Muse has become heated under the inspiration of wine; he attacks the Cottas' foul loves in his verse, while beautiful Lydia is warm on his own lap; Horace condemns Roman morals with biting poetry, while he himself is a more fitting target for his own satire.

Text: ms. L, p. 103

17 The passage is puzzling; possibly the urn is introduced as a joke (on the disturbance caused by emptying chamber pots).

Title: Hor., *Serm.* 1. 3. 23. Either three separate poems on the theme, or a single poem in three parts.
7 Bavius: a bad author attacked at Virg., *Ecl.* 3. 90.   15 Cf. Hor., *Serm.* 1. 2. 25.   16 Cf. Hor., *Carm.* 3. 21.
12, 'mero caluisse'.   17 Cotta: not, apparently, in Hor.; the name occurs in Juvenal, Ovid, and Martial: see n. on Alsop 3. 9. 32.

4.16 'NEMPE HAEC ASSIDUE—'

Usque adeone scelus renovas cum luce,
                diurnis
  Et vitam culpis annumerare juvat?
An fatale malum serpentis pectore nutris?
  Et parit assidue se, velut Hydra, nefas?
5 An? qualis tunica Alcidae quae tincta
                veneno
  Haeret, et avellit dilacerata cutem:
Aut qualis fixa est lateri lethalis arundo,
  Et secum vitam cuspis acuta trahit:
Sic haeret vitium fibris et amabilis error?
10   Quem mente haud Lethes diluet unda tua.
Heu! sero obstabis scelerum demersus in alto
  Exerere Oceano terque quaterque caput.
Si veniam repetita semel vix culpa meretur;
  Quam poenam, assidue quae repetita,
                luet?
15 Te fugis, Ixion, sequerisque fugisque
                sequentem;
  Dum praeceps rapido volvitur axe rota.
Te fugis, Ixion, quod Te reus ipse timeres,
  Te sequeris vindex criminis ipse tui:
Talis erat sceleris repetiti poena; rotanti
20   Nulla datur gyro meta, nec ulla Tibi.

Translation: 'Surely this is going on for ever . . .'

Do you continually renew your crime each day, and do you enjoy counting your life by daily faults? Or do you nourish the serpent's fatal evil in your breast? And does wickedness, like a Hydra, continually give birth to itself? Is it like Hercules' poisoned tunic, which sticks, and pulls away the skin when torn; or like a lethal dart stuck in your side, with a sharp point that draws life out with it? (9) Does vice and attractive error stick thus in your entrails? The waters of Lethe could hardly wash it from your mind. Alas! submerged in a deep ocean of crimes, it will be too late when you stop to raise your head three or four times. If a crime once repeated scarcely deserves pardon, what punishment is called for, when it is continually repeated? You flee from yourself, Ixion; you pursue and flee from the pursuer, while the wheel is rolled headlong on its swift axle. You flee from yourself, Ixion, because in your guilt you should fear yourself; you pursue yourself, as an avenger of your own crime. Such was the punishment for a repeated crime; no limit is given to the turning wheel, or to him.

Text: ms. L, p. 105.

4.17 AN BRUTA SINT AUTOMATA? NEGATUR

En! agilem saltator Equus plaudente caterva
  Exercet varia mobilitate pedem.
En! notos repetit, Domino nutante, labores,
  Et coeptum verso pollice sistit iter.
5 Commonstrat Nymphae quos inclementia
                torquet,

Translation: 'Are brute beasts automatons? No'

Look, as the crowd applauds, the leaping horse shows off its agility in varied motion. Look, at its master's command it repeats its familiar tasks, and stops what it has begun when he gives the signal. (5) He shows those whom a girl's unkindness tortures, and has

Title: Persius 3. 1.   5 Hercules and the shirt of Nessus; Hor., *Epod.* 17. 32, etc.   9 Cf. Hor., *Carm.* 3. 4.
5–6, 'amabilis insania'.   17 Ixion: cf. Alsop's English poem, 4. 3.

5 Ms. E reads *Commonstrant* for -at.

Et novit Juvenes queis favet alma Venus.
Se parat in pugnam Gulielmi ad nomina promptus;
    Poscit opem Lodoix; languida membra trahit.
Ad saltantis equi motus stupet inscia turba,
10   Sed novit Domini signa monentis Equus.

known young men whom kind Love favours. One prepares himself keenly for battle in William's name; when Louis asks for help, he drag his limbs slowly. The ignorant crowd is amazed at the motions of the leaping horse; but the horse knows its master's signals.

Text: ms. L, p. 149; ms. E, pp. 76–7 [= fo. 41^v–42^r]. This rather puzzling poem is perhaps about life-like mechanical figures, or automatons (turning round the question, to ask 'are automatons just brutes?'). For interest in subtle machinery, cf. 4. 23.

4.18 AN EX AERE GENERARI POSSIT ALIUD CORPUS? AFFIRMATUR

Vere novo ut primum notus redit ossibus ignis,
    Obversam Zephyrus flatibus implet
                                        equam.
Illa maritales non frustra experta calores,
    Maturum tenero gramine ponit onus.
5   Emicat, et cursu Pullus volat alite: Dices
        Ex alio nasci non potuisse Patre.

Translation: 'Can any body be generated from air? Yes'
As soon as, in spring, the familiar fire first returns to her bones, the west wind fills a mare with its breath. She does not feel the heat of marriage in vain, and places her burden in due time on the soft grass. The foal comes out, and flies off running; you might say that it could not have been born from any other father.

Text: ms. L, p. 149.

4.19 AN, MOTUS SIT IN MOBILI? AFFIRMATUR

Belgicus in turpi dum potat Nauta taberna,
    Et crassum invadit sordida vappa caput;
Ebibit, eructat, nutat, titubatque, caditque,
    Et terra recubans, ne cadat inde, timet.
5   Attonitus tandem tremulos circumvolat orbes,
        Et gemina socios fronte rubere videt.
Jam credit mensam et calices rubigine ferri
    Insolita, et metuit ne ruat ipsa domus.
Quin tu fide solo, manet inconcussa Popina;
10   In cerebro motus volvitur ille tuo.

Translation: 'Is motion in what is mobile? Yes'
While a Dutch sailor drinks in a sleazy tavern, and sour wine goes to his head, he drinks, belches, nods, totters, and falls; and, lying on the ground, he is afraid of falling off. (5) He flies, astonished, around trembling globes, and sees his companions red and double. Now he believes that the table and cups are carried off likewise, and fears lest the house itself might collapse. You rely on the ground: the inn remains unshaken. The motion is in your own head.

Text: ms. E, p. 73 [fo. 40^r].

7–8 Ms. E reads *Sic* for *Se*, *Poscat* for *-it*, *Lodois* for *-ix*. Mention of William suggests a date before 1702.

1–2 Alluding to a common Greek belief; see, e.g., Homer, *Il*. 16. 150–1, 20. 221–5.   6 *Alio*: the text is unclear (*alvo*?), but *alio* seems to make sense.

1–2 Probably alluding to Hor., *Serm*. 1. 5. 16, 'multa prolutus vappa nauta'.   7 Ms. clearly reads *rubigine*: perhaps a mistake for *vertigine* (cf. *rubere* in 6).

4.20 AN, UBICUNQUE SIT TRINA DIMENSIO, IBI SIT CORPUS? NEGATUR

Per noctem fatuos sequitur dum Rusticus
                  ignes,
  Et temere ignotum devius urget iter;
Per montes sylvasque ruit praeruptaque
                  saxa,
  Quoque magis properat, longius ignis
                  abit.
5 Usque tamen properans flammis ductricibus
                  instat,
  Atque avido captat lumina falsa sinu.
Dum veros sperat captare amplexibus ignes,
  Elusa spatium claudit inane manu.

Translation: 'Is there a body wherever there is a third dimension? No'

While a peasant follows will-o'-the-wisps through the night, and rashly strays from his path on an unknown route, he rushes through mountains and forests and rugged rocks: the more he hurries on, the farther the fire flees. (5) Yet still he continues hurrying, led by the flames, and eagerly hopes to touch false lights. While he hopes to embrace true fires, he clutches empty space as his hand is deceived.

Text: ms. E, p. 74 [fo. 40ᵛ].

4.21 AN, LOCUS SIT SUPERFICIES CORPORIS AMBIENTIS? AFFIRMATUR

Est in quadrivio pravis bene nota Columna,
  Cui geminum claudunt ligna forata latus.
Huc nebulo adductus circumplaudente
                  caterva
  Submittit tereti colla manusque jugo.
5 Sublimem plebs insultans putri oblinit ovo,
  Undique et infami polluit ora luto.
Interior ligni inclusum dum circuit orbis,
  Quam mallet spatio liberiore frui?

Translation: 'Is a place the surface of a surrounding body? Yes'

At the crossroads there is a column, well known to the wicked, which pierced wood closes in on both sides. Hither a scoundrel is brought, as the crowd applauds, and submits his neck and hands to the smooth stocks. The common people insult his head, throwing rotten eggs, and cover his face in foul mire. While the inner circle of wood surrounds him, how much would he prefer to enjoy a freer space!

Text: ms. E, p. 74 [fo. 40ᵛ]. On the stocks; a humorous picture of the rougher side of everyday life.

1 Ms. has *pravis* written over *improbulis*.

4.22 AN, NATURA INTENDAT MONSTRUM? NEGATUR

Tympana pulsa strepunt, raucum dat Buccina
                      signum,
   Mox in quadrivium sordida turba ruit.
Ridicula ostentat se Mimus imagine, risus
   Incertum moveat veste vel ore magis.
5   Ingens caeruleam subnectit fibula vestem
   Pileolo tegitur multicolore caput.
Gibbosus varia distendit bracchia forma;
   Atque jocos praebet, materiamque jocis.
Tandem elephas prodit, quem protulit Africa
                     tellus,
10   Foecunda horrendis Africa terra feris:
Innocuum populo commonstrat Mauria brutum,
   Sed Mimum potius spissa corona stupet.
Quod natura negat, portentum Scena ministrat;
   Et monstri plus, quam bellua, Mimus habet.

Translation: 'Does nature intend a monster? No'

The drums are beaten, the trumpet gives a harsh signal, soon the squalid crowd rushes into the crossroads. The clown shows himself, appearing absurd, unsure whether to rouse laughter by his face or costume. (5) A huge brooch joins his blue coat, and his head is covered by a multicoloured hat. Hunchbacked, he distorts his arms in various shapes; he offers jokes, and a subject for joking. (9) Finally an elephant comes forth, born in Africa: Africa is fertile with horrendous beasts. A Moorish girl shows off the harmless beast to the people; but the thick crowd is more amazed at the mime. The stage provides the marvel that nature denies; and there is more of the monster in the mime than in the beast.

Text: ms. E, p. 79 [fo. 43ʳ].

4.23 AN, ALIQUID SIT CAUSA SUI IPSIUS? NEGATUR

Commonstrant certis labantes motibus horas,
   Et nova Daedalea machina facta manu.
Artificem ducunt momenta latentia cursum,
   Subtilesque regunt conscia fila rotas;
5   Aptatur vario rigidi libramine ferri
   Et circum fixa mobilitate ruit.
Quam spirante putas anima . . . moveri,
   Molem fila regunt, et regit illa faber.

Translation: 'Can anything be the cause of itself? No'

They show hours slipping by with certain movements, and there is a new machine made by a scientific hand. Hidden weights lead on their artificial course, and knowing threads rule their subtle rotations. (5) It is adjusted by the varied balance of hard iron, and goes around in fixed motion. You might think that it is moved by a breathing soul; but threads rule the mass, and the workman rules the threads.

Text: ms. E, p. 80 [fo. 43ᵛ]. On the mechanism of a clock.

13 Cf. Juv. 1. 79.

7 Gap in ms.   8 *Molem*: I tentatively emend ms. *Mollem*; but I am not quite sure of the point here.

4.24 AN OMNE VIVENS, QUANDIU VIVIT, NUTRIATUR? AFFIRMATUR

Ecce inter plenas jejunum Erisicthona mensas,
    Quo plura absumit, fercula plura petit.
Devorat hic quod pontus habet, quod terra,
                              quod aer,
    Pellere quae solita est, provocat Esca, famem.
5 Hinc avido proprios morsu depascitur artus,
    Deficiente cibo fit satur ipse sui;
Postulat usque nova esuriens alimenta; suoque
    Corpore corpus alens, se minuendo fovet.

Translation: 'Is every living thing nourished as long as it lives? Yes'

    See Erysichthon, hungry among full tables; the more he eats, the more courses he seeks. He devours all that sea, earth, and air produce. A piece of food, that generally removes hunger, sharpens it. (5) Hence he eats his own limbs with greedy bites, and when food fails is sated on himself. Always hungry, he keeps asking for more; and, feeding his body on his own body, he nourishes himself by diminishing himself.

Text: ms. E, p. 198 [fo. 144ᵛ]. The story is taken from Ovid, *Met.* 8. 738–884 [= O], with several allusions and direct borrowings.

4.25 AN QUODLIBET FIERI POSSIT EX QUOLIBET? AFFIRMATUR

Dum simulacra notat pictos signantia fastos
    Daedaleae lustrans Zoilus artis opus,
Commenta arcanae sibi deprensisse tabellae
    Visus, et obscuros explicuisse dolos:
5 En! Cives, pictura loquax, praesaga malorum,
    Et quae Saxonidis fata minantur, ait.
Hic luce effulgens, positoque Britannia luctu
    Aspicit exultans Caesaris ora novi:
Hic grandi assurgit pompa venerabile bustum,
10   Relliquiasque tenens urna, Jacobe, tuas:
Dum solii infelix Rivalis moestus et exspes
    Volvitur, inque imas praecipitatur aquas:
Belgicus inde Leo—Quin tu damnabere
                        flammis
    Impia Niliacis foeta tabella notis.
15 O cerebrum felix! et divinare peritum!
    O lepidum ingenii luxuriantis opus!

Translation: 'Can anything come from anything at all? Yes'

    While Zoilus notes images that indicate our festival days in pictures, surveying the work of a marvellous art, he seems to have caught out the fictions of an ancient tablet, and to explain obscure tricks. (5) 'Look, citizens, here is a speaking picture, a foreteller of evils, that tells of the fates threatening us Saxons. Here Britannia, shining with light and with grief laid aside, looks joyfully at the face of a new Caesar; here a venerable tomb rises with great pomp, and an urn holding your remains, James, while the unlucky, sad, and hopeless rival for the throne is carried along and hurled into deep waters. (13) Thence the Dutch lion— but you will be condemned to the

2 Cf. O 834, 'quo plura'; 839 'plura petit.'   3 ms. original text: 'Terra parit, quodque educat Aer': alteration written above. Alluding to O 830, 'quod pontus habet, quod terra, quod educat aer'.   8 Cf. O 878, 'minuendo corpus alebat'.

2 *CQ*: 'Kalendarium Oxoniense anno 1702 editum' [the 1702 Oxford almanack]. Zoilus: critic and cynic philosopher, famous for attacks on Homer; cf. Ovid, *Remed. Am.* 366.   14 Cf. Ovid, *Ars Am.* 3. 318, 'Niliacis'; 'tabella' frequently in Ovid.

Quin pergas, bone Vir; nondum extricata
                                    latescit
    Materia auguriis plurima digna tuis.
Macte sagax, repete examen, quae praebuit
                                    unum
20   Chartula figmentum, Zoile, mille dabit.

flames, blasphemous image pregnant with marks of the Nile.' O happy mind, that is skilled in augury; o clever work of a flourishing intellect! Go on, good man; there is much work worthy of your prophecies that lies hidden, not yet disentangled. Carry on, wise man, continue your examination; the canvas that has offered one invention, Zoilus, will give you a thousand.

Text: *Carmina Quadragesimalia* (1723), p. 110; BL ms. Add. 36663, fo. 522. *Date*: *c.* 1702. The background to this poem is discussed in Ch. 4.

Other poems

Three further poems from the *Carmina Quadragesimalia* may possibly be Alsop's; the attributions seem quite flimsy (and largely rely on information only available after this book went to the publishers: see note preceding 4. 13). Since they can be consulted by scholars in the original edition, I do not swell this section further by reprinting them in full. Nevertheless they deserve at least a passing mention among the 'doubtful' poems, and I allocate numbers to them, to facilitate further discussion:

4.26 (= p. 33, 'An Natura sit perfectior Arte? Affirmatur'): 'Aspicis ut frondet . . .' (8 lines of elegiacs): a painting of a vine, and real wine.

4.27 (= pp. 96–7, 'An Natura aliquem Finem intendat? Affirmatur'): 'Impatiens irae . . .' (14 lines of elegiacs): the usefulness of a cat, alive and dead.

4.28 (= p. 158, 'An Simile agat in Simile? Affirmatur'): 'Carmina dum meditans . . .' (10 lines of elegiacs): musical resonance.

4. 28. 10, 'Et poterit fidicen dicier ipsa fides.' [and the lyre itself will be able to be called a lyre-player], is quite a neat ending: the resonance from another lyre makes it appear that the instrument plays itself: cf. 2. 5. 3–4 (also mentioning cat-gut, cf. 4. 27); on 4. 28. 1, 'et totus in illis', cf. 3. 8. 11. These may suggest Alsopian wit and style: but many of the other authors of elegiac poetry could equally well have produced them.

Also, recently discovered:
4.29: 'Hermogenes cantor . . .' (Nott. PwV 1314/1); thanks to Mss. Dept., and S. Corcoran in particular, for this and other Nott. items.

Bibliography

The bibliography is divided into three parts: manuscripts (and unique or annotated printed items); primary sources (chiefly Neo-Latin texts); and secondary sources. It does not contain all the sources cited in the book (those used only to illustrate a minor point are generally omitted here); but it does add some other material which I have found useful. For a more detailed list of primary sources, the reader should consult the works of L. Bradner (see 'secondary sources'). I have, however, given a detailed list of the Oxford and Cambridge verse collections (discussed in Chapter 9); these are listed in chronological order (in 'primary sources', under 'Cambridge' and 'Oxford': place of publication, unless stated otherwise, is Cambridge or Oxford respectively). Outside these lists of university volumes, the place of publication is London, unless stated otherwise.

MANUSCRIPTS

Berkshire County Record Office
  D/P 25 1/2

Bodleian Library
  ms. Ballard 2, fo. 6, 10
  ms. Ballard 12, fo. 110
  ms. Ballard 13, fo. 41
  ms. Ballard 19, fo. 23, 26, 33, 38, 47–8, 160, 162, 166–7, 174
  ms. Ballard 20, fo. 120, 135
  ms. Ballard 21, fo. 62, 139, 166–8
  ms. Ballard 24, fo. 25–6, 38, 98
  ms. Ballard 25, fo. 15
  ms. Ballard 29, fo. 55, 60, 137–8, 147
  ms. Ballard 30, fo. 54
  ms. Ballard 35, fo. 158–9
  ms. Ballard 38, fo. 4, 15, 87, 133
  ms. Ballard 47, fo. 52–4
  ms. Carte 208, 62, fo. 397
  ms. Don. e. 53
  ms. Eng. poet. f. 13
  ms. Eng. misc. e. 184

  ms. Lat. misc. c. 14
  ms. Lat. misc. e. 19, fo. 152–6, 172–7
  ms. Mus. sch. c. 121
  ms. Rawl. D. 697, fo. 1
  ms. Rawl. D. 742, fo. 7
  ms. Rawl. J. fol. 2, fo. 58
  ms. Rawl. J. quarto 2, fo. 180
  ms. Rawl. letters 31, fo. 142–4
  ms. Rawl. letters 108, fo. 245
  ms. Tanner 40, fo. 7, 10, 14, 29, 109, 112, 118
  ms. Tanner 44, fo. 274, 278
  ms. Top. Oxon. a. 76

British Library
  printed book, 11409. h. 30 (copy of Alsop's odes, 1752, with copious ms. additions: referred to as 'the British Library ms.')
  ms. Add. 3516, fo. 157, 199
  ms. Add. 4457, fo. 204, 208
  ms. Add. 6666, fo. 240

ms. Add. 22911, fo. 65
ms. Add. 24120, fo. 252–61
ms. Add. 29601, fo. 258–9
ms. Add. 30162
ms. Add. 34744, fo. 65–6
ms. Add. 36663, fo. 522
ms. Add. 37684, fo. 39–40, 43–50
ms. Add. 40836, fo. 42
ms. Add. 51441, fo. 108
ms. Add. 64125
ms. Egerton 2618, fo. 197
ms. Lansdowne 825, fo. 35–6

Cambridge University Library
ms. Ii. 5. 37
ms. Add. 2615, fo. 30–73
ms. Add. 7908
ms. Add. 8915

Chetham's Library, Manchester
printed broadsheet, BY 215–48 (13)

Christ Church, Oxford
ms. 346
ms. 353
ms. 618
ms. 619
ms. 621
ms. Wake 16, no. 73
ms. Wake 17, no. 133
ms. Wake 18, no. 514
ms. Wake 24, no. 6
archives: Caution and Disbursement
books; card index of college members
compiled by E. G. W. Bill
Gaudy commemoration speech, 1844,
by C. Conybeare

Derbyshire County Record Office
XM 1/ 109
8792/ P1

Emmanuel College, Cambridge
ms. 52
ms. 78
ms. 79
ms. 105
ms. 171

ms. 175
ms. 178

Folger Shakespeare Library
ms. V. a. 232, pp. 127–31

Huntington Library
printed book, RB 316448 (copy of
Alsop's odes, 1752, with ms. note on
last page)
[Brydges family papers: a large archive
of material, some of it related to Henry
Brydges, Alsop's addressee; I have not
had an opportunity to examine these]

Northamptonshire County Record Office
Dolben (Finedon) archive, D (F) 1, 11,
86
Isham Longden archive, no. 1586

Nottingham University Library, Portland
collection
Pw V 141
Pw V 142
Pw V 143
Pw V 144
Pw V 145/ 1–3
Pw V 146
Pw V 147
Pw V 148/ 1–3
Pw V 149/ 1–5
Pw V 150
Pw V 151/ 1–8

Royal College of Music
ms. 995, fo. 119–31

Royal Society
Boyle correspondence, ms. 1, fo. 20;
ms. 4, fo. 6–7

Trinity College, Cambridge
printed book, H. 5. 17 (copy of Alsop's
odes, 1752, with some ms. additions)
ms. 615 (= R. 3. 35, 36, 39, 40, 45
bound together)

Yale University Library
ms. Osborn c. 233

PRIMARY (Chiefly Neo-Latin)

Alsop, A., ed., *Fabularum Aesopicarum Delectus* (Oxford, 1698)
——— *Charlettus Percivallo suo* (1706)
——— *Charissimo suo duci de Vendosme Tallardus* (1708)
——— (ed. Sir F. Bernard), *Odarum Libri Duo* (1752)
Anon. ed., *Musarum Anglicanarum Analecta* (1698; new edition, ed. J. Addison, 1699; repr. 1714, 1721; further volume 1717; new edition, ed. V. Bourne, 1741; repr. 1761)
Anon. ed., *Examen Poeticum Duplex* (1698)
Anon. ed., *Musae Britannicae* (1711)
Atterbury, F., ed., *ἈΝΘΟΛΟΓΙΑ* (1684; rev., ed. A. Pope, 1740, as *Selecta Poemata Italorum*)
Bagshawe, E., *A True and Perfect Narrative of the differences between Mr Busby and Mr Bagshawe . . .* (1659)
Bourne, V., ed., *Carmina Comitialia* (1721)
——— *Poematia* (1734; many reprints)
Browne, I. H., *De Animi Immortalitate* (1754)
Brydges, H., *A Sermon Preach'd before the Queen, at St James' Chapel, on Monday, January 31. 1708/9. Being the Anniversary of the Martyrdom of King Charles I* (1709)
——— *A Speech to the Clergy of the Diocese of Rochester at the Archidiaconal Visitation begun on Wednesday May 31. 1721* (1721)
Burton, J., *Sacerdos paroecialis rusticus* (1757)
——— *Opuscula miscellanea* (1771)
'G. G. C.', ed., *Fasciculus carminum stylo Lucretiano* (Eton, 1839)

Cambridge verse collections:

Academiae Cantabrigiensis Lachrymae Tumulo . . . Philippi Sidneii (London, 1587)
Threno-thriambeuticon . . . luctuosus triumphus (1603)
Epicedium Cantabrigiense in obitum . . . Henrici . . . Principis Walliae (1612)
Lachrymae Cantabrigienses in obitum . . . Reginae Annae (1619)
Gratulatio Academiae Cantabrigiensis de . . . principis reditu (1623)
Cantabrigiensium Dolor et Solamen (1625)
Epithalamium . . . Principum Caroli Regis et H. Mariae . . . a Musis Cantabrigiensibus decantatum (1625)
Genethliacum . . . Caroli et Mariae a Musis Cantabrigiensibus celebratum (1631)
Anthologia in regis Exanthemata seu Gratulatio Musarum Cantabrigiensium . . . (1632)
Rex Redux . . . post receptam Coronam comitiaque peracta in Scotia (1633)
Ducis Eboracensis Fasciae a Musis Cantabrigiensibus raptim contextae (1633)
Carmen natalitium ad cunas . . . Principis Elisabethae decantatum . . . per humiles Cantabrigiae Musas (1635)
ΣΥΝΩΔΙΑ, sive Musarum Cantabrigiensium concentus et congratulatio . . . de quinta sua sobole . . . nata (1637)
Voces votivae . . . pro novissimo Caroli et Mariae principe filio emissae (1640)
Irenodia Cantabrigiensis ob paciferum . . . e Scotia reditum (1641)
Oliva Pacis ad . . . Oliverum . . . de Pace . . . feliciter sancita, carmen Cantabrigiense (1654)

Musarum Cantabrigiensium Luctus et Gratulatio: Ille in funere Oliveri Angliae, Scotiae et Hiberniae Protectoris, Haec de Ricardi successione felicissima ad eundem (1658)

Academiae Cantabrigiensis ΣΩΣΤΡΑ sive ad Carolum II reducem, de regnis ipsi, Musis per ipsum feliciter restitutis Gratulatio (1660)

Threni Cantabrigienses in funere duorum prinicipum Henrici Glocestrensis et Mariae Arausionensis . . . Caroli II fratris et sororis (1661)

Epithalamia Cantabrigiensia in nuptias . . . Caroli II . . . et illustrissimae principis Catharinae . . . (1662)

Threni Cantabrigienses in exequiis serenissimae Reginae Henriettae Mariae augustissimi Caroli II matris (1669)

Musarum Cantabrigiensium Threnodia in obitum incomparabilis herois et ducis illustrissimi Georgii Ducis Albaemarlae, regiarum copiarum Archistrategi . . . (1670)

Lacrymae Cantabrigienses in obitum . . . Henriettae Caroli I regis et martyris filiae Ducissae Aurelianensis (1670)

Epicedia Cantabrigiensia in obitum illustrissimae principis Annae Ducissae Eboracensis (1671)

Epithalamium in desideratissimis nuptiis . . . principum Guilielmi-Henrici Arausii et Mariae Britanniarum ab Academia Cantabrigiensi decantatum (1677)

Hymenaeus Cantabrigiensis (1683)

Moestissimae et Laetissimae Academiae Cantabrigiensis Affectus decedente Carolo II succedente Jacobo II . . . (1684/5)

Illustrissimi principis Ducis Cornubiae et Comitis Palatini &c Genethliacon (1688)

Musae Cantabrigienses serenissimis principibus Wilhelmo et Mariae . . . publicae salutis et libertatis vindicibus . . . (1689)

Lacrymae Cantabrigienses in obitum serenissimae Reginae Mariae (1694/5)

Gratulatio Academiae Cantabrigiensis de reditu . . . Gulielmi III post pacem et libertatem Europae feliciter restitutam (1697)

Threnodia Academiae Cantabrigiensis in immaturum obitum . . . Principis Gulielmi Ducis Glocestrensis (1700)

Academiae Cantabrigiensis Carmina quibus decedenti augustissimo regi Wilhelmo III parentat; et succedenti optimis auspiciis Annae gratulatur (n.d.: 1701/2)

Epicedium Cantabrigiense in serenissimum Daniae principem Georgium . . . Reginae Anna conjugem . . . rei navalis ac maritimae praefectum &c (1708)

Gratulatio Academiae Cantabrigiensis de pace Reginae Annae auspiciis feliciter constituta (1713)

Moestissima et Laetissima Academiae Cantabrigiensis Carmina Funebria et Triumphalia. Illis . . . Annam repentina morte abreptam deflet. His . . . Georgio . . . solium optimis auspiciis ascendenti gratulatur (1714)

Academiae Cantabrigiensis Luctus in obitum . . . Georgii I . . . et Gaudia ob . . . Georgii II patriarum virtutum ac solii haeredis accessionem pacificam simul ac auspicatissimam (1727)

Gratulatio Academiae Cantabrigiensis . . . Gulielmi Principis Auriaci et Annae . . . nuptias celebrantis (1733)

Gratulatio Academiae Cantabrigiensis . . . Frederici Walliae Principis et Augustae Principissae Saxo-Gothae nuptias celebrantis (1736)

Pietas Academiae Cantabrigiensis in funere . . . Wilhelminae Carolinae et luctu . . . Georgii II . . . (1738)

Gratulatio Academiae Cantabrigiensis de reditu . . . regis Georgii II post pacem et libertatem Europae feliciter restitutam (1748)

Academiae Cantabrigiensis Luctus in obitum Frederici celsissimi Walliae Principis (1751)

Carmina ad nobilissimum Thomam Holles Ducem de Newcastle inscripta, cum Academiam Cantabrigiensem Bibliothecae restituendae causa inviseret (1755)

Academiae Cantabrigiensis Luctus in obitum Regis Georgii II et Gratulationes in Regis Georgii III inaugurationem (1760)

Gratulatio Academiae Cantabrigiensis auspicatissimas Georgii III . . . et Charlottae Principis de Mecklenbergh-Strelitz nuptias celebrantis (1761)

Gratulatio Academiae Cantabrigiensis natales . . . Georgii Walliae Principis . . . celebrantis (1762)

Gratulatio Academiae Cantabrigiensis in pacem Georgii III . . . auspiciis Europae feliciter restitutam (1763)

Christ Church, *Carmina Quadragesimalia* (ed. C. Este, Oxford, 1723, repr. London 1741; new collection, Oxford, 1748, repr. with first volume, Glasgow [in fact printed at Oxford], 1757; new collection, London, 1812)

Dillingham, W., *Poemata varii argumenti* (1678)

Dodsley, R., ed., *Collection of Poems* (1748; many reprints; continuation, ed. Pearch, 1770)

Duport, J., ΣΟΛΟΜΩΝ ΈΜΜΕΤΡΟΣ, *sive tres libri Solomonis . . . Graeco carmine donati* (Cambridge, 1646)

———— ΔΑΒΙΔΗΣ ΈΜΜΕΤΡΟΣ, *sive Metaphrasis libri Psalmorum* (Cambridge, 1666)

———— *Musae Subsecivae* (Cambridge, 1676)

Eton College, *Musae Etonenses* (1755; 2nd series, 1795; 3rd series, 1869)

Fisher, P., *Irenodia Gratulatoria, sive . . . Oliveri Cromwelli Epinicion* (1652)

Freind, J., *History of Physick from the time of Galen . . . chiefly with regard to practice* (1725–6)

The Gentleman's Magazine, or Trader's Monthly Intelligencer (1731–)

Gibbs, J. A., *Carmina* (Rome, 1665; 2nd edn., 1668)

Hardinge, N., *Poemata* (1780; 2nd edn., 1818)

Harvard University, *Pietas et Gratulatio* (Cambridge, MA, 1761)

Hill, T., *Nundinae Sturbrigienses* (1709)

Hogg, W., *Victoria Gulielmi III Namurae* (1695)

———— *Ad regem de pace carmen triumphale* (1697)

Holdsworth, E., *Muscipula* (1709)

Jortin, J., *Lusus Poetici* (1722; other editions, 1724, 1748)

King, W., *Miltonis Epistola ad Pollionem* (1738)

———— *Sermo Pedestris* (1739)

———— *Scamnum, ecloga* (1740)

———— *Templum Libertatis, liber primus* (1742)

———— *Antionetti ducis Corsorum epistola* (1744)

———— *Elogium famae inserviens Jacci Etonensis* (1750) [an attack on J. Burton]

———— *Opera* (1754)

———— *Aviti Epistola ad Perillam* (1760)

Landor, W. S., *Poems* (1795)

———— *Poemata et inscriptiones* (1847)

[Loveling, B.], *Latin and English Poems by a Gentleman of Trinity College, Oxford* (1738; 2nd edn., 1741)

Maittaire, M., *Senilia* (1742)

Oxford verse collections:

[Lincoln College], *In adventum . . . Lecestrensis Comitis ad Collegium Lincolniense Carmen gratulatorium* (1585)

[New College], *Peplus . . . Philippi Sidnaei supremis honoribus dicatus* (1587)

Exequiae . . . Philippi Sidnaei Gratissimae memoriae ac nomini impensae (1587)

Oxoniensium ΣΤΕΝΑΓΜΟΣ . . . in obitum . . . Christophori Hatton . . . (1592)

Epicedium in obitum . . . Henrici comitis Derbiensis (1593) [two authors only]

Funebria . . . Henrici Untoni . . . (1596)

Oxoniensis Academiae Funebre officium in memoriam . . . Elisabethae . . . (1603)

Academiae Oxoniensis Pietas erga . . . Iacobum . . . legitime et auspicatissime succedentem (1603)

[Christ Church], *Musa Hospitalis Ecclesiae Christi . . . in adventum . . . Jacobi Regis, Annae Reginae, et Henrici Principis ad eandem Ecclesiam* (1605)

[New College], *Encomion Rodolphi Warcoppi ornatissimi, quem habuit Anglia, Armigeri, qui communi totius patriae luctu extinctus est* (1605)

[Magdalen College], *Beatae Mariae Magdalenae Lachrymae in obitum . . . Gulielmi Grey . . . Baronis de Wilton . . . filii natu minoris* (1606)

Ilium in Italiam. Oxonia ad protectionem Regis sui, omnium optimi filia, pedisequa (1608) [this book is probably the work of a single author, but includes poems on behalf of each college]

[New College], *Musae Hospitales Wicchamicae in adventum . . . Frederici-Ulrici . . .* (1610)

[Broadgates Hall], *Eidyllia in obitum . . . Henrici . . . Romaeque ruentis Terroris maximi* (1612)

[Magdalen College], *Luctus Posthumus sive erga defunctum . . . Henricum Walliae principem . . . Magdalenensium officiosa pietas* (1612)

Justa Oxoniensium (1612)

Epithalamia sive Lusus Palatini in nuptias . . . Frederici . . . et serenissimae Elisabethae . . . (1613)

[Merton College], *Bodleiomnema* (1613)

Iusta Funebria Ptolemaei Oxoniensis Thomae Bodleii . . . (1613)

[Exeter College], *Threni Exonensium in obitum . . . Iohannis Petrei . . .* (1613)

[Corpus Christi College], *Carmina Funebria in obitum . . . Georgii de Sancto Paulo . . .* (1614)

Jacobi Ara . . . in . . . reditum e Scotia in Angliam . . . (1617)

Academiae Oxoniensis Funebria sacra aeternae memoriae . . . Annae . . . dicata (1619)

Ultima Linea Savilii . . . (1622)

Votiva, sive ad . . . Jacobum . . . de . . . Caroli . . . in Regiam Hispanicam adventu, Pia et Humilis Oxoniensium Gratulatio (London, 1623)

Carolus Redux (1623)

Camdeni Insignia (1624)

Schola Moralis Philosophiae Oxon. in funere Whiti pullata (1624)

Oxoniensis Academiae Parentalia . . . memoriae . . . Iacobi . . . fidei orthodoxae defensoris . . . dicata (1625)

Epithalamia Oxoniensia in . . . Caroli . . . cum Henrietta Maria . . . connubium (1625)

Britanniae Natalis (1630)

Ad magnificum et spectatissimum virum dominum Ioannem Cirenbergium proconsulem civitatis Gedanensis, ob acceptum synodalium epistolarum Concilii Basileensis ΑΥΤΟ-ΓΡΑΦΟΝ sigillo eiusdem in plumbum impresso obsignatum, quod . . . Thomas Roe . . . Oxoniensi Bibliothecae transmisit ac dono dedit, Carmen Honorarium (1631)

Solis Britannici Perigaeum sive Itinerantis Caroli auspicatissima Periodus (1633)

Musarum Oxoniensium pro rege suo Soteria (1633)

Vitis Carolinae Gemma Altera sive . . . Ducis Eboracensis Genethliaca decantata ad vada Isidis (1633)

Coronae Carolinae Quadratura sive perpetuandi imperii Carolini ex quarto pignore feliciter suscepto captatum Augurium (1636)

Flos Britannicus veris novissimi Filiola Carolo et Mariae Nata (1636)

[Christ Church], *Death Repeal'd by a Thankfull Memoriall sent from Christ-Church in Oxford, celebrating the Noble Deserts of . . . Paule, Late Lord Vis-Count Bayning of Sudbury . . .* (1638)

Musarum Oxoniensium Charisteria pro . . . Maria recens e nixus laboriosi discrimine recepta (1638)

Horti Carolini Rosa Altera (1640)

Eucharistica Oxoniensia in . . . Caroli . . . e Scotia Reditum Gratulatoria (1641)

ΠΡΟΤΕΛΕΙΑ Anglo-Batava pari plusquam virgineo, Gulielmo Arausi, et Mariae Britanniarum, Academia Oxoniensi procurante (1641)

Musarum Oxoniensium ΕΠΙΒΑΤΗΡΙΑ . . . Mariae ex Batavia feliciter reduci (1643)

Verses on the Death of . . . Sir Bevill Grenvill, Knight, Who was slaine by the Rebells, on Landsdown-hill neare Bath, Iuly. 5. 1643 (1643; repr. 1684)

Musarum Oxoniensium ΕΛΑΙΟΦΟΡΙΑ, sive ob foedera, auspiciis serenissimi Oliveri . . . foeliciter stabilata, Gentis Togatae ad vada Isidis celeusma metricum (1654)

Britannia Rediviva (1660)

Epicedia Academiae Oxoniensis in obitum celsissimi principis Henrici Ducis Glocestrensis (1660)

Epicedia Academiae Oxoniensis in obitum serenissimae Mariae principis Arausionensis (1661)

Domiduca Oxoniensis, sive . . . Gratulatio ob auspicatissimum principis Catharinae Lusitanae regi suo desponsatae in Angliam appulsum (1662)

Epicedia Universitatis Oxoniensis in obitum augustissimae principis Henriettae Mariae Reginae Matris (1669)

Epicedia Universitatis Oxoniensis in obitum invictissimi herois Georgii Ducis Albemarliae (1670)

Epicedia Universitatis Oxoniensis in obitum illustrissimae principis Henriettae Mariae Ducissae Aurelianensis (1670)

Epicedia in obitum Annae Ducissae Eboracensis (1671)

Comitia Philologica . . . in gratulatione solenni ob adventum . . . Ormondiae Ducis . . . (1677)

Supplex recognitio et Gratulatio Solennis . . . et Pietas . . . in obitum . . . Caroli II (1685)

Strenae Natalitiae Academiae Oxoniensis in celsissimum Principem (1688)

Vota Oxoniensia pro serenissimis Guilhelmo rege et Maria regina M. Britanniae &c nuncupata (1689)

Academiae Oxoniensis Gratulatio pro exoptato serenissimi regis Gulielmi ex Hibernia reditu (1690)

Pietas Universitatis Oxoniensis in obitum augustissimae et desideratissimae Reginae Mariae (1695)

Exequiae desideratissimo principi Gulielmo Glocestriae Duci ab Oxoniensi Academia solutae (1700)

Pietas Universitatis Oxoniensis in obitum augustissimi regis Gulielmi III et Gratulatio in exoptatissimam . . . Annae reginae inaugurationem (1702)

Epinicion Oxoniense sive solennis gratulatio ob res feliciter terra marique gestas . . . contra Gallos pariter ac Hispanos (1702)

Plausus Musarum Oxoniensium . . . ob res prospere terra marique gestas . . . (1704/5)

Academiae Francofurtanae ad Viadrum Encaenia Secularia (1706)

Exequiae celsissimo principi Georgio Principi Daniae ab Oxoniensi Academia solutae (1708)

Academiae Oxoniensis Comitia philologica . . . in honorem Reginae Annae Pacificae (1713)

Pietas Universitatis Oxoniensis in obitum serenissimae reginae Annae et Gratulatio in augustissimi regis Georgii inaugurationem (1714)

Exequiae clarissimo viro Johanni Radcliffe M.D. ab Oxoniensi Academia solutae (1715)

Pietas Universitatis Oxoniensis in obitum serenissimi regis Georgii I et Gratulatio in augustissimi regis Georgii II inaugurationem (1727)

Epithalamia Oxoniensia . . . in Gulielmi . . . Arausionensis, Annaeque Britannicae nuptias (1734)

Gratulatio Academiae Oxoniensis in nuptias . . . Frederici Principis Walliae et Augustae Principissae de Saxo-Gotha (1736)

Pietas Academiae Oxoniensis in obitum augustissimae et desideratissimae reginae Carolinae (1738)

Epicedia Oxoniensia in obitum . . . Frederici Principis Walliae (1751)

Pietas . . . in obitum . . . Georgii II et Gratulatio in . . . Georgii III inaugurationem (1761)

Epithalamia Oxoniensia, sive gratulationes in . . . Georgii III et illustrissimae principissae Sophiae Charlottae nuptias auspicatissimas (1761)

Gratulatio Solennis Universitatis Oxoniensis ob celsissimum Georgium Fredericum Augustum principem Walliae . . . auspicatissime natum (1762)

An Account of the visit of HRH the Prince Regent . . . June MDCCCXIV (1815) [some poems at end]

Congratulatory Addresses recited in the theatre, Oxford, at the Installation of his grace the Duke of Wellington, Chancellor of the University, MDCCCXXXIV (1834)

Pitcairne, A., *Selecta Poemata* (Edinburgh, 1727)

Popham, E., ed., *Selecta Poemata Anglorum Latina* (Bath, 1774–6; 2nd edn., London, 1779)

Ramsay, A. B., *Inter Lilia* (Cambridge, 1920)

———— *Ros Rosarum* (Cambridge, 1925)

———— *Frondes Salicis* (Cambridge, 1935)

———— *Flos Malvae* (Cambridge, 1946)

[Richards, T.], *Hoglandiae Descriptio* (1709)

The Student, or Oxford and Cambridge monthly miscellany (1750–1)

Tate, R. W., *Carmina Dublinensia* (Dublin and London, 1946)

Westminster School, *Duci Glocestriae . . . Scholae Westmonasteriensis alumni regii haec carmina consecrant* (1700)

Westminster School, *Lusus Westmonasterienses* (1730; later editions, 1734, 1740, 1750; *Lusus Alteri*, 1863; later editions, 1867, 1906)

SECONDARY (Literary and Historical Background)

Adams, J. N., *The Latin Sexual Vocabulary* (1982)

Adams, J. W. L., 'Scottish Neo-Latin Poetry', in Kinsley, J. ed., *Scottish Poetry* (1955)

Anselment, R. A., 'The Oxford University poets and Caroline Panegyric', *John Donne Journal* 3 (1984), pp. 181–201

Bailey, J. L. H., *Finedon otherwise Thingdon* (Finedon, 1975)

Baldwin, B., 'On some Latin and Greek poems by Thomas Gray', *International Journal of the Classical Tradition* 1 (1994), pp. 71–88

————— *The Latin and Greek Poems of Samuel Johnson* (1995)

Baldwin, T. W., *William Shakspere's Small Latine and Lesse Greeke* (Urbana, IL, 1944)

Barker, N., *The Oxford University Press and the spread of learning, 1478–1978* (Oxford, 1978)

Bate, J., *Shakespeare and Ovid* (Oxford, 1993)

Baxter, S. B., *William III* (1966)

Beattie, J. M., *The English Court in the reign of George I* (1967)

Bennett, G. V., *White Kennet (1660–1728), Bishop of Peterborough* (1957)

————— *The Tory Crisis in Church and State, 1688–1730: the career of Francis Atterbury, Bishop of Rochester* (Oxford, 1975)

Bill, E. G. W., *Education at Christ Church, Oxford, 1660–1800* (Oxford, 1988)

Binns, J. W., ed., *The Latin Poetry of English Poets* (1974)

Binns, J. W., *Intellectual Culture in Elizabethan and Jacobean England: the Latin writings of the age* (Leeds, 1990)

————— *Harriot and the Latin culture of his time* (Durham, 1993)

Blackett-Ord, M., *Hell-Fire Duke: the life of the Duke of Wharton* (1982)

Bliss, P., ed., *Reliquiae Hearnianae* (Oxford, 1857; rev. J. Buchanan-Brown, 1966)

Bloxam, J. R., ed., *Register of Magdalen College* (Oxford, 1853–5)

Bloxam, J. R., *Magdalen College and King James I, 1686–88* (Oxford, 1886)

Bolgar, R. R., ed., *Classical Influences on European Culture, A.D. 1500–1700* (Cambridge, 1976)

Bond, D. F., ed., *The Spectator* (Oxford, 1965)

Bond, R. P., *English Burlesque Poetry, 1700–50* (Cambridge, MA, 1932)

Boucé, P. G., *Sexuality in 18th century Britain* (Manchester, 1982)

Bradner, L., *Musae Anglicanae: a history of Anglo-Latin poetry, 1500–1925* (New York and London, 1940)

————— 'Musae Anglicanae, a supplemental list', *The Library*, 5th Ser., 22 (1967), pp. 93–101

Brink, C. O., *English Classical Scholarship: historical reflections on Bentley, Porson, and Housman* (Cambridge, 1986)

Broich, U., *The 18th century Mock-heroic poem* (Cambridge, 1990)

Bruère, R. T., 'The Latin and English versions of Thomas May's *Supplementum Lucani*', *Classical Philology* 44 (1949), pp. 145–63

Burnet, G., *History of his own time* (1724–34; ed. O. Airy, Oxford, 1897–1900)

Burnett, J., *A History of the cost of living* (1969)

Butler, H. Montagu, *Some remarks on the teaching of Greek and Latin verses . . .* (1913)

Cannon, J., *Aristocratic Century: the peerage of 18th century England* (Cambridge, 1984)

Carter, H., *A History of the Oxford University Press, vol. 1, to 1780* (Oxford, 1975)

Clark, A., ed., *The Life and times of Anthony à Wood . . .* (Oxford, 1891–2)

Clark, G. N., *The Later Stuarts* (Oxford, 1934)

Clark, J. C. D., *Samuel Johnson* (Cambridge, 1994)

Clark, S. H., '"Pendet Homo Incertus": Gray's Response to Locke', *18th century Studies* 24 (1991), pp. 273–91 (pt. 1) and 484–503 (pt. 2)

Clarke, M. L., *Greek Studies in England, 1700–1830* (Cambridge, 1945)

———— *Classical Education in Britain, 1500–1900* (Cambridge, 1959)

Colley, L., *Britons* (New Haven and London, 1992)

Cook, H. J., *The Decline of the Old Medical Regime in Stuart London* (Ithaca and London, 1986)

Cruickshanks, E., *Political Untouchables: the Tories and the '45* (1979)

Cruickshanks, E., ed., *Ideology and Conspiracy: Aspects of Jacobitism, 1689–1759* (Edinburgh, 1982)

Cruickshanks, E., Black, J., eds., *The Jacobite Challenge* (Edinburgh, 1988)

Davies, G., (rev. M. F. Keeler), *Bibliography of British History, Stuart Period, 1603–1714* (Oxford, 1970)

DeMaria, R. (jun.), *The Life of Samuel Johnson: a critical biography* (Oxford and Cambridge, MA, 1993)

Diggle, J., *Phaethon* (Cambridge, 1970)

Dilke, O., Townend, G., eds., *Acta Omnium Gentium ac Nationum Conventus Sexti Latinis Litteris Linguaeque Fovendis* (Kendal, 1986)

Doble, C. E., *et al.*, eds., *The Remarks and Collections of Thomas Hearne* (Oxford, 1885–1921)

Donaldson, W., *The Jacobite Song* (Aberdeen, 1988)

Ecton, J., *Liber Valorum et Decimarum* (1711)

Ecton, J., Willis, B., *Thesaurus Rerum Ecclesiasticarum* (1754)

Erskine-Hill, H. H., *The Social Milieu of Alexander Pope* (New Haven, 1975)

———— *The Augustan Idea in English Literature* (1983)

———— *Poetry and the Realm of Politics* (Oxford, 1996)

Feiling, K., *A History of the Tory Party, 1640–1714* (Oxford, 1924; repr., 1950)

———— *The Second Tory Party, 1714–1832* (1938)

Field, J., *The King's Nurseries* (1987)

Forcellini, E., *et al.*, *Totius Latinitatis Lexicon* (Padua, 1771)

Ford, P. J., *George Buchanan, Prince of Poets* (Aberdeen, 1982)

Forrester, E. G., *Northamptonshire county elections and electioneering, 1695–1832* (1941)

Forster, H., 'The rise and fall of the Cambridge Muses (1603–1763)', *Transactions of the Cambridge Bibliographical Society* 8 (1982), pp. 141–72

Foster, J., *Alumni Oxonienses, 1715–1886* (Oxford, 1888); *1500–1714* (Oxford, 1891–2)

Foxon, D., *Libertine Literature in England, 1600–1745* (1964)

Garrison, J. D., *Dryden and the tradition of panegyric* (Berkeley, 1975)

Godman, P., Murray, O., eds., *Latin Poetry and the Classical Tradition* (Oxford, 1990)

Grant, W. L., *Neo-Latin Literature and the Pastoral* (Chapel Hill, 1965)

Greenwood, D., *William King, Tory and Jacobite* (Oxford, 1969)

Hardin, R. F., 'Recent Studies in Neo-Latin Literature', *English Literary Renaissance* 24 (1994), pp. 660–98

Hawkins, J., *A General History of the Science and Practice of Music* (1776)

Highet, G., *The Classical Tradition* (Oxford, 1949)

Hiscock, W. G., *David Gregory, Isaac Newton and their circle* (Oxford, 1937)

———— *Henry Aldrich of Christ Church, 1648–1710* (Oxford, 1960)

Holmes, G., *The trial of Dr Sacheverell* (1973)

———— *Augustan England* (1982)

Hopkins, K., *The Poets Laureate* (1954; 3rd edn., Wakefield, 1973)

Horne, C. J., 'The Phalaris controversy; King vs. Bentley', *Review of English Studies* 22 (1946), pp. 289–303

Humphreys, A. R., *The Augustan World: Life and Letters in 18th century England* (1954)

Hyam, R., ed., *A History of Magdalene College, Cambridge, 1428–1988* (Cambridge, 1994)

IJsewijn, J., *A Companion to Neo-Latin Studies* (Amsterdam, 1977; 2nd edn., Louvain, 1990)

Jarrett, D., *England in the age of Hogarth* (1974)

Johnson, A., ed., *Dictionary of American Biography* (London and New York, 1928–37)

Johnson, J. W., *The Formation of English Neo-Classical Thought* (Princeton, 1967)

Jones, G. H., *The Main Stream of Jacobitism* (Cambridge, MA, 1954)

Kaiser, L. M., *Early American Latin Verse, 1625–1825* (Chicago, 1984)

Kay, W. D., *Ben Jonson: A Literary Life* (London and Basingstoke, 1995)

King, L. S., *The Medical World of the 18th century* (Chicago, 1958)

Kramnick, I., *Bolingbroke and his circle* (Cambridge, MA, 1968)

Langford, P., *A Polite and Commercial People: England 1727–1783* (1989)

Leedham-Green, E. S., 'The Cult of the Horatian Ode in the 19th century' (unpublished D.Phil. thesis, Oxford, 1970)

Lelièvre, F. J., *Cory's Lucretilis* (Cambridge, 1964)

Le Neve, J., revised T. D. Hardy, *Fasti Ecclesiae Anglicanae* (Oxford, 1854)

Lenman, B., *The Jacobite Risings in Britain, 1689–1746* (1980)

———— *The Jacobite Cause* (Glasgow, 1986)

Levine, J. M., *Dr Woodward's Shield* (Berkeley and Los Angeles, 1977)

———— *The Battle of the Books* (Ithaca and London, 1991)

Lodge, R., *History of England . . . 1660–1702* (1910)

Loewe, V., *Ein Diplomat und Gelehrter Ezechiel Spanheim* (Berlin, 1924)

Love, H., *Scribal Publication in 17th century England* (Oxford, 1993)

Lytton Sells, A. L., *The Paradise of Travellers* (1964)

———— *Thomas Gray* (1980)

McFarlane, I. D., *Renaissance Latin Poetry* (Manchester, 1980)

McFarlane, I. D., ed., *Acta Conventus Neo-Latini Sanctandreani* (Binghamton, NY, 1985)

McKeown, J. C., *Ovid: Amores: text, prolegomena and commentary* (Liverpool, 1987)

McQueen W. A., Rockwell, K. A., *The Latin Poetry of Andrew Marvell* (Chapel Hill, NC, 1964)

Maddison, C., *Apollo and the nine* (1960)

Maslen, K., Lancaster, J., *The Bowyer Ledgers* (London and New York, 1991)

Midgley, G., *University Life in 18th century Oxford* (New Haven and London, 1996)

Money, D. K., Olszowy, J., 'Hebrew Commemorative Poetry in Cambridge, 1564–1763', *Transactions of the Cambridge Bibliographical Society* 10 (1995), pp. 549–76

————, Swan, H. T., 'Doctors as Poets: laudatory verses addressed to Antonio Molinetti by British Medical Students at Padua, 1650–4', *Journal of Medical Biography* 3 (1995), pp. 139–47

Monk, J. H., *Life of Richard Bentley, D.D.* (1830; 2nd edn., 1833)

Monod, P. K., *Jacobitism and the English People, 1688–1788* (Cambridge, 1989)

Moynihan, Lord, *Truants* (Cambridge, 1936)

Munk, W., *Roll of the Royal College of Physicians of London* (1878)

Nichols, F. J., *Anthology of Neo-Latin Poetry* (New Haven, 1979)

Nichols, J., ed., *The Epistolary Correspondence of Francis Atterbury* (1789–90)

Nichols, J., *Literary Anecdotes of the 18th century* (1812–16; repr. New York 1966)

———— *Illustrations of the literary history of the 18th century* (1817–58; repr. New York 1966)

Nisbet, R. G. M., Hubbard, M., *A Commentary on Horace: Odes, Book 1* (Oxford, 1970); *Book 2* (Oxford, 1978)

Noel, T., *Theories of the Fable in the 18th century* (New York and London, 1975)

Oxenden, G. C., *Railway Horace* (1862)

Pargellis, S., Medley, D. J., *Bibliography of British History, the 18th century, 1714–89* (Oxford, 1951)

Parker, R., *Memoirs of Military Transactions, 1683–1718* (Dublin, 1746–7)

Patterson, A., *Fables of Power* (Durham and London, 1991)

Perosa, A., Sparrow, J., *Renaissance Latin Verse: an anthology* (1979)

Philips, J. E., Allen, D. C., *Neo-Latin Poetry of the 16th and 17th centuries* (Los Angeles, 1965)

Pittock, M. G. H., *Poetry and Jacobite Politics in 18th century Britain and Ireland* (Cambridge, 1994)

Poole, R. L. (Mrs), *Catalogue of Oxford Portraits . . .* (Oxford, 1912–25)

Porter, R., *English Society in the 18th century* (1982)

Postgate, J. P., *Prosodia Latina: an introduction to classical Latin verse* (Oxford, 1923)

Postlethwaite, N., Campbell, G., 'Edward King, Milton's *Lycidas*: Poems and Documents', *Milton Quarterly* 28 (1994), pp. 77–111

Quarrell, W. H., Mare, M., *London in 1710, from the travels of Z. C. von Uffenbach* (1934)

Quicherat, L., *Thesaurus Poeticus Linguae Latinae* (Paris, 1850)

Raven, D. S., *Latin metre: an introduction* (1965)

Reddick, A., *The Making of Johnson's Dictionary* (Cambridge, 1990)

Rigg, A. G., *A History of Anglo-Latin Literature, 1066–1422* (Cambridge, 1992)

Rivers, I., *The Poetry of Conservatism, 1660–1745* (Cambridge, 1973)

Rivers, I., ed., *Books and their readers in 18th century England* (Leicester, 1982)

Robson, R. J., *The Oxfordshire Election of 1754* (Oxford, 1949)

Rogers, P., *Literature and Popular Culture in 18th century England* (Brighton, 1985)

Røstvig, M. S., *The Happy Man; studies in the metamorphoses of a classical ideal* (Oslo, 1954–8)

———— *The Background of English Neo-Classicism* (Oslo, 1961)

Sandys, J. E., *History of Classical Scholarship* (Cambridge, 1903–8)

Schleiner, L., *Tudor and Stuart Women Writers* (Bloomington and Indianapolis, 1994)

Scudi, A. T., *The Sacheverell Affair* (New York, 1939)

Sedgwick, R., ed., *History of Parliament: Commons 1715–54* (1970)

Smith, M., 'A study of the administration of the Diocese of Exeter during the Episco-
pate of Sir Jonathan Trelawny, baronet, 1689–1707' (unpublished BD thesis, Oxford,
1964)

Souter, A., *A Glossary of Later Latin* (Oxford, 1949)

Spanheim, E. (ed. E. Bourgeois), *Relation de la cour de France en 1690, et Relation de la cour
d'Angleterre en 1704* (Paris and Lyon, 1900)

Sparrow, J., *Poems in Latin* (London and Oxford, 1941)

Spence, J., *Anecdotes . . . collected from the conversation of Mr Pope . . .* (1820; ed. J. M.
Osborn, Oxford, 1895)

Stanwood, P. G., ed., *Of Poetry and Politics: New essays on Milton and his world* (Bing-
hamton, NY, 1995)

Stewart, A. G., *The Academic Gregories* (Edinburgh, 1901)

Stone, L., ed., *The University in Society* (Princeton and London, 1975)

Sutherland, L. S., Mitchell, L. G., eds., *History of the University of Oxford, vol. 5, the 18th
century* (Oxford, 1986)

Sykes, N., *Church and State in England in the 18th century* (Cambridge, 1934)

Thackray, A., *Atoms and Powers* (Cambridge, MA, 1970)

Thompson, D'Arcy W., *A Glossary of Greek Birds* (Oxford, 1895)

Trevelyan, G. M., *England under Queen Anne* (1930–34)

Trowles, T. A., 'The Musical Ode in Britain, *c.* 1670–1800' (unpublished D.Phil. thesis,
Oxford, 1992)

Tufte, V., *The Poetry of marriage: the epithalamium in Europe . . .* (Los Angeles, 1970)

Turner, A. T., 'Milton and the Convention of the Academic Miscellanies', *Yearbook of
English Studies* 5 (1975), pp. 86–93

Venn, J., Venn, J. A., *Alumni Cantabrigienses* (Cambridge, 1922)

Wagner, P., *Eros Revived: Erotica of the Enlightenment in England and America* (1988)

Ward, R., ed., *Historical Mss. Commission, Report on the Mss. of his Grace the Duke of
Portland, K.G., at Welbeck Abbey, vol. 7* (1901)

Ward, W. R., *Georgian Oxford* (Oxford, 1958)

Watterson, W. C., '"Once more, O ye Laurels": *Lycidas* and the Psychology of Pastoral',
Milton Quarterly 27 (1993), pp. 48–57

Wedeck, H. E., 'Casimir, the Polish Horace', *Philological Quarterly* 16 (1937), pp. 307–16

Wedgwood, C. V., *Poetry and politics under the Stuarts* (1960)

Welch, J., *List of Scholars of St Peter's College, Westminster* (1788)

White, R. J., *Dr Bentley, a study in academic scarlet* (1965)

Williams, B., *The Whig Supremacy* (Oxford, 1939; rev. C. H. Stuart, 1960)

Williams, R. D., Kelsall, M., 'Critical Appreciations 5: Joseph Addison, *Pax Gulielmi
Auspiciis Europae Reddita, 1697 . . .*', *Greece and Rome*, 2nd ser., 27 (1980), pp. 48–59

Winn, J. A., *John Dryden and his world* (1987)

Wordsworth, C., ed., *Correspondence of Richard Bentley* (1842)

Wordsworth, C. *Social Life in the English Universities in the 18th century* (Cambridge, 1874)

———— *Scholae Academicae: some accounts of studies at the English Universities in the 18th
century* (Cambridge, 1877; repr. London, 1968)

Wright, F. A., Sinclair, T. A., *A History of Later Latin Literature* (1931)

Index

The index is in four parts: index of first lines; index of passages cited from Alsop's works; index of passages cited from classical authors; and general index. The index of first lines covers all of Alsop's poems in Part II (both the Latin poems of books 1–3, and the English and doubtful Latin poems of book 4, including 4. 26–9, which are not printed in full). References are to the poem numbers used in Part II. In the lists of cited passages, references to a whole poem precede references to individual lines: for example, Alsop's poem 1. 1 is mentioned on p. 91, and printed in full on pp. 270–1; line 20 of poem 1. 1 is cited in a note on p. 323. In the general index, modern scholars are indexed only selectively: e.g. when mentioned in the main text, or when a footnote contains a citation or criticism of a particularly important work.

INDEX OF FIRST LINES

INDEX OF PASSAGES CITED FROM ALSOP'S WORKS

INDEX OF PASSAGES CITED FROM CLASSICAL AUTHORS

GENERAL INDEX